COMMERCIAL LAW

AUSTRALIA AND NEW ZEALAND
The Law Book Company Ltd.
Sydney : Melbourne : Perth

CANADA AND U.S.A.
The Carswell Company Ltd.
Agincourt, Ontario

INDIA
N.M. Tripathi Private Ltd.
Bombay
and
Eastern Law House Private Ltd.
Calcutta
M.P.P. House
Bangalore

ISRAEL
Steimatzky's Agency Ltd.
Jerusalem : Tel Aviv : Haifa

MALAYSIA : SINGAPORE : BRUNEI
Malayan Law Journal (Pte.) Ltd.
Singapore

PAKISTAN
Pakistan Law House
Karachi

COMMERCIAL LAW

by

ROBERT LOWE, LL.B.

*Solicitor; formerly Director of Continuing
Education at the College of Law*

SIXTH EDITION

LONDON
SWEET & MAXWELL
1983

First edition 1964
Second edition 1967
Third edition 1970
Fourth edition 1973
Fifth edition 1976
Second impression 1978
Sixth edition 1983

Published by
Sweet & Maxwell Ltd.
of 11 New Fetter Lane, London
Computerset by Promenade Graphics Ltd; Cheltenham
and printed
by Richard Clay (The Chaucer Press) Ltd.,
Bungay, Suffolk

British Library Cataloguing in Publication Data
Lowe, Robert
    Commercial Law.—6th ed.
    1. Commercial law—England
    I. Title
    344.206'7   KD1629
    ISBN 0–421–29870–7
           0–421–29880–4 Pbk

PREFACE

MORE than seven years have passed since the publication of the Fifth Edition—more than twice as long as the gap between any previous editions. Needless to say a great deal of legal water has flowed under the bridges since the Fifth Edition appeared in 1976. Perhaps the two most important developments have been the Unfair Contract Terms Act 1977 and the Supply of Goods and Services Act 1982. Since both of them are common to most of the other topics discussed in the book I have taken the opportunity of dealing with them in two new chapters. In addition there has been a lot of activity in the field of consumer protection (which is discussed in Chapter Nine), regulations on consumer credit have finally begun to appear and the Civil Jurisdiction and Judgments Act 1982 has made major changes in the rules governing the jurisdiction of the English courts and the enforcement of foreign judgments. There has also been the usual crop of important recent cases.

Faced with this mass of new law I had to decide how I could incorporate it in such a way that the book (and the price) did not get out of hand. I finally decided to leave out altogether the chapter on Employment Law; this is now a major subject in its own right which no longer forms part of general courses on Commercial Law. In the result the new edition is only three pages longer than its predecessor.

I should like to thank my friend Geoffrey Woodroffe for reading three of the chapters (including the two new ones) and making a number of valuable suggestions. I should also like to thank my proof readers Justyna Szczpanek and Pamela Ashby. Both of them found errors which had escaped the glazed eyes of an author suffering from the common problem of reading only the words which he had originally written and not the words which the typist or printer had reproduced from his illegible scrawl! Finally I would like to thank the publishers for their endless patience and for preparing the index, the table of contents and the tables of cases and statutes.

The law is never static for very long and it is likely that further regulations under the Consumer Credit Act 1974 are likely to be laid before Parliament in the autumn and to come into force within the next two years. A note on this topic is to be found on page 246. Subject to this I have tried to state the law as at July 29, 1983.

July 29, 1983.   Robert Lowe

CONTENTS

TABLE OF CASES

xi

TABLE OF STATUTES

CHAPTER ONE

SOME COMMON THREADS

WHAT is commercial law? In the words of a learned writer[1] it is:

> "that branch of law which is concerned with rights and duties arising from the supply of goods and services in the way of trade."

It is a vast subject and it is clearly impossible within the scope of a single volume, to do justice to all of its many constituent parts. At first glance each of the topics chosen for inclusion in this book appears to be governed by its own set of rules. Nevertheless there are some common threads (many of which are of recent origin) and it might be helpful to begin the book by drawing these strands together.

1. The "business-to-business" and "business-to-consumer" dichotomy

The main principles of English commercial law were developed in the eighteenth and nineteenth centuries to regulate contracts between businessmen—contracts of agency, sale, loan, carriage, bills of exchange and insurance. They were never designed to cater for the enormous "business-to-consumer" explosion which took place at the turn of the century and for which, in particular, the Victorian ideas of laissez-faire were clearly inappropriate. Parliament has intervened from time to time in order to protect the consumer from unfair exploitation but essentially the two very different types of transactions are governed by the same sets of rules; thus the same rules will regulate the purchase of an oil-tanker by a multinational company and the purchase of a jar of coffee by an individual. The question of consumer protection is briefly considered in Chapter Nine but it has rapidly become a subject in its own right and it is more fully considered elsewhere.[2]

---

[1] Professor R.M. Goode, *Commercial Law*, p. 35.
[2] See, *e.g.* Lowe and Woodroffe, *Consumer Law and Practice*.

1

2. Statutory controls

As methods of marketing and distribution became more sophisticated it became clear that controls were needed for business customers as well as for private customers. Accordingly the large battery of controls (civil, criminal and administrative) which were introduced by the Consumer Credit Act 1974 will benefit not only private individuals but also sole traders and partnerships. Similarly the restrictions on exemption clauses which are considered in Chapter Eight (*post*, p. 429) are not confined to consumer transactions. Finally, there are a number of Acts which imply various terms into contracts and once again they apply equally to consumer and to non-consumer transactions. The most recent of these Acts is considered below.

3. Standardisation

The law of contract is based upon a bargain being struck between two persons—whether they be individuals, firms or companies. In modern conditions, however, the concept of individual negotiation of all the terms of a contract on every occasion is wholly impracticable and economically wasteful.

Accordingly the "contract" between the two parties is increasingly based upon a standard set of trading terms which have been drafted by the lawyers of one party and are largely non-negotiable. In many cases the terms appear in a catalogue, brochure or quotation and are not even looked at (let alone understood) before the contract has been made. The trend towards standardisation is not limited to the contracts of individual traders. Many trade associations have developed codes of practice and standard terms of business for their members. In addition there has been strong pressure for the harmonisation of the laws of different states and this has led to international conventions on such matters as the international sale of goods (*post*, p. 485) and the international carriage of goods by road, sea and air. This trend received a new dimension on January 1, 1973 when the United Kingdom became a member of European Economic Community; Article 100 of the EEC Treaty provides that:

> the Council shall. . . . issue directions for approximation of such provisions laid down by law, regulation or administrative action in Member States as directly affect the establishment or functions of the Common Market.

4. General duties owed by the supplier of a service

Until recently the duties owed by the supplier of a service had to be gleaned from common-law cases (some of which were of considerable antiquity) and the scope of those duties were uncertain. The problem was clearly of great practical importance since it covered a vast number of transactions including agency, finance, insurance, storage, repair, cleaning, maintenance, installation, transport, building, holidays, entertainment and the whole battery of legal, accountancy, medical, dental, banking and other professional services. Fortunately, the task of finding the law on three particular topics—skill, time and price—has been made easier by Part II of the Supply of Goods and Services Act 1982 and since these provisions affect virtually all of the contracts which are described in this book it may be helpful to consider them at this point.

Scope of the new provisions

The provisions of Part II of the 1982 Act (which are declaratory of, and hence a codification of, the relevant common law rules) apply to "a contract for the supply of a service" and this is defined—perhaps not very surprisingly—as "a contract under which a person ("the supplier") agrees to carry out a service" (s.12(1)). Contracts of service (*i.e.* employment and apprenticeships) are, however, expressly excluded (s.12(2)). In addition, the Secretary of State has power to provide by Order that all or any of the obligations described below shall not apply to services of a description specified in the Order (s.12(4)). The idea behind this provision is that the Act is essentially declaratory and is not designed to impose a liability which did not exist before. An order has already been made[3] that section 13 of the Act (see below) shall not apply to:

(a) the services of an advocate in court or before any tribunal, inquiry or arbitration or in carrying out any preliminary work directly affecting the conduct of the hearing; or

(b) the services rendered to a company by a director of the company in his capacity as such.

---

[3] Supply of Services (Exclusion of Implied Terms) Order 1982, No. 1771. For the limits of an advocate's immunity at common law see *Rondel* v. *Worsley* [1969] 1 A.C. 197 and *Saif Ali* v. *Sidney Mitchell & Co.* [1980] A.C. 198; [1978] 3 All E.R. 1033, H.L.

Care and skill
By section 13:

> In a contract for the supply of a service where the supplier is acting in the course of a business there is an implied term that the supplier will carry out the service with reasonable care and skill.

This section puts into statutory form what every customer, whether business or private, would reasonably expect—namely that a person who offers to carry out work in the course of a business will carry out that work with reasonable care and skill.[4] The supplier will be expected to conform to the standards of the relevant trade or profession and he will be in breach of his duty if he falls below that standard.[5]

Quite apart from section 13, the person who negligently performs a service may well be liable in tort. There has recently been a major increase in the extent of liability[6] and in the range of persons to whom a duty is owed.[7]

Time for performance
By section 14:

> (1) Where, under a contract for the supply of a service by a supplier acting in the course of a business, the time for the service to be carried out is not fixed by the contract, left to be fixed in a manner agreed by the contract or determined by the course of dealing between the parties, there is an implied term that the supplier will carry out the service within a reasonable time.
>
> (2) What is a reasonable time is a question of fact.

The wording of this provision follows the model of section 8 of the Sale of Goods Act 1979 (*post*, p. 88) but it does not deal with the remedies which are available to the other party if performance is delayed. Research carried out by the National Consumer Council showed that, as might have been expected, a large number of complaints related to builders and many consumers were

---

[4] For a selection of the many illustrations of the rule see the commentary to section 13 in the Current Law Statutes Annotated 1982.

[5] See, *e.g. Roe* v. *Minister of Health* [1954] 2 Q.B. 66 for a discussion of this topic.

[6] See, *e.g. Junior Books Limited* v. *Veitchi* [1982] 3 W.L.R. 477; [1982] 3 All E.R. 201.

[7] See, *e.g. Ross* v. *Caunters* [1980] Ch. 297; [1979] 3 W.L.R. 605; [1979] 3 All E.R. 580.

completely unaware that a legal remedy might be available to them.

Reasonable charges for the work
By section 15:

> (1) Where, under a contract for the supply of a service, the consideration for the service is not determined by the contract, left to be determined in a manner agreed by the contract or determined by the course of dealing between the parties, there is an implied term that the party contracting with the supplier will pay a reasonable charge.
>
> (2) What is a reasonable charge is a question of fact.

This section unlike the two previous sections, is not confined to services provided in the course of a business but in practice the distinction is likely to be slight. The section is largely aimed at the problem which arises where, for example, a plumber is called out to carry out emergency work but no price is mentioned until the work has been done. In this situation expert evidence as to what is a reasonable charge will clearly be highly relevant (although not conclusive). The National Consumer Council and the Consumers' Association have both described cases where a consumer has been compelled to pay what he considered to be an unreasonable charge; in a number of these cases the consumer has successfully taken county court proceedings to recover the excess over a reasonable charge from the supplier. Once again the Act applies equally to private and business customers.

Exemption clauses
The extent to which liability can be excluded is considered in Chapter Eight (*post*, p. 429).

Additional obligations
Section 16(3) provides that:

> Nothing in this Part of this Act prejudices—
>
> (a) any rule of law which imposes on the supplier a duty stricter than that imposed by section 13 or 14 above;

For examples of this see the duties owed by a carrier at common law (*post*, p. 423) and by statute (*post*, p. 428).

CHAPTER TWO

AGENCY

INTRODUCTION

THE concept of agency is fundamental to modern commercial law; it lies at the very heart of the subject and without it modern commerce would not exist. An example will illustrate the point. Suppose that A wishes to open a business for the manufacture and sale of toys. He will have to acquire premises and machinery, engage staff, obtain supplies of the necessary materials and then he must sell the finished product to buyers at home and perhaps abroad. To do these things he will have to make a great many contracts and clearly it will be physically impossible for him to make all the contracts personally. He therefore employs other persons to make them on his behalf. These other persons are called agents. Then he may decide to take in one or more partners, in which case each partner will be an agent for the others in the running of the business of the firm.[1] Alternatively he may decide to form a limited company by filing certain documents at Companies House. A company registered under the Companies Act 1948 is a distinct legal person apart from its members[2] and being an artificial person it can only do business through agents.

The foregoing paragraph should have revealed the essential nature of the agency relationship. It can be defined as the relationship which arises whenever one person (the agent) acts on behalf of another person (the principal) and has power to affect the principal's legal position with regard to a third party.[3] In practice the two most important functions of an agent are (*a*) making contracts on his principal's behalf and (*b*) disposing of his property.

---

[1] Partnership Act 1890, s.5.
[2] *Salomon* v. *Salomon and Co.* [1897] A.C. 22.
[3] See an interesting article by Dowrick, (1954) 17 M.L.R. 24, where the history of agency and its development in the courts of equity and common law are skilfully traced.

Since an agent usually brings his principal into relationship with a third party it is necessary to consider three different relationships.

(1) Principal and Agent.
(2) Principal and Third Party.
(3) Agent and Third Party.

This order will be followed in this chapter, but it is first necessary to make some general observations.

When is an agent not an agent?

In this book the word agent is used to describe a person who acts on behalf of another in his dealings with third parties. In commerce, however, the word is very often used in a different sense. For example, a "sole agent" may be simply a person who is given sole selling rights by a particular manufacturer. When such a person contracts with third parties he does so as principal. This distinction is fundamental and must be borne in mind. In *Lamb (W.T.) & Sons* v. *Goring Brick Co. Ltd.*[4]:

> The defendants appointed the plaintiffs sole selling agents of their goods for a fixed period. Before the end of that period they informed the plaintiffs that they would henceforth sell the goods themselves. Had this been a genuine agency contract, it would not have prevented the defendants from selling their own goods.[5] It was held, however, that this was a contract giving sole selling rights for a fixed period and that the defendants' letter amounted to a breach of that contract.

The power to act through an agent

The common law rule is that any person can act through an agent—*qui facit per alium facit per se*,[6] the reason being the obvious one of practical convenience. The only exceptions to the rule occur where a person occupies a position requiring personal performance or where the parties make a contract which expressly or impliedly prohibits delegation to an agent.[7] So far as statute is

---

[4] [1932] 1 K.B. 710, followed in *Nolan* v. *Watson* (1965) 109 S.J. 288, C.A. Such contracts are essentially distributorship agreements.

[5] See *Bentall, Horsley & Baldry* v. *Vicary* [1931] 1 K.B. 253.

[6] See, *e.g. Bevan* v. *Webb* [1901] 2 Ch. 59, 77, *per* Stirling J.

[7] *Bevan* v. *Webb, supra,* and see *post*, p. 16, for an important example of non-delegation.

concerned, some statutes expressly adopt the common law rule[8] while others are silent. In the latter case there is a presumption in favour of the common law rule,[9] but this presumption cannot apply if it would be inconsistent with the clear and explicit words of the statute,[10] which is in each case a question of construction.

Agency distinguished from other relationships

(1) *Agents and trustees*

Agents resemble trustees in that both stand in a fiduciary position so that they must not make a secret profit and must not allow their interest to conflict with their duty.[11] Again if a principal entrusts property to an agent who misappropriates it, the agent can be regarded as a trustee for the purposes of the Limitation Act 1980.[12] On the other hand an agent differs from a trustee in various ways. A trustee is the legal owner of property while an agent has, at most, a legal power to dispose of it. Again, an agent genuinely represents his principal, whereas it cannot be said that a trustee represents his beneficiaries. Finally there are many cases where the principal-agent relationship is merely that of creditor and debtor. Thus an agent who receives a bribe from a third party is under a personal duty to pay it over to his principal, but this does not give the principal any proprietary interest in the bribe nor in any property bought with it.[13]

(2) *Agents, servants and independent contractors*

In many areas of law (including tax, national insurance, employer's liability and employment protection) there is a major distinction between a "servant" and an "independent contractor"—between a contract of service and a contract for services. The distinction is not an easy one to apply in particular cases and a

---

[8] *e.g.*, Bills of Exchange Act 1882, s.91, *post*, p. 265; Sale of Goods Act 1979, s.62(1) *post*, p. 73; Law of Property Act 1925, s.40, *post*, p. 35.

[9] *R.* v. *Kent Justices* (1873) L.R. 8 Q.B. 305; *Re Whitley Partners Ltd.* (1886) 32 Ch.D. 337.

[10] *Hirst* v. *West Riding Union Banking Co.* [1901] 2 K.B. 560. (Statute of Frauds (Amendment) Act 1828.) *Re Blucher* [1931] 2 Ch. 70 (s.16(1), Bankruptcy Act 1914). As to Consumer Credit Act 1974 see *post*, p. 222.

[11] *Post*, p. 18.

[12] s.21. See *Burdick* v. *Garrick* (1870) L.R. 5 Ch. 233.

[13] *Lister* v. *Stubbs* (1890) 45 Ch.D. 1, C.A.

number of tests have been suggested from time to time. The one currently favoured is to treat a person as an independent contractor if he is "in business on his own account."[14] The distinction between servants and independent contractors on the one hand and agents on the other is essentially one of function, in that agents are mainly employed to make contracts and to dispose of property, while servants and independent contractors are often employed for other tasks. It is not surprising therefore that in the law of contract agency is all important while the distinction between servants and independent contractors has little significance, whereas in the law of tort the employer's liability turns primarily on the distinction between servants and independent contractors and the doctrine of agency has little importance except in relation to torts connected with contracts[15] or with the transfer of property.[16]

Some statutory provisions refer to both servants and agents while others (notably the Factors Act 1889) refer exclusively to agents. The cases suggest that an agent is a person with greater independence and freedom from control than a servant.[17] While this is no doubt so in many cases, it is not universally true, because the concepts overlap. Thus a person may be (1) a servant only, *e.g.* chauffeur, (2) an independent contractor only, *e.g.* an electrician, (3) a servant and an agent, *e.g.* a sales representative, (4) an independent contractor and an agent, *e.g.* a free-lance commercial traveller.

There has been much discussion as to whether there can be agents who are neither servants nor independent contractors.[18] The discussion appears to have little practical importance since, as already pointed out, the concept of agency appears principally in one branch of the law (contract) while the distinction between servant and contractor is of importance in another (tort). It is clear

---

[14] See, *e.g. Warner Holidays Ltd.* v. *Secretary of State for Social Services, The Times* January 3, 1983.

[15] *e.g.*, deceit (*Armstrong* v. *Strain* [1952] 1 K.B. 232; [1952] 1 All E.R. 139), *post*, p. 54. See generally *Street on Torts*, (7th ed.), pp. 392–393.

[16] *e.g.* conversion (*Hilbery* v. *Hatton* (1864) 2 H. & C. 822, *post*, p. 46).

[17] *Hayman* v. *Flewker* (1863) 13 C.B.(N.S.) 519; *R.* v. *Negus* (1873) L.R. 2 C.C.R. 34; *Baillie* v. *Goodwin* (1886) 33 Ch.D. 604.

[18] See, *e.g.* Powell, *Law of Agency*, (2nd ed.), pp. 7–24 (the learned author concludes that there is no such third category); Fridman, *Law of Agency*, (5th ed.), 26–32.

however that partners are agents of their fellow-partners (*post*, p. 67) without at the same time being either servants or independent contractors.

(3) *Agents and bailees*

A bailee is a person who receives possession of goods from (or for) the owner for a specific purpose. The concept of bailment overlaps with agency where the agent receives possession, as in the case of factors and other mercantile agents. On the other hand many agents, such as brokers and estate agents, are not bailees since they do not receive possession. Conversely, many bailees are not agents since they in no way represent their bailors. Examples include bailees for storage, hire and work and materials. The subject of bailments is dealt with in Chapter Seven.

The key feature of agency

The key feature of agency is the agent's power to alter his principal's legal position, by making contracts on his behalf or disposing of his property. This power to bind the principal can arise in three ways:

(1) By consent.
(2) By operation of law.
(3) By the doctrine of apparent authority.

In the vast majority of cases the agent's power to bind his principal is based on consent. The principal authorises the agent to do an act on his behalf and the agent does it. The authority can be express or implied,[19] and it can be precedent or subsequent (when it is known as ratification). In two special cases, however, the principal is bound by his agent's act even if he did not consent to it. The first of these cases is of limited importance and is confined to agents of necessity.[20] The second case, however, is far more interesting and important. When a third party deals with an agent he clearly cannot be expected to concern himself with the precise limits of the agent's actual authority. He relies instead on the appearance of authority. This has crystallised into the maxim that

---

[19] For a modern statement of the principles involved, see *Garnac Grain Co. Inc.* v. *H. M. F. Faure & Fairclough Ltd.* [1968] A.C. 1130, 1137; [1968] 2 All E.R. 353, 358, *per* Lord Pearson.

[20] *Post*, p. 64.

so far as the third party is concerned, the apparent authority is the real authority.[21] Used in this sense the expression "apparent authority" means any authority which the agent appears to have, so that it overlaps with actual authority if the agent does an authorised act. It is more convenient, however, to use the words "apparent authority" to mean authority which appears to exist but does not exist in fact, and this meaning is the one used in this book. The doctrine of apparent authority is discussed more fully below.[22]

PRINCIPAL AND AGENT

This section deals with the relationship between a principal and his agent in those cases where the relationship is a consensual one.

Formalities

The general rule is that no formalities are required for the appointment of an agent. As Lord Cranworth put it in an early case:

> "No one can become the agent of another person except by the will of that other person.[23] His will may be manifested in writing or orally or simply by placing another in a situation in which . . . according to the ordinary usages of mankind that other is understood to represent and act for the person who has so placed him."[24]

To the general rule there is one major exception—an agent appointed to execute a deed (such as a conveyance on the sale of land) must be authorised to do so by a deed—the latter being known as a power of attorney.[25] It should be noted, however, that even if the agent is not appointed by deed he can validly execute a deed if he does so in his principal's presence and by his authority.[26] Further, section 53 of the Law of Property Act 1925 provides that, subject to exceptions, an interest in land cannot be granted or

---

[21] See *per* Scrutton L.J., in *Reckitt* v. *Barnett Pembroke and Slater Ltd.* [1928] 2 K.B. 244, 257.

[22] *Post*, p. 41.

[23] His Lordship was not dealing with agency of necessity.

[24] *Pole* v. *Leask* (1863) 33 L.J.Ch. 155, 161–162. See also *Garnac Grain Co. Inc.* v. *H. M. F. Faure & Fairclough* [1968] A.C. 1130; [1968] 2 All E.R. 353.

[25] *Steiglitz* v. *Egginton* (1815) Holt N.P. 141.

[26] *R.* v. *Longnor (Inhabitants)* (1833) 4 B. & A. 647.

disposed of except by writing signed by the person creating or disposing of it or by his agent authorised in writing.[27]

Capacity

The extent to which a minor[28] can appoint an agent is not free from doubt. In *Re Shepherd*[29] Denning L.J. declared that a minor could never appoint an agent or be bound by the agent's acts. "He is all too likely to choose the wrong man." While one can sympathise with this tender regard for youthful pop-stars and boxers there are several cases which do not support such a sweeping proposition and it has been forcefully criticised by academic writers. Lord Denning has himself admitted that the statement was too wide; the true principle was that a minor could not appoint an agent to dispose of property so as to bind him irrevocably.[30] A minor cannot, however, give a valid power of attorney, unless the minor happens to be a married woman.[31]

The problem of the principal's mental disorder is also an interesting one. The general rule, of course, is that where a party to a contract is of unsound mind the contract is nevertheless binding upon him unless he can prove that he was so insane as not to know what he was doing and that this was known to the other party.[32] In *Yonge* v. *Toynbee*,[33] however, the insanity of a principal was held to terminate his agent's authority automatically, although the agent was unaware of the insanity. From this case it seems that the rule in *Imperial Loan Co.* v. *Stone* does not apply to agency contracts and that the contract is void if the principal is of unsound mind. The matter, however, is not free from doubt.[34]

So far as an agent is concerned, there is no need for him to have full contractual capacity because he will normally be a mere link

---

[27] Contrast s.40 of the same Act—an agent who signs a memorandum of a *contract* for the sale of land need not be appointed in writing.

[28] Throughout this book the word "minor" is used to refer to a person who is not of full age, *i.e.* under 18 (see Family Law Reform Act 1969, s.12).

[29] [1953] Ch. 728, 755; [1953] 2 All E.R. 608, 618–619.

[30] *G.* v. *G.* [1970] 2 Q.B. 643, 652.

[31] Law of Property Act 1925, s.129.

[32] *Imperial Loan Co.* v. *Stone* [1892] 1 Q.B. 599.

[33] [1910] 1 K.B. 215, *post*, p. 63.

[34] See *Taylor* v. *Walker* [1958] 1 Lloyd's Rep. 490, 574. Hudson, 37 Can. B.R. 497.

between two contracting parties. An agent for one party can also act as agent for the other if this does not involve any breach of the duties which he owes to the first principal.[35] An example is that of a solicitor acting for both vendor and purchaser on a sale of land.[36] Another example is that of an auctioneer who has authority to sign the memorandum required by section 40 of the Law of Property Act 1925, on behalf of both the vendor and the purchaser.[37] It is well established, however, that one party cannot sign the memorandum as agent of the other.[38]

Consideration

Although in most cases there is an express or implied agreement to pay remuneration, it is perfectly possible for agency to be gratuitous. The most common case of gratuitous agency is in the domestic sphere, as where a wife buys goods on her husband's behalf (or vice versa).

Ratification

The relationship of principal and agent can be created by ratification, which occurs where an agent acting without authority does an act on behalf of his principal and the principal adopts what the agent has done. This interesting and important doctrine raises a number of problems concerning third party rights and fuller discussion is therefore reserved until the section dealing with the agent's authority.[39] Here it is sufficient to point out that ratification is retrospective, so that the relationship between principal and agent is the same as if authority had existed from the beginning.[40]

---

[35] For a recent case on breach of duty, see *North and South Trust Co.* v. *Berkeley* [1971] 1 W.L.R. 470; [1971] 1 All E.R. 980 (insurance broker).

[36] The circumstances where this is permitted are now considerably restricted (Solicitors Practice Rule 2; *Law Society's Gazette*, November 22, 1972).

[37] *Chaney* v. *Maclow* [1929] 1 Ch. 461.

[38] *Farebrother* v. *Simmons* (1822) 5 B. & A. 333.

[39] *Post*, p. 43.

[40] *Keay* v. *Fenwick* (1876) 1 C.P.D. 745 (agent's right to claim commission from ratifying principal).

Duties of agent

(1) *Obedience*

If the agency is contractual, an agent who agrees to act is bound to perform his agency and is liable in damages if he fails to do so. In *Fraser* v. *B.N. Furman (Productions), Ltd.*[41]:

> The plaintiff obtained damages for personal injuries from his employers. The employers claimed an indemnity from a broker who had agreed to effect an employers' liability policy but had failed to do so. *Held*, the employers were entitled to the indemnity.

The agent will not, of course, be liable if he fails to perform an act which is illegal or void.[42]

If the agency is a purely gratuitous one, the agent incurs no liability for not embarking on the agency at all, but if he does embark on it he will be in the same position as a paid agent. It has been suggested than an agent who decides not to perform must notify the principal of this fact[43] but there appear to be no English cases to support this view.

An agent must keep within his authority, express or implied, and cannot disregard his instructions[44] even if this might benefit the principal. In *Bertram Armstrong & Co.* v. *Godrey*[45]:

> An agent was instructed to sell stock when it stood at £85 or above that price. The price did come up to £85 but the agent failed to sell. It was held that the agent had no general discretion to wait for a higher price and was liable for not having sold as instructed.

If, however, the principal's instructions are ambiguous, the agent will not be liable if he acts reasonably and in the interests of his principal, even though the principal never intended to authorise the particular act.[46]

(2) *Care and skill*

Some early cases appear to draw a distinction between a paid agent and a gratuitous one. The latter is only bound to show such

---

[41] [1967] 1 W.L.R. 898; [1967] 3 All E.R. 57, C.A.
[42] *Cohen* v. *Kittell* (1889) 22 Q.B.D. 680 (agent not liable for failing to place bets).
[43] Powell, *op. cit.* at pp. 302–303.
[44] Apart from agency of necessity, *post*, p. 64.
[45] (1830) 1 Knapp 381, P.C.
[46] *Pariente* v. *Lubbock* (1856) 8 De G.M. & G.5.

skill as he in fact possesses[47] while the former must show the degree of skill which an agent in his position usually shows. This distinction has been criticised as being "entirely unsound in principle,"[48] and the modern distinction is likely to be somewhat different. Under a business contract for the supply of a service the agent must exercise reasonable care and skill (Supply of Goods and Services Act 1982, s.13 *ante*, p. 4). If, however, he is a member of an excluded class (*ante*, p. 3) the standard of care may well be lower[49] and the same may be true if the agency is gratuitous (and therefore non-contractual). The basic principle which regulates the standard of care has already been mentioned—a person professing a particular calling must show the degree of skill appropriate thereto. In *Hart and Hodge* v. *Frame, Son & Co.*, a case concerning negligent attorneys, the matter was put in the following way:

> "Their employers had a right to their diligence, their knowledge and their skill and whether they had not so much of these qualities as they were bound to have or having them neglected to employ them, the law properly makes them liable for the loss which has accrued to their employers."[50]

Where it is the agent's duty to communicate material facts to his principal he must do so with reasonable diligence. In *Proudfoot* v. *Montefiore*[51]:

> The plaintiff's ship was lost. His agent knew of this but deliberately failed to inform his principal in order that the principal could insure it. In an action on the policy it was held that the agent's knowledge must be treated as the principal's knowledge since it ought to have been communicated. Consequently the policy was voidable for non-disclosure of a material fact which was deemed to be known by the principal.

---

[47] See, *e.g. Giblin* v. *McMullen* (1868) L.R. 2 P.C. 317.

[48] Powell, *op cit.* at p. 304. See also Fridman, *op. cit.* pp. 140–144 for a somewhat different view.

[49] See, *e.g. Re City Equitable Fire Insurance Co. Ltd.* [1925] Ch. 407.

[50] (1839) 6 Cl. & Fin. 193. See also *Kenney* v. *Hall, Pain and Foster* (1976) 239 E.G. 355—liability of estate agents for overvaluing a house.

[51] (1867) L.R. 2 Q.B. 511.

In recent years there has been a massive increase in the legal liability of professional persons—not only to their principals (both in contract and in tort) but also in tort to third parties.[52]

(3) *Personal performance*

Since the relationship of principal and agent is essentially one where the personal quality and skill of the agent are of the essence, the general rule is that the agent must perform personally and cannot delegate—*delegatus non potest delegare*.

There are, however, three exceptions to this rule. The first, which requires no comment, arises where the principal expressly authorises the agent to delegate his powers. The second is where a power to delegate can be implied from the circumstances of the case. As Thesiger L.J. put it in *De Bussche* v. *Alt*[53]:

> "An authority [to delegate] may and should be implied where from the conduct of the parties to the original contract of agency, the usage of trade or the nature of the particular business which is the subject of the agency it may reasonably be presumed that the parties to the contract of agency originally intended that such authority should exist or where, in the course of the employment, unforeseen emergencies arise which impose upon the agent the necessity of employing a substitute."

The final exception concerns purely ministerial acts. The basic rule is based on the reliance by the principal on the agent's skill and discretion and does not therefore apply to acts, such as signature, where no skill or discretion is required. The physical act of signing can, therefore, be delegated[54] unless a contrary intention appears.[55]

There remains the important question of the effect of delegation, assuming it to be lawful in accordance with the rules set out above. The position is not free from doubt, but it is probably safe to say that where an agent (A) of a principal (P) has power to appoint a delegate (D) the delegate becomes the agent of A and

---

[52] See, *e.g. Ross* v. *Caunters* [1979] 3 W.L.R. 605 and *Yianni* v. *Edwin Evans & Sons* [1981] 3 W.L.R. 843.

[53] (1878) 8 Ch.D. 286, 311. The quotation was *obiter* because the case was one of express authority.

[54] *Marsh* v. *Joseph* [1897] 1 Ch. 213. See also *Allam* v. *Europa Poster Services* [1968] 1 W.L.R. 638; [1968] 1 All E.R. 826.

[55] See *Bell* v. *Balls* [1897] 1 Ch. 663 (signature by auctioneer's clerk insufficient).

not of P[56] unless P gave A authority not merely to appoint a delegate but to appoint someone to act as agent for P.[57] The latter situation, which Professor Powell has called the appointment of a substitute rather than a sub-agent,[58] is a matter requiring precise proof.[59] In the ordinary case, therefore, no privity exists between the principal and the delegate and consequently the delegate cannot sue the principal for remuneration,[60] nor can the principal sue the delegate for failing to carry out the terms of the original agency.[61] The delegate can, however, be liable to the principal for those duties which do not depend on the existence of privity, so that the principal might be able to sue him for breach of his fiduciary duties or for negligence in the performance of his work.[62]

While there is no privity between the principal and the delegate, the original agent will remain liable to the principal for the due performance of the agency, and will be liable for the defaults of himself or of his delegate,[63] although in the latter case he would, of course, have an action against his own agent, the delegate.

If the delegate does become the agent of the principal, the rules discussed in this part of this chapter will govern his rights and duties, so that (for example) he cannot without the principal's consent buy for himself property which he received from his principal for sale.[64]

It remains to add that in *McCann* v. *Pow*[65] the Court of Appeal has re-affirmed the general non-delegation rule. In that case an agent was appointed "sole agent" for the sale of land and he passed on the work to other agents. It was held that delegation was unauthorised and consequently the owner was not liable to pay commission when one of the "delegates" introduced a purchaser.

---

[56] See *per* Wright J. in *Calico Printers Assn.* v. *Barclays Bank* (1931) 145 L.T. 51, 55.

[57] See *Schwensen* v. *Ellinger, Heath Western & Co.* (1949) 83 Ll.L.R. 79.

[58] Powell, *op. cit.* pp. 307–311. For a somewhat different approach see Seavey (1955) 68 Harvard L.R. 658.

[59] See note 56, above.

[60] *Schmaling* v. *Tomlinson* (1815) 6 Taunt. 147.

[61] *Calico Printers Assn.* v. *Barclays Bank, supra.*

[62] Consider the sub-contractor case of *Junior Books Ltd.* v. *Veitchi Co. Ltd.* [1982] 3 W.L.R. 477, H.L.—sub-contractor liable to the building owner for the negligent construction of a floor.

[63] *Swire* v. *Francis* (1877) 3 App. Cas. 106.

[64] *De Bussche* v. *Alt, supra.*

[65] [1974] 1 W.L.R. 1643.

(4) *Good faith*

An agent stands in a fiduciary position to his principal and like other persons in such a position (*e.g.* employees,[66] trustees,[67] company directors[68] and promoters[69]) he must act in good faith and he must not allow his interest to conflict with his duty. The law enforces this duty strictly, as can be seen from an examination of the rules concerning bribes. If an agent receives a bribe or secret commission from a third party, he is liable to prosecution under the Prevention of Corruption Acts 1889–1916, forfeits all rights to remuneration (which if paid is repayable[70]) and indemnity, and is liable to instant dismissal even if the principal has suffered no loss.[71] The principal can, within a reasonable time, repudiate any contract made by an agent who was bribed.[72] He can also recover the bribe from the agent in an action for money had and received, and in addition he has an action against the agent and the third party if he has suffered any loss. Such loss is usually presumed to be the amount of the bribe, and it is immaterial that the principal has already recovered the bribe from the agent.[73] The curious result is that the principal can make a profit out of the bribe by recovering more than his actual loss. In the words of Sir Frederick Pollock:

> "The morality of the law is, much to the benefit of the world, decidedly above the morality of ordinary mercantile life as regards the duties of agents."[74]

Secret profit. If an agent were to be allowed to make a secret profit from his agency, his interest would be likely to conflict with his duty. Hence, in the absence of full disclosure, he must account for such profit. In *Hippisley* v. *Knee Brothers*[75]:

---

[66] See, *e.g. Sanders* v. *Parry* [1967] 1 W.L.R. 753; [1967] 2 All E.R. 803.
[67] See Hanbury, *Modern Equity*, (9th ed.), pp. 366 *et seq.*
[68] See, *e.g. Prudential Assurance Co.* v. *Newman Industries (No. 2)* [1982] 2 W.L.R. 31; [1982] 1 All E.R. 354, C.A.
[69] See, *e.g. Gluckstein* v. *Barnes* [1900] A.C. 240.
[70] *Andrews* v. *Ramsay* [1903] 2 K.B. 635.
[71] *Cf. Boston Deep Sea Fishing and Ice Co.* v. *Ansell* (1889) 39 Ch.D. 339.
[72] *Shipway* v. *Broadwood* [1899] 1 Q.B. 369.
[73] *Salford Corpn.* v. *Lever* [1891] 1 Q.B. 168.
[74] (1891) 7 L.Q.R. 99.
[75] [1905] 1 K.B. 1.

A principal appointed an auctioneer to sell goods and agreed (*inter alia*) to pay the auctioneer's advertising and printing expenses. The auctioneer charged the full price of these items to his principal, without disclosing that he (the auctioneer) had received certain trade discounts. It was held that he must account for the difference.

Although in a sense the term "secret profit" is wide enough to include a bribe, it would seem preferable to confine the term to a profit made by the agent without the connivance of the other party to the transaction, and to use the term bribe where such connivance exists. The distinction is an important one because while an agent receiving a bribe can never claim commission[76] an agent who merely receives a secret profit can usually claim his commission if there was no fraud. The agent in *Hippisley* v. *Knee* genuinely thought that his conduct was not unlawful and it was held that although he had been guilty of breach of duty in making a secret profit (for which he had to account) the breach did not prevent him from claiming his commission. It has also been held that if an agent performs several acts, some of which are unlawful, he may still be entitled to commission if the doctrine of severance can be invoked. In *Nitedals Taendstikfabrik* v. *Bruster*[77]:

> P appointed A to sell P's goods. A did so, but in breach of contract he also sold goods for P's competitors. In an action by A for commission it was held that A's acts were severable, with the result that (1) A was entitled to commission on sales for P but (2) A had to account to P for all profit made on the other sales.

The question whether the liability to account extends to cases where the acts were totally unconnected with the agent's duties received an affirmative answer in the remarkable case of *Reading* v. *Attorney-General*.[78]

> A sergeant in the British Army in Egypt agreed to accompany lorries carrying illicit spirits. Since he was in uniform the vehicles were not searched. He was paid £20,000 for his trouble. It was held that as he had made this profit through the use of his position, he was bound to account to his employer, the Crown.

There are many other cases illustrating the agent's duty, and they all rest on the principle of conflicting interests. In the absence

---

[76] *Andrews* v. *Ramsay* [1903] 2 K.B. 635.
[77] [1906] 2 Ch. 671.
[78] [1951] A.C. 507; [1951] 1 All E.R. 617. The case also illustrates the point already mentioned that the fiduciary duties are not confined to agents.

of full disclosure an agent employed to sell cannot sell to himself[79] or act for the purchaser,[80] and conversely an agent employed to buy cannot without full disclosure buy from himself.[81] Finally, an agent cannot make use of confidential information for his own benefit as by compiling a list of his principal's customers.[82]

It will have been apparent from the above that an agent can sell his own property to his principal on making full disclosure, and if this occurs the relationship ceases to be that of principal and agent and becomes that of vendor and purchaser. Anything short of full disclosure is not enough. In *Regier* v. *Campbell-Stuart*[83]:

> An agent, A, instructed to give particulars of a house suitable for purchase by his principal, P, bought a house through a nominee for £2,000 and then "bought" it from the nominee for £4,500. He then informed P that he himself had bought for £4,500 a house suitable for P and P agreed to buy it from A for £5,000. On discovering the true facts, P sued A for fraud and for an account of his profit.
>
> A argued that on informing P that he owned the house, the agency relationship ceased and that the profit made by him was made as vendor and not as agent. This argument was rejected and it was held that A could not terminate the agency relationship without disclosing *all* the material facts (including the hidden £2,500 profit) and since he had not done this he was liable to account for the hidden profit.

Duration of duty. On principle the duty of good faith should not automatically terminate on the termination of the agency and there are early cases which suggest it does not do so.[84] More recently, however, Lord Evershed considered that the point was still an open one.[85] Much, of course, depends on the nature of the agency relationship and on the facts of the particular case. Thus an agent who acquires confidential information cannot obtain a right to use it by the simple process of terminating the agency.[86]

---

[79] *De Bussche* v. *Alt, supra.*
[80] *Fullwood* v. *Hurley* [1928] 1 K.B. 498.
[81] *Armstrong* v. *Jackson* [1917] 2 K.B. 822.
[82] *Lamb* v. *Evans* [1893] 1 Ch. 218.
[83] [1939] Ch. 766; [1939] 3 All E.R. 235.
[84] *e.g. Carter* v. *Palmer* (1842) 8 Cl. & Fin. 657.
[85] *Nordisk Insulinlaboratorium* v. *Gorgate Products, Ltd.* [1953] Ch. 430, 442; [1953] 1 All E.R. 986, 991, and see Powell, *op. cit.* p. 314.
[86] *Marshall (Thomas) (Exporters)* v. *Guinle* [1978] Ch. 227; 3 W.L.R. 116; [1978] 3 All E.R. 193.

(5) *Duty to account*

An agent is bound to pay over to his principal all sums received by him for the use of his principal.[87] He is bound to do this even if the transaction giving rise to the payment to the agent was illegal or void[88] but not if the contract of agency is itself illegal.[89] A number of other duties are supplementary to this basic one, and they include a duty to keep the principal's property distinct from that of the agent, a duty to keep an account of transactions entered into on behalf of the principal and a duty to produce this account to the principal or someone appointed by him.[90]

Quite apart from these general rules there are a number of statutes and regulations dealing with property received by certain types of agents and specifying the accounts to be kept. The Solicitors Act 1974, and the Solicitors Accounts Rules made thereunder are obvious examples.

(6) *Estoppel*

Just as an agent is bound to account to his principal, so also he is not allowed to deny the title of his principal to any property or money which is the subject-matter of the agency.[91] If he is faced with competing claims—one by his principal and one by a third party—he is estopped from setting up the title of the third party as a defence to an action brought by his principal[91] even if he defends the action by the authority of the third party.[92] There is, however, one exception to this rule and it arises where the agent is in possession of goods as bailee for his principal. In this case, he is entitled to set up the third party's title if he defends the action with the third party's authority—a rule common to all bailments.[93] In practice, of course, an agent may well be reluctant to deny the title of either claimant because he runs the risk of liability if that claimant happens to be the true owner. His best course in such a case is to take interpleader proceedings under Order 17 of the Rules of the Supreme Court.

---

[87] *Blaustein* v. *Maltz, Mitchell & Co.* [1937] 2 K.B. 142, 151; [1937] 1 All E.R. 497, at p. 502, *per* Slesser L.J.

[88] *De Mattos* v. *Benjamin* (1894) 63 L.J.Q.B. 248 (turf commission agent).

[89] *Harry Parker Ltd.* v. *Mason* [1940] 2 K.B. 590; [1940] 4 All E.R. 199.

[90] *Dadswell* v. *Jacobs* (1887) 34 Ch.D.278.

[91] *Dixon* v. *Hammond* (1819) 2 B. & Ald. 310, 313, *per* Abbott C.J.

[92] *Blaustein* v. *Maltz, Mitchell & Co.*, *supra*.

[93] See *e.g. Biddle* v. *Bond* (1865) 6 B. & S. 225, *post*, p. 415.

Remedies of principal for agent's breach of duty

These have been dealt with over the past few pages and can be briefly listed for purposes of convenience.

(1) If the agency is contractual the principal can sue the agent for damages for breach of contract.[94]

(2) If the agent has committed a tort against the principal (*e.g.* the tort of conversion in refusing to return the principal's property or conspiracy with a third party resulting in a bribe) the principal can sue him for damages in tort.

(3) If the agent has received a bribe, a secret profit or money for the principal, the principal can sue the agent for money had and received or for an account. The latter remedy is also available where the agent fails to keep proper accounts of his agency transactions.

(4) The principal can dismiss an agent guilty of a serious breach of duty and is not bound to pay him compensation.[95]

(5) Whether the principal can refuse to indemnify or to pay remuneration to an agent who has earned it depends on the terms of the contract and the nature of the agent's breach of duty (see *ante*, p. 19).

Rights of agent

(1) *Indemnity*

If an agent incurs liability or is forced to expend money in the performance of his agency, the general rule is that he is entitled to an indemnity from his principal unless the contract excludes this right. In *Adamson* v. *Jarvis.*[96]

> P instructed A, an auctioneer, to sell goods by auction. A did so. P did not in fact own the goods and A had to pay damages for conversion to the owner. *Held*, A was entitled to an indemnity from P.

---

[94] An injunction can also be obtained in appropriate cases (*e.g.* to restrain a breach of the duty of good faith).

[95] See *L. S. Harris* v. *Power Packing Services, Ltd.* [1970] 2 Lloyd's Rep. 65 (disclosure of confidential information).

[96] (1827) 4 Bing. 66.

The right to indemnity is subject to three qualifications. In the first place there is no right of indemnity unless the agent's acts are authorised or ratified by the principal. In *Barron* v. *Fitzgerald*[97]:

> An agent was employed to effect some policies of life insurance and to do so in his own name or in that of his principal. He insured in the names of himself and X and claimed indemnity. *Held*, he was not entitled to it.

Secondly, there can be no right of indemnity if the agent is in breach of his duties to the principal or if the loss in question is due to the agent's own default. In *Duncan* v. *Hill*[98]:

> A stockbroker bought goods for his principal who asked him to defer payment until the next account. The stockbroker became insolvent and consequently the stock was sold at a loss. It was held that the principal was not bound to indemnify the stockbroker in respect of this, since the cause of the loss was the agent's own insolvency.

The position might, however, have been different if it could have been shown that it was the principal's own default, *viz.*, his delay in paying for the shares, which caused the insolvency.[99]

The third qualification is the obvious one that no indemnity can generally be claimed in respect of an illegal act. The agent can, however, claim indemnity by showing that he was unaware of the illegality and that the act in question was not manifestly unlawful.[1] Similarly, no indemnity can be claimed where the subject-matter of the agency is a wagering contract,[2] a rule which has given rise to problems in connection with speculations on the Stock Exchange. It is clear that if a broker incurs a liability to accept shares from a jobber he will be entitled to an indemnity from his principal even though the principal intended to gamble and never intended to take up the shares.[3]

(2) *Remuneration*

Three problems arise:

---

[97] (1840) 6 Bing.(N.S.) 201.
[98] (1873) L.R. 8 Ex. 242.
[99] *Cf. Lacey* v. *Hill* (1874) L.R. 18 Eq. 182.
[1] *Adamson* v. *Jarvis, supra*, and see *Smith* v. *Lindo* (1858) 5 C.B.(N.S.) 587, and contrast *Gregory* v. *Ford* [1951] 1 All E.R. 121.
[2] Gaming Act 1892, s.1.
[3] *Thacker* v. *Hardy* (1878) 4 Q.B.D. 685.

(a) Is the agent entitled to remuneration?
(b) If so, how much?
(c) Has he earned it?

Entitlement. The agent can only claim remuneration if there is an express or implied agreement to pay it. Such an agreement will be implied wherever a person is employed to act as agent in circumstances which raise the presumption that he would, to the knowledge of his principal, have expected to be paid.[4] Obviously an agent employed in a normal commercial transaction will expect remuneration. Estate agents are now under a statutory duty to inform their clients as to the event upon which remuneration is payable and also the amount (or the method of calculation) of that remuneration. This must be done before the contract is made and a failure to do so can result in the agent being deprived of his commission.[5]

Quantum. The amount of remuneration depends on the express terms of the contract and on any relevant trade usage. In default of such guidance, a reasonable sum is payable.[6] Where, however, an agent agreed to accept £50 to cover expenses and in addition "a commission which I have agreed to leave to the discretion of the company" it was held that the court could not fix the rate of commission, for to do so would be to make a new contract for the parties.[7]

Has remuneration been earned? Frequently payment is by commission, and claims for commission, especially by estate agents, have occupied much of the time of the courts in recent years. Before examining the voluminous mass of case law, it is as well to remember that the courts are faced with two basic questions:

(a) Has the event happened on which the contract provided for payment of commission?

(b) Was the agent the effective cause of the happening of that event?

---

[4] *Way* v. *Latilla* [1937] 3 All E.R. 759.

[5] Estate Agents Act 1979, s.18.

[6] *Way* v. *Latilla* (*supra*) and see now Supply of Goods and Services Act 1982, s.15 *ante*, p. 5.

[7] *Obu* v. *Strauss* [1951] A.C. 243, P.C. See also *Gilbert and Partners* (*A Firm*) v. *Knight* [1968] 2 All E.R. 248, C.A.

The first of these questions will now be discussed with reference to the much litigated subject of estate agents' commission, but it should be remembered that the problem is a general one and is not confined to estate agents.

The event. When an owner of property appoints an agent to find a purchaser in return for a commission, his object is, of course, to sell the property and then to pay commission out of the proceeds of the sale. The agent's view of the matter is naturally somewhat different. The remarkable features of a commission contract are that on the one hand the agent is not bound to do anything at all, while on the other hand he may do a great deal, and expend much time, money and trouble without any reward whatsoever if no purchaser appears.[8] There is no room in such a case for a *quantum meruit* because this would be inconsistent with the express terms of the contract. Worst of all from the agent's point of view, the agent may succeed in introducing someone who is prepared to purchase, only to see the cup of commission dashed from his lips if for some reason the sale does not go through. Agents have accordingly sought to protect themselves against such hazards by appropriate words in the contract.

The modern law and practice has developed as a result of the leading case of *Luxor (Eastbourne), Ltd.* v. *Cooper*,[9] where the following facts arose:

> A company appointed A to find a purchaser for certain cinemas in return for £10,000 payable on completion. A introduced B who offered to buy, but the company decided not to proceed. Clearly no commission was payable since no completion had taken place. A therefore claimed damages for breach of an implied term that the company would not without just cause act so as to prevent him from earning his commission.

The House of Lords, overruling an earlier case,[10] held that no such term could be implied. Lord Wright tested the suggested implied term by reference to the normal course of business in these matters. He said:

---

[8] For an unusual case where the contract gave the agent a right to recover advertising expenses regardless of a sale see *Bernard Thorpe & Partners Ltd.* v. *Flannery* (1977) 244 E.G. 129, C.A.

[9] [1941] A.C. 108; [1941] 1 All E.R. 33. The case did not concern an estate agent.

[10] *Trollope (George)* v. *Martyn Brothers* [1934] 2 K.B. 436.

"It is well known that in the ordinary course a property owner intending to sell may put his property on the books of several estate agents with each of whom he makes a contract for payment of commission on a sale. If he effects a sale to the client introduced by one, is he to be liable in damages to all the others for preventing them from earning their commission? Common sense and ordinary business understanding clearly give a negative answer."[11]

Lord Russell of Killowen, however, pointed the way to the future when he said:

"If according to the true construction of the contract the event has happened on the happening of which the agent has acquired a vested right to the commission . . . then no act or omission by the principal or anyone else can deprive the agent of that right."[12]

This led agents to redraft their contracts so as to give a vested right to commission at an earlier date than completion.

Illustrations. It must be remembered that basically every case depends on the construction of the words used, and judges have deprecated attempts to put forward a decision on a particular contract as a rule of law.[13] Nevertheless the contracts of estate agents, many of which are standardised, are in practice drafted in the light of such decisions.

"*Introduce a purchaser.*" If commission is payable on introducing a purchaser, the agent must introduce someone who signs a legally binding contract[14] and who is ready, able and willing to complete.[15] Where the contract signed by the purchaser is avoided by him for misrepresentation it is not a "binding" contract and no commission is payable.[16]

"*Introduce a person ready, able and willing to purchase.*" Commission is not earned if the person introduced merely offers to buy "subject to contract" or "subject to survey."[17] He must enter into a legally binding contract, or at least make an unqualified firm

---

[11] [1941] A.C. 108, 139; [1941] 1 All E.R. 33, 54.
[12] [1941] A.C. 108, 129; [1941] 1 All E.R. 33, 46–47.
[13] See Lord Wright in the *Luxor* case, *ibid.* at p. 130 and p. 48.
[14] Not a mere agreement "subject to contract": *McCallum* v. *Hicks* [1950] 2 K.B. 271; [1950] 1 All E.R. 864.
[15] *Poole* v. *Clarke & Co.* [1945] 2 All E.R. 445.
[16] *Peter Long* v. *Burns* [1956] 1 W.L.R. 1083; [1956] 3 All E.R. 207.
[17] *Graham & Scott (Southgate) Ltd.* v. *Oxlade* [1950] 2 K.B. 275.

offer.[18] Further, he must be ready, able and willing to complete.[19]

In both the above cases the agent has a vested right to be paid commission on completion, once he has performed what the contract required him to do. If the principal subsequently does anything to deprive the agent of that right, he is liable in damages to the agent.[19] The agent's vested right is, however, liable to be divested if the sale goes off owing to the purchaser's default, because the purchaser is no longer "ready, able and willing" at the moment fixed for completion.[20]

"Introduce a purchaser who signs a legally binding contract." If these words are used, commission is earned when such a contract is signed, and there is no question of divesting if the purchaser fails to complete. The agent may, however, be liable to his principal for fraud or for negligence if he introduces a "man of straw."[21]

"Secure an offer." If these words are used, the agent has earned his commission, and cannot be divested of it, if a firm offer is made by a person introduced by him. An offer "subject to contract" is not enough.[22] The words "prepared to purchase" apparently have a similar meaning to the words "on securing an offer."[23]

"On finding a prospective purchaser." These words give the agent a vested and indefeasible right to commission when he introduces a person who has the question of buying the property bona fide in prospect or contemplation and is prepared to make a bona fide offer for it.[24]

"Introducing a person willing to sign a document capable of becoming a contract to purchase." This immensely wide clause—

---

[18] *Christie Owen and Davies Ltd.* v. *Rapacioli* [1974] Q.B. 781; [1974] 2 All E.R. 311, C.A.

[19] For a recent example see *Alpha Trading* v. *Dunnshaw-Patten* [1981] Q.B. 290, [1981] 2 W.L.R. 169; (1980) 124 S.J. 827, C.A. Failure by the principal to make title does not automatically give the agent a right to commission (*Blake* v. *Sohn* [1969] 1 W.L.R. 1412; [1969] 3 All E.R. 123).

[20] See note 15, above.

[21] *Midgley Estates Ltd.* v. *Hand* [1952] 2 Q.B. 432; [1952] 1 All E.R. 1394.

[22] *Bennett Walden & Co.* v. *Wood* [1950] W.N. 329; [1950] 2 All E.R. 134.

[23] *Ackroyd* v. *Hasan* [1960] 2 Q.B. 144; [1960] 2 All E.R. 254; discussed in (1960) 76 L.Q.R. 482; (1960) 23 M.L.R. 561. Contrast *Wilkinson* v. *Brown* [1966] 1 W.L.R. 194; [1966] 1 All E.R. 509.

[24] *Drewery & Drewery* v. *Ware-Lane* [1960] 1 W.L.R. 1204; [1960] 3 All E.R. 529.

easily the widest so far considered by the courts—has been held to be void for uncertainty.[25]

Conclusion. Most readers will agree that the law is unsatisfactory in two respects. In the first place, the obligations of agents and house owners should not be made to depend on narrow and technical distinctions between particular words. Secondly, the cases where commission is earned on securing an offer seem hard on the owners. An answer to the argument that the parties are free to agree on what they please was given by Denning L.J.[26] when he said:

> "Such a claim [*i.e.* commission on securing an offer] is, indeed, so contrary to the ordinary understanding on these matters, that I think that the agent who desires it should bring it specifically to the notice of the house owner and get his specific agreement to it."

Effective cause. Even if the event happens upon which remuneration is to be payable, the agent is only entitled to it if he was the effective cause of the happening of that event. Questions of causation are notoriously difficult to apply to particular cases, and all that can be done is to give some illustrations. An agent employed to find a tenant or purchaser was entitled to commission when he introduced someone who became a tenant, but not to further commission when that tenant subsequently purchased.[27] Similarly an agent who received commission for introducing a person who provided capital for the principal's business was not entitled to further commission when that person later entered into partnership with the principal and provided further capital.[28] An agent employed to sell property is entitled to commission if the relation of buyer and seller is really brought about by his act, even if the actual sale has not been effected by him,[29] but is not entitled if the result of his efforts is a compulsory purchase order.[30]

---

[25] *Jaques* v. *Lloyd George & Partners Ltd.* [1968] 1 W.L.R. 625; [1968] 2 All E.R. 187.

[26] *Dennis Reed Ltd.* v. *Goody* [1950] 2 K.B. 277 at p. 288. For a similar approach to the problem under German Law see Cohn, *Manual of German Law*, Vol. 1 at p. 97.

[27] *Toulmin* v. *Millar* (1887) 12 App.Cas. 746.

[28] *Tribe* v. *Taylor* (1876) 1 C.P.D. 505.

[29] See, *e.g. Green* v. *Bartlett* (1863) 14 C.B.(N.S.) 681; *Taplin* v. *Barrett* (1889) 6 T.L.R. 30; *Windle* v. *Brierley* [1952] 1 All E.R. 398.

[30] *Hodges* v. *Hackridge Park Residential Hotel* [1940] 1 K.B. 404; [1939] 4 All E.R. 347.

Restrictions on principal's freedom. It has just been seen that until the agent's right to remuneration becomes a vested right, there is no implied term that the principal will do nothing to prevent the agent earning his commission. An interesting problem arose in *Nelson (E.P.) Ltd.* v. *Rolfe*[31]:

> P appointed A and others to find a person "ready, able and willing" to purchase P's bungalow. A introduced T, who made a firm offer. P refused it because he had already granted an option (not legally binding) to a prospective purchaser introduced by another agent. It was conceded by counsel that no commission would be payable if, before the introduction of T, P had (1) sold the bungalow, or (2) agreed to sell it, or (3) revoked A's authority. As none of these events had taken place the Court of Appeal held that the introduction of T gave A a vested right to commission.

The agent's position is somewhat stronger if he is appointed "sole agent." Such wording gives the agent a right to damages if, the principal accepts an offer or the renewal of an offer by a purchaser introduced by other agents,[32] but it does not prevent the principal from selling the property himself.[33]

Discontinuance of business. A somewhat similar problem has arisen in the case of a commission agent employed by a principal who sells or discontinues his business and thereby deprives the agent of earning the commission. The principal incurs no liability for doing this unless he had agreed so to conduct his business as to enable the agent to earn his commission. The cases on this topic are not easy to reconcile. In *Rhodes* v. *Forwood*.[34]

> The contract provided that for seven years F would be R's agent at Liverpool for the sale of coal produced at R's colliery. R undertook not to appoint other agents, and F undertook not to sell coal for anyone else without R's consent. The contract provided for determination if the amount of coal supplied or sold in any year fell short of a specified figure. Three and a half years later R sold the colliery. F claimed damages for breach of contract, alleging an implied term that R would send coal to Liverpool for seven years. The House of Lords held that no such term could be implied.

---

[31] [1950] 1 K.B. 139; [1949] 2 All E.R. 584.

[32] *Hampton & Sons Ltd.* v. *George* [1939] 3 All E.R. 627.

[33] *Bentall, Horsley & Baldry* v. *Vicary* [1931] 1 K.B. 253, *ante*, p. 7; Gower, (1950) 13 M.L.R. 491, esp. 497.

[34] (1876) 1 App.Cas. 256; followed in *French Ltd.* v. *Leeston Shipping Co. Ltd.* [1922] A.C. 451.

On the other hand in *Turner* v. *Goldsmith*[35]:

> The contract began: "Whereas . . . the company agree to employ the said A. S. T. as their agent, canvasser and traveller . . . and in consideration of the premises the said A. S. T. hereby agrees with the said company that he . . . shall and will diligently, faithfully and honestly serve the said company." Then followed clauses providing that—(1) the contract was to run for five years, (2) the said A. S. T. would do his utmost to obtain orders for and sell goods *manufactured or sold* by the company, (3) payment was to be by commission. Before the five years had expired the company's premises were destroyed by fire and they decided to discontinue their business. The plaintiff (A. S. T.) claimed damages.
>
> The Court of Appeal held that (a) there was an agreement to employ the plaintiff for five years, (b) it had been broken, (c) since the agency was not confined to goods manufactured by the company the contract was not frustrated, (d) the plaintiff was entitled to damages.

The court found no difficulty in distinguishing *Rhodes* v. *Forwood* on the ground that "that case went on the ground that, there not being an express contract to employ the agent, such a contract could not be implied. In the present case we find an express contract to employ him."[36]

Not everyone would find the two cases so easy to distinguish and many would agree with Phillimore J. that the distinction between the two cases was "too fine."[37] His Lordship then proceeded to lay down his own test, namely, to distinguish between pure agency on the one hand and a contact where there was "service or subordination" on the other. He considered than an employer who discontinued his business during the contract term would be bound to pay compensation in the latter case but not in the former. This distinction, which has been followed in a more recent case,[38] seems reasonable enough in theory but far from easy to apply in practice, especially if it is remembered that in *Rhodes* v. *Forwood* itself, where no damages were payable, the agents were forbidden to sell for anyone else.

---

[35] [1891] 1 Q.B. 544.

[36] *Ibid.* at p. 549, *per* Lindly L.J. See also *Nolan* v. *Watson & Co.* (1965) 109 S.J. 288, C.A.

[37] *Northey* v. *Trevillion* (1902) 18 T.L.R. 648.

[38] *Bauman* v. *Hulton Press Ltd.* [1952] W.N. 556 (photographer sent by employer on world tours, payment by commission and salary, no right to accept other work, *held* contract not terminable without reasonable notice).

Enough has been said to indicate that no businessman should be content to rely on the subtle distinction drawn in these cases, and an express provision should always be included.

Post-termination commission. If the agency is terminated, the question arises whether the liability to pay commission is also terminated at the same time. What is the position of, say, a commercial traveller with regard to customers introduced by him who give repeat orders after his agency has been terminated? This once again depends on what the parties have agreed. In one case commission was payable on any business transacted with a customer introduced by the agent and it was held that commission was payable even after the agency had been terminated.[39] In another case where the principal agreed to pay commission "on all orders . . . and all repeats" these words were construed to mean orders and repeats given during the agency.[40] In a third case,[41] an agent was employed to obtain orders for advertising space, but was only entitled to be paid commission when orders obtained by him were accepted and executed by his employers. The Court of Appeal, by a majority, held that the agent was entitled to be paid commission (*inter alia*) in respect of orders for advertisements obtained by him before the termination of his agency, even though they were not published until after such termination. These cases show that it is difficult, if not impossible, to extract a general principle. In practice the contract frequently contains an express clause that commission is not payable on post-termination business, even though the negotiations took place during the agency.

If the court finds that post-termination commission is payable, what is the agent's remedy if the principal refuses to pay? The Court of Appeal has held that in most cases the appropriate remedy is an award of compensation but not a declaration nor an account. The assessment of compensation can be a difficult matter; it is based on the present value of repeat orders in the future,

---

[39] *British Bank for Foreign Trade* v. *Novinex* [1949] 1 K.B. 623; [1949] 1 All E.R. 155.

[40] *Crocker Horlock, Ltd.* v. *B. Lang & Co.* [1949] W.N. 97; [1949] 1 All E.R. 526.

[41] *Sellers* v. *London Counties Newspapers* [1951] 1 K.B. 784; [1951] 1 All E.R. 544.

bearing in mind the general uncertainties of trade and the fact that
the agent is normally free to canvass his old customers on behalf of
a new principal.[42]

Repayments. The question occasionally arises of an agent who is
paid a sum "on account of commission" or "to be set against
commission" and then fails to earn enough commission to cover
such payments. In the absence of express agreement, the payment
is only recoverable by the principal if the contract shows that this
was the intention of the parties. There are conflicting cases on the
application of this principle to particular facts.[43]

(3) *Lien*

A lien is a right to retain possession of the goods of another as
security for payment of a debt. The lien may be particular, *i.e.*
limited to moneys outstanding in the particular transaction, or
general, in which case it extends to a general balance of account.
The law does not favour general liens because they give one
creditor an undue advantage over the other creditors, but some
agents have a general lien by the usage of their profession or trade.
Among the more important of these are factors,[44] stockbrockers,[45]
bankers[46] and solicitors.[47]

A lien is generally founded on possession and an agent can
therefore only claim the lien if he has lawful possession of the
goods. In *Taylor* v. *Robinson*[48]:

> A bought goods from T on behalf of P. It was agreed that the
> goods should remain on the premises of T. Subsequently, and
> without the authority of P, A removed the goods on to his own

---

[42] *Roberts* v. *Elwells Engineers Ltd.* [1972] 2 Q.B. 586; [1972] 2 All E.R. 890.

[43] *Clayton Newbury Ltd.* v. *Findlay* [1953] 1 W.L.R. 1194; [1953] 2 All E.R. 826.
Rivoli Hats Ltd. v. *Gooch* [1953] 1 W.L.R. 1190; [1953] 2 All E.R. 823. *Bronester*
v. *Priddle* [1961] 1 W.L.R. 1294; [1961] 3 All E.R. 471, C.A. (Pearson L.J.
dissenting).

[44] *Baring* v. *Corrie* (1818) 2 B. & A. 137.

[45] *Hope* v. *Glendinning* [1911] A.C. 419.

[46] *London Chartered Bank of Australia* v. *White* (1879) 4 App.Cas. 413.

[47] *Cowell* v. *Simpson* (1809) 16 Ves. 275, and see s.73 of the Solicitors Act 1974.
The scope of the lien in litigation was recently considered in *Gamlen Chemical Co.*
(U.K.) v. *Rochem* [1980] 1 W.L.R. 614; [1980] 1 All E.R. 1049, C.A.

[48] (1818) 8 Taunt. 648. The possession must also have been acquired as agent:
Dixon v. *Stansfield* (1850) 10 C.B. 398. See also *Langley Beldon & Co.* v. *Morley*
[1965] 1 Lloyd's Rep. 297.

premises. P became bankrupt and A claimed a lien. *Held*, he was not entitled to it because the goods had at all times remained in the possession of P.

No lien can be claimed if the contract excludes it nor if the goods are delivered for a special purpose inconsistent with the alleged lien.[49]

The agent's lien is lost in a number of ways, of which perhaps the most common is that of voluntarily parting with possession. A change in the character of the possession may also have this result. In *Barrett* v. *Gough-Thomas*[50]:

> A solicitor acted for A and had possession of (and a lien over) the title deeds to A's land. A mortgaged the land to B and the deeds remained with the solicitor who acted for both parties. It was held by the Court of Appeal that as soon as the mortgage was executed the solicitor held the deeds as agent for B and this destroyed any lien which he (the solicitor) might have over the deeds as against A.

If, however, the goods are obtained from the agent by fraud the lien survives[51] and it also survives if at the time of transfer of possession the lien is expressly reserved.[52]

A lien is also lost if the agent waives it. One example of such waiver occurs where the agent takes a security which is inconsistent with the lien. In *Re Morris*[53]:

> A client who owed money to solicitors deposited some share certificates as security for disbursements in certain matters. *Held*, this was not inconsistent with the solicitors' lien over other papers in respect of outstanding profit costs.

Finally, a lien is lost if the principal pays or tenders the sum due.

Sub-agent.[54] A sub-agent has, of course, a lien against the agent and also against the principal where the principal expressly or impliedly authorises the agent to appoint a sub-agent,[55] as in the case of country solicitors appointing a town agent. It has been held

---

[49] *Brandao* v. *Barnett* (1846) 12 Cl. & Fin. 787.

[50] [1951] Ch. 242; [1951] 2 All E.R. 48.

[51] *North Western Bank* v. *Poynter, Son and Macdonalds* [1895] A.C. 56.

[52] *Caldwell* v. *Sumpters* [1972] Ch. 478; [1972] 1 All E.R. 567 (solicitor's lien).

[53] [1908] 1 K.B. 473. Kennedy L.J. and Lord Alverstone C.J. both emphasised the solicitor's duty to explain the legal position to his client if he desires to preserve his lien.

[54] See (1951) 18 *The Solicitor* 101.

[55] See, *e.g* *Fisher* v. *Smith* (1878) 4 App.Cas. 1.

that the lien of the town solicitor is general as against the country solicitor,[56] but merely particular (*i.e.* in respect of the costs and disbursements of the matter in question) as against the lay client.[57]

THE AGENT'S AUTHORITY

This section is concerned with what is undoubtedly the most important and the central feature of the agency relationship—the power of the agent to affect his principal's relations with third parties. In the vast majority of cases this power flows from what is known as authority—the principal authorises the agent to do an act and the agent does it. Sometimes, however, the power arises as the result of conduct of the principal which creates the appearance of authority although it does not in fact exist. If the principal induces a third party to believe that the agent has authority and the third party relies and acts upon this so-called "apparent authority,"[58] the principal will be estopped from denying the authority and will be liable accordingly.

It is convenient to divide this section into five parts:

(1) Express authority.
(2) Implied authority.
(3) Usual authority.
(4) Apparent authority.
(5) Ratification.

(1) *Express authority*

Express authority may be given by a principal to his agent orally or in writing, and in the latter case it may be under hand or under seal. If the authority is given under seal it is known as a power of attorney. The construction of a written authority is governed by the normal construction rules. In *Danby* v. *Coutts & Co.*[59]

> The operative part of a power of attorney was silent on the question of duration but the recitals stated that it was only to operate

---

[56] *Re Jones and Roberts* [1905] 2 Ch. 219.
[57] *Lawrence* v. *Fletcher* (1879) 12 Ch.D. 858.
[58] Professor Hanbury prefers "ostensible authority"; *Principles of Agency*, (2nd ed.), p. 110. The distinction, of course, is purely verbal.
[59] (1885) 29 Ch.D. 500.

while the donor was abroad. *Held*, the recital was effective, because it was not positively repugnant to anything in the operative part.

Where the instructions given to the agent are ambiguous, the agent will not be liable, and the principal will be bound, if the agent acts in accordance with a reasonable construction of his instructions, even if that construction is not the one intended by the principal.[60] It has,however, been suggested that if the agent is aware of the ambiguity he should ask for clarification if this is commercially practicable.[61]

(2) *Implied authority*

The scope of the agent's authority is not in practice confined to the performance of those acts which are specified in the express words of authority. In addition the agent has authority (known as implied authority) to do everything necessary for, or incidental to, the execution of his express authority. Thus, to take an obvious example, an agent employed to "sell" a house has implied authority to sign a memorandum of the contract under section 40 of the Law of Property Act 1925.[62] This implied authority is a real authority and it arises from the construction of the express authority. It is important to remember that the words of express authority must be examined in every case. In *Keen* v. *Mear*[63] an agent who was employed to sell was held to have no authority to sign a contract containing special conditions, but merely to sign an open contract. On the other hand in *Wragg* v. *Lovett*[64] the Court of Appeal, while agreeing that an authority to make a contract containing special conditions was not lightly to be inferred, emphasised that *Keen* v. *Mear* had not laid down any general rule, and then went on to hold that the agent in *Wragg* v. *Lovett* had implied authority to make a contract on any terms he thought fit.

(3) *Usual authority*

The usual authority of an agent links up neatly with his implied authority, because it forms part of the implied authority unless it is restricted. This topic can be conveniently subdivided into three

---

[60] *Weigall & Co.* v. *Runciman & Co.* (1916) 85 L.J.K.B. 1187.
[61] Powell, *op. cit.* at p. 40.
[62] *Rosenbaum* v. *Belson* [1900] 2 Ch. 276.
[63] [1920] 2 Ch. 574.
[64] [1948] 2 All E.R. 968.

parts—the general rules, particular cases and finally the problem of restricted usual authority.

General rules. Where an agent carries on a trade, profession or business as an agent (*e.g.* factor, auctioneer, stockbroker, estate agent) he has an implied authority to perform such acts as are usual in that trade, profession or business. What is usual will often be a matter for expert evidence. Another aspect of usual authority is that where an agent is employed to act in a particular place (*e.g.* the London Stock Exchange) where certain customs prevail, the agent has implied authority to act in accordance with such customs, provided that they are reasonable and lawful. A custom will not bind the principal if it is fundamentally inconsistent with the relationship of principal and agent[65] or if it brings the agent's interest into conflict with his duty. In *Blackburn* v. *Mason*[66]:

> P instructed a country broker, A, to sell shares for him and A sold them to T, a member of the London Stock Exchange. T alleged a custom of the Exchange whereby a member owing money to a country broker could set off debts owed by the broker personally in respect of previous transactions. *Held*, this custom was unreasonable and was not binding on P.

Particular cases

Auctioneers. Since an auctioneer is instructed to sell, he has authority to sign a memorandum of the contract of sale. There are three points which should be noted with regard to this authority. First, it is irrevocable.[67] Secondly, the auctioneer is deemed to be the agent of the purchaser as well as of the vendor for the purposes of such signature so that he can sign the memorandum of behalf of the purchaser. This signature must, however, take place at the time of the sale or so soon thereafter that it can reasonably be regarded as part of the transaction.[68] Thirdly, the power to sign extends to a licensed auctioneer employed by the auctioneers in

---

[65] *Robinson* v. *Mollett* (1875) L.R. 7 H.L. 802 (custom whereby agent acted as principal *vis-à-vis* his own principal held unreasonable).

[66] (1893) 68 L.T. 510. For further problems relating to Stock Exchange regulations and illegal customs see Powell, *op. cit.* pp. 44–46.

[67] *Phillips* v. *Butler* [1945] Ch. 358; [1945] 2 All E.R. 258.

[68] *Chaney* v. *Maclow* [1929] 1 Ch. 461; contrast *Bell* v. *Balls* [1897] 1 Ch. 663.

question,[69] but not (in the absence of express authority from the principal) to the auctioneer's clerk.[70]

It is also well established that one party to the contract cannot sign the memorandum as agent for the other, so that a seller cannot sign the memorandum as agent for the buyer and then use that signature as evidence in an action against the buyer for the price.[71] In the case of an auctioneer, however, it has been suggested that his power to sue the buyer for the price is based on his lien and special property and not on the contract, in which case his signing of the memorandum as agent for the buyer would not prevent him from suing the buyer for the price.[72]

Factors and brokers. A factor is "an agent entrusted with the possession of goods for the purpose of sale"[73] and has implied authority to sell in his own name.[74] He may also warrant the goods if it is customary to warrant the type of goods in question.[75] Where a factor pledges goods which he receives for sale, the position is that, as between principal and factor, the factor has committed a breach of duty but that as between principal and pledgee the pledgee may have acquired a good title under section 2 of the Factors Act 1889 (*post*, p. 148). A broker differs from a factor in that he has no authority to sell in his own name, and in addition he is generally not entrusted with possession of the principal's goods.[76] It has already been seen that a broker has authority to observe all reasonable and lawful customs prevailing at the place where he works (*ante*, p. 36). With the development of the doctrine of apparent authority and the passing of the Factors Act, the distinction between factors and brokers has lost much of its importance.

Estate agents.[77] An estate agent who is instructed to find a purchaser has no authority to sign a contract on behalf of the

---

[69] *Wilson* v. *Pike* [1949] 1 K.B. 176; [1948] 2 All E.R. 267.

[70] *Bell* v. *Balls, supra.*

[71] See, *e.g. Farebrother* v. *Simmons* (1822) 5 B. & A. 333.

[72] *Benton* v. *Campbell, Parker & Co.* [1925] 2 K.B. 410, cited with approval in *Wilson* v. *Pike, supra.*

[73] *Stevens* v. *Biller* (1883) 25 Ch.D. 31, 34, *per* Cotton L.J.

[74] *Ibid.*

[75] See, *e.g. Benmag Ltd.* v. *Barda* [1955] 2 Lloyd's Rep. 354.

[76] *Baring* v. *Corrie* (1818) 2 B. & A. 137.

[77] The conduct of "estate agency work" is now controlled by the Estate Agents Act 1979.

vendor,[78] but if he is employed to sell property he has such a right.[79] It has already been seen that in the latter case it is a question of construction as to whether he has power to make a contract containing special conditions or merely an open contract (*ante*, p. 35). On the thorny question of pre-contract deposits it has finally been held by the House of Lords in *Sorrell* v. *Finch*[80] that an estate agent has no usual authority to receive such a deposit. There may, of course, be particular cases of express, implied or apparent authority but in other cases a prospective purchaser who decides not to proceed can only sue the agent to recover the deposit; if the agent is unable to return it (whether through insolvency or otherwise) the prospective purchaser cannot claim it from the vendor. The receipt and control of such deposits is now regulated by statute.[81]

Del credere agents.[82] A *del credere* agent is usually a broker and like other brokers he has implied authority to make contracts on his principal's behalf. The special feature of this type of agency is that the agent agrees, in return for a commission, to guarantee payment of the price. Pickford J. put the matter thus:

> "Where there is an ascertained or certain sum due as a debt from the buyer to the seller and the buyer fails to pay that amount either through insolvency or something that makes it as impossible to recover it as in the case of insolvency the broker has to answer for that default by reason of his having received a *del credere* commission."[83]

Three points should be noted with regard to an agent of this type. In the first place, the contract does not have to be evidenced in writing as a guarantee under section 4 of the Statute of Frauds, because the guarantee merely forms part of a larger transaction.[84] Secondly, he merely guarantees payment and not the performance of other obligations, such as failure under an f.o.b. contract to

---

[78] Nor has he any authority to give a warranty that the premises can be used for any particular purpose (*Hill* v. *Harris* [1965] 2 Q.B. 601; [1965] 2 All E.R. 358).

[79] *Rosenbaum* v. *Belson, ante,* p. 35.

[80] *Sorrell* v. *Finch* [1977] A.C. 728, H.L.; [1976] 2 All E.R. 371.

[81] Estate Agents Act 1979, ss.14, 16 and 19 and Estate Agents (Accounts) Regulations 1981 No. 1520.

[82] See (1929) 45 L.Q.R. 221.

[83] *Gabriel (Thomas) and Sons* v. *Churchill & Sim* [1914] 3 K.B. 1272, 1278–1279.

[84] *Sutton* v. *Grey* [1894] 1 Q.B. 285.

name an effective ship.[85] Finally, he is a guarantor of the buyer's solvency and not a guarantor of the seller's duty to supply merchantable goods, so that if he (the agent), having accounted to the principal, then draws a bill of exchange on the buyer for the price, the buyer cannot escape liability to the agent on such a bill by alleging that he is entitled to reject the goods which the seller supplied and which formed the consideration for the bill.[86]

Confirming houses. A confirming house, which is important in some sections of the export trade, performs duties similar in some ways to those of a *del credere* agent. An English exporter might be unwilling to deal directly with a foreign importer whose reputation and financial standing might be unknown. The foreign importer may therefore instruct an English confirming house to assume personal responsibility for the price and also to make the necessary shipping arrangements. The liability of the confirming house is a primary one so that a purported cancellation of the order by the foreign buyer would not absolve the confirming house from its duty under the contract to pay for the goods if the sellers are ready and willing to deliver.[87] On payment of such price the confirming house can then claim to be indemnified by the foreign importer and can also claim the agreed commission.[88]

Restriction of usual authority.[89] If a principal restricts the usual authority of his agent, this restriction will not affect a third party who is unaware of it. This rule is similar to the principle of apparent authority (discussed below) and, sometimes, restricted usual authority is treated as apparent authority.[90] Nevertheless it is distinguishable because in the case of apparent authority both the fact of agency and the identity of the principal must be apparent to the third party, whereas in the case of restricted usual authority the principal may be liable even though the third party was

---

[85] *Gabriel (Thomas) & Sons* v. *Churchill & Sims, supra.*

[86] *Churchill & Sim* v. *Goddard* [1937] 1 K.B. 92; [1936] 1 All E.R. 675.

[87] *Rusholme & Bolton & Roberts Hadfield Ltd.* v. *Read & Co. (London) Ltd.* [1955] 1 W.L.R. 146; [1955] 1 All E.R. 180.

[88] *Anglo-African Shipping Co. of New York* v. *J. Mortner Ltd.* [1962] 1 Lloyd's Rep. 610, C.A.

[89] See Powell, *op. cit.* pp. 74–78; Stoljar, *The Law of Agency*, pp. 49–59; [1961] C.L.J. 239.

[90] See the judgments in *Edmunds* v. *Bushell, infra,* and the article in 4 C.L.J. 320 based on *Watteau* v. *Fenwick.*

unaware of his identity or existence. The following three cases
illustrate the problem and its solution.

> *Edmunds* v. *Bushell & Jones* (1865) L.R. 1 Q.B. 97. P appointed
> A as manager of P's business carried on under the name of A & Co.
> A was forbidden to accept bills of exchange, an act which was
> incidental to his duties. He did accept a bill in the name of A & Co.,
> and an indorsee sued P. *Held*, he was liable. *Per* Cockburn C.J. (at
> p. 99); "if a person employs another as agent in a character which
> involves a particular authority, he cannot be secret reservation divest
> him of that authority."
>
> *Daun* v. *Simmins* (1879) 41 L.T. 783. P was owner and licensee of
> a public-house and A was his manager. A had authority to buy spirits
> only from X but he bought them from T, who sued P. *Held*, P was
> not liable. It was a well known fact that a manager's authority in this
> particular field was restricted and T should therefore have inquired.
>
> *Watteau* v. *Fenwick* [1893] 1 Q.B. 346. P appointed A as manager
> of his public-house but the licence was taken out in A's name and
> accordingly A's name appeared over the door. A bought cigars from
> T on credit. Although this appears to have been considered part of
> the usual authority of a manager P had in fact forbidden A to do it.
> On discovering that P owned the public-house, T sued P. *Held*, P was
> liable.[91]

The reader may ask why P should be liable in a case like *Watteau*
v. *Fenwick* since he had not conferred any authority on A. T had
not been misled by any representation of authority by P because T
had never heard of P. T thought he was contracting with A and, of
course, he did have a right to sue A. Why then should he be
allowed to sue P? The answer is given in the following extract from
an American judgment which appears in Dr. Stoljar's book on
agency:

> "A man conducting an apparently prosperous and profitable
> business obtains credit thereby, and his creditors have a right to
> suppose that his profits go into his assets for their protection in case
> of a pinch or an unfavourable turn in the business. To allow an
> undisclosed principal to absorb the profits and then when the pinch
> comes to escape responsibility on the ground of orders to his agent
> not to buy on credit would be a plain fraud on the public."[92]

---

[91] This case has been much discussed and criticised. See Goodhart and Hamson,
(1932) 4 C.L.J. 320; Wright, 13 Can.B.R. 116; Montrose, 17 Can.B.R. 693, and the
standard works on partnership, *e.g.* Lindley, Pollock.

[92] *Hubbard* v. *Tenbrook* (1889) Pa. 291; Stoljar, pp. 88–89.

(4) Apparent authority[93]

The topic of restricted usual authority links up neatly with apparent authority because in both cases a principal is liable for acts done by his agent without real authority. The following judicial pronouncement forms a convenient starting point:

> "Ostensible or apparent authority which negatives the existence of actual authority is merely a form of estoppel and a party cannot call in aid an estoppel unless three ingredients are present (1) representation, (2) a reliance on that representation and (3) an alteration of his position resulting from such reliance."[94]

The representation must be made by the principal since it is the belief produced in the mind of the third party by the act of the principal which gives rise to his liability. It may be by words or conduct. An example of the former is a letter written by a principal to his bank informing the bank that the agent has authority to draw cheques, while examples of the latter include placing an agent in a position where he normally has authority to do a particular act[95] and a husband creating the appearance of authority by paying for goods supplied to his wife (*post*, p. 65). The representation may be intentional or negligent; thus if P mistakenly but negligently signed a document giving authority to A, it is thought that P would be liable to a third party who relied on that document.[96] Two further points should be noted with regard to the representation. The first is that it must convey the clear message that the agent has authority to do a particular act on the principal's behalf. In *Colonial Bank* v. *Cady*[97]:

> The deceased owned shares which could be transferred by using a transfer form on the back of the share certificates. On his death the executors, wishing to get themselves registered in the books of the company, signed the transfer in blank and sent it to a broker. The broker fraudulently pledged them with a bank who made no inquiry

---

[93] See (1959) 75 L.Q.R. 469, (1960) 76 L.Q.R. 115 and the judgment of Diplock L.J. in *Freeman & Lockyer* v. *Buckhurst Park Properties* [1964] 2 Q.B. 480; [1964] 1 All E.R. 630.

[94] Slade J. in *Rama Corpn.* v. *Proved Tin and General Investments Ltd.* [1952] 2 Q.B. 147, 149–150; [1952] 1 All E.R. 554, 556. For a recent example of holding-out see *Swiss Air Transport Co.* v. *Palmer* [1976] 2 LL.L.R. 604.

[95] *Lloyd* v. *Grace, Smith & Co.*, *post*, pp. 53–54.

[96] Consider *Saunders* v. *Anglia Building Society* [1971] A.C. 1004; [1970] 3 All E.R. 961, H.L.

[97] (1890) 15 App.Cas. 267.

as to his authority. On discovering the fraud the executors sued the bank to recover the shares. *Held*, they were entitled to recover the shares.

The House of Lords pointed out that the transfer was ambiguous, since it might mean that the executors were authorising the broker to sell or pledge, or merely that the executors wanted to get themselves registered. In view of the ambiguity the bank was under a duty to inquire and the document did not raise an estoppel. The clear inference is that if the transfer had been executed in blank by *the deceased* the position would have been different.

Secondly, the representation must be made to the person seeking to hold the principal liable. In *Farquharson Bros.* v. *King & Co.*, the facts of which appear on p. 145, the buyer's plea of apparent authority failed for the simple reason that the buyer had never even heard of the principal or of the clerk. The only holding out which took place was by the principal to the dock company, and if they had been sued by the plaintiffs the agent's apparent authority would have provided a good defence.

The third party's plea of apparent authority is based on the belief that the agent had authority and therefore it is clearly not available if the third party had actual or constructive notice or if the facts should have aroused suspicion. In *Reckitt* v. *Barnett, Pembroke and Slater Ltd.*[98]:

> A had a power of attorney drawn in wide terms which enabled him (*inter alia*) to draw cheques "without restriction" for the purposes of P's business. A bought a car from T for his own purposes and paid for it by drawing a cheque on P's account and signing it "P by his attorney A." P sued T for conversion or for money had and received. The House of Lords held that: (1) The circumstances, *viz.*, that A was paying his own debt with P's money should have put T on inquiry, and (2) accordingly T was liable.

This case also illustrates the further point that a principal can be held liable on the basis of apparent authority, even though the agent acted fraudulently and for his own benefit.[99]

---

[98] [1929] A.C. 176. See also *Overbrooke Estates Ltd.* v. *Glencombe Properties Ltd.* [1974] 1 W.L.R. 1335; [1974] 3 All E.R. 511 (statement in auction particulars that auctioneer had no authority to make representations).

[99] See also *Lloyd* v. *Grace, Smith & Co.* [1912] A.C. 716, *post*, pp. 53–54.

It should also be noted that where an agent is known to act under a written authority such as a power of attorney, the third party should examine the document, because the principal will not be liable for the agent's unauthorised act if the lack of authority was apparent from the document.[1] Further, there are certain statutory provisions which impose on the third party a duty of inquiry.[2]

Finally, it is not enough to show that a representation was made by P and believed by T. It must also be shown that the representation caused T to alter his position.[3]

(5) *Authority by ratification*

Having considered the cases of real authority (express, implied and usual) and the cases where the principal is liable despite the absence of authority (restricted usual authority and apparent authority) it remains to consider the problem of ratification. This occurs where an initially unauthorised act is subsequently affirmed (or ratified) by the principal and thereupon becomes binding. It is a case of real authority given after the event has taken place.[4]

Necessary conditions. For ratification to be effective a number of conditions must be satisfied.

(1) *Principal in existence.* The person on whose behalf the agent purported to act must have been in existence when the act was done. In *Kelner* v. *Baxter*[5]:

> B, C and D bought wine on behalf of a company which had not yet been formed. On formation the company purported to ratify the contract made by B, C and D. *Held*, it could not do so.

In a case of this type the further question arises as to whether the agent for the non-existent principal can be treated as a contracting party, so that he can sue and can be sued personally on the contract. Until January 1, 1973, the rules of English Law were

---

[1] *Jacobs* v. *Morris* [1902] 1 Ch. 816.
[2] *e.g.* s.25 of the Bills of Exchange Act 1882, *post*, p. 265.
[3] See, *e.g. Re Lewis* [1904] 2 Ch. 656.
[4] For a recent illustration see *Re Mawcon Ltd.* [1969] 1 W.L.R. 78; [1969] 1 All E.R. 188.
[5] (1866) L.R.2 C.P. 174.

somewhat anomalous[6] and out of line with the law of other EEC countries. Now, however, section 9(2) of the European Communities Act 1972 provides that:

> "Where a contract purports to be made by a company, or by a person as agent for a company, at a time when the company has not been formed, then subject to any agreement to the contrary the contract shall have effect as a contract entered into by the person purporting to act for the company or as agent for it, and he shall be personally liable on the contract accordingly."[7]

Although the section does not expressly say so, it seems clear from the context that the "agent" can sue on the contract as well as be liable on it.

(2) *Principal ascertainable.* The principal on whose behalf the agent purported to act must have been named or been ascertainable by the third party when the act was done; an undisclosed principal can never ratify. In the leading case of *Keighley, Maxsted & Co.* v. *Durant*.[8]

> An agent authorised to buy wheat at a certain price was unable to do so. He therefore *in his own name* bought wheat at a higher price. The principal purported to ratify but later failed to take delivery. The seller sued the principal. *Held*, by the House of Lords, (1) A's act was unauthorised, (2) since P's identity was not disclosed P could not ratify, (3) accordingly P was not liable.[9]

Lord Macnaghten's dictum that "civil obligations are not to be created by or founded upon undisclosed intentions"[10] is clearly too wide since it leaves out of account the case of the undisclosed principal. Nevertheless, as Lord Davey pointed out,[11] there is a clear difference between an undisclosed agency which can be proved to exist and an undisclosed intention in the mind of one of the contracting parties.

The position as it appears to the third party is all important, a fact which is well illustrated by *Re Tiedemann and Ledermann*

---

[6] See *Newborne* v. *Sensolid (Great Britain) Ltd.* [1954] 1 Q.B. 45; [1953] 1 All E.R. 708, and Jenkins Committee on Company Law, Cmnd. 1749, para. 44.

[7] For a recent illustration see *Phonogram* v. *Lane* (1981) 125 S.J. 527, C.A.

[8] [1901] A.C. 240. For criticism see Stoljar, *op. cit.* p. 199 *et seq.*

[9] The non-ratification rule here worked to the benefit of P. If P wanted to take the benefit of the contract he would have to take an assignment of it from A.

[10] *Ibid.* at p. 246.

[11] At p. 256.

Freres[12] where the facts were the exact converse of those in *Keighley, Maxsted* v. *Durant*:

> A sold wheat on behalf of P. The market rose and A then re-bought the wheat and sold it to T at a profit. This purchase and sale was made by A on his own behalf but in his dealing with T he used the name of P for financial reasons. Later P purported to ratify the contract. *Held*, he could do so.

(3) *Principal capable.* The principal must have had capacity to do the act at the time the agent did it. Thus if an act done on behalf of a company is void as being *ultra vires*, the company cannot ratify it even if before the purported ratification it has altered its memorandum of association to give itself power to do the act in question.[13] He must also have capacity at the time of the purported ratification.[14]

(4) *Act ratifiable.* The act in question must be one capable of ratification. Thus an *ultra vires* act done on behalf of a company cannot be ratified,[15] nor, it seems, can a forgery.[16] These acts are said to be void *ab initio*. Acts which are merely voidable, on the other hand, can be ratified. In *Danish Mercantile Co. Ltd.* v. *Beaumont*[17]:

> Legal proceedings were started in the name of a company. Later, the liquidator of the company purported to ratify the steps taken in the proceedings. *Held*, he could do so.

(5) *Principal aware of facts.* A principal cannot ratify unless he is aware of all material facts. In *Freeman* v. *Rosher*[18]:

> L let premises to T. When T fell into arrears with his rent, L instructed A to levy distress. A wrongly seized and sold a shed which T used as a workshop. He then accounted to L. T sued L in trespass. *Held*, as L was not aware of the wrongful seizure, his acceptance of the money did not amount to ratification of the tort. Consequently L was not liable.

---

[12] [1899] 2 Q.B. 66.

[13] The European Communities Act 1972 has greatly reduced the scope of *ultra vires*. See *post*, p. 71.

[14] *Grover & Grover Ltd.* v. *Matthews* [1910] 2 K.B. 401 (ratification of fire policy not possible after loss had occurred).

[15] *Ashbury Railway Carriage and Iron Co.* v. *Riche* (1875) L.R. 7 H.L. 653.

[16] *Brook* v. *Hook* (1871) L.R. 6 Exch. 89. Professor Hanbury suggests that a forgery can be adopted (*The Principles of Agency*, p. 102). See *post*, p. 264.

[17] [1951] Ch. 680; [1951] 1 All E.R. 925.

[18] (1849) 18 L.J.Q.B. 340.

On the other hand in *Hilbery* v. *Hatton*[19]:

> A bought a ship on behalf of P without authority. When he heard
> of this P said to A "You had better make a hulk of her." The ship
> belonged to T and A's purchase was unlawful. T sued P for
> conversion. *Held*, P was liable.

In the tort of conversion therefore it is sufficient if the ratifying
principal knows of the act of conversion. He need not know that
the act is a conversion. The position might well be different in the
case of a tort requiring a more positive mental element.

Effect of ratification. Although, as will be seen shortly, a valid
ratification is generally retrospective to the date of the original act,
this is subject to the important qualification that vested rights
cannot be divested. In *Bird* v. *Brown*[20]:

> P sent goods to T. Hearing of T's insolvency P's agent A gave an
> unauthorised notice to the carrier to stop the goods *in transitu*. T's
> trustee in bankruptcy seized the goods. Then P purported to ratify
> A's notice. *Held*, too late.

In *Dibbins* v. *Dibbins*[21]:

> The principal, a partner, had an option to purchase the share of his
> fellow partner, exercisable within three months of the latter's death.
> The other partner died, and within three months A purported to
> exercise the option on behalf of the principal. This was not
> authorised but at a date outside the three months period P purported
> to ratify. *Held*, he could not do so, since by then other persons had
> acquired a vested right in the property.

Subject to this, however, ratification is retrospective and this
may have surprising results. In *Bolton Partners* v. *Lambert*[22]:

> A acting on behalf of P but without authority agreed to sell land to
> T. T purported to repudiate. P then ratified. The Court of Appeal
> held that the ratification dated back to the time of the original
> contract so that T's withdrawal was inoperative.

The decision has had a mixed reception, because between A's
act and P's ratification T is stranded in a sort of no-man's land—he
has no contract with P and yet he cannot withdraw from it. In

---

[19] (1864) 2 H. & C. 822.
[20] (1850) 4 Ex. 486.
[21] [1896] 2 Ch. 348.
[22] (1889) 41 Ch.D. 295, 302.

Fleming v. *Bank of New Zealand*[23] Lord Lindley (who as Lindley L.J. had been a party to the decision) must have had second thoughts because he said:

> "The decision . . . presents difficulties and their Lordships reserve the liberty to reconsider it if on some further occasion it should become necessary to do so."

Viewed practically the decision is not likely to lead to great hardship and injustice. If the contract is favourable to T he will not be anxious to repudiate. If it is unfavourable and T wishes to get out of it, then if P does not ratify he can do so, while if P does ratify T should surely be bound by the very contract which he intended to, and did in fact, make. There are, moreover, two exceptions to the rule in *Bolton* v. *Lambert*. The first is that vested rights cannot be divested (see above). The second is the rule in *Watson* v. *Davies*[24] that if an offer is accepted "subject to ratification" the offeror can withdraw before ratification and if he does so there is nothing left to ratify.

RELATIONSHIP BETWEEN PRINCIPAL AND THIRD PARTY

Having considered the powers of an agent to alter his principal's legal relations with third parties, we now consider exactly what are the principal's rights and liabilities *vis-à-vis* the third party.

Contracts

The position with regard to contracts made by the agent on the principal's behalf depends on whether the principal was named, disclosed or undisclosed.

Principal named

If an agent makes a contract on behalf of a named principal, the only contracting parties are the principal and the third party, and

---

[23] [1900] A.C. 577, 587, P.C. See also *Warehousing and Forwarding Co. of East Africa Ltd.* v. *Jafferali & Sons Ltd.* [1964] A.C. 1 and articles 83 *Law Notes* 47 and 29 Yale L.J. 859.

[24] [1931] 1 Ch. 455. Where the third party knows that the agent has no authority the courts will imply a term that the acceptance is subject to ratification, *Warehousing and Forwarding Co. of East Africa* v. *Jafferali, supra.*

the agent, his work done, usually drops out.[25] The principal will be liable if the agent had authority (express, implied, usual or apparent) or if he ratifies the agent's act. Conversely, the principal can sue the third party where the agent had actual authority (precedent or subsequent). There appear to be no reported cases where a principal who had clothed his agent with apparent authority or with a restricted usual authority has sought to sue a third party who has acted upon it. Since these rules are designed for the protection of the third party there seems no reason why the principal should be allowed to sue.

To the rule that the principal can sue and can be sued there is one exception. By an old and highly technical rule, a principal cannot sue on a deed made by his agent unless he (the principal) is described in the deed as a party and the deed is executed in his name.[26] There are, however, two modifications. The first is equitable and is to the effect that if the agent entered into the contract as trustee for his principal, the principal can sue the third party by joining the agent as a party to the action—as co-plaintiff if he consents and co-defendant if he does not.[27] The second is statutory and relates to an agent executing a deed in pursuance of a power of attorney. Section 7 of the Powers of Attorney Act 1971 provides that a donee of a power of attorney (*viz.* the agent) may sign or seal any instrument with the authority of the donor (*viz.* the principal) and that such execution is to be as effective as if the donee had executed in the name of the donor.[28]

Principal disclosed

An agent may inform the third party that he is acting on behalf of a principal but he may not disclose the principal's identity. The principal is then said to be unnamed. The legal rights and liabilities of principal and third party are the same as if the principal was named. The difference concerns the position of the agent (*post*, p. 57).

---

[25] Formerly an agent contracting on behalf of a foreign principal was presumed to contract personally, unless a contrary intention appeared (*Rusholme & Bolton & Roberts Hadfield Ltd.* v. *Read* [1955] 1 W.L.R. 146, 150; [1955] 1 All E.R. 180, 183). It is clear, however, that this presumption no longer applies (*Teheran-Europe Co.* v. *S.T. Belton (Tractors), Ltd.* [1968] 2 Q.B. 545; [1968] 2 All E.R. 886, C.A.).

[26] See, *e.g. Re International Contract Co.* (1871) L.R. 6 Ch. 525.

[27] *Harmer* v. *Armstrong* [1934] Ch. 65; [1933] All E.R. Rep. 778.

[28] See further Powell, *op. cit.* 178–179; Fridman, *op. cit.* 192–193.

Principal undisclosed[29]

Where an agent while acting within his express, implied or usual authority makes a contract on behalf of a principal but does not disclose the existence of the principal to the third party, the principal is said to be undisclosed, and the general rule is that he can sue and can be sued on the contract which the agent made with the third party. This doctrine has been described as anomalous and contrary to principle by some authorities,[30] while others have praised the doctrine on practical grounds.[31] In *Keighley, Maxsted* v. *Durant* Lord Lindley, after describing the doctrine as anomalous, went on thus:

> "But middlemen, through whom contracts are made, are common and useful in business transactions and in the great mass of contracts it is a matter of indifference to either party whether there is an undisclosed principal or not. If he exists it is, to say the least, extremely convenient that he should be able to sue and be sued as a principal and he is only allowed to do so upon terms which exclude injustice."[32]

There are three exceptional cases where the undisclosed principal cannot sue, or be sued by, the third party. The first is where the contract between the agent and the third party expressly provides that the agent is the sole principal.[33] The second is where the terms of the contract are inconsistent with agency. In *Humble* v. *Hunter*[34]:

> An agent signed a charterparty in his own name and described himself as "owner" of the ship. *Held*, his undisclosed principal could not sue.

Opinions have differed as to the *ratio decidendi*. In *Formby Bros.* v. *Formby* (where it was followed) and in *Killick* v. *Price (W.R.) & Co.*[35] (where it was doubted) it was said to turn on the rule that parol evidence cannot vary the terms of a written contract. On the other hand, in *Drughorn (F.), Ltd.* v. *Rederiak-*

---

[29] For recent surveys see (1965) 28 M.L.R. 167 and [1967] J.B.L. 122.

[30] See, *e.g.* Pollock, (1887) 3 L.Q.R. 359.

[31] See, *e.g.* (1953) 16 M.L.R. 299.

[32] [1901] A.C. 240, 261–262.

[33] *U.K. Mutual Steamship Assurance Association* v. *Nevill* (1887) 19 Q.B.D. 110.

[34] (1848) 12 Q.B. 310, followed in *Formby Bros.* v. *Formby* (1910) 102 L.T. 116 ("proprietor").

[35] (1896) 12 T.L.R. 263.

tiebolaget Trans-Atlantic[36] it was said to turn on the fact that the agent had impliedly contracted that he was the sole principal. The case was distinguished on the facts in the *Drughorn* case where the agent contracted as "charterer," and in *Danziger* v. *Thompson*[37] where he contracted as "tenant." In both these cases the court allowed the undisclosed principal in.

The third case where an undisclosed principal cannot sue is where the identity of the principal is material to the third party. This is clearly what Lord Lindley had in mind when he spoke of injustice. One such case is where the contract made between the agent and the third party is too personal to permit an undisclosed principal to intervene. Contracts for personal service are obvious examples. Another illustration is afforded by the case of *Said* v. *Butt*[38]:

> P wanted a ticket for the first night of a new play. Owing to personal differences with the managing director of the company who owned the theatre he was unable to get one. He therefore persuaded a friend, A, to buy a ticket for him. A bought a ticket in his own name and gave it to P. On arrival at the theatre P was not allowed to occupy his seat, and he left and brought an action. McCardie J. held that: (1) the personal identity of the ticket holder was of great importance to the theatre; (2) since the ticket holder was a person with whom the theatre would not have contracted directly, he could not contract with them indirectly by acting through an agent.

If, however, the contract is not of a personal nature, the undisclosed principal can sue even though the third party would not have dealt with him directly, unless[39] the agent misrepresented the existence or identity of his principal.[40]

Miscellaneous contractual matters

Settlement with agent. Where a principal who owes a debt to the third party pays his own agent, the question arises whether the principal can be made to pay again if the agent fails to account to the third party. On principle the answer is clearly yes, because a

---

[36] [1919] A.C. 203.
[37] [1944] K.B. 654; [1944] 2 All E.R. 151.
[38] [1920] 3 K.B. 497; and see 4 C.L.J. 320.
[39] *Dyster* v. *Randall & Sons* [1926] Ch. 932 (sale of land).
[40] *Archer* v. *Stone* (1898) 78 L.T. 34.

debtor must seek out his creditor and pay him.[41] Are there any exceptions to this fundamental rule? In *Thomson* v. *Davenport*[42] there is a wide dictum that the principal should not have to pay twice if this would be unjust. Normally, of course, justice requires that the third party should be paid and accordingly the injustice to the principal was confined in *Heald* v. *Kenworthy* to cases where the third party had by his own conduct led the principal to settle with the agent, *e.g.* by leading the principal to believe that he (the third party) had already been paid.[43] However, in *Armstrong* v. *Stokes*[44] the Court of Queen's Bench created a further exception to the general rule by holding that where an undisclosed principal paid the agent before the third party discovered his existence, the principal could not be made to pay again. In a judgment delivered by Blackburn J. (who clearly regretted the whole doctrine of undisclosed principal) the court was prepared to push the "injustice" exception to the general rule further than the court in *Heald* v. *Kenworthy*. However, in *Irvine* v. *Watson*[45] the authority of *Heald* v. *Kenworthy* was affirmed and *Armstrong* v. *Stokes* was severely criticised, and must therefore be regarded as doubtful.

In the converse case a third party cannot in general escape liability for a debt which he owes to the principal merely by paying the agent, unless the agent has actual, usual or apparent authority to receive payment.

Where the agency is undisclosed it would seem on principle that the third party can safely pay the agent, but in *Drakeford* v. *Piercy*[46] it was held that such payment was only good as against the principal if the agent had authority to act in his own name.

Set-off. Can a third party dealing with an agent set off a debt due from the agent to the third party against a debt due from the third party to the principal? The general rule is obvious enough—where the principal is disclosed the third party must pay the principal (or his agent) in full irrespective of any debt which the agent owes to the third party. Set-off, therefore, is not allowed, unless autho-

---

[41] *Heald* v. *Kenworthy* (1855) 10 Ex. 739.
[42] (1829) 9 B. & C. 78.
[43] Or by the third party taking a security from the agent: *Smith* v. *Anderson* (1849) 7 C.B. 21, cited in *Heald* v. *Kenworthy, supra.*
[44] (1872) L.R. 7 Q.B. 598.
[45] (1880) 5 Q.B.D. 414, C.A.
[46] (1866) 7 B. & S. 515.

rised by the principal.[47] If, however, the principal is undisclosed and the debt owed by the agent arises before the third party discovers that the agent is not the principal, the position is different. When T contracted with A believing him to be the sole principal, T could set off A's debt in an action brought by A against T. It would clearly be unjust to let the sudden and unexpected appearance of the undisclosed principal destroy T's right of set-off. P must take the contract between A and T as he finds it and is therefore bound by T's right of set-off.[48] There is, however, another possible source of injustice and that is where P requires A to contract expressly on behalf of P (so that T cannot set off A's debt) but A in fact contracts in his own name (so that P may find himself saddled with a set-off claim by T). To avoid this possible hardship, some cases suggest that an undisclosed principal will only be bound by a third party's set-off where the agent had actual or apparent authority to contract as principal. Thus in *Cooke* v. *Eshelby*[49]:

> A, who was acting for an undisclosed principal P, sold cotton to T. P sued T, who claimed to set off a debt due from A to T on general account. In answer to interrogatories T admitted that he dealt with A as brokers without knowing whether they were acting for principals or for themselves. The House of Lords held that the plea of set-off failed.

Lord Watson said (at p. 278): " . . . it is not enough to show that the agent sold in his own name. It must be shown that he sold the goods as his own . . . and it must also be shown that the agent was enabled to appear as the real contracting party by the conduct, or by the authority, express or implied, of the principal."

Third Party's Election. The general rule, as already stated, is that where an agent brings his principal into contractual relationship with a third party, the agent drops out. It will be seen in the next section of this chapter that there are some exceptional cases where the agent does not in fact drop out. One such case is where he signs the contract personally as a contracting party,[50]

---

[47] As in *Barker* v. *Greenwood* (1837) 2 Y. & C. Ex. 414.
[48] See, *e.g. George* v. *Claggett* (1797) 7 Term Rep. 359.
[49] (1887) 12 App.Cas. 271, H.L.
[50] *Priestley* v. *Fernie* (1865) 3 H. & C. 977.

while another is where the principal is undisclosed. In the latter case the third party believes that he has a contract with the agent, and his right to sue the agent on that contract cannot be destroyed by the sudden emergence of the undisclosed principal. In these exceptional cases the third party has a choice whether to sue the principal or the agent. Once he has made an unequivocal election to look to the agent, the principal is discharged from liability to the third party. The clearest example of unequivocal election is where the third party sues the agent to judgment. This extinguishes the principal's liability, even if the judgment is unsatisfied, since the cause of action is merged in the judgment.[51] On the other hand, it has been held that demanding payment from the agent and threatening him with proceedings was not necessarily an unequivocal choice,[52] nor proving in the agent's bankruptcy.[53] The question of whether such choice has been made is one of fact.[54]

In the case of an undisclosed principal it is obvious that no effective election can take place until the third party knows that a right to elect exists, *i.e.* discovers the existence of the principal.[55]

Torts

There is very little case law on the liability of a principal for his agent's tort. The reason is that an agent's main tasks are to make contracts and to dispose of property, and in these transactions the claims against the principal are likely to be contractual and proprietary rather than tortious.[56] Recently, however, the courts have started to demolish the rigid contract-tort classification and in many cases there is now substantial overlap between them.[57]

One of the few agency-type torts which have occupied the attention of the courts has been deceit. The general rule is that where an agent, while acting within his actual, usual or apparent authority, commits the tort of deceit the principal (as well as the

---

[51] *Kendall* v. *Hamilton* (1879) 4 App.Cas. 504.

[52] *Calder* v. *Dobell* (1871) L.R. 6 C.P. 486.

[53] *Addison* v. *Gandassequi* (1812) 4 Taunt. 574.

[54] *Calder* v. *Dobell, supra* and see *Clarkson Booker* v. *Andjel* [1964] 2 Q.B. 775; [1964] 3 All E.R. 260.

[55] *Thomson* v. *Davenport* (1829) 9 B. & C. 78.

[56] For a recent case on liability of the negligence of an agent see *Nelson* v. *Raphael* [1979] R.T.R. 437, C.A.

[57] See, *e.g. Midland Bank Trust Co.* v. *Hett Stubbs & Kemp* [1978] Ch. 384; [1978] 3 All E.R. 571.

agent) will be liable, whether the agent acted for the principal's benefit or for his own.[58] What is the position, however, where an agent makes a statement believing it to be true while his principal (or a fellow agent) knows that the statement is untrue? After much judicial conflict[59] the following principles now appear firmly established:

(1) If the principal, knowing that the statement is going to be made, deliberately keeps the agent ignorant of the true facts, the principal is liable for fraud.[60]

(2) If an agent (or the principal himself) makes the statement as the result of information supplied by another agent who knows that it is untrue and that it is going to be passed on to a third party the principal is liable for fraud.[61]

(3) If the agent makes a statement believing it to be true, and neither the principal nor any other agent knowing the facts knows that the statement is being made, neither the principal nor the agent can be guilty of fraud[62] but a learned writer has pointed out that the position is not finally settled.[62a]

Motor-car cases

A group of cases show that if one person owns a motor-vehicle and another person drives it for the owner's purposes under a delegation of a task or duty, the owner is liable for the driver's negligence.[63] In these cases the driver is sometimes described as

---

[58] *Lloyd* v. *Grace Smith* [1912] A.C. 716 (managing clerk defrauds client). The position is different if the agent exceeds his authority (see the recent negligence case of *Kooragang Investment Pty.* v. *Richardson and Wrench* [1981] 3 W.L.R. 493 P.C.

[59] For a full review of the earlier authorities see the judgment of Devlin J. (as he then was) in *Armstrong* v. *Strain* [1951] 1 T.L.R. 856. The Court of Appeal subsequently took a different view of the *London Freehold and Leasehold* case.

[60] *Ludgater* v. *Love* (1881) 44 L.T. 694.

[61] *Pearson* v. *Dublin Corpn.* [1907] A.C. 351; *London County Freehold & Leasehold Properties Ltd.* v. *Berkeley Property & Investment Co. Ltd.* [1936] 2 All E.R. 1039, as explained in *Armstrong* v. *Strain, infra.*

[62] *Cornfoot* v. *Fowke* (1840) 6 M. & W. 358; *Armstrong* v. *Strain* [1952] 1 K.B. 232; [1952] 1 All E.R. 139, C.A.

[62a] *Street on Torts* (7th ed.), pp. 292–293 and cases there cited.

[63] See now *Morgans* v. *Launchbury* [1973] A.C. 127; [1972] 2 All E.R. 606, H.L. and cases there cited and *Norwood* v. *Nevan* [1981] R.T.R. 457, C.A.

the owner's "agent." These cases can equally well be explained without reference to the law of agency and the reader is referred to the standard works on tort for further discussion.

Property

A principal will be bound by dispositions of his property made by his agent if the agent had express, implied,[64] usual or apparent authority to make the disposition. In the vast majority of cases where a dispute arises the agent has acted fraudulently and for his own benefit, but this does not affect the position as between the principal and the third party.

Many of the cases on the disposition of property by agents involve the sale of goods and the various problems which arise both at common law and under the Factors Act 1889 will be discussed when dealing with that subject (see *post*, p. 147). It will be seen there that the mere delivery of possession of goods by the owner to someone else will not, as a general rule, give rise to any estoppel. The delivery of title deeds or a blank transfer of shares may, however, operate as an estoppel, especially if the agent receiving them has authority to deal with them. Three cases illustrate the principle of estoppel at work:

Brocklesby v. *Temperance Building Society* [1895] A.C. 173. P owned land the deeds of which were deposited with the X bank. Wishing to borrow money P gave A (his son) documents which enabled him to obtain the deeds from that bank and told him to pledge the deeds with Y bank in return for a loan. Having obtained the deeds A deposited them with the Z bank as security for a larger loan, keeping the excess for himself. Later, by means of forged documents, A purported to "sell" the land to a building society who paid off the debt to the Z bank. P sued the building society to recover the land. The society claimed that he must pay them the sum which they had paid to the Z bank. *Held*, (1) P was estopped by his conduct from denying to the Z bank that A had authority to raise the money. (2) Consequently the Z bank had had a valid claim against P. (3) The building society could be regarded as an assignee of this claim and accordingly (4) P was bound to pay this sum to the building society.

Rimmer v. *Webster* [1902] 2 Ch. 163. An agent fraudulently induced his principal to execute transfers of certain bonds into the

---

[64] See *Lloyd and Scottish Finance Co.* v. *Williamson* [1965] 1 W.L.R. 404; [1965] 1 All E.R. 641.

agent's name, the intention being that the agent should deal with the bonds. The agent (using the transfers as proof of title) pledged them with a third party. *Held*, the principal was bound.

Spiro v. *Lintern* [1973] 1 W.L.R. 1002; [1973] 3 All E.R. 319. H asked his wife to instruct agents to find a buyer for his house. The agents introduced P and, acting on the instructions of the wife, they signed a contract of sale and handed it to P. The court found that H had not authorised this sale but when he discovered what had happened he took no steps and allowed P to alter his position. When he later sought to argue that the contract had been made without authority the Court of Appeal held that he was estopped by his conduct from doing so.

As Mr. Fridman correctly points out the matter will always turn on the apparent authority of the agent in each particular case.[65] A solicitor receiving the title deeds of land for safe custody could not, it is submitted, bind his principal by pledging them. Again if the form of blank transfer is such as to put the third party on inquiry it has already been seen that no question of estoppel will arise.[66]

RELATIONSHIP BETWEEN AGENT AND THIRD PARTY

Contracts

The general rule, as already stated, is that the agent can neither sue, nor can he be sued, on a contract concluded between his principal and a third party.[67] The exceptions to this rule will now be considered and it will be convenient to consider his liabilities first.

Liability on the contract

If the agent is in fact the principal he is clearly liable. Thus in *Schmalz* v. *Avery*[68] a person who was described in a charterparty as "agent for the freighters" was held personally liable on proof that he himself was the freighter. Such a result was clearly necessary to give business efficacy to the contract. For the same reason the courts are ready to hold an agent liable if he contracts

---

[65] Fridman, *op. cit.* pp. 98–99.

[66] *Colonial Bank* v. *Cady, ante*, p. 41.

[67] *Paquin Ltd.* v. *Beauclerk* [1906] A.C. 148. The House of Lords was evenly divided on the facts.

[68] (1851) 16 Q.B. 655.

on behalf of a non-existing principal if on a true construction of the contract it is possible to reach this result.[69]

An agent is also liable if he signs the contract in such a way as to assume personal responsibility. The obvious example is the contract made on behalf of an undisclosed principal. In the case of such a contract evidence is generally (but not universally[70]) admissible to prove that another person, *viz.*, the undisclosed principal, is liable as well as the agent.[71] If, however, an agent is sued on a written contract in which he appears as a contracting party he cannot escape liability by proving that he was merely acting as agent for someone else.[72] This is a further illustration of the basic rule that parol evidence is inadmissible to vary the terms of a written contract.

Even if the fact of agency is disclosed the agent may still be liable as a contracting party if this is the correct inference to be drawn. In *Hall* v. *Ashurst*[73]:

> A solicitor acting in a bankruptcy case agreed "on behalf of the London creditors" to be responsible for certain expenses. *Held*, he was personally liable.

The court was influenced by the fact that the principals were a large body of persons. If the contract had been made on behalf of a specific individual the result might have been different.[74]

The matter of the agent's personal liability is essentially a question of construction of the contract, having regard to the body of the contract as well as to the signature.[75] Thus in *Gadd* v. *Houghton*[76] a sales note ran:

---

[69] *Kelner* v. *Baxter* (1866) L.R. 2 C.P. 174 and see now s.9(2) of the European Communities Act 1972, *ante*, p. 44.

[70] *Ante*, pp. 49–50.

[71] See, *e.g. Basma* v. *Weeks* [1950] A.C. 441; [1950] 2 All E.R. 146.

[72] *Higgins* v. *Senior* (1841) 8 M. & W. 834. See also *Sika Contracts* v. *Gill, The Times* April 27, 1978—a signature by agent followed by his professional qualification is not of itself sufficient to avoid personal liability.

[73] (1833) 1 Cr. & M. 714.

[74] See, *e.g. Wakefield* v. *Duckworth & Co.* [1915] 1 K.B. 218 (solicitor not personally liable for photographs ordered on behalf of client).

[75] See *per* Lindley L.J. in *Royal Albert Hall* v. *Winchelsea* (1891) 7 T.L.R. 362 at p. 364.

[76] (1876) 1 Ex.D. 357. See also *Universal Steam Navigation Co.* v. *McKelvie* [1923] A.C. 492; and *The Swan* [1968] 1 Lloyd's Rep. 5, discussed in (1969) 85 L.Q.R. 92.

"We have this day sold you on behalf of M 2,000 cases of Valencia
oranges, (Signed) H."
It was held that H were not personally liable.

If a custom imposes personal liability on an agent, proof of such
custom is admissible provided that it does not contradict the
express words of the written contract. Two cases illustrate this
point. The first is *Hutchinson* v. *Tatham*[77]:

> The agents signed "as agents for principals." There was a custom
> that the agents were personally liable unless the name of the
> principal was forthcoming within a reasonable time. It was held that
> evidence of this custom was admissible.

The second is *Barrow & Bros.* v. *Dyster, Nalder & Co.*[78]:

> Brokers agreed (*inter alia*) to arbitrate in disputes between their
> principal and a third party. Evidence of a custom that the brokers
> were to be personally liable was not admitted, because it would
> contradict the express terms of the contract.

The final case where an agent is personally liable is where he
contracts in a dual capacity. Such cases are likely to be rare but an
important modern example occurs where a dealer makes a
representation relating to goods which are then sold to a finance
company and let out on hire purchase. Such representation may be
made by the dealer not only as agent for the finance company but
also on his own behalf as part of a collateral contract. The matter is
examined in Chapter Four (*post*, p. 219).
Where the agent is liable the principal will often also be liable,
and just as a principal may be discharged if the third party, with
knowledge of the facts, unequivocally elects to pursue his rights
against the agent, so conversely the agent will be discharged if the
third party unequivocally elects to enforce his rights against the
principal. It has been held that the issue of a writ against the
principal does not necessarily exonerate the agent.[79]

---

[77] (1873) L.R. 8 C.P. 482.
[78] (1884) 13 Q.B.D. 635. See also *Vlassopulos* (*N. & J.*) v. *Ney Shipping Co.*
[1977] 1 W.L.R. 478—no evidence of custom—agent not liable.
[79] *Clarkson Booker* v. *Andjel* [1964] 2 Q.B. 775; [1964] 3 All E.R. 260.

Liability for breach of warranty of authority

If an agent warrants an authority which he in fact does not possess, a third party who relies on such warranty can sue the agent for breach of warranty of authority. In *Collen* v. *Wright*[80]:

> A, purporting to act on behalf of P, granted a lease of P's land to T. A had no authority to do this and P was not bound by his acts. *Held*, A's personal representatives were liable to T for A's breach of warranty of authority.

There has been some discussion as to the basis of this liability. According to one view it is contractual,[81] while another regards it as based on quasi-contract.[82] Whichever view is correct the third party cannot sue the agent if he knew the agent was not warranting his authority or if he ought to have known it from the surrounding circumstances.[83]

If the third party sues the principal who denies that the agent had authority to bind him, the plaintiff can join the agent as a co-defendant and can claim damages for breach of warranty of authority if it should be held that such authority did not in fact exist. What happens if in such a case the plaintiff fails against the principal but obtains an unsatisfied judgment against the agent? The Court of Appeal has held[84] that this judgment does not prevent an appeal being brought by the plaintiff against the dismissal of his claim against the principal; presumably, if the appeal is successful, the Court of Appeal would set aside the inconsistent judgment against the agent.

Agent's right to sue

The principles governing the agent's right to sue on the contract are similar to those governing his contractual liability. Thus he can sue if he is in fact the principal although the contract describes him

---

[80] (1857) 8 E. & B. 647; *cf.* the case of *Smout* v. *Ilbery* (1842) 10 M. & W. 1 which must now be regarded as doubtful. See also *Yonge* v. *Toynbee, post,* p. 63.

[81] Buckley L.J. in *Yonge* v. *Toynbee* [1910] 1 K.B. 215, 228; Seavey (1920) 29 Yale L.J. 859, 886.

[82] Fridman (1956) 34 Can.B.R. 393, 395.

[83] Compare *Lilly, Wilson & Co.* v. *Smales Eeles & Co.* [1892] 1 Q.B. 456 with *Smart* v. *Haigh* (1893) 9 T.L.R. 488. It is uncertain whether the plaintiff must prove that he has suffered damage from the breach (*V/0 Rasnoimport* v. *Guthrie & Co.* [1966] 1 Lloyd's Rep. 1).

[84] *Barclays Bank* v. *Williams* (1971) 115 S.J. 674, C.A.

as agent.[85] He can also sue if he is a party to the contract which, as already seen, depends on the form of the contract and above all on the signature.

Apart from these cases some agents can sue the third party by reason of their lien or so-called "special property" in the goods. It has already been seen that an auctioneer comes within this rule.[86] It is also noteworthy that although a settlement between principal and third party will affect the agent's right to sue, this is not so where the agent has a lien.[87]

Tort

An agent is, of course, liable to a third party who is injured by the agent's tort. The principal's liability has already been considered.

TERMINATION OF AGENCY

Methods of termination

The relationship of principal and agent is determinable in the following ways:

(1) By agreement.

(2) By withdrawal of the original agreement, as where the principal revokes the agent's authority.[88]

(3) By performance.

(4) By death of either party.

(5) By bankruptcy of the principal.[89]

(6) By bankruptcy of the agent if (as is usually the case) it renders him unfit to perform his duties.[90]

(7) By frustration.

---

[85] *Harper & Co.* v. *Vigers Brothers* [1909] 2 K.B. 549.

[86] *Ante*, p. 37.

[87] *Robinson* v. *Rutter* (1855) 4 E. & E. 954; contrast *Grice* v. *Kenrick* (1870) L.R. 5 Q.B. 340.

[88] In a number of Continental countries, an agent who has built up his principal's business will be entitled to compensation. See Schmitthoff, *The Export Trade*, (7th ed.) at p. 182 and authorities there cited.

[89] See Bankruptcy Act 1914, s.37. The Act provides, however, that acts done by the agent before the making of a receiving order are valid in favour of a third party taking in good faith and without notice of an available act of bankruptcy (see s.45).

[90] But see *McCall* v. *Australian Meat Co. Ltd.*, cited in Powell, *op. cit.* at p. 392.

(8) By the insanity of either party if such as to prevent them from entering into a contract.

Restriction on termination

Vested rights

Whether termination occurs by act of party or by operation of law it will not affect rights which became vested before the terminating event. Thus where an agent has a right to commission or indemnity the principal cannot deprive the agent of such right by revoking his authority for the future.[91] Conversely, where an agent has been guilty of a breach of duty and the principal revokes the agent's authority, the principal can still sue the agent for damages for such breach.[92] It has also been seen that the revocation itself may be a breach of contract.[93]

Notice

The question of whether reasonable notice is required to terminate the agency depends on the nature of the agency relationship. In the case of an estate agent, for example, the owner can usually revoke the agency summarily, but if the contract approximates to a contract of employment reasonable notice must be given.[94]

Authority coupled with an interest

If the authority is coupled with an interest it cannot be revoked. The "interest" is usually a debt due from the principal to the agent and the authority is given as security for that debt. In *Raleigh* v. *Atkinson*[95]:

> P entrusted goods to A for sale. From time to time A made advances to P and received authority to dispose of the goods at

---

[91] See, *e.g. Read* v. *Anderson* (1884) 13 Q.B.D. 779—the principle of this case has not been affected by the Gaming Act 1892.

[92] *Ante*, p. 22.

[93] *Ante*, pp. 27, 29.

[94] See, *e.g. Martin-Baker Aircraft Co.* v. *Canadian Flight Equipment Ltd.* [1955] 2 Q.B. 556; [1955] 2 All E.R. 722.

[95] (1840) 6 M. & W. 870. The mere fact that the agent has both an authority and an interest is insufficient—the authority must be given as security for the interest (*Smart* v. *Sanders* (1848) 5 C.B. 895).

market value and to repay himself the advances out of the proceeds.
Held, his authority was coupled with an interest and was irrevocable.

It is important to note that if the authority is irrevocable it is not
affected by the principal's bankruptcy, death or unsoundness of
mind. Further, if P tries to revoke the authority he can be
restrained by injunction from so doing.

Irrevocable powers of attorney

Where a person is appointed agent under a power of attorney,
the normal revocation rules (especially revocation by operation of
law) could clearly cause considerable hardship and practical
difficulty to the donee of the power and to persons dealing with
him. The law on this topic was amended by the Powers of
Attorney Act 1971,[96] which embodied recommendations made by
the Law Commission. The basic rules on revocation can be
summarised as follows:

(1) A third party dealing with the donee of the power is
protected if, at the time of the disposition, he had no knowledge of
any revocation or of any event giving rise to revocation, *e.g.* the
donor's death.[97]

(2) A purchaser from the third party can safely assume that the
third party had no knowledge of revocation etc. if (a) the
disposition to the third party took place within twelve months of
the power coming into operation or (b) the third party makes a
statutory declaration before or within three months after completion that he had no such knowledge.[98]

(3) If the power is given to secure some proprietary interest of
the donee and if it is expressed to be irrevocable, it cannot be
revoked (even by operation of law) without the donee's consent.[99]
This would be relevant on an equitable mortgage of land or shares
where the mortgagor gives the mortgagee a power of attorney to
enable the mortgagee to execute a transfer under seal of the
mortgaged property.

---

[96] See articles in (1971) 68 L.S.Gaz. 434 (C.K. Liddle) and 437 (J.E. Adams).
[97] s.5(2) and (5). The donee of the power is also protected if he had no
knowledge of the revocation (s.5(1)).
[98] s.5(4).
[99] s.4(1).

Effect of termination

As between principal and agent the termination is effective for the future although (as already stated) it does not extinguish vested rights. As regards third parties, however, the problem is not so straightforward because an agent who is stripped of actual authority may still have an apparent authority with which to bind his principal. If the termination was due to the principal's voluntary act, it is only right and proper that if he has held out the agent as having authority he should remain liable until the third party has notice that the authority is at an end. The justice of making an insane principal liable is more dubious but this is what the courts have done. In *Drew* v. *Nunn*[1]:

> A husband held out his wife as having authority to pledge his credit. She had such authority but it terminated when he became insane. Nevertheless she continued to pledge his credit. On recovery the husband was sued for the price of goods supplied during his insanity. *Held*, he was liable.

The Court of Appeal based their decision on the fact that there had been a representation of authority given to the third party and that this representation had not been withdrawn. It was immaterial that the husband was in no fit condition to withdraw it.

On the other hand, it would seem that the principal's personal representatives are not liable on contracts made by the agent after the principal's death. The authority for this proposition is the early case of *Blades* v. *Free*[2] but it is noteworthy that the question of holding out does not appear to have been raised although the case clearly was one involving holding out.

Is the agent liable to the third party on post-termination contracts? The leading case is *Yonge* v. *Toynbee*[3]:

> Solicitors acting for a client entered an appearance and took certain other steps in an action. Unknown to them the client was insane. On discovering this the plaintiff in the action successfully applied to have the appearance and subsequent pleadings struck out. He then applied for an order that the solicitors who had warranted their authority should pay the costs personally. *Held*, the order should be made.

---

[1] (1879) 4 Q.B.D. 661.
[2] (1829) 9 B. & C. 167.
[3] [1910] 1 K.B. 215, and see further Hudson, 37 Can.B.R. 497.

How can this case be reconciled with *Drew* v. *Nunn*? A passage
in the judgment of Brett L.J. in *Drew* v. *Nunn* provides the
answer[4]:

> "In my opinion, if a person *who has not been held out as agent*
> assumes to act on behalf of a lunatic the contract is void as against
> the supposed principal and the pretended agent is liable to an action
> for misleading an innocent person."

Therefore if there has been holding out so that the agent has
power to bind the principal, the third party can still sue the
principal (who can presumably sue the agent). In this case the
third party cannot sue the agent for breach of warranty of
authority, either because he had authority (even though only
apparent) or because the third party has suffered no damage as a
result of the breach. If, however, the agent has no power to bind
the principal—and in *Yonge* v. *Toynbee* it was for this reason that
the action was struck out—the third party can sue the agent for
breach of warranty of authority.

SPECIAL TYPES OF AGENCY

Agency of necessity

There are a few (but not many) cases where an agent can bind
his principal in case of necessity[5] even though the agent had no
actual, usual or apparent authority to do the act in question. In an
early case Parke B. cited two examples: (a) a master of a ship who
has wide powers to purchase necessaries and to sell cargo and even
the ship itself if the need is sufficiently great, and (b) a person who
accepts a bill of exchange for the honour of the drawer.[6] In more
recent times carriers on land have been added to the list.[7]

For the agent's act to be binding on his principal four conditions
must be satisfied. First there must be a genuine emergency. Many
of the pleas of agency of necessity have failed on this ground.[8]

---

[4] (1879) 4 Q.B.D. 661, 686.
[5] *i.e.* emergency. *Sachs* v. *Miklos* [1948] 2 K.B. 23, 34; [1948] 1 All E.R. 67, 68,
per Lord Goddard C.J.
[6] *Hawtayne* v. *Bourne* (1841) 7 M. & W. 595 at p. 599 and see *post*, p. 301.
[7] *Sims* v. *Midland Ry.* [1913] 1 K.B. 103.
[8] *e.g. Prager* v. *Blatspiel, Stamp and Heacock Ltd.* [1924] 1 K.B. 566; *Sachs* v.
Miklos [1948] 2 K.B. 23; [1948] 1 All E.R. 67.

Secondly it must be commercially impracticable to get the owner's instructions before the act is done[9] (a factor which greatly minimises the importance of the doctrine in these days of telegram and telex). Thirdly, the act must be done in good faith[10] and finally it must be done for the benefit of the owner and not merely for the convenience of the agent.[11]

Whether the doctrine will be carried beyond acceptors for honour, masters and carriers remains to be seen. McCardie J. in *Prager* v. *Blatspiel* was all for extension, and expressed the view that "an expanding society demands an expanding common law."[12] The general trend, however, has been much more conservative than this.[13] In particular Scrutton L.J., in *Jebara* v. *Ottoman Bank*,[14] considered that the doctrine should only be applied where there was a subsisting principal-agent relationship at the time of the act in question. This reluctance to allow a stranger to claim to be an agent of necessity can be seen from the early case of *Binstead* v. *Buck*[15] where the finder of a pointer dog fed it for 20 weeks and was unsuccessful in an action for the cost against the owner. "Liabilities," said Bowen L.J. in a later case,[16] "are not to be forced upon people behind their backs."

Agency of married women

A husband is liable on contracts which his wife makes as his agent if she had actual or apparent authority to make them or if he ratifies her act. An example of apparent authority arises where a husband pays a tradesman for goods supplied to his wife. If the tradesman supplies further goods to the wife in reliance on such holding out he will be able to hold the husband liable until he receives actual notice that the wife's authority is at an end.[17] Apart

---

[9] *Springer* v. *G.W.R.* [1921] 1 K.B. 257.

[10] *Prager* v. *Blatspiel, supra.*

[11] *Sachs* v. *Miklos, supra. Munro* v. *Willmott* [1949] 1 K.B. 295; [1948] 2 All E.R. 983.

[12] [1924] 1 K.B. 566, 570.

[13] See *per* Lord Goddard C.J. in *Sachs* v. *Miklos* [1948] 2 K.B. 23, 26; [1948] 1 All E.R. 67, 68.

[14] [1927] 2 K.B. 254, 271 and cases there cited.

[15] (1776) 2 Wm.Bl. 1117.

[16] *Falcke* v. *Scottish Imperial Insurance Co.* (1886) 34 Ch. 234, 238.

[17] See *Drew* v. *Nunn, ante,* p. 63 for an illustration of this.

from this, the relationship of husband and wife gives rise to one special agency problem which must now be briefly examined.

Presumed agency

Where a man co-habits with his wife in a domestic establishment she is presumed to have his authority to pledge his credit for necessaries falling in that sphere of domestic management which is normally under her control.[18] The onus of proving that the goods are necessaries will be on the tradesman and the matter will be judged by reference to the wife's actual requirements and to the standard of living which the husband chooses to adopt.[19] The rule grew up at a time when a wife had no contractual capacity so that without such a rule the tradesman would have been entirely without a remedy. Even now his position is not a very strong one because the so-called "presumed agency" is merely a presumption of fact and from the illuminating judgment of McCardie J. in *Miss Gray Ltd.* v. *Cathcart*[20] it seems that the husband can escape liability in the following ways:

(1) By proving that the goods were excessive in extent.

(2) By proving that the wife already had an adequate allowance for the goods in question.

(3) By proving that he had told the tradesman not to give credit to the wife.

(4) By proving that the tradesman had relied on the wife's credit to the exclusion of that of her husband.

(5) By proving that he had forbidden his wife to pledge his credit. A prohibition will not, however, be effective if there has been a holding out and the tradesman is unaware of the restriction.

It will be apparent from the above that a tradesman who gives credit to the wife without confirmation by the husband may well be acting at his peril.[21]

Unmarried couples

The rules described in the previous section apply equally to an unmarried couple.

---

[18] See *Debenham* v. *Mellon* (1880) 6 App.Cas. 24.

[19] *Phillipson* v. *Hayter* (1870) L.R. 6 C.P. 38.

[20] (1922) 38 T.L.R. 562.

[21] The "presumed agency" must not be confused with the wife's "agency of necessity." This was abolished by the Matrimonial Proceedings and Property Act 1970.

PARTNERSHIPS AND LIMITED COMPANIES

Any discussion of agency would be unrealistic without some reference to partnerships and companies. What follows is only the barest outline, and readers requiring more detailed information are referred to the standard works on these important subjects.[22]

Partners

The legal rules regulating the rights and duties of partners towards outsiders are contained in the Partnership Act 1890, and, as regards limited partners, in the Limited Partnership Act 1907. The Act of 1907 has not been widely used and is not further considered here. References to a section of an Act are to the Act of 1890.

Scope of partner's authority

General. Section 5 states the general position thus:

> Every partner is an agent of the firm and his other partners for the purpose of the business of the partnership; and the acts of every partner who does any act for carrying on in the usual way business of the kind carried on by the firm of which he is a member bind the firm and his partners, unless the partner so acting has in fact no authority to act for the firm in the particular matter, and the person with whom he is dealing either knows that he has no authority or does not know or believe him to be a partner.

The liability of partners for the acts of their fellow partners rests basically on normal agency rules. There is clearly liability if the partner had express authority, and section 5 in effect provides that there is also liability where the partner had implied (or usual) authority—the authority being inferred where the partner's act is one usually done in the course of the type of business carried on by the firm.

It has been held that a member of a trading partnership[23] has implied authority to do any of the following things:

(1) Drawing, accepting or indorsing negotiable instruments in the firm name in the ordinary course of the partnership business.

---

[22] *Lindley on Partnership*; Gower, *Modern Company Law.*

[23] It was suggested in *Higgins* v. *Beauchamp* [1914] 3 K.B. 1192 that a trading partnership was one which involved the purchase and sale of goods. It is thought that a modern court would take a broader view.

(2) Selling, pledging or insuring goods of the firm.

(3) Receiving money for the firm.

(4) Assigning or releasing debts due to the firm.

(5) Borrowing money to meet expenses incurred for partnership purposes.

(6) Hiring employees.

Usual authority. Subject to one exception, the rules as to usual authority are the same as those already discussed. If a partner does an act which he is not authorised to do (as where his usual authority is restricted) a third party knowing of the restriction clearly cannot sue the other partners (see sections 5 and 8). If, however, the third party is unaware of the restriction, an act within the usual authority of the partner will bind his co-partners unless the third party "does not know or believe him to be a partner." These somewhat obscure words raise the question of whether a partner is liable to someone unaware of his existence. Thus:

> A buys goods from B. A has in fact a partner C but B does not know this. Can B sue C?

(1) If A acted within his actual authority B can clearly sue C under the opening words of section 5.

(2) If A acted outside his actual but within his usual authority, the second part of section 5 applies, and the position depends on whether A had other partners whose existence was known to B. If he had, then A was "known to be a partner" and if B was unaware of the restriction on A's authority B can sue all the partners including C. If, however, B did not know that A had any partners, the closing words appear to prevent B from suing C. In other words decisions like *Watteau* v. *Fenwick* (*ante*, p. 40), do not apply in the case of undisclosed partnership.

Nature of liability. By section 9 of the Act every partner is liable jointly[24] with the other partners for all debts and obligations of the firm incurred while he is a partner, and after his death his estate is also severally liable for such debts or obligations. The joint liability in contract should be contrasted[25] with liability in tort, which is joint and several.

---

[24] Judgment against one partner discharges the others even if the judgment is unsatisfied: *Kendall* v. *Hamilton* (1879) 4 App.Cas. 504.

[25] See ss.10 and 12.

Duration of liability

In general a partner is only liable for debts incurred while he is a member of the firm, and his retirement does not extinguish his liabilities for such debts. He is not, however, liable for debts incurred before he became a member or incurred after his retirement, unless he has agreed with the creditors to make himself liable or unless the holding-out rules operate to make him liable.

Holding-out. Section 14 provides that:

(1) Everyone who by words spoken or written or by conduct represents himself, or knowingly suffers himself to be represented, as a partner in a particular firm is liable as a partner to anyone who has on the faith of any such representation given credit to the firm, whether the representation has or has not been made or communicated to the person so giving credit by or with the knowledge of the apparent partner making the representation or suffering it to be made.

(2) Provided that where after a partner's death the partnership business is continued in the old firm's name, the continued use of that name or of the deceased partner's name as part thereof shall not of itself make his executors' or administrators' estate or effects liable for any partnership debts contracted after his death.

This section in effect provides that a person who is not a partner at all may nevertheless be liable as if he were one if his conduct has caused another person to believe him to be one. A rather similar principle governs the position of a partner who has retired from the firm. The matter is governed by section 36 of the Act of 1890, a section designed to protect third parties from the full rigour of the general rule that a partner is not liable for post-retirement debts. Section 36 provides that:

(1) Where a person deals with a firm after a change in its constitution he is entitled to treat all apparent members of the old firm as still being members of the firm until he has notice of the change.

(2) An advertisement in the *London Gazette* as to a firm whose principal place of business is in England or Wales . . . shall be notice as to persons who had no dealings with the firm before the date of the dissolution or change so advertised.

(3) The estate of a partner who dies or who becomes bankrupt or of a partner who, not having been known to the person dealing with the firm to be a partner, retires from the firm, is not liable for

partnership debts contracted after the date of the death, bankruptcy or retirement respectively.

The section divides creditors into two groups—those who did and those who did not deal with the firm before the partner's retirement. So far as creditors in the first class are concerned, the retiring partner must give individual notice of retirement to each of these creditors, and if he fails to do this he will be liable for post-retirement debts to any creditor who dealt with the firm while he was a partner, knew him to be a partner and did not know of his retirement. As to the creditors in the second class, a notice in the *London Gazette* is sufficient notice of retirement, even if the new firm continues to use the old name. Even if such notice is not given, the retiring partner will not be liable for post-retirement debts to a creditor who did not know that he was a partner.[26]

On a dissolution, section 38 provides that a partner can only bind the firm for purposes of winding up the affairs of the partnership and completing transactions begun but unfinished at the time of dissolution. In any event the firm is not bound by the acts of a bankrupt, but an individual person may be liable if he has represented himself or caused himself to be represented, as a partner of the bankrupt.

Liability of partners inter se

Although this is essentially a matter for agreement, the Partnership Act 1890, contains provisions governing such matters in default of agreement. Many of the provisions, such as those against secret profits (s. 29) and those against competition (s. 30), merely reproduce in statutory form the agency rules discussed earlier in this chapter.

Agents of companies

The most important agents of a limited company are the directors, in whom management is usually vested.

A company formed by registration under the Companies Act 1948, must file certain documents including the Memorandum of Association which sets out, *inter alia*, the objects for which the company is formed. Any act not expressly or impliedly authorised by the objects clause is *ultra vires* and void and no ratification is

---

[26] See *Tower Cabinet Co.* v. *Ingram* [1949] 2 K.B. 397; [1949] 1 All E.R. 1033.

possible (see *ante*, p. 45). Until recently an *ultra vires* transaction was not enforceable against the company. Now however section 9(1) of the European Communities Act 1972, provides that:

> In favour of a person dealing with a company in good faith, any transaction decided on by the directors shall be deemed to be one which it is within the capacity of the company to enter into, . . . and a party to a transaction so decided on shall not be bound to enquire as to the capacity of the company to enter into it . . . and shall be presumed to have acted in good faith unless the contrary is proved.

The opening words make it clear that the section merely protects the third party. It does not protect the directors who will be liable to the company for having applied its property for *ultra vires* purposes.

If a transaction is *intra vires* the further question arises as to whether the agent acting on the company's behalf had actual or apparent authority to bind the company.

This vast subject cannot be fully treated here but the following points should be noted:

(1) The company is liable if the agent has actual authority or if it ratifies his act.[27]

(2) The company will also be liable if the agent had apparent authority to do the act in question (as to apparent authority see *ante*, p. 41). If the persons having actual authority to manage the company's affairs have held out a person as occupying a particular position (*e.g.* managing director) and the act is within the usual authority of someone in that position, an outsider can hold the company liable if he has relied on such holding out.[28]

(3) A person dealing with the company is not prejudiced by any defect of internal management into which he cannot inquire and can hold the company liable despite such defect[29] unless he knew of the defect[30] or unless the circumstances should have put him on inquiry.[31]

---

[27] See *Irvine* v. *Union Bank of Australia* (1877) 2 App.Cas. 366. The actual authority may, of course, be express or implied. For recent cases on implied authority, see *Hely-Hutchinson* v. *Brayhead* [1968] 1 Q.B. 549; [1967] 3 All E.R. 98, C.A. and *Mitsui & Co.* v. *Mapro Industrial and another* [1974] 1 Ll.L.R. 386.

[28] *Freeman & Lockyer* v. *Buckhurst Park Properties (Mangal) Ltd.* [1964] 2 Q.B. 480; [1964] 1 All E.R. 630: 83 *Law Notes*, 124.

[29] *Royal British Bank* v. *Turquand* (1856) 6 E. & B. 327.

[30] *Morris* v. *Kanssen* [1946] A.C. 459; [1946] 1 All E.R. 567.

[31] *Houghton* v. *Nothard, Lowe & Wills* [1927] 1 K.B. 246.

(4) Section 9(1) of the European Communities Act 1972, provides that, in favour of a person dealing with a company in good faith the power of the directors to bind the company shall be deemed to be free of any limitation under the memorandum or articles of association. If the words "the directors" refer to the board of directors collectively, the section will be of limited practical application; the problems usually arise where a person deals with a single director or someone who is not a director at all.[32]

---

[32] A number of articles have been written on the effect of s.9. See 32 C.L.J. 1; 116 S.J. 851; (1973) 36 M.L.R. 270.

CHAPTER THREE

SALE OF GOODS

INTRODUCTION

THE contract of sale of goods is probably the best known and most common of all commercial contracts. Millions of them are concluded each day and the overwhelming majority gives rise to no problems at all. Until the end of the nineteenth century the principles governing sales lay embedded in the general mass of contract case law, but in 1893 the Sale of Goods Act was passed to codify the common law and this Act remained on the statute book for more than 80 years. A few amendments were made in 1954, 1967, 1973 and 1977 and finally the statute law was consolidated in the Sale of Goods Act 1979 which is the basis of the modern law.[1]

Sale of Goods Act 1979

Three points should be noted about the Act.

(1) *Savings*

The Act is not fully comprehensive because by section 62(1):

> The rules of the common law,[2] including the law merchant, except in so far as they are inconsistent with the provisions of this Act, and in particular the rules relating to the law of principal and agent and the effect of fraud, misrepresentation, duress or coercion, mistake,[3] or other invalidating cause, apply to contracts for the sale of goods.

It follows that the practitioner or student considering a sale of goods problem must consider the Act within the framework of the general law of contract.[4]

---

[1] In this chapter, unless otherwise stated, a reference to "the Act" is to the Sale of Goods Act 1979 and a reference to a section (*e.g.* s.55) is to that section of the Act .

[2] In New Zealand and Victoria it has been held that this term does not include the rules of equity. See (1959) 22 M.L.R. 76 and (1963) 26 M.L.R. 272 and consider the observations of Atkin L.J. in *Re Wait* [1927] 1 Ch. 606, 636. See also *post*, p. 189.

[3] See, *e.g. Ingram* v. *Little* [1961] 1 Q.B. 31; [1960] 3 All E.R. 332, *post*, p. 152.

[4] In a recent case involving specific performance the Act was not referred to at all even though it was directly relevant to the point in issue (*Sky Petroleum* v. *VIP Petroleum* [1974] 1 W.L.R. 576; [1974] 1 All E.R. 954), *post*, p. 189.

(2) *Restrictions on freedom of contract*

The 1893 Act did not seek to make a contract for the parties—it merely defined their obligations where the matter was not governed by agreement. Section 55, as originally drafted, provided that:

> Where any right, duty, or liability would arise under a contract of sale by implication of law, it may be negatived or varied by express agreement or by the course of dealing between the parties, or by usage, if the usage be such as to bind both parties to the contract.

Thus the Act preserved the common law rule that, in the words of Blackburn J.:

> "there is no rule of law to prevent the parties from making such contract as they please."[5]

A usage will bind both parties if it is reasonable, and is known or taken to be known at the time of contract, and is not inconsistent with the express terms of the contract.[6] In *Cointat* v. *Myham*[7]:

> A meat salesman sold a carcass of pig to a retailer butcher at Smithfield market. The meat was seized as being unfit for human consumption. Normally there would have been a claim by the buyer under what is now s.14(3) (*post*, p. 119) but evidence was admitted of a usage prevailing at the market that no term of fitness for food was implied. The buyer's action therefore failed.

Where a dispute is referred to arbitration, the House of Lords has held that the arbitrator has jurisdiction to inquire into and adjudicate upon the existence of an alleged custom.[8]

The widespread exclusion of the statutory conditions and warranties was severely criticised by judges, writers and the Law Commissioners for England and Scotland; it was clearly capable of causing considerable hardship, especially as the buyer generally

---

[5] *Calcutta and Burmah Steam Navigation Co.* v. *De Mattos* (1863) 32 L.J.Q.B. 322, 328. More recently this philosophy has been greatly modified by recognition of the need to protect the consumer—see the new rules discussed in Chapter Eight.

[6] *Re Sutro (L.) and Heilbut, Symons* [1917] 2 K.B. 348; *London Export Corpn.* v. *Jubilee Coffee Roasting Co.* [1958] 1 W.L.R. 661; [1958] 2 All E.R. 411, C.A.

[7] (1914) 110 L.T. 749, C.A. In theory such a usage is presumably a "term" of the contract and therefore caught by the Unfair Contract Terms Act 1977 (*post*, p. 434) in its application to non-consumer sales. It is thought that the courts would be very reluctant to interfere.

[8] *Produce Brokers Co.* v. *Olympia Oil & Cake Co.* [1916] 1 A.C. 314.

had no choice in the matter and in most cases did not appreciate the true position at the time of the contract. Accordingly, the Supply of Goods (Implied Terms) Act 1973 severely curtailed the use of exclusion clauses and this process was continued and extended by the Unfair Contract Terms Act 1977 which repealed, re-enacted and extended the relevant provisions of the 1973 Act. The 1977 Act is considered in Chapter Eight.

(3) *Construction*

The correct approach to the construction of a codifying Act is to

" . . . examine the language of the statute and to ask what is its natural meaning, uninfluenced by any consideration derived from the previous state of the law."[9]

A reference to the law before the Act is, however, justified if a provision of the Act is ambiguous or of doubtful import, or if it is thought to show that words used in the Act had previously acquired a technical meaning different from their natural meaning.

Professor Gower has said[10] that "despite the praise justly lavished on Sir Mackenzie Chalmers' draftsmanship, the Sale of Good Act[11] was perhaps his least happy effort." The reason partly is that while each section read by itself is a model of simplicity and clarity, difficulties arise when it is sought to link two or more sections together, because there is a certain amount of overlap[12] and at times direct conflict between them. Thus it is necessary to consider the Act as a whole, if the subject is to become clear.

Standardisation. The modern trend towards standardisation of contracts is to be found in the sale of goods as elsewhere. Many trade organisations[13] have produced their standard form of contract of sale and these are widely used in many sections of commerce, and particularly in the export trade.[14] In the private sphere, however, and in particular in the ordinary retail trade,

---

[9] *Bank of England* v. *Vagliano Bros.* [1891] A.C. 107 at p. 145, *per* Lord Herschell (a case on the Bills of Exchange Act 1882).

[10] In his foreword to Atiyah's *The Sale of Goods.*

[11] The reference is to the 1893 Act.

[12] *e.g.* ss.25 and 47, *post*, p. 178.

[13] *e.g.* the London Corn Trade Association, the London Jute Association and the London Rubber Trade Association.

[14] The subject of export is considered in Chapter Ten, *post*, p. 460.

standard form contracts are the exception rather than the rule, and the rights and duties of the parties are governed by the general law of sale.

WHAT ARE GOODS?

Definition

The definition section, section 61, provides that in the Act:

> "Goods" includes all personal chattels other than things in action and money . . . and, in particular, "goods" includes emblements, industrial growing crops, and things attached to or forming part of the land which are agreed to be severed before sale or under the contract of sale.

Thus the Act does not apply to freehold land nor to chattels real, such as leases. Nor does it apply to things (or choses) in action, a term used to describe

> "all personal rights of property, which can only be claimed or enforced by action and not by taking physical possession."[15]

Examples include stocks and shares, trade marks and debts. Negotiable instruments[16] are also choses in action, although, as will be seen, they are subject to special rules of their own.

Money

Section 6 excludes "money" from the definition of "chattels personal" and this means that where a coin is transferred as currency in the normal way, it will not be a sale of goods. If, however, a coin is sold as a curio or as an investment it seems that this will be a sale of goods and the Act will therefore apply.[17]

Emblements

This term, borrowed from ancient real property law, comprises crops and vegetables (such as corn and potatoes) produced by the labour of man and ordinarily yielding a present annual profit.[18]

---

[15] *Torkington* v. *Magee* [1902] 2 K.B. 427, 430.

[16] See Chapter Five.

[17] *Cf. Moss* v. *Hancock* [1899] 2 Q.B. 111—criminal law case concerning a jubilee five-pound gold piece. *Esso Petroleum Co.* v. *Customs and Excise Commissioners* [1976] 1 W.L.R. 1; [1976] 1 All E.R. 117, H.L. (World Cup coin supplied to buyers of petrol was held not to be "sold" to them; such arrangements are now within Part I of the Supply of Goods and Services Act 1982 (*post*, p. 125).

[18] To encourage good farming a tenant who had planted "emblements" was allowed to reap them even though his tenancy had expired before the crop matured.

Industrial growing crops

This term has not been judicially defined, but presumably it is wider than emblements and may include crops[19] not maturing within a year, such as clover.

Things attached to the land

Before the 1893 Act, the main distinction was between *fructus industriales* and *fructus naturales*. The former, largely co-extensive with emblements, were generally regarded as goods, but the position with regard to the latter was far from certain. The expression *"fructus naturales"* was used to refer to the natural produce of the soil such as grass, and also to products (such as fruit trees) where the annual crop was "natural" in the sense that it naturally recurred year after year. The question of whether a contract for the sale of *fructus naturales* was a contract for sale of goods or sale of land, produced a mass of confusing and conflicting case law, so that:

> "No general rule is laid down in any of them that is not contradicted by some other."[20]

The reason for all the trouble was the notorious Statute of Frauds which required different formalities for a contract for the sale of an interest in land[21] and for a contract for the sale of goods.[22] One line of cases suggested that if property passed before severance it was sale of land and in the converse case it was sale of goods.[23] Another view was that where the contract provided for immediate severance it was sale of goods, whereas if the buyer was to derive benefit from the retention of the crops in the soil it was sale of land.[24] Fortunately for sale of goods purposes this case law is now largely irrelevant, because section 61 declares to be goods

---

[19] Chalmers, *Sale of Goods* (18th ed.), p. 268; Fridman, *Sale of Goods,* pp. 11–12 and authorities there cited.

[20] *Rodwell* v. *Phillips* (1842) 9 M. & W. 501, 505, *per* Lord Abinger C.B.

[21] s.4 re-enacted in s.40 of the Law of Property Act 1925.

[22] s.17, re-enacted in s.4 of the Sale of Goods Act 1893 which was repealed by the Law Reform (Enforcement of Contracts) Act 1954.

[23] This view was favoured by Lord Blackburn, *Blackburn on Sale,* (2nd ed.), pp. 4–6. See also *Smith* v. *Surman,* 7 L.J.(o.s.)K.B. 296.

[24] *Marshall* v. *Green* (1875) 1 C.P.D. 35 approved in *Kauri Timber Co.* v. *Commissioner of Taxes (N.Z.)* [1913] A.C. 771, a taxation case. The Sale of Goods Act was not referred to.

anything "forming part of the land which are agreed to be severed before sale or under the contract of sale." In other words the time of severance is irrelevant and the overwhelming majority of contracts for the sale of *fructus naturales* will now be sale of goods.[25]

This, however, is not the end of the matter because there is still one unsettled problem of considerable practical importance. It has just been seen that the 1893 Act brought within the ambit of "goods" many types of product which were not goods before. Does that mean that these products are now goods only or are they both goods under section 61 and also "land" within section 205 of the Law of Property Act 1925, so that (*inter alia*) a contract for their sale must still be evidenced in writing so as to comply with section 40 of that Act? The majority of academic opinion favours the latter view.[26] Persuasive arguments have been presented on both sides and it is clearly open for the court to decide either way. This being so, it may well be that, as part of its general policy of construing the Statute of Frauds and its successors narrowly, the court will come down in favour of the view that section 40 of the Law of Property Act does not apply to any property which is declared by the Sale of Goods Act to be "goods."[27]

Things

The Act applies to "things," forming part of the land but not to the land itself. In *Morgan* v. *Russell & Sons*[28]:

> The seller agreed to sell all the slag and cinders lying on a particular piece of land or so much thereof as the buyer should require. After the buyer had taken some of the slag, third parties claimed that the slag belonged to them and effectively prevented the buyer from collecting further supplies. The buyer sued the seller for damages for non-delivery under the Sale of Goods Act. It was held on the facts that the cinders and slag were not an identifiable heap

---

[25] Before the Act a contract whereby a purchaser agreed to buy a piece of land and the crops thereon was held to be one entire contract for the sale of land only (*Falmouth* v. *Thomas* (1832) 1 Cr. & M. 89). Presumably this is unchanged.

[26] The "double classification" view is suggested by Megarry & Wade, *The Law of Real Property*, (4th ed.), p. 549; Hudson, 22 *The Conveyancer*, 137; Cheshire and Fifoot regard the point as still open *Law of Contract*, (10th ed.), p. 184.

[27] This possible solution is suggested by Anson, *Law of Contract*, (25th ed.), p. 78.

[28] [1909] 1 K.B. 357.

but had become part of the land itself and were therefore not "goods." The action therefore failed.[29]

Classification of goods

Specific, ascertained and unascertained

Many of the rules[30] of the Act depend upon whether the goods which are the subject-matter of the contract of sale are "specific" or "unascertained." Section 61 defines specific goods as "goods identified and agreed on at the time a contract of sale is made." Thus the ordinary retail sale, where a buyer goes into a shop, selects an article and agrees to buy it, is a sale of specific goods.

The Act does not define unascertained goods but it clearly covers two distinct transactions. The first is a sale of purely generic goods where the subject-matter of the sale is not a specific chattel, but goods of a particular type. An example is a contract for the sale of "100 boxes of canned fruit" or "a washing machine." The second case where goods are unascertained is where the contract relates to part of a larger quantity of goods, as, for example, a contract for the sale of "50 tons of wheat out of the consignment of 200 tons now on board *SS. London.*" The failure of the Act to distinguish between these two types of unascertained goods has been criticised.[31]

Ascertained goods. This expression is again not defined in the Act, but it probably means goods identified in accordance with the agreement after the contract is made.[32] If a man on becoming engaged agreed to buy from a jeweller "a diamond ring to be selected by me from your stock" the contract would initially be for unascertained goods but on the selection being made the goods would become ascertained. The expression "ascertained goods" only appears to be important in connection with the passing of property (*post*, p. 129) and with the court's power to order specific performance.[33]

---

[29] Since the property was held to be land, a claim for general damages was precluded by the rule in *Bain* v. *Fothergill* (1874) L.R. 7 H.L. 158.

[30] *e.g.* those relating to the perishing of goods (ss.6 and 7) and to the passing of property (ss.16–18).

[31] Atiyah, *Sale of Goods*, (6th ed.), p. 38.

[32] *Per* Atkin L.J. (as he then was) in *Re Wait* [1927] Ch. 606, 630; [1926] All E.R. Rep. 433.

[33] See s.52 and *Re. Wait, post,* p. 189.

Existing and future goods

A further classification made by the Act is that of existing and future goods.[34] Section 61 defines future goods as:

> Goods to be manufactured or acquired by the seller after the making of the contract of sale.

It will be apparent that this classification cuts across the previous one, in that the contract can be for the sale of unascertained future goods or specific future goods. If the goods do not yet exist, as in the case of a crop to be grown or a propeller to be manufactured, they will clearly be unascertained. If they do exist, they may be unascertained or specific. An example of the former would be sale of "a Rolls-Royce car" where the parties know that the seller will have to obtain one from a dealer. An example of the latter would be a sale of a specific machine where the parties know that it belongs to a third party at the time of sale.[35]

THE CONTRACT OF SALE

Definition

Section 2 of the Act is the basis of all that is to follow. It opens with these words:

> "(1) A contract of sale of goods is a contract by which the seller transfers or agrees to transfer the property in goods to the buyer for a money consideration, called the price.
> (2) There may be a contract of sale between one part owner and another."

Five elements must be considered—seller, buyer, property, goods and price.

(1) *Seller* is defined as "a person who sells or agrees to sell goods."[36]

---

[34] The distinction is chiefly important in connection with the passing of property. See s.5 (*post*, p. 82) and s.18, rule 5 (*post*, p. 133).

[35] The writer respectfully disagrees with the view that "future goods are always unascertained goods" (Schmitthoff, *The Sale of Goods*, 2nd ed., p. 53). If in this example the machine was destroyed after the making of the contract, it is thought that s.7 (which only applies to specific goods—*post*, p. 141) would apply.

[36] s.61.

(2) *Buyer* is defined as "a person who buys or agrees to buy goods."[37] It follows from section 2(1) that there must be both a seller and a buyer, but a person can validly buy his own goods if, for example, he buys them from a sheriff who has seized them under a writ of *fi.fa.*

(3) *Property* is defined as "the general property in the goods and not merely a special property."[38] In other words it means ownership.

(4) *Goods.* The meaning of this term has already been considered.

(5) *Price.* The price is of course the consideration given by the buyer for the property in the goods. It follows that if he fails to get the property, he can recover the price because the consideration for it has wholly failed.[39]

It is to be noted that section 2(1) uses the expression "money consideration," the point being to distinguish a contract of sale from a contract of exchange. The price need not, however, be wholly in money. In *Aldridge* v. *Johnson*[40] a contract for the sale of 52 bullocks valued at £6 each against 100 quarters of barley valued at £2 per quarter, the difference to be paid in cash, was treated without argument as sale of goods. Further the buyer may have an option of paying an agreed price or of supplying goods in lieu of payment. In *G. J. Dawson (Clapham) Ltd.* v. *H. & G. Dutfield*[41]:

> Sellers agreed to sell two lorries for £475, of which £250 was to be paid in cash, and two other lorries were to be delivered by the buyers within one month in satisfaction of the remaining £225. The buyers failed to deliver. *Held*, the contact was a single contract of sale at a price of £475 and the seller's remedy was not an action in detinue but an action for the outstanding £225 as a debt.[42]

Sale and agreement to sell

Where a vendor of land sells it to a purchaser the disposition takes place in two stages—the contract, conferring rights which to

---

[37] *Ibid.* A person with a mere option to buy is not a buyer (see below).

[38] *Ibid.* "Property" is not used in the Act as a synonym for goods.

[39] *Rowland* v. *Divall, post,* p. 106.

[40] (1857) 7 E. & Bl. 885.

[41] [1936] 2 All E.R. 232.

[42] The whole subject of exchange and part—exchange must now be considered in the light of the Supply of Goods and Services Act 1982. See Woodroffe, *Supply of Goods and Services—The New Law* at p. 61 *et seq.*

some degree are purely personal, and the conveyance, when the vendor vests in the purchaser the legal title to the property. The Roman Law of sale of goods contained similar provisions.[43] Under the Sale of Goods Act however, contract and conveyance are sometimes merged into one. Section 2 provides that:

> "(4) Where under a contract of sale the property in the goods is transferred from the seller to the buyer the contract is called a sale.[44]
>
> (5) Where under a contract of sale the transfer of the property in the goods is to take place at a future time or subject to some condition later to be fulfilled the contract is called an agreement to sell."[45]

Further, section 2(6) provides that:

> "An agreement to sell becomes a sale when the time elapses or the conditions are fulfilled subject to which the property in the goods is to be transferred."

In other words the expression "contract of sale" covers both a sale and an agreement to sell. Under a sale the property passes immediately to the buyer,[46] whereas under an agreement to sell the buyer acquires merely personal rights. In theory this distinction is fundamental, but its practical results are surprisingly small. The matter will be more fully discussed when the rules governing the passing of property are dealt with (*post*, pp. 126–128).

A contract whereby a seller purports to effect a present sale of future goods operates as an agreement to sell them.[47]

A contract of sale may be absolute or conditional.[48]

Sale distinguished from other transactions

(1) *Hire-purchase agreement*

Commercially the object of a contract of sale of goods and a contract of hire-purchase is the same, but legally the two types of contract are very different. Under the modern form of hire-purchase agreement, the hirer is given possession of the goods

---

[43] See an interesting comparative study by Mr. F. H. Lawson in (1949) 65 L.Q.R. 352.

[44] See s.18, r.1, *post*, p. 130.

[45] See s.18, rr. 2–5, *post*, pp. 130–136.

[46] This is the normal rule for retail sales.

[47] s.5(3).

[48] s.2(3).

together with an option to purchase them. Since he is not bound to exercise the option, he has not "agreed to buy"[49] them and is therefore not a buyer. Having regard to the words "to the buyer" in section 2(1) it seems clear that the Act does not apply to a hire-purchase agreement.[50]

(2) *Mortgage*
Section 62(4) provides that:

> The provisions of this Act about contracts of sale do not apply to a transaction in the form of a contract of sale which is intended to operate by way of mortgage, pledge, charge, or other security.

In the words of Lord Halsbury:

> "a colourable sale where an attempt is made to conceal a loan under the disguise of a sale is not governed by the provisions of the Act."[51]

This is clear enough, but what is not clear is whether section 62(4) goes beyond colourable sales and also applies to a genuine sales transaction entered into with the ulterior motive of providing security for advances.[52] At all events the form of the transaction is not conclusive.

(3) *Work and materials*
Until 1954[53] it was necessary to draw a sharp distinction between a contract for the sale of goods (where formalities were required where the price was £10 and upwards) and a contract for work and materials, which could be in any form. It was at one time thought that whenever the contract would result in the sale of a chattel it was sale of goods.[54] This view, however, is now out of favour and a more realistic attitude can be seen in the following quotation from Greer L.J.:

---

[49] *Helby* v. *Matthews* [1895] A.C. 471.

[50] Obiter dicta to the contrary in *Felston Tile Co. Ltd.* v. *Winget* [1936] 3 All E.R. 473, C.A., can presumably be disregarded as being inconsistent with the House of Lords decision in *Helby* v. *Matthews, supra.* But see (1972) 88 L.Q.R. 21 for a contrary view.

[51] *Maas* v. *Pepper* [1905] A.C. 102, 104.

[52] See *Benjamin's Sale of Goods*, (2nd ed.), pp. 46–48.

[53] The year in which s.4 of the 1893 Act was repealed by the Law Reform (Enforcement of Contracts) Act 1954.

[54] *Lee* v. *Griffin* (1861) 30 L.J.Q.B. 252.

"If you find . . . that the substance of the contract was the production of something to be sold . . . then it is a sale of goods. But if the substance of the contract, on the other hand, is that skill and labour have to be exercised for the production of the article and that it is only ancillary to that that there will pass . . . some materials, the substance of the contract is the skill and experience."[55]

These words were spoken in a case where an order for a portrait to be painted at a price of 250 guineas was held by the Court of Appeal to be a contract for work and materials. On the other hand a contract for the construction of a ship's propeller was held to be a contract of sale of goods[56] and so also was a contract for the supply of a fur coat costing 900 guineas to be made from fur supplied by the furrier.[57]

In *Samuels* v. *Davis*[58] the Court of Appeal had to consider the case of a denture which had been made in such a way that it did not fit. The court found it unnecessary to classify the contract because, whatever view was taken, there was an implied term that the goods should be reasonably fit for their purpose. With the repeal, in 1954, of the formality provisions, and with the recent statutory assimilation of the implied terms (*post*, p. 125) the distinction has clearly lost some of its importance. Nevertheless there are still areas where the distinction may be crucial; they include the perishing of specific goods,[59] purchase of goods from a non-owner (*post*, p. 143 *et seq.*) and criminal sanctions for the use of certain void exemption clauses.[60]

(4) *Exchange*

It has already been seen that a transfer of one chattel for another is a contract of exchange or barter. There is no "money consideration" and therefore the Act does not apply. There are however various implied terms which apply to such contracts and these are considered later in this chapter (*post*, pp. 125–126).

---

[55] *Robinson* v. *Graves* [1935] 1 K.B. 579, 589.
[56] *Cammell Laird & Co. Ltd.* v. *Manganese Bronze & Brass Co.* [1934] A.C. 402.
[57] *Marcel (Furriers) Ltd.* v. *Tapper* [1953] 1 W.L.R. 49; [1953] 1 All E.R. 15.
[58] [1943] K.B. 526; [1943] 2 All E.R. 3.
[59] The Law Reform (Frustrated Contracts) Act 1943 is excluded if the contract is one for the sale of specific goods which perish.
[60] Under the Consumer Transactions (Restrictions on Statements) Order 1976 *post*, p. 454.

FORMATION OF CONTRACT

Offer and acceptance

The general law of contract governs this matter and difficult questions can arise if the "contract" has to be gleaned from a mass of letters, telexes, conversations and telephone calls. This is particularly troublesome where the seller and the buyer each seek to incorporate their own terms of business into the contract. This is commonly known as the "battle of the forms" and can present difficult problems if, for example, the quotation contains the seller's terms, the order contains the buyer's terms and the acknowledgment of order again contains the seller's terms. On these facts there may well be no contract at all because the acknowledgment is merely a counter-offer.[61] The position is different if the seller signs a tear-off slip on the order form whereby he agrees to supply on the buyer's terms.[62]

Capacity

Section 3 provides that:

> (1) Capacity to buy and sell is regulated by the general law concerning capacity to contract and to transfer and acquire property.
>
> (2) Where necessaries are sold and delivered to a minor or to a person who by reason of mental incapacity or drunkenness is incompetent to contract, he must pay a reasonable price for them.
>
> (3) In subsection (2) above "necessaries" mean goods suitable to the condition in life of the minor or other person concerned and to his actual requirements at the time of the sale and delivery.

Buyer or seller a minor

Buyer a minor. Despite the vast sums spent by industry to attract the teenage market, and despite the vast numbers of sale contracts made with minors (records, clothes, magazines, sweets, etc.) there is virtually no modern case law on the topic and nearly all of the decided cases are more than 50 years old.

The position where goods are sold to a minor depends upon whether the goods are "necessaries" as defined in section 3. The

---

[61] This was one of the points in issue in *Re Bond Worth* [1980] Ch. 228; [1979] 3 W.L.R. 629.

[62] See *Butler Machine Tool Co. Ltd.* v. *Ex-Cell-O Corporation (England) Ltd.* [1979] 1 W.L.R. 401, C.A.

burden of proving that they are necessaries is on the person seeking to enforce the contract which will usually be the seller.[63] A finding by a judge that goods were or were not necessaries will not be varied on appeal unless there was no evidence to support that finding.[64] On the wording of section 3 the obligation to pay a reasonable price only arises where the necessaries have been "sold and delivered" which suggests that the supplier's claim is based on quasi-contract[65] and that he could not bring a claim for damages (or for a reasonable price) if the minor failed to take delivery. Presumably even on a cash sale (as opposed to a credit sale) the minor could claim the return of part of the price in so far as it exceeded a reasonable price. If the goods are not necessaries the law is clearly "archaic and out of touch with the present day."[66] The Infants Relief Act 1874 roundly declares such contracts to be "absolutely void" but it is generally accepted that such contracts are not devoid of all legal effect.[67] Two points are clear:

(1) The minor cannot be sued on the contract.

(2) If the minor obtained the goods by misrepresenting his age he cannot be sued in deceit as this would be an indirect way of enforcing the contract.[68]

Four other points are less clear:

(1) Can a minor, who has fraudulently obtained and disposed of non-necessary goods, be made liable to pay over the proceeds of sale received by him? The reasoning in *R. Leslie* v. *Sheill*[69] suggests that the minor is not accountable, but a learned writer[70] has argued that the minor may be liable to a proprietary judgment if the proceeds of sale can be traced into a clearly identifiable fund.

(2) Can the minor sue on the contract? The words "absolutely void" appear at first sight to preclude this, but the minor could do so before the Act and it seems strange that an Act called the Infants Relief Act should remove this right.

---

[63] See, *e.g. Nash* v. *Inman* [1908] 2 K.B. 1.
[64] See, *e.g. Elkington & Co. Ltd.* v. *Amery* [1936] 2 All E.R. 86.
[65] See dicta in *Nash* v. *Inman (supra,) per* Fletcher Moulton L.J. Presumably those dicta do not prevent the minor enforcing the contract.
[66] Mr. W. H. Thomas in his commentary to the Act (Current Law Statutes).
[67] See, *e.g.* (1957) 73 L.Q.R. 194 and a reply in (1958) 74 L.Q.R. 97.
[68] *Stocks* v. *Wilson* [1913] 2 K.B. 235; *R. Leslie Ltd.* v. *Sheill* [1914] 3 K.B. 607.
[69] [1914] 3 K.B. 607.
[70] Treitel, *Law of Contract*, (5th ed.), at pp. 435–436.

(3) Can the minor recover money paid under the contract? It was clearly open to the courts to interpret the words "absolutely void" literally, so as to permit recovery, but the authorities favour the view that money is only recoverable if there has been a total failure of consideration.[71] From what has been said it is clear that a person selling to a minor should, if at all possible, insist on immediate payment in cash.

(4) Does the property in non-necessary goods pass to the minor? There are conflicting dicta[72] on the point which must await judicial decision. It would certainly be an odd result, capable of working hardship on third parties buying the goods from the minor, if the property did not pass, at all events if the goods are delivered and paid for.

Seller a minor. The Act of 1874 does not apply where the minor sells the goods, and the contract there is governed by the general law, under which a contract is not binding on the minor unless it is for his benefit. As a result he is liable on contracts of education and apprenticeship but not trading contracts.[73]

Conclusion

It is clear that the present law is archaic and riddled with anomalies. In a recent working paper[74] the Law Commission has canvassed the possibility of full contractual capacity at 16 or alternatively the retention of the present law with fairly minor changes. It is to be hoped that, after consultation, their Report will recommend a complete overhaul and modernisation of the law on this topic.

Formalities

In general the contract can be made in any form. Section 4 reads:

---

[71] *Valentini* v. *Canali* (1889) 24 Q.B.D. 166; *Pearce* v. *Brain* [1929] 2 K.B. 310. Mr. Treitel, in (1957) 73 L.Q.R. 94, suggests that the principle laid down in *Pearce* v. *Brain* was wider than necessary for the decision and that it is open to the courts to allow recovery in any case where a minor is able to make restitution.

[72] *Stocks* v. *Wilson* [1913] 2 K.B. 235, 246, *per* Lush J. *obiter*—property passes; *contra Pearce* v. *Brain, supra,* where Swift J. considered that the words "absolutely void" precluded this.

[73] *Cowern* v. *Nield* [1912] 2 K.B. 419.

[74] Working Paper No. 81—Minors' Contracts.

(1) Subject to the provisions of this Act and of any statute in that behalf, a contract of sale may be made in writing (either with or without seal), or by word of mouth, or partly in writing and partly by word of mouth, or may be implied from the conduct of the parties.

(2) Provided that nothing in this section shall affect the law relating to corporations.

Statutes in that behalf

A few statutes require formalities. Thus the Merchant Shipping Act 1894 requires a transfer of a British ship or any share therein to be made in writing, while section 61 of the Consumer Credit Act 1974 provides that certain conditional sale and credit-sale agreements are unenforceable unless they are in writing and comply with formal requirements laid down by the Act and by regulations (see *post*, p. 222).

Corporations

The closing words of section 3 are no longer of importance because a corporation can now contract in the same way as a private person.[75]

Price[76]

Section 8 reads:

(1) The price in a contract of sale may be fixed by the contract, or may be left to be fixed in a manner agreed by the contract, or may be determined by the course of dealing between the parties.

(2) Where the price is not determined as mentioned in sub-section (1) the buyer must pay a reasonable price.

(3) What is a reasonable price is a question of fact, dependent on the circumstances of each particular case.

In *May and Butcher* v. *The King*[77] Viscount Dunedin considered that section 8(2) could only be invoked if the contract was silent on the question of price, and would not apply if the contract contained an express provision as to the price—for example, a clause that "the price is to be agreed by the parties from time to time." If such a clause is used, it is a question of construction of

---

[75] Companies Act 1948, s.32; Corporate Bodies (Contracts) Act 1960, s.1. The statement in the text is, of course, only intended to refer to formalities.

[76] On the question of trading stamps see Trading Stamps Act 1964. See also s.16 of the Supply of Goods (Implied Terms) Act 1973.

[77] [1934] 2 K.B. 17, H.L.

the relevant documents as to whether the parties have shown an intention to be bound. If the court finds that they have done so, it may, in order to give business efficacy to the contract, imply a term that, failing agreement, a reasonable price is to be paid.[78] If, on the other hand, it appears that the parties have not progressed beyond the negotiating stage, they are clearly not bound, having regard to the well-known rule that there can be no agreement to make an agreement.[79] The application of the above principles to particular cases may be a difficult matter, and the cases themselves are hard to reconcile. Since, however, each case is essentially one of construction, no useful purpose would be served in trying to reconcile them.

Price maintenance

A retailer may find that goods which he buys for resale are subject to conditions as to the price at which they can be sold to the public. Until 1956 a manufacturer who wished to impose such conditions found it impossible to enforce them legally against a retailer with whom he was not in contractual relationship. The reason for this was, of course, the time-hallowed privity of contract rule.[80] The existence of this rule led manufacturers to resort to extra-legal means of enforcement, such as placing a defaulting retailer on a stop-list or extracting a fine in lieu.[81] The Restrictive Trade Practices Act 1956 dealt with both these matters in opposing ways—section 24 made collective enforcement unlawful while section 25 for the first time made individual enforcement possible. Section 25(1) provides that a supplier of goods which are subject to resale price conditions can enforce these conditions against anyone "not a party to the sale who subsequently acquires the goods with notice[82] of the conditions as if he has been party thereto." The remainder of the section imposes certain qualifications to the general rule. Now, however, the Resale Prices Act 1964, makes it unlawful for a supplier to impose minimum resale

[78] *Foley* v. *Classique Coaches Ltd.* [1934] 2 K.B. 1, C.A. The Sale of Goods Act was not even referred to. See also *Smith* v. *Morgan* [1971] 1 W.L.R. 803 for a similar problem on sale of land (criticised in (1971) L.S. Gaz. at p. 484).

[79] *May and Butcher* v. *The King, supra.*

[80] *Taddy* v. *Sterious* [1904] 1 Ch. 358.

[81] *Ware and De Freville* v. *Motor Trade Association* [1924] 3 K.B. 40.

[82] *Goodyear Tyre and Rubber Co.* (*Great Britain*) v. *Lancashire Batteries, Ltd.* [1958] 1 W.L.R. 655; [1958] 3 All E.R. 7, and see [1958] C.L.J. 857.

price conditions and makes such conditions void, unless the Restrictive Practices Court makes an order exempting the goods from the operation of the Act, which it can do on certain specified grounds. The Act also prevents a supplier withholding supplies from a dealer on the ground that the dealer is reselling below a specified price.[83] If a notice is given to the Director-General of Fair Trading, the position prior to the hearing is the same as if an order had been made.[84]

Valuation

Section 8(1) provides that the price can be fixed in a manner agreed upon by the parties. The parties sometimes provide that the price is to be fixed by valuation, and section 9 deals with the position where no valuation takes place. it provides as follows:

> (1) Where there is an agreement to sell goods on the terms that the price is to be fixed by the valuation of a third party, and he cannot or does not make such valuation, the agreement is avoided; but if the goods or any part of them have been delivered to and appropriated by the buyer he must pay a reasonable price for them.
> (2) Where the third party is prevented from making the valuation by the fault of the seller or buyer, the party not at fault may maintain an action for damages against the party at fault.

A few points remain unsettled. In the first place section 9(1) refers to "an agreement to sell." What is the position in the case of a "sale" where the price is to be fixed by valuation? Does the valuer's inability or unwillingness to carry out the valuation discharge the contract? It has been suggested that if the property has actually passed to the buyer the contract will not be discharged and he will be bound to pay a reasonable price.[85] It may well be that since the main object of the contract, *viz.* the passing of property, had been achieved the courts would readily construe the clause as collateral and would require the buyer to pay a reasonable price in default of valuation. Secondly, it will be noted that section 9(1) only refers to valuation "by a third party" so that it is uncertain whether a contract would be discharged if, for

---

[83] See *Comet Radiovision Services* v. *Farnell-Tandberg* (1971) L.R. 7 R.P. 168; [1971] 3 All E.R. 230.

[84] For an excellent survey of the 1964 Act see Lever, *The Law of Restrictive Practice and Resale Price Maintenance.* See also the Competition Act 1980.

[85] See Benjamin, *op. cit.* p. 105.

example, the price was to be fixed by the seller or by the buyer and that person died before valuation had taken place. Presumably the remarks made in dealing with the previous point are equally relevant here.

Section 9(2) enables one party to maintain an action for damages where the other party prevents the valuer from making a valuation. An obvious example is where the seller refuses to let the valuer see the goods for the purpose of valuing them.[86] With regard to default by the buyer, it may be that the draftsman had in mind a case like *Clarke* v. *Westrope*[87] where during a dispute between two valuers the buyer consumed the goods and thereby rendered valuation impossible. In such a case the buyer would in any event be liable under the proviso to section 9(1) to pay a reasonable price and he might also be liable in damages under section 9(2) if, for example, the seller had incurred expense in connection with the abortive valuation.

TERMS OF THE CONTRACT

Introduction

Having examined the nature of a contract of sale and the rules governing its formation, it is now necessary to consider some of its more important terms. The terms of the contract may be express or implied, and by far the most important of the implied terms are those contained in sections 12–15 of the Act which are incorporated into the contract of sale with very limited powers of exclusion. Before examining them closely, however, it is first necessary to distinguish between those statements which form part of the contract and those which do not.

A person hoping to effect a contract of sale is likely to make a number of statements during the negotiations, and the courts have the difficult task of determining the precise nature of such statements and the legal consequences if they prove to be untrue. For a long time the law on this topic, and particularly the law relating to the buyer's remedies, was unsatisfactory but the

---

[86] A mandatory injunction compelling the seller to admit the valuer can be obtained (*Smith* v. *Peters* (1875) L.R. 20 Eq. 511).

[87] (1856) 18 C.B. 765.

Misrepresentation Act 1967 has ironed out a number of the former anomalies.

Classification and Remedies

Statements can be broadly classified into:

(1) Mere puff.
(2) Condition precedent.
(3) Representation.
(4) Contractual term.

The test of deciding the true nature of the statement is ultimately one of intention. This is notoriously vague, but it must be appreciated that here, as in other branches of the law of contract, the intention of the parties is judged from their acts. In *Heilbut, Symons* v. *Buckleton*[88] Lord Moulton said:

> "The intention of the parties can only be deduced from the totality of the evidence."

More recently in *Oscar Chess Ltd.* v. *Williams*[89] Denning L.J., said:

> "The question . . . depends on the conduct of the parties, on their words and behaviour, rather than on their thoughts."

(1) *Mere puff*

The tendency of traders to praise their wares in glowing terms has been part of the language of commerce for centuries. Such praise in general does not give rise to any legal liability—*simplex commendatio non obligat*—because the prospective seller is not regarded in law as making a positive representation as to the existence of a fact.[90] It must, however, be noted that the words must be construed in their context. In *Smith* v. *Land and House Property Corporation*,[91] a statement in auction particulars that the tenant of the property was "most desirable" was held by the Court of Appeal to imply that the vendors were unaware of facts making

---

[88] [1913] A.C. 30, 51.
[89] [1957] 1 W.L.R. 370, 375; [1957] 1 All E.R. 325, 329.
[90] See, *e.g. Dimmock* v. *Hallett* (1866) L.R. 2 Ch.App. 21 where land was described as "very fertile and improvable."
[91] (1884) 28 Ch.D. 7, and see also *Brown* v. *Raphael* [1958] Ch. 636; [1958] 2 All E.R. 79.

him undesirable, with the result that since they were aware of such facts the buyer was entitled to rescind.

(2) *Condition precedent*

A statement made during negotiations may be held to form the basis of the entire contract, if the parties intended it to have this effect. The leading case is *Bannerman* v. *White*[92]:

> During negotiations for the sale of hops, the buyer asked if they had been treated with sulphur, adding that if they had he would not even bother to ask the price. On being told that sulphur had not been used he bought the hops but on delivery he discovered that some of them had been treated with sulphur and he repudiated the contract. The seller sued for the price.

It was held that the statement as to sulphur was a condition precedent underlying the whole contract. The facts showed a clear intention that the contract should be null and void if the stipulation was untrue. Consequently, the buyer was not bound to pay the price.

(3) *Representation*

A representation is a statement made at or before the making of the contract but not forming part of that contract or any other contract. A representation is often contrasted with a "warranty" and to avoid serious confusion it must be emphasised at once that the word "warranty" is used in two different senses. It is used, first, to refer to a minor contractual term as opposed to a condition, which is a major term. This meaning which appears in section 61 is not further considered here. The second and more common meaning of the word "warranty" is any statement which the maker warrants to be true. It is this assumption of responsibility which distinguishes a warranty from a representation.[93]

---

[92] (1861) 10 C.B.(N.S.) 844. In *John Bowron & Sons Ltd.* v. *Rodema Canned Foods Ltd.* [1967] 1 Lloyd's Rep. 183 the contract was made "subject to approval [by buyers] of 25 cases to be shipped by first available steamer." Widgery J. held that this was *not* a condition precedent, and that the contract was binding even though the buyers rejected the 25 cases.

[93] The liability in tort of the maker of a careless statement is likewise based on assumption of responsibility (*Hedley Byrne & Co.* v. *Heller & Partners* [1964] A.C. 465; [1963] 2 All E.R. 575, H.L.; *Esso Petroleum* v. *Mardon*, [1976] Q.B. 801; [1976] 2 All E.R. 5.

A person giving a warranty assumes responsibility for it and intends it to form part of the contract[94] or of a collateral contract.[95] A person making a mere representation, on the other hand, does not assume responsibility for it and does not therefore make it part of his contractual promise.

The difficulty, of course, is to decide when a statement is a representation and when it is a warranty, using that word in the sense of contractual term. Ultimately, as already stated, the question turns on intention, but this depends on what view the court takes of all the facts and is not particularly helpful. Three modern cases, however, throw some light on the problem. The first was *Routledge* v. *McKay*[96]:

> A person wishing to buy a motor-cycle combination asked the seller how old it was. The seller replied that it was a late 1941 or 1942 model and produced the registration book which was dated 1941. The vehicle was, unknown to both parties a 1930 model. A written contract was drawn up which did not refer to the age. On discovering the facts the buyer claimed damages for breach of warranty. The Court of Appeal held that the statement was intended as a mere representation and not a warranty.

Two points emerge. In the first place, the conclusion of a written contract containing no reference to the statement is some evidence that no warranty was intended. Secondly, a person with no direct personal knowledge who merely passes on a statement appearing in the registration book will not normally be taken to warrant its accuracy.

This second point was reaffirmed in *Oscar Chess Ltd.* v. *Williams*[97]:

> The defendant owned a Morris car which he desired to sell to the plaintiffs, car dealers, in part exchange for a new Hillman car. On being asked the age of the Morris the defendant (who had no personal knowledge) informed the plaintiffs that it was a 1948 model and produced the registration book which confirmed this. Thereupon the plaintiffs allowed him £290 for the Morris. It was in fact a 1939 model and the plaintiffs sued the defendant for breach of warranty.

---

[94] *Harling* v. *Eddy* [1951] 2 K.B. 739; [1951] 2 All E.R. 212.

[95] *Routledge* v. *McKay* [1954] 1 W.L.R. 615; [1954] 1 All E.R. 855.

[96] *Ibid.*

[97] [1957] 1 W.L.R. 370; [1957] 1 All E.R. 325. Lord Denning suggested that had the buyers come sooner the contract could have been set aside on the grounds of mistake.

A majority of the Court of Appeal (Morris L.J. dissenting) dismissed the claim on the grounds that the defendant was merely stating his opinion on a matter of which he had no special knowledge and was not warranting it to be true.[98]

The relevance of special knowledge was underlined in the third case, *Dick Bentley Productions Ltd.* v. *Harold Smith Motors Ltd.*[99]

> In answer to an inquiry for a well-vetted Bentley car, a motor dealer informed a potential customer that he had such a car and that the engine had done 20,000 miles. In fact it had done 100,000 but the dealer was unaware of this. The Court of Appeal held that
> (1) the dealer was in a position to know or discover the history and mileage of this car;
> (2) consequently his statement amounted to a warranty and the buyer was entitled to damages.

Remedies for misrepresentation. In the previous discussion the reader may have wondered why it was so important for the innocent party to allege warranty. The reason was that, as the law then stood, no damages could be obtained for a mere representation unless there was fraud. Thus in *Oscar Chess Ltd.* v. *Williams* (*supra*) where, on the facts, it was too late to rescind the contract, the plaintiff was left with no remedy at all. Clearly this result was unsatisfactory and the Misrepresentaiton Act 1967 was passed to improve the law by making a number of important changes.[1] As a result of these changes, the present position can be summarised as follows:

(1) *Fraudulent misrepresentation.* If a party is induced to make a contract (*e.g.* a contract to buy or to sell goods) as a result of a fraudulent misrepresentation made by the other party to the contract, he can claim damages for the tort of deceit. He can also rescind the contract, but this remedy is subject to various bars similar to those discussed on page 97. Thus, for example, it will not be available where an innocent third party has acquired rights

---

[98] The classic exposition of the law of warranty is that of Lord Moulton in *Heilbut, Symons* v. *Buckleton* [1913] A.C. 30, 50. For a recent example, see *Wells (Merstham) Ltd.* v. *Buckland Sand and Silica Co. Ltd.* [1965] 2 Q.B. 170; [1964] 1 All E.R. 41.

[99] [1965] 1 W.L.R. 623; [1965] 2 All E.R. 65. The result would presumably have been exactly the same if the buyer had sued in tort for negligence (*cf. Hedley Byrne & Co.* v. *Heller & Partners*, n. 93 *supra*).

[1] For a criticism of the Act, see (1967) 30 M.L.R. 369 (Treitel and Atiyah).

over the subject-matter of the contract.[2] The law relating to fraudulent misrepresentation has not been affected by the 1967 Act. In practice, fraud is difficult to establish and requires a very high standard of proof.

(2) *Non-fraudulent misrepresentation.* (a) It has already been seen that before the Act damages for non-fraudulent misrepresentation were generally not available. This was subject to an exception under section 43 of the Companies Act 1948, which applied where a person had acquired shares or debentures as a result of a misrepresentation in a company prospectus. Such a person could claim damages from the persons issuing the prospectus unless they could prove that they had reasonable ground for believing the statement to be true. The principle underlying this section has now been applied to the whole law of contract by section 2(1) of the Misrepresentation Act 1967, which reads:

> Where a person has entered into a contract after a misrepresentation has been made to him by another party thereto and as a result thereof he has suffered loss, then, if the person making the representaiton would be liable to damages in respect thereof had the misrepresentation been made fraudulently, that person shall be so liable notwithstanding that the misrepresentation was not made fraudulently, unless he proves that he had reasonable ground to believe and did believe up to the time the contract was made that the facts represented were true.[3]

This section therefore creates a right to claim damages for negligent misrepresentation, and the onus is on the defendant to disprove negligence. If he has no specialist knowledge of the matter in question it may be relatively easy for him to do this; it is thought that the private seller in *Routledge* v. *McKay* (*supra*) and in *Oscar Chess Ltd.* v. *Williams* (*supra*) would be able to escape liability on this ground.

(b) The innocent party can rescind the contract,[4] but this is an equitable remedy and is barred in certain cases. Thus it will not be

---

[2] See, *e.g. Phillips* v. *Brooks* [1919] 2 K.B. 243 and s.23 of the Act, *post*, p. 152.

[3] For an example of a successful claim under s. 2(1) see *Howard Marine & Dredging Co. Ltd.* v. *A. Ogden & Sons (Excavations) Ltd.* [1978] 2 All E.R. 1134, C.A.

[4] The right to rescission and the right to damages under s.2(1) appear to be cumulative and not alternative. It seems, therefore, that the right to damages under s.2(1) must be treated as a claim in tort.

available where the party seeking to rescind has affirmed the contract,[5] or been guilty of unreasonable delay,[6] nor will it be available if third parties have acquired rights over the subject-matter of the contract,[7] nor where the parties can no longer be restored to their previous positions. The Act of 1967 has made three changes in the law relating to rescission:

(i) A misrepresentation inducing the contract will sometimes be incorporated into that contract (*e.g.* if a car is described as a 1948 Morris both during negotiations and in the contract itself). In such a case the buyer's rights depended entirely on the contract itself and he could not go outside it to claim rescission for misrepresentation. Section 1 repeals this rule by providing that the right to rescind is available even though the representation has become a term of the contract. Thus the buyer would now have both contractual rights and misrepresentation rights and the latter can sometimes be more valuable than the former.[8]

(ii) Under the so-called rule in *Seddon* v. *North-Eastern Salt Co. Ltd.*[9] the right to rescind was lost once the contract had been performed. The rule was developed in relation to the sale of land and there was much controversy as to whether it ever applied to goods. Section 1 disposes of the matter by providing that the right to rescind shall be available even though the contract has been performed. This does not, of course, affect other bars to rescission, *e.g.* unreasonable delay.

(iii) While the remedy of rescission is fair and reasonable for the innocent party it can sometimes cause very real hardship to the other party. The most obvious example is in relation to the sale of land. If, for example, the vendor of a house makes an innocent misrepresentation that there is no dry rot, it can be extremely embarrassing for him if the purchaser seeks to rescind the sale after the vendor has invested the entire proceeds of the sale in a new house and has moved in with his wife and family. To deal with this type of case section 2(2) breaks new ground by giving the court

---

[5] *Long* v. *Lloyd* [1958] 1 W.L.R. 753; [1958] 2 All E.R. 402.
[6] *Leaf* v. *International Galleries* [1950] 2 K.B. 86; [1950] 1 All E.R. 753.
[7] See, *e.g. Phillips* v. *Brooks* [1919] 2 K.B. 243 and s.23 of the Act, *post*, p. 152.
[8] See Atiyah, *op. cit.* pp. 358–359.
[9] [1905] 1 Ch. 326.

a discretionary power to refuse rescission and award damages instead.[10] It reads:

> Where a person has entered into a contract after a misrepresentation has been made to him otherwise than fraudulently, and he would be entitled, by reason of the misrepresentation, to rescind the contract, then, if it is claimed, in any proceedings arising out of the contract, that the contract ought to be or has been rescinded, the court or arbitrator may declare the contract subsisting and award damages in lieu of rescission, if of opinion that it would be equitable to do so, having regard to the nature of the misrepresentation and the loss that would be caused by it if the contract were upheld, as well as to the loss that rescission would cause to the other party.

Two points call for brief comment. First, the power to award discretionary damages under section 2(2) is quite distinct from the right to claim damages under section 2(1) and is available even though the representation was neither fraudulent nor negligent. Such damages will, however, be taken into account if the court is asked to award damages under section 2(1) (see section 2(3)). Secondly, section 2(2) only applies if the innocent party "would be entitled, by reason of the misrepresentation, to rescind the contract." Although the point is not free from doubt it would seem that the innocent party must be "entitled" to rescission at the time of the proceedings. If this is correct, it follows that the loss of the right to rescind (*e.g.* by unreasonable delay) will prevent the court awarding damages under section 2(2). It may well be, therefore, that a car dealer like the one in *Oscar Chess Ltd.* v. *Williams* (*ante*, p. 94) would still be without a remedy.

Contracting out. Section 3 of the 1967 Act[11] which deals with exemption clauses is considered in a later chapter.[12]

(4) *Contractual term*

If a statement made by one party is found to be a contractual term it will be necessary to classify the term in order to consider the remedies available to the other party if that term is broken. The Act distinguishes between a "warranty" (defined in section 61

---

[10] Compare the power to award damages in lieu of an injunction (Supreme Court Act 1981, s.50).

[11] As re-drafted by section 8 of the Unfair Contract Terms Act 1977.

[12] Chapter Eight, *post*, p. 442.

as an agreement collateral to the main purpose of the contract) and a more important type of term called a "condition." Section 11(3) reads as follows:

> Whether a stipulation in a contract of sale is a condition, the breach of which may give rise to a right to treat the contract as repudiated, or a warranty, the breach of which may give rise to a claim for damages but not to a right to reject the goods and treat the contract as repudiated, depends in each case on the construction of the contract; and a stipulation may be a condition, though called a warranty in the contract.

It has already been seen that the question of distinguishing a representation from a contractual term depends on the intention of the parties, as ascertained from their behaviour. The distinction between conditions and warranties reveals a similar judicial approach. Thus in *Harling* v. *Eddy*[13] the owner of a heifer at an auction sale said to a prospective but somewhat dubious buyer "I guarantee her in every respect." In classifying this statement Lord Evershed M.R. said:

> "It has been said many times . . . that whether any statement is to be regarded as a condition or warranty must depend on the intention to be properly inferred from the particular statement made. A statement that an animal is sound in every respect would prima facie be a warranty but in this case the learned judge found as a fact that the defendant went further and promised that he would take the animal back if she was no good . . . it seems to me plain that the language he used could not have been intended to be a warranty, for a warranty would give no right of rejection to a purchaser."

In other branches of the law of contract there is a general distinction between those breaches which frustrate the commercial object of the contract and those which do not. In other words, the rights of the other party depend not merely on the term itself but also on its consequences. Until recently it was thought that there was no room for this doctrine in sale of goods cases because the "condition-warranty" classification was exhaustive. It is now clear, however, that this is not so. Although the Act only refers to conditions and warranties the rules of the Common Law are preserved by section 62(2). Accordingly a term may be (a) a condition or (b) an intermediate stipulation or (c) a warranty. If a term is classified as an intermediate stipulation the position is as

---

[13] [1951] 2 K.B. 739; [1951] 2 All E.R. 212.

set out above, *i.e.* the right to reject for breach depends on whether it is so serious that the commercial object of the contract is frustrated.[14]

If a term is classified as a condition the innocent party usually has an option. Section 11(2) provides that:

> Where a contract of sale is subject to any condition to be fulfilled by the seller, the buyer may waive the condition, or may elect to treat the breach of such condition as a breach of warranty, and not as a ground for treating the contract as repudiated.
>
> *Example.* A dealer in shoes buys 1,000 pairs of Wellington boots, subject to a condition that they are merchantable. On delivery they are unmerchantable. In the absence of a valid exemption clause he has two alternatives:
>
> 1. He can treat the contract as repudiated by the breach, in which case
>   - (a) He can reject the goods.
>   - (b) He is not bound to pay the price.
>   - (c) If he has paid the price he can recover it because the consideration for it has failed (s.54 *post*, p. 184).
>   - (d) If he has suffered damage through the breach he can maintain an action for damages for non-delivery (s.51 *post*, p. 185).[15]
> 2. He may elect to treat the breach of condition as a breach of warranty, in which case
>   - (a) He retains the goods, and
>   - (b) He claims damages either by action, or by set-off against the price, or both (s.53 *post*, p. 184).

The right to reject for breach of condition is, however, cut down by section 11(4). The section[16] provides that:

> Where a contract of sale is not severable and the buyer has accepted the goods or part of them, the breach of a condition to be fulfilled by the seller can only be treated as a breach of warranty, and not as a ground for rejecting the goods and treating the contract as repudiated, unless there is an express or implied term of the contract to that effect.

A contract is said to be severable if it is capable of being split, and is in fact split, into smaller contracts, as where delivery is by

---

[14] *Cehave N.V.* v. *Bremer Handelsgesellschaft mbH*[1975] 3 W.L.R. 447, C.A.

[15] A claim under s.54 would not be appropriate if the buyer was claiming damages but the price to the defaulting seller could be taken into account as part of the damages (see, *e.g. Mason* v. *Burningham, post*, p. 107).

[16] Re-enacting section 11(1)(c) of the 1893 Act (as amended by section 4 of the Misrepresentation Act 1967).

instalments which are to be separately paid for.[17] In such a case the acceptance of one or more instalments would not prevent the buyer from rejecting future instalments for breach of condition. If, on the other hand, the contract is indivisible, as in practice most contracts are, the acceptance of any part of the goods will prevent any right of rejection from being exercised. A buyer should always endeavour to inspect the goods before accepting them because the loss of his right to reject can be a serious matter. The Act contains a number of rules, which are discussed below, but in practice the task of advising a client, especially in consumer cases, whether he has "accepted" the goods is extremely difficult and there is virtually no modern authority on the point.

What constitutes acceptance? Section 34 provides that:

> (1) Where goods are delivered to the buyer, and he has not previously examined them, he is not deemed to have accepted them until he has had a reasonable opportunity of examining them for the purpose of ascertaining whether they are in conformity with the contract.
> (2) Unless otherwise agreed, when the seller tenders delivery of goods to the buyer, he is bound on request to afford the buyer a reasonable opportunity of examining the goods for the purpose of ascertaining whether they are in conformity with the contract.

This section must be read in conjunction with section 35, which reads as follows:

> The buyer is deemed to have accepted the goods when he intimates to the seller that he has accepted them, or (except where section 34 otherwise provides) when the goods have been delivered to him and he does any act in relation to them which is inconsistent with the ownership of the seller, or when after the lapse of a reasonable time he retains the goods without intimating to the seller that he has rejected them.

The words in brackets did not form part of the original section 35. There was, therefore, a clear conflict between sections 34 and 35; what happened if the buyer did an act inconsistent with the seller's ownership (*e.g.* delivery to a sub-purchaser) without having had a reasonable opportunity for examination? In at least

---

[17] If the contract provides that "each shipment shall be regarded as a separate contract" and the seller in fact sends all the goods on one ship under two separate bills of lading, the contract as performed is *not* severable (*Rosenthal & Sons Ltd.* v. *Esmail* [1965] 1 W.L.R. 117; [1965] 2 All E.R. 860).

two cases[17a] the courts decided that section 35 prevailed and that, accordingly, the right of rejection was lost. This was clearly unsatisfactory at a time when goods were increasingly being supplied in sealed containers and when it was often commercially impractical for the buyer to examine the goods. Accordingly the law was changed by the insertion of the words in brackets and the resale, etc., will not of itself destroy the right to reject. Theoretically the seller could argue that the buyer had waived his right to inspect but this argument is unlikely to succeed unless it was clearly within the contemplation of the parties that the buyer would do so.

Particular terms[18]

Time clauses

Section 10 of the Act reads as follows:

> (1) Unless a different intention appears from the terms of the contract, stipulations as to time of payment are not deemed to be of the essence of a contract of sale.
> (2) Whether any other stipulation as to time is of the essence of the contract or not depends on the terms of the contract.
> (3) In a contract of sale "month" means prima facie calendar month.

In contrast to time for payment, other time stipulations have frequently been regarded as being of the essence, or, in other words, conditions of the contract. In the words of McCardie J.:

> "In ordinary commercial contracts for the sale of goods the rule clearly is that time is prima facie of the essence with respect to delivery."[19]

Likewise time for shipment[20] and time for opening a commercial credit[21] have been held to be, and are usually, of the essence in commercial contracts. In these cases the courts have allowed a

---

[17a] *Hardy (E.) & Co.* v. *Hillerns and Fowler* [1923] 2 K.B. 490; *E. & S. Ruben* v. *Faire Bros. & Co.* [1949] 1 K.B. 254; [1949] 1 All E.R. 215.

[18] For a survey of the previous law and the changes see the 24th Report of the Law Commission and comments in [1970] J.B.L. and [1973] J.B.L. 135.

[19] *Hartley* v. *Hymans* [1920] 3 K.B. 475.

[20] *Thomas Borthwick (Glasgow)* v. *Faure Fairclough* [1968] 1 Lloyd's Rep. 16.

[21] *Ian Stach Ltd.* v. *Baker Bosley Ltd.* [1958] 2 Q.B. 130; [1958] 1 All E.R. 542.

buyer to reject for breach of a time clause without having to prove that he had suffered any damage.[22]

If time is not of the essence, the innocent party cannot treat the contract as repudiated by breach of a time clause, but he can sometimes make time of the essence by giving reasonable notice to the defaulting party.[23] Likewise, if the breach of an essential time clause has been waived, the innocent party can again make time of the essence by giving reasonable notice.[24] In *Charles Rickards Ltd.* v. *Oppenheim*[25]:

> The defendant wished to have a body built on to a Rolls-Royce chassis and he instructed the plaintiffs to do the work on the basis that the work had to be completed on March 20 at the latest. On that date the car was not ready. The defendant continued to press for delivery but at the end of June he informed the plaintiffs that he would refuse the car unless it was delivered by July 25. The car was tendered in October and the defendant rejected it.

The Court of Appeal held that he was entitled to do so, because, having waived the initial breach, his notice in June had again made time of the essence.

The strictness of these rules make it important for a seller to protect himself by suitable drafting, especially where the delay in delivery may be due to circumstances beyond his control.[26]

Title

Section 12 of the Act reads as follows:

> (1) In a contract of sale, other than one to which subsection (3) below applies, there is an implied condition on the part of the seller that in the case of a sale, he has a right to sell the goods, and in the

---

[22] See *Bowes* v. *Shand* (1877) 2 App.Cas. 455, where the goods were shipped too soon. Perhaps the new doctrine of "intermediate stipulation" (*ante*, p. 99) could lead to a more commercially realistic approach whereby rejection would not be available if the buyer had suffered no loss.

[23] *e.g.* under s.48(3) as explained in *R. V. Ward* v. *Bignall*, *post*, p. 179.

[24] See, *e.g. Hartley* v. *Hymans* [1920] 3 K.B. 475. If, however, it is clear that the party in default cannot perform the contract during the notice period, the notice need not be given (*Etablissements Chainbaux S.A.R.L.* v. *Harbormaster Ltd.* [1955] 1 Lloyd's Rep. 303).

[25] [1950] 1 K.B. 616; [1950] 1 All E.R. 420. If, however, a party to a contract waives his rights he cannot afterwards insist on those rights if his waiver has induced the other party to alter his position (see *W. J. Alan & Co.* v. *El Nasr Export and Import Co.* [1972] 2 Q.B. 189; [1972] 2 All E.R. 127, C.A.).

[26] But see Unfair Contract Terms Act 1977, s.3 *post*, p. 438.

case of an agreement to sell, he will have a right to sell the goods at the time when the property is to pass.

(2) In a contract of sale, other than one to which subsection (3) below applies, there is also an implied warranty that—

    (a) the goods are free, and will remain free until the time when the property is to pass, from any charge or encumbrance not disclosed or known to the buyer before the contract is made, and

    (b) the buyer will enjoy quiet possession of the goods except so far as it may be disturbed by the owner or other person entitled to the benefit of any charge or encumbrance so disclosed or known.

(3) This subsection applies to a contract of sale in the case of which there appears from the contract or is to be inferred from its circumstances an intention that the seller should transfer only such title as he or a third party may have.

(4) In a contract to which subsection (3) above applies there is an implied warranty that all charges or encumbrances known to the seller and not known to the buyer have been disclosed to the buyer before the contract is made.

(5) In a contract to which subsection (3) above applies there is also an implied warranty that none of the following will disturb the buyer's quiet possession of the goods, namely:

    (a) the seller;

    (b) in a case where the parties to the contract intend that the seller should transfer only such title as a third party may have, that person;

    (c) anyone claiming through or under the seller or that third person otherwise than under a charge or encumbrance disclosed or known to the buyer before the contract is made.

History. In the early nineteenth century, dominated by the spirit of *laissez-faire*, the basic rule was *caveat emptor*. In the words of Baron Parke the seller was:

> "not liable for a bad title unless there was an express warranty or an equivalent to it by declaration or conduct."[27]

Later cases, however, were very ready to find that the conduct of the parties did give rise to an implied undertaking as to title. Section 12 now enacts the modern law in a way diametrically opposite to the former common law rule—there is an undertaking that the seller has a right to sell, unless the conduct of the parties shows that only a limited title is being sold.

---

[27] *Morley* v. *Attenborough* (1849) 3 Exch. 500, 512.

Right to sell. The meaning of "right to sell" is wider than "right to pass the property." In *Niblett* v. *Confectioners' Materials Co.*[28]:

> Sellers sold 3,000 tins of preserved milk, and some of the tins bore a wrapping which infringed the trade-mark of a third party. On complaint by the third party the tins (which were imported) were detained at the customs and the buyers were compelled to remove the labels, which reduced the sale value. In an action for damages the Court of Appeal held that although the property had passed, the sellers were in breach of section 12(1) because "if a vendor can be stopped by process of law from selling, he has no right to sell."

One problem which has not yet been decided concerns a "sale" by a non-owner.

> Suppose that H, holding goods belonging to O, sells them in market overt[29] to T and confers on him a good title. After a while T, who regrets having bought the goods, discovers that before the sale to him they belonged to O and that the sale by H was not authorised by O. Can T claim damages from H on the ground that H had no *right* to sell?

The practical answer is that even if the courts would allow such an action, it would usually be difficult, if not impossible, for T to prove that he had suffered damage. If, of course, T was involved in expensive litigation in order to establish his title, he might have a claim.

Quiet possession. The warranty of quiet possession and freedom from incumbrances appears to have little practical importance, since there will be many cases in practice when a breach of section 12(1) will not also involve a breach of section 12(2). One situation where section 12(2) could be useful is where B buys goods from S without paying for them and then resells to B2 who is unable to obtain possession because S claims an unpaid seller's lien. A further distinction was confirmed by the case of *Microbeads A.G.* v. *Vinhurst Road Markings Ltd.*[30] In that case S sold goods to B and after the sale T acquired a patent involving interference with B's user. It was held that S was not in breach of the condition (since he had a right to sell) but that he was in breach of the continuing warranty for quiet possession.

---

[28] [1921] 3 K.B. 387, C.A.
[29] *Post*, p. 151.
[30] [1975] 1 W.L.R. 218, C.A.

Title paramount. It is clear from the *Microbeads* case and from the wording of the Act that the warranty for quiet possession under section 12(2) will be broken if the buyer is evicted, not only by the seller or someone claiming under him, but by anyone with a better title. This is clearly in line with the commercial object of the contract and is in sharp contrast to the much more limited warranty which applies in section 12(3) case.

Remedies for breach. If the seller is in breach of section 12(1) and as a result of this no property passes to the buyer, the buyer can claim that there has been a total failure of consideration and can recover the price which he has paid. This is so even if he has used the goods for some time and even though he has done an act amounting to "acceptance." The leading case dealing with this remarkable state of affairs is *Rowland* v. *Divall*[31] where the following facts arose:

> The defendant sold a car to the plaintiff who used it for several months. The defendant was not the true owner and the plaintiff had to return it to the owner. The plaintiff sued for the return of his price as money paid on a consideration which had failed.

The defendant argued that since the plaintiff had accepted the goods he was limited to a claim for damages for breach of warranty, and that in assessing these damages an allowance should be made for the use of the car which the plaintiff had enjoyed. Both these arguments failed. Atkin L.J. considered that there could not be acceptance if there was nothing to accept. The fact that the plaintiff had had the use of the car was also irrelevant, because in the first place the user exposed the plaintiff to an action for conversion and secondly the plaintiff had paid for the property in the car and not merely the right to use it. Consequently he was entitled to recover the whole price because it had been paid for a consideration which had failed.

This rule, which has been criticised,[32] can work very beneficially in favour of the buyer. If he discovers that no property has passed and repudiates the contract, his right to the return of the price

---

[31] [1923] 2 K.B. 500.

[32] Atiyah, *op. cit.* pp. 64, 66. A change was recommened by the Law Reform Committee in their Twelfth Report, but the Law Commission in their 24th Report pointed out a number of practical difficulties (see pp. 4–5 of the report).

crystallises and nothing done by the seller after this can deprive him of that right. In *Butterworth* v. *Kingsway Motors*[33]:

> The hirer of a car under a hire-purchase agreement sold it when he had no right to do so. After several sales, the car reached the defendant who sold it to the plaintiff for £1,275. After 11 months' use, the plaintiff received a letter from the original owners claiming that the car was theirs. He thereupon wrote to the defendant and demanded the return of the whole price which he had paid. The car at that time had a value of only £800. Meanwhile the original hirer who had continued paying his instalments, paid a final instalment which passed the property to him, and this in turn fed the later titles. The plaintiff insisted on recovering his price and it was held that although his claim was somewhat lacking in merit, it was sound in law and he was therefore entitled to succeed.

Pearson J. (as he then was) left open the question of whether the result would have been the same if the property had passed before the notice of rejection was given. It is thought that rejection would not have been possible. It has already been seen from *Niblett's* case that a breach of section 12(1) is not always the same thing as a failure to transfer the property. Now what the buyer is paying for is the property in the goods and it cannot be said that there has been a total failure of consideration if, before he repudiates, he does acquire the property. It is though that *Rowland* v. *Divall*[34] would be confined to its own facts, *i.e.* to a situation where the buyer never gets the property. Bankes L.J. indicated that a buyer who had "accepted" the goods might be confined to an action for damages if he got some part of what he contracted for. This principle would clearly cover a case where he actually gets the property in the goods (although he gets it late).[35]

A buyer who has been dispossessed can also claim general damages, such as the cost of necessary repairs carried out by him.[36]

---

[33] [1954] 1 W.L.R. 1286; [1954] 2 All E.R. 694. On the facts of this case the buyer might now acquire title under Part III of the Hire-Purchase Act 1964 (see *post*, p. 157).

[34] [1923] 2 K.B. 500.

[35] The courts of New South Wales have decided in favour of this view (see *Patten* v. *Thomas Motors Pty. Ltd.* (1965) N.S.W.R. 1457 cited in Atiyah, *op. cit.* at p. 63).

[36] *Mason* v. *Burningham* [1949] 2 K.B. 545; [1949] 2 All E.R. 134. See also *Greenwood* v. *Bennett* [1973] 1 Q.B. 195; [1972] 3 W.L.R. 691, where a car belonging to O was sold by B (a rogue) to B2 who spent money on repairs. The police seized the car and interpleader proceedings took place between O and B2. The Court of Appeal held that on general equitable principles O should compensate B2 for the cost of repairs. The principle of this case is now to be found in section 6 of the Torts (Interference with Goods) Act 1977.

Limited titles and exemption clauses. Section 12(3) which has been in force for some nine years, has not been considered by the courts in any reported case. It can clearly cover such matters as sales by a Sheriff under a distress warrant where he does not guarantee the debtor's title; in such cases the risk of defects in the title is on the buyer.[37] Presumably it can also apply where the seller makes it clear to the buyer that he (the seller) is in the process of acquiring title from a third party (such as a supplier with retention of title). Apart from limiting the section 12 obligations in the manner allowed by section 12(3) the title obligations cannot be excluded or limited at all (see section 6 of the Unfair Contract Terms Act 1977, *post*, p. 440).

Description[38]

Section 13, provides that:

> (1) Where there is a contract for the sale of goods by description, there is an implied condition that the goods shall correspond with the description.
> (2) If the sale is by sample, as well as by description it is not sufficient that the bulk of the goods corresponds with the sample if the goods do not also correspond with the description.
> (3) A sale of goods is not prevented from being a sale by description by reason only that, being exposed for sale or hire, they are selected by the buyer.

This section gives rise to three problems:
(1) What is a sale by description?
(2) What are the buyer's remedies?
(3) Can liability under section 13 be excluded?

(1) Sale by description. A sale can be said to be by description if words are used to identify the goods sold. Dealing first with unascertained goods, in the sense of purely generic goods, it is clear that they can be identified in one of three ways:
(1) By description. An example would be flooring sold as "solid oak wood flooring."

---

[37] See *Payne* v. *Elsden* (1900) 17 T.L.R. 161 (sale by auctioneer under invalid distress warrant).

[38] A false trade description may lead to criminal liability under the Trade Descriptions Act 1968–1972 and the criminal court can award compensation on convicting the accused (Powers of Criminal Courts Act 1973, s.35 *post*, p. 449).

(2) By sample and description. An example would be a contract for the sale of "foreign refined rape oil, warranted equal to sample."
(3) By sample only, as where a seller simply produces a sample of a new product and the buyer says, "Send me one thousand pairs of those."

Section 13 applies to the first two of these cases but not to the third.

Turning now to specific goods, these can also be sold by description, but it is a question of construction as to whether the words in question were used to identify the things sold or whether they were merely collateral. In *Varley* v. *Whipp*[39]:

> The seller agreed to sell a second-hand reaping machine which he described as new the previous year. The buyer had not seen the machine. On arrival it was found to be much older and he purported to reject it. The seller sued for the price.

The case turned on the rather fine point of whether the words relating to the age of the machine formed part of the description. It was held that they did, and as the seller had broken the condition implied under section 13 the buyer could reject.

Channell J. said[40]:

> "The term 'sale of goods by description' must apply to all cases where the purchaser has not seen the goods but is relying on description alone. The most usual application of that section, no doubt, is to unascertained goods, but I think it must also be applied to cases such as this where there is no identification otherwise than by description."

This is not the end of the matter, because specific goods may be sold by description even if the buyer has seen them, provided that they are sold not as specific goods but as goods answering a description. Thus a buyer who goes into a shop and asks for a pair of woollen underpants[41] or a catapult[42] buys by description even though he sees the article in front of him. The same result usually

---

[39] [1900] 1 Q.B. 513.
[40] At p. 516. Note that there must be *reliance* on the descriptive words, *i.e.* the buyer must buy them *because* their identity is as described (*Travers (Joseph)* v. *Longel, Ltd.* (1948) 64 T.L.R. 150).
[41] *Grant* v. *Australian Knitting Mills, post*, p. 120.
[42] *Godley* v. *Perry, post*, p. 124.

follows from subsection (3) where the buyer selects goods in a self-service store or shop.

On the other hand a customer who agrees to buy a specific article *as* a specific article and without using any descriptive words does not buy by description unless the goods can be said to describe themselves. It now seems clear from the remarkable case of *Beale* v. *Taylor*[43] that this is indeed possible. In that case:

> The plaintiff saw an advertisement for a 1961 Herald convertible. When he went to see it he saw a "1200" disc at the back of the car and he agreed to buy it. When he drove the car away he found that the steering wheel was defective and he took it into a garage. The garage found that the so-called "1200" car was, in fact, a combination of two cars—the back portion of a 1961 "1200" model having been welded on to the front part of a much older car. The buyer (a minor suing through his next friend) claimed damages.

The seller (who appeared in person) argued that it was not a sale by description at all but a sale of a particular thing seen by the buyer and bought by him on his own assessment of its value. The Court of Appeal rejected this view. The advertisement of a 1961 Herald, and the disc which confirmed it, was the basis of the buyer's offer to buy and accordingly the seller must be taken as agreeing to sell a car answering that description. Since the car did not correspond to the description the seller was in breach of section 13 and was liable to pay damages. As the buyer had kept the car the damages were assessed at the difference between the price paid by the buyer and the value of the car in his hands.

In view of this decision and in view of subsection (3) (*ante*, p. 108) the section is, in the words of the Law Commission,[44] "to all intents and purposes comprehensive." A sale which is not a sale by description must now be extremely rare.

Meaning of description. It has already been seen that whether words form part of the description is a question of construction in each case, but the tendency of the courts is to construe the word "description" widely. Thus it has been held to include not only the class or type to which the goods belong but also such matters as

---

[43] [1967] 1 W.L.R. 1193; [1967] 3 All E.R. 253.
[44] 24th Report at p. 8.

ingredients,[45] thickness,[46] packing,[47] quantity,[48] and date of shipment.[49] Recently, however, the House of Lords has strongly hinted (in a case not directly involving the sale of goods) that a number of these cases dealing with the meaning of "description" might require reconsideration.[50] Lord Wilberforce was clearly unhappy at the rigid condition–warranty classification (*ante,* p. 99) and at the possibility that a relatively minor deviation from the contract "description" would enable the buyer to reject for breach of condition (see below).[51]

(2) Buyer's remedies. On breach of section 13 the buyer has received goods different from those which he contracted to receive, and accordingly he can either claim damages or he can reject the goods. In *Arcos* v. *Ronaasen.*[52]

> Buyers ordered a quantity of staves half an inch thick. Most of those delivered were between half an inch and nine-sixteenths of an inch thick, and an umpire found that they were merchantable under the contract specification. Despite this, the House of Lords held that the buyers were entitled to reject.

Lord Atkins said (at p. 479):

> "A ton does not mean about a ton, or a yard about a yard. Still less when you descend to minute measurements does half an inch mean about half an inch. If a seller wants a margin he must, and in my experience does, stipulate for it."

In practice sellers often seek to evade the strict consequences of section 13 by the use of words such as "about," "approximately," "little more or less." If these words are used it is a question of construction whether the seller's deviation is sufficiently small to come within the margin.[53]

---

[45] *Ashington Piggeries* v. *Christopher Hill* [1972] A.C. 441.
[46] [1933] A.C. 470.
[47] *Manbre Saccharine Co.* v. *Corn Products Co.* [1919] 1 K.B. 198.
[48] *Green* v. *Arcos* (1931) 47 T.L.R. 336, C.A.
[49] *Macpherson Train* v. *Ross* [1955] 1 W.L.R. 640; [1955] 2 All E.R. 445.
[50] See note 45 above.
[51] *Reardon Smith Lines Ltd.* v. *Hansen Tangen* [1976] 1 W.L.R. 989; [1976] 3 All E.R. 570.
[52] [1933] A.C. 470.
[53] Presumably a clause in a standard-form contract requiring the buyer to pay for the surplus would have to be "reasonable" within the Unfair Contract Terms Act 1977, s.3(2)(*b*)(i) *post,* p. 438.

The question of remedies is also dealt with by section 30 which provides as follows:

> (1) Where the seller delivers to the buyer a quantity of goods less than he contracted to sell, the buyer may reject them,[54] but if the buyer accepts the goods so delivered he must pay for them at the contract rate.
>
> (2) Where the seller delivers to the buyer a quantity of goods larger than he contracted to sell, the buyer may accept the goods included in the contract and reject the rest, or he may reject the whole.
>
> (3) Where the seller delivers to the buyer a quantity of goods larger than he contracted to sell and the buyer accepts the whole of the goods so delivered he must pay for them at the contract rate.
>
> (4) Where the seller delivers to the buyer the goods he contracted to sell mixed with goods of a different description not included in the contract, the buyer may accept the goods which are in accordance with the contract and reject the rest, or he may reject the whole.
>
> (5) This section is subject to any usage of trade, special agreement, or course of dealing between the parties.

Section 30(1) can be illustrated by *Behrend* v. *Produce Brokers Co.*[55]

> Sellers sold a quantity of cotton seed *ex* the *Port Inglis* in London. On arrival, the ship discharged a small part of this, and then went on to Hull, returning to London three weeks later to discharge the remainder. It was held that under section 30(1) the buyers were entitled to retain the seed originally supplied and to reject the rest.

It will be apparent that section 30 overlaps with section 13. In *Re Moore & Co. and Landauer & Co.*[56]:

> On a sale of canned fruit, delivery was to be in boxes containing 30 tins. Some of the boxes supplied contained only 24 tins. The market value of the consignment was in no way affected, but the Court of Appeal, affirming Rowlatt J., held that (1) the packing formed part of the description, (2) the sellers were accordingly in breach of section 13, (3) the buyer was entitled under section 30(4) to reject the entire consignment.

---

[54] Conversely if S agrees to sell to B a specified quantity of a crop to be grown, and if part of the crop fails, B may be able to insist on delivery of the remainder (see *Sainsbury* v. *Street* [1972] 1 W.L.R. 834).

[55] [1920] 3 K.B. 530.

[56] [1921] 2 K.B. 519. The subsection numbers in the 1893 Act were slightly different.

Three other points are worthy of note in connection with section 30. The first is that trifling breaches will be ignored—*de minimis non curat lex.*[57] Secondly, it will be observed that section 30(3) enables the buyer to retain the non-contractual goods whereas section 30(4) does not in terms confer such a right. Presumably if the buyer accepted the non-contractual goods there would be a new contract and he would be bound under section 8(2) to pay a reasonable price. Thirdly, although section 30 overlaps with section 13, it does give distinct rights to the buyer. Under the general rule governing a non-severable contract a buyer cannot accept part and reject part (section 11(4) *ante*, p. 100). If, however, the breach comes within section 30 he can do so. Accordingly, section 30 can be regarded as an exception to section 11(4). In one case[58] a buyer inspected and selected timber and thereby "accepted" it. The sellers sent him a consignment consisting partly of the timber selected by the buyer and partly of other timber. It was held that under what is now section 30(4) the buyer could reject the whole consignment.

(3) Exclusion of liability under section 13. This topic is considered *post*, pp. 440–441.

Quality and fitness

Until comparatively recent times the maxim *caveat emptor* reigned supreme[59] in the field of sale of goods as it did (and still does) in the sale of land. Although eaten away by many exceptions, it is not entirely extinct. Section 14 of the Act opens with these words:

> (1) Except as provided by this section, and section 15 below and subject to the provisions of any other enactment, there is no implied condition or warranty as to the quality or fitness for any particular purpose of goods supplied under a contract of sale.
> *Example.* A buys from his friend B a computer which turns out to be useless. B does not sell in the course of a business. Result: A has no claim against B. *Caveat emptor.*

---

[57] *Shipton, Anderson* v. *Weil Bros.* [1912] 1 K.B. 574.

[58] *London Plywood and Timber Co.* v. *Nasic Oak Extract Factory and Steam Sawmills Co.* [1939] 2 K.B. 343. See Fridman, *Sale of Goods*, pp. 208–211; Atiyah, *op. cit.* pp. 354–355.

[59] See (1952) 15 M.L.R. 425 and (1953) 16 M.L.R. 174.

There are, however, a number of very important exceptions to the general rule, namely:

(1) An implied condition of merchantable quality (s.14(2)).
(2) An implied condition of fitness (s.14(3)).
(3) Conditions and warranties implied by usage (s.14(4)).
(4) A condition of freedom from latent defects on a sale by sample (s.15(2)(c)).

Scope of exceptions. The first two exceptions in section 14 only apply to a sale *in the course of a business*, a term which includes a profession and the activities of a government department, local or public authority (see s.61(1)). The business does not have to consist of buying and selling the type of goods which are actually sold; thus if a coal-merchant sold off one of his lorries this would be a sale "in the course of a business."

What happens if the person who sells the goods does so as agent for another? Section 14(5) provides the answer:

> The preceding provisions of this section apply to a sale by a person who in the course of business is acting as agent for another as they apply to a sale by a principal in the course of a business except where that other is not selling in the course of a business and either the buyer knows that fact or reasonable steps are taken to bring it to the notice of the buyer before the contract is made.

Accordingly if A (a car dealer) is instructed by P (a non-trader) to sell P's car and he then sells it to B, the latter will have the benefit of the statutory terms unless he knows that the car was being sold on behalf of a non-trader or unless A took reasonable steps to bring this to B's notice.

Merchantable quality. Section 14(2) reads as follows:

> Where the seller sells goods in the course of a business, there is an implied condition that the goods supplied under the contract are of merchantable quality, except that there is no such condition—
>
> (a) as regards defects specifically drawn to the buyer's attention before the contract is made; or
> (b) if the buyer examines the goods before the contract is made, as regards defects which that examination ought to reveal.

The first point to notice is that the condition is not confined to the goods which are actually "sold"; it applies to all goods "supplied under the contract." Thus if lemonade is supplied in a defective bottle the "goods" may be unmerchantable even if the contract provides that the bottle is to be returned after use.[60] Again, in the remarkable case of *Wilson* v. *Rickett Cockerell & Co. Ltd.*[61]

> A lady ordered Coalite. The Coalite supplied was unhappily mixed with a detonator, which exploded in the fireplace. When sued under what is now s.14(2) the sellers argued that the Coalite was merchantable quality and that the detonator was superfluous and could be disregarded. Amazingly enough this argument prevailed in the county court. Fortunately the Court of Appeal would have none of it. The goods "supplied" under the contract of sale were not of merchantable quality, because coal accompanied by a detonator could not be said to be fit for burning. The sellers were liable.

Surprisingly enough the key phrase "merchantable quality" was not defined in the 1893 Act but a definition was inserted by the Supply of Goods (Implied Terms) Act 1973 and this definition now appears in section 14(6). It reads:

> Goods of any kind are of merchantable quality within the meaning of subsection (2) above if they are as fit for the purpose or purposes for which goods of that kind are commonly bought as it is reasonable to expect having regard to any description applied to them, the price (if relevant)[62] and all the other circumstances.

The reference to "purpose or purposes" recognises the fact that goods can have several purposes. What is less clear is whether this definition has (perhaps unwittingly[63]) changed the law. In 1970 the House of Lords had held in *Brown* v. *Craiks*[64] that where goods were unfit for *one* of their purposes this did not make them unmerchantable, provided that a buyer would accept them without a substantial abatement in price. In that case:

---

[60] *Geddling* v. *Marsh* [1929] 1 K.B. 668; *Morelli* v. *Fitch and Gibbons* [1928] 2 K.B. 636.

[61] [1954] 1 Q.B. 598; [1954] 1 All E.R. 868.

[62] If goods of a general description can be sold in different qualities which are reflected in the price "it could not be right that if the contract price is appropriate for the better quality the seller should be entitled to tender the lower quality and say that, because the lower quality is commercially saleable under the contract description, he has fulfilled his contract by delivering goods of the lower quality" (*per* Lord Reid in *Brown* v. *Craiks Ltd.* [1970] 1 W.L.R. 752, 755; [1970] 1 All E.R. 823).

[63] No change was intended by the Law Commission.

[64] [1970] 1 W.L.R. 752; [1970] 1 All E.R. 823, H.L.

B ordered cloth from S at 36p per yard. The cloth supplied by S was not fit for B's particular purpose (dressmaking) but was perfectly suitable for industrial purposes, although the price of industrial cloth was only 30p per yard. The House of Lords held that the difference of 6p per yard did not make the goods unmerchantable.

How would this case be decided today? A learned writer[65] has commented that the statutory wording is ambiguous; does it mean that multi-purpose goods must be fit for *all* their normal purposes or is it sufficient that they are fit for *all* or *any* of those purposes? The first construction (which would alter the law in favour of the buyer) seems the more natural one and the position will depend on whether the courts will be prepared to go behind the actual wording to find out whether Parliament intended to change the law. In view of the prevailing uncertainty a buyer of multi-purpose goods would be well advised to make his particular purpose known to the seller. This may enable him to invoke section 14(3) (*post*, p. 119) if the goods turn out to be unfit for that purpose.

There have been very few reported cases on the statutory definition of merchantable quality but the following points, decided under the previous law, must be borne in mind.

(1) If goods have only one purpose (*e.g.* underpants) they are unmerchantable if they have defects rendering them unfit for that purpose.[66]

(2) The packing of the goods can, in appropriate cases, make them unmerchantable. Thus in *Niblett* v. *Confectioners' Materials Co.* (*ante*, p. 105) Bankes and Atkin L.JJ. considered that the sellers were in breach of section 14(2) as well as section 12(1). On the other hand the mere fact that the goods are unsaleable at one particular place does not make them unmerchantable.[67]

(3) The concept of "merchantable quality" is a relative one. Thus a second-hand car may be "merchantable" even if its condition is less than perfect; regard must be had to its age, the price paid and all other relevant circumstances.[68]

---

[65] Professor Aubrey Diamond in (1970) 33 M.L.R. 78.
[66] *Grant* v. *Australian Knitting Mills* [1936] A.C. 85.
[67] *Sumner Permain* v. *Webb* [1922] 1 K.B. 55.
[68] *Bartlett* v. *Sidney Marcus Ltd.* [1965] 1 W.L.R. 1013; [1965] 2 All E.R. 753; *Lee* v. *York Coach and Marine* [1977] R.T.R. 35 (right to reject lost by non-acceptance).

The above points are reasonable enough but the statutory definition has raised one unexpected problem in relation to new manufactured goods—and in particular new motor cars. The section uses the words "as fit . . . as it is reasonable to expect." It is well known that many new goods have minor defects; accordingly the argument has been advanced (and, amazingly, accepted by some courts) that such defects do not make goods unmerchantable because a buyer can reasonably expect such defects. This point has usually arisen in cases where a buyer has sought to reject the goods altogether (a remedy which the court might be reluctant to grant) but if pressed to its logical conclusion it would leave the unfortunate buyer with no remedy whatever (unless some kind of "intermediate stipulation" (*ante*, p. 99) could be invented by the courts). It is felt that the argument is unsound and that a buyer who spends, say £5,000 on a new car can claim that it was "reasonable to expect" a trouble-free car having regard to the price and all other relevant circumstances. The whole question of merchantable quality (and fitness for purpose) has been referred to the Law Commission.

Time. If goods are intended for immediate use they must be merchantable when they are sold and delivered and it is no defence that they could have been made merchantable by a simple process.[69] If, on the other hand, both parties contemplate some action before use, the goods must be merchantable after this has been done but not necessarily before. In *Heil* v. *Hedges*[70]:

> A lady bought pork chops, ate them only half-cooked and became ill. The cause of the illness was a parasitic worm in the pork, which would have been killed if the pork had been properly cooked. It was held that the sellers were not liable under section 14.

Not only must the goods be of merchantable quality when they are appropriated to the contract, but they must remain so for a reasonable time.[71] Where perishable goods are sold under a

---

[69] *Grant* v. *Australian Knitting Mills* [1936] A.C. 85 (excessive sulphite in underpants); *Jackson* v. *Rotax Motor and Cycle Co. Ltd.* [1910] 2 K.B. 937 (motor horns scratched and dented).
[70] [1951] 1 T.L.R. 512.
[71] *Per* Atkin J. (as he then was) in *Ollett* v. *Jordan* [1918] 2 K.B. 41, 47.

contract which involves transit before use, the goods must remain merchantable throughout a normal journey and for a reasonable time thereafter. In *Beer* v. *Walker*[72]:

> Sellers of rabbits sent them by train from London to Brighton. When they were put onto the train at London they were merchantable, but on arrival at Brighton they were putrid and useless. The journey was a perfectly normal one. It was held that the sellers were liable.

The sellers will not, however, be liable if they supply goods which can remain merchantable throughout a normal journey but become unmerchantable by reason of the journey being abnormal.[73] One unsettled point concerns the durability of non-perishable goods—what happens if (for example) a dishwasher with a normal working life of four years breaks down irreparably after two years? In the absence of any direct authority there are *dicta*[74] to suggest that a buyer could successfully argue that the article was "unmerchantable"—provided that he can link the failure of the machine with its condition when he bought it. The position however is not free from doubt and this may help to explain the interest shown in long term "guarantees" promoted by finance companies under arrangements with insurers.

Examination. Section 14(2)(*b*) makes it clear that a buyer who actually examines the goods will not be protected as regards defects which "that examination" ought to have revealed. In *Thornett and Fehr* v. *Beers & Sons*[75]:

> A buyer of barrels of glue inspected the outside of the barrels only. Had he looked inside he would have discovered the defect. Held: the examination by the buyer exempted the seller from liability.

---

[72] (1877) 46 L.J.Q.B. 677; for a possible qualification, see s.33, *post*, p. 138.

[73] *Mash & Murrell* v. *Joseph Emanuel* [1962] 1 W.L.R. 16; [1962] 1 All E.R. 77 as explained in *Cordova Land Co.* v. *Victor Bros. Inc.* [1966] 1 W.L.R. 793.

[74] See, *e.g.* Lord Diplock in *Lambert* v. *Lewis* [1981] 2 W.L.R. 713; [1981] 1 All E.R. 1185, 1191 (the point was not directly in issue in that case and his remarks must be read in their context) see further Goode, *Commercial Law* at p. 288.

[75] [1919] 1 K.B. 486. It is doubtful whether the decision is correct. Unlike s.15(2)(*c*), which refers to "a reasonable examination," s.14(2) (as originally drafted) used the term "such examination," which seems to refer to the examination actually made. The learned judge proceeded on the basis that "such examination, *if made in the ordinary way*, would have revealed the defect" (italics are mine). The section now uses the words "that examination" and this lends support to the argument that *Thornett* should not be followed.

If on the other hand, the defect is not discoverable on examination, the seller will still be liable.[76]

Condition of fitness. Section 14(3) reads as follows:

> (3) Where the seller sells goods in the course of a business and the buyer expressly or by implication, makes known—
> (*a*) to the seller, or
> (*b*) where the purchase price or part of it is payable by instalments and the goods were previously sold by a credit-broker to the seller, to that credit-broker,
> any particular purpose for which the goods are being bought, there is an implied condition that the goods supplied under the contract are reasonably fit for that purpose, whether or not that is a purpose for which such goods are commonly supplied, except where the circumstances show that the buyer does not rely, or that it is unreasonable for him to rely, on the skill or judgment of the seller or credit-broker.

The condition of fitness will only be implied if the buyer notifies the seller of the particular purpose for which he requires the goods. In *Priest* v. *Last*[77]:

> A customer went to a chemist's shop to buy a hot water bottle. He asked whether it would stand boiling water and was told that it would take hot water but not boiling water. He thereupon bought it. After only five days it burst while being used and he claimed damages under what is now s.14(3). The jury found that the bottle was not fit for use as a hot water bottle. Thereupon judgment was given for the plaintiff, and the Court of Appeal affirmed it.

Counsel for the seller argued that the bottle was only required for its normal purpose and did not therefore come within the subsection which required notification of a "particular" purpose. This argument was swept aside. Collins M.R. said[78]:

> "There are many goods which . . . are capable of general use for a multitude of purposes. . . . In the case of a purchase of goods of that kind in order to give rise to the implication of warranty[79] it is necessary to show that . . . it was sold with reference to a particular purpose. But in a case where the discussion begins with the fact that

---

[76] *Wren* v. *Holt* [1903] 1 K.B. 610 (arsenic in beer).
[77] [1903] 2 K.B. 148; followed in *Frost* v. *Aylesbury Dairy Co.* [1905] 1 K.B. 608.
[78] *Ibid.* at p. 153.
[79] *i.e.* condition.

the description of the goods by which they were sold[80] points to one particular purpose only, it seems to me that the first requirement of the subsection is satisfied, namely, that the particular purpose for which the goods are required should be made known to the seller."

Thus where the purpose is obvious as in the case of a hot water bottle,[81] undergarments[82] or food[83] the mere fact of asking for the goods amounts to an implied notification of the purpose for which they are required. If goods have several purposes, the buyer must indicate the one for which he requires them.[84] Finally, if there are special circumstances connected with the buyer, these again must be made known. In *Griffiths* v. *Peter Conway Ltd.*[85]

> A lady bought a coat without disclosing that her skin was particularly sensitive. She contracted dermatitis and sued for damages under what is now section 14(3). It was proved that the coat was suitable for wearing by a person whose skin was normal. The Court of Appeal, affirming Branson J., dismissed the action, on the ground that the particular purpose, *viz.* wearing by an abnormal buyer, had not been disclosed.

Under the law as it stood before the 1973 Act, the buyer had to prove that he relied on the seller's skill or judgment but this requirement was generously construed in favour of the buyer. As Lord Wright put it in *Grant* v. *Australian Knitting Mills*[86]:

> "To take the case . . . of a purchaser from a retailer the reliance will in general be inferred from the fact that a buyer goes to the shop in the confidence that the tradesman has selected his stock with skill and judgment."

The courts have been prepared to find "reliance" even in a case where the seller and the buyer were traders in the same line of business.[87] They also held that partial reliance was sufficient[88]

---

[80] The sale need not, of course, be by description.

[81] See n. 77, *supra*.

[82] *Grant* v. *Australian Knitting Mills* [1936] A.C. 85.

[83] *Chaproniere* v. *Mason* (1905) 21 T.L.R. 633, C.A.

[84] See, *e.g. Manchester Lines Ltd.* v. *Rea* [1922] 2 A.C. 74 (coal for bunkering a particular ship) and *Brown Ltd.* v. *Craiks Ltd., ante*, p. 115.

[85] [1939] 1 All E.R. 685; compare *Ingham* v. *Emes* [1955] 2 Q.B. 366; [1955] 2 All E.R. 740 (work and labour).

[86] [1936] A.C. 85, 99 and see *Godley* v. *Perry, post*, p. 124.

[87] *Hardwick Game Farm* v. *Suffolk Agricultural Assn.* [1969] 2 A.C. 31; [1968] 2 All E.R. 444, H.L.

[88] See, *e.g. Cammell Laird* v. *Manganese Bronze and Brass Co.* [1934] A.C. 402.

unless the seller could prove that the defect fell outside the area of reliance. In *Ashington Piggeries* v. *Christopher Hill Ltd.*[89]:

> S a manufacturer of animal foodstuffs was asked by B to make up a particular foodstuff for feeding to mink. S had never previously made up mink food and B knew this. The court found that B relied on S to see that the food was suitable for animals generally but that he relied on his own judgment in relation to any special requirements of mink. The food was unsuitable for the mink and many of them died.

If the seller had been able to prove that the food was satisfactory for animals other than mink this would have meant that the defect was a special "mink" defect and therefore fell outside the area of reliance. Unfortunately the evidence on this was vague and inconclusive. Accordingly the House of Lords held that the seller was liable.

It seems clear from the present wording of section 14(3) that cases such as those discussed above will still be relevant. The seller can escape liability if the court is satisfied[90] that (a) the buyer did not rely on the seller's skill or judgment or (b) it was not reasonable for him to do so.[91] Accordingly a seller who receives an order for goods which he does not normally handle (*e.g.* the mink food in the *Hill* case) should always make it clear to the buyer that the buyer must rely on his own judgment. It would then be unreasonable for the buyer to rely on the seller's judgment.

Credit-brokers

The term credit-broker (which first appeared in this context in the Consumer Credit Act 1974) is defined in section 61(1) as "a person acting in the course of a business of credit-brokerage carried on by him, that is a business of effecting introductions of individuals[92] desiring to obtain credit—

---

[89] [1972] A.C. 441; [1971] 1 All E.R. 847.

[90] The Law Commission assume that the onus of disproving reliance will be on the seller (24th Report, para. 37); the section, however, does not say so.

[91] See, *e.g. Teheran-Europe Co. Ltd.* v. *S. T. Belton* (*Tractors*) *Ltd.* [1968] 2 Q.B. 545; [1968] 2 All E.R. 886 (Persian buyer orders goods from English sellers; unfit for use in Persia; *held*, no reliance).

[92] Presumably a dealer who only arranges credit for limited companies would *not* be a credit-broker although the Act is silent on the point.

(*a*) to persons carrying on any business so far as it relates to the provision of credit, or

(*b*) to other persons engaged in credit-brokerage."

A common financing situation is to be found where a dealer ("credit-broker") introduces a credit-seeking customer to a finance company. If the finance company agrees to the proposal it will buy the goods from the dealer and will then sell them to the customer who will repay by instalments. In such a case the finance company will be the seller but the buyer will have the benefit of the condition of fitness if he has made his purpose known to the dealer.

Relationship between sections 14(2) *and* 14(3)

Four matters are common to both subsections. In both cases:

(1) The seller must sell in the course of a business (*ante*, p. 114).
(2) The condition applies to all goods "supplied" (*ibid.*).
(3) In deciding whether goods are "merchantable" and "reasonably fit" regard must be had to the age of the goods, the price (if relevant) and other relevant circumstances (see *Bartlett* v. *Sidney Marcus*, *ante*, p. 116).
(4) The condition is absolute; in other words, the absence of negligence on the part of the seller is no defence. In *Frost* v. *Aylesbury Dairy Co.*[93]:

> S supplied milk to B. It contained some germs and B's wife contracted typhoid and died. B sued S in contract and S argued that no amount of reasonable care on his part could have discovered the germs. The Court of Appeal held that the clear wording of the Act left no room for such an argument. S was therefore liable.

There is a considerable overlap between sections 14(2) and 14(3); if goods have basically only one purpose and if they are unfit for that purpose a buyer can normally succeed under both subsections.[94] On the other hand, the goods may be unfit for the buyer's particular purpose while perfectly usable for other

---

[93] [1905] 1 K.B. 608. A claim in tort on behalf of B's estate or dependants would have failed because B's personal representatives would have had to prove negligence on the part of S.

[94] *Godley* v. *Perry*, *post*, p. 124. The Law Commission suggest that a buyer who cannot use s.14(2) because he had examined the goods and should have discovered the defect can still succeed under s.14(3) (24th Report, para. 39). *Quaere* whether such an examination could negative "reliance" on the seller's skill or judgment.

purposes. In such a case the buyer will have a remedy under section 14(3); it will be recalled that the position under section 14(2) is doubtful.[95]

Conditions implied on a sale by sample
Section 15 of the Act is largely self-explanatory. It provides as follows:

> (1) A contract of sale is a contract for sale by sample where there is a term in the contract, express or implied, to that effect.[96]
> (2) In the case of a contract for sale by sample—
> (*a*) There is an implied condition that the bulk shall correspond with the sample in quality:
> (*b*) There is an implied condition that the buyer shall have a reasonable opportunity of comparing the bulk with the sample:
> (*c*) There is an implied condition that the goods shall be free from any defect rendering them unmerchantable, which would not be apparent on reasonable examination of the sample.

It will be recalled that where the sale is by sample and by description, it is an implied condition that the goods correspond both with the sample and with the description. In *Nichol* v. *Godts*[97]:

> Sellers sold "foreign refined rape oil, warranted only equal to sample." They delivered oil which did not answer the description of foreign refined rape oil. It was held that the exemption clause related only to quality[98] and did not excuse the sellers from their duty to supply goods answering the description.

The first condition implied by section 15(2), namely that the bulk shall correspond with the sample, is an example of the general rule that if a seller contracts to deliver goods of a particular quality, he does not perform his contract by delivering goods of a different quality. Again, a contract that the goods are to be supplied "with all faults" will not assist a seller who supplied a bulk not corresponding with the sample.[99] The second condition is

---

[95] *Ante*, p. 115.
[96] The mere showing of a sample during negotiations does not necessarily make the sale a sale by sample (*Gardiner* v. *Gray* (1815) 4 Camp. 144).
[97] (1854) 10 Exch. 191.
[98] *i.e.* it might have excluded the condition now implied in s.15(2)(*c*).
[99] *Champanhac* v. *Waller* [1948] 2 All E.R. 724. The exemptive words might have been effective to exclude the condition implied by s.15(2)(*c*).

an illustration of section 34 (*ante*, p. 101). The third condition and others were considered in *Godley* v. *Perry*[1]:

> A small boy went into a shop and asked for a catapult. He was sold one for 6d. It broke almost at once and he lost the sight of one eye. The shopkeeper had bought it from a wholesaler by sample, and had inspected the sample catapult by pulling the elastic. Edmund Davies J. held that (1) the boy succeeded against the shopkeeper under section 14(2) and under 14(3); (2) the retailer succeeded against the wholesaler under section 15(2)(*c*) because the defect would not have been revealed by a "reasonable examination" as that phrase would be understood by the commonsense standards of ordinary life. No doubt a more elaborate examination, such as taking the catapult to pieces, might have revealed the defect, but this was not required.

Overlap between sections 14 and 15. In view of the amended wording of section 14(2) there appears to be an overlap between that subsection and section 15(2)(*c*).[2] Thus if the defect is not apparent from the sample a buyer could normally succeed under sections 14(2) or 15(2)(*c*). If, however, the defect was discoverable from a reasonable examination of the sample, a buyer might have rights under section 14(2) even though he has no right under section 15(2)(*c*).[3]

Express terms

An express term of the contract (*e.g.* to repair goods free of charge within a specified period) is in addition to, and does not negative, the terms implied by the Act unless it is inconsistent with those terms (s.55(2)). If it does purport to negative the implied terms its validity will depend on the rules discussed in Chapter Eight.

Terms implied into other contracts

A person may acquire goods not only under a contract of sale but also under (1) a hire-purchase agreement or (2) a contract of barter or exchange or (3) a contract for work and materials. He

---

[1] [1960] 1 W.L.R. 9; [1960] 1 All E.R. 36.

[2] Formerly s.14(2) only applied to a sale "by description."

[3] On the other hand a claim under s.14(2) might fail if the buyer actually examined the sample and the court treated this as an examination of the goods.

may also decide that, instead of buying them, he will hire or lease them. In the latter case the supplier's obligations as to title will clearly be of a limited nature because the property in the goods is not being transferred. Apart from this it is clearly desirable that the terms as to quality, fitness, etc., should be essentially identical whichever form of contract is used. This process of assimilation has largely been achieved and, for the sake of completeness, it will now be briefly considered.[4]

(a) **Hire-purchase.** Sections 8–11 of the Supply of Goods (Implied Terms) Act 1973 contain conditions and warranties as to title,[5] description, quality, fitness and sample which are virtually identical to those in sections 12–15 of the Sale of Goods Act (*ante*, pp. 103–124).

(b) **Work and materials, barter and exchange.** These contracts, which can be conveniently called "quasi-sales"[6] were formerly governed entirely by common law rules and the nature and extent of these rules was a matter of some doubt. Fortunately, in response to a Law Commission proposal, the law is now clearly set out in sections 1–5 of the Supply of Goods and Services Act 1982 which came into force on January 4, 1983. The new rules apply to a "contract for the transfer of goods." Subject to five exceptions, this means a contract under which one person transfers or agrees to transfer to another the property in goods" (s. 1(1)). The five exceptions are listed in section 1(2) as follows:

(a) a contract of sale of goods;
(b) a hire-purchase agreement;
(c) a contract under which the property in goods is (or is to be) transferred in exchange for trading stamps on their redemption;
(d) a transfer by deed without consideration; and
(e) a contract intended to operate by way of mortgage, pledge, charge or other security.

In practice the most important type of contract within section 1(1) is undoubtedly a contract for work and materials; examples

---

[4] Where goods are acquired by the redemption of trading stamps the Trading Stamps Act 1964 contains a number of implied terms. These are not further considered in this book.
[5] Suitably adapted to reflect the fact that property will pass at a future time.
[6] The term is used by Mr. G. F. Woodroffe in Chapter Two of his book *Goods and Services—The New Law.*

include building, construction, repairs, and contracts for the installation of central heating, double glazing and burglar alarms. In these cases the supplier undertakes a dual obligation, namely (i) an obligation relating to the goods (now governed by sections 2–5 of the 1982 Act) and (ii) an obligation relating to the work (now governed by ss. 13–15 of the 1982 Act, *ante*, pp. 4–5).

Obligations as to title, description, quality, fitness and sample are once again virtually identical to what the Law Commission has described as the Sale of Goods Act model (see ss. 2–5 of the 1982 Act).

Contracts of hire. Apart from the more limited obligations as to title (Act of 1982 s. 7) the conditions and warranties implied in favour of the hirer are once again virtually identical to those discussed earlier in this chapter (see ss. 8–10 of the 1982 Act).

Remedies

In practice, the obligations set out above only become important if something goes wrong with the goods and at that point the question of remedies becomes crucial. On this topic there appear to be two differences between a contract of sale of goods and the various other contracts discussed in this section. In the first place, section 11(4) of the 1979 Act is not mirrored in the other legislation. It may well be, therefore, that the right to reject may be available for a somewhat longer period under these various other contracts. Secondly the Acts of 1973 and 1982 use the words "condition" and "warranty" without defining them. This follows a Law Commission recommendation and leaves it open to a robust judge to deny a right to reject for a breach of condition in a case where the customer has suffered no loss.

Exemption clauses

The vitally important subject of exemption clauses is considered in a later chapter.[7]

PASSING OF PROPERTY

Introductory

The main object of a contract of sale is the transfer of property from seller to buyer and in this section we shall examine the rules

---

[7] Chapter Eight, *post*, p. 429.

which determine when such transfer takes place. Before doing so, however, it may be useful to examine the practical consequences which flow from the property passing. It will be seen that in some respects the transfer of possession is as important (perhaps even more important) than the transfer of property and the two concepts must not be confused. Thus:

(1) Unless otherwise agreed the risk of accidental loss or damage passes to the buyer as soon as the property passes to him (*post*, p. 137) (and such loss or damage will only have insurance cover if the buyer has made the necessary arrangements).

(2) The passing of property gives the seller the right to sue the buyer for the price (s.49 *post*, p. 180).

(3) If the property has passed to the buyer he can re-sell the goods to a third party without incurring any liability to the seller (even if the seller is unpaid).

(4) The passing of property does not automatically give the buyer a right of possession—a rule which is clearly of great importance if the buyer is in financial difficulty. Under section 28 (*post*, p. 161) unless otherwise agreed, delivery and payment are concurrent conditions. This means that the buyer can only claim the goods if he is ready and willing to pay the price or if he can prove that the seller has agreed to allow him credit. Further, the unpaid seller may have a lien (*post*, p. 170) or a right of stoppage *in transitu* (*post*, p. 173) and in these cases it seems that the buyer must pay or tender the price before he can claim possession.

(5) If property and possession pass at different times a disposition by the non-owning party in possession may nevertheless pass a good title to a third party taking in good faith (ss.24 and 25, *post*, pp. 154–155).

(6) If a third party wrongfully interferes with the goods an action in tort under the Torts (Interference with Goods) Act 1977 can only be brought by a party having either possession or an immediate right to possess. Thus in *Lord v. Price*[8] it was held that a buyer could not sue a third party who had wrongfully removed the goods at a time when the seller still had a lien over them.

---

[8] (1874) L.R. 9 Ex. 54.

(7) In recent times the issue of insolvency has become increasingly important as creditors have sought to protect themselves against the risk of the debtor becoming insolvent. The rules are somewhat complex but broadly they operate in the following way:

(a) If the seller becomes insolvent while the goods are still in his possession the buyer can only claim the goods if (i) the property has passed or (ii) the goods are specific or ascertained and the court exercises its discretion to grant specific performance (s.52 *post*, p. 189). If the seller is unpaid the trustee, receiver or liquidator will have the usual rights of an unpaid seller (see note (4) above).

(b) If the seller becomes insolvent after the buyer has obtained possession the trustee, etc., can only recover possession if, under the terms of the contract, the seller could have done so. He will, however, be able to bring an action for the price if the property has passed.

(c) If the buyer becomes insolvent and the seller still has possession the seller can exercise his unpaid seller's rights (see note (4) above).

(d) If the buyer becomes insolvent after obtaining possession the unpaid seller may be able to recover the goods if the contract so provides. A typical clause might provide that

(i) the risk shall pass to the buyer on delivery but the property shall not pass to the buyer until the full price for the goods has been paid and

(ii) if the buyer shall default in payment, or if (being an individual) he commits an act of bankruptcy or if (being a company) a receiver is appointed . . . the rights of the buyer under this agreement shall terminate and the seller shall be entitled to recover possession of the goods.

(e) In the case of individuals and partnerships (but not companies) the Bills of Sale Act 1878 and the "reputed ownership" rules contained in section 38(*c*) of the Bankruptcy Act 1914 could defeat the claims of an owner out of possession (*i.e.* the buyer's claim in (a) above and the seller's claim in (d) above) but these provisions are of limited importance in practice.

When does property pass?

The rules governing the passing of property depend primarily on whether the goods are specific or unascertained and these terms have already been considered (*ante*, p. 79).

Two basic rules

The first basic rule concerns unascertained goods. By section 16:

> Where there is a contract for the sale of unascertained goods no property in the goods is transferred to the buyer unless and until the goods are ascertained.

Thus on a contract for the sale of "10 bottles of wine" or "10 bottles of wine from the crate in my cellar" no property can pass until the goods have been ascertained, *i.e.* earmarked or appropriated to the contract with the consent of both parties, express or implied. The contract may, of course, postpone the passing of property until a later time, *e.g.* the time of payment.

The second basic rule concerns specific or ascertained goods. Section 17 provides that:

> (1) Where there is a contract for the sale of specific or ascertained goods the property in them is transferred to the buyer at such time as the parties to the contract intend it to be transferred.

Thus the key factor is intention. The section continues:

> (2) For the purpose of ascertaining the intention of the parties regard shall be had to the terms of the contract, the conduct of the parties, and the circumstances of the case.

If, therefore, the contract contains an express provision as to when the property is to pass, this concludes the matter. In most cases, however, the contract is silent on the point and in these cases section 18 becomes all-important. It opens with these words:

> Unless a different intention appears, the following are rules for ascertaining the intention of the parties as to the time at which the property in the goods is to pass to the buyer.

In considering the five rules which follow, the opening words "unless a different intention appears" must constantly be kept in mind.

The five rules of section 18

The first four rules relate to specific goods.

Rule 1. Where there is an unconditional contract for the sale of specific goods in a deliverable state, the property in the goods passes to the buyer when the contract is made, and it is immaterial whether the time of payment or the time of delivery, or both, be postponed.

Section 18, rule 1, applies even if the time for payment is postponed. In practice, however, many sale agreements are so drafted that the property is not to pass until the payments have been completed.[9] Such contracts are governed by the opening words "unless a contrary intention appears." To be effective, however, the contrary intention must be shown at or before the making of the contract. In *Dennant* v. *Skinner and Collom*[10]:

> X, a swindler, bid for a car at an auction, and it was knocked down to him. He gave a false name and address and was allowed to take the car away in return for a cheque, on signing a form that no property in the car would pass until the cheque was met. He then sold the car, which was resold to the defendant. When the cheque was dishonoured, the original owners sought to recover the car. Hallett J. held that (1) when X signed the form the property had already passed to him under section 18, rule 1, so that the form which he signed had no legal effect, and accordingly (2) the defendant had acquired a good title to the car and was entitled to retain it.

It remains to add that, in the words of Diplock L.J.:

> "In modern times very little is needed to give rise to the inference that the property in specific goods is to pass only on delivery or payment."[11]

Rule 2. Where there is a contract for the sale of specific goods and the seller is bound to do something to the goods, for the purpose of putting them into a deliverable state, the property does not pass until such thing is done, and the buyer has notice that it has been done.

By section 61(5):

> Goods are in a "deliverable state" within the meaning of this Act when they are in such a state that the buyer would under the contract be bound to take delivery of them.

---

[9] See *Re Anchor Line, Ltd.* [1937] Ch. 1; [1936] 2 All E.R. 941, and see *post*, p. 136.

[10] [1948] 2 K.B. 164; [1948] 2 All E.R. 29. The contract was "made" when the hammer fell (s.58(2)). The defendant may also have been protected under s.25 *post*, p. 155.

[11] *R. V. Ward Ltd.* v. *Bignall* [1967] 1 Q.B. 534, 545; [1967] 2 All E.R. 449. In many supermarkets sales no property passes until payment of the price (*Lacis* v. *Cashmarts* [1969] 2 Q.B. 400).

If, therefore, the seller sells a second-hand car and agrees that he will respray it and exchange the tyres, the property does not pass until the buyer has notice that this work has been done. The definition was considered in *Underwood Ltd.* v. *Burgh Castle Brick and Cement Syndicate*[12]:

> Sellers sold a 30-tone condensing engine "free on rail London." At the time of the sale it was embedded in the floor of a factory. The sellers dismantled it and proceeded to load it on to a truck, but in doing so part of the machine was accidentally broken. The Court of Appeal held that the buyers could reject it because (1) at the time of the contract the machine was not in a deliverable state so that section 18, rule 1 did not apply; (2) section 18, rule 2 did apply so that the risk was still on the sellers; (3) as an alternative to (2) above, the parties intended that no property should pass until the engine was safely on rail.

Rule 3. Where there is a contract for the sale of specific goods in a deliverable state, but the seller is bound to weigh, measure, test, or do some other act or thing with reference to the goods for the purpose of ascertaining the price, the property does not pass until such act or thing is done, and the buyer has notice that it has been done.

It should be noted that, like the previous rule, rule 3 only applies where something has to be done by the *seller*. In *Turley* v. *Bates*[13]:

> S sold B a heap of clay at a price of £x per ton and it was agreed that the buyer would load the clay and weigh it to ascertain the price. The court held that the property passed to the buyer when the contract was made.

Rule 4 deals with goods sent on approval or on sale or return.[14] It provides that:

> When goods are delivered to the buyer on approval or on sale or return or other similar terms the property therein passes to the buyer:
> (a) When he signifies his approval or acceptance to the seller or does any other act adopting the transaction:

---

[12] [1922] 1 K.B. 343.

[13] (1863) 2 H. & C. 200.

[14] To avoid misunderstanding, it should be pointed out that this rule refers to goods sent on approval *at the buyer's request* and not where the seller unilaterally sends goods which the "buyer" has not ordered. The latter situation is governed by the Unsolicited Goods and Services Act 1971 (as amended).

(b) If he does not signify his approval or acceptance to the seller but retains the goods without giving notice of rejection, then, if a time has been fixed for the return of the goods, on the expiration of that time, and if no time has been fixed, on the expiration of a reasonable time. What is a reasonable time is a question of fact.

In the words of Lopes L.J.:

"The position of a person who has received goods on sale or return is that he has the option of becoming the purchaser of them, and may become so in three different ways. He may pay the price, or he may retain the goods beyond a reasonable time for their return, or he may do an act inconsistent with his being other than a purchaser."[15]

Accordingly it has been held that the act of pledging the goods is an act adopting the transaction, because it is inconsistent with the buyer's power to return the goods.[16] Such pledging will pass the property even if the buyer was fraudulent in obtaining the goods, provided that the "sale or return contract" was voidable only and not void.[17]

It is again important to remember the opening words "unless a different intention appears." If the contract provides, as it should, that no property is to pass until the goods are paid for, the pledging of the goods by the buyer will not pass the property under section 18, because that section has been excluded.[18] The pledgee will acquire no title unless he is protected by one of the exceptions to the *nemo dat* rule.[19] It should be noticed in this connection that the name given to the transaction by the parties is not conclusive.[20]

Damage. The combined effect of section 18, rule 4, and section 20 is that the goods are at the seller's risk while they are on approval, so that if, for example, S sends to B an electric shaver on approval within seven days and the shaver is accidentally damaged during this period B will be entitled to return the shaver to S

---

[15] *Kirkham* v. *Attenborough* [1897] 1 Q.B. 201, 204.

[16] *Ibid.*

[17] See *London Jewellers Ltd.* v. *Attenborough* [1934] 2 K.B. 206; [1934] All E.R. Rep. 270, where the principles and authorities are fully discussed.

[18] *Weiner* v. *Gill* [1906] 2 K.B. 574.

[19] It is doubtful whether s.25 applies. *Edwards* v. *Vaughan* (1910) 26 T.L.R. 545 decides that it does not, but see the views of Scrutton L.J. in the *London Jewellers* case *supra* at p. 215.

[20] *Weiner* v. *Harris* [1910] 1 K.B. 285. A retailer received jewellery on "sale or return" but had no power to buy himself. It was held to be a contract of agency.

without having to pay any compensation for the damage.[21] The position can, of course, be varied by contract or trade usage. In any event section 20 only applies to accidental loss so that if the buyer negligently damages the goods he (being a bailee) will be liable in accordance with the general law of bailments (*post*, p. 410).

A contract can be one for sale or return even if the buyer never intends to buy the goods for himself. In *Poole* v. *Smith's Car Sales (Balham) Ltd.*[22]:

> A Vauxhall car was sent by the plaintiff to the defendants (both car dealers) for storage and it was agreed that the defendant could sell the car, provided that the plaintiff received £325 for it. The car remained unsold for three months. When the plaintiff demanded the return of the car it was tendered in a damaged condition, whereupon the plaintiff refused to accept it and sued for the price. The Court of Appeal held that: (1) since both parties had treated the contract as one of sale or return it must be regarded as such; (2) the defendants had retained the car beyond a reasonable time; (3) accordingly, under section 18, rule 4, the property had passed to them and they were liable for the price.

Finally, it should be noted that "retained" means "retained by the buyer." In *Re Ferrier*[23] furniture was handed to Mrs. Ferrier for sale or return in seven days. Before the seven days had expired execution was levied on her property and the sheriff retained the furniture for some time. It was held that no property had passed.

Rule 5 deals with future or unascertained goods. It provides that:

> (1) Where there is a contract for the sale of unascertained or future goods by description,[24] and goods of that description and in a deliverable state are unconditionally appropriated to the contract, either by the seller with the assent of the buyer, or by the buyer with

---

[21] *Elphick* v. *Barnes* (1880) 5 C.P.D. 321 (horse dies while on approval). If the article is accidentally destroyed during the approval period, the contract would presumably be frustrated at common law.

[22] [1962] 1 W.L.R. 744; [1962] 2 All E.R. 482. It is rather surprising that a person in the position of the defendant could be described as a "buyer." Could it really be said that the goods had been "delivered to the buyer" when he had neither bought nor agreed to buy as required by s.61?

[23] [1944] Ch. 295.

[24] See *Philip Head & Sons Ltd.* v. *Showfronts Ltd.* [1970] 1 Lloyd's Rep. 140, where carpeting which was to be laid by the seller was not in a "deliverable state" unitl the laying had taken place.

the assent of the seller, the property in the goods then passes to the buyer; and the assent may be express or implied, and may be given either before or after the appropriation is made.

(2) Where, in pursuance of the contract, the seller delivers the goods to the buyer or to a carrier or other bailee or custodier (whether named by the buyer or not) for the purpose of transmission to the buyer, and does not reserve the right of disposal, he is to be taken to have unconditionally appropriated the goods to the contract.

Therefore in the absence of contrary agreement, the key factor is unconditional appropriation. This means that some act must be done by the seller, or (unlike rules 2 or 3) by the buyer, whereby the goods are irrevocably earmarked to the contract. In this connection, the following passage taken from a judgment of Pearson J. is instructive:

> "A mere setting apart or selection by the seller of the goods which he expects to use in performance of the contract is not enough. If that is all, he can change his mind and use those goods in performance of some other contract and use some other goods in performance of this contract. To constitute an appropriation of the goods to the contract, the parties must have had or be reasonably supposed to have had an intention to attach the contract irrevocably to those goods so that those goods and no others are the subject of the sale and become the property of the buyer."[25]

One example of such appropriation is given in rule 5(2) above, *i.e.* delivery to a carrier, but there can be many other ways. If, for example, a seller agrees to sell 10 television sets out of his present stock to be selected by the buyer, the buyer's selection will amount to appropriation. Again in *Wardar's (Import & Export) Ltd. v. W. Norwood & Sons Ltd.*[26]

> Cartons of frozen kidneys belonging to S were stored in a warehouse. S sold 600 of these cartons to B and gave B a delivery order addressed to the warehouseman W. When B's carrier arrived at the warehouse W had already set aside 600 cartons. The carrier handed the delivery order to W who gave instructions for loading to commence. At that time the kidneys were in good condition but during the loading they deteriorated because (a) the porters had a very long tea-break and (b) the carrier failed to turn on the

---

[25] *Carlos Federspiel & Co. S.A.* v. *Twigg (Charles) Ltd.* [1957] 1 Lloyd's Rep. 240, 255, where the authorities are fully reviewed.
[26] [1968] 2 Q.B. 663; [1968] 2 All E.R. 602.

refrigeration. The Court of Appeal held that (1) where unascertained goods were in the possession of a third person, the property and risk passed to the buyer when that third person, having selected an appropriate part of the goods, acknowledged that he held them on the buyer's behalf. (2) In the present case the property and risk passed when W received the delivery order and acted on it by ordering loading to commence. (3) As the goods had deteriorated after that time the risk was on the buyer and he was liable to pay the price.

It will be noted that there must be assent to the appropriation, but the assent may come before or after the appropriation, and may be express or implied. If, therefore, a buyer having seen the seller's stock of wine orders "100 bottles of champagne" he impliedly assents to the seller's subsequent appropriation,[27] so that, for example, the property and risk would pass to the buyer when the seller handed the goods to the carrier. Again in *Pignatoro* v. *Gilroy*[28]:

> A seller of bags of rice to be delivered at the seller's place of business informed the buyer that the bags were ready. On receipt of this information the buyer did nothing further for over three weeks, during which time the bags were stolen. *Held,* the buyer had by his conduct assented to the seller's appropriation and accordingly the property (and with it the risk) had passed to the buyer.

On an f.o.b. contract no appropriation occurs until the goods are shipped.[29]

Section 18, rule 5(2), must be read subject to section 16. In *Healy* v. *Howlett & Sons*[30]:

> Buyer ordered 20 boxes of fish from seller, an Irish fish exporter. The seller consigned 190 boxes by railway and directed the railway officials to set aside 20 for the buyer's contract. At the same time he sent the buyer an invoice stating that the goods were at his "sole risk." The train was delayed and before the 20 boxes had been

---

[27] *Cf. Aldridge* v. *Johnson, supra.* The position where the buyer has not seen the goods is uncertain. See Atiyah, *op. cit.* at p. 200. It is significant that in *Healy* v. *Howlett, infra,* the court proceeded on the basis that delivery to the carrier would pass the property and risk, if the goods were then ascertained. This would suggest that (especially in sales between traders) the buyer's assent to appropriation may be readily inferred.

[28] [1919] 1 K.B. 459.

[29] See n. 25 *supra.*

[30] [1917] 1 K.B. 337. If at the time of delivery of the 190 boxes 20 of them had been marked with the buyer's name, the delivery could have constituted an unconditional appropriation passing the property and risk (*ibid.*).

appropriated to the contract the fish had deteriorated and was no longer merchantable. It was held that (1) the invoice formed no part of the contract, (2) the property in the 20 boxes did not pass to the buyer until appropriation, (3) at the moment of appropriation the fish was not merchantable and accordingly the buyer was not bound to accept it.

Romalpa clauses

It must be emphasised once again that the provisions of section 18 yield to a contrary intention. Although the opening words of section 18 reached the statute book in 1894 very few sellers took advantage of them and it was not until 1976 that the trading terms of a Dutch supplier of aluminium foil highlighted the possible benefits of a retention of title clause.[31] Since then the floodgates have opened and Romalpa clauses (as they have come to be known) have become much more common. The case has not escaped criticism and two 1979 cases have somewhat restricted its scope.[32] Nevertheless with careful drafting a Romalpa clause can give the hard-pressed unsecured creditor a degree of insolvency protection.

Reservation of right of disposal

It will be recalled that the delivery to a carrier will only pass the property in unascertained goods where the seller does not "reserve the right of disposal." These words are dealt with in section 19 which provides as follows:

(1) Where there is a contract for the sale of specific goods or where goods are subsequently appropriated to the contract, the seller may, by the terms of the contract or appropriation,[33] reserve the right of disposal for the goods until certain conditions are fulfilled. In such case, notwithstanding the delivery of the goods to the buyer, or to a carrier or other bailee or custodier for the purpose of transmission to the buyer, the property in the goods does not pass to the buyer until the conditions imposed by the seller are fulfilled.

(2) Where goods are shipped, and by the bill of lading the goods

---

[31] *Aluminium Industrie B.V.* v. *Romalpa Aluminium Ltd.* [1976] 1 W.L.R. 676 [1976] 2 All E.R. 552; C.A. On the special facts the seller succeeded in recovering unsold foil *and* the identifiable proceeds of sold foil from the buyer's liquidator.

[32] *Borden (U.K.) Ltd.* v. *Scottish Timber Products Ltd.* [1981] Ch. 25; [1979] 3 W.L.R. 672; [1979] 3 All E.R. 961; *Re Bond Worth* [1980] Ch. 228; [1979] 3 W.L.R. 629; [1979] 3 All E.R. 919.

[33] The appropriation in such a case would not be "unconditional" within rule 5(1).

are deliverable to the order of the seller or his agent, the seller is prima facie to be taken to reserve the right of disposal.

(3) Where the seller of goods draws on the buyer for the price, and transmits the bill of exchange and bill of lading to the buyer together to secure acceptance or payment of the bill of exchange, the buyer is bound to return the bill of lading if he does not honour the bill of exchange, and if he wrongfully retains the bill of lading the property in the goods does not pass to him.

A bill of lading is a document signed by the master of a ship and operates in three ways—as a receipt, as evidence of the contract of carriage and perhaps most important of all as a document of title.[34] If a bill of lading is made out to the order of the buyer or his agent the general rules will apply, but if it is made out to the seller or his agent (in which case it will usually only be indorsed over to the buyer when he pays the price) section 19(2) applies and despite the shipping of the goods the property does not pass to the buyer.

Section 19 is subject to section 25 and is further considered on p. 156, *post*.

RISK[35]

General Rule

By section 20(1):

> Unless otherwise agreed, the goods remain at the seller's risk until the property in them is transferred to the buyer, but when the property in them is transferred to the buyer the goods are at the buyer's risk whether delivery has been made or not.

A number of illustrations of the general rule have already been given. The maxim *res perit domino* means in effect that the risk of accidental loss or damage falls on the owner of the goods, whether he is in possession or not.[36]

---

[34] The bill represents the goods and ownership of the goods can be transferred by transferring the bill.

[35] See 31 C.L.J. 225.

[36] In *Tarling* v. *Baxter* (1827) 6 B. & C. 360, S sold to B a haystack which was to remain on the seller's premises until the following May. Before May arrived, the haystack was destroyed in an accidental fire. *Held*, property and risk had passed to the buyer who remained liable to pay the price.

Contrary agreement

Once again the provisions of the Act can be varied by agreement or by trade custom. In some cases the parties may agree that the risk passes before property. In *Sterns Ltd.* v. *Vickers, Ltd.*[37]

> Seller agreed to sell 120,000 gallons of spirit out of 200,000 in a tank on the premises of a third party. A delivery warrant was issued to the buyer, but was not acted upon for some months during which time the spirit deteriorated. *Held*, although no property had passed (because no appropriation had taken place) the parties must have intended the risk to pass when the delivery order was delivered, and consequently the buyer remained liable to pay the price.

At other times the property may pass before the risk, as where the seller agrees to send specific goods to the buyer at the seller's risk. If the seller does agree to deliver goods at his own risk, his liability is governed by section 33, which reads:

> Where the seller of goods agrees to deliver them at his own risk at a place other than that where they are when sold, the buyer must, nevertheless, unless otherwise agreed, take any risk of deterioration in the goods necessarily incident to the course of transit.

The seller must, however, take the risk of extraordinary or unusual deterioration or loss.

Relationship between section 33 and section 14

A point which does not appear to have been decided in any case heard since the passing of the 1893 Act is whether section 33 must be read subject to section 14 or vice versa. An example will illustrate the problem:

> A agrees to sell some carcasses of meat to B and to deliver them, at his own risk, by sea to B in Cairo. When the goods are shipped in London the meat is of merchantable quality but on arrival in Cairo it is not. Expert evidence shows that this particular type of meat can never withstand a sea journey to Cairo without becoming unmerchantable. In other words the deterioration is necessarily incidental to the transit.

It is thought that section 33 would apply and that the seller would not be liable in damages. If the courts were to insist that the

---

[37] [1923] 1 K.B. 78. A similar result was reached in *Margarine Union GmbH* v. *Cambay Prince Steamship Co.* [1969] 1 Q.B. 219; [1967] 3 All E.R. 775. C.I.F. contracts provide another exception to s.20. See *post,* p. 469. See also *post,* p. 489.

goods *must* remain merchantable until the end of the journey, they would be demanding the impossible. Cases like *Beer* v. *Walker* (*ante*, p. 118) which appear to decide that the goods must be merchantable on arrival, can be treated as merely an illustration of the rule that the goods must remain merchantable for a reasonable time after appropriation (*ibid.*). If the point were to arise, the court would be justified in looking at the early case of *Bull* v. *Robison*[38] which is not only directly in point but also contains a judgment by Alderson B. which was "lifted" by Chalmers almost verbatim and now appears in section 33 of the Act. This case supports the view put forward in the text. On principle, section 33 should also apply, by analogy, where the risk passes on shipment, as in the case of an f.o.b. and c.i.f. contract.[39]

Delayed delivery

Section 20(2) makes it clear that delay in delivery can displace the basic rule. It reads:

> But where delivery has been delayed through the fault of either buyer or seller the goods are at the risk of the party in fault as regards any loss which might not have occurred but for such fault.

Suppose that A sells to B a car on Monday and agrees to deliver it on Wednesday. He fails to do so and the car is destroyed in an accidental fire on A's premises on the Thursday. The proviso applies and A bears the loss, so that B is discharged from his obligation to pay the price and can sue for damages for non-delivery. Again in *Demby Hamilton* v. *Barden*[40]:

> A buyer of 30 tons of apple juice agreed to give delivery instructions but failed to do so. The juice went bad and it was held that the deterioration was due to the buyer's delay in taking delivery and consequently the loss fell on the buyer.

Duties of bailee

Section 20(3) is straightforward. It provides that:

---

[38] (1854) 10 Ex. 342.

[39] In other words, the seller is prima facie liable if the goods fail to remain merchantable throughout a normal journey but he is not liable for any inevitable deterioration which all such goods are bound to undergo. See (1965) 28 M.L.R. 189.

[40] [1949] W.N. 73; [1949] 1 All E.R. 435.

Nothing in this section affects the duties or liabilities of either seller or buyer as a bailee or custodier[41] of the goods of the other party.

Thus if A sells furniture to B and agrees to store it until B is ready to move into his house, the seller has become a bailee of the goods and will be liable as such for negligence.

PERISHING OF GOODS

Definition

Goods can be said to perish when they physically or commercially[42] cease to exist. In considering the legal effect of their perishing it is necessary once again to distinguish sharply between specific[43] and unascertained goods and then to consider precisely when the perishing occurred.

Specific goods

Before contract. By section 6:

Where there is a contract for the sale of specific goods, and the goods without the knowledge of the seller have perished at the time when the contract is made, the contract is void.

If the man on the Clapham omnibus were asked "What is the position if A sells to B goods which unknown to A have already perished?" he would reply "The contract is off." This is the effect of section 6, although as a learned writer forcefully argues[44] the matter is essentially one of construction. Thus it would seem that the seller could sue the buyer if the buyer agreed to pay the price regardless of whether the goods had perished or not, and conversely the buyer could sue the seller for damages for non-delivery if the seller in effect promised that the goods did exist.

---

[41] The Scots equivalent to a bailee.

[42] Consider *Asfar* v. *Blundell* [1896] 1 K.B. 123 and contrast dicta of Morris J. in *Horn* v. *Minister of Food* (1948) 65 T.L.R. 106; [1948] 2 All E.R. 1036.

[43] For a case on the perishing of specific goods, see *Couturier* v. *Hastie* (1856) 5 H.L.Cas. 673.

[44] Mr. P. S. Atiyah in (1957) 73 L.Q.R. 340.

The perishing of part of the goods may bring section 6 into operation if the contract is indivisible. In *Barrow, Lane and Ballard* v. *Phillip Phillips & Co.*[45]:

> The sellers sold 700 specific bags of Chinese nuts. Subsequently it was discovered that at the time of the contract 109 of the bags had been fraudulently removed. Wright J. held that section 6 applied, because the contract was an indivisible one for 700 bags. Consequently the buyers were not bound to pay the price, although they were bound to pay for goods actually delivered.

After contract. By section 7:

> Where there is an agreement to sell specific goods, and subsequently the goods, without any fault on the part of the seller or buyer, perish before the risk passes to the buyer, the agreement is avoided.

It will be noted that section 7 only applies where neither the property nor the risk have passed to the buyer. It can therefore have little practical importance, because in the vast majority of cases, the property and risk pass immediately under rule 1 of section 18. It does, however, apply to a contract governed by section 18, rules 2 and 3. Thus if in the example given on p. 131, the car was destroyed after the respraying had been completed but before the buyer had notice thereof, section 7 would apply and the contract would be avoided.

Section 7 is an illustration of the doctrine of frustration. Most frustrated contracts are governed by the Law Reform (Frustrated Contracts) Act 1943, which (*inter alia*) allows a party to make a claim for expenses incurred or for benefits conferred on the other party. This Act, however, does not apply to cases within section 7, which are governed by the common law rules of frustration. These rules provide that money paid is only repayable if there has been a total failure of consideration, and no adjustments are allowed.[46] Thus in our example the position would be that:

(a) The seller would not be liable for non-delivery.

(b) The seller could not sue for the price, and if he has received it he is liable to repay it.

---

[45] [1929] 1 K.B. 574.
[46] *Fibrosa Spolka Akcyjna* v. *Fairbairn Lawson Combe Barbour Ltd.* [1943] A.C. 32; [1942] 2 All E.R. 122.

(c) The seller has no claim at all for the respraying charges.

Frustration being again a matter of construction, section 7 can give way to a contrary agreement.

It need scarcely be added that if the goods perish after the risk has passed to the buyer, the buyer bears the loss.

Unascertained goods

If the goods are purely generic, as on a sale of "25 bottle of Scotch whisky," no question of perishing can arise—*genus numquam perit*. The mere fact that the source from which the seller had intended to obtain the goods has ceased to exist in no way affects the contract, and the seller must obtain the goods from somewhere else or pay damages for non-delivery. If, of course, goods have been appropriated to the contract, the risk of their perishing will be on the buyer (unless the contract otherwise provides) and he will remain liable to pay the price.

If, however, the contract specifies the source from which the goods are to come,[47] the position is different. If the entire source has, unknown to the seller, been destroyed before the making of the contract the matter would be governed by common law rules analogous to section 6 of the Act and the contract would be void unless a contrary intention could be inferred from the agreement made between the parties. If the source is destroyed after the making of the contract but before the risk has passed to the buyer, the contract will be avoided either by treating it as conditional within section 5(2)[48] or by reason of the frustration rules preserved by section 62(2).[49] In the latter case, the Law Reform (Frustrated Contracts) Act 1943 would govern the rights of the parties so that adjustments for expenses and benefits would be possible.[50]

---

[47] As in *Sterns Ltd.* v. *Vickers Ltd.* (*ante*, p. 138).

[48] The section reads: "There may be a contract for the sale of goods, the acquisition of which by the seller depends on a contingency which may or may not happen."

[49] *Howell* v. *Coupland* (1876) 1 Q.B.D. 258 (crop to be grown on particular field) as explained in *Re Wait* [1927] 1 Ch. 606. In *H. R. and S. Sainsbury Ltd.* v. *Street* [1972] 1 W.L.R. 834, the contract provided for the delivery of 275 tons of barley to be grown on a farm but the harvest produced only 140 tons. McKenna J. held that (1) a term could be implied that S should not be liable to pay damages if any part of the crop failed, but (2) he remained liable to deliver the 140 tons to B.

[50] For a recent discussion of the statutory adjustment rules see *B.P. Exploration Co.* (*Libya*) *Ltd.* v. *Hunt* [1982] 2 W.L.R. 253, H.L.

TRANSFER OF TITLE BY A NON-OWNER[51]

In an earlier part of this chapter the rules governing the passing of property were discussed. The discussion proceeded on the basis that the seller was the person in whom the property was vested. Sometimes, however, the buyer can acquire a good title to the goods even though the seller had neither the property nor a right to dispose of the property,[52] and it is with this important topic that this section is concerned. The matter is dealt with in sections 21–26 of the Act under the general heading "Transfer of Title."

> "In the development of our law, two principles have striven for mastery. The first is for the protection of property: no one can give a better title that he himself possesses. The second is for the protection of commercial transactions: the person who takes in good faith and for value without notice should get a good title."[53]

This short passage perfectly summarises the topic about to be discussed—the maxim *nemo dat quod non habet* and the exceptions thereto. The exceptions were slowly evolved to make the common law suitable to a dynamic economy instead of a merely static one. Although the exceptions are now numerous, it is as well to remember that they are exceptions and that the basic rule is still of great importance. It will be seen that the courts have at times shown an undue tendency to protect property at the expense of commercial transactions and have paid little regard to the negligence of the owner in parting with possession. The problem which comes before the courts is usually an old one; namely, which of two innocent people is to suffer for the fraud of a third.[54]

Nemo dat

Section 21(1) reads as follows:

> Subject to this Act, where goods are sold by a person who is not their owner, and who does not sell them under the authority or with the consent of the owner, the buyer acquires no better title to the

---

[51] See the Twelfth Report of the Law Reform Committee (Cmnd. 2958), which is referred to in appropriate places.

[52] Either as owner or as pledgee.

[53] *Bishopsgate Motor Finance Corpn.* v. *Transport Brakes Ltd.* [1949] 1 K.B. 322, 336–337; [1949] 1 All E.R. 37, 46, *per* Denning L.J.

[54] Recent cases show a strong swing in favour of the buyer. See *Lewis* v. Averay (*post*, p. 153); the *Worcester Works* case (*post*, p. 154) and *Barker* v. *Bell* (*post*, p. 158). Lord Denning M.R. presided in all three cases.

goods than the seller had, unless the owner of the goods is by his conduct precluded from denying the seller's authority to sell.

Exceptions

To the general *nemo dat* rule there are the following nine exceptions:

(1) Sale under order of court.
(2) Sale under a common law or statutory power.
(3) Estoppel.
(4) Agency.
(5) Sale in market overt.
(6) Sale under a voidable title.
(7) Disposition by seller in possession.
(8) Disposition by buyer in possession.
(9) Disposition under Part III of Hire-Purchase Act 1964.

(1) Sale under order of court. Section 21(2)(*b*) provides that nothing in the Act is to affect the validity of any sale under the order of a court of competent jurisdiction. The High Court is given power to order a sale of goods if they are of a perishable nature, or likely to deteriorate if kept, or if for any other good reason it is desirable to sell forthwith.[55]

This power is a wide one and can be used, for example, where a bailee wishes to enforce a lien which he has over goods in his possession.[56]

(2) Sales under a common law or statutory power. The validity of these is also preserved by section 21(2)(*b*). There are numerous powers whereby a non-owner is enabled to pass a good title. At common law a pledgee can do so if the pledgor makes default[57] and so can a mortgagee,[58] while another example can be found in the case of an agent of necessity (*ante*, p. 64). Persons having a

---

[55] R.S.C., Ord. 29, r. 4. This power is exercisable in respect of any property other than land, and an application for an order for sale can be made by any party to the action. See also C.C.R., Ord. 13, r. 12.

[56] *Larner* v. *Fawcett* [1950] W.N. 342; [1950] 2 All E.R. 727.

[57] *Re Morritt* (1887) 18 Q.B.D. 222, 232, *per* Cotton L.J.

[58] *Ibid.* at p. 233.

statutory power include landlords,[59] bailees,[60] innkeepers[61] and unpaid sellers.[62]

(3) Estoppel. Section 21 provides that the *nemo dat* rule is not to apply where the owner is by his conduct precluded from denying the seller's authority to sell. In *Henderson* v. *Williams*[63] Lord Halsbury stated the position thus:

> "The question here is whether the true owner of the goods has so invested the person dealing with them with the *indicia* of property as that when an innocent person entered into negotiation with the person to whom these things have been entrusted with the *indicia* of property, the true owner of the goods cannot afterwards complain that there was no authority to make such a bargain."

The facts in *Henderson* v. *Williams* were as follows:

> Sugar bags belonging to O were stored in the warehouse of W. F fraudulently induced O to sell the sugar to him, the "contract" being void for mistake. O instructed W to hold the sugar to the order of F and, in response to an inquiry from H, W informed H that the sugar was held to the order of F. H thereupon bought the sugar from F. On discovering the fraud, O instructed W to detain the bags and indemnified him for doing so.

It was held by the Court of Appeal that O (through whom W claimed) had held out F as having a right to sell and could not therefore deny F's right as against H who had acted on the holding out. H was therefore entitled to damages for conversion of his goods.

There must, however, be some form of holding out to the person claiming to have acquired a title. In *Farquharson* v. *King*[64]:

> The plaintiffs who owned timber lying at docks authorised a dock company to honour delivery orders signed by C. C, calling himself B, fraudulently sold timber to the defendants. He then in his own name directed the dock company to transfer the timber to the order of B, and then in the name of B he directed them to hold it to the order of the defendants. The defendants *who had not heard of the plaintiffs or*

---

[59] Distress for Rent Act 1689, as amended.
[60] Torts (Interference with Goods) Act 1977, p. 419.
[61] Innkeepers Act 1878.
[62] Sale of Goods Act 1979, s.48, *post*, p. 178.
[63] [1895] 1 Q.B. 521, 525. For a good modern illustration of estoppel see *Moorgate Mercantile Co.* v. *Twitchings* [1975] 3 W.L.R. 286, C.A.
[64] [1902] A.C. 325.

C then paid C (alias B) the price and obtained delivery. The House of Lords held that the plaintiffs were not precluded from setting up their ownership as against the defendants.

An estoppel usually operates to prevent a person from denying the truth of a fact which he has represented and which has been acted upon. Thus where a warehouseman acknowledges to a buyer that he holds goods to the buyer's order, he will be estopped from denying this.[65] If, however, an owner gives a seller the appearance of ownership and a buyer acts upon it, he acquires not merely a personal "title by estoppel" as against the owner, but a full title binding on third parties.[66]

Possession. It is of the greatest importance to appreciate that the mere delivery of possession does not give rise to an estoppel, even though possession was transferred with a view to sale and even though the owner was careless. In *Central Newbury Car Auctions* v. *Unity Finance Ltd.*[67]:

> A distinguished-looking swindler called Cullis entered the showroom of a motor dealer and wished to buy a Hillman car on hire-purchase terms. He filled up a proposal form for a hire-purchase agreement with a finance company and was then allowed to take away the car and its registration book. He sold it to X. The finance company declined the proposal for hire-purchase because the answers were dishonest, whereupon the dealers sued X for the return of the car. A majority of the Court of Appeal (Denning L.J. dissenting) held that the dealers were not precluded by their conduct from setting up their ownership.

Negligence. It may sometimes occur that the owner of goods (A) signs a blank form which contains a representation that the goods are owned by another person (B) and on the strength of that signature B completes the form and sells the goods to C. To what extent is A estopped from asserting his ownership if B in some way exceeds his authority? Clearly if B completes the form in a duly

---

[65] If the warehouseman merely receives a delivery order and gives no acknowledgment, no estoppel arises (*Laurie and Morewood* v. *Dudin (John)* [1926] 1 K.B. 223).

[66] *Eastern Distributors* v. *Goldring* [1957] 2 Q.B. 600; [1957] 2 All E.R. 525.

[67] [1957] 1 Q.B. 371; [1956] 3 All E.R. 905. As Cullis was only a prospective hirer who had neither "bought" nor "agreed to buy" there was no room for the operation of s.23 (*post*, p. 152), or s.25 (*post*, p. 155) and since no hire-purchase agreement was ever made there was no room for Part III of the Hire-Purchase Act 1964 (*post*, p. 157).

authorised manner A will be bound by B's acts and will be estopped from denying B's right to sell.[68] If, however, B completes the form in an unauthorised manner the question arises: can A be estopped by his negligence from denying B's right to sell? In *Wilson & Meeson* v. *Pickering*[69] the view was expressed that the doctrine of estoppel by negligence only applied to negotiable instruments, and in *Campbell Discount Co.* v. *Gall*[70] this was apparently accepted as a correct statement of the law. The distinction is clearly anomalous and it now seems clear that it no longer represents the law. It follows that the negligent signature of any document can give rise to an estoppel if (1) the signer owed a duty of care, (2) the signer broke that duty, and (3) the negligence was the proximate cause of the loss.[71]

(4) Agency. *At common law.* a sale by an agent will bind his principal if the agent had actual, apparent or usual authority, or authority by operation of law. These principles have already been discussed (*ante*, p. 55).

Section 2 Factors Act 1889. The Factors Acts were passed to protect third parties dealing with what might loosely be called "professional" agents. The Acts partly consolidated the common law of apparent authority and partly extended it.[72] The 1889 Act is the one at present in force and section 2 deals with dispositions by a "mercantile agent." Section 1 defines this term as follows:

> " . . . mercantile agent" shall mean a mercantile agent having in the customary course of his business as such agent authority either to sell goods or to consign goods for the purpose of sale, or to buy goods, or to raise money on the security of goods.

In spite of the word "business" it has been held that a person can be a mercantile agent even if he only acts for one principal,[73] and even though he only acts on one occasion, provided that he does so in a business capacity.[74] An employee, however, is not a

---

[68] See *ante*, p. 145.

[69] [1946] K.B. 422; [1946] 1 All E.R. 394.

[70] [1961] 1 Q.B. 431; [1961] 2 All E.R. 104.

[71] *Mercantile Credit Co. Ltd.* v. *Hamblin* [1965] 2 Q.B. 242; [1964] 3 All E.R. 592; *U.D.T. Ltd.* v. *Western* [1976] 2 W.L.R. 64, C.A.

[72] See *per* Devlin J. in the *Eastern Distributors* case [1957] 2 Q.B. 600, 609; [1957] 2 All E.R. 525, 530.

[73] *Weiner* v. *Harris* [1910] 1 K.B. 285; *Lowther* v. *Harris* [1927] 1 K.B. 393.

[74] *Budberg* v. *Jerwood & Ward* (1934) 51 T.L.R. 99.

mercantile agent,[75] nor is a person who merely sells goods on his own behalf and not as agent for others.[76]

The key provisions for present purposes is section 2(1) which reads as follows:

> Where a mercantile agent is, with the consent of the owner, in possession of goods or of the documents of title to goods, any sale, pledge or other disposition of the goods, made by him when acting in the ordinary course of business of a mercantile agent, shall, subject to the provisions of this Act, be as valid as if he were expressly authorised by the owner of the goods to make the same, provided that the person taking under the disposition acts in good faith, and has not at the time of the disposition notice that the person making the disposition has not authority to make the same.
>
> *Example.* A gives B his car and instructs B not to sell it at a price below £500. B sells the car to C for £300 and absconds. If B is a private person no title passes,[77] but if he is a mercantile agent it does pass, if C took in good faith and without notice of the excess of authority.[78]

Possession. The agent must receive possession in his capacity as mercantile agent, so that a buyer from a car dealer would not get a good title if the dealer was only in possession for the purposes of repairing the car,[79] or if the dealer did not become a dealer until after he received possession.[80] Where goods are received ostensibly on "sale or return" it is a question of construction as to whether it is a genuine sale or return contract or a contract of agency, because in the latter case the Factors Act 1889 can apply.[81]

Consent. The Act only applies if the agent obtains possession with the owner's consent. Consent is presumed in the absence of evidence to the contrary[82] and the termination of consent does not affect a person taking under a disposition from the agent, unless he knows of it.[83]

---

[75] See note 73, above.

[76] *Belvoir Finance Co. Ltd.* v. *Harold (G.) Cole & Co. Ltd.* [1969] 1 W.L.R. 1877; [1969] 2 All E.R. 904.

[77] The reason is that there is no estoppel, either by negligence or otherwise (*Heap* v. *Motorists Advisory Agency Ltd.* [1923] 1 K.B. 577, 587).

[78] *Folkes* v. *King*[1923] 1 K.B. 282.

[79] *Staffs. Motor Guarantee* v. *British Wagon* [1934] 2 K.B. 305, followed in *Astley Industrial Trust* v. *Miller (infra)* and in *Belvoir Finance Co.* v. *Harold Cole (supra).*

[80] *Heap* v. *Motorists Advisory Agency, supra.*

[81] *Weiner* v. *Harris* [1910] 1 K.B. 285.

[82] s.2(4).

[83] s.2(2).

Since the sort of transaction envisaged by the Act frequently involves some element of fraud on the part of the agent, it is not surprising that the courts have had on a number of occasions to consider whether the apparent "consent" of the owner was vitiated by some fraud or trick on the part of the agent. After some earlier doubts,[84] it now seems clear that the Act can apply if, on the particular facts, the owner consented to that particular agent having possession. It is immaterial that the consent was obtained by fraud or by a trick.[85] It has however been suggested in *Folkes* v. *King*[86] that a trick as to the agent's identity might nullify consent.

Motor-cars. Many of the modern cases have been concerned with the sale of secondhand cars by fraudulent agents, and an owner may wish to know how he can prevent the Factors Act from operating. The answer given by the courts is: retain the registration document. The reason, of course, is that while the registration document is not a document of title, it is the best evidence of title, and a sale by the dealer without it would not be a sale in the ordinary course of business.[87] Even if the owner accidentally leaves the document with the dealer, this will not prejudice him, because the Court of Appeal has twice held that for the Factors Act to apply the owner must have consented to the dealer having possession of the document as well as the car.[88] The position may be different in the case of a new car.[89]

Owner. The word "owner" in section 2 sometimes includes a person with only a limited right over the goods. In *Lloyds Bank* v. *Bank of America National Trust and Savings Association*[90]:

---

[84] *Oppenheimer* v. *Frazer and Wyatt* [1907] 2 K.B. 71, *per* Fletcher Moulton L.J.; *Whitehorn Bros.* v. *Davison* [1911] 1 K.B. 463.

[85] *Folkes* v. *King* [1923] 1 K.B. 282; *Pearson* v. *Rose & Young* [1951] 1 K.B. 275; [1950] 2 All E.R. 1027.

[86] *Ibid.* at p. 298 (Bankes L.J.); p. 305 (Scrutton L.J.).

[87] *Pearson* v. *Rose & Young* [1951] 1 K.B. 275; [1950] 2 All E.R. 1027. Until the mid-1970s a registration book was given to the "keeper" of the car.

[88] *Pearson* v. *Rose & Young, supra; Stadium Finance* v. *Robbins* [1962] 2 Q.B. 664; [1962] 2 All E.R. 633, where the Court of Appeal did not follow a dictum of Denning L.J. in the earlier case that a car without its registration book was not "goods." It seems that the consent must also extend to the ignition key (*ibid*).

[89] *Astley Industrial Trust* v. *Miller* [1968] 2 All E.R. 36.

[90] [1938] 2 K.B. 147. Where a bank is a pledgee of a bill of lading, the bank generally releases the bill to the buyer in return for a "trust receipt," which is an acknowledgment by the buyer that he holds the goods (and the proceeds) on trust for the bank.

The plaintiffs who were pledgees of bills of lading released them to the pledgor to enable him to sell the goods as trustee for the plaintiffs. The pledgor, who was a mercantile agent, fraudulently pledged them with the defendants. The Court of Appeal held that (1) the pledgor and the plaintiffs were jointly the owners, and (2) the defendants had acquired a good title under the Factors Act as against the plaintiffs.

Document of title. It will be noted that the Factors Act covers dealings with the documents of title as well as with the goods. Section 1(4) provides that:

> The expression "document of title" shall include any bill of lading, dock warrant, warehousekeeper's certificate, and warrant or order for the delivery of goods, and any other document used in the ordinary course of business as proof of the possession or control of goods, or authorising or purporting to authorise, either by endorsement or delivery, the possessor of the document to transfer or receive goods thereby represented.

Ordinary course of business. The agent must act in the ordinary course of business of "a" mercantile agent, but it is not necessary that the act should be a usual one in his particular trade. In *Oppenheimer* v. *Attenborough*[91]:

> A mercantile agent fraudulently obtained possession of diamonds from a diamond merchant and pledged them with a pawnbroker. The agent was a diamond broker, and it was proved that diamond brokers did not usually pledge. It was held, nevertheless, that the agent's act was in the ordinary course of business of "a" mercantile agent, and the pawnbroker was therefore protected.

Good faith and without notice. The burden of proving these matters is on the person claiming the protection of the Factors Act.[92]

Antecedent debt. Although the foregoing examples have shown that the Factors Act applies to a pledge as well as to a sale, section 4 provides that where the agent pledges goods as security for a debt or liability due from the pledgor to the pledgee before the time of the pledge, the pledgee acquires no further right to the goods than could have been enforced by the pledgor at the time of the pledge. Thus the pledgee becomes, in effect, the assignee of

---

[91] [1908] 1 K.B. 221.
[92] *Heap* v. *Motorists Advisory Agency, ante,* p. 148.

any rights which the agent had against the principal, *e.g.* a lien for unpaid commission.

(5) Sale in market overt. Sale in market overt is probably the most ancient of the exceptions to the *nemo dat* rule. It dates from the sixteenth century when trading took a much simpler form than the complex commercial transactions of today. It is astonishing that this ancient rule still forms part of the English law[93] in the second half of the twentieth century, but it was duly incorporated into the Sale of Goods Act, and it must now be considered. Section 22 provides that:

> (1) Where goods are sold in market overt, according to the usage of the market, the buyer acquires a good title to the goods, provided he buys them in good faith and without notice of any defect or want of title on the part of the seller.

What is market overt? The expression "market overt" covers an open, public and legally constituted market.[94] It may be held by charter, or prescription of under statutory powers, and in addition every shop in the City of London is market overt as regards any goods usually sold there. A sale in such a shop is, however, only protected if it takes place in the public part of the shop and if it is by, and not to, the shopkeeper.[95]

Usage of the market. The sale must be of goods normally dealt with in the market and the sale must take a form which is usual in the market. In *Bishopsgate Motor Finance Corpn.* v. *Transport Brakes Ltd.*[96]

> A hirer of a car under a hire-purchase agreement took it to Maidstone market. He tried to sell it by auction but failed and then sold it there privately. The Court of Appeal held that (1) Maidstone market was market overt, having been established since 1747, (2) a private sale was not contrary to the usage of the market, (3) the buyer got a good title.

Since the essence of the rule is that the sale must be public and open it has been held that the goods themselves must be displayed

---

[93] It does not form part of the law of Scotland (s.22(2)) or of Wales (The Laws in Wales Act 1542).

[94] *Lee* v. *Bayes* (1856) 18 C.B. 599, 560, *per* Jervis C.J.

[95] *Ardath Tobacco Co.* v. *Ocker* (1931) 47 T.L.R. 177. As to whether an auction room for unredeemed pledges is a shop, see *Clayton* v. *Le Roy* [1911] 2 K.B. 1031.

[96] [1949] 1 K.B. 322; [1949] 1 All E.R. 37.

in the market, so that a mere sale by sample would not be protected.[97] Presumably for the same reason, the sale must take place between sunrise and sunset.[98]

Where goods were stolen section 24 of the 1893 Act encouraged the owner to prosecute the thief by providing that on a conviction for larceny the property in the goods revested in the original owner nothwithstanding any dealing with them whether in market overt or otherwise. This section was repealed by the Theft Act 1968.[99] The result is that any title acquired in market overt will not be divested on conviction of the thief.

Law Reform Committee. The Committee unanimously recommended the repcal of section 22 and, with the exception of Lord Donovan, the introduction of a new provision that a person buying goods by retail at trade premises or by public auction should acquire a good title, if be bought in good faith and without notice of any defect in the seller's title.[1]

(6) Sale under a voidable title. Section 23 provides as follows:

> When the seller of goods has a voidable title to them, but his title has not been avoided at the time of the sale, the buyer acquires a good title to the goods, provided he buys them in good faith and without notice of the seller's defect of title.

This section is declaratory of the general rule that a party cannot avoid a voidable contract (*e.g.* for misrepresentation, *ante*, p. 97) once third party rights have been acquired. The essential point is to distinguish between a contract of sale which is void and one that is merely voidable, because section 23 protects the third party in the latter case, but not in the former. Thus in *Ingram* v. *Little*[2]:

> Three old ladies wishing to sell a Renault Dauphine car were approached by a swindler describing himself as P. G. M. Hutchinson (a reputable man). The ladies thereupon sold the car to "Hutchinson" and allowed him to take it away in return for a cheque which was dishonoured. They sued an innocent third party who had bought the car from "Hutchinson." The Court of Appeal (Devlin L.J.

---

[97] *Hill* v. *Smith* (1812) 4 Taunt. 520.
[98] *Reid* v. *Commissioner of Police* [1973] Q.B. 551; [1973] 2 All E.R. 97.
[99] s.33 and Sched. 3, Part III.
[1] This is a highly controversial proposal which may explain why this 1966 Report has not been implemented.
[2] [1961] 1 Q.B. 31; [1960] 3 All E.R. 332.

dissenting) held that there was no contract between the ladies and the rogue, because their offer to sell was addressed to the real Hutchinson and could not be accepted by anyone else. Consequently the *nemo dat* rule applied and the third party was liable.

The Law Reform Committee recommended that a mistake as to identity should make the contract voidable only, so that section 23 would protect a third party (see para. 15). There has been no legislation on this proposal but the Court of Appeal has gone a long way towards achieving this result. In *Lewis* v. *Averay*[3] where the facts were rather similar to those in *Ingram* v. *Little* (*supra*) the original contract was held to be voidable so that the innocent buyer was protected. The court made it clear that this was the normal inference to be drawn when the parties were face to face, and that the onus was on the original seller to show that the identity of the first buyer was crucial. The court treated the case of *Ingram* v. *Little* (*supra*) as a very special one.

The third party will only be protected if he buys before the original contract has been avoided. In *Car & Universal Finance Co.* v. *Caldwell*[4]:

C was persuaded by the fraud of N to sell his car to N in return for a worthless cheque. On discovering the facts, C informed the police and asked them to get his car back. Shortly afterwards the car was sold to X, who took in bad faith, and X in turn sold to the plaintiff, who bought in good faith. The Court of Appeal held that: (1) although an innocent party rescinding a voidable contract must normally communicate this to the other party, this was not so where (as here) that other party was a rogue who had acquired a voidable title and had then disappeared; (2) C's action in going to the police showed a clear intention to avoid the contract; (3) accordingly N's title had been effectively avoided before the sale to the plaintiff who therefore acquired no title.[5]

The practical value of avoiding the contract has, however, been cut down by a later decision indicating that, even after avoidance the buyer may still be able to pass a good title under another section of the Act (*post*, pp. 155–156).

---

[3] [1972] 1 Q.B. 198; [1972] 3 All E.R. 907, C.A. See (1972) 35 M.L.R. 306.
[4] [1965] 1 Q.B. 525; [1964] 1 All E.R. 290.
[5] The Law Reform Committee recommended that no avoidance should be possible without notice to the other contracting party (*op. cit.* para. 16). Such notice will of course be impossible in many cases.

(7) Disposition by a seller in possession. The position of a seller who sells goods, retains possession and then disposes of them again is governed by two sections which are in virtually identical terms—section 8 of the Factors Act 1889, and section 24 of the Sale of Goods Act. Section 8 reads:

> Where a person having sold goods continues or is in possession of the goods, or the documents of title to the goods, the delivery or transfer by that person, or by a mercantile agent acting for him, of the goods or documents of title under any sale, pledge, or other disposition thereof [or under any agreement for sale, pledge or other disposition thereof], to any person receiving the same in good faith and without notice of the previous sale, shall have the same effect as if the person making the delivery or transfer were expressly authorised by the owner of the goods to make the same.

Section 25(1) is identical, except that the words in square brackets are omitted.

To illustrate the operation of the above, suppose that A sells furniture to B and agrees to deliver in a week's time. During the week A sells and delivers the same furniture to C who buys in good faith and without notice of the sale to B. The result is that C gets a good title as against B who is left with a merely personal action against A.

Character of seller's possession. Does the seller have to remain in possession "as seller"? the Act does not require this but in 1957 the Court of Appeal rather surprisingly held in *Eastern Distributors* v. *Goldring*[6] that this was an essential requirement. Accordingly they held that the second buyer was not protected where the seller, having sold the goods, entered into a hire-purchase agreement and retained possession "as hirer." In *Pacific Motor Auctions* v. *Motor Credits Ltd.*[7] the Privy Council held that there was no justification for putting this gloss on the Act; they expressed the view that *Goldring's* case was wrongly decided. In 1971 the matter again came before the Court of Appeal. In *Worcester Works Finance Co.* v. *Cooden Engineering Co.*[8]:

> B bought a car from S and resold it to F, a finance company. B paid for the car with a "dud" cheque and his title was voidable. After

---

[6] *Eastern Distributors* v. *Goldring* [1957] 2 Q.B. 600; [1957] 2 All E.R. 525.
[7] *Pacific Motor Auctions* v. *Motor Credits Ltd.* [1965] A.C. 867; [1965] 2 All E.R. 105.
[8] [1972] 1 Q.B. 210, C.A.; [1971] 3 All E.R. 708; see also (1972) 35 M.L.R. 186.

the resale B should have delivered the car to H who had entered into a hire-purchase agreement with F. Instead B wrongly retained possession and, when S came to see him following the dishonouring of B's cheque, B allowed S to retake the car [S of course having no idea that B had already resold it]. F sued S for conversion. The Court of Appeal held that: (1) it was not bound by the *Goldring* decision since the Privy Council had disapproved it; (2) After the resale to F, B was a seller in possession and the character of that possession was immaterial; (3) By allowing S to take the car away in return for their promise not to sue B on the cheque B had delivered the car to S under some "other disposition"; (4) accordingly S acquired title under section 24 and the action by F failed.

The section only operates if the original seller, having retained possession, delivers or transfers the goods or documents under the second contract.[9]

(8) Disposition by a buyer in possession. The converse situation to the previous one is again covered by two virtually identical sections. Section 9 of the Factors Act 1889, provides as follows:

> Where a person having bought or agreed to buy goods obtains, with the consent of the seller, possession of the goods or the documents of title to the goods, the delivery or transfer by that person, or by a mercantile agent acting for him, of the goods or documents of title, under any sale, pledge, or other disposition thereof [or under any agreement for sale, pledge or other disposition thereof], to any person receiving the same in good faith and without notice of any lien or other right of the original seller in respect of the goods, has the same effect as if the person making the delivery or transfer were a mercantile agent in possession of the goods or documents of title with the consent of the owner.

Section 25(1) of the Sale of Goods Act is in identical terms except that the words in square brackets are omitted.

The operation of these sections can best be seen by an example. A agrees to sell goods to B and it is agreed that property shall pass on payment. B obtains possession of the goods or documents of title with A's consent[10] and delivers them to C, who takes in good faith and is unaware of A's ownership. Subject to the mercantile agency point (*post*, p. 156) C acquires title.

---

[9] See *Nicholson* v. *Harper* [1895] 2 Ch. 414. It seems that some form of physical transfer is necessary if the section is to apply (*ibid*).

[10] This term includes consent obtained by fraud (*Du Jardin* v. *Beadman Bros.* [1952] 2 Q.B. 712; [1952] 2 All E.R. 160).

Sections 9 and 25(1) may override section 19(3) so that where a buyer, on receiving the bill of exchange and bill of lading together, wrongly retains the bill of lading and then transfers it to a third party, the third party acquires title even though the seller had none.[11]

There are two puzzling features. The first is that the section applies where a person has "bought" or "agreed to buy" goods. The reference to "bought" is puzzling because a buyer who owns the goods can pass title anyway and the transferee from him does not have to rely on one of the *nemo dat* exceptions. The section can however be relevant where the buyer acquires something less than full unencumbered ownership, such as a voidable title (*ante*, p. 152) or ownership subject to a charge or lien in favour of a third party (*e.g.* an unpaid seller). The real importance of sections 9 and 25(1) is in relation to a person who has "agreed to buy." This term includes a person who has conditionally agreed to buy[12] but not one having a mere option to do so.[13] It should be noted that a conditional sale agreement regulated by the Consumer Credit Act 1974 is expressly taken outside sections 9 and 25(1)[14] and consequently the sections have lost some of their importance. The sections do, however, apply to a person in possession under a voidable title even after avoidance (see below).

The second puzzling feature is contained in the concluding words "shall have the same effect as if the person making the delivery or transfer were a mercantile agent in possession . . . with the consent of the owner." Until 1964 no one seriously thought that the sections could only apply if the disposition made by the buyer was in the ordinary course of business of a mercantile agent.[15] It was a great surprise, therefore, when in *Newtons of Wembley Ltd.* v. *Williams*[16] the Court of Appeal held that they did have this effect. The facts of this case, which must be sharply distinguished from those in *Car & Universal Finance Co. Ltd.* v. *Caldwell* (*ante*, p. 153), were as follows:

---

[11] *Cahn* v. *Pocketts Bristol Channel Steam Packet Co.* [1899] 1 Q.B. 643 and see *ante*, p. 137 and *post*, p. 178.
[12] *Marten* v. *Whale* [1917] 2 K.B. 480.
[13] *Helby* v. *Matthews* [1895] A.C. 741.
[14] s.25(2).
[15] There was no suggestion of such a restriction in the leading case of *Lee* v. *Butler* [1893] 2 Q.B. 318.
[16] [1965] 1 Q.B. 560; [1964] 2 All E.R. 135 (1964) 27 M.L.R. 472.

The plaintiffs sold a Sunbeam Rapier to A, who paid by cheque and agreed that no property should pass until the cheque was cleared. When A's cheque was dishonoured the plaintiffs informed the police and sought to repossess the car. A, who was not a mercantile agent, took the car to Warren Street, where there was an established street market for second-hand cars, and sold it to B for cash. B took in good faith[17] and sold to the defendants. The car was then seen and claimed by the plaintiffs. The Court of Appeal held that (1) A was a person who, having bought or agreed to buy goods, had obtained possession with the seller's consent, and the operation of sections 9 and 25(1) was not cut down by the avoidance of the original contract; (2) these sections, however, only applied if, assuming the buyer to have been a mercantile agent, the disposition by him was in the ordinary course of business of a mercantile agent; (3) this test was satisfied in the present case as the sale had taken place in an established market for second-hand cars; (4) consequently, as B took in good faith, he, and through him the defendants, acquired title.

The final point to note is that there must be a delivery or transfer under the second contract. From a reading of the sections it would seem that the same document must pass from seller to buyer and from buyer to transferee. It has, however, been suggested that the transferee will be protected even if he takes a different document from the one given to the buyer.[18] It is doubtful whether this can be regarded as correct.

(9) Disposition under Part III of Hire-Purchase Act 1964. This Act came into force on January 1, 1965, and Part III was not affected by the consolidating Act of 1965. The statutory provisions are now reproduced in the Consumer Credit Act 1974, Schedule 4, paragraph 22 with minor changes of terminology but not of substance.

Background. There was much public concern at the number of buyers who bought a car in perfectly good faith, only to find that it was the subject of an unexpired hire-purchase agreement. This led the Government to propose new measures whereby the owners of vehicles were to retain the registration books while the hirers were to be issued with licensing cards. The finance houses disliked this

---

[17] It was this factor which distinguished the case from *Caldwell's* case. It will be recalled that in that case the immediate transferee from the rogue took in bad faith.
[18] *Mount* v. *Jay & Jay (Provisions) & Co. Ltd.* [1960] 1 Q.B. 159; [1959] 3 All E.R. 307, *post*, p. 178.

scheme for administrative reasons, and the Government then brought forward much more radical buyer-protection provisions. To these provisions the finance houses were prepared to agree provided that the protection was confined to private buyers, since motor dealers and finance house should be better able to discover whether a car was or was not subject to hire-purchase, and should not therefore be in need of statutory protection. The legislation, therefore, protects private purchasers but not "a trade or finance purchaser," who is defined as a purchaser who at the time of the disposition to him carries on a business consisting wholly or partly[19] in buying motor vehicles for re-sale or of providing finance by buying motor vehicles for the purpose of letting them out under hire-purchase agreements or agreeing to sell them under conditional sale agreements (Act of 1964, s.29). A purchaser not carrying on such a business is a private purchaser (*ibid*).

Basic provisions. Section 27 (in its amended form) applies where a motor vehicle is held under a hire-purchase or conditional sale agreement[20] (see *post*, p. 206) and the debtor disposes of the vehicle before the property has passed to him. If the disposition (defined below) is made in favour of a private purchaser who takes in good faith and without notice[21] of the agreement, the disposition takes effect as if the title of the creditor[22] had been vested in the hirer or buyer immediately before the disposition. Thus if A the owner of a car lets it to H on hire-purchase and H sells it to P, a bona fide purchaser without notice of the agreement, P gets a good title. The Act does not, however, affect any liability of H whether civil (*e.g.* in contract or for conversion) or criminal.

If, however, the disposition by the debtor is made to a trade or finance purchaser the section has no application, so that the purchaser has no title unless he can invoke one of the other exceptions to the *nemo dat* rule, such as sale in market overt. If further dispositions take place the Act protects the first private

---

[19] See *Stevenson* v. *Beverley Bentinck Ltd., The Times,* February 5, 1976.

[20] Note that Part III may apply even though the agreement is outside the Act of 1974 because the debtor is a body corporate or because the credit exceeds £5,000.

[21] This means *actual* notice of the relevant agreement (*Barker* v. *Bell* [1971] 1 W.L.R. 983; [1971] 2 All E.R. 867, C.A.).

[22] This being the creditor in relation to the hire-purchase or conditional sale agreement. Thus if in a hire-purchase agreement the person letting out the goods and described as creditor has in fact no title, there is nothing that can be notionally vested in the debtor and therefore nothing to pass to the purchaser.

purchaser if he takes in good faith and without notice of the original agreement. In such a case the disposition takes effect as if the title of the creditor under the original agreement had been vested in the debtor immediately before the disposition by him.

Example. O (the owner) lets a car to H on hire-purchase. H sells to D a motor dealer. D sells to P a private purchaser who buys in good faith and without notice. *Result* (1) O can sue H in contract and for conversion, (2) O can sue D in conversion, (3) P gets a good title.

Where the first disposition is to a trade or finance purchaser and a subsequent disposition to the first private purchaser takes the form of a hire-purchase agreement under which the "owner" transfers the property to the private purchaser (or to a person claiming under him) under a clause in the agreement, the protection provisions operate as to both the hire-purchase agreement and the transfer of property, even though the transferee is not a purchaser in good faith and without notice when the property is transferred.

Example. O (the owner) lets to H (hirer) who sells to D (motor dealer). D lets the vehicle to P (private purchaser) under a hire-purchase agreement which allows P to buy on paying all outstanding instalments. P initially is unaware of the original hire-purchase agreement but later discovers it. He then tenders the balance which is accepted. P acquires a good title.

Disposition. This term includes any sale, contract of sale (including conditional sale agreement), letting under a hire-purchase agreement and transfer of property under a provision in such agreement. Thus if, in the previous example, O had claimed the goods before P had completed his payments, he would not have been successful since P was in possession under a lawful hire-purchase agreement.

It goes without saying that once a private purchaser has acquired a title under the Act, his title passes to any subsequent purchaser, whether private, finance or trade and whether such subsequent purchaser has knowledge of the original agreement or not.

Presumptions. It may sometimes be difficult in practice for the innocent private purchaser to prove the vital facts, and section 28 of the Act of 1964 as amended lays down certain presumptions to assist him. Where in any proceedings it is proved (a) that a motor vehicle was let under a hire-purchase agreement or agreed to be sold under a conditional sale agreement and (b) a person became a private purchaser in good faith and without notice of the agreement, the following presumptions apply unless the contrary is proved:

(1) A presumption that the disposition to that purchaser was made by the debtor.

(2) If it is proved that it was not made by the debtor, then a presumption that the debtor disposed of the vehicle to a previous private purchaser in good faith and without notice and that the purchaser in (b) above is or was a person claiming through such previous purchaser.

(3) If it is proved that the original purchaser was a trade or finance purchaser, then a presumption that the first private purchaser took in good faith and without notice and that the purchaser in (b) above is or was a person claiming through such original purchaser.

> *Example.* P a private purchaser buys a car from Q, another private purchaser (who has vanished). The car is now claimed by F & Co. a finance company who can prove (a) they let it to H under a hire-purchase agreement (b) that H sold it to X and Co., a motor dealer. P can prove that he bought in good faith and without notice of the agreement. It is presumed in his favour (a) that Q took in good faith and without notice and (b) that Q bought from X & Co. (so that P also claims through X & Co.). P is therefore protected unless the finance company can rebut the presumptions.

Unjust enrichment

If a buyer from a non-owner fails to acquire title he will usually have a claim against the seller under section 12 of the Act (*ante*, p. 103). In addition if the true owner claims the return of the goods from the innocent buyer the court may in its discretion order the owner to give credit for money spent by the buyer in improving it. In *Greenwood* v. *Bennett*[23] Lord Denning M.R. based his judgment on the principle of unjust enrichment. Although the principle is a novel one and not without difficulties[24] it seems a fair one and is in line with earlier cases on the assessment of damages

---

[23] [1973] Q.B. 195; [1972] 3 All E.R. 586.
[24] *Munro* v. *Willmott* [1949] 1 K.B. 295; [1948] 2 All E.R. 983.

for conversion.[25] The principle of this case now appears in statutory form.[26]

Sections 27 to 37 of the Act are headed "Performance of the Contract" and they deal with the three topics of delivery, acceptance and payment. Section 27 reads:

> It is the duty of the seller to deliver the goods, and of the buyer to accept and pay for them in accordance with the terms of the contract of sale.

The relationship between delivery and payment has already been noted (*ante*, p. 127). Section 28 provides that:

> Unless otherwise agreed, delivery of the goods and payment of the price are concurrent conditions, that is to say, the seller must be ready and willing to give possession of the goods to the buyer in exchange for the price and the buyer must be ready and willing to pay the price in exchange for possession of the goods.

Property and possession

It will be recalled that property can pass to the buyer before delivery, but the right of property does not entitle him to possession. To claim possession he must either be ready and willing to pay the price or he must show that (as very often happens) section 28 has been varied by contract. In practice the contract frequently allows the buyer to have possession immediately and provides for payment at a later date. Such a contract is called a sale on credit. Even in this case, however, the buyer's right to possession is not absolute, because it is liable to be defeated if he becomes insolvent.[27]

It is now proposed to consider separately the topics of delivery, acceptance and payment.

Delivery

The rules governing delivery are essentially a matter for agreement and the rules contained in the Act only apply in so far as no contract agreement has been made.

---

[25] (1973) 36 M.L.R. 89.
[26] Torts (Interference with Goods) Act 1977, s.6.
[27] *Bloxham* v. *Sanders* (1825) 4 B. & C. 941, 948, and see s.41(1)(*c*), *post*, p. 171.

Definition

Section 61 defines delivery as:

> Voluntary transfer of possession from one person to another.

Methods

There are five ways in which delivery can take place. The first and unquestionably the most common is by a physical transfer of the goods themselves. Secondly, there may be delivery of the means of control, as where the seller hands to the buyer the key to the warehouse where the goods are stored. Such a transaction:

> consists of such a transfer of control in fact as the nature of the case admits, and as will practically suffice for causing the new possessor to be recognised as such.[28]

The third form of delivery is by what is called "attornment." Section 29(4) provides that:

> Where the goods at the time of sale are in the possession of a third person, there is no delivery by seller to buyer unless and until such third person acknowledges to the buyer that he holds the goods on his behalf; provided that nothing in this section shall affect the operation of the issue or transfer of any document of title to goods.

If, therefore, A sells to B a crate of wine stored at the warehouse of C, the property may pass as soon as the contract is made but delivery will not take place until C "attorns" to B, *i.e.* acknowledges that he holds the goods on behalf of B. Such acknowledgment can be inferred from conduct.[29]

The closing words of section 29(4) disclose the fourth method of delivery, namely the delivery of a document of title. In a c.i.f. contract it will be seen that payment and delivery of the shipping documents are concurrent conditions.[30]

The final method of delivery is constructive delivery, an example being where the buyer is already in possession at the time of the sale, but once the sale is effected the character of his possession changes from possession as bailee to possession as

---

[28] Pollock and Wright, *Possession in the Common Law*, p. 61.

[29] *Wood* v. *Tassell* (1844) 6 Q.B. 234. Such acknowledgment may also constitute an "unconditional appropriation" passing the property and risk (*ante*, pp. 133–134).

[30] See *post*, p. 468.

buyer. Conversely, the seller may agree to retain the goods as bailee until such time as the buyer requires them. This again could operate as constructive delivery.

Place

Section 29 begins with these words:

> (1) Whether it is for the buyer to take possession of the goods or for the seller to send them to the buyer is a question depending in each case on the contract, express or implied, between the parties.
>
> (2) Apart from any such contract, express or implied, the place of delivery is the seller's place of business, if he has one, and if not, his residence; except that if the contract is for the sale of specific goods which to the knowledge of the parties when the contract is made are in some other place, then that place is the place of delivery.

Thus if nothing is said the seller's sole duty is to have the goods available at his place of business or residence and he is not bound to send them to the buyer. In practice, of course, this is varied in a great many inland sales and in virtually all export sales.

The exception would apply where, for example, A sold to B an aircraft which both parties knew was on a piece of waste land at the time of the contract. That land would then be the place of delivery.

A duty to deliver at the buyer's premises is discharged if the seller delivers the goods at those premises to a person who appears to be authorised to receive them even though in fact he was not so authorised.[31]

Time

By section 29(3):

> Where under the contract of sale the seller is bound to send the goods to the buyer, but no time for sending them is fixed, the seller is bound to send them within a reasonable time.

Further by section 29(5):

> Demand or tender of delivery may be treated as ineffectual unless made at a reasonable hour and what is a reasonable hour is a question of fact.

It has already been seen that time for delivery is usually of the essence in commercial contracts. A seller may often find his

---

[31] *Galbraith & Grant* v. *Block* [1922] 2 K.B. 155.

attempts at delivery hindered by events beyond his control, such as strikes, restrictive legislation or default on the part of his own supplier. It is therefore of the greatest importance that the seller should stipulate in the contract that such events should relieve him from strict performance of his duty to deliver.[32]

In the absence of such a clause, the seller will be liable for non-delivery unless the doctrine of frustration can be invoked.[33]

Expenses
Section 29(6):

> Unless otherwise agreed, the expenses of and incidental to putting the goods into a deliverable state must be borne by the seller.

This follows logically from section 61(5) which provides, in effect, that goods are not in a deliverable state until they are in such a state that the buyer is bound to accept them.

Delivery of wrong quantity
This matter is governed by section 30 which has already been considered (see *ante*, pp. 112–113).

Delivery by instalments
Section 31 reads as follows:

> (1) Unless otherwise agreed, the buyer of goods is not bound to accept delivery of them by instalments.
>
> (2) Where there is a contract for the sale of goods to be delivered by stated instalments, which are to be separately paid for, and the seller makes defective deliveries in respect of one or more instalments, or the buyer neglects or refuses to take delivery of or pay for one or more instalments, it is a question in each case depending upon the terms of the contract and the circumstances of the case, whether the breach of contract is a repudiation of the whole contract or whether it is a severable breach giving rise to a claim for

---

[32] A typical clause is "should the sellers be prevented from delivering the goods sold by reason of riots, strikes, lock out, or any other cause comprehended in the term *force majeure* at the place of delivery, the time for delivery shall be extended until the operation of the cause preventing delivery has ceased." For the possible effect of section 3 of the Unfair Contract Terms Act 1977 see *post*, p. 438.

[33] *Re Shipton, Anderson & Co. and Harrison Bros. and Co.* [1915] 3 K.B. 676 (goods requisitioned by Government). Contrast *Tsakiroglou & Co.* v. *Noblee Thorl GmbH* [1962] A.C. 93; [1961] 2 All E.R. 170 (closure of Suez Canal—contracts not frustrated).

compensation[34] but not to a right to treat the whole contract as repudiated.

Where nothing is said in the contract about instalments it is clear that the commercial object of the contract would frequently be frustrated if a seller who had agreed to supply an entire quantity of goods were to be allowed to tender an instalment. Therefore, if the contract was for "10 tons of coal" and the seller tendered an "instalment" of six tons, the seller would be in breach of section 13 (*ante*, p. 108) and the buyer's remedies would be governed by section 30(1) (*ante*, p. 112). This is the effect of section 31(1).

If, however, the contract does provide for instalment deliveries, a distinction must be drawn between a contract for delivery by instalments at a single lump sum price, and a contract for deliveries which are to be separately paid for. If the instalments are not to be separately paid for, section 31(2) does not apply. In this case a breach with regard to any one instalment can be treated as a breach of the entire contract, subject, of course, to the *de minimis* rule. Therefore, if an instalment is defective or short, this will usually amount to a breach of either section 13 or 14 and will entitle the buyer to treat the contract as repudiated. It must, however, be remembered that as the contract is "not severable"[35] a buyer who has accepted any part of the goods is obliged by section 11(4) to treat a breach of condition as a breach of warranty, and cannot therefore reject the goods, unless the case is governed by section 30 (*ante*, p. 113).

If, on the other hand, the instalments are to be separately paid for, section 31(2) applies. Such a contract can be regarded as "severable" and two results flow from this. The first is that the acceptance of one or more instalments does not, under section 11(4), prevent rejection of future instalments.[36] Secondly, a breach with regard to one or more instalments cannot automatically be regarded as a breach of the whole contract. Section 31(2) provides that it depends in each case upon the terms of the contract and the circumstances of the case. In the words of Lord Hewart:

---

[34] *i.e.* a claim for unliquidated damages or for the instalment in arrear (*Workman Clark* v. *Lloyd Brazileño* [1908] 1 K.B. 968, 979).

[35] Whether the contract is severable or not depends in some cases on how the seller chooses to perform it (see *Rosenthal & Sons Ltd.* v. *Esmail, ante,* p. 101).

[36] See, *e.g. Jackson* v. *Rotax Motor and Cycle Co.* [1910] 2 K.B. 937.

"The true test will generally be . . . the relation in fact of the default to the whole purpose of the contract . . . the main tests to be considered . . . are first, the ratio quantitatively which the breach bears to the contract as a whole, and secondly the degree of probability or improbability that such a breach will be repeated."[37]

In the case in which these words were spoken the seller supplied 18 instalments of rag flock, one of which was defective. The Court of Appeal held that this was a severable breach only and did not entitle the buyers to refuse further deliveries. On the other hand, in *Munro (Robert A.) and Co. Ltd.* v. *Meyer*[38]:

Under a contract for the sale of 1,500 tons of bone meal, the sellers, who were middle-men, delivered 611 tons which were seriously adulterated. It was held that the size of this breach and the likelihood that further supplies would be similarly defective entitled the buyers to treat the contract as repudiated and to refuse further supplies.

Since time for payment is normally not of the essence, it is unlikely that a default with regard to one or more instalments will entitle the seller to treat the contract as repudiated, unless it is reasonably clear that the buyer regards himself as no longer bound. If, however, the seller wishes to insist on punctual payment, he can stipulate that "all payments to be made on due date as a condition precedent to future deliveries." If he does this and the buyer defaults he can refuse unconditionally to make any further deliveries.[39]

Some instalment contracts contain a provision that "each instalment is to be considered a separate contract." Speaking of such a clause in *Smyth (Ross T.) & Co.* v. *Bailey & Co.*[40] Lord Wright said[41]:

"Such clauses are subsidiary clauses which generally have effect upon questions of performance, there is still only one contract and one contract quantity, though, for certain purposes, in the way of performance, particular instalments or shipments and parcels may be treated in separation from the others."

---

[37] *Maple Flock Co.* v. *Universal Furniture Products (Wembley) Ltd.* [1934] 1 K.B. 148.

[38] [1930] 2 K.B. 312.

[39] *Ebbw Vale Steel, Iron and Coal Co.* v. *Blaina Iron Co.* (1901) 6 Com.Cas. 33, C.A.

[40] (1940) 45 Com.Cas. 292; [1940] 3 All E.R. 60.

[41] *Ibid.* at p. 73.

Delivery to carrier

Section 32(1) provides that:

> Where, in pursuance of a contract of sale, the seller is authorised or required to send the goods to the buyer, delivery of the goods to a carrier (whether named by the buyer or not) for the purpose of transmission to the buyer is prima facie deemed to be a delivery of the goods to the buyer.

The presumption of delivery can be rebutted if, for example, a seller sending goods abroad makes out the bill of lading to himself or to his own agent.

Effect of section 32(1)

Delivery to a carrier under section 32(1) usually operates as performance of the seller's duty to deliver (s.27 *ante*, p. 161) and it may also constitute an unconditional appropriation passing the property and risk where the goods were originally unascertained (see s.18, r. 5(2) *ante*, p. 134 and s.20 *ante*, p. 137). It usually destroys the unpaid seller's lien (s.43(1), *post* p. 172) but not his right of stoppage in transit (s.44 *post*, p. 173). Finally, delivery to a carrier does not destroy the buyer's right to reject for breach of condition. It has already been seen that the right to reject is only lost when the buyer accepts the goods (*ante*, p. 100).

Contract of carriage

Section 32(2) provides that:

> Unless otherwise authorised by the buyer, the seller must make such contract with the carrier on behalf of the buyer as may be reasonable having regard to the nature of the goods and the other circumstances of the case. If the seller omit so to do, and the goods are lost or damaged in course of transit, the buyer may decline to treat the delivery to the carrier as delivery to himself or may hold the seller responsible in damages.

In *Thomas Young & Sons Ltd.* v. *Hobson & Partners*[42]:

> Sellers of electric engines agreed to send them to buyers by rail. They were sent at "owner's risk," and were damaged during the journey because they were insufficiently secured. On arrival the buyers refused to accept them. It was proved that the sellers could have consigned the goods at identical rates at "company's risk" in

---

[42] (1949) 65 T.L.R. 365.

which case the railway authorities would have ensured that they were properly secured. The Court of Appeal held that (1) the sellers had failed to make a reasonable contract of carriage and accordingly (2) the buyers were entitled to reject.

It may be useful to group together the cases where a buyer can have a claim against the seller if goods which are sent to him arrive in a defective condition. He may have a claim in at least five cases:

(1) If the seller has agreed to send the goods at his own risk and the deterioration is not necessarily incidental to the transit (s.33, *ante*, p. 138).

(2) If the goods deteriorate before there has been an unconditional appropriation (*Healy* v. *Howlett ante*, p. 135).

(3) If the seller is in breach of section 14 (see *ante*, p. 114).

(4) If the seller has failed to make a reasonable contract of carriage (s.32(2), *supra*).

(5) If the journey involves sea transit and the seller has failed to give the buyer particulars to enable the buyer to insure (s.32(3), *post*, p. 464).

Examination and acceptance

This topic has already been considered.[43] It will be recalled that by accepting the goods the buyer loses his right to reject for breach of condition. The acceptance of goods will not normally operate to pass the property to the buyer[44] nor will it make him liable to pay the price.[45]

If the buyer validly refuses to accept goods he is not bound to send them back to the seller and it is sufficient if he intimates his refusal to the seller.[46]

Payment

It has already been seen that, as a general rule, the buyer must pay the price in return for delivery. It follows that a seller cannot sue for the price unless he is ready and willing to deliver. There is, however, one exception to this rule. If the goods, while still in the seller's possession, are destroyed after the risk has passed to the buyer, the seller will still be able to sue for the price even though

---

[43] *Ante*, pp. 101–102.
[44] For rules as to passing of property, see *ante*, pp. 126–137.
[45] For rules as to payment of price, see *post*, p. 180.
[46] s.36.

he is unable to effect delivery. In other words, section 28 must be read subject to section 20.

If, having received and paid for the goods, the buyer lawfully rejects them, he can, of course, sue under section 54 to recover the price because the consideration for it has failed.

REMEDIES

Remedies of seller

It has already been seen that by section 27 the buyer's duty is to accept and pay for the goods. A seller who is unpaid has the following six remedies to compel performance of these duties.

(1) A lien (ss.41–43).

(2) A right of stoppage in transit (ss.44–46).

(3) Where the property has not passed to the buyer, a right of retention co-extensive with the right of lien and stoppage (s.39(2)).

(4) A right of resale (s.48).

(5) An action for the price (s.49).

(6) An action for damages for non-acceptance (s.50).

The remedies over the goods themselves ((1)–(4)) are likely to prove of greater value in practice than the merely personal remedies ((5) and (6)) and will therefore be considered first.

Rights against the goods

Part IV of the Act is headed "Rights of Unpaid Seller against the Goods" and it begins by defining "unpaid seller." Section 38 reads as follows:

(1) The seller of goods is deemed to be an "unpaid seller" within the meaning of this act—

(a) when the whole of the price has not been paid or tendered:

(b) when a bill of exchange or other negotiable instrument has been received as conditional payment, and the condition on which it was received has not been fulfilled by reason of the dishonour of the instrument or otherwise.

(2) In this Part of this Act the term "seller" includes any person who is in the position of a seller, as, for instance, an agent of the seller to whom the bill of lading has been indorsed, or a consignor or agent who has himself paid, or is directly responsible for, the price.

Conditional payment. Where a buyer pays by drawing a cheque, accepting a bill or making a promissory note, it is a question of fact whether the payment is absolute or conditional. In the former case, the seller's rights under the contract are extinguished and he can only sue on the instrument. In the latter case, however, the seller's rights to sue on the contract are merely suspended and revive if the instrument is dishonoured. For obvious commercial reasons, the courts are far more likely in practice to hold that the payment was conditional only. The following quotation from an early case is instructive on this point and on the general question of unpaid seller's rights:

> "Whoever heard of such a thing in a mercantile contract, when it is said that payment is to be made by buyer's acceptance of seller's drafts, that if the acceptance was dishonoured, the right to sue under the original contract did not revive? . . . No doubt if the buyer does not become insolvent, that is to say, if he does not openly proclaim his insolvency, then credit is given by taking the bill and during the time that the bill is current there is no vendor's lien, and the vendor is bound to deliver. But if the bill is dishonoured before delivery had been made, then the vendor's lien revives; or if the purchaser becomes openly insolvent before delivery actually takes place, then the law does not compel the vendor to deliver to an insolvent purchaser."[47]

Illustration of section 38(2). A Japanese importer instructs an English confirming house to obtain goods from an English manufacturer. The confirming house is personally responsible for the price. Having paid it, the confirming house has the rights of an unpaid seller *vis-à-vis* the importer.[48]

A buyer who validly rejects goods, having paid the price, is not deemed to be an "unpaid seller" as against the seller so that he has no lien over them.[49]

Lien. Section 41 provides that an unpaid seller has a lien in three cases. The section reads as follows:

> (1) Subject to this Act, the unpaid seller of goods who is in possession of them is entitled to retain possession of them until payment or tender of the price in the following cases, namely:

---

[47] *Gunn* v. *Bolckow, Vaughan & Co.* (1875) 10 Ch. App. 491, 501 *per* Mellish L.J. The last sentence quoted illustrates the words "or otherwise" in s.38(1)(*b*).

[48] This example presupposes that the contract is governed by English law.

[49] *J. L. Lyons* v. *May and Baker* [1923] 1 K.B. 685.

(a) where the goods have been sold without any stipulation as to credit;
(b) where the goods have been sold on credit, but the term of credit has expired;
(c) where the buyer becomes insolvent.
(2) The seller may exercise his right of lien notwithstanding that he is in possession of the goods as agent or bailee or custodier for the buyer.

The lien conferred by the section is a right whereby an unpaid seller is entitled to retain possession of goods the property in which has passed to the buyer. It is a valuable security for him, especially when it is linked with the power of sale conferred by section 48. The section follows from the basic rule that delivery and payment are concurrent conditions. There is, however, one important difference between the two rules. Under section 28 a buyer suing for non-delivery must merely be "ready and willing" to pay the price, whereas under section 41, if the seller claims his lien, the buyer must apparently go further and must actually pay or tender the price before becoming entitled to delivery.

Section 41(1)(b) is likely to be of little practical importance, because the buyer will usually have obtained possession (thereby destroying the lien under section 43) before expiry of the credit term.

Section 41(1)(c) is important, and it should be noted that "insolvent" is wider than "bankrupt." Section 61(4) reads:

> A person is deemed to be insolvent within the meaning of this Act who either has ceased to pay his debts in the ordinary course of business, or cannot pay his debts as they become due, whether he has committed an act of bankruptcy or not. . . .

On the buyer's insolvency the seller can claim a lien, even if the sale is on credit and the credit term has not expired.

Extent of lien. The lien can be claimed for the price of the goods, but it is doubtful whether it extends to any other charges. It has been held that where a buyer neglects to pay, whereupon the seller stores the goods, the seller cannot claim for the storage charges because he incurred them for his own benefit (*viz.* to preserve his lien) and not for the benefit of the buyer.[50] There appears to be no

---

[50] *Somes* v. *The British Empire Shipping Co.* (1860) 8 H.L.C. 338—a shipwright case but seller's lien discussed. The seller can, of course, recover by action a reasonable charge for custody where the buyer has refused to accept (s.37).

reported case where a seller has incurred expense for the benefit of the buyer as by garaging a car or feeding an animal. Presumably the best practical step is to stipulate in the contract that any necessary storage and maintenance charges shall be added to the price.

Part delivery. By section 42:

> Where an unpaid seller has made part delivery of the goods, he may exercise his right of lien or retention on the remainder unless such part delivery has been made under such circumstances as to show an agreement to waive the lien or right of retention.

Where the contract is for delivery by instalments which are to be separately paid for, the buyer's default with regard to one instalment does not confer a right to refuse to deliver future instalments, but the buyer's insolvency does give such a right.[51] Even if the buyer becomes insolvent, however, the seller has no lien over goods which have actually been paid for.[52]

Loss of lien. By section 43:

> (1) The unpaid seller of goods loses his lien or right of retention in respect of them—
> (*a*) when he delivers the goods to a carrier or other bailee or custodier for the purpose of transmission to the buyer without reserving the right of disposal of the goods;
> (*b*) when the buyer or his agent lawfully obtains possession of the goods;
> (*c*) by waiver of the lien or right of retention.
> (2) The unpaid seller of goods, who has a lien or right of retention thereon, does not lose his lien or right of retention by reason only that he has obtained judgment or decree for the price of the goods.

Delivery to a carrier destroys the lien (but not the right of stoppage *in transitu*) provided that the seller does not "reserve the right of disposal."

It will be recalled that these words appeared in sections 18, rule 5(2), and 19,[53] and in that context they clearly referred to the seller reserving his right of property. It is clear, however, that they cannot have the same meaning in section 43, because the word

---

[51] *Ex p. Chalmers* (1873) 8 Ch.App. 289.
[52] *Merchant Banking Co. of London* v. *Phoenix Bessemer Steel Co.* (1877) 5 Ch.D. 205.
[53] *Ante,* pp. 134–136.

"lien" itself presupposes that the property has already passed. In this context, therefore, they must be taken to refer to the reservation of the right of possession, as where the seller hands the goods to his own agent for transmission to the buyer.

The provisions of section 43(1)(*b*) follow from the basic rule that a lien is founded on possession. The buyer does not acquire possession of the goods merely because he has some degree of control over them. Therefore, if the seller can effectively prevent the buyer having access to the goods, the lien continues.[54] The word "lawfully" presumably means that if the buyer obtains possession by stealing, by fraud or by a trick, the seller can sue to recover them and then resume his lien.

A lien can also be lost by waiver, which can be express or implied. One instance of waiver is where the seller takes a security which is inconsistent with the lien, as where the price is initially payable immediately but subsequently the seller takes a 30-day bill. Another example of waiver occurs where the seller does a wrongful act such as consuming the goods or transferring them to a third party. If he does this the buyer can sue in conversion without tendering the price, but the damages will be limited to the difference (if any) between the value of the goods and the unpaid balance of the price.[55] A final example of waiver is where the unpaid seller assents to a sub-sale by the buyer.[56]

Effect of lien. The exercise of the unpaid seller's lien does not rescind the contract.[57]

Stoppage in transit. Section 44 provides that:

> Subject to this Act, when the buyer of goods becomes insolvent, the unpaid seller who has parted with the possession of the goods has the right of stopping them in transit, that is to say, he may resume possession of the goods as long as they are in course of transit, and may retain them until payment or tender of the price.

This remedy was at one time of considerable importance in the export trade, but today this is no longer so. The reason is that the

---

[54] See, *e.g. Great Eastern Ry.* v. *Lord's Trustee* [1909] A.C. 109.
[55] *Chinery* v. *Viall* (1860) 5 H. & N. 288 (damages); *Mulliner* v. *Florence* (1878) 3 Q.B.D. 484 (destruction of lien).
[56] s.47 *post*, p. 176, and see *Mount Ltd.* v. *Jay and Jay* (*Provisions*) *Co. Ltd.* [1960] 1 Q.B. 159; [1959] 3 All E.R. 307.
[57] s.48(1).

majority of export sales are financed by means of banker's commercial credits, whereby a bank in the seller's country pays the seller or accepts bills of exchange drawn by him in return for the shipping documents. When this occurs he ceases to fulfil the definition of an "unpaid seller." The other form of finance which is still of some importance is that of sending a bill of exchange together with a bill of lading (see s.19(3), *ante*, p. 137). Even here the shipping documents are frequently handled by a bank so that there is no question of the buyer being able to obtain the bill of lading (and thereby the goods) unless he honours the bill of exchange. The right of stoppage is not, of course, confined to export sales, but the period of transit in inland sales is usually fairly short, so that the remedy of stoppage is likely to be comparatively rare. The rules governing the duration of transit are set out in section 45 which reads as follows:

(1) Goods are deemed to be in course of transit from the time when they are delivered to a carrier or other bailee or custodier for the purpose of transmission to the buyer, until the buyer, or his agent in that behalf, takes delivery of them from such carrier or other bailee or custodier.

(2) If the buyer or his agent in that behalf obtains delivery of the goods before their arrival at the appointed destination, the transit is at an end.

(3) If, after the arrival of the goods at the appointed destination, the carrier or other bailee or custodier acknowledges to the buyer, or his agent, that he holds the goods on his behalf and continues in possession of them as bailee or custodier for the buyer, or his agent, the transit is at an end, and it is immaterial that a further destination for the goods may have been indicated by the buyer.

(4) If the goods are rejected by the buyer, and the carrier or other bailee or custodier continues in possession of them, the transit is not deemed to be at an end, even if the seller has refused to receive them back.

(5) When goods are delivered to a ship chartered by the buyer it is a question depending on the circumstances of the particular case whether they are in the possession of the master as a carrier, or as agent to the buyer.

(6) Where the carrier or other bailee or custodier wrongfully refuses to deliver the goods to the buyer, or his agent in that behalf, the transit is deemed to be at an end.

(7) Where part delivery of the goods has been made to the buyer, or his agent in that behalf, the remainder of the goods may be stopped in transit, unless such part delivery has been made under such circumstances as to show an agreement to give up possession of the whole of the goods.

The key feature of transit, therefore, is that the goods are in the possession not of the seller, nor of the buyer, but of the carrier acting as such. As Cairns L.J. put it in one case: "The essential feature . . . is that goods should be . . . in the possession of a middleman."[58] It will be recalled that by section 61 delivery involves transfer of possession and that by section 32(1) the delivery to a carrier for transmission to the buyer is prima facie delivery to the buyer. Section 32 must, however, be read subject to section 45: in other words, the mere delivery to a carrier does not give the buyer possession[59] so as to destroy the right of stoppage in transit.

It will be apparent from subsection (4) that goods may be in transit even though they are no longer in motion.

Perhaps the most difficult problem arises (or arose) where the transit covers several stages and several carriers, and where the transit is interrupted. In the former case, the transit is deemed to continue if the goods are merely on the way to their contractual destination, and it is immaterial that the carrier is instructed by the buyer. If, however, the buyer gives instructions to the carrier to undertake a new transit, the original transit is at an end.[60] If the buyer instructs the seller to suspend the transit and it cannot be resumed without further orders from the buyer, the transit again is at an end.[61]

Methods of stoppage. There are two methods in which stoppage can take place. Section 46 reads as follows:

> (1) The unpaid seller may exercise his right of stoppage in transit either by taking actual possession of the goods, or by giving notice of his claim to the carrier or other bailee or custodier in whose possession the goods are.
> (2) The notice may be given either to the person in actual possession of the goods or to his principal.
> (3) If given to the principal, the notice is ineffective unless given at such time and under such circumstances that the principal, by the

---

[58] *Schotsmans* v. *Lancs. & Yorks. Ry.* (1867) 2 Ch. App. 332, 338.

[59] For those readers who approve of "constructive" doctrines, the buyer may during the transit be said to have constructive possession (see *per* Brett L.J. in *Kendall* v. *Marshall, Stevens and Co.* (1883) 11 Q.B.D. 356, 364–365).

[60] See *Bethell* v. *Clark* (1888) 20 Q.B.D. 615.

[61] *Reddall* v. *Union Castle Mail Steamship Co.* (1914) 84 L.J.K.B. 360. See the principles summarised in Benjamin (2nd ed.), pp. 587–597 and cases there cited.

exercise of reasonable diligence, may communicate it to his servant or agent in time to prevent a delivery to the buyer.

(4) When notice of stoppage in transit is given by the seller to the carrier, or other bailee or custodier in possession of the goods, he must re-deliver the goods to, or according to the directions of, the seller; and the expenses of the re-delivery must be borne by the seller.

Where the carrier claims to have a lien over the goods, the position is that:

(a) the lien for freight for the consignment in question has priority over the unpaid seller's right to resume possession,[62] but

(b) the unpaid seller will usually have priority over any further lien which the contract purports to give to the carrier, e.g. a lien for all sums due from the buyer to the carrier.[63]

Stoppage does not of itself rescind the original contract (section 48(1)).

Retention. It has already been seen that an unpaid seller who is still the owner of the goods has a right of retention co-extensive with the right of lien and stoppage.

Restriction on seller's rights. The previous discussion has dealt with the rights of seller and buyer *inter se.* Frequently, however, the buyer resells or pledges the goods, and it is necessary to consider how far this affects the unpaid seller's rights. Section 47 provides that:

> (1) Subject to this Act, the unpaid seller's right of lien or retention or stoppage in transit is not affected by any sale or other disposition of the goods which the buyer may have made, unless the seller has assented to it.

To amount to "assent" the unpaid seller must, in effect, renounce his rights against the goods, as, for example, by selling goods and agreeing to be paid out of the proceeds of a resale by

---

[62] *Booth S.S. Co.* v. *Cargo Fleet Iron Co.* [1916] 2 K.B. 570.
[63] *U.S. Steel Products Co.* v. *G.W.R.* [1916] 1 A.C. 189, H.L. It seems that if the carrier wishes his general lien to have priority over the unpaid seller's lien, the contract of carriage must contain a clause to this effect.

the buyer.[64] The case of *Mordaunt* v. *British Oil and Cake Mills*[65] shows that a mere knowledge of the sub-contract is not enough:

> Buyers of oil (which was unascertained) resold part of it to the plaintiff and gave the plaintiff a delivery order addressed to the sellers and asking them to supply the plaintiff "*ex* our contract." The sellers made some deliveries but subsequently refused to make further deliveries on the ground that they had not been paid by the buyers and were exercising their unpaid seller's lien. Pickford J. held that they were entitled to the lien because they had not assented to the sub-sale.

There is, however, an important qualification to the basic rule. Section 47(2) provides that:

> Where a document of title to goods has been lawfully transferred to any person as buyer or owner of the goods and that person transfers the document to a person who takes it in good faith and for valuable consideration, then:
> (a) if the last mentioned transfer was by way of sale the unpaid seller's right of lien or retention or stoppage in transit is defeated; and
> (b) if the last mentioned transfer was made by way of pledge or other disposition for value, the unpaid seller's right of lien or retention or stoppage in transit can only be exercised subject to the rights of the transferee.

The subsection applies even if goods are unascertained. In *Ant. Jurgens Margarinenfabriken* v. *Louis Dreyfus & Co.*[66]:

> Buyer bought 2,400 bags of seed forming part of a large consignment and paid by cheque. Seller handed buyer a delivery order and buyer indorsed this to the plaintiff who took it in good faith and for value. The buyer's cheque was dishonoured. It was held that the transfer of the document from the buyer to the plaintiff destroyed the unpaid seller's lien.

Section 47(2) only operates where a single document passes *twice*—once from the unpaid seller to the buyer and once from the buyer to the third party. If, therefore, a seller transfers a delivery order to the buyer who then transfers a different delivery order to his sub-buyer the proviso will not apply. In such a case, however, it

---

[64] *Mount Ltd.* v. *Jay and Jay* (*Provisions*) *Co. Ltd.* [1960] 1 Q.B. 159; [1959] 3 All E.R. 307.
[65] [1910] 2 K.B. 502. Assent might have been more readily inferred had the goods been specific (*ibid*).
[66] [1914] 3 K.B. 40.

has been suggested that the sub-buyer can rely on section 25 (*ante,* p. 155) to defeat the unpaid seller's lien.[67] It is also interesting to note that section 25, which covers much of the same ground as section 47(2), only protects a third party who takes "in good faith and without any notice of any lien or other right of the original seller in respect of the goods," whereas under section 47(2) the third party need only take the document "in good faith."

Resale. The foregoing rights of lien, stoppage and retention are frequently exercised with a view to the ultimate resale of the goods. Section 48 deals with the question of resale:

> (1) Subject to this section, a contract of sale is not rescinded by the mere exercise by an unpaid seller of his right of lien or retention or stoppage in transit.
>
> (2) Where an unpaid seller who has exercised his right of lien or retention or stoppage in transit resells the goods, the buyer acquires a good title to them as against the original buyer.
>
> (3) Where the goods are of a perishable nature, or where the unpaid seller gives notice to the buyer of his intention to resell.[68] and the buyer does not within a reasonable time pay or tender the price, the unpaid seller may resell the goods and recover from the original buyer damages for any loss occasioned by his breach of contract.
>
> (4) Where the seller expressly reserves the right of re-sale in case the buyer should make default, and on the buyer making default, resells the goods, the original contract of sale is rescinded but without prejudice to any claim the seller may have for damages.

This section deals first with the rights of the second buyer and then with the position as between the seller and the original buyer and the same order will be adopted here.

Rights of second buyer. Where an unpaid seller resells the goods the second buyer will acquire a good title as against the original buyer in at least three cases:

(1) If the seller was still the owner of the goods at the time of the resale.

(2) Under section 48(2) if the seller resells after exercising his lien or right of stoppage. This, as has already been mentioned, is

---

[67] By Salmon J., *obiter,* in *Mount* v. *Jay and Jay, supra.* The actual decision in that case was that the unpaid seller's rights had disappeared in any event because he had "assented" to the sub-sale.

[68] The Court of Appeal has held that the service of this notice makes time for payment of the essence (*R. V. Ward* v. *Bignall* [1967] 1 Q.B. 534; [1967] 2 All E.R. 449).

an exception to the *nemo dat* rule because the seller can pass a good title even if the property has passed to the defaulting buyer. The second buyer under section 48(2) is protected even if the seller's resale is wrongful as against the original buyer.

(3) Under section 8 of the Factors Act 1889, and section 24 (as to which see *ante*, p. 154).

Position as between seller and original buyer. The resale by the seller is lawful if it comes within section 48(3) or section 48(4). Even if it is unlawful, so that the original buyer can sue the original seller for damages, it has just been seen that if section 48(2) applies the title of the second buyer prevails over that of the first.

Section 48(4) expressly states that resale rescinds the original contract. What is the effect of a resale under section 48(3)? Since the subsection does not refer to rescission it was formerly held in *Gallagher* v. *Shilcock*[69] that a resale did not rescind the original contract. The Court of Appeal have now overruled this decision[70] and have held that by reselling the goods the unpaid seller necessarily rescinds the contract, because he puts it out of his power to perform it. Accordingly any resale under section 48(3) or section 48(4) does rescind the contract. It follows that:

1. The unpaid seller cannot, after the resale, sue the first buyer for the price.

2. If the resale results in a loss the unpaid seller can sue the first buyer for damage for non-acceptance.

3. If the resale results in a profit, the unpaid seller can keep it.

4. If the first buyer has paid a deposit, the unpaid seller can keep it, but if he brings an action for damages he must bring the deposit into account in measuring his loss.

Quite apart from the Act an unpaid seller can resell if the buyer repudiates the contract. This is a rule of the common law[71] and as such it is preserved by section 62. It should, however, be remembered that the courts will be slow to infer repudiation from

---

[69] [1949] 2 K.B. 765; [1949] 1 All E.R. 921.
[70] *R. V. Ward* v. *Bignall* [1967] 1 Q.B. 534; [1967] 2 All E.R. 499. This case was concerned solely with a lawful resale under s.48(3) so that the observation made by the court would not necessarily apply to a wrongful sale.
[71] *Ogg* v. *Shuter* (1875) 1 C.P.D. 47.

mere non-payment since time for payment is generally not of the essence.[72]

Personal remedies

The unpaid seller has two personal remedies against the buyer—an action for the price and an action for damages for non-acceptance.

Action for the price. Section 49 reads as follows:

> (1) Where, under a contract of sale, the property in the goods has passed to the buyer, and he wrongfully neglects or refuses to pay for the goods according to the terms of the contract, the seller may maintain an action against him for the price of the goods.
>
> (2) Where, under a contract of sale, the price is payable on a day certain irrespective of delivery, and the buyer wrongfully neglects or refuses to pay such price, the seller may maintain an action for the price, although the property in the goods has not passed, and the goods have not been appropriated to the contract.

The seller can only claim the price if it is due and if the buyer is liable to pay it. Thus he cannot claim it during the currency of a credit period, nor where the buyer validly rejects the goods for breach of condition.

Action for damages. Section 50(1) reads as follows:

> Where the buyer wrongfully neglects or refuses to accept and pay for the goods, the seller may maintain an action against him for damages for non-acceptance.

Further, section 37 provides that:

> (1) When the seller is ready and willing to deliver the goods, and requests the buyer to take delivery, and the buyer does not within a reasonable time after such request take delivery of the goods, he is liable to the seller for any loss occasioned by his neglect or refusal to take delivery, and also for a reasonable charge for the care and custody of the goods.

---

[72] s.10, *ante*, p. 102 and see *Financings Ltd.* v. *Baldock* [1963] 2 Q.B. 104; [1963] 1 All E.R. 443, C.A. where default by a hirer under a hire-purchase agreement did not, on the facts, amount to repudiation. See, however, *R. V. Ward* v. *Bignall* (*supra*), where time was made of the essence by service of a notice of intention to resell. In such a case failure to comply with the notice would constitute repudiation by the buyer.

(2) Nothing in this section affects the rights of the seller where the neglect or refusal of the buyer to take delivery amounts to a repudiation of the contract.

Where the property has passed, or where the price is payable on a day certain, and the buyer refuses to accept and pay for the goods, the seller can elect whether to sue for the price under section 49 or for damages under section 50. In either case the claim can be linked with a claim under section 37. In deciding whether it is more beneficial to claim the price or damages, it should be remembered that a seller suing for the price must generally be ready and willing to deliver, which on a rising market he might be reluctant to do. It has already been seen that an unpaid seller who has resold the goods cannot claim the price from the first buyer (*ante*, p. 179).

Measure of damages. If the seller claims damages for non-acceptance, the assessment of his damages will be governed by the well-known rule in *Hadley* v. *Baxendale*,[73] which has been incorporated in the Act. The first limb of the rule appears in section 50(2) as follows:

> The measure of damages is the estimated loss directly and naturally resulting, in the ordinary course of events, from the buyer's breach of contract.

Section 50(3) amplifies this by setting out a prima facie rule for calculating the damages. It reads:

> Where there is an available market for the goods in question the measure of damages is prima facie to be ascertained by the difference between the contract price and the market or current price at the time or times when the goods ought to have been accepted or (if no time was fixed for acceptance) at the time of the refusal to accept.

The term "available market" has been examined in a number of cases. In an early case James L.J. considered that it connoted a "fair market where they [the sellers] could have found a purchaser."[74] This view was readily understandable at a time when the marketplace was the centre of so much commerce, but in modern times this definition is not likely to be followed. In

---

[73] (1854) 9 Exch. 341 as explained in *Victoria Laundry (Windsor) Ltd.* v. *Newman Industries Ltd.* [1949] 2 K.B. 528; [1949] 1 All E.R. 997.
[74] *Dunkirk Colliery* v. *Lever* (1878) 9 Ch.D. 20, 25.

Thompson (W. L.) v. Robinson (Gunmakers) Ltd.,[75] Upjohn J. considered that the word "market" was of no fixed legal significance and that, apart from authority, there was an available market if the conditions in the trade were such that the goods could be freely sold. This case and the later one of *Charter* v. *Sullivan*[76] were both concerned with motor-cars which at the time could only be sold at a fixed retail price, and in *Charter* v. *Sullivan* Jenkins L.J., after stating that he did not find the definition propounded by Upjohn J. entirely satisfactory, considered that the word "market" in section 50(3) involved a market where the price was fixed by the law of supply and demand. In his view, therefore, there could not be an available market where goods could only be sold at a price fixed in advance by the manufacturer.

The market must, of course, be ascertained by reference to the level of trade in question so that on a sale to a retailer "market" connotes other retailers. The market must also be "available" in the sense that the seller is not bound to go globe-trotting to find buyers.[77]

Illustration of section 50(3). A sells goods to B for £100, delivery May 1. On May 1 the goods are tendered and B refuses to accept. At that date there is an available market but the market price has fallen to £80. Damages £20. The market price is, of course, a matter of evidence, and the amount for which the seller has resold the goods is a relevant factor in ascertaining the market price. Any increase or decrease in the market price after the refusal to accept is generally immaterial, so that in one case a seller recovered as damages the difference between the market price and the contract price, even though some time after the buyer's non-acceptance he actually sold above the contract price.[78]

Exclusion of section 50(3). If there is no available market or, if for some other reason the market test is inappropriate, section 50(3) will not apply and instead the matter will be governed by

---

[75] [1955] Ch. 177; [1955] 1 All E.R. 154.

[76] [1957] 2 Q.B. 117.

[77] *Lesters Leather & Skin Co.* v. *Home and Overseas Brokers* (1948) 64 T.L.R. 569 C.A. (a case on s.51). As to anticipatory breach see *Tredegar Iron & Coal Co. Ltd.* v. *Hawthorn Bros.* (1902) 18 T.L.R. 716.

[78] *Campbell Mostyn (Provisions) Ltd.* v. *Barnett* [1954] 1 Lloyd's Rep. 65. Mr. Fridman suggests that the position might be different if the seller's resale took place immediately on the buyer's breach (Fridman, *Sale of Goods*, at p. 244).

section 50(2). One problem of importance is whether a seller (if he is a manufacturer or dealer) can recover the profit which he would have made had the sale gone through. The answer depends on whether the state of demand is such that as a result of the buyer's default the seller has in fact lost a sale. In *Thompson (W. L.) v. Robinson (Gunmakers) Ltd.*[79]:

> Sellers, who were car dealers, sold a new car to the buyer, who later repudiated. The cars were in plentiful supply and demand was slack. The sellers returned the car to their suppliers. Upjohn J. held that having regard to the lack of demand, the sellers had lost a sale and were entitled to claim their loss of profit from the buyer.[80]

On the other hand in *Charter v. Sullivan*[81]:

> The buyer of a Hillman car repudiated, whereupon the sellers, who were dealers, resold it elsewhere at the same fixed price. The cars were in short supply and the demand was very great. On these facts the Court of Appeal held that the buyer's default had not robbed the sellers of a sale and accordingly they were only entitled to nominal damages.

Special damage. The second "limb" of *Hadley v. Baxendale*[82] is preserved by section 54, which is set out below (*post*, p. 187).

Remedies of buyer

The buyer has six remedies to compel performance of the seller's duties. Some of these have already been considered, but for convenience they are set out again.

(1) *Rejection*

A buyer can reject the goods for breach of a condition[83] to be performed by the seller. The restrictions on this right have already been examined (see *ante*, p. 100).

---

[79] [1955] Ch. 177; [1955] 1 All E.R. 154.

[80] Even if the sellers had succeeded in selling the same car to someone else at the same price, the result would still have been the same, because had the first buyer not defaulted, the sellers would have sold two cars. The position is different if the goods are second-hand (*Lazenby Garages Ltd. v. Wright* [1976] 1 W.L.R. 459; [1976] 2 All E.R. 770, C.A.).

[81] See n. 76, *supra.*

[82] See *Koufos v. C. Czarnikow (The Heron II)* [1969] 1 A.C. 350; [1967] 3 All E.R. 686, H.L.

[83] Or for breach of intermediate stipulation (*ante*, p. 99) where rejection is justified by the consequences of breach for the buyer.

(2) *Recovery of price*

If the buyer has paid the price, section 54 preserves his right to recover it if the consideration has failed, as where the seller has no title or delivers goods which the buyer validly rejects.

(3) *Action for damages for breach of warranty*

Section 53 provides that:

> (1) Where there is a breach of warranty by the seller, or where the buyer elects (or is compelled) to treat any breach of a condition on the part of the seller as a breach of warranty, the buyer is not by reason only of such breach of warranty entitled to reject the goods; but he may
>> (*a*) set up against the seller the breach of warranty in diminution or extinction of the price; or
>> (*b*) maintain an action against the seller for damages for the breach of warranty.
>
> (2) The measure of damages for beach of warranty is the estimated loss directly and naturally resulting, in the ordinary course of events, from the breach of warranty.
>
> (3) In the case of warranty of quality such loss is prima facie the difference between the value of the goods at the time of delivery to the buyer and the value they would have had if they had fulfilled the warranty.[84]
>
> (4) The fact that the buyer has set up the breach of warranty in diminution or extinction of the price does not prevent him from maintaining an action for the same breach of warranty if he has suffered further damage.
>
> (5) Nothing in this section shall prejudice or affect the buyer's right of rejection in Scotland as declared by this Act.

It will be appreciated that section 53(3) is again a prima facie rule only and higher damages are often awarded. In *Jackson* v. *Watson*[85] a man who bought poisoned salmon which killed his wife was entitled, *inter alia,* to medical expenses (£4), funeral expenses (£29) and an amount for the loss of his wife's services (£200). So also in *Mason* v. *Burningham*[86] where a typewriter turned out to have been stolen the buyer's damages for breach of the implied warranty of quiet enjoyment included sums spent by her in overhauling it.

---

[84] Applied in *Aryeh* v. *Lawrence Kostoris & Son Ltd.* [1967] 1 Lloyd's Rep. 63.

[85] [1909] 2 K.B. 193.

[86] [1949] 2 K.B. 545; [1949] 2 All E.R. 134. See also *Bowmaker (Commercial)* v. *Day* [1965] 1 W.L.R. 1396; [1965] 2 All E.R. 856n.

(4) *Action for damages for non-delivery*

Section 51, which is the exact counterpart of section 50, provides that:

> (1) Where the seller wrongfully neglects or refuses to deliver the goods to the buyer, the buyer may maintain an action against the seller for damages for non-delivery.
>
> (2) The measure of damages is the estimated loss directly and naturally resulting, in the ordinary course of events, from the seller's breach of contract.
>
> (3) Where there is an available market for the goods in question the measure of damages is prima facie to be ascertained by the difference between the contract price and the market or current price of the goods at the time or times when they ought to have been delivered, or if no time was fixed, then at the time of the refusal to deliver.

A seller is guilty of non-delivery not only when he fails to deliver at all, but also where he delivers goods which the buyer is entitled to and does reject.[87]

It will be seen from section 51 that the measure of damage depends primarily on whether there is an available market where the buyer can obtain goods of the type which the seller has failed to supply.[88] The meaning of available market has already been considered. If there is no such market the buyer, if he is a manufacturer or dealer, can sometimes recover his loss of profit.[89]

Sub-contracts. A question of considerable practical importance arises where the buyer has actually effected a sub-sale which goes off owing to the seller's default. Can the loss of profit on the sub-sale, or the damages which the buyer had had to pay to the sub-buyer, can be recovered from the original seller? The general answer is that they cannot. As Lord Esher M.R. put if:

> "It is well settled that in an action for non-delivery or non-acceptance of goods under a contract of sale, the law does not take into account in estimating the damages anything that is accidental as between the plaintiff and the defendant, as for instance an

---

[87] See n. 77, *supra*.

[88] In *R. Pagnan & Fratelli* v. *Corbisa Industrial Agropacuaria* [1970] 1 W.L.R. 1306; [1971] 1 All E.R. 165, B lawfully rejected goods supplied by S and later he repurchased them from S at a reduced price in accordance with a course of dealing between them. It was held that B was not entitled to damages as he had not suffered any loss.

[89] See n. 77, *supra*.

intermediate contract entered into with a third party for the purchase or sale of the goods."[90]

In the leading case of *Williams* v. *Agius*[91] the facts were as follows:

> Coal was sold at 16s. 3d. per ton. Buyers resold at 19s. 6d. per ton. Sellers refused to deliver and at the date of refusal the market price had risen to 23s. 6d. per ton. The House of Lord held that in assessing damages for non-delivery the sub-contract should be ignored; consequently buyers were entitled to the difference between 16s. 3d. and 23s. 6d., *viz.* 7s. 3d. per ton.

The general rule can, however, be displaced if the parties must have contemplated sub-sales of those very goods. In *Chao* v. *British Traders and Shippers*, Devlin J., after dealing with the general rule, said this:

> "There are of course cases where the prima facie measure of damages is not applicable because something different is contemplated. If, for example, a man sells goods of a special manufacture and it is known that they are to be resold, it must also be known that they cannot be bought in the market, being specially manufactured by the seller. In such a case the loss of profit becomes the appropriate measure of damage. Similarly it may very well be that in the case of string contracts, if the seller knows that the merchant is not buying merely for resale generally but upon a string contract where he will resell those specific goods and where he could only honour his contract by delivering those goods and no others, the measure of loss of profit on resale is the right measure."[92]

If in this type of case the buyer is sued by his sub-buyer and settles the claim, the sum paid in settlement is recoverable from the seller if the court considers that the compromise was a reasonable one.[93]

Section 51(3), like section 50(3) is a prima facie rule only and even if there is an available market it does not necessarily provide an exclusive measure of the buyer's loss. Thus in a recent case

---

[90] *Rodocanachi* v. *Milburn* (1887) 18 Q.B.D. 67, 77.

[91] [1914] A.C. 510. Followed in *Aryeh* v. *Lawrence Kostoris & Son Ltd.* [1967] 1 Lloyd's Rep. 63, C.A.

[92] [1954] 2 Q.B. 459, 489–490; [1954] 2 W.L.R. 365. See also *Patrick* v. *Russo-British Grain Export Co.* [1927] 2 K.B. 533 and *Aryeh* v. *Lawrence Kostoris & Son Ltd. supra.*

[93] *Biggin Ltd.* v. *Permanite Ltd.* (*Wiggins and Co. Third Parties*) [1951] 2 K.B. 314; [1951] 2 All E.R. 191, C.A., reversing Devlin J.

concerning the non-delivery of a ship Mocatta J. held that under the general principal of section 51(2) the buyers could claim compensation for the profits which they were prevented from making by the non-delivery.[94]

Delayed delivery. The basic rule that sub-contracts are to be ignored applies to cases of non-delivery. If the seller is merely guilty of delayed delivery and the buyer accepts the goods and sues for damages, a different rule prevails. In general, damages for delayed delivery are assessed on the basis of the difference between the value of the goods when they should have been delivered and the value at the time of actual delivery. Thus if the latter is higher than the former damages will merely be nominal, whereas if the market is falling the drop in value is the measure of damages. If, however, the buyer realising that the market is falling resells the goods at a price which is higher than the market price when the goods are finally delivered, he is only entitled to the difference between the value when the goods should have been delivered and the price obtained by him on resale.[95]

This rule can be justified on the simple ground that the damages represent what the buyer has in fact lost, and he should not be allowed to make a profit from the seller's breach.

Where the seller's default is followed by devaluation, any loss resulting from the devaluation will normally be too remote unless the question of devaluation was within the contemplation of the parties when the contract was made.[96]

Special damage. The right of a party to recover special damage is preserved by section 54, which provides as follows:

> Nothing in this Act shall affect the right of the buyer or the seller to recover interest or special damages in any case where by law interest or special damages may be recoverable, or to recover money paid where the consideration for the payment of it has failed.

In this way this section preserves, *inter alia*, the second limb of *Hadley* v. *Baxendale.*

---

[94] *The Ile Aux Moines* [1974] 2 Lloyd's Rep. 502.
[95] *Wertheim* v. *Chicoutimi Pulp Co.* [1911] A.C. 301, P.C. This decision was cited without disapproval in *Williams* v. *Agius, supra,* but was criticised by Scrutton L.J. in *Slater* v. *Hoyle and Smith* [1920] 2 K.B. 11; [1918–19] All E.R. Rep. 654.
[96] *Aruna Mills* v. *Dhanrajmal Gobindram* [1968] 1 Q.B. 655; [1968] 1 All E.R. 113.

Anticipatory breach. An anticipatory breach occurs (*inter alia*) where before the time of performance has arrived one party informs the other that he does not intend to perform. As with every other case of repudiation,[97] the innocent party has an option. He may, if he wishes, ignore the repudiation and wait until the date fixed for performance, in the hope that the other party will perform after all.[98] Alternatively he can accept the repudiation and sue for damages. The question of mitigation is relevant in the latter case but not in the former.

> *Example.* Sale of goods for £1,000, to be delivered on May 1. On April 15 the seller informs the buyer that he will not deliver. The market is rising. On April 15 the market price is £1,200. On May 1 it is £1,400.
>
> (1) If the buyer ignores the repudiation and on May 1 no delivery takes place, he is entitled under section 51(3) to the difference between £1,000 and £1,400. He is not under any duty to buy goods before May 1 at a cheaper price.
>
> (2) If the buyer accepts the repudiation, he must act reasonably to mitigate his loss. In the words of Cockburn J.:
>
> "he will be entitled to such damages as would have arisen from non-performance of the contract at the appointed time,[99] subject, however, to abatement in respect of any circumstances which may have afforded him the means of mitigating his loss."[1]

Thus in the example the court might well find that it was the buyer's duty to buy as cheaply as he could as soon as he accepted the repudiation. If he did buy the goods elsewhere, the damages will be the difference between the original contract price and the repurchase price. If he did not, the damages will be the difference between the original contract price and the market value of the goods not on May 1 but on such earlier date as the buyer ought to have bought other goods.[2]

Mitigation. An innocent party must act reasonably to mitigate his loss, but he is not bound to do more. A seller need not hunt

---

[97] *Avery* v. *Bowden* (1855) 5 E. & B. 714.

[98] In which case the contract remains open for the benefit of both parties, so that a subsequent frustrating event may excuse performance.

[99] And not the time of repudiation (*Millett* v. *Van Heek & Co.* [1921] 2 K.B. 369 where it was held that the words "time of the refusal" in s.51(3) did not cover the case of an anticipatory breach). See also *Garnac Grain Co.* v. *H. M. Faure Fairclough Ltd.* [1968] A.C. 1130; [1968] 2 All E.R. 353, H.L.

[1] *Frost* v. *Knight* (1872) L.R. 7 Ex. 111, 113.

[2] *Per* Bailhache J. in *Melachrino* v. *Nickoll and Knight* [1920] 1 K.B. 693.

the globe looking for other buyers[3] nor need a buyer sue his sub-buyers if this would damage his commercial reputation.[4]

(5) *Action for specific performance*
 By section 52:

> (1) In any action for breach of contract to deliver specific or ascertained goods the court may, if it thinks fit, on the plaintiff's application, by its judgment or decree direct that the contract shall be performed specifically, without giving the defendant the option of retaining the goods on payment of damages.
> (2) The plaintiff's application may be made at any time before judgment or decree.
> (3) The judgment or decree may be unconditional, or on such terms and conditions as to damages, payment of the price and otherwise as seem just to the court.

In accordance with the well-known principles of equity, the remedy of specific performance will only be awarded where damages are an inadequate remedy.[5] Thus it will usually only be ordered where the goods are of a special value to the buyer, *e.g.* a valuable painting. Another case where damages would be inadequate is where the seller has become bankrupt. It should be noted, however, that the section only applies to specific or ascertained goods. In *Re Wait*[6]:

> Wait bought 1,000 tons of wheat ex motor vessel Challenger and resold 500 tons to a buyer who paid the price in advance. Before the goods had been appropriated Wait became bankrupt, whereupon the buyer claimed delivery of the wheat as owners or alternatively specific performance. The Court of Appeal held that as the goods were unascertained the buyer's sole remedy was to prove in the bankruptcy for the price.

(6) *Action in tort*
 The final remedy available to a buyer is to sue the seller and third parties in tort if he is entitled to possession of the goods and

---

[3] *Lesters Leather & Skin Co.* v. *Home and Overseas Brokers*, n. 77, *supra*.
[4] *James Finlay & Co.* v. *N.V. Kwik Hoo Tong Handel Maatschappij* [1929] 1 K.B. 400.
[5] In *Sky Petroleum Ltd.* v. *VIP Ltd.* [1974] 1 W.L.R. 576; [1974] 1 All E.R. 954 Goulding J. granted an interlocutory mandatory injunction which, in effect, ordered specific performance of a contract to supply petrol (unascertained goods). Neither section 52 nor the case of *Re Wait* [1927] Ch. 606 nor the case there cited were referred to in the judgment.
[6] [1927] 1 Ch. 606.

possession is withheld. If the seller is sued in conversion the damages are apparently[7] the same as on a contractual claim for non-delivery, so that, for example, a buyer who has resold the goods cannot recover the loss of profit in tort if he cannot recover it in contract.[8]

AUCTION SALES

By section 57:

(1) Where goods are put up for sale by auction in lots, each lot is prima facie deemed to be the subject of a separate contract of sale.

(2) A sale by auction is complete when the auctioneer announces its completion by the fall of the hammer or in other customary manner,[9] and until the announcement is made, any bidder may retract his bid.

(3) A sale by auction may be notified to be subject to a reserve or upset price, and a right to bid may also be reserved expressly by or on behalf of the seller.

(4) Where a sale by auction is not notified to be subject to a right to bid on behalf of the seller, it is not lawful for the seller to bid himself or to employ any person to bid at such sale, or for the auctioneer knowingly to take any bid from the seller or any such person.

(5) A sale contravening subsection (4) alone may be treated as fraudulent by the buyer.

(6) Where in respect of a sale by auction, a right to bid is expressly reserved (but not otherwise) the seller, or any one person on his behalf, may bid at the auction.

Knockout agreement

The Auction (Bidding Agreement) Acts 1927–1969 make it a criminal offence for dealers to give or receive consideration or a reward for abstaining or having abstained from bidding.[10] Where the buyer was a party to such an agreement and there has been a

---

[7] See *The Arpad* [1934] P. 189, C.A. (Scrutton L.J. dissenting), where the authorities are reviewed.

[8] *Ibid.*

[9] See *Dennant* v. *Skinner and Collom, ante,* p. 130. Some auction particulars vary this rule by providing that where any dispute as to the bidding arises, the goods shall immediately be re-auctioned. See *Richards* v. *Phillips* [1969] 1 Ch. 39; [1968] 2 All E.R. 859, C.A.

[10] See also Mock Auctions Act 1961.

prosecution and conviction, the seller may treat the sale as fraudulent. In practice such arrangements are very hard to prove.

Position of auctioneer

The auctioneer has a lien over the goods as against the seller for commission and the expenses of the sale and he has a personal right to sue the buyer for payment of the price. As between himself and the buyer the auctioneer undertakes the following obligations:

(a) he warrants his authority;
(b) he warrants that he knows of no defects in his principal's title;
(c) he undertakes to give possession in return for the price;
(d) he undertakes that such possession will not be disturbed by his principal or by himself.

As a general rule, however, the auctioneer does not warrant his principal's title. If, therefore, the seller has no title and the buyer has to return the goods to the true owner, the buyer can sue the seller under section 12 but has no claim against the auctioneer, unless the latter expressly warranted the seller's title or failed to disclose that he was acting for a principal.[11]

Sale "subject to reserve"

In practice many goods sold at an auction are expressed to be "subject to reserve"; this means that the auctioneer has no authority to knock the goods down to a buyer until the seller's minimum (or "reserve") price has been reached. If he inadvertently knocks the goods down before then, the courts have held that, he can (and must) refuse to proceed as soon as he discovers his mistake.[12] In such a case he will not be liable to the disappointed buyer for warranting his authority because the words "subject to reserve" in the auction particulars made it clear that his authority was limited.

If, however, the existence of the reserve price was not notified to prospective buyers, the position would probably be different. In that case a buyer to whom the goods were knocked down in breach

---

[11] See *Benton* v. *Campbell Parker & Co.* [1925] 2 K.B. 410 at pp. 415–416, *per* Salter J. and s.12(3) *ante*, p. 104.
[12] *McManus* v. *Fortescue* [1907] 2 K.B. 1.

of the secret reserve would have a remedy; he could either sue the auctioneer for wrongly warranting his unlimited authority or he could sue the auctioneer's principal for holding out the auctioneer as having such authority.

Sale "without reserve"

If the auction is incorrectly expressed to be "without reserve" and if goods are withdrawn from the sale because the reserve has not been reached, it has been suggested that the auctioneer may be liable for breach of an implied promise to sell to the highest bidder.[13] There are, however, a number of difficulties here; in particular it is not easy to find any consideration for the promise unless the very act of attending the auction can be treated as consideration.

Export Sales

This topic together with Bankers' Commercial Credits, is considered in Chapter Ten.

---

[13] Consider *Warlow* v. *Harrison* (1859) 1 E. & E. 309; (1952) 68 L.Q.R. 238, 457; (1953) 69 L.Q.R. 21.

CHAPTER FOUR

CONSUMER CREDIT

INTRODUCTION

IN the first four editions of this book this chapter was entitled "Hire-Purchase Conditional Sale and Credit Sale." The reason for the change is the passing of the Consumer Credit Act 1974 which is by far the most radical, wide-ranging and comprehensive statute in this important and rapidly expanding field.

Background

The provision of consumer credit can take various forms—hire-purchase, conditional sale, credit sale, personal loans (with or without security), Barclaycards, overdrafts, budget accounts in stores, check trading and so on. Basically they are all examples of a single transaction—a loan of money to enable goods or services to be acquired. One of the deficiencies of the previous law was that there were numerous different statutes imposing differing rules to govern essentially the same transaction. These different rules were based on the form which the transaction took. Thus hire-purchase, conditional sale and credit sale were regulated by the Hire-Purchase Acts; money-lending contracts were regulated by the Moneylenders Acts (although banks were not covered); mortgages of personal chattels were (and still are) regulated by the Bills of Sale Acts; contracts of hire were not regulated at all. These different rules produced numerous anomalies which were clearly illogical and indefensible and the Crowther Committee resolved to make a fresh start. They recommended two statutes—one regulating loans and security generally (including registration of security interests) and a further statute protecting the consumer in consumer transactions. The Government has so far accepted only the second of these recommendations and the Consumer Credit Act 1974 gives effect to many (but not all) of the Committee's proposals for consumer protection. Thus:

(1) The Director-General of Fair Trading is required to supervise the consumer credit scene and to make recom-

mendations when the law is found to be inadequate to deal with particular business practices.

(2) There is a licensing system administered by the Director.

(3) There are regulations governing advertising and canvassing for business.

(4) Contracts with consumers are regulated by the Act itself and by regulations.

(5) The courts are given wide powers of suspending obligations, granting extensions of time, and re-opening extortionate bargains.

It will be seen that the term "consumer" is given an extended meaning and is not confined to private consumers.

Finding the law[1]

Although the Consumer Credit Act 1974 received the Royal Assent as long ago as July 31, 1974 there are still large parts of the Act which are not yet in force. Although the Act itself is extremely detailed and complex a great deal of the law is to be found in regulations and it has taken a very long time for these regulations to be finalised. Even when the Act is fully operational it will not cover the whole ground and various other sources of law may have to be consulted in particular cases. Among these are the following:

1. *Common law*
   (a) Apart from the formalities required by the Act and regulations the common law rules will govern the formation of the contract and will deal with such matters as offer and acceptance, illegality, and mistake.
   (b) The common law rules, based upon the freedom of the parties to make their own contract, will be relevant in cases where the Consumer Credit Act does not apply because the debtor is a body corporate, or because the credit exceeds £5,000, or because the agreement is an exempt agreement.
   (c) Common law rules may be relevant in disputes involving third party rights (as, for example, where a garage claims a lien for repairs to a car held on hire-purchase (*post*, p. 418).

---

[1] The three leading looseleaf works are Goode, *Consumer Credit Legislation*, Guest, *Consumer Credit Act* 1974 and Bennion *Consumer Credit Control*. The legal controls exist side by side with a voluntary code as to which see Goode, *op. cit.* at p. V/104.

2. *Bills of Sale Acts* 1878–1882. These highly technical Acts regulate the granting of mortgages and other security interests over personal property. If the stringent provisions of the Acts are not complied with the lender may lose all his security.

3. *The Sale of Goods Act* 1979 applies to all sales including conditional sales and credit sales.

4. *The Supply of Goods (Implied Terms) Act* 1973 (as redrafted by the 1974 Act) implies terms as to title, description, quality, fitness and sample into all hire-purchase agreements (see ss.8–11). The terms are virtually identical to those in the Sale of Goods Act (*ante*, pp. 103–124).

5. *The Supply of Goods and Services Act* 1982 contains similar provisions in relation to contracts of hire (*ante*, p. 126).

6. *Part III of the Hire-Purchase Act* 1964. This has already been considered (*ante*, p. 157).

7. *Hire-Purchase Act* 1965. This Act, which was the model for many of the provisions of the 1974 Act, will continue to be important for some time because it will continue to govern agreements made before the appropriate appointed day under the 1974 Act. The 1965 Act applies to hire-purchase and conditional sale agreements where the total price does not exceed £7,500 and where the hirer or buyer is not a body corporate. Its main provisions relate to formation, cancellation, termination and restrictions on the right of the owner or seller to repossess. A few of its provisions also apply to credit sale agreements.

8. *Unfair Contract Terms Act* 1977. This very important act, which controls exemption clauses and notices, is considered in detail in Chapter Eight (*post*, p. 429).

9. *Fair Trading Act* 1973 (*post*, p. 450).

The remainder of this chapter will be devoted to an examination of the 1974 Act, and the various Orders and Regulations made under it.

CONSUMER CREDIT ACT 1974

It is proposed to divide this chapter into nine parts namely:

I. Definitions, and examples of their use.

It will be seen that control takes two forms namely:

(a) control of the credit industry generally through the licensing system, the restrictions on advertising, quotations and canvassing and the general supervisory powers of the Director-General and

(b) control of individual agreements on such matters as formalities, termination, cancellation and default.

I. DEFINITIONS, AND EXAMPLES OF THEIR USE

It has been seen that the Act sweeps away and replaces the Moneylenders Acts and the Hire-Purchase Acts. In addition, in the words of two learned writers

> It extends to cover transactions which were previously unregulated by any enactment. It thus affects banks, finance houses, building societies, local authorities, life insurance offices, moneylenders, pawnbrokers, check and voucher traders, issue of credit cards, mail order companies, retailers, service industries, first and second mortgage companies and other businesses providing financial accommodation. It also affects mortgage, finance and insurance brokers, solicitors, estate agents, debt collectors, factors, companies engaged in block discounting, debt counsellors, debt adjusters, credit insurers and credit reference bureaux.[2]

It was obviously necessary at some points to distinguish between the very many different types of agreement and for this purpose the draftsman has devised a number of entirely new terms, some of which appear to be needlessly complex. Fortunately the reader is not left unaided in his efforts to master the new terminology. In a most welcome development, which one sincerely hopes will be

---

[2] Guest and Lloyd, introduction to annotated copy of *Consumer Credit Act 1974* published by Sweet and Maxwell.

followed by draftsmen of Finance Acts and others, Schedule 2 contains no less than 24 examples showing how the new terminology operates in particular cases. Some of the examples will be referred to at appropriate places in this chapter. The definitions are most usefully collected together in section 189.

Parties

Under a consumer credit agreement the supplier of the credit is the "creditor" and the recipient of the credit is the "debtor." In a consumer hire agreement the Act uses the terms "owner" and "hirer." These terms will be used throughout this chapter.

Regulated agreements

Apart from advertisements, quotations and extortionate bargains the protective provisions of the Act only apply to a *regulated agreement*. If one turns to section 189 this term is defined as a consumer credit agreement or consumer hire agreement other than an exempt agreement. This definition is cental to the working of the Act and it must be more closely examined.

(1) *What is a consumer credit agreement?*

Section 8 provides that a consumer credit agreement is an agreement between an individual (the debtor) and any other person (the creditor) whereby the creditor provides the debtor with credit not exceeding £5,000. It will be appreciated that the debtor must be an individual, a term which includes a partnership (s.189) but not a body corporate. The term "consumer" in this context is wider than under the Unfair Contract Terms Act (*post*, p. 439) or the Fair Trading Act 1973 (*post*, p. 452). As long as the debtor is not a body corporate the Act and the regulations apply equally to private and business transactions—although this is subject to an exception in relation to advertisements (*post*, p. 214).

Section 8 refers to credit and by section 9 this term is widely defined to include a cash loan and any other form of financial accommodation. Thus in hire-purchase cases the price of the goods is no longer the determining factor. An agreement with a price of £10,000 or a price of £100,000 will be treated in exactly the same way if the *credit* does not exceed £5,000. By section 9(3) the credit in hire-purchase cases is deemed to be "the total price of the goods less the aggregate of the deposit (if any) and the total charge for credit."

Illustration (Schedule 2 example 10)

> Hire-purchase price £7,500 including £1,000 down payment and £1,500 charge for credit. Total credit is (£7,500—£1,000—£1,500) =£5,000.
> The agreement is a consumer credit agreement.

The task of measuring the credit can be difficult in a case where the debtor has power from time to time to obtain money, goods or services up to a specified limit and where the amount outstanding varies according to payments made by and to the debtor. Such agreements are referred to in section 10(1)(a) as agreements for "running account credit" and a bank overdraft agreement is an obvious example. The section then provides that:

> (2) "Credit Limit" means, as respects any period, the maximum debit balance which, under the credit agreement, is allowed to stand on the account during that period, disregarding any term of the agreement allowing that maximum to be exceeded merely temporarily.
> (3) For the purposes of section 8(2) [the £5,000 limit] running account credit shall be taken not to exceed the amount specified in that subsection (the specified amount) if
> (a) the credit limit does not exceed the specified amount; or
> (b) whether or not there is a credit limit, and if there is, notwithstanding that it exceeds the specified amount—
> > (i) the debtor is not enabled to draw at any one time an amount which, so far as . . . it represents credit, exceeds the specified amount, or
> > (ii) the agreement provides that, if the debit balance rises above the given amount (not exceeding the specified amount), the rate of the total charge for credit increases or any other condition favouring the creditor or his associate comes into operation or
> > (iii) at the time when the agreement is made it is probable, having regard to the terms of the agreement and any other relevant consideration, that the debit balance will not at any time rise above the specified amount.

Illustrations

> 1. The G Bank grants H an unlimited overdraft with an increased rate of interest on so much of the debit balance as exceeds £2,000.

Under paragraph (ii) above the agreement is a consumer credit agreement—see Schedule 2 example 6. 2. J owns a shop which normally carries a stock worth about £1,000. K undertakes to provide, on short term credit, the stock needed by J without any specified limit. Under paragraph (iii) above, the agreement is a consumer credit agreement—see Schedule 2 example 7.

The distinction is important in relation to a number of matters including the supply of information (s.78 *post*, p. 230), advertisements relating to the true cost of borrowing (*post*, p. 215) and the fundamental question of whether the transaction is regulated or exempt (*post*, p. 204).

(2) *What is a consumer hire agreement?*

This is defined in section 15 as an agreement made by a person (the owner) with an individual (the hirer) for the bailment of goods to the hirer where (a) it is not a hire-purchase agreement and (b) can subsist for more than three months and (c) does not require the hirer to make payments exceeding £5,000.

Thus if the hirer has to pay £2,000 per year for three years this would not be a consumer hire agreement (see Sched. 2 example 20) but if he has a contractual right of termination which will bring his maximum liability down to £5,000 or less it would be a consumer hire agreement (see Sched. 2 example 24). In considering this matter any *statutory* right of termination (*post*, p. 235) is disregarded.

(3) *When is an agreement exempt?*

It will be recalled that a consumer credit agreement or a consumer hire agreement is a regulated agreement unless it is exempt. The definition of "exempt agreement" in section 16 and in regulations is considered *post*, p. 203.

Restricted use and unrestricted use credit[3]

The Act is largely about loans and section 11 draws a distinction between loans where the debtor gets his hands on the money

---

[3] This classification is based upon the Crowther Committee distinction between "Purchase money loans" and Non-purchase-money loans (Crowther Report Vol. 1, p. 241).

(unrestricted use credit) and loans where he does not (restricted use credit). Section 11 provides that:

> (1) a restricted use credit agreement is a regulated consumer credit agreement—
> (*a*) to finance a transaction between the debtor and the creditor, whether forming part of that agreement or not, (*b*) to finance a transaction between a debtor and a person (the "supplier") other than the creditor, or (*c*) to refinance any existing indebtedness of the debtor's whether to the creditor or another person . . .
> (2) An unrestricted use credit agreement is a regulated consumer credit agreement not falling within subsection (1) . . .
> (3) An agreement does not fall within subsection (1) if the credit is in fact provided in such a way as to leave the debtor free to use it as he chooses, even though certain uses would contravene that or any other agreement.
> (4) An agreement may fall within subsection (1)(*b*) although the identity of the supplier is unknown at the time the agreement is made.

The key provision is subsection (3). Thus a loan which reaches the debtor's hands is an agreement for unrestricted use, even though the debtor is contractually bound to apply the money in a particular way. On the other hand a hire-purchase agreement would be "restricted use credit" and so would an agreement where the money was paid by the creditor (*e.g.* a finance house or a credit card company) direct to a third party (*e.g.* a person supplying goods or services to the debtor).

The distinction appears in various parts of the Act including sections 49 (canvassing for business), 58 and 67 (mortgages of land) and 71 (repayment of credit after cancellation).

Debtor-creditor-supplier and debtor-creditor agreements

Closely linked with the previous classification based on the form of the loan is a further classification based on the relationship between the creditor and the supplier. The debtor may use the credit to obtain goods or services:

(a) from the creditor himself or

(b) from a supplier who is connected with the creditor or

(c) from a supplier who is not connected with the creditor.

In cases (a) and (b) the agreement is rather confusingly referred to as a "debtor-creditor-supplier" agreement (s.12) while in case (c) it is referred to as a "debtor-creditor" agreement (s.13). It must be emphasised that the word "connected," which is used in the Crowther Report (Vol. I at p. 242) does not appear in the Act. Instead section 12 provides that:

> A debtor-creditor-supplier agreement is a regulated consumer credit agreement being:
> (a) a restricted use credit agreement which falls within section 11(1)(a), or
> (b) a restricted use credit agreement which falls within section 11(1)(b) and is made by the creditor under pre-existing arrangements, or in anticipation of future arrangements between himself and the supplier or
> (c) an unrestricted-use credit agreement which is made under pre-existing arrangements between himself and a person "the supplier" other than the debtor in the knowledge that the creditor is being used to finance a transaction between the debtor and the supplier.

Four examples can now be given to clarify the position:

(1) C lets out goods on hire-purchase to D. This is a two-party debtor-creditor-supplier agreement.

(2) C (a store) supplies goods to D (a customer) under a budget account whereby D makes monthly payments to C. This again is a two-party debtor-creditor-supplier agreement within section 12(a) above.

(3) C agrees with S to finance sales of goods made by S to his customers. S sells goods to D and C provides the loan (either to D or direct to S). This is a three-party debtor-creditor-supplier agreement within section 12(b) above. A bank "credit card" is a common example.

(4) C agrees to make a loan to D and D uses it to buy goods from S. There are no "pre-existing arrangements" between C and S. This is a debtor-creditor agreement even though C, at the request of D, pays the money direct to S (see s.13(a)).

The terms set out above appear in various parts of the Act including sections 16 (exempt agreements), 56 (antecedent negotiations), 70 (cancellations) and 75 (liability of creditor for supplier's default.) The underlying principle is that the supplier of the goods or services and the "connected lender" should assume joint responsibility towards the debtor on such matters as (a) defects in the goods or services supplied and (b) repayment obligations if the agreement is cancelled by the borrower.

Credit-token agreements

The Act has a number of specific provisions relating to credit-token agreements, a term which cuts across some of the other definitions already considered. Section 14 provides that:

> (1) a credit token is a card, check, voucher, coupon, stamp, form, booklet or other document or thing given to an individual by a person carrying on a consumer credit business who undertakes—
> > (a) that on the production of it (whether or not some other act is also required) he will supply cash, goods and services (or any of these) on credit, or
> > (b) that where, on the production of it to a third party (whether or not any other act is required) the third party supplies cash, goods or services (or any of them), he will pay the third party for them (whether or not deducting any discount or commission) in return for payment to him by the individual.
>
> (2) A credit-token agreement is a regulated agreement for the provision of credit in connection with the use of a credit token.

Thus a bank "credit card" would normally qualify as a regulated credit-token agreement since the credit limit is invariably well short of £5,000 (see Sched. 2 example 16). On the other hand a cheque card will usually be a regulated consumer credit agreement but not a credit-token agreement because payment by the bank to suppliers would be payment of cheques and not a payment for goods or services. (See Sched. 2 example 21.)

Multiple agreements

An agreement may come within more than one of the above classifications; if this is so section 18 makes it clear that it is to be treated as an agreement in each of the categories in question. It is also possible for part of the agreement to be classified one way and for another part to be classified in a different way.

Illustration (Sched. 2 example 16)

> A (credit) an associate of X Bank, gives B a credit card for use in obtaining cash on credit from A (credit) to be paid by branches of X bank, or goods or cash from suppliers or banks who have agreed to honour credit cards issued by A (credit). The credit limit is £30. *Analysis.* (1) As regards cash this is a debtor-creditor agreement for unrestricted use credit; (2) as regards goods it is a debtor-creditor-supplier agreement for restricted use credit; (3) it is therefore a multiple agreement.

Exempt agreements

Section 16 and the Orders made under it are of fundamental importance because an "exempt" agreement is subject to none of the controls laid down in the Act except extortionate credit bargains (*post*, p. 244) and, in some cases, advertising and quotations (*post*, pp. 215–216).

1. Land mortgages

General. Before examining this topic it may be helpful to summarise the present position. If one disregards for the moment sections 137–140 (*post*, p. 244) the position is as follows:

(1) If the credit exceeds £5,000 or if the debtor is a body corporate the transaction will not be a consumer credit agreement at all;

(2) If the agreement does not fall within (1) above it will be a *regulated* consumer credit agreement unless it is *exempt* under section 16 or by an Order made under that section (see below). It will be seen that the exemption requires both (a) an exempt lender and (b) an exempt purpose.

(3) Even if the agreement is *regulated* the normal rules are modified in that the usual right of post-contract cancellation is not available—although in some cases this is replaced by a period of pre-contractual reflection and isolation (*post*, p. 219).

Regulated or exempt? By Section 16(1) and (2) the Act (except ss. 137–140) does not apply where a Building Society or Local Authority:

(a) enters into a debtor-creditor-supplier agreement to finance the purchase of land, or the provision of dwellings on that land, and takes a mortgage of that land as security; or

(b) makes a loan (*i.e.* debtor-creditor agreement) secured by a land mortgage; under this provision the purpose of the loan is immaterial.

The section also enables the Secretary of State to grant exempt status to consumer credit agreements entered into by particular bodies falling within one of the descriptions set out in the section (*e.g.* insurance companies, friendly societies, charities). The agreements must also fall within one of the purposes set out in (a) or (b) above and these purposes can be further cut down by the

Order. If one turns to the Consumer Credit (Exempt Agreements) Order 1980 (as amended by S.I. 1982 No. 1029) one finds a list of more than 250 insurance companies and other bodies—the list is not closed. One also finds that the general category set out in (b) above is limited to cases where the agreement finances or refinances:

(i) the purchase of land or the provision of dwellings or business premises on land or

(ii) the alteration, enlargement, repair or improvement of a dwelling-house or business premises on any land. In other words, a general purpose "second mortgage" would not be covered. In the light of recent developments it is also significant that the list of "exempt lenders" does not include banks.

2. Instalment exemption

The Act is wide enough to cover short term credit such as the supply of milk or newspapers to householders who pay at the end of each week or month. Clearly it would be absurd (and hopelessly burdensome) to subject all such agreements to control. Accordingly Article 3 of the 1980 Order (as amended) removes a number of agreements from control. The list of exempt agreements includes:

(1) a debtor-creditor-supplier agreement for fixed sum credit under which the total number of payments to be made by the debtor *in respect of the credit* does not exceed four;

(2) a debtor-creditor-supplier agreement for periodic running account credit under which the debtor is bound to discharge the total credit for that period by a single payment.[4] Neither of these exemptions applies to (a) a hire-purchase or conditional sale agreement nor (b) an agreement secured by pledge nor (c) an agreement to finance land purchase (but see below).

(3) a debtor-creditor-supplier agreement financing the purchase of land where the total of payments to be made by the debtor *in respect of credit and in respect of the total charge for credit* does not exceed four. It will be apparent that this exemption is narrower than exemption (1) above because

---

[4] This exemption applies to many budget accounts in shops and also to the credit cards issued by Diners Club and American Express.

of the nature of the payments; thus an agreement falling within (1) above (*e.g.* sale of goods on deferred terms) can be exempt if the loan itself is repayable in four or fewer instalments even though further payments have to be made in respect of interest or other charges.

One point needs to be stressed throughout; the Act will not apply at all unless the "credit" is contractual. Thus if A supplies goods to B for immediate payment in cash and then, without consideration, allows B to pay by instalments the Act would not apply.

3. *Low-cost loans*

The Act draws a fundamental distinction between "Credit" and "the Total Charge for Credit" and article 4 of the 1980 Order (as amended by S.I. 1982 No. 1029) gives exempt status to a debtor-creditor agreement where the "total charge for credit" does not exceed the higher of:

(1) One per cent. plus the highest of any base rate published by a number of specified banks, *e.g.* Bank of England, Bank of Scotland and the "Big Four" Clearing Banks, being the latest rates in operation 28 days before the making of the agreement; and

(2) 13 per cent.

Several points need to be noted.

(1) The exemption will not apply if the amount payable by the debtor in respect of *credit* can vary according to a formula or index.

(2) If the "total charge for credit" is within the maxima set out above the exempt status will not be lost by any later fluctuation in the base rate.

Example

On April 1, 1983 the highest of the Bank base rates is 10 per cent. On April 29 a debtor-creditor agreement is made under which the total charge for credit is fixed at "2 per cent. above Finance House rate." At the date of the agreement that rate is 11 per cent. but a month later it is increased. *Result* at the date of the agreement the contractual rate (13 per cent. is within the permitted maxima; therefore the agreement is, and remains, exempt.

(3) Apart from index linking no other increase is permissible but the 1982 amendment modified this rule to meet the common case where an employer grants a loan to an

employee (*e.g.* for a house purchase) on very favourable terms but includes a provision that a higher rate of interest shall become payable on termination of employment.

(4) In deciding whether or not the exemption applies the "total charge for credit" must be calculated in accordance with the Consumer Credit (Total Charge for Credit) Regulations 1980 which are considered later in this chapter (*post,* p. 207).

Linked transactions

Various provisions of the Act (*e.g.* the cancellation provisions) refer to linked transactions and the definition in section 19 makes it clear that it is in some way ancillary to the principal transaction. Examples would include (a) an agreement by the debtor to maintain or to insure the goods or (b) the purchase of goods with money supplied under a debtor-creditor-supplier agreement or (c) an agreement by the debtor to take out a policy of insurance (see Sched. 2 example 11). Section 19(3) provides that a linked transaction entered into before the making of the principal agreement has no effect until such time (if any) as the principal agreement is made. Section 69 also provides that the cancellation of the principal agreement will also operate to cancel any linked transaction.

Other definitions

All the technical terms used in the Act are collected together in section 189—another most helpful innovation. Some of them will be mentioned later in this chapter but four of them can usefully be set out at this point:

Hire-purchase agreement

An agreement, other than a conditional sale agreement, whereby goods are bailed in return for periodical payments and the property in the goods is to pass on the excercise of an option to purchase, or the doing of some other specified act, or the happening of some other specified event.

Conditional sale agreement

An agreement for the sale of goods or land under which the purchase price or part of it is payable by instalments and the property in the goods or land is to remain in the seller, notwithstanding that the buyer is to have possession of the goods or land, until such conditions as may be specified in the agreements are fulfilled.

Credit sale agreement
   An agreement for the sale of goods under which the price is payable by instalments but which is not a conditional sale agreement. It follows from this that under a credit sale agreement the property passes to the buyer immediately.

Notice
   Notice in writing.

II. The Total Charge for Credit

One of the main objects of the Act is to ensure what is known as "truth in lending"—an accurate statement as to the true cost of the credit facility which will enable a prospective borrower to make meaningful comparisons between the costs of the various sources of credit available to him—bank loan, overdraft, budget account, credit card, finance company loan, hire purchase, moneylender's loan and so on. A meaningful comparison can only be made if the rate incoporates not merely interest charges but also other borrowing costs. Further, in many cases the borrower will be repaying the loan over a period and a "true" rate of interest must reflect this fact. Finally, many loans provide for compounding (whereby unpaid interest becomes capitalised) and a stated rate of interest will be seriously misleading if this fact is ignored.
   The law on this topic is largely to be found in the Consumer Credit (Total Charge for Credit) Regulations 1980 and the matter is also dealt with in the regulations which relate to Advertising and to Quotations (*post*, p. 213). It will be apparent that, quite apart from disclosure, the calculation of the true rate of interest is vitally important in deciding whether a debtor-creditor agreement is regulated or exempt (*ante*, p. 205). The topic is extremely complex and the summary that follows is, of necessity, an over-simplification.

1. Items included

As might be expected, regulation 4 provides that the total charge for credit includes:

(a) the total of the interest on the credit which may be provided under the agreement; and

(b) other charges at any time payable under the transaction by or on behalf of the debtor (or a relative of his) to the creditor or to some other person. A sum must be included even though the whole or part of the charge may be repayable at any time and even though the consideration may include matters not within the transaction or subsisting at a time not within the duration of the agreement.

The term "transaction" is widely defined so as to include certain types of linked transactions (*e.g.* a compulsory maintenance or installation contract) and also security transactions. Thus legal costs, survey fees, installation charges, insurance premiums and stamp duty must all be included in appropriate cases—*unless* they are excluded by regulation 5.

2. Items excluded

The all-embracing provisions of regulation 4 are cut down by a long list of exceptions in regulation 5. They include:

(a) sums only payable on default;

(b) sums payable under a restricted-use agreement (*ante*, p. 200) which would be equally payable in a non-credit transaction;

(c) sums which are payable under a maintenance contract and which only become payable when the repairs, etc., become necessary;

(d) insurance premiums in various cases, *e.g.*

(i) motor vehicle insurance, or

(ii) where the contract was made before the debtor applied to enter into the credit agreement, or

(iii) where the insurance contract is not required by the creditor as a condition of the making of the agreement, or

(iv) where the insurer was selected by the debtor in a case where comparable arrangements were available elsewhere.

3. Calculating the rate

Having considered the items to be included and excluded, the next stage is to calculate the total charge for credit and to express it as an "annual percentage rate" (APR) even where the interest etc. is expressed by reference to a shorter period.

Example

A loan of £1,000 is repayable by four equal instalments over one year, with interest at 10 per cent. every three months and no other charges. By regulation 7 the following formula must be applied.

$$100 \left[(1 + \frac{x}{100}) \, y - 1 \right]$$

where x is the period rate of charge and y is the appropriate number of periods in a year.
Thus

$$100 \left[(1 + \frac{10}{100}) \, 4 - 1 \right] = 45 \text{ per cent.}$$

Conversely a single lump sum payment in respect of more than one year may have to be dissected to produce the APR and regulation 8 contains a formula for this. The really difficult task is to dissect regular mixed payments (*e.g.* under a hire-purchase agreement) where these are made over an extended period. Regulation 9 does not provide a formula; it merely states that the APR is a rate per annum, compounding annually at which (a) the present value of the credit matches (b) the present value of credit repayments and of the total charge for credit. This can be a soul-destroying task of trial-and-error—unless a suitably-programmed computer is available. Fortunately the Government have produced 15 sets of Rate Tables (complete with Correction Slips!) and these can readily produce the necessary APR if the "charge per pound lent" or the "flat rate" is matched by an identical item in the tables. For further explanation and illustration see Goode *op. cit.* at p. I/151 *et seq.*

4. Assumptions

The previous paragraphs have proceeded on the basis that all the relevant facts (the amount of credit, the amount of charges, the duration of credit and so on) are clearly ascertainable from the agreement. In many cases, however, this will not be so and in such cases a number of assumptions have to be made. Thus, to take just one example, where the earliest date on which credit is to be provided cannot be ascertained at the date of the agreement, it must be assumed that the credit will be provided as at that date (see regulation 17). It may be that, at the date of the agreement, the amount of a particular item is unknown and is not covered by one of the assumptions. In this case the APR cannot be ascertained and accordingly the exemption for low-cost loans (*ante*, p. 205) cannot be claimed.

III. The Director-General

The Crowther Committee recommended the setting up of a Consumer Credit Commissioner and originally the Government accepted their recommendation. It was then decided that this would involve unnecessary duplication and accordingly the task of enforcing the Act and surveying the whole field of consumer credit was given to the Director-General of Fair Trading appointed under the Fair Trading Act 1973 (*post*, p. 450). One of his most important functions is the granting, renewing, varying, suspending and revoking of licences under Part III and Part X of the Act (see below). Apart from this his main powers and duties can be summarised as follows:

(1) To supervise the Act and regulations.

(2) To enforce the Act and regulations where this is necessary or expedient.

(3) To make orders dispensing with the statutory formalities in appropriate cases or allowing agreements with unlicensed traders to be enforced.

(4) To disseminate information and advice.

(5) To make an annual report to the Secretary of State.

(6) By section 1(2) he must, so far as to him appears practicable, and having regard to the national interest and the interests of persons carrying on businesses to which this Act applies and their customers, keep under review and from time to time advise the Secretary of State about

(a) social and commercial developments in the United Kingdom and elsewhere relating to the provision of credit or bailment or (in Scotland) hiring of goods to individuals, and related activities and

(b) the working and enforcing of the Act and orders and regulations made under it.

IV. LICENSING

Before the passing of the Act the only persons who had to be licensed were moneylenders and it was an area of law containing many anomalies, many technicalities and severe penalties for non-compliance—notably that the moneylender might find himself prevented by some minor technicalities from recovering the money which he had lent. The 1974 Act sets up a comprehensive licensing system, administered by the Director, and gives him very wide powers to grant, refuse, suspend or revoke licences. There is no doubt that this "loss of livelihood" sanction (or the threat of it) is by far the strongest sanction provided by the Act.

The figures of refusals, etc., are not large (for 1979–1981 there were 157 whereas the total number of licenced traders was in excess of 90,000) but, as previously stated, it is the threat of refusal or withdrawal which can encourage traders to maintain high standards.

Who needs a licence?

A licence is required by any person (other than a local authority) carrying on a consumer credit or consumer hire business (s.21) or an ancillary credit business under section 145, *i.e.* credit brokerage (as defined in section 145(2)), debt adjusting, debt counselling, debt collection, or a credit reference agency. In relation to consumer credit and consumer hire (but not in relation to the other types of business) a licence is only required if the proposed licensee makes "regulated" agreements (*ante*, p. 197) and if he does this more than "occasionally" (see s.189(2)).

> Suppose that John sells television sets for cash but from time to time he sells on credit. If the credit sales are covered by the four-instalment exemption (*ante*, p. 204) no licence is required. If the exemption does not apply, John *will* need a licence unless the credit sales are only made "occasionally." This is a narrow concept *but* if it applies John will not need a licence (although the agreements themselves will be controlled).

A dealer who introduces his customers to a person offering credit (*e.g.* finance company) will require a credit-brokers licence and the finance company may find that their own credit agreements with the customer are unenforceable unless the broker was duly licenced.

The two types of licence

By Section 22 a licence may be:

(a) a standard licence, that is a licence issued by the Director to a person named in it on an application made by him which, during the prescribed period, covers such activities as are described in the licence; or

(b) a group licence, that is a licence issued by the Director (whether on the application of any person or of his own motion) which, during such period as the director thinks fit or (if he thinks fit) indefinitely, covers such person's activities as are described in the licence.

A group licence has been issued to The Law Society authorising solicitors "to carry on the business of consumer credit, credit brokerage, debt adjusting and debt counselling and debt collecting, limited to activities arising in the course of practice as a solicitor." Other group licencees include the Institute of Chartered Accountants, the Association of Certified Accountants and the National Association of Citizens Advice Bureaux.

A standard licence authorises the trader to carry on a business under a particular name but not otherwise.

Application, issue, refusal

An application for a standard licence must be in writing in the form specified by the Director (s.6). The Director must then satisfy himself that the applicant is a fit person to engage in activities covered by the licence and that the name which he proposes to use is not misleading or otherwise undesirable (s.25(1)). If the Director proposes to refuse the licence, or to grant it on different terms, he must first send a notice to the applicant inviting him to make representations (s.27(1)). A licence can be varied on request (s.30) and the Director has power, on his own initiative, to vary, suspend or revoke a licence (ss.31, 32), although he must give the licensee notice of his intention to do so and invite him to make representations (*ibid.*). These powers are very wide and provide a powerful weapon for the raising of trading standards.

If a licence is refused, suspended or is revoked the applicant or licensee can appeal to the Secretary of State (s.41) and there is a further appeal, on a point of law, to the High Court (s.42).[5]
The Director is required to maintain a register of licence applications, etc., and this is open to public inspection (see s.35).

Agreements made by unlicensed trader
Regulated agreements made by unlicensed traders can only be enforced if the Director by order so directs (ss.40, 148, 149). There is a right of appeal (as set out above) against the Director's refusal to make an order. In addition these are criminal penalties.

V. SEEKING BUSINESS

Sections 43–54 and 151–153 seek to protect customers by regulating advertisements, quotations and canvassing for business. Here again the Act is merely a skeleton and the regulations provide most of the meat.

The Consumer Credit (Advertisements) Regulations 1980 and the Consumer Credit (Quotations) Regulations 1980 have been in force since October 6, 1980; they are highly complex and can provide a nasty trap for the unwary. Fortunately the Office of Fair Trading has produced a very readable pictorially-illustrated guide which can serve as a useful introduction to the Regulations themselves.

1. Advertising

Scope of control
The various exemptions from control are scattered between the Act itself, the Advertising Regulations and the Consumer Credit (Exempt Advertisements) Order 1980 (as amended). In one respect the advertising controls go beyond the rest of the Act because they can apply whenever the advertiser carries on "a business in the course of which he provides credit to individuals secured on land"—even if it is not a consumer credit business (see

---

[5] For details of the Act in operation see the 1981 Report of the Director-General and Lawson (1982) 132 N.L.J. 1033.

s.43(2)(*b*)). In another respect, however, the main advertising controls are narrower than the rest of the Act. It has been seen earlier (*ante*, p. 197) that there is basically no distinction between private and business customers. To this basic rule there is one exception—the Advertising Regulations do not apply to an advertisement which clearly indicates (expressly or by implication) that credit or hire facilities are only available "for the purposes of a person's business" (reg. 2(2)). Other exemptions include the following:

1. A credit advertisement which indicates that the credit will exceed £5,000 and that no security is required or that the only security is on property other than land.
2. A credit agreement which indicates that the credit is only available to a body corporate.
3. An advertisement offering credit for an agreement which falls within section 16(2) or which would have done so if the credit had been £5,000 or less.[6] It will be recalled that section 16(2) grants exempt status for certain land transactions involving building societies, local authorities and the other specified bodies (*ante*, p. 203).
4. An advertisement offering credit for agreements which fall within the first and second of the "instalment exemptions" (*ante*, p. 204) or which would have done so if the credit had been £5,000 or less.
5. A hire advertisement which indicates that the advertiser is not willing to enter into a consumer hire agreement.

General provisions

The first point to note is that the term "advertisement" is defined as including "every form of advertising" (s.189) so that films, circulars and even sales-talk are covered. Secondly, the Act imposes criminal liability on the advertiser in two cases namely:

(1) If the advertisement indicates that he is willing to provide credit under a restricted-use agreement (*ante*, p. 200) relating to any goods or services to be supplied by any person, but at the time of publication that person does not

---

[6] Such agreements may still be controlled by the advertising provisions of the Act but they are expressly exempted from the Regulations.

hold himself out as prepared to sell the goods or services for
cash;
(2) If the advertisement contains information which is false or
misleading in a material respect. An example may be "two
years to pay" but failing to mention that a 50 per cent.
down-payment is required.

Now if Fred, a dealer, advertises that credit is available from the
Razorsharp Finance Company it might have been thought that
Fred was the "advertiser" but this is not so—it is the finance
company (see s.189). The criminal liability can however extend to
the publisher, the advertising agency and the person who procured
the advertisements (s.47(1)). Various defences are available (see
s.47(2) and 168).

The advertising regulations

The overriding obligation is that the information must be
provided clearly and as a whole (reg. 17) and due prominence
must be given to the total charge for credit where this is stated
(reg. 20). As regards content the Regulations provide for no less
than six different categories—simple, intermediate and full credit
advertisements and simple, intermediate and full hire advertisements. The key factor for the advertiser is to decide how much
information he wants to include because a criminal offence can be
committed if he includes too little or too much. The following
examples of credit advertisements may be helpful:
(1) A poster bears the words "A. Smith—Moneylender." This
is a simple advertisement within regulation 6. It must not
indicate any price or any other indication of willingness to
enter into credit agreements.
(2) A newspaper advertisement reads "A. Smith—Moneylender—Telephone 123–4567 for full details of credit terms."
This is an intermediate advertisement within regulation 7.
Some additional information is compulsory,[7] and some
additional voluntary information may be given. Thus for
example the creditor may give (and in some cases he must
give) the annual percentage rate of credit (APR) and in
such a case he may also state the repayment period *or* the

---

[7] Thus if security and insurance is required for a specified type of agreement, this
must be stated.

frequency of the instalments *or* the total sum payable by the debtor.

(3) If the advertisement contains anything more than the information required or permitted under (1) or (2) above it will be a full credit advertisement within regulation 8 and it must contain a great deal of additional information.

2. Quotations

As part of the policy of giving customers pre-contractual information the Act enables quotation regulations to be made (see ss.52 and 152) and the Consumer Credit (Quotations) Regulations 1980 have been in force since October 6, 1980.

Scope

Like the Advertisement Regulations the Quotation Regulations go beyond the rest of the Act because they apply not only to consumer credit or consumer hire but also to all agreements for the provision of credit (regardless of amount) to individuals secured on land. In addition, the Regulations apply equally to regulated and exempt agreements— the only exception being the section 16(2) land exception for building societies, local authorities and specified bodies (*ante*, p. 203). Unlike the Advertising Regulations there is no distinction between private and business customers.

The trader's obligations

The Regulations deal with the situation where a trader receives a request from an individual asking for written information about the terms on which the trader is prepared to do business with the customer in relation to a particular transaction. In such a case the trader must (presumably within a reasonable time although the Regulations do not say so) provide the necessary information as set out in the Regulations. The information is similar in many respects to that required in the case of a "full advertisement" (see above). Indeed, the request need not be complied with at all if, *inter alia*, it is made in writing at the business premises of the creditor or credit-broker where a full advertisement is conspicuously displayed. Three further points are worthy of note:

(1) The request need not be complied with if the creditor or credit broker informs the customer within a reasonable time that he is not prepared to do business with him.

(2) If the information given by the customer is incomplete the creditor or credit-broker can either ask the customer for the missing information or he can send a quotation based on certain assumptions (which must be stated).

(3) The sending of a quotation does not necessarily amount to an offer which is capable of being turned into a binding contract, because by regulation 6

"every quotation . . . (c) may be framed as an offer or in any other way."

Thus the quotation can say "if this is of interest to you please complete the enclosed application form.

3. Canvassing

With regard to canvassing there are four distinct offences:

(1) If an individual visits premises other than business premises of the creditor, owner, supplier, canvasser, debtor or hirer and there makes oral representations to induce another individual to enter into a debtor-creditor agreement (*ante*, p. 200) he commits an offence unless the visit takes place in response to a request in writing made on a previous occasion and signed by the person making it (ss. 48, 49).

(2) Sections 153 and 154 contain somewhat similar provisions relating to the canvassing off trade premises of the services of a person carrying on the business of credit-brokerage, debt-adjusting or debt-counselling.

(3) By section 50(1) a person commits an offence if, with a view to financial gain, he sends to a minor any document containing an invitation to borrow money, obtain goods on credit or hire, obtain services on credit, or apply for information or advice relating to the above matters. A defence is available if he did not know, and had no reasonable cause to suspect that the addressee was a minor (s.50(2)).

(4) Section 51 deals with the much criticised practice of sending unsolicited credit tokens (*ante*, p. 202) by making it an offence to give a person such a token if he has not asked for it.[8]

Section 168 may provide a defence if all due care was taken.

---

[8] If the wording on the card satisfies the conditions of a "credit token" the statutory controls will apply even if the wording is untrue (*Elliott* v. *D.G.F.T. The Times*, May 17, 1980).

VI. REGULATION OF THE AGREEMENT

In this section it is proposed to consider sections 56–103 but before examining them in detail three general observations can be made.

(1) If an agreement is said to be "improperly executed" it can only be enforced against the hirer or debtor on an order of the court (see s.65(1)).

(2) When a right is enforceable on an order of the court only this does not prevent an act being done with the consent of the debtor or hirer (s.173(3)).

(3) As might have been expected the Act severely curtails exemption clauses. Section 173(1) provides that:

> A term . . . is void if, and to the extent that it is inconsistent with a provision for the protection of the debtor or hirer or any relative or any surety contained in the Act or in any regulation made under the Act.

It will be recalled that in a consumer credit agreement the parties are referred to as "creditor and debtor" while in a consumer hire agreement they are referred to as "owner and hirer."

A. *Pre-Contractual Matters*

Pre-contractual disclosure

Regulations may specify what matters have to be disclosed before any regulated agreement is made (s.55). Clearly one matter of particular importance to the debtor is the true cost of borrowing. At the present it is difficult if not impossible for him to work this out in a meaningful way so that he can make comparisons. This topic has already been considered in relation to exempt agreements (*ante*, p. 205) and in relation to advertising (*ante*, p. 215) and it will also be covered in the section 55 regulations.

Antecedent negotiations

Where a person acquires goods or services under a debtor-creditor-supplier agreement (*ante*, p. 201) he will normally negotiate with a dealer and the dealer will then (a) sell the goods or services to the debtor with finance provided by the creditor or

(b) sell the goods to the creditor who then lets them out to the debtor on hire-purchase or conditional sale.

By section 56(2) negotiations with the debtor

> shall be deemed to be conducted by the negotiator in the capacity of agent of the creditor as well as in his actual capacity.

In *Andrews* v. *Hopkinson*[9] a dealer said to a prospective hirer-purchaser "it's a good little bus—I'd stake my life on it." This statement induced the customer to take the car from the finance company to whom the dealer had sold it. Unfortunately the car had a serious defect and the customer was injured when the steering failed. As the law then stood, the customer's claim against the company was blocked by an exemption clause. He therefore sued the dealer; the court held that the dealer was liable to him (1) for breach of a collateral contract and (2) in tort for negligence. If the facts of this case were to recur today the customer would still have the same rights against the dealer but he would also, under section 56 above, have non-excludable rights against the finance company.

Section 56(3) makes void a clause which excludes the liability of the creditor for the defaults of the negotiator of the formation of the agreement or which provides that such a negotiator is to be treated as the agent of the debtor.

Pre-contractual reflection and isolation

To meet criticisms of high pressure door-step selling the hire-purchase legislation in 1965 gave the hirer a right to cancel the agreement in certain cases. This right is carried across into the consumer credit legislation (*post*, p. 223) but its application to transactions secured on land could cause considerable administrative problems. Accordingly the Act excludes the right of post-contractual cancellation (s.67(*a*)) and instead sections 58 and 61 give the debtor a pre-contractual right of reflection and isolation in certain cases. The rules on this topic can be summarised as follows:

(1) Before sending the agreement itself for signature the creditor or owner must send to the debtor or hirer a copy of the

---

[9] [1957] 1 Q.B. 229; [1956] 3 All E.R. 422. Note that the term "negotiations" is widely defined so that *e.g.* the payment of a deposit to the negotiator will be treated as a payment to him as agent of the finance company (see an interesting article by Mr. A. P. Dobson in [1975] J.B.L. 208).

unexecuted agreement containing a notice in the prescribed form
setting out his right to withdraw (s.58(1)) together with a copy of
any other document referred to in the agreement.

(2) The creditor or owner must then wait seven days before
sending the agreement for signature (s.61(2)(*b*)) and if he receives
a notice of withdrawal during this period he must not send the
agreement for signature at all (s.61(2)(*d*)). This is apparently so
even where the debtor or hirer changes his mind and decides to go
ahead after all (see Goode, *Consumer Credit Act Legislation* at p.
II/43 where a similar view is expressed).

(3) During the "consideration period" the creditor or owner
must not approach the debtor or hirer in any way except in
response to a specific request made during the consideration
period (s.61(2)(*c*)). This period begins with the service of the
withdrawal copy in (1) above and ends seven days after service of
the signature copy in (2) above or on its return duly signed,
whichever first occurs. Thus in most cases the consideration period
will be at least 14 days.

(4) An agreement which fails to comply with the above
requirements is "improperly executed" (*ante*, p. 218).

(5) The scope of sections 58 and 61 is limited. They will not
apply:

(a) If the agreement is not a "regulated agreement" because the
credit or hire payments exceed £5,000 (*ante*, pp. 197 and 199) or
because the debtor or hirer is a body corporate or because it is
"exempt" under section 16 *ante*, p. 203, nor

(b) if it is a restricted use credit agreement to finance the
purchase of the mortgaged land (s.58(2)) nor

(c) if it is an agreement for a bridging loan in connection with
the purchase of the mortgaged land or other land (*ibid.*).

The reason for the exclusion of cases (b) and (c) above is that
the money may be required quickly so that a 14-day delay could
cause serious complications (Goode *op. cit.* at p. I/193). In
practice the prospective mortgagor is almost certain to be advised
by a solicitor in this type of case and accordingly the need for
statutory consumer protection is far less strong.

Withdrawal from prospective agreement

On general contractual principles a party can withdraw from a
prospective agreement. No special form is necessary, although if

an offer has been made it must be effectively revoked before it is accepted. Section 57 confirms the general law and goes on to state that withdrawal will operate in the same way as cancellation of a concluded agreement (*post*, p. 223). What is surprising is the general rule in section 57(3) which appears again in the section dealing with cancellation (*post*, p. 225) and rescission (s.102). Section 57(3) reads:

> Each of the following shall be deemed to be the agent of the creditor or owner for the purpose of receiving a notice under subsection (2)—
> (a) a credit-broker or supplier who is the negotiator in antecedent negotiations and
> (b) any person who, in the course of a business carried on by him, acts on behalf of the debtor or hirer in any negotiations for the agreement.

Thus the debtor can effectively withdraw by informing his own solicitor or other negotiating agent.

Pre-contractual agreement

The above rules as to withdrawal are reinforced by section 59 which makes void an agreement whereby the debtor or hirer binds himself to enter into a regulated agreement. This rule can be modified by regulations in appropriate cases.

B. *Formation of the Agreement Itself*

In this section it is proposed to deal with sections 60–64 which deal with formalities and copies. They are modelled on the previous hire-purchase legislation but they merely provide a skeleton which will be clothed by regulations which, at the time of writing, have not yet been made.

Information and signature

One of the main problems in the consumer protection field is to make sure that the consumer understands his rights and obligations (including the true cost of credit). Regulations under sections 60 and 61 are designed to assist the debtor or hirer in this respect although the Director is given power to waive compliance in any particular case where he is satisfied that compliance would be impracticable (s.60). Section 61(1) specifies the scope of the regulations as follows:

A regulated agreement is not properly executed unless

    (*a*) a document in the prescribed form itself containing all the prescribed terms and conforming to regulations under section 60(1) is signed in the prescribed manner both by the debtor or hirer and by or on behalf of the creditor or owner, and

    (*b*) the document embodies all the terms of the agreement, other than implied terms, and

    (*c*) the document is, when presented or sent to the debtor or hirer for signature, in such a state that all its terms are readily legible.

If the debtor or hirer were to sign a blank form leaving the details to be filled in later, this would not satisfy section 61(1) and consequently the creditor or owner may be unable to enforce it (see s.127(3) *post*, p. 241).[10]

Copy provisions

The rules here are taken, with modifications, from the hire-purchase legislation and they may depend on:

(i) whether the document which the debtor or hirer signs is an agreement or only an offer;

(ii) whether it is presented to him personally or sent to him; and

(iii) whether it is a cancellable agreement.

The rules can be summarised as follows:

(1) If a document is presented personally to the debtor or hirer for signature and then becomes an executed agreement a copy of the agreement and of any agreement referred to therein must be delivered to him there and then (s.63(1)). There is no obligation to supply a second one (s.63(2)(*a*)). If, however, the document does not become an executed agreeement there and then, the creditor or owner must (a) deliver to the debtor or hirer a copy of the document there and then (s.62(1)) *and* (b) give him a copy of the executed agreement (s.63(2)) and any document referred to therein within seven days of the making of the agreement.

(2) If the document is sent to the debtor or hirer for signature a copy of the document (and any other document referred to in it) must be sent at the same time (s.62(2)). If it then becomes an executed agreement no further copy is required (s.63(2)(*b*)). If it does not, a copy of the executed agreement, and any document

---

[10] For a similar decision on the somewhat different wording of the Hire-Purchase Acts see *Eastern Distributors* v. *Goldring* [1957] 2 Q.B. 600; [1957] 2 All E.R. 525.

referred to in it, must be given to the debtor or hirer within seven days of the making of the agreement (s.63(2)).

(3) In cancellation cases (see below) the copy required by section 63(2) must be sent by post.

(4) In cancellation cases (a) each copy must give details of the cancellation rights in a form prescribed by the regulations and (b) if only one copy of the agreement has to be supplied (see (1) and (2) above) the creditor or owner must also send by post a notice giving details of the cancellation rights; this must be done within seven days of the making of the agreement—section 64(1).

(5) In cancellation cases a failure to comply with the above provisions relating to copies renders the agreement completely unenforceable by the creditor or owner, *i.e.* the court has no power to make an enforcement order unless the defect is rectified before commencement of proceedings (s.127(3)). If the creditor or owner is in breach of section 64(1) (*supra*) no such rectification is possible.

Apart from these basic requirements sections 77–79 give the debtor or hirer the right to ask for additional information and copies (*post*, p. 230) while section 80 confers such a right on the creditor or owner (*ibid.*).

C. *Cancellation*

The debtor's right of cancellation has already been mentioned at various points and it is now proposed to consider it in more detail. The law is contained in sections 66–73 of the Act which are modelled on the previous hire-purchase legislation. The right of cancellation must be distinguished from:

(1) Withdrawal from a prospective agreement (*ante*, p. 220).

(2) The rescission of an agreement (*e.g.* for misrepresentation).

(3) Termination (*post*, p. 234).

When available

By section 67 the right of cancellation is available if two conditions are satisfied:

(a) the antecedent negotiations included oral representations made in the presence of the debtor or hirer by an individual acting as, or on behalf of, the negotiator and

(b) the debtor or hirer signed the unexecuted agreement at a place other than a place of business of (i) the creditor or owner or (ii) a party to a linked transaction (other than the debtor or hirer or any relative of his) or (iii) the negotiator in any antecedent negotiations.

Thus if the debtor signs in his own home or office or in his solicitor's office or anywhere else not listed above, the right of cancellation is available, provided that oral representations were made in his presence. If everything was done by letter or telephone the risk of high pressure salesmanship is clearly reduced and no right of cancellation exists even though, for example, the debtor signed at home.

Exclusion of cancellation in land transactions

No cancellation is possible where the agreement (i) is secured on land, or (ii) is a restricted-use credit agreement to finance the purchase of land or (iii) is a bridging loan in connection with the purchase of land. It will be recalled that in case (i) above the debtor or hirer is given instead a pre-contractual right of reflection and isolation (*ante*, p. 219). In cases (ii) and (iii) above neither section 58 nor section 67 will apply.

Time for cancellation

The debtor or hirer can exercise his right of cancellation from the date when he signs the unexecuted agreement until the end of the fifth day following the day on which he received the second copy or notice (see pp. 222–223, paras. (1) to (4)). Thus if he receives the second copy or notice on February 1 the last day for cancellation is February 6. If he never receives the second copy or notice at all (*e.g.* if it is lost in the post) the right of cancellation will remain open until he receives another one and the statutory period expires.

The creditor's duty to send a notice setting out the right of cancellation can be waived by the Director in particular cases laid down in the regulations (s.64(4)). In such a case the cancellation period ends at the end of the fourteenth day following the day on which the debtor or hirer signed the unexecuted agreement (s.68(*b*)).

Method of cancellation

The debtor or hirer must serve notice in writing (s.189) on (i) the creditor or owner or (ii) the person specified in the notice served under section 64(1) or (iii) the agent of the creditor or owner (s.69(1)). The notice need not be in any particular form as long as it indicates the intention of the debtor or hirer to withdraw from the transaction (*ibid.*). The special "deemed agency" rules already discussed in withdrawal cases (*ante*, p. 221) also apply in cancellation cases (s.69(*b*)) although they are not exhaustive. If the notice of cancellation is sent by post it takes effect from the date of the posting whether it reaches the addressee or not (s.69(1)).

Effect of cancellation

The rules in sections 69–70 can be summarised as follows:

(1) The service of a notice of cancellation operates to cancel the agreement and any linked transaction and to revoke an offer by the debtor or hirer or his relative to enter into a linked transaction.

(2) The cancelled agreement is to be treated as though it had never been entered into.

(3) All sums paid by the debtor or hirer or his relative under or in contemplation of the agreement or transaction are repayable. This would include a deposit, an instalment and an insurance premium paid under a linked insurance policy. Further, any sums which are or may become payable cease to be payable.

(4) The obligation to repay under (3) above is on the person to whom it was originally paid but under a three-party debtor-creditor-supplier agreement a creditor who pays the credit direct to the supplier is liable jointly and severally with the supplier, although he is entitled to be indemnifed by him. Thus if for example the supplier had become insolvent the debtor could look to the creditor for repayment of the deposit which he, the debtor, had paid to the supplier.

(5) In the type of agreement described in (4) above the credit paid by the creditor to the supplier is repayable to the creditor. This would apply where a creditor makes a loan to the debtor by paying the money straight to the supplier. The debtor's cancellation wipes out both the contract of loan and the linked contract whereby he uses the loan to buy goods from the supplier.

(6) If the total charge for credit includes a fee, commission, or

other sum payable to a credit-broker the excess over £1 is repayable to the debtor or hirer.

Repayment of credit

It has been seen that on cancellation any sums payable by the debtor or hirer cease to be payable. This can cause problems in a case where the debtor obtains the loan during the cancellation period and then cancels the agreement. It would clearly be unreasonable if the debtor was relieved of his obligation to repay the loan and section 71 therefore deals with this type of situation. It provides that (except in the case of a debtor-creditor-supplier agreement for restricted use credit) the cancellation of a regulated consumer credit agreement does not destroy the debtor's obligation to repay the credit and interest. If however the debtor repays the whole or part of the credit within one month of cancellation or, if the credit is repayable by instalments, before the first instalment is due, no interest is payable on the amount repaid. Further, if (as is usually the case) the credit is repayable by instalments and the debtor does not repay it before the first instalment is due, he is not liable to repay anything at all except on receipt of a request in writing in the prescribed form, signed by or on behalf of the creditor, recalculating the instalments due without extending the repayment period and without including anything other than principal and interest. Since the repayment period is limited to the period between service of the repayment notice and the final contractual repayment date the instalments are likely to be larger (see Goode *op. cit.* p. I/207).

The moral is clear; in unrestricted use cases the creditor should not provide the credit until after the expiry of the cancellation period.

One final point; credit can be repaid to the creditor or to his agent but not to a person who is deemed to be the creditor's agent under section 69(2)(*b*), *i.e.* a person conducting negotiations on behalf of the debtor. Repayment to such a person would not extinguish the debtor's repayment obligation under section 71.

Return of goods and the duty of care

The basic effect of cancellation is to restore the parties to their precontractual position. Section 72 applies this principle to a case where:

(a) the transaction is a restricted-use debtor-creditor-supplier agreement, or consumer hire agreements or a linked transaction to which the debtor or hirer under any regulated agreement is a party; or

(b) a linked transaction to which a relative of the debtor or hirer under a regulated agreement is a party; and

(c) the debtor, hirer or relative has acquired possession before cancellation.

The person in possession under the above rules is to be treated as having been under a pre-cancellation duty to retain possession and to take reasonable care of the goods; subject to what is said below, this duty continues after cancellation and until redelivery. On the question of redelivery section 72 provides that the possessor is only under a duty to redeliver at his own premises in pursuance of a written request signed by or on behalf of the other party and served at or before the time of collection. The duty of retention and redelivery is discharged if the possessor:

(1) delivers the goods to any person to whom a notice of cancellation could have been sent (other than his own negotiating agent); or

(2) sends the goods at his expense to such a person.

With regard to the post-cancellation duty of care the section contains three provisions:

(a) if the possessor redelivers under (1) above his duty to take care comes to an end;

(b) if he sends the goods under (2) above he must take reasonable care to see that they are received by the other party and are not damaged in transit;

(c) subject to this, the duty of care comes to an end 21 days after cancellation unless within that time the debtor has received a written request for redelivery and has unreasonably failed to comply with it.

Breach of any of the duties imposed by section 72 is actionable as a breach of statutory duty.

Part exchange allowance

In accordance with the general principle of restoring the parties to their pre-contractual position section 73 deals with a case where the negotiator has received goods in part-exchange. It is clearly necessary to deal specifically with this situation because the negotiator may quite lawfully have disposed of the goods. The section provides that unless the goods are redelivered to the debtor or hirer in substantially the same condition within ten days of cancellation the debtor or hirer can recover the part-exchange allowance from the negotiator. In the case of a debtor-creditor-supplier agreement for restricted use credit he can also recover it from the creditor who is then entitled to be indemnified by the negotiator.

Lien

The debtor or hirer who cancels a regulated agreement has a lien over the goods for the return of sums paid by him and for the return of the part-exchange goods or allowance (sections 70(1) and 73(5)). A relative who is in possession under the agreement or a linked transaction has a similar lien for the return of sums paid by him.

Special cases

Cancellation can clearly cause hardship to the supplier in a case where a debtor-creditor-supplier agreement for restricted-use credit was used to finance goods supplied in an emergency or the supply of goods which, before cancellation, had by the act of the debtor or his relative become incorporated in any land or thing not comprised in the agreement or any linked transaction. In such a case the effect of section 69(2) is that cancellation only operates to extinguish the credit arrangements and it does not affect the debtor's obligation to pay for the said work or goods. Section 72(9) confirms that the duty of reasonable care and redelivery does not apply in this type of case. This seems fair enough but what is much more remarkable is the further provision in section 72(9) that the duty of reasonable care and redelivery does not apply to perishable goods nor to goods which by their nature are consumed by use and were so consumed before cancellation. Thus the debtor can consume the goods, cancel the agreement and get his money back! In this type of case it is vital for the creditor not to let the debtor have possession until the cancellation period has expired.

D. General Exclusions

Sections A B and C above were concerned with part V of the Act (ss.55–73) and before leaving this topic a few exclusions must be mentioned—they appear in section 74.

(1) If the agreement is a non-commercial agreement (*i.e.* not made by the creditor or owner in the course of a business), the agency provisions of section 56 will apply but the rest of part V will not.

(2) If the agreement is a small debtor-creditor-supplier agreement for restricted use credit the only provisions of part V to apply are sections 55 and 56. A small agreement is defined in section 17 as (i) a regulated consumer credit agreement for credit not exceeding £30 other than a hire-purchase or conditional sale agreement or (ii) a regulated consumer hire agreement which does not require the hirer to make payments exceeding £30. In either case the agreement must be unsecured or secured by a guarantee or an indemnity only (*ibid.*). There are anti-avoidance provisions to prevent a transaction being split into a number of small agreements.

(3) The Director may determine that part V (except section 56) shall not apply to (a) any overdraft arrangement nor (b) a debtor-creditor agreement to finance the making of such payments on or in connection with the death of a person as may be prescribed.

E. *Matters Arising during the Currency of the Agreement*

Liability of creditor for breaches by supplier

In the section on cancellation it was seen that the creditor and the connected supplier were jointly and severally liable to refund sums paid by the debtor and the part-exchange allowance. Another and potentially much more important consequence of their business association is found in section 75 which provides that if the debtor under a three-party debtor-creditor-supplier agreement has, in relation to a transaction financed by the agreement, any claim against the supplier in respect of misrepresentation or breach of contract he will have a similar[11] claim against the creditor; the creditor is however entitled to be indemnified by the supplier unless otherwise agreed. The practical importance of

---

[11] In *U.D.T.* v. *Taylor* 1980 S.L.T. 28 a Scottish court held that a breach of the sale contract gave the debtor a right to rescind not only that contract but also the credit contract. The decision has been criticised (see (1982) 132 N.L.J. 1024, 1026 and in the opinion of the author the decision is clearly wrong.

section 75 is in cases where the debtor buys defective goods with the aid of a personal loan or Barclaycard. If the supplier is in breach of one of the terms implied by the Sale of Goods Act 1979 the debtor may have a claim for damages against the creditor or alternatively he can set up the breach as a defence to an action brought by the creditor on the loan contract. The section applies even though the debtor exceeded the credit limit or contravened some other term of the regulated agreement (s.75(4)) but by section 75(3) it does not apply to a claim (a) under a non-commercial agreement, nor (b) so far as the claim relates to any single item to which the supplier has attached a cash price not exceeding £30 nor more than £10,000.

Additional information

Sections 77–79 supplement the earlier information provisions (*ante*, p. 221) by giving the debtor or hirer the right, on tendering 15 p, to make a written request for an additional copy of the executed agreement, any document referred to in it, and a statement signed by or on behalf of the creditor or owner giving details of the total sum due, sums accrued due, and details of future instalments. Section 77 relates to consumer credit agreements for fixed term credit, section 78 deals with running account credit and section 79 deals with consumer hire agreements. Four matters are common to all of them:

(1) They do not apply to non-commercial agreements.
(2) If the creditor or owner fails to comply with the request within the prescribed period he cannot, while the default continues, enforce the agreement.
(3) If the default continues for one month he commits an offence punishable on summary conviction with a fine not exceeding £200 (s.167 and Sched. 1).
(4) They do not apply in case where no sums are payable, nor if a request is made within one month of the date when a previous request was complied with.

Just as the debtor may wish to know how much he has to pay, the creditor may wish to know where the goods are. Section 80 accordingly provides that where, under a regulated agreement other than a non-commercial agreement, the debtor or hirer is required to keep goods in his possession or control he shall, within seven working days after he has received a request in writing to that effect from the creditor or owner, tell the creditor or owner where the goods are. If he defaults for 14 days he commits an offence punishable on summary conviction with a fine not exceeding £50 (s.167 and Sched. 1).

Appropriation of payments

Where a debtor who owes two or more debts to the same creditor makes a payment which is insufficient to cover all the sums due the position at common law is that the debtor can appropriate the payment (*i.e.* indicate the debt or debts to which the money is to be applied) and if he fails to do so the creditor can do so. If however the sums are due under two or more regulated agreements the common law rules are replaced by section 81 of the Act. The section preserves the debtor's right to appropriate at the time of payment but it goes on to provide that if he fails to do so where one or more of the agreements is (i) a hire-purchase or conditional sale agreement or (ii) a consumer hire agreement or (iii) any agreement in relation to which security is provided, the payment *must* be appropriated towards satisfaction of the sums due in the proportion which those sums bear to each other.

> *Example.* £10 is due under a regulated agreement for a radio and £5 under a regulated agreement for a tape-recorder. The debtor sends a cheque for £12. If he fails to appropriate at the time of payment the £12 will be split in the proportion 10:5 so that £8 will go towards the radio and £4 towards the tape-recorder.

Variation of regulated agreements

A regulated agreement may contain a clause giving the creditor or owner the right to vary the agreement (whether by altering the repayments or in any other way). It is clearly reasonable that the debtor should be given notice of any such variation and accordingly section 86(1) provides that the variation shall not take effect before notice has been given to the debtor or hirer "in the prescribed manner." The form of the notice is to be found in the Consumer Credit (Notice of Variation of Agreements) Regulations 1977 (as amended) which originally came into force on April 1, 1977. In general the notice must be served on the debtor or hirer not less than seven days before the variation takes effect (regulation 2). This could cause serious complications in a case where the variation relates to the rate of interest payable on the debtor's daily outstanding balance (*e.g.* bank overdraft interest). In such a case the creditor need not send notice to all his customers every time that the interest rate changes. Instead, regulation 3 provides that the notice requirements are to be treated as satisfied where:

(i) The notice of variation is published in at least three national daily newspapers, in each case being printed in a type not less than 3mm in height and occupying a space of not less than 100 sq. cm. *or* (if this is not reasonably practicable) it is published in the *Gazette*; and

(ii) If it is reasonably practicable to do so, the notice of variation is prominently displayed, so that it may easily be read in a part (if any) open to the public of the premises of the creditor where the agreement is maintained.

The seven-day notice period could also cause complications in the case of a regulated consumer hire agreement where the variation relates to the rate of value added tax. Each payment by the hirer is a chargeable supply and the owner is clearly anxious to alter the hirer's contractual obligations before the next payment is made. Accordingly by regulation 4 the notice requirements are to be treated as satisfied where, before the variation takes effect:

(a) The notice of variation is served on the hirer; or

(b) the notice of variation is prominently displayed so that it may easily be read in the part of the premises of the owner where the hirer or a person on his behalf ordinarily makes payments under the agreement in person.

If a regulated agreement is varied by a later agreement this operates as a revocation of the earlier agreement and the incorporation of the unamended terms into the later one (s.82). The section then goes on to make sure that this device is not used to deprive the debtor or hirer of rights which he would otherwise have enjoyed. Thus if the earlier agreement is regulated but the later one is not (*e.g.* credit limit in excess of £5,000) the later one must nevertheless be treated as a regulated agreement unless it is for running-account credit (s.82(3)). Further, if the earlier agreement is cancellable but the later one is not (*e.g.* no oral representations) the right of cancellation, and the time limit for cancellation, continue to apply to the earlier agreement as though it had not been modified. The section does not apply to a non-commercial agreement. See also section 90(3) *post*, p. 239.

Special rules relating to credit-token agreements

Dealing first with two small points on formalities section 63(4) provides that the second copy need not be given to the debtor within seven days of the making of the agreement, provided that it is given to him at or before the credit-token itself is given to him. Further, if a new credit-token is given to the debtor the creditor must at the same time give him a copy of the executed agreement (if any) and any other document referred to in it (s.85). If he fails to do so he cannot enforce the agreement while the default continues and if it continues for one month he commits an offence punishable on summary conviction with a maximum fine of £200 (s.167 and Sched. 1).

Turning now to substantive matters section 83 lays down the general rule that the debtor under a regulated consumer credit agreement (other than a non-commercial agreement) is not to be liable to the creditor for loss arising from the use of the credit facility by another person not acting, or to be treated as acting, as the debtor's agent. The obvious example is where a credit card issued to A is used by B. This situation is expressly dealt with in section 84 which removes the protection of section 83 in certain cases and limits it in others. Thus (1) if the person using the token acquires possession of it with the debtor's consent the debtor may be liable to the creditor without limit for loss caused to the creditor by that person's use of the token (s.84(2)); (2) apart from this, the debtor may be liable for up to £30 (or the credit limit if lower) for loss to the creditor caused by the use of the token by other persons during a period when the token was not in the possession of any authorised person (s.84(1)). The term "authorised person" means the creditor, the debtor or anyone authorised by the debtor to use the token (s.84(1)). In view of the risky nature of credit-tokens section 84(3) provides that liability under (1) or (2) above is not to arise after the debtor has given written or oral notice to the creditor that the token has been stolen or is otherwise liable to misuse. To enable such notice to be given the token itself must contain, in the prescribed form, the name, address and telephone number of a person to whom notice can be given (s.84(4)). An oral notice must be confirmed in writing within seven days (s.84(5)). If the debtor alleges that the token was used by an unauthorised person the onus is on the creditor to prove that it was not so used or that the unauthorised use occurred before notification under section 84 (s.171(*b*)).

F. *Termination and Related Matters*

Termination by the debtor or hirer

The debtor or hirer can terminate the agreement either by completing his payments or by exercising his statutory right to terminate under sections 99–101.

If the debtor wishes to discharge his liability ahead of time section 94 gives him a statutory non-excludable right to do this, and section 95 enables regulations to be made providing for a rebate in such a case[12]—or indeed in any other case where a sum becomes payable to the creditor earlier than it would otherwise have done.

These rules are supplemented by three other provisions. Thus section 96 provides that early settlement will operate to terminate any future liability of the debtor or his relative under a linked transaction. Section 97 requires the creditor to furnish the debtor with a statement giving details of the sum needed to discharge the debtor's indebtedness; he must supply this statement within a period to be specified in regulations. Finally section 103 enables the debtor or hirer to demand a statement from the creditor or owner confirming that the debtor or hirer has discharged his indebtedness and that the agreement is no longer operative. The creditor must then, within a period to be specified in regulations, comply with the request or serve a counter-notice to the effect that the matter is disputed.

Statutory right of termination by debtor

Sections 99 and 100, which are similar to previous hire-purchase law, give the debtor under a regulated hire-purchase or conditional sale agreement the right to terminate it at any time before the final instalment falls due. The right can be exercised by giving notice in writing to the person entitled or authorised to receive

---

[12] At the time of writing no regulations have been made.

payments under the agreement (s.99(1)). There are two exceptions:

(1) In the case of a conditional sale of land there could be considerable practical problems if the agreement were to be terminated after title had passed to the debtor. Consequently the right of termination is excluded in his situation (s.99(3)).

(2) Under a conditional sale of goods the property may have passed to the debtor. If he then vests it in a third person (*e.g.* a buyer) who does not become the debtor under the agreement it would clearly be wrong to allow termination, because the debtor would be unable to return the goods to the creditor. Accordingly no termination is possible under a conditional sale agreement if the property, having become vested in the debtor, is transferred to a third person (s.99(4)).

If the debtor lawfully terminates a regulated hire-purchase or conditional sale agreement his liability is as follows:

(1) He remains liable to pay all sums accrued due (s.99(2)).

(2) Unless the agreement is more favourable to him he must bring his total payments up to one-half of the total price immediately before termination. If, however, the court is satisfied that some smaller sum is sufficient to compensate the owner the court may order such smaller sum to be paid (s.100(3)). This could be important if, for example, the debtor sought to terminate an agreement for a very expensive article after only a few weeks' use. He would presumably tender a smaller sum and leave it to the creditor to take court proceedings if he was not satisfied with it.

(3) If the debtor is in breach of a duty to take reasonable care he must compensate the creditor for this (s.100(4)).

(4) He must allow the owner to retake the goods—this is the effect of section 100(5).

If the creditor is required to carry out installation work and if the price for this forms part of the total price the "one half" in section 100(1) is calculated by taking the installation charge *in full* and then adding one-half of the balance (s.100(2)). This seems reasonable enough since the owner will usually have paid a contractor and he should be entitled to be reimbursed by the debtor.

Statutory right of termination by the hirer
Section 101 gives a hirer under a regulated consumer hire

agreement a right to terminate it by giving written notice to any person entitled or authorised to receive payments. As with the case of hire-purchase and conditional sale the termination will not affect liability to pay sums which have already accrued due (s.101(2)). The question then arises as to the length of notice. The section provides that:

(1) The agreement can never be made to terminate less than 18 months after the making of the agreement.

(2) Subject to this, the minimum period for notice (unless the contract is more favourable to the hirer) is as follows:

  (a) If sums are payable by the hirer to the owner at equal intervals, the minimum period is one interval or 3 months whichever is the less.

  (b) If sums are payable at unequal intervals, the minimum period is the shortest interval or 3 months, whichever is less.

  (c) In any other case the minimum period of notice is 3 months.

Termination of hiring agreements can cause problems, especially in the case of goods or equipment let out for business purposes. To deal with this problem the section provides that the right of termination does not apply at all in the following cases:

  (a) If the agreement requires the hirer to make payments which in total (and without breach of the agreement) exceed £300 in any year;

  (b) If the goods are bailed to the hirer for the purposes of a business carried on by him, or if he holds himself out as requiring them for business purposes, and the goods were selected by the hirer and acquired by the owner (at the hirer's request) from any person other than the hirer's associate;

  (c) If the hirer requires, or holds himself out as requiring, the goods for the purposes of bailing or hiring them out in the course of a business carried out by him;

  (d) If, on the application of a person carrying on a consumer hire business, the Director decides that the termination rules should not apply to agreements made by him.

Although the section does not expressly refer to the hirer's duty of care there will invariably be such a duty, either at common law or under the term of the contract, and if the hirer is in breach of the duty at any time before the termination notice expires this would presumably be a "liability . . . which has accrued before the termination" for which the hirer would remain liable.

Restrictions on the rights of creditor or owner in default cases

If the debtor or hirer defaults the creditor or owner may wish to (a) increase the sums payable under the agreement and/or (b) terminate the agreement and recover possession of the goods or land. All these matters are regulated by the Act. The various rules, all of which are designed to protect the debtor or hirer, can be summarised as follows:

(1) By section 93 a clause increasing the rate of interest in the event of default is void.

(2) Before taking any step in a default case to terminate the whole or part of the agreement, or to demand early payment, or to enforce any security (*e.g.* guarantee), or to recover possession of the goods or land, the creditor or owner must serve a notice of default under section 87 unless regulations otherwise provide. The notice must specify:

(a) The nature of the alleged breach;
(b) If the breach is capable of remedy, what action is required to remedy it and the date before which that action is to be taken;
(c) If the breach is not capable of remedy, the sum (if any) required to be paid as compensation for the beach and the date before which it is to be paid;
(d) The consequences of failure to comply with the notice.

The date specified in (b) and (c) above must be not less than seven days from the date of service of the notice of default (s.88(2)) and even if the breach is an irremediable one for which no compensation is required the creditor or owner must wait for seven days before exercising the rights specified in section 87. The case of *Eshun* v. *Moorgate Mercantile Co.* [1972] 1 W.L.R. 722; [1972] 2 All E.R. 402 emphasises that the notice must be clear and unambiguous; no doubt the regulations will be drafted on that basis.

Where the debtor or hirer remedies the breach or pays the compensation before the specified date the breach must be treated as never having occurred (s.89). The service of the notice also enables the debtor or hirer to apply to the court for a time order (s.129, *post*, p. 241).

(3) Section 90, which is one of the most important provisions in the Act, protects the debtor against "snatch-back." It applies where (a) the debtor is in breach under a regulated hire-purchase or conditional sale agreement relating to goods and (b) the debtor has paid one-third or more of the total price of the goods and has not terminated the agreement and (c) the property in the goods remains in the creditor. The goods are referred to as "protected goods" and by section 90(1), in such a case:

> "the creditor is not entitled to recover possession of the goods from the debtor except on an order of the court."

If the owner contravenes this requirement the consequences are severe; by section 91 the agreement terminates (if it has not already done so) and the debtor can recover all sums paid by him under the agreement (s.91).

The wording of section 90 is somewhat similar to that in the Hire-Purchase Acts and four points have been established by the courts.

(1) Since the agreement is terminated the debtor has no right to get the goods back.[13]

(2) For the same reason the creditor cannot unilaterally revive the agreement by returning the goods to the debtor.[14]

(3) If the debtor genuinely consents to the recovery of possession by the creditor there is no infringement of section 90 (see s.173(3).)[15]

(4) Section 90 only refers to recovery "from the debtor." Thus there is no infringement where the creditor repossesses goods which the debtor has abandoned,[16] or which are in the wrongful possession of a third party.[17]

Where the creditor agrees to install goods and the installation charge forms part of the total price the fraction of one-third in (b) above is calculated by adding the installation charge in full to one-third of the balance (s.90(2)). Further, to prevent the avoidance of section 90(e.g. by "tacking on" other goods so that the total paid by the debtor drops below the one-third), section

---

[13] *Carr* v. *Broderick* [1942] 2 K.B. 275; [1942] 2 All E.R. 441.

[14] *Capital Finance Co.* v. *Bray* [1964] 1 W.L.R. 323; [1964] 1 All E.R. 603.

[15] *Mercantile Credit Ltd.* v. *Cross* [1965] 2 Q.B. 205; [1965] 1 All E.R. 577.

[16] *Bentinck* v. *Cromwell Engineering Co.* [1971] 1 Q.B. 324; [1971] 1 All E.R. 33.

[17] *Cf. Eastern Distributors* v. *Goldring* [1957] 2 Q.B. 600; [1957] 2 All E.R. 525.

90(3) provides that where, after goods have become protected goods, they are comprised in a new agreement (with or without other goods) in respect of which less than one-third has been paid, the provision of section 90 will apply to *all* the goods in the new agreement even though one-third has not been paid.

Restrictions on rights of creditor or owner in non-default cases

The agreement may contain a clause allowing the creditor or owner to call in money at any early date, or terminating a particular right of the debtor or hirer, or giving the creditor or owner a right to re-possess. In a non-default case such a term cannot be enforced until the creditor or owner has given to the debtor or hirer at least seven days' notice of his intention to do so (s.76). Section 98 contains a similar provision where the creditor or owner wishes to terminate the agreement altogether in a non-default case. Service of either of these notices will enable the debtor or hirer to apply for a time order under section 129 (*post*, p. 241). There seems no reason in principle why the two notices should not be incorporated into a single seven-day document. The form of notice will be prescribed by regulations. Both sections only apply where the agreement specifies a term for its duration and that term has not expired.

A further restriction in a non-default case is contained in section 86 which curtails the right of the creditor or owner to exercise any of the rights specified in section 87(1) (*ante*, p. 237) in the event of the death of the debtor or hirer. The rights cannot be exercised at all, if the agreement is "fully secured"; in any other case an order of the court is required and such an order can only be made if the creditor or owner proves that he has been unable to satisfy himself that the present and future obligations of the debtor or hirer are likely to be discharged (s.128). Section 86 only applies if the agreement is to run for a fixed term and if this term has not expired.

Entry on land

Two other provisions restrict the rights of the creditor or owner. Section 92(1) provides that, except by order of court, the creditor or owner cannot enter premises to recover goods comprised in a hire-purchase, conditional sale or consumer hire agreement. Similarly where the debtor is in breach under a conditional sale agreement relating to land the creditor cannot recover possession of that land from the debtor or any person claiming under him except by order of court (s.92(2)). In either case, however, a genuine consent by the debtor or hirer at the time of entry will obviate the need for a court order (s.173(3)). If the creditor or owner contravenes section 92 he is liable to an action for breach of statutory duty (s.92(3)).

VII. SECURITY

Part VIII of the Act is headed Security and it contains some important provisions. The following points are among the most important.

(1) The "security" includes not only mortgages and similar documents but also guarantees and indemnities (see s.189).

(2) Sections 105 and 111 regulate the formalities of documents securing regulated agreements. They are similar in many ways to the provisions governing the agreement itself.

(3) Section 113 breaks new ground by providing that the liability of the person giving the security (*e.g.* a person signing a guarantee or indemnity at the request of the debtor or hirer) is not to exceed the liability of the debtor or hirer. Thus if the debtor terminates the agreement under section 100 his liabilities (apart from arrears and damages) cannot exceed one-half of the total price (*ante*, p. 235); the creditor cannot sidestep this limit by suing the guarantor or indemnifier for a larger amount.

(4) The creditor or owner is not allowed to take a negotiable instrument (other than a cheque) in payment of or as security for, a sum due under a regulated agreement. Likewise, if he receives a cheque as payment he is not allowed to negotiate it except to a banker (s.123).

(5) A land mortgage securing a regulated agreement is enforceable by order of court only (s.126).

VIII. JUDICIAL CONTROL

The courts are given wide discretionary powers in connection with the enforcement of regulated agreements. They can also reopen extortionate credit bargains whether regulated or not.

Enforcement orders

It will be recalled that if a regulated agreement is improperly executed it can only be enforced by the creditor or owner by order of court (s.65(1) *ante*, p. 218) and that in certain cases no order can be made at all. Thus if the agreement is not duly signed the court cannot make an enforcement order unless some other document containing all the prescribed terms was signed by the debtor (s.127(3)). If the power to make an enforcement order does exist the court can exercise it if it considers that it would be just to do so, having regard to (a) the prejudice (if any) caused to any person by the contravention and (b) the powers conferred on the court by sections 135 and 136 (as to which see *post*). The court can also in an enforcement order reduce or discharge any sum payable by the debtor or hirer in order to compensate him for the prejudice caused by the contravention (s.127(2)). In practice the prejudice will often be negligible or non-existent. Alternatively, a time order can be made (see below).

Time orders

The court can make a time order under section 129 if (a) the creditor or owner (i) applies for an enforcement order or (ii) brings an action to enforce a regulated agreement or any security to recover possession of any goods or land to which the agreement relates or (b) the debtor or hirer applies for a time order after he has been served with a notice under section 76 (*ante*, p. 239), 87 (*ante*, p. 237) or 98 (*ante*, p. 239). The term "time order" is defined in section 129(2) as an order providing for:

(a) the payment by the debtor or hirer or any surety of any sum owed under a regulated agreement or a security by such instalments and at such times as the court, having regard to the means of the debtor or hirer and any surety, thinks just and/or

(b) the remedying by the debtor or hirer of any breach (other than non-payment of money) within such period as the court may specify.

This provision is a new one and goes far beyond the power to make a "postponed" order in hire-purchase and conditional sale cases, a power which has been widely used. The section must be read together with the remaining sections of Part IX of the Act so that the general picture becomes clear. In particular section 130 provides that in hire-purchase and conditional sale cases the time order can relate to future instalments as well as to instalments which have already accrued due. Further, in the case of non-money breaches the creditor or owner cannot take any enforcement step until the specified period has run out and if the breach is rectified during that period it must be treated as never having occurred.

Protection orders

Section 131, which is in line with previous legislation, gives the court power to make orders protecting any property of the creditor or owner, or property subject to any security, from damage or depreciation pending the determination of any proceedings under the Act, including orders restricting or prohibiting use of the property or giving directions as to its custody. This is in addition to the general power under rules of court to order a sale (*ante*, p. 144).

Financial relief for hirer

It will be recalled that in the case of hire-purchase or conditional sale agreements the creditor cannot recover possession of protected goods otherwise than by action (s.90 *ante*, p. 238). There is no corresponding provision for regulated hire agreements but section 132 provides that where the owner recovers possession otherwise than by action the court may, on the hirer's application, order that the whole or part of any sum paid by the hirer to the owner in respect of the goods shall be repaid and that the hirer's obligation to pay sums which have accrued due shall cease. Such an order can also be made where the owner brings an action to recover possession. The court can make a section 132 order if it considers it just, having regard to the extent of the enjoyment of the goods by the hirer. Perhaps the power might be used where a hirer paid a very large deposit or rentals in advance and the agreement then came to an end after a very short time. It is uncertain whether the section can be invoked by a hirer who has exercised his statutory right of termination under section 101 (*ante*, p. 235).

Hire-purchase and conditional sale cases

Apart from the power to make time orders and protection orders section 133 gives the court power to make certain other orders in hire-purchase and conditional sale cases. These orders can be made in an action for an enforcement order or for a time order or in an action to recover possession (whether the goods are protected goods or not). In any such proceedings the court may:

(a) order the debtor to return to the creditor goods to which the agreement relates (a "return" order) or

(b) order the debtor to return some of the goods to the creditor and vest the remaining goods in the debtor (a "transfer" order). The maximum transferable to the debtor is found by taking the "paid-up sum" and deducting one-third of the unpaid balance.

The section then goes on to make certain supplemental provisions. If the debtor pays the price at any time before the creditor has recovered possession the creditor's title will vest in him and this will override and extinguish any return or transfer order (see s.133(4) and (5)). Conversely, if the debtor fails to comply with a return or transfer order, the creditor can ask the court to cancel the order and substitute an order for payment of the price of the unrecovered goods (s.133(6)). This power, which is not a new one, could be useful where the debtor has disposed of the goods.

Conditional and suspended orders

Section 135 enables the court (a) to make any term of an order conditional on the doing of a specified act by a party to the proceedings and/or (b) to suspend the operation of any term of the order until such time as the court directs or until the occurrence of a specified act or omission. The only qualifications are that (a) an order for delivery of goods by any person is not to be suspended unless the court is satisfied that the goods are in that person's possession or control and (b) in a consumer hirer agreement the court cannot extend the hiring period. One combined effect of sections 129, 133 and 135 is to give the court power, in a hire-purchase or conditional sale case, to order the debtor to return the goods and then postponing the operation of the order on condition that he pays the balance on terms fixed by the court. In the past this power has been widely exercised in relation to "protected" goods; it is now of general application.

Variation of agreements by the court

Section 136, which is widely drafted, provides that the court may in an order made by it under this Act include such provisions as it considers just for amending any agreement or security in consequence of a term of the order. Presumably the court will regard this power as ancillary to their other powers under Part IX.

Extortionate credit bargains[18]

Sections 137 to 140, which are based on a principle formerly found in the Moneylenders Acts, give the court power to reopen an extortionate credit bargain so as to do justice between the parties. These provisions apply to a "credit bargain" whether regulated by the Act or not. The definition of credit bargain in section 137 makes it clear that the debtor must be an individual.

When can the matter be raised?

Section 139 allows the debtor or any surety to raise the matter (a) in proceedings specifically brought for this purpose or (b) in proceedings brought to enforce the agreement, or any linked agreement, or any security or (c) in any proceedings in which the amount paid or payable under the credit agreement is relevant. Further, the power to re-open applies to any agreement whenever made (Sched. 3, para. 42).

When is a bargain extortionate?

Section 138 contains a non-exhaustive list of factors, some of which are personal to the parties while others are not. A bargain is to be treated as extortionate if it requires the debtor or his relative to pay sums which are grossly exorbitant, or if it otherwise grossly contravenes ordinary principles of fair dealing. In deciding this matter the court must take into account:

(a) interest rates prevailing when the agreement was made;
(b) matters personal to the debtor—age, health, experience, business capacity and financial pressures;
(c) matters personal to the creditor—the risk, his relationship to the debtor and whether the rate of interest was artificially reduced by a colourable cash price;
(d) any other relevant consideration.

---

[18] The leading case is *Ketley Ltd.* v. *Scott* [1981] I.C.R. 241 where a lender agreed to lend £25,000 (at 48 per cent. interest) to a prospective house buyer at a few hours' notice. The borrower's claim that the bargain was extortionate was rejected by Foster J. For an analysis of this and other cases see (1982) 132 N.L.J. 1041.

What can the court do?

The court can, predictably, rewrite the credit bargain, extinguish liabilities, order repayment of sums paid and order accounts to be taken (s.139(2)). It cannot, however, make an order which affects a judgment (s.139(4)).

Burden of proof

If the debtor alleges that the bargain is extortionate the onus is on the creditor to prove that it is not (s.171(7)). It would seem, as Guest and Lloyd suggest, that this burden will only be cast on the creditor if the debtor proves at least some evidence that the bargain is extortionate.

IX. MISCELLANEOUS MATTERS

Proceedings by the creditor or owner to enforce a regulated agreement or any linked transaction or security must be brought in the county court (s.141). All the parties to the agreement and any surety must be made parties to the proceedings unless rules of court otherwise provide (*ibid.*). The court is given power to give a declaratory judgment that the creditor or owner is not entitled to take a particular step (s.142).

Section 170(1) provides that a breach of any requirement made by or under the Act is to incur no civil or criminal sanction over and above those specifically provided by the Act, although this does not prevent the granting of an injunction (s.170(3)). Thus if the agreement was formally defective (so that the creditor could not enforce it without an order of the court), and if the creditor then repossessed the goods without court proceedings, the debtor could presumably obtain an injunction for the return of these goods but he could not sue for damages for breach of statutory duty.

The strongest sanction against breaches is provided by section 170(3) which provides that the Director can take the breaches into account in exercising "his functions under this Act." The revocation of a licence may well be the ultimate and most powerful sanction (*ante*, p. 212).

The Act and regulations impose a large number of duties and obligations and section 161 provides that the Director and the local

Weights and Measures Authorities are responsible for the enforcement of these duties.

X. The Future

It has been explained earlier in this Chapter that many parts of the Act are not yet in force and that many of its provisions will not become effective until regulations have been made. It is likely that a large batch of regulations will be laid before Parliament in the autumn of 1983 and that they, together with the provisions to which they relate, will come into force some 18 months thereafter.

The regulations which arc likely to be of the greatest practical importance are those relating to the formalities of the agreement itself (*ante*, pp. 221–222). It is likely that they will be modelled on the regulations made under the Hire-Purchase Act 1965 so that (1) the agreement must contain a great deal of information (2) the agreement must draw the attention of the debtor or hirer to a number of their statutory rights (*e.g.* cancellation, termination, early settlement) and (3) there will be a special form of wording in the box where the debtor or hirer has to sign. In addition the debtor or hirer will be invited to consult the Citizens Advice Bureau or the Trading Standards Department if he wishes to know more about his rights.

Other regulations in the batch referred to above will deal with:

1. Cancellation formalities and the repayment of credit.
2. Information relating to early settlement.
3. Rebates on early settlement.
4. Linked transactions.
5. Pawn transactions.
6. Sums payable on death.

CHAPTER FIVE

NEGOTIABLE INSTRUMENTS

INTRODUCTION

THE negotiable instrument, and especially the bill of exchange, has had a very long history, and has for long occupied a central place in the finance of industry and commerce. At the present time the traditional form of bill of exchange is seldom seen in inland sales, but is still of the greatest importance in export sales. In addition there is one form of bill of exchange in everyday use, namely the cheque.

Nature of a negotiable instrument

Property which cannot be reduced into physical possession is called a chose in action. Examples of choses in action are shares, rights under a contract and debts. A person having such property may wish to transfer (or assign) it to someone else. At common law choses in action were unassignable, but equity permitted assignment in most cases.[1] There were, however, two restrictions on assignment. In the first place notice usually had to be given to the debtor, because if he paid the assignor without notice of the assignment he could not be called upon to pay the assignee. Secondly, an equitable assignment was always "subject to equities" so that the debtor could raise against the assignee any defence or set-off which he could have raised against the assignor. In some cases these restrictions on transfer were found to be undesirable by the mercantile community who proceeded to ignore them. There grew up, in relation to certain mercantile documents, a custom that they could be freely transferred from one person to another without notice being given, and that if the transferee took in good faith and for value and without notice of any defect of title he would obtain a full legal title although his

---

[1] Assignment is now possible at law under s.136, Law of Property Act 1925, as well as in equity.

transferor had no title or a defective one. These documents came to be known as negotiable instruments.

Thus a negotiable instrument is a chose in action which can be freely transferred and in respect of which a transferee can acquire a better title than his transferor. As Blackburn J. put it:

> "when an instrument is by the custom of the trade transferable, like cash, by delivery and is also capable of being sued upon by the person holding it *pro tempore*, than it is entitled to the name of a negotiable instrument and the property in it passes to a bona fide transferee for value, although the transfer may not have taken place in market-overt."[2]

What instruments are negotiable

Historically the law of negotiable instruments has evolved through three stages—commercial practice, judicial recognition and finally legislation. Originally an instrument was negotiable merely as part of commercial usage, but in due course these usages of the law merchant were recognised by, and incorporated into, the common law.[3] To qualify for recognition the usage did not have to be of great antiquity but there had to be evidence that it was widespread and well recognised. At the present time the list of negotiable instruments includes bills of exchange, cheques, promissory notes, dividend warrants,[4] bearer bonds, bearer scrip, debentures payable to bearer, share warrants to bearer and Treasury Bills. On the other hand, a bill of lading is not a negotiable instrument, so that the transfer of a bill of lading by a non-owner does not give the transferee a good title to the goods, unless he is protected by one of the exceptions to the *nemo dat* rule (as to which see *ante*, p. 144 *et seq.*). By far the most important types of negotiable instrument in use today are bills of exchange, cheques and promissory notes, and the remainder of this chapter will be devoted to a study of them. The law is mainly to be found in the Bills of Exchange Act 1882. This Act, which, like the Sale of Goods Act 1893, was the work of Sir Mackenzie Chalmers, is a codifying Act and has not given rise to the same problems of interpretation as the Sale of Goods Act.

---

[2] *Crouch* v. *Crédit Foncier of England* (1873) L.R. 8 Q.B. 374, 381.
[3] See the full historical survey in the judgment of Cockburn C.J. in *Goodwin* v. *Robarts* (1875) L.R. 10 Ex. 337, 338, *et seq.*
[4] These are almost invariably in the form of a cheque.

SCHEME OF THIS CHAPTER

The chapter is divided into three parts. The first examines the function of a bill and then considers a number of rules relating to bills. Many of these rules also apply to cheques. The second part is headed "cheques" and deals with a number of matters relating exclusively to cheques. The final part deals with promissory notes.

BILLS OF EXCHANGE

Functions of bill

A seller of goods is clearly anxious to obtain payment as soon as possible, while a buyer may be equally anxious to defer payment, at any rate until he has been able to re-sell the goods and collect the proceeds. By using a bill of exchange it is possible for the seller to have payment and for the buyer to have credit at the same time. Ignoring for the moment the question of bankers' commercial credits (as to which see *post*, p. 471), suppose that Brown in London sells steel to Schmidt in Bonn, who requires credit of 30 days. Brown will draw a bill of exchange "on" (*i.e.* addressed to) Schmidt ordering him to pay in 30 days' time. The bill would appear as follows:

£500	London
	1st July 1983
30 days after date pay to my order Five Hundred Pounds (£500) value received.	
To Schmidt	Brown.
37 Hochstrasse, Bonn	

If Schmidt agrees to the terms of the bill, he will show his agreement by signing (or "accepting") the bill and returning it to Brown. Brown can then sell the bill to his bank in London at its face value less a small discount.

It will be seen that Brown now has his money while Schmidt has his credit for 30 days. When the time for payment arrives, the bill is said to "mature" and the bank, or the person to whom the bank has transferred it, will then seek to enforce payment from

Schmidt, who may meanwhile have obtained the goods and re-sold them. In practice Schmidt is more likely to make an arrangement whereby a London bank accepts the bill. This, of course, greatly adds to the value of the bill in the market.

A bill can also be used to enable a trader to obtain short-term capital where he wishes to purchase raw materials or (perhaps) finance his own hire-purchase. If his credit is good he can arrange for an accepting house to accept bills drawn on them (in return for a commission) and on such acceptance he will be able to "discount" the bill with a discount house, *i.e.* sell the bill to them.

In both these two examples, the bill has been used for what is perhaps its primary function—credit.[5]

£1,000	London
	1/7/83
3 months after date pay to	
my order the sum of £1,000	
To A. House Ltd.	T. R. Ader
Accepted	

The other main function of a bill of exchange is that it serves as a convenient method of settling a debt, or, sometimes, two debts. If Brown owes £100 to Black who in his turn owes £100 to White, Black can order Brown to pay White, and if Brown does this both debts are extinguished.

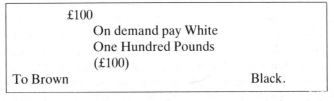

£100	
On demand pay White	
One Hundred Pounds	
(£100)	
To Brown	Black.

If in this example the name of Black's bank were substituted for Brown as the person to whom the order was addressed, the instrument would be a cheque, *i.e.* in effect a document where one person (the customer) orders his debtor (the bank) to pay a sum of money to his creditor.

---

[5] As to regulated consumer credit or consumer hire agreements see *ante*, p. 240, (4).

Parties

Initially there are three parties to every bill. The person who gives the order is called the *drawer*; the person to whom the order is given is called the *drawee*[6] and when he signs the bill, *i.e.* accepts it, he is called the *acceptor*. Finally, the person to whom the bill is payable is called the *payee*. The liabilities and the obligations of the various parties will be fully examined later, but very broadly, the principal debtor is the acceptor while the drawer and any indorsers are in the position of guarantors.

Definition

It is now proposed to examine the definition of a bill of exchange. It may assist readers to remember that all cheques are bills of exchange, and that with certain exceptions (notably all provisions about acceptance, because a bank does not "accept" a cheque) the rules about to be discussed apply to cheques as well as to other bills. A reference to a section is to that section in the Bills of Exchange Act 1882, unless otherwise stated.

Section 3(1) defines a bill of exchange as:

> An unconditional order in writing, addressed by one person to another, signed by the person giving it, requiring the person to whom it is addressed to pay on demand, or at a fixed or determinable future time, a sum certain in money to or to the order of a specified person, or to bearer.

Section 3(2) goes on to provide that any instrument which does not come within the above definition is not a bill of exchange.[7]

It is now necessary to examine the definition more closely.

(1) It must be an order, as opposed to a mere request. The most common order is the word "Pay" but other words are equally effective. Words of politeness will not prevent the instrument from being a bill of exchange,[8] provided that they do not deprive it of its imperative character. Thus "Please pay" would be a valid bill, whereas "I would be pleased if you would kindly pay" probably would not.

---

[6] In the case of a cheque the bank on whom the cheque is drawn is the "drawee."

[7] It may still be a chose in action and assignable as such.

[8] *Ruff* v. *Webb* (1794) 170 E.R. 30.

(2) The order must be unconditional as between drawer and drawee. In *Bavins Junr. and Sims* v. *London and S.W. Bank*[9] a document which directed payment "provided that the receipt form at the foot hereof is duly signed" was held to be conditional, and therefore not a valid bill. If, however, the order to complete a receipt is addressed solely to the payee (as where a document reads "Pay X £100" and then, at the foot, "the receipt on the back must be signed") it has been held that the order to pay is unconditional and therefore a valid bill.[10] The distinction is clearly a fine one and in practice bankers usually obtain an indemnity from their customer to protect them if they wrongly treat an instrument requiring a receipt as a cheque. Section 3(3) provides that an order to pay out of a particular fund is not unconditional but that an order is unconditional even though coupled with:

(a) An indication of the fund out of which the drawee is to reimburse himself (as, for example, pay X £100 and debit my No. 1 A/c); or

(b) A statement of the transaction giving rise to the bill (*e.g.* Pay X £1,000 being purchase price of Blackacre).

It is important to remember that an order which is initially unconditional remains a valid bill even though it is conditionally delivered,[11] or conditionally accepted,[12] or conditionally indorsed.[13]

(3) It must be in writing, which, by section 2, includes printing. Even a bill written in pencil is possible, but is strongly discouraged by banks, because of the risk of fraudulent alteration.[14]

(4) It must be addressed by one person[15] to another.[16] Thus a document addressed to no one cannot be a bill, although a person who subsequently writes an acceptance on it may make himself liable as the maker of a promissory note.[17] Again if the drawer and

---

[9] [1900] 1 Q.B. 270. Some provisions of the Act and of the Cheques Act 1957 apply, however, to conditional orders. See *post*, pp. 316, 319 and 320.

[10] *Nathan* v. *Ogdens Ltd.* (1905) 94 L.T. 126.

[11] *Post*, p. 267.

[12] *Post*, p. 261.

[13] *Post*, p. 274.

[14] The bill need not be on any particular substance. Thus in 1970 *The Times* carried a photograph showing the British Davis Cup team receiving their cheques written on tennis balls.

[15] This includes a body of persons whether incorporated or not.

[16] Or, in the case of a cheque, by one person to a bank.

[17] *Mason* v. *Lack* (1929) 45 T.L.R. 363.

the drawee are the same person (as in the case of a banker's draft) the instrument is strictly not a bill as it is not addressed "to another." The holder in this case may at his option treat the instrument either as a bill of exchange or as a promissory note made by the drawer. He may also do this where the drawee is fictitious or without capacity to contract (s.5(2)).

(5) It must be signed by the person giving it. An instrument which is not signed by the drawer cannot be a bill, although if his signature is forged, a party can sometimes acquire rights by estoppel (see *post*, p. 293). If the drawer's signature is written on the bill by his duly authorised agent, this, of course, is perfectly valid (s.91(1), *post*, p. 265).

(6) It must require payment of a sum certain in money. The first point to note is that by section 3(2) an instrument which orders any act to be done in addition to the payment of money is not a bill of exchange.[18] Secondly, section 9(1) provides that a sum is certain even if required to be paid:

(a) With interest[19];

(b) By stated instalments;

(c) By stated instalments with a provision that on default the whole shall become due:

(d) According to a specified rate of exchange.

Finally, section 9(2) provides that where there is a discrepancy between the sum stated in words and the sum stated in figures the sum stated in words prevails.[20]

This emphasis on "certainty" is a notable feature of the law relating to bills of exchange. They are intended to circulate freely from hand to hand and uncertainties on the face of the bill would seriously hamper this. There must be certainty as to the sum payable (*supra*), the time of payment (s.11, *infra*), the identity of the drawee (s.6(1), *post*, p. 258) and the identity of the payee (s.7(1), *post*, p. 259).

(7) It must be payable on demand or at a fixed or determinable future time.

---

[18] *Martin* v. *Chauntry*, 93 E.R. 1175.

[19] As to interest on dishonour see s.57 *post*, p. 297.

[20] In the case of a cheque the banker on whom it is drawn will in practice return it unpaid marked "words and figures differ." Presumably the cheque would not be "complete and regular on the face of it" (*post*, p. 275).

On demand

Section 10 provides that:

> (1) A bill is payable on demand
>   (*a*) Which is expressed to be payable on demand or at sight, or on presentation; or
>   (*b*) In which no time for payment is expressed.
> (2) Where a bill is accepted or indorsed when it is overdue, it shall, as regards the acceptor who so accepts, or any indorser who so indorses it, be deemed a bill payable on demand.

The effect of a bill being payable on demand is that the holder can demand payment immediately. By far the most important type of bill payable on demand is the cheque, which is:

> a bill of exchange drawn on a banker and payable on demand (s.73).

The words "on demand" do not normally appear on the cheque form used in practice, but by virtue of section 10(1)(*b*) they will be implied.

Time bills

If the bill is not payable on demand it must be payable at a fixed or determinable future time, which means:

(a) at a fixed period after date or sight, or
(b) on or at a fixed period after the occurrence of a specified event which is certain to happen, though the time of happening may be uncertain (s.11).

Examples

"30 days after date."
"30 days after sight"[21] [*i.e.* after the bill is first seen by the drawee].
"30 days after A's death."

All these are valid but an instrument requiring payment "30 days after A's marriage" is not a valid bill because the event, *i.e.* A's marriage, is not certain to occur. Section 11 further provides that:

> An instrument expressed to be payable on a contingency is not a bill, and the happening of the event does not cure the defect.

---

[21] An instrument requiring payment 90 days after "acceptance" (the word "sight" being deleted) is not a bill of exchange (*Korea Exchange Bank* v. *Debenhams* (*Central Buying*) [1979] 1 Ll.L.R. 538 C.A.

The courts have held that the words "on or before" a certain date involve an element of contingency so that an instrument requiring payment in this way is not a valid bill.[22]

(8) It must be payable to or to the order of a specified person or to bearer. A direction to pay an impersonal payee such as "Wages" or "Cash" is not a valid bill because it is not payable to "a specified person."[23] Bankers in practice treat such a document as a mandate from their customer authorising them to pay the bearer of the document, and have been held entitled to do so.[24] If the mandate is revoked the instrument becomes valueless.[25]

Types of bill

Section 8 divides bills into three types:

(a) Non-transferable bills.

(b) Order bills.

(c) Bearer bills.

Non-transferable bills. Section 8(1) reads:

> When a bill contains words prohibiting transfer, or indicating an intention that it should not be transferable, it is valid as between the parties thereto, but is not negotiable.

What is the meaning of this subsection? The answer depends on the meaning of the word "negotiable." The normal meaning of this word (and the one used in this book) is "transferable free from equities." Sometimes, however, the word is used as a synonym for "transferable" and it is clear that in section 8(1) the draftsman has given it that meaning. If, therefore, A draws a bill on B in favour of "C only" and the bill contains on its face the words "not negotiable" the bill is valid as between A, B and C but cannot be transferred by C.[26] The words "not negotiable" on a crossed cheque have a different meaning (*post*, p. 315).

---

[22] *Williamson v. Rider* [1963] 1 Q.B. 89; [1962] 2 All E.R. 268. An Irish court has refused to follow it (*Creative Press v. Harman and Harman* [1973] I.R. 313).

[23] *North and South Insurance Corpn. v. National Provincial Bank* [1936] 1 K.B. 328. See also *Orbit Mining and Trading Co. Ltd. v. Westminster Bank* [1963] 1 Q.B. 794 *post*, pp. 316 and 322.

[24] *Ibid.*

[25] *Cole v. Milsome* [1951] W.N. 49; [1951] 1 All E.R. 311.

[26] *Hibernian Bank v. Gysin and Hanson* [1939] 1 K.B. 483; [1939] 1 All E.R. 166, C.A.

Order bills. Section 8(4) provides that:

> A bill is payable to order which is expressed to be so payable, or which is expressed to be payable to a particular person, and does not contain words prohibiting transfer or indicating an intention that it should not be transferable.

Thus if a bill is drawn "Pay X or order" it is an order bill, and so is a bill drawn "Pay X" because the words "or order" are implied. It follows that if the drawer of a cheque writes "Pay X" and strikes out the printed words "or order" the striking out has no legal effect, because the words "or order" will, in any event, be implied. If, in the example, X wishes to enforce payment he can do so. Alternatively, if he wishes to negotiate the bill to someone else, he can do so by indorsement coupled with delivery (s.31, *post*, p. 272). The words "Pay to the order of X" have the same meaning and effect as the words "Pay X or order" (s.8(5)).

Bearer bills. Section 8(3) provides that:

> A bill is payable to bearer which is expressed to be so payable, or on which the only or last indorsement is an indorsement in blank.

Thus if a bill is drawn "Pay bearer" or "Pay X or bearer" and is given to X in settlement of a debt, the bill is a bearer bill and X can either obtain payment or he can negotiate the bill by mere delivery without indorsement.

The fundamental distinction, therefore, between a bearer bill and an order bill is that:

A bill payable to bearer is negotiated by delivery[27] (s.31(2)) whereas:

A bill payable to order is negotiated by the indorsement of the holder coupled with delivery (s.31(3)).

A bill is also a bearer bill if the last or only indorsement on an order bill is an indorsement in blank (as to which see *post*, p. 273), or if the payee named in an order bill is fictitious or non-existing (as to which see *post*, p. 280).

Contents of a bill

It has already been seen that a bill must specify the drawer, the drawee and the payee and also the sum payable. It remains to

---

[27] This clearly makes a bearer bill much more risky since a thief can easily pass ownership to a bona fide transferee (*post*, p. 273).

consider certain other matters which may sometimes appear on bills.

Date

The Act provides that a bill is not invalid merely because:
    (a) It is not dated (s.3(4)), or
    (b) It is ante-dated, or
    (c) It is post-dated (as to post-dated cheques, see *post*, p. 311), or
    (d) It is dated on a Sunday (s.13(2)).

Where a bill is payable at a fixed time after date or sight, the date of the bill or of the acceptance is clearly of the greatest importance. Section 12 deals with the position where such date is omitted. It reads:

> Where a bill expressed to be payable at a fixed period after date is issued undated, or where the acceptance of a bill payable at a fixed period after sight is undated, any holder may insert therein the true date of issue or acceptance, and the bill shall be payable accordingly.
>
> Provided that (1) where the holder in good faith and by mistake inserts a wrong date, and (2) in every case where a wrong date is inserted, if the bill subsequently comes into the hands of a holder in due course the bill shall not be avoided thereby, but shall operate and be payable as if the date so inserted had been the true date.

Finally, section 13(1) provides that where a bill, acceptance or indorsement is dated, the date is presumed to be the correct date unless the contrary can be proved.

Other matters

A bill frequently indicates the place of drawing, the place of payment and the fact that value has been given. Section 3(4), which is much more liberal than the law of many European countries, provides that a bill is valid even though none of these matters is specified. In practice, where bills are used in connection with export sales, the bank or discount house generally prefers the bill to contain a short narrative indicating the transaction.

The holder of the bill

Already there have been several references to "the holder" and a great many more will be made in the following pages. Section 2 defines a holder as:

The payee or indorsee of a bill or note who is in possession of it, or the person in possession of a bill or note which is payable to bearer.

If A draws a bill on B in favour of C or order and hands the bill to C, C, as the payee in possession, is the holder. If C negotiates the bill to D by indorsement coupled with delivery, D, as the indorsee in possession, is now the holder. If D likewise negotiates to E, E becomes the holder and so on.

Bearer bill

If a bill is payable to bearer, the person for the time being in possession of it is the holder even though he has no title. Thus a thief in possession of a bearer bill would be the holder of it.

Holder for value

This means a holder, as above defined, who has given, or is deemed to have given, valuable consideration for a bill, as to which see section 27, *post*, pp. 269–270.

Holder in due course

This means a holder, as above defined, who satisfies the definition specified in section 29, *post*, p. 275.

Parties

It has already been stated that the three principal parties are the drawer, the drawee and the payee.

Drawee[28]

The drawee must be named or otherwise indicated in the bill with reasonable certainty (s.6(1)). In *Gray* v. *Milner*[29]:

> A bill directed payment at "No. 1 Wilmot Street, London" and B, who lived there, accepted it. It was held that he could not subsequently repudiate on the grounds that he had not been indicated with reasonable certainty.

Although a bill may be addressed to more than one drawee, an order addressed to two drawees in the alternative or to two or more drawees in succession is not a valid bill (s.6(2)).

---

[28] The bank on whom a cheque is drawn is the drawee.

[29] (1819) 8 Taunt. 739. (See also *ante*, p. 252 for further points as to the drawee.)

Payee

Although in many cases the payee will be someone distinct from the drawer and the drawee, this is not always so. Section 5(1) provides that:

> a bill may be drawn payable to, or to the order of, the drawer; or it may be drawn payable to, or to the order of, the drawee.
>
> *Examples.* (1) A draws on Y to "Pay to my order." Drawer and payee are the same person.
>
> (2) X, a customer of Y bank, draws a cheque on that bank in favour of the bank to reimburse them for purchasing travellers cheques on his behalf. Drawee and payee are the same person.

Section 7(1) provides that unless the bill is payable to bearer, the payee must be named or indicated with reasonable certainty. Whether this has been complied with is a question of construction. Extrinsic evidence is admissible to cure a latent defect, as, for example, where the name of the payee is misspelt. If, however, the document reads "Pay —— or order," it seems that it is not a bill because no payee is indicated.[30] On the other hand, the words "Pay to —— order" have been held to mean "Pay to my [*i.e.* the drawer's] order."[31]

Joint payees

Section 7(2) provides that:

> A bill may be made payable to two or more payees jointly, or it may be made payable in the alternative to one of two, or one or some of several payees. A bill may also be made payable to the holder of an office for the time being.

Alternative payees (Pay A or B) are possible, therefore, whereas alternative drawees are not.

Indorser

This, as the name implies, is a person who writes his name on the back of the bill. Usually he will do this to negotiate an order bill to another person. Another possibility is that to strengthen the credit of a bill a person may write his name on the back, even though he is strictly not a party. Section 56 provides that:

---

[30] *R.* v. *Randall* (1811) R. & R. 195; *Chamberlain* v. *Young* [1893] 2 Q.B. 206, *per* Lord Esher and Bowen L.J.

[31] *Chamberlain* v. *Young, supra.*

> Where a person signs a bill otherwise than as drawer or acceptor, he thereby incurs the liabilities of an indorser to a holder in due course.

If, for example, a bill is drawn on a company to secure a loan made to the company, the lender may insist that the bill be indorsed by the company's directors. These directors will in effect "guarantee" payment of the bill. In such a case it seems that in order to give effect to the intention of the parties, the court will allow the original payee to enforce his rights against the indorsers[32] even though the original payee cannot be a holder in due course.[33]

Acceptance[34]

By section 17 acceptance is:

> the signification by the drawee of his assent to the order of the drawer.

It must be written on the bill and signed by the drawee, and it must not express that the drawee will perform his promise by any other means than the payment of money (*ibid.*). If the bill is drawn on A, any of the following will constitute a valid acceptance:

"Accepted 1/7/75. A." or
"Accepted payable at Lombank Ltd. A." or
"Accepted. A." or
"A."

Once the drawee accepts the bill, he becomes liable upon it.

General and qualified

If the drawee assents without qualification to the order as drawn, he is said to give a "general" acceptance. If, however, his acceptance in some way varies the effect of the bill as drawn, it is called a "qualified" acceptance. Section 19 proceeds to specify five types of qualified acceptance:

---

[32] *McDonald* v. *Nash* [1924] A.C. 625, followed in *Lombard Banking Co. Ltd.* v. *Central Garage and Engineering Co. Ltd.* [1963] 1 Q.B. 220; [1962] 2 All E.R. 949 and in *Yeoman Credit Ltd.* v. *Gregory* [1963] 1 W.L.R. 343; [1963] 1 All E.R. 245.

[33] *Jones* v. *Waring & Gillow* [1926] A.C. 670. In so far as the two recent cases cited in the last note held that the payee was a holder in due course, they must be regarded as wrongly decided.

[34] This topic does not apply to cheques.

(a) A conditional acceptance, *e.g.* "I accept if the bills of lading are handed over."

(b) Partial, *e.g.* if a bill is drawn for £500 and the drawee accepts £400.

(c) Local, *i.e.* an acceptance to pay *only* at a particular place. "Accepted payable at Lombank Ltd., Fetter Lane" is a general acceptance, whereas "Accepted payable at Lombank Ltd., Fetter Lane, only" is a qualified acceptance.

(d) Qualified as to time, as where a bill drawn payable "30 days after date" is accepted payable "40 days after date."

(e) Acceptance of one or more of the drawees but not of all.

On receiving a qualified acceptance the holder has an option to refuse it or to take it. The matter is more fully discussed when dealing with the duties of a holder (*post*, p. 283).

Capacity, signature and delivery

Before any person can be liable on a bill three conditions must be satisfied:

(a) He must have capacity.

(b) He must sign the bill.

(c) (Generally) he must deliver the bill.

Capacity

Section 22 provides that:

> (1) Capacity to incur liability as a party to a bill is co-extensive with capacity to contract.
>
> Provided that nothing in this section shall enable a corporation to make itself liable as drawer, acceptor, or indorser of a bill unless it is competent to it so to do under the law for the time being in force relating to corporations.
>
> (2) Where a bill is drawn or indorsed by an infant . . . or corporation having no capacity or power to incur liability on a bill, the drawing or indorsement entitles the holder to receive payment of the bill, and to enforce it against any other party thereto.

The general rule is that where a person without capacity draws or indorses a bill, that person is not liable on it, but his incapacity does not prevent the holder from suing other parties to the bill who are liable in the ordinary way. In addition, sections 54(2), 55(1) and 55(2) contain provisions whereby the acceptor, drawer and indorser of a bill are estopped from denying to a holder in due course the capacity of certain other parties, but these estoppel provisions do not appear to add anything to the general rule formulated in section 22(2):

> *Example.* Henry, a minor, buys necessaries from Smart and pays by cheque. The payee, Smart, indorses the cheque to Philip. The cheque is dishonoured. Philip cannot sue Henry because a minor is not liable on a negotiable instrument.[35] He can, however, sue Smart on his indorsement. Smart, again, cannot sue Henry on the cheque but he can sue him on the consideration for the cheque and can claim a reasonable price for necessaries sold and delivered (section 3 of the Sale of Goods Act 1979 (*ante*, p. 85).

It will be recalled that if the *drawee* is without capacity, the holder may treat the instrument as a bill of exchange or as a promissory note (s.5(2), *ante*, p. 253).

Companies. A company formed for the purposes of trade has implied power to draw, accept or indorse bills of exchange, as such a power is incidental to the performance of its objects.[36] A non-trading corporation cannot do so, however, unless such a power is expressly or impliedly conferred by its memorandum or other constitution.[37] It has been suggested, however, that the practice of drawing cheques is now so common that a power to draw them should be implied.[38] In any event a third party may be protected if the act in question (*e.g.* signing a cheque) is decided on by the directors (see the European Communities Act 1972, s.9(1) *ante*, p. 71).

Signature

Section 23 opens with these words:

> No person is liable as drawer, indorser, or acceptor of a bill who has not signed it as such.

This fundamental rule is of the greatest importance in the law relating to bills. It follows from section 23 that:

(1) The drawee of a bill cannot be sued on it until he has signed (or "accepted") it.

---

[35] *Re Soltykoff* [1891] 1 Q.B. 413.

[36] As to incidental powers see *Deuchar* v. *Gas Light & Coke Co.* [1925] A.C. 691.

[37] Compare *Re Peruvian Railways Co.* (1867) L.R. 2 Ch. 617 (power implied) and *Bateman* v. *Mid-Wales Ry.* (1866) L.R. 1 C.P. 499 (power not implied).

[38] Chalmers, *Bills of Exchange* (13th ed.), p. 65.

(2) The bank on which a cheque is drawn is not liable to the holder of a cheque if payment is refused.[39]

(3) An undisclosed principal cannot be liable on a bill signed by his agent in his (the agent's) own name.

Where a person signs a bill in the mistaken belief that it was an entirely different document he may be able to escape liability by pleading "*non est factum*," but the House of Lords has recently held that this doctrine must be confined within very narrow limits.[40]

Proviso. There are two provisos to section 23:

> (1) Where a person signs a bill in a trade or assumed name, he is liable thereon as if he had signed it in his own name.
>
> (2) The signature of the name of a firm is equivalent to the signature by the person so signing of the names of all persons liable as partners in that firm.

Thus, if the firm of Hook & Co. has three partners, Hook, Line and Sinker, and one partner, Hook, draws a bill in the name of Hook & Co., he is deemed to have signed the names of all three partners.[41] The question whether Line and Sinker will be bound by Hook's act will, of course, depend on normal rules of agency and partnership and on whether it was a trading firm (*ante*, p. 67).

Exception in the case of companies. Section 97(3) provides that the Act is not to affect the provisions of the Companies Acts and accordingly section 23 must be read subject to an important exception which is contained in section 108(4) of the Companies Act 1948. This subsection, which is designed to protect persons dealing with companies, provides that where officers of the company have signed or authorised the signature of the company on any bill, cheque or note on which the company's name does not appear in legible characters, the officers are themselves to be liable to the holder of the bill, cheque or note if it is not duly paid by the company. Thus the officer might be personally liable if, for example, the word "limited" were omitted from the company's

---

[39] The bank *is* however liable to the payee under the collateral contract created by the use of a cheque card if the necessary conditions are satisfied.

[40] *Saunders* v. *Anglia Building Society* [1971] A.C. 1004; [1970] 3 All E.R. 961.

[41] See also *Ringham* v. *Hackett, The Times* February 9, 1980 C.A. (partner signs his own name below printed name of firm. *Held*: his co-partner was liable on the cheque).

name on the bill.[42] The holder cannot, however, enforce this liability if he himself was responsible for the incorrect name appearing on the bill; he cannot take advantage of his own wrong.[43]

Forged signature. From the basic rule of section 23 it should logically follow that a forged or unauthorised signature has no legal effect, and subject to the ratification of an unauthorised signature and subject also to estoppel section 24 says precisely that. It reads:

> Subject to the provisions of this Act, where a signature on a bill is forged or placed thereon without the authority of the person whose signature it purports to be, the forged or unauthorised signature is wholly inoperative, and no right to retain the bill or to give a discharge therefor or to enforce payment thereof against any party thereto can be acquired through or under that signature, unless the party against whom it is sought to retain or enforce payment of the bill is precluded from setting up the forgery or want of authority.
>
> Provided that nothing in this section shall affect the ratification of an unauthorised signature not amounting to a forgery.

Example of general rule. A draws a bill on B in favour of C. B accepts. D steals the bill, forges C's indorsement and transfers the bill to E. The position is that:

(1) the forged indorsement is wholly inoperative and accordingly

(2) E has no title to the bill, which still belongs to C. If, in ignorance of the forgery, B pays the bill to E, he will not obtain a good discharge, and remains liable to pay the true owner, C. C in this example can also sue E for money had and received.[44]

(3) B may be entitled to recover money which he has wrongly paid to E; he must however act promptly (*post*, p. 298).

Ratification. It is clear that an unauthorised signature can be ratified if the usual conditions for ratification are present (as to

---

[42] *Penrose* v. *Martyr* (1858) E.B. & E. 499. See also *Hendon* v. *Adelman, The Times*, June 16, 1973 (omission of "ampersand" in company's name—signing directors liable under s.108; and, more recently, *British Airways Board* v. *Parish* [1979] 2 Ll.L.R. 361.

[43] *Durham Fancy Goods Ltd.* v. *Michael Jackson (Fancy Goods) Ltd.* [1968] 2 Q.B. 839; [1968] 2 All E.R. 987.

[44] See *Brook* v. *Hook* (1871) L.R. 6 Ex. 89. Hanbury, *Principles of Agency*, pp. 101–103.

which see *ante*, p. 43). A forgery, however, cannot be ratified on the ground, *inter alia*, that the forger was not purporting to act as agent for the person whose signature he forged. It does seem, however, that a forgery can be adopted if the person whose signature was forged acknowledges it as his own.[44] Such adoption may give rise to liability if it is supported by valuable consideration[45] or if it induces a subsequent party to alter his position.[46]

Estoppel. Although a forged signature generally confers no rights, there may sometimes be liability by estoppel. Thus a person who discovers that his signature is forged should usually take speedy action; if his failure to do so causes another person to alter his position he may be estopped from setting up the forgery at a later stage.[47] Estoppel is not confined to the person whose signature was forged. Thus by sections 54 and 55 the acceptor and indorsers are sometimes estopped, as against a subsequent party, from setting up a forgery (see *post*, pp. 293–294).

Signature by agents. Section 91(1) provides that where the Act requires the bill to be signed by any person, it is sufficient if his signature is written thereon by some other person by or with his authority.

Procuration signature. In practice many agents sign a bill by the use of words such as:

per pro [the principal],[48]
for and on behalf of [the principal],
pp. [the principal],[48]

followed by their own signature. This is known as a signature by procuration and it operates as notice that the agent's authority may be limited. Section 25 provides that:

> A signature by procuration operates as notice that the agent has but a limited authority to sign, and the principal is only bound by such signature if the agent in so signing was acting within the actual limits of his authority.

---

[45] See *Greenwood* v. *Martins Bank* [1933] A.C. 51, 57, *per* Lord Tomlin.
[46] *Brook* v. *Hook, supra.*
[47] *Greenwood* v. *Martins Bank* [1933] A.C. 51, *post*, p. 309.
[48] Technically, this form of wording is probably incorrect: see *Law Notes*, Vol. 89, at pp. 82, 110, 138, 166.

Thus in *Morison* v. *Kemp*[49]

> A clerk, authorised to draw cheques *"per pro"* his employer for the employer's business, drew a cheque in this form in favour of a bookmaker in settlement of the clerk's private debt. The bookmaker persuaded someone to cash it. *Held*, the employer was not bound and could recover the money from the bookmaker. [The clerk would, of course, be liable for falsely warranting his authority.]

Section 25 does not, of course, prevent a person being liable under the normal rules of holding out. Where a bill is signed on behalf of a company, a third party is entitled to rely on the apparent authority of the signer (and if he deals with the directors any restrictions in the memorandum or articles will not prejudice him—see *ante*, p. 72). In practice a company's banker usually insists on express instructions as to who is to sign.[50]

Representative signature. Section 26 provides that:

> (1) Where a person signs a bill as drawer, indorser, or acceptor, and adds words to his signature, indicating that he signs for or on behalf of a principal, or in a representative character, he is not personally liable thereon; but the mere addition to his signature of words describing him as an agent, or as filling a representative character, does not exempt him from personal liability.
>
> (2) In determining whether a signature on a bill is that of the principal or that of the agent by whose hand it is written, the construction most favourable to the validity of the instrument shall be adopted.

If a person signs "A. director of B. Ltd." the concluding words (being words of description) will not prevent personal liability.[51] On the other hand a signature "for and on behalf of X Ltd. Y Director" will not normally involve personal liability although extrinsic evidence is admissible to show personal liability was intended.[52]

---

[49] (1912) 29 T.L.R. 70.

[50] See *Paget on Banking*, 9th ed., at pp. 44–46, and cases there cited.

[51] *Courtauld* v. *Sanders* (1867) 16 L.T.(N.S.) 562. For further illustrations, see Chalmers, *op. cit.* at pp. 83–84. This is merely an illustration of the general principle of agency law, as to which see *The Swan* [1968] 1 Lloyd's Rep. 5, discussed in 85 L.Q.R. 92.

[52] *Rolph Lubell & Co.* v. *Keith* [1979] 1 All E.R. 860.

Delivery

Every contract on a bill, whether it be that of the drawer, acceptor or indorser, is incomplete and revocable until delivery (s.21(1)). The Act, however, provides that where an acceptance is written on the bill and the drawee gives notice to or according to the directions of the person entitled to the bill that he has accepted it, the acceptance then becomes complete and irrevocable (*ibid*). Where the bill is no longer in the possession of a party who has signed as drawer, acceptor or indorser, a valid and unconditional delivery by that party is presumed until the contrary is proved (s.21(3)). Section 2 defines delivery as the transfer of possession, actual or constructive, from one person to another.

Rules as to delivery. By section 21(2):

> As between immediate parties, and as regards a remote party other than a holder in due course, the delivery—
> (*a*) in order to be effectual must be made either by or under the authority of the party drawing, accepting, or indorsing, as the case may be;
> (*b*) may be shown to have been conditional or for a special purpose only, and not for the purpose of transferring the property in the bill.
> But if the bill be in the hands of a holder in due course a valid delivery of the bill by all parties prior to him so as to make them liable to him is conclusively presumed.

This subsection illustrates what is a common feature of the Act—the statement of a general rule, followed by a modification of it in favour of a holder in due course (see, for example, ss.20, 48, 64 and 71).

> *Example.* A draws a cheque in favour of B or order. B indorses it in blank, thereby converting it into a bearer cheque. A thief steals it from B. The thief has no title because there has been no delivery. The thief negotiates the cheque to H. a holder in due course. H can sue all prior parties because in his favour a delivery from B to the thief is conclusively presumed.[53]

The posting of a bill or note will amount to a valid delivery if the sender had express or implied authority to use the post.[54]

---

[53] See on rather similar facts the case of *Ingham* v. *Primrose* (1859) 7 C.B.(N.S.) at p. 85.

[54] *Ex p. Cole* (1873) L.R. 9 Ch. 27.

Delivery of inchoate instruments. Section 20(1) provides that:

> Where a simple signature on a blank stamped paper is delivered by the signer in order that it may be converted into a bill, it operates as a prima facie authority to fill it up as a complete bill for any amount the stamp will cover,[55] using the signature for that of the drawer, or the acceptor, or an indorser; and, in like manner, when a bill is wanting in any material particular, the person in possession of it has a prima facie authority to fill up the omission in any way he thinks fit.
>
> *Example.* A, who owes £100 to B, writes an acceptance for £100 on a piece of paper and hands it to B. B (or his administrator after his death) can write in B's name as drawer and as payee and can then sue A.[56]

The subsection, however, only applies if an instrument is delivered to someone for the purpose of being converted into a bill. In *Baxendale* v. *Bennett*[57]:

> B put a blank acceptance of his own into his desk. It was stolen, completed and negotiated. It was held that B was not liable.

Section 20(2) deals with the position where the instrument is wrongly completed. It provides that:

> In order that any such instrument when completed may be enforceable against any person who became a party thereto prior to its completion, it must be filled up within a reasonable time, and strictly in accordance with the authority given. Reasonable time for this purpose is a question of fact.
>
> Provided that if any such instrument after completion is negotiated to a holder in due course it shall be valid and effectual for all purposes in his hands, and he may enforce it as if it had been filled up within a reasonable time and strictly in accordance with the authority given.

The operation of this subsection can best be illustrated by an example. Suppose that P instructs A to buy a block of opera tickets on P's behalf and that he gives A a blank cheque, with instructions not to fill in an amount in excess of £40. If A then writes in his own name as payee and the amount of £100, it is clear that he cannot sue P. If, however, after completing the cheque in this way he

---

[55] These words are now superfluous since stamp duty on bills of exchange has been abolished.

[56] *Scard* v. *Jackson* (1875) 34 L.T.(N.S.) 65.

[57] (1878) 3 Q.B.D. 525. The concluding words of s.21(2) would not apply to a case of this type since the document signed by B was a blank piece of paper and not a negotiable instrument.

negotiates it to B, a holder in due course, B is not affected by the fact that A exceeded his authority and can sue P for the full £100 if the cheque is dishonoured.

If, in the example, A had inserted B's name as the payee, the proviso to section 20(2) would not have protected B, because the payee cannot be a holder in due course.[58] If, however, B had altered his position in reliance on P's signature, P would have been estopped from denying that A had an unlimited authority, and would have been liable under the normal common law estoppel rules which have not been cut down by section 20.[59]

The above discussion shows that signing a blank cheque can be risky, but disaster can be avoided if the drawer crosses the cheque and adds the words "not negotiable." In this case he will not be liable, either under section 20 or at common law, if the instrument is wrongly completed.[60]

Consideration

General rule

Valuable consideration is essential for a bill of exchange, as it is for any other contract not under seal.[61] Thus if A gives B a cheque as a gift, neither A, nor after A's death his personal representative, is liable to B on the cheque.

Special rules

The consideration rules for a bill differ in three respects from those governing other contracts.

(1) By section 30(1) consideration is presumed until the contrary is proved.

(2) The effect of section 27(2) is that consideration need not move from the promisee.[62] It provides that:

---

[58] *Jones* v. *Waring & Gillow* [1926] A.C. 670, *post*, p. 277.

[59] *Lloyds Bank* v. *Cooke* [1907] 1 K.B. 794.

[60] *Wilson & Meeson* v. *Pickering* [1946] K.B. 422; [1946] 1 All E.R. 394 and see s.81 *post*, p. 315.

[61] For a recent case on consideration see *Pollway Ltd.* v. *Abdullah* [1974] 1 W.L.R. 493—auctioneer accepted buyer's cheque as a deposit on sale; buyer stopped the cheque and seller then treated the contract as repudiated; the Court of Appeal held that the auctioneer (as payee of the cheque) could enforce it against the drawer because (*inter alia*) the auctioneer's warranty of authority was sufficient consideration.

[62] In addition, on general contractual principles, the consideration need not move to the promisor. Thus if A draws a cheque in favour of B in consideration of B paying money to C, B has given value and can sue A on the cheque.

Where value has at any time been given for a bill, the holder is deemed to be a holder for value as regards the acceptor and all parties to the bill who became parties prior to such time.

Example. A draws a cheque in favour of B or order as a gift. B indorses it to C, his landlord, in payment of his rent. If the cheque is dishonoured C, having given value, can sue A and B who became parties before value was given. Suppose, however, that instead of seeking payment C indorses the cheque over to his daughter D as a gift. Pictorially the position is:

A—*No Value*→B—*Value*→C—*No Value*→D

Thus if the cheque is dishonoured D would be a holder for value as regards A and B who became parties before value was given. She cannot, of course, sue C because as between immediate parties (*e.g.,* indorser and indorsee) the absence of consideration is always a defence.

In the above example the person giving value (C) was a party to the cheque, but it is now clear that this is not essential.[63]

Example. H draws a cheque in favour of G in consideration of G drawing a cheque in favour of D. As value has been given for G's cheque (by H), D is a holder for value of that cheque and can sue the drawer G.

(3) Consideration may be past. Section 27(1) provides that:

Valuable consideration for a bill may be constituted by:
(*b*) Any consideration sufficient to support a simple contract.
(*b*) Any antecedent debt or liability.

The reason for this departure from the general rule is that so many cheques are drawn (and bills accepted) in settlement of past debts, with the result that, but for section 27(1)(*b*), many actions on a cheque would be met with a defence of "no consideration."

Where the debt is that of the person who draws, accepts or indorses the bill, the debt itself will usually be the consideration. Where, however, the debt is that of a third party (as where A owes B £100 and subsequently C draws a cheque in favour of B for that amount), there will not be consideration unless there is some relationship between the receipt of the cheque and the antecedent debt or liability—as, for example, where the creditor agrees to take the cheque in satisfaction of the debt.[64]

---

[63] *Diamond* v. *Graham* [1968] 1 W.L.R. 1061; [1968] 2 All E.R. 909, C.A. Some doubts were cast on the decision in *Pollway Ltd.* v. *Abdullah* [1974] 1 W.L.R. 493 although no reasons were given for these doubts.

[64] *Oliver* v. *Davis* [1949] 2 K.B. 727.

Lien

Section 27(3) provides that:

> Where the holder of a bill has a lien on it, arising either from contract or by implication of law, he is deemed to be a holder for value to the extent of the sum for which he has a lien.

At common law a banker has a general lien over papers which his customer hands to him, otherwise than for safe custody.[65] This lien could arise, for example, where the customer has an overdraft. The bank will be a holder for value of any bills and cheques which they hold under their lien.

The precise meaning of the words "to the extent of the sum for which he has a lien" is obscure. It seems that if a previous party to the bill has given full value the holder can use that value under section 27(2) and can sue the drawer for the full amount of the cheque. If, however, the *only* value is the amount of the lien the holder will only be able to claim that amount *unless* he goes on to prove that he is a holder in due course, in which case he can claim the full amount of the cheque.[66]

Accommodation parties

In the first example on p. 25, it was seen that a bill of exchange could be used to raise money if it contained the signature of someone whose credit was good. The use of accommodation parties is another example of this. Section 28 provides:

> (1) An accommodation party to a bill is a person who has signed a bill as drawer, acceptor, or indorser, without receiving value therefor, and for the purpose of lending his name to some other person.
>
> (2) An accommodation party is liable on the bill to a holder for value; and it is immaterial whether, when such holder took the bill, he knew such party to be an accommodation party or not.
>
> *Example.* A is a young man just starting in business and requires capital. He persuades a wealthy friend B to accept a bill drawn on him in favour of A payable "90 days after date." B accepts this bill without receiving value, solely to enable A to raise money by using his signature. A then negotiates the bill to his bank, and as the bill bears B's signature, he will obtain a good price for it, thus obtaining

---

[65] *Brandao* v. *Barnett* (1846) 3 C.B. 519, H.L.

[66] See *Barclays Bank* v. *Astley Industrial Trust* [1970] 2 Q.B. 527; [1970] 1 All E.R. 719, and the Australian case of *Bank of New South Wales* v. *Ross, Stuckey and Morawa* [1974] 2 Lloyd's Rep. 110.

the capital he requires. As between A and B, A will (hopefully) have agreed to meet the bill at maturity or to put B in funds. This, of course, is of no concern to a holder for value who can sue B on his acceptance, even if he knew that B was an accommodation party. B, of course, is not liable to A because A did not furnish any consideration for B's acceptance.

Accommodation bill

Although an accommodation party may be the drawer, acceptor or indorser, the expression accommodation bill should only be used where the accommodation party is the acceptor.[67]

Negotiation

Section 31 provides that negotiation means

the transfer of a bill by one person to another so as to constitute the transferee the holder of the bill.

It has already been noted that a bearer bill is negotiated by delivery and that an order bill is negotiated by indorsement coupled with delivery (*ante*, p. 256).

Thus indorsement is essential for the negotiation of an order bill.[68] If the holder transfers an order bill for value but omits to indorse it, the transferee acquires the same title as the transferor and in addition he acquires a right to have the transferor's indorsement (s.31(4)). If in such a case the transferor refuses to indorse, the court has power, under the Supreme Court Act 1981, s. 39, to order some other person to sign on his behalf. If the transferor's title is defective, the transferee cannot get a better one as a holder in due course unless he proves that he was unaware of the defect when he obtained the indorsement. If should be noted that section 31(4) only applies where the transfer was for value.

Indorsement

Section 32 contains the requirements for a valid indorsement. It provides that:

(1) It must be written on the bill itself and be signed by the indorser. The simple signature of the indorser on the bill, without additional words, is sufficient.

---

[67] The distinction is of importance in connection with the discharge of the bill by payment in due course. See s.59(3), *post*, p. 298.

[68] For an exception, see s.2 of the Cheques Act 1957, *post*, p. 324.

An indorsement written on an allonge, or on a "copy" of a bill issued or negotiated in a country where "copies" are recognised, is deemed to be written on the bill itself.

(2) It must be an indorsement of the entire bill. A partial indorsement, that is to say, an indorsement which purports to transfer to the indorsee a part only of the amount payable, or which purports to transfer the bill to two or more indorsees severally, does not operate as a negotiation of the bill.

(3) Where a bill is payable to the order of two or more payees or indorsees who are not partners all must indorse, unless the one indorsing has authority to indorse for the others.

(4) Where, in a bill payable to order, the payee or indorsee is wrongly designated, or his name is misspelt, he may indorse the bill as therein described, adding, if he thinks fit, his proper signature.

(5) Where there are two or more indorsements on a bill, each indorsement is deemed to have to have been made in the order in which it appears on the bill, until the contrary is proved.

These rules appear straightforward and self-explanatory. A partial indorsement (*e.g.* Pay X £80 of the within £100) does not operate as a negotiation, but it may operate as an authority entitling X to receive the £80 and to that extent he will have a lien on the bill.

Types of indorsement

Sections 33–35 deal with four different types of indorsement.

(1) **Indorsement in blank.** This is one which specifies no indorsee.

(2) **Special indorsement.** This specifies the person to whom or to whose order the bill is payable.

> *Example.* A draws a cheque in favour of B or order. B negotiates it to C by writing on the bank "Pay to the order of C. B." This is a special indorsement and the bill is still an order bill in the hands of C. C then negotiates it to D by simply writing on the back "C." This is an indorsement in blank and the bill is now a bearer bill, negotiable by delivery.

An indorsement in blank is risky. If A, the payee of an order bill, indorses it in blank and delivers it to B, a thief who steals it from B can pass a good title by delivery to a holder in due course. To eliminate this risk section 34(4) permits any holder to convert an indorsement in blank into a special indorsement by writing above the indorser's signature a direction to pay the bill to or to the order of himself or another person.

(3) **Conditional indorsement**. If the holder A indorses the bill "Pay B if he hands over the bill of lading" this is a conditional indorsement. It does not invalidate the bill, but section 33 provides that the payer may disregard the condition if he wishes, and payment to the indorsee is valid whether the condition is fulfilled or not. Alternatively the payer may, if he wishes, refuse payment until the condition is satisfied.

(4) **Restrictive indorsement.** Section 35 is largely self-explanatory. It provides that:

> (1) An indorsement is restrictive which prohibits the further negotiation of the bill, or which expresses that it is a mere authority to deal with the bill as thereby directed and not a transfer of the ownership thereof, as, for example, if a bill be indorsed "Pay D only," or "Pay D for the account of X," or "Pay D or order for collection."
>
> (2) A restrictive indorsement gives the indorsee the right to receive payment of the bill and to sue any party thereto that his indorser could have sued, but gives him no power to transfer his rights as indorsee unless it expressly authorises him to do so.
>
> (3) Where a restrictive indorsement authorises further transfer, all subsequent indorsees take the bill with the same rights and subject to the same liabilities as the first indorsee under the restrictive indorsement.
>
> *Examples of use.* If the payee of a cheque owes a debt to a supplier P who may be in a foreign country, the payee may wish to indorse the bill over to P's English agent A, and at the same time make it clear that A is not the beneficial owner. He can indorse "Pay A for the account of P." A can obtain payment, and must then account to P. He cannot transfer the bill. Again, suppose that a cheque is drawn on a French bank and sent to an English trader P. P may wish to authorise A (his French agent) to collect payment on his behalf. He can indorse "Pay A for collection" or "Pay A or order for collection." A can obtain payment and must then account to the person who authorised him to collect. If the words "or order" are used, A can transfer his rights (and liabilities) to another person, but such person cannot obtain a better title than A because the restriction on A's ownership passes with the cheque.

Irregular indorsement

This is not mentioned in the Act and is a matter largely of banking practice.[69] If, for example, John Smith, trading as "John

---

[69] *Arab Bank* v. *Ross, infra,* at p. 276, *per* Denning L.J. His Lordship suggested that an indorsement was irregular if it gave rise to doubt whether it was the indorsement of the person entitled to indorse.

Smith & Co." receives a cheque in that name and negotiates it by signing "Smith" and delivering it to Brown, the indorsement is valid but irregular. The result is that if Smith has a good title, Brown also gets a good title, but if Smith has a defective title Brown cannot get a better one by claiming to be a holder in due course, because the bill is not "complete and regular on the face of it." The significance of this will become apparent in the section which follows.

The holder in due course

It has already been seen that the holder of a bill is the payee or indorsee in possession of it or the bearer of a bearer bill (s.2) and that a holder for value is any holder who has given, or is deemed to have given, valuable consideration for a bill. A holder for value will always acquire the same title as his transferor, and if his transferor had an unimpeachable title no problem will arise. If, however, the title was in some way defective (as, for example, where a signature was procured by fraud, misrepresentation or duress, or where the consideration for a bill was illegal) a holder will only get a better title than his transferor if he is not merely a holder for value but a holder in due course. This exception to the general *nemo dat* rule lies at the very heart of the law relating to negotiable instruments, and section 29 which defines a holder in due course, is accordingly of the greatest importance. It reads as follows:

> (1) A holder in due course is a holder who has taken a bill, complete and regular on the face of it, under the following conditions; namely,
>
> (a) That he became the holder of it before it was overdue, and without notice that it had been previously dishonoured, if such was the fact.
>
> (b) That he took the bill in good faith and for value, and that at the time the bill was negotiated to him he had no notice of any defect in the title of the person who negotiated it.
>
> (2) In particular the title of a person who negotiates a bill is defective within the meaning of this Act when he obtained the bill, or the acceptance thereof, by fraud,[70] duress, or force and fear, or other

---

[70] The mere fact that the bill amounts to a "fraudulent preference" under the Companies Act 1948, s.320 is not "fraud" for this purpose (*Osterreichische Länderbank* v. *S'Elite* [1980] 3 W.L.R. 356.

unlawful means, or for an illegal consideration, or when he negotiates it in breach of faith, or under such circumstances as amount to a fraud.

Complete and regular

A blank cheque or bill would clearly not be "complete" before completion nor would a bill bearing an obvious uninitialled alteration. The word "face" includes the back of the bill. In *Arab Bank Ltd.* v. *Ross*[71]

> A promissory note made in favour of a firm "F and FN Co." was indorsed by one of the partners "F and FN" and discounted with the plaintiffs. The note was dishonoured and the plaintiffs sued the maker[72] of the note, claiming that they were holders in due course. The Court of Appeal held that (1) they were not holders in due course because the indorsement was irregular, but (2) despite this, they were holders for value and (3) as there was no defect in their title the maker had no defence to the claim.

Overdue

A bill payable on demand is deemed to be overdue when it appears on the face of it to have been in circulation for an unreasonable length of time, the question of unreasonableness being one of fact (s.36). Other bills are overdue when the due date for payment has passed. An overdue bill is only negotiable subject to equities.[73]

Good faith

Section 90 provides that:

> A thing is deemed to be done in good faith within the meaning of this Act, where it is in fact done honestly, whether it is done negligently or not.

Value

To be a holder in due course the holder must have given value himself[74] and cannot rely on value given by a prior party.

---

[71] [1952] 2 Q.B. 216; [1952] 1 All E.R. 709.

[72] The maker of a note corresponds to the acceptor of a bill, *post*, p. 327.

[73] An overdue bill must be distinguished from a "stale" cheque. It is the practice of bankers to treat a cheque as stale if it has been in circulation for six months. They will return the cheque unpaid marked "stale cheque."

[74] This includes value which is deemed to have been given under s.27(3). (*Barclays Bank Ltd.* v. *Astley Industrial Trust* [1970] 2 Q.B. 527; [1970] 1 All E.R. 719).

Without notice of defect

"Notice" in this context means actual notice of the defect or actual knowledge of facts giving rise to a suspicion that there may be a defect, coupled with a deliberate abstention from further inquiry.[75]

Payee

The words "at the time the bill was negotiated to him" indicate that a holder in due course must be someone to whom the bill is "negotiated." Accordingly, as a bill is not "negotiated" to the original payee but is merely issued to him, the House of Lords decided in *Jones* v. *Waring & Gillow*[76] that the original payee could not be a holder in due course. The facts in that case were as follows:

> X, who owed money to W, fraudulently induced J to draw a cheque in favour of W by representing that he was W's agent. He handed the cheque to W who obtained payment from J's bank. On discovering the facts J sued W for the amount of the cheque as money paid under a mistake of fact. The House of Lords held that as W were not holders in due course they were liable. [It will be appreciated that if X had obtained J's signature to a cheque in favour of X and had then negotiated the cheque to W, W would have been holders in due course and would have acquired a good title free from the fraud and could have kept the money.]

Burden of proof

Section 30(2) provides that:

> Every holder of a bill is prima facie deemed to be a holder in due course; but if in an action on a bill it is admitted or proved that the acceptance, issue, or subsequent negotiation of the bill is affected with fraud, duress, or force and fear, or illegality, the burden of proof is shifted, unless and until the holder proves that, subsequent to the alleged fraud or illegality, value has in good faith been given for the bill.[77]
>
> *Example.* A draws a cheque in favour of B in settlement of a gaming debt. Under the Gaming Acts B cannot sue A. B negotiates

---

[75] *Cf. Raphael* v. *Bank of England* (1855) 17 C.(N.S.) at p. 174, *per* Willes J.

[76] [1926] A.C. 670.

[77] In *Barclays Bank Ltd.* v. *Astley Industrial Trust* (*supra*), it was held that the bank could sidestep the presumption under s.30(2) and could base their claim on the fact that they satisfied the requirements of s.29. A claim based purely on ss.27(3) and 30(2) could break down if no value was given *after* the fraud.

to C. On presentation to A's bank the cheque is dishonoured. C can only sue A if he has a better title than B, *i.e.* if he is a holder in due course. Initially it is presumed that he is one, but once A pleads the Gaming Acts the onus shifts to C to prove that he gave value for the bill without notice of its illegality. In other words he must prove that he is a holder in due course.

Rights of holder in due course

By section 38(2) a holder in due course:

> holds the bill free from any defect of title of prior parties, as well as from mere personal defences available to prior parties among themselves and may enforce payment against all parties liable on the bill.

Rights of subsequent parties

Section 29(3) provides:

> A holder (whether for value or not), who derives his title to a bill through a holder in due course, and who is not himself a party to any fraud or illegality affecting it, has all the rights of that holder in due course as regards the acceptor and all parties to the bill prior to that holder.

This subsection is similar to section 27(2). That subsection permits a holder for value to transmit his rights to subsequent parties, while section 29(3) enables a holder in due course to do likewise.

> If, for example, A, having obtained a cheque by fraud, negotiates it to B who is a holder in due course, and B negotiates it as a gift to C who knows of the original fraud, C can take over the mantle of B as a holder in due course and can enforce the cheque against any person whom B could have sued. If, however, C was a party to the fraud he could not enforce the cheque.

Effect of forged indorsements

Order bills

It has been seen that title to an order bill passes by indorsement completed by delivery and that a forged indorsement (like any other forged signature) is wholly inoperative. It follows that where an order bill bears the forgery of an essential indorsement, no subsequent party can acquire a title to the bill. The holder in due course provisions do not apply here, because the person in possession of such a bill is not even a holder.[78]

> *Example.* A draws a bill on B in favour of C or order. B accepts. C negotiates to D. A thief steals the bill, forges D's indorsement and negotiates the bill to E who indorses it over to F. Viewed pictorially the chain of title is:
>
> C———▶D   E———▶F
>
> There is clearly a break in the chain and accordingly D is still the true owner. He can recover the bill from F, by suing him in tort if necessary, and can enforce the bill against A, B and C.[79] It is immaterial that F took the bill in good faith for value without notice of the forgery.

Although no title can pass under a forged indorsement, persons subsequent to the forgery may have certain rights as between themselves. Section 55(2) provides, *inter alia*, that the indorser of a bill by indorsing it:

> is precluded from denying to a holder in due course the genuineness and regularity in all respects of the drawer's signature and all previous indorsements.

The term "holder in due course" is used here in a rather special sense as meaning "the person who would be a holder in due course but for the forgery." In the example F could sue E, because by section 55 E is estopped from setting up the forgery of D's indorsement. The result is the usual one that the ultimate loss falls on the victim of the fraud, *i.e.* in this case E who will have no rights at all except an action against the thief which may well be valueless.

Bearer bills

A forged indorsement on a bearer bill is, of course, completely superfluous, since such a bill does not require indorsement, and it does not prevent a holder in due course acquiring a title free from prior defects. In the ordinary case, of course, no thief of a bearer bill is going to go to the trouble of forging an unnecessary indorsement. The only cases where such a problem has arisen have

---

[78] For the definition of holder see *ante*, p. 258.

[79] If he cannot find the bill he can take advantage of the lost bill provisions of ss.69 and 70, *post*, p. 302. The position in the case of a cheque is exactly the same except of course, that there is no "acceptor." Thus D on recovering the cheque could sue A (drawer) and C (indorser) if the cheque was not met on presentation.

been those where a bill appeared on the face of it to be an order bill, but the payee was either fictitious or non-existing. Section 7(3) provides that such a bill may be treated as payable to bearer. This subsection has been considered in a number of cases in which innocent transferees have taken bills bearing forged indorsements. The following propositions can be gleaned from the cases:

(1) If the drawer signs a bill in favour of a person whose existence is entirely unknown to him, the payee is non-existing, and the bill is a bearer bill. In *Clutton* v. *Attenborough*[80]

> A fraudulent clerk wrote out a cheque in favour of B, a name he had invented, and persuaded his employer to sign it by falsely representing that "B" had done work for the firm. The clerk forged B's indorsement and negotiated the cheque to the defendant who obtained payment from the employer's bank. In an action by the employer against the defendant to recover the money, the House of Lords held that (a) the payee was non-existing so that the bill was a bearer bill, and (2) the defendant was a holder in due course and was entitled to retain the money.

(2) If the payee is a real person known to the drawer, he is fictitious if the drawer inserted his name as a pretence and did not intend him to receive payment. In *Bank of England* v. *Vagliano Brothers*[81]:

> V Bros. who were in the habit of accepting bills of exchange drawn by A in favour of C & Co., received what appeared to be such a bill and accepted it. In fact, the name of the drawer had been written in by a fraudulent clerk, who then proceeded to forge the indorsement of C & C. and obtained payment from V Bros.' bankers. The question of whether the bankers could debit V Bros.' account turned on whether the bills were payable to bearer. The House of Lords held that they were, because the drawer (*i.e.* the clerk) never intended C & Co. to receive payment, with the result that C & Co. were fictitious.

This case was distinguished in *Vinden* v. *Hughes*[82]:

> A clerk fraudulently represented to his employers that money was due to certain customers, who were well known to the employers. In

---

[80] [1897] A.C. 90.
[81] [1891] A.C. 107.
[82] [1905] 1 K.B. 795, followed in *North and South Wales Bank* v. *Macbeth* [1908] A.C. 137. It is thought that the principle in *Vagliano's* case can never apply to a cheque, since the drawer of a cheque must always intend the payee to receive payment. Thus s.7(3) would only apply in the case of a cheque if the payee was non-existent.

fact no money was due. The employers drew the cheques, and the clerk forged the payees' indorsements and negotiated them to the defendants. It was held that as the drawer had intended the payees to receive payment, the payees were not fictitious. Consequently the defendants held order bills, and the forged indorsements meant that they had no title.

Rights of the holder

Section 38 summarises much of what has been said before:

The rights and powers of the holder of a bill are as follows:

(1) He may sue on the bill in his own name.

(2) Where he is a holder in due course he holds the bill free from any defect or title of prior parties, as well as from mere personal defences available to prior parties among themselves, and may enforce payment against all parties liable on the bill.

(3) Where his title is defective (a) if he negotiates the bill to a holder in due course, that holder obtains a good and complete title to the bill, and (b) if he obtains payment of the bill the person who pays him in due course gets a valid discharge for the bill.

Duties of the holder

It is now necessary to examine sections 39–52 which impose four duties on the holder, namely:

(a) A duty to present for acceptance.[83]

(b) A duty to present for payment.

(c) A duty to give notice of dishonour.

(d) A duty to note and protest.

The sections dealing with these matters are detailed but straightforward.

Duty to present for acceptance

This duty only arises where the holder receives a bill (other than a cheque) which has not yet been accepted. In such a case he usually presents the bill to the drawee for his acceptance, and then when the bill matures he presents it again, this time for payment. If, however, the bill is payable on demand, there is clearly no point in making a formal presentation for acceptance, followed immediately by a presentation for payment, and in such a case the

---

[83] This duty does not of course apply to cheques, because cheques are not accepted.

holder simply presents the bill for payment. Accordingly the rules about to be discussed only apply to time bills.

The effect of section 39 is that presentation for acceptance is only essential[84] in three cases:

(1) Where a bill is payable after sight, presentation for acceptance is necessary to fix the maturity of the instrument (s.39(1)).

(2) Where a bill is drawn payable elsewhere than at the residence or place of business of the drawee.

(3) Where it expressly stipulates that it shall be presented for acceptance (s.39(2)).

Even if a time bill falls outside section 39, there are two very good reasons why it should be presented for acceptance. The first is that once the drawee accepts he becomes liable. The second is that a refusal to accept gives the holder an immediate right of recourse against prior parties[85] without having to wait for the date of maturity.

Failure to present. Section 40 provides that where a bill payable after sight is negotiated, the holder must either present it for acceptance or negotiate it within a reasonable time and that if he does not do so the drawer and all indorsers prior to that holder are discharged. In deciding what is a reasonable time regard must be had to the nature of the bill, the usage of trade with respect to similar bills and the facts of the particular case.

In the other two cases where presentment is essential (*i.e.* cases (2) and (3) above) the holder cannot present the bill for payment until he has presented it for acceptance. It will be seen shortly that a failure to make a due presentation for payment discharges the drawer and all prior indorsers.

Rules as to presentment. Section 41(1) requires presentment to be made to the drawee (or, if dead, to his personal representative) or to his authorised agent. It must be made:

(a) by or on behalf of the holder,

(b) at a reasonable hour,

(c) on a business day,

(d) before the bill is overdue.

---

[84] Unless excused (see below).
[85] *e.g.* the drawer and any indorser. See s.55, *post,* p. 293.

A bill addressed to two or more drawees (not being partners) must be presented to all of them, unless one has authority to accept on behalf of all in which case presentation to that one is sufficient.

A presentation through the post is sufficient, if authorised by agreement or usage.

Excuses. Section 41(2) specifies certain circumstances in which presentment is excused. They include cases where the drawee is bankrupt, fictitious or without capacity, or where after the exercise of reasonable diligence presentment cannot be effected.

Acceptance. It has already been seen that once the drawee accepts he becomes known as the acceptor and is primarily liable to pay the bill.

Non-acceptance. Section 42 provides that:

> When a bill is duly presented for acceptance and is not accepted within the customary time,[86] the person presenting it must treat it as dishonoured by non-acceptance. If he does not, the holder shall lose his right of recourse against the drawer and indorsers.

Further by section 43(1):

> A bill is dishonoured by non-acceptance—
> (a) When it is duly presented for acceptance, and such an acceptance as is prescribed by this Act is refused or cannot be obtained; or
> (b) When presentment for acceptance is excused and the bill is not accepted.

Qualified acceptance. It will be recalled that a qualified acceptance is one which varies the operation of the bill as drawn.[87] Where the holder receives a qualified acceptance, section 44 provides that he may either refuse it and treat the bill as dishonoured by non-acceptance, or he may take it. With one exception, the holder is well advised to refuse a qualified acceptance, because if he takes it any drawer or indorser is discharged from liability unless he has expressly or impliedly authorised the holder to take a qualified acceptance, or unless he

---

[86] 24 hours.

[87] Thus it may be conditional, partial, local, qualified as to time or acceptance by one or more drawees but not all (see *ante*, pp. 260–261).

subsequently assents thereto (s.44(2)). To discover whether the drawer and any indorser are prepared to assent to the qualified acceptance the holder must give them notice. Section 44(3) provides that a person receiving such notice who does not notify his dissent within a reasonable time is deemed to have assented.

The one exception concerns partial acceptance. In this case the holder is still perfectly free to refuse it but if he decides to take it and gives due notice of having done so, the other parties remain liable in full whether they consent or not.

> *Example.* A draws on B a bill for £200 payable to C 30 days after date. C indorses to D. On presentation by D, B accepts "as to £150 only." D can refuse this, in which case he can serve notice of dishonour and then proceed against A (as drawer) and C (as indorser). Alternatively he may take the partial acceptance. If he does this and gives notice thereof to A and C, he can hold them liable immediately for the £50 for which the bill has been dishonoured, and they will also remain liable for the other £150 in the event of non-payment by B.

Duty to present for payment

General. It will be recalled that presentation for acceptance is only necessary in three cases and that it does not apply to bills payable on demand. Presentation for payment, on the other hand, is essential for all bills (including cheques) and is essential in every case, unless excused.

Failure to present. If a bill is not duly presented, the drawer and indorsers are discharged (s.45). The acceptor, however, is not discharged (s.52), because it is his duty to seek out his creditor and pay him.

Rules as to presentment.[88] These rules, which are set out in section 45, are fairly similar to those governing presentment for acceptance, except that whereas presentment for acceptance is essentially personal, presentment for payment is essentially local. The bill must be presented at "the proper place," which is defined in the Act as follows:

---

[88] See *Ringham* v. *Hackett, The Times* February 9, 1980 where the Court of Appeal gave a broad interpretation to the section by holding that a crossed cheque could be validly presented by the holder personally at the paying bank.

Section 45(4):

A bill is presented at the proper place:

(a) Where a place of payment is specified in the bill[89] and the bill is there presented.

(b) Where no place of payment is specified, but the address of the drawee or acceptor is given in the bill, and the bill is there presented.

(c) Where no place of payment is specified and no address given, and the bill is presented at the drawee's or acceptor's place of business if known, and if not, at his ordinary residence if known.

(d) In any other case if presented to the drawee or acceptor wherever he can be found, or if presented at his last known place of business or residence.

Section 45(5):

Where a bill is presented at the proper place, and after the exercise of reasonable diligence no person authorised to pay or refuse payment can be found there, no further presentment to the drawee or acceptor is required.

Time. Where a bill is payable on demand, it must be presented for payment within a reasonable time of issue to make the drawer liable and within a reasonable time of indorsement to make the indorsers liable (s.45(2)). This provision is modified with regard to the drawer[90] of a cheque, because section 74 provides that:

Subject to the provisions of this Act—

(1) Where a cheque is not presented for payment within a reasonable time of its issue, and the drawer or the person on whose account it is drawn had the right at the time of such presentment at between him and the banker to have the cheque paid and suffers actual damage through the delay, he is discharged to the extent of such damage, that is to say, to the extent to which such drawer or person is a creditor of such banker to a larger amount than he would have been had such cheque been paid.

(2) In determining what is a reasonable time regard shall be had to the nature of the instrument, the usage of trade and of bankers, and the facts of the particular case.

---

[89] This includes the acceptance, so that if the bill is accepted "payable at National Provincial Bank, Fleet Street," it must be presented there. *Yeoman Credit Ltd.* v. *Gregory* [1963] 1 W.L.R. 343; [1963] 1 All E.R. 245.

[90] But not an indorser—if the chque is not presented within a reasonable time of indorsement, he is discharged.

(3) The holder of such cheque as to which such drawer or person is discharged shall be a creditor, in lieu of such drawer or person, of such banker to the extent of such discharge, and entitled to recover the amount from him.

The reason for this difference between bills and cheques is that the drawer of a bill is a mere guarantor for the debtor (*i.e.* the acceptor), whereas the drawer of a cheque usually draws it to pay his own debt. The effect of section 74 is that the drawer of a cheque will be liable on his signature for the normal limitation period, *i.e.* six years, and he will only be discharged before then if the holder fails to present for payment within a reasonable time and the drawer suffers actual damage through the delay. This will seldom occur but an example might arise where D draws a cheque for £1,000 in favour of P when there is enough money at D's bank to cover the cheque. P delays in presenting for payment beyond a reasonable time and when he does finally present, the bank has gone into liquidation and is only paying a dividend of 25p in the £ (*i.e.* £750 of D's money has been lost). The effect of section 74, is that this loss, quite rightly, falls on P. D must pay to P the £250 which he receives from the liquidator and is discharged as to the balance of the cheque. P becomes a creditor of the bank to the extent of that balance, *i.e.* £750.

Where a bill is not payable on demand, it must be presented on[91] the day it falls due (s.45(1). The bill falls due on the last day of the period or, if this is a non-business day on the first business day thereafter. Thus a bill dated January 1, and payable "30 days after date" will be due and payable on January 31 if this is a business day (Banking and Financial Dealings Act 1971, s.3 which replaces section 14 of the Bills of Exchange Act).

It is important to distinguish between a bill payable "*at* sight" which is a bill payable on demand (*ante*, p. 254) and one payable "*after* sight" which is a time bill (*ibid.*).

Once the due date has passed, the bill is said to be overdue, and failure to present on that date discharges the drawer and indorsers,[92] unless the holder can bring himself within the

---

[91] Presentation *before* the due date is ineffective (*Hamilton Finance Co. Ltd.* v. *Coverley Westray Walbaum & Tosetti Ltd.* [1969] 1 Lloyd's Rep. 53).

[92] Even if they have suffered no damage: *Yeoman Credit Ltd.* v. *Gregory* [1963] 1 W.L.R. 343, 354; [1963] 1 All E.R. 245, 255 *per* Megaw J. It will be recalled that once a bill is overdue it cannot be negotiated to a holder in due course (*ante*, p. 275).

exemptive provisions of section 46, which must now be considered.

Delay and excuses. Delay in making presentment for payment is excused when the delay is caused by circumstances beyond the control of the holder and not imputable to his default, misconduct or negligence. When the cause of delay ceases to operate, presentment must be made with reasonable diligence (s.46(1)). Further, in some cases presentment is dispensed with altogether as where, for example, after the exercise of reasonable diligence presentment cannot be effected, or where the drawee is fictitious (s.46(2)). In *Cornelius* v. *Banque Franco-Serbe*[93]:

> A bill was drawn on a bank in Amsterdam, and was sent to the plaintiff in England. Shortly afterwards Amsterdam was occupied by the German forces. It was held that (quite apart from any question of illegality) presentation for payment was excused by section 46(2).

The section also provides that, as regards the drawer, the duty to present is dispensed with if the drawee owes no duty to the drawer to pay the bill.

Non-payment. Section 47(1) provides that:

> A bill is dishonoured by non-payment (*a*) when it is duly presented for payment and payment is refused or cannot be obtained, or (*b*) when presentment is excused and the bill is overdue and unpaid.

Such dishonour gives the holder an immediate right of recourse against the drawer and indorsers, in the same way as dishonour by non-acceptance. In either case, before proceeding further the holder must generally serve notice of dishonour under the provisions set out below.

Duty to give notice of dishonour[94]
Section 48 provides that:

> Subject to the provisions of this Act, when a bill has been dishonoured by non-acceptance or by non-payment, notice of dishonour must be given to the drawer and each indorser, and any drawer or indorser to whom such notice is not given is discharged:

---

[93] [1942] 1 K.B. 29; [1941] 2 All E.R. 728.
[94] This duty applies to cheques, although it is frequently excused under s.50 (see *post*, p. 290).

Provided that—

(1) Where a bill is dishonoured by non-acceptance, and notice of dishonour is not given, the rights of a holder in due course subsequent to the omission, shall not be prejudiced by the omission.

(2) Where a bill is dishonoured by non-acceptance and due notice of dishonour is given, it shall not be necessary to give notice of a subsequent dishonour by non-payment unless the bill shall in the meantime have been accepted.

If a bill drawn by A on B in favour of C and indorsed to D is dishonoured by non-acceptance, D must give notice of dishonour to A and to C before enforcing his rights against them. If he fails to give due notice, A and C will be discharged, but if subsequently he negotiates the bill to a holder in due course,[95] the holder in due course can sue A and C and is not prejudiced by D's failure to serve due notice.

Notice can be given by or on behalf of the holder (in which case it enures for the benefit of all subsequent holders and all prior indorsers who have a right of recourse against the party to whom it is given) or it can be given by or on behalf of an indorser who at the time of giving it is himself liable on the bill (in which case it enures for the benefit of the holder and for all indorsers subsequent to the party to whom it is given) (s.49(1)(3)(4)).

The notice can be oral or in writing, or partly oral and partly in writing, and the mere return of a dishonoured bill to the drawer or an indorser[96] is deemed, in point of form, to be a sufficient notice (s.49(5)(6)(7)).

The time for giving notice is dealt with in section 49(12) which provides that:

> The notice may be given as soon as the bill is dishonoured and must be given within a reasonable time thereafter.
>
> In the absence of special circumstances notice is not deemed to have been given within a reasonable time, unless—
>
> (a) where the person giving and the person to receive notice reside in the same place, the notice is given or sent off in time to reach the latter on the day after the dishonour of the bill.
>
> (b) where the person giving and the person to receive notice reside in different places, the notice is sent off on the day after the

---

[95] To be a holder in due course he must, of course, take the bill "without notice that it had been previously dishonoured" (s.29 *ante*, p. 275). If the bill has been dishonoured by non-payment, there cannot be a subsequent holder in due course, because the bill is overdue.

[96] This practice is commonly followed by collecting banks.

dishonour of the bill, if there be a post at a convenient hour on that day, and if there be no such post on that day then by the next post thereafter.

Until 1969 there was not a single modern authority on the meaning of the words "reside in the same place." This can be explained partly by the decline in the use of time bills, and partly by the fact that notice of dishonour is seldom necessary in practice in the case of cheques (see s.50(2)(*c*), below). When the point eventually came before MacKenna J. he considered that the two parties resided at the same place if it was reasonable in all the circumstances to deliver the notice by hand instead of relying on the post.[97]

If notice is required, the rules as to time must be strictly complied with, and in the absence of special circumstances a delay of as little as one day may deprive the holder of his rights against drawer and indorsers.[98] In applying these rules the House of Lords has recently held that if the notice is posted it will be treated as given when it is received. If the notice is received *before* the bill has been dishonoured this will be ineffective and the holder will lose his rights. On the other hand the mere fact of *posting* the notice before the day of actual dishonour is not fatal.[99]

To obtain complete protection the holder should serve notice of dishonour on all prior parties, but if he only gives notice to one party (as, for example, his own immediate indorser) that party has the same time, as from the receipt of notice, to give notice to prior parties as the holder had on dishonour (s.49(14)). Thus if A draws a bill on B in favour of C who indorses to D (all residing in the same place) and B fails to accept on May 1, and D serves notice on C which reaches him on May 2, C has a further 24 hours (or longer if there are special circumstances) in which to give notice to A.

Where a notice of dishonour is duly addressed and posted, the sender is deemed to have given due notice, notwithstanding any miscarriage by the post office (s.49(15)).

---

[97] *Hamilton Finance Co. Ltd.* v. *Coverley Westray Walbaum & Tosetti Ltd.* [1959] 1 Lloyd's Rep. 53.

[98] *Yeoman Credit Ltd.* v. *Gregory, supra.* As to special circumstances see *Lombard Banking Co. Ltd.* v. *Central Garage and Engineering Co. Ltd.* [1963] 1 Q.B. 220; [1962] 2 All E.R. 949.

[99] *Eaglehill Ltd.* v. *J. Needham Builders Ltd.* [1973] A.C. 992; [1972] 3 W.L.R. 789.

Delay and excuses. Section 50 specifies the circumstances in which delay in giving notice is excused and in which the giving of notice is excused altogether. Thus the holder is excused if after the exercise of reasonable diligence, notice cannot be given or does not reach the person sought to be charged (s.50(2)(a)). The section also dispenses with the need for notice to be given to the drawer:

(1) Where the drawer and the drawee are the same person.[1]

(2) Where the drawee is fictitious or without capacity.[1]

(3) Where the drawer is the person to whom the bill is presented for payment.

(4) Where the drawee or acceptor is as between himself and the drawer under no obligation to accept or pay the bill.[2]

(5) Where the drawer has countermanded payment (s.50(2)(c)).

(6) Where the drawer has expressly or impliedly waived the right to notice.[3]

Acceptor. Failure to give notice of dishonour does not discharge the acceptor.

Duty to note and protest the bill

In many foreign countries a bill must be noted and protested by a notary public if it has been dishonoured. In English law, however, noting and protest is only necessary in a few cases, of which the most important is the dishonour of a foreign bill. The object of noting and protesting is to obtain formal evidence of dishonour which will be universally recognised and respected.

Noting. Where a bill has been dishonoured, the holder takes it to a notary public who re-presents the bill. If it is again dishonoured he "notes" on the bill the date, a reference to his register, the noting charges and his initials, and he attaches a ticket stating the answer given to the notary's clerk when presentment was made.

---

[1] The holder can treat such an instrument as a bill of exchange or as a promissory note made by the drawer (*ante*, p. 253).

[2] Thus if a cheque is countermanded or is drawn on a bank at which the drawer had insufficient funds, notice of dishonour need not be given to the drawer.

[3] The drawer and any indorser may expressly waive some or all of the holder's duties (s.16(2)).

Protest. This is a formal declaration signed by the notary public and giving details of the re-presentation and the result (s.51(7)).

Form. The form of a protest is as follows:

> On the—day of— I AB public notary by lawful authority and sworn, dwelling in Blanktown in the county of—in the United Kingdom of Great Britain and Northern Ireland at the request of CD did exhibit the original bill of exchange whereof a true copy is on the other side written unto EP at his business premises, the person upon whom the same is drawn, and demanded acceptance thereof and he answered that he would not accept.
>
> Wherefore I, the said notary, at the request aforesaid, did and do by these presents protest against the drawer of the said bill and all other parties thereto and all others concerned for all costs of exchange, re-exchange and all costs, damages and interest, present and to come, for want of acceptance of the said bill. Thus protested in the presence of G.H and J.K. witnesses.
>
> Which I attest
MM
>
> Notary public of—

Time. Noting must take place on the day of dishonour or on the following business day. Protest can take place later (s.93).

Where required. Noting and protest is only essential

(1) Where a foreign bill, appearing on the face of it to be such, is dishonoured (s.51(2)).[4]

(2) Before resorting for payment to a referee in case of need (see *post*, p. 295).

(3) Before a bill can be accepted or paid for honour (see *post*, pp. 301–302).

Foreign bills. By section 4:

> (1) An inland bill is a bill which is or on the face of it purports to be (*a*) both drawn and payable within the British Islands, or (*b*) drawn within the British Islands upon some person resident therein. Any other bill is a foreign bill.
>
> For the purposes of this Act "British Islands" mean any part of the United Kingdom of Great Britain and Ireland, the islands of Man, Guernsey, Jersey, Alderney, and Sark, and the islands adjacent to any of them being part of the dominions of Her Majesty.

---

[4] The reason why noting and protest are made essential in this case is to bring English law into line with the many foreign legal systems under which protest is essential. In practice an English collecting bank will take its customer's instructions on noting and protesting before it collects a cheque drawn on an overseas bank.

(2) Unless the contrary appear on the face of the bill the holder may treat it as an inland bill.

Failure to protest. Failure to note and protest a foreign bill discharges the drawer and indorsers (s.51(2)) unless protest is excused.

Delay and excuses. Section 51(9) provides that:

> Protest is dispensed with by any circumstance which would dispense with notice of dishonour. Delay in noting or protesting is excused when the delay is caused by circumstances beyond the control of the holder, and not imputable to his default, misconduct, or negligence. When the cause of delay ceases to operate the bill must be noted or protested with reasonable diligence.

Liability of parties

Nature of liability

A bill of exchange is designed to be freely transferable, *i.e.* the transferee should be able to regard it as cash. Accordingly the defences which can be raised are very limited and the liabilities discussed below are very different from those arising under the original transaction.

> Example. Suppose that B. buys goods from S and pays by accepting a bill of exchange (or by drawing a cheque). B finds that the goods are defective and refuses to honour the bill of exchange. Unless there is a total failure of consideration he cannot raise the defects either as a defence or by way of set-off or counterclaim.[5] It follows that S. can obtain judgment on the bill and can enforce that judgment unless the court grants a stay of execution.

Drawee

A drawee who does not accept is not liable on the bill (s.53).[6] He may, of course, be liable on the original debt for which the bill was drawn or on a collateral contract (*e.g.* cheque card).

Acceptor

By section 54:

---

[5] *Nova (Jersey) Knit* v. *Kammgarn Spinnerei* [1977] 1 W.L.R. 713 H.L.
[6] s.23, *ante*, p. 262.

The acceptor of a bill, by accepting it—

(1) Engages that he will pay it according to the tenor of his acceptance:

(2) Is precluded from denying to a holder in due course:

(*a*) The existence of the drawer, the genuineness of his signature, and his capacity and authority to draw the bill;

(*b*) In the case of a bill payable to drawer's order, the then capacity of the drawer to indorse, but not the genuineness or validity of his indorsement;

(*c*) In the case of a bill payable to the order of a third person, the existence of the payee and his then capacity to indorse, but not the genuineness or validity of his indorsement.

Operation of section 54(2)

A bill appearing to be drawn by A on B in favour of C is accepted by B. In fact C (the payee) has forged A's signature as drawer. C negotiates the instrument to D. If D is a holder in due course, D can sue B, because B is estopped from setting up the forgery. [Technically, of course, the instrument is not a bill at all, since it is not signed by the person giving it (*ante*, p. 253), but in reading section 54(2) the word "bill" must be read as "instrument which would be a bill but for the forgery."]

Drawer

By section 55(1):

The drawer of a bill by drawing it—

(*a*) Engages that on due presentment it shall be accepted and paid according to its tenor, and that if it be dishonoured he will compensate the holder or any indorser who is compelled to pay it, provided that the requisite proceedings on dishonour be duly taken;

(*b*) Is precluded from denying to a holder in due course the existence of the payee and his then capacity to indorse.

Indorser

By section 55(2):

The indorser of a bill by indorsing it—

(*a*) Engages that on due presentment it shall be accepted and paid according to its tenor, and that if it be dishonoured he will compensate the holder or a subsequent indorser who is compelled to pay it, provided that the requisite proceedings on dishonour be duly taken;

(*b*) Is precluded from denying to a holder in due course the genuineness and regularity in all respects of the drawer's signature and all previous indorsements;

(*c*) Is precluded from denying to his immediate or a subsequent indorsee that the bill was at the time of his indorsement a valid and subsisting bill, and that he had then a good title thereto.

If in the previous example D had indorsed to E who was also a holder in due course, E could have sued B under section 54(2) and D under section 55(2). For another illustration where an indorser is estopped from denying the validity of previous indorsements the reader is referred back to pp. 278–279.

Section 55 enables the holder to sue the drawer and indorsers, and if an indorser is compelled to pay, he can in turn sue parties prior to himself, and the liability will pass down the line until it reaches the drawer.

> *Example.* A draws on B for £100 in favour of C or order and the bill passes by special indorsement to D, E and F. If B fails to accept, F can sue E, who can sue D, who can sue C, who can sue A. F of course is not bound to take this course, because A, C, D and E are all liable to him.[7]

Exclusion

Section 16(1) provides that the drawer and any indorser can add words expressly limiting or excluding his liability on the bill. Common expressions which have this effect are "*sans recours*" or "without recourse to me."

A rather similar provision relating to indorsement is to be found in section 31(5):

> Where any person is under obligation to indorse a bill in a representative capacity, he may indorse the bill in such terms as to negative personal liability.

This section could, for example, be used where personal representatives are compelled to indorse a cheque on behalf of the estate.[8] This could happen if the deceased had transferred an

---

[7] This illustration would be equally applicable to a cheque if B were A's bank who refused to honour the cheque.

[8] Another example would be where solicitors receive a cheque in their favour from a client which they endorse over "sans recours" to a third party to avoid the delay of clearing the client's cheque before they send their own cheque to the third party.

unindorsed order cheque either for value (as to which see section 31(4), *ante*, p. 272), or as a valid *donatio mortis causa*. The words "so far as assets only" are sometimes used.

Transferor by delivery

By section 58:

> (1) Where the holder of a bill payable to bearer negotiates it by delivery without indorsing it, he is called a "transferor by delivery."
>
> (2) A transferor by delivery is not liable on the instrument.
>
> (3) A transferor by delivery who negotiates a bill thereby warrants to his immediate transferee being a holder for value that the bill is what it purports to be, that he has a right to transfer it, and that at the time of transfer he is not aware of any fact which renders it valueless.[9]
>
> *Example.* A draws a cheque in favour of B or order. B indorses it in blank and hands it to C who transfers it for value to D who transfers it for value to E. Neither C nor D indorses the cheque, which on presentation at A's bank is dishonoured. E can sue A (section 55(1)(*a*)), and he can also sue B on his indorsement (section 55(2)(*a*)). He cannot sue C because C has not signed the bill and because he is not C's *immediate* transferee. E cannot sue D on the bill but he will be able to sue him under section 58, if he can prove that D has broken one of the three warranties. Thus if D knew at the time of the transfer that the bill was valueless, he will be liable. It will be appreciated that the liability of a transferor by delivery is less stringent than that of an indorser.[10]

Referee in case of need

This person is strictly not a party to the bill at all (since he does not sign it) but as his name sometimes appears on a bill it might be convenient to mention him at this point. Section 15 provides that:

> The drawer of a bill and any indorser may insert therein the name of a person to whom the holder may resort in case of need, that is to say, in case the bill is dishonoured by non-acceptance or non-payment. Such person is called the referee in case of need. It is in the option of the holder to resort to the referee in case of need or not as he may think fit.

The bill must generally be protested for dishonour before being presented to the referee for payment (s.67(2)).

---

[9] This section should not be confused with s.31(4) which relates to unindorsed order bills.

[10] If the transferee insists on indorsement, the transferor will undertake the stricter indorser liability in favour of a holder in due course (s.56).

The reader may recall the first example in this chapter in which goods were shipped to Schmidt in Bonn and the bill of lading was released to him on his accepting the bill of exchange. This form of export finance may run into difficulties where the drawee refuses to accept the bill of exchange, in which case the goods must be shipped back to the seller. To avoid this, the seller, as drawer, may insert in the bill the name of a referee in case of need, who may perhaps be the seller's agent in the buyer's country. If, on dishonour by the drawee, the holder approaches the referee, the latter may pay it, obtain the shipping documents and dispose of the goods locally.

Measure of damages[11]

Section 57 provides that:

> Where a bill is dishonoured, the measure of damages which shall be deemed to be liquidated damages, shall be as follows:
>
> (1) The holder may recover from any party liable on the bill, and the drawer who has been compelled to pay the bill may recover from the acceptor, and an indorser who has been compelled to pay the bill may recover from the acceptor or from the drawer, or from a prior indorser—
>
> (*a*) The amount of the bill:
>
> (*b*) Interest thereon from the time of presentment for payment if the bill is payable on demand, and from the maturity of the bill in any other case:
>
> (*c*) The expenses of noting, or, when protest is necessary, and the protest has been extended, the expenses of protest.
>
> (2) [Repealed by section 4 of the Administration of Justice Act 1977].[12]
>
> (3) Where by this Act interest may be recovered as damages, such interest may, if justice require it, be withheld wholly or in part, and where a bill is expressed to be payable with interest at a given rate, interest as damages may or may not be given at the same rate as interest proper.

This section is straightforward. It will be appreciated that the expenses of protest will normally only be recoverable in practice

---

[11] In the case of a cheque this section regulates the damages recoverable as between the drawer, the payee and subsequent holders. It does not, however, regulate damages for breach of the contractual duties owed by a banker to his customer (see *post*, p. 307).

[12] The subsection dealt with bills dishonoured abroad and the purpose of the repeal was to enable the court to exercise its power to give judgment in a foreign currency (as to which see *post*, p. 526).

where a foreign bill is dishonoured, whereas the (much lighter) noting expenses can be recovered on the dishonour of any bill, whether inland or foreign.

Interest

If the bill specifies payment of interest, *e.g.* "Pay X £100 with interest at 10 per cent." such interest is recoverable as of right as a debt.[13] In other cases, the court may award interest, as part of the damages and in practice the rate will be the current rate for the High Court Short-Term Investment Account (presently 12 per cent.) from the date of dishonour until judgment. Interest will not be awarded, however, unless the failure to pay involves breach of duty.[14]

Discharge of bill

A bill is said to be discharged when all rights of action on it are extinguished.

Payment in due course

The overwhelming majority of bills (including cheques) are discharged in this way. Section 59 provides that:

(1) A bill is discharged by payment in due course by or on behalf of the drawee or acceptor.

"Payment in due course" means payment made at or after the maturity of the bill to the holder thereof in good faith and without notice that his title to the bill is defective.

(2) Subject to the provisions hereinafter contained, when a bill is paid by the drawer or an indorser it is not discharged; but

(*a*) Where a bill payable to, or to the order of, a third party is paid by the drawer, the drawer may enforce payment thereof against the acceptor, but may not re-issue the bill.

(*b*) Where a bill is paid by an indorser, or where a bill payable to drawer's order is paid by the drawer, the party paying it is remitted to his former rights as regards the acceptor or antecedent parties, and he may, if he thinks fit, strike out his own and subsequent indorsements, and again negotiate the bill.

---

[13] Contrast *Cato* v. *Cato* (1972) 116 S.J. 138 where an American promissory note provided for an attorney's fee of 15 per cent. to be paid on default; it was held that by English law such a clause was a penalty and irrecoverable in an action brought in England.

[14] *N.V. Ledeboter* v. *Hibbert* [1947] K.B. 964, where a bill payable in 1940 was not paid until 1945, the reason being that the holder was in enemy-occupied territory with the result that payment would have been a criminal offence.

> (3) Where an accommodation bill is paid in due course by the party accommodated the bill is discharged.

The bill must be paid by or on behalf of the drawee or (in the case of an accommodation bill) by the party accommodated, so that in the example on p. 271 payment by A would discharge the bill. Payment by the accommodation acceptor would not discharge the bill because he would still have a right to claim indemnity from the party whom he accommodated.

The bill must be paid to the holder. Thus:

> A draws a bearer bill and hands it to B. It is accepted by C. A thief steals the bill. C pays the thief at maturity, in good faith and without notice of the theft. C has paid the holder and the bill is discharged. B's only right is to sue the thief for conversion or for money had and received.[15]

If, in the example, the bill had been an order bill payable to B, stolen by D and transferred to E by means of a forged indorsement, a payment by C to E would not have discharged the bill, because E was not the holder.[16] On these facts, B the true owner could, of course, sue D and E for conversion, but in addition he could enforce the bill against C. The question of whether C could recover the money from E as money paid under a mistake of fact would depend on how quickly he acted, because money can only be recovered if prompt action is taken.[17]

Acceptor the holder at maturity

By section 61:

> When the acceptor of a bill is or becomes the holder of it at or after its maturity, in his own right, the bill is discharged.

This is straightforward and seldom likely to arise in practice. Quite apart from the section there is a common law rule that where the acceptor becomes the executor of the holder the debt is extinguished.[18] The section cannot apply to cheques.

---

[15] This illustration is equally valid in the case of a cheque if C is regarded as A's bank and if the words "it is accepted by C" are deleted.

[16] The position would be different in the case of a cheque (see *post*, p. 317).

[17] *London and River Plate Bank* v. *Bank of Liverpool* [1896] 1 Q.B. 7, where a delay of six weeks was held to prevent the acceptor from recovering money paid to the wrong person.

[18] *Jenkins* v. *Jenkins* [1928] 2 K.B. 501.

Express waiver or renunciation

By section 62:

> (1) When the holder of a bill at or after its maturity absolutely and unconditionally renounces his rights against the acceptor the bill is discharged.
>
> The renunciation must be in writing, unless the bill is delivered up to the acceptor.
>
> (2) The liabilities of any party to a bill may in like manner be renounced by the holder before, at, or after its maturity; but nothing in this section shall affect the rights of a holder in due course without notice of the renunciation.

At common law, a renunciation must be under seal or supported by consideration or it must have induced the debtor to alter his position. This, however, is not necessary in many foreign countries, and in view of the international character of bills of exchange section 62 brings English law into line with the foreign systems. It will be noted that a holder in due course is again protected and he can enforce the bill against all parties if he was unaware of the renunciation.

Cancellation

By section 63:

> (1) Where a bill is intentionally cancelled by the holder or his agent, and the cancellation is apparent thereon, the bill is discharged.
>
> (2) In like manner any party liable on a bill may be discharged by the intentional cancellation of his signature by the holder or his agent. In such case any indorser who would have had a right of recourse against the party whose signature is cancelled is also discharged.
>
> (3) A cancellation made unintentionally, or under a mistake, or without the authority of the holder is inoperative; but where a bill or any signature thereon appears to have been cancelled the burden of proof lies on the party who alleges that the cancellation was made unintentionally, or under a mistake, or without authority.

Section 63(2) is clearly necessary to prevent the rights of a party being taken away from him without his consent. To illustrate this point suppose that A draws a bill on B in favour of C who indorses to D who indorses to E. After B has accepted, E cancels the name of A as the drawer. In doing so he not only discharges A but also C and D, both of whom would have had a right of recourse against A under section 55(1)(a).

Material alteration

Section 64 is important for all bills, including cheques. It provides that:

> (1) Where a bill or acceptance is materially altered without the assent of all parties liable on the bill, the bill is avoided except as against a party who has himself made, authorised, or assented to the alteration, and subsequent indorsers.
> Provided that,
> Where a bill has been materially altered, but the alteration is not apparent, and the bill is in the hands of a holder in due course, such holder may avail himself of the bill as if it had not been altered, and may enforce payment of it according to its original tenor.
> (2) In particular the following alterations are material, namely, any alteration of the date, the sum payable, the time of payment, the place of payment, and, where a bill has been accepted generally, the addition of a place of payment without the acceptor's assent.

The effect of this section can best be illustrated by two examples:

> (1) A draws a bill on B for £50 in favour of C. B accepts. C fraudulently alters the amount of the bill to £150. Although the alteration is apparent C persuades D to give him £150 for the bill which he then indorses to D. D indorses to E. *Result*: E has no rights as against A and B because the bill is void as against them. He can, however, sue C and D on their indorsements (C being the person who made the alteration, and D being a subsequent indorser).
> (2) The facts are as above but alteration is not apparent. Here, if E is a holder in due course, he is given additional rights. Not only can he enforce the bill against C and D for £150, but he can enforce the bill against A and B as drawer and acceptor of a bill for £50. This might be useful if, for example, C and D were both insolvent.

Negligence. If in the above example the instrument had been drawn and accepted in such a way as to facilitate alteration, this would not have affected the acceptor's liability, because the House of Lords has decided that the acceptor of a bill owes no duty of care to a holder to guard against alteration after acceptance.[19] The position is the same in the case of a cheque, *i.e.* no duty is owed to the holder, but the drawer of a cheque does owe a contractual duty of care to his bank.[20]

---

[19] *Scholfield* v. *Londesborough* [1896] A.C. 514.
[20] *London Joint Stock Bank* v. *Macmillan and Arthur* [1918] A.C. 777, *post*, p. 306.

Accident. Section 64 does not apply to an unintentional alteration, as, for example, where the bill is inadvertently torn by the holder or is accidentally washed while in a garment.[21]

Acceptance and payment for honour

Acceptance

Where a bill is dishonoured, the holder can sue the drawer and the previous indorsers. If there are several indorsers there will clearly be a large number of claims with each indorsee suing his indorser, the payee suing the drawer and so on. To avoid the practical inconvenience of this a stranger can intervene and accept the bill for the honour of someone already liable thereon. This is called acceptance for honour *supra* protest and the object is to prevent action being taken against the person for whose honour the bill is accepted. By section 65:

(1) Where a bill of exchange has been protested for dishonour by non-acceptance, or protested for better security, and is not overdue, any person, not being a party already liable thereon, may, with the consent of the holder, intervene and accept the bill *supra* protest, for the honour of any party liable thereon, or for the honour of the person for· whose account the bill is drawn.

(2) A bill may be accepted for honour for part only of the sum for which it is drawn.

(3) An acceptance for honour *supra* protest in order to be valid must—

(*a*) be written on the bill, and indicate that it is an acceptance for honour;

(*b*) be signed by the acceptor for honour.

(4) Where an acceptance for honour does not expressly state for whose honour it is made, it is deemed to be an acceptance for the honour of the drawer.

The holder is not bound to take an acceptance for honour and his rights on the bill are not prejudiced if he refuses it.

Liability of acceptor for honour

Section 66 provides that:

(1) The acceptor for honour of a bill by accepting it engages that he will, on due presentment, pay the bill according to the tenor of his

---

[21] *Hong Kong and Shanghai Banking Corpn.* v. *Lo Lee Shi* [1928] A.C. 181, P.C.

acceptance, if it is not paid by the drawee, provided it has been duly presented for payment, and protested for non-payment, and that he receives notice of these facts.

(2) The acceptor for honour is liable to the holder and to all parties to the bill subsequent to the party for whose honour he has accepted.

Payment for honour

Where a bill has been dishonoured by non-payment and protested, any person can intervene and pay it for the honour of any person liable on the bill or for the honour of the person for whose account the bill is drawn (s.68(1)). This is called payment for honour *supra* protest, and to operate as such it must be attested by a document prepared by a notary public and called "a notarial act of honour" (s.68(3)). Such payment discharges all persons subsequent to the person for whose honour the bill is paid, and the payer takes over the rights of that person against prior parties (s.68(5)). If the holder refuses such payment, he loses his rights against all persons who would have been discharged by such payment (s.68(7)).

Lost bills

Section 69 provides that:

> Where a bill has been lost before it is overdue, the person who was the holder of it may apply to the drawer to give him another bill of the same tenor, giving security to the drawer if required to indemnify him against all persons whatever in case the bill alleged to have been lost shall be found again.
>
> If the drawer on request as aforesaid refuses to give such duplicate bill, he may be compelled to do so.

Further by section 70:

> In any action or proceeding upon a bill, the court or a judge may order that the loss of the instrument shall not be set up, provided an indemnity be given to the satisfaction of the court or judge against the claims of any other person upon the instrument in question.

If will be appreciated that section 70 is far more beneficial to the holder, since section 69 only gives a right to the drawer's signature and not to that of other parties. The holder will not be required to give an indemnity if the bill has been accidentally destroyed. Loss of the bill does not excuse the holder from giving notice of dishonour.

Bill in a set

Occasionally to guard against loss in transit a bill is drawn in several parts and the various parts are sent by different mails. The following is an example of the first part of a three-part bill:

£1,000   1/5/83 30 days after date pay this first of exchange (second and third of the same tenor being unpaid) to G. Green or order the sum of one thousand pounds. To S. Scarlett   B. Brown

The law as to bills in a set is to be found in section 71 which reads:

(1) Where a bill is drawn in a set, each part of the set being numbered, and containing a reference to the other parts, the whole of the parts constitute one bill.

(2) Where the holder of a set indorses two or more parts to different persons, he is liable on every such part, and every indorser subsequent to him is liable on the part he has himself indorsed as if the said parts were separate bills.

(3) Where two or more parts of a set are negotiated to different holders in due course, the holder whose title first accrues is as between such holders deemed the true owner of the bill; but nothing in this subsection shall affect the rights of a person who in due course accepts or pays the part first presented to him.

(4) The acceptance may be written on any part, and it must be written on one part only.

If the drawee accepts more than one part, and such accepted parts get into the hands of different holders in due course, he is liable on every such part as if it were a separate bill.

(5) When the acceptor of a bill drawn in a set pays it without requiring the part bearing his acceptance to be delivered up to him, and that part at maturity is outstanding in the hands of a holder in due course, he is liable to the holder thereof.

(6) Subject to the preceding rules, where any one part of a bill drawn in a set is discharged by payment or otherwise, the whole bill is discharged.

CHEQUES

General

By section 73:

> A cheque is a bill of exchange drawn on a banker payable on demand.
>
> Except as otherwise provided in this Part, the provisions of this Act applicable to a bill of exchange payable on demand apply to a cheque.

Thus, amalgamating this definition with the definition of a bill in section 3 we find that a cheque is:

> An unconditional order in writing addressed by one person to a bank signed by the person giving it requiring the bank to pay on demand a sum certain in money to or to the order of a specified person or to bearer.

The following is the form of a cheque:

M. Bank Ltd.	1st October 1983
Cheapside	
Pay James Jones or order	
Ten Pounds only	£10.00
	A. Drawer

Procedure

If James Jones (or his indorsee) wishes to obtain payment, he can either present it at the M. Bank, Ltd., and obtain payment over the counter, or he can pay it into his own bank, who will present the cheque to the M. Bank, Ltd., for payment.[22] If all is well, the M. Bank, Ltd., will pay the cheque, cancel the drawer's signature and debit his account, while the bank which has collected payment will credit the account of its customer with the amount of the cheque.

In the absence of contrary agreement the cheque need not take any particular form, and cheque forms issued by one branch can be altered so as to constitute a mandate to another branch. Having regard to the increasing use of computers, strenuous effects will no

---

[22] In the case of the "Big Four" banks this is done in bulk through a "Clearing House."

doubt be made by the banks to exclude this possibility. A printed statement on the cover of the cheque book is not necessarily sufficient.[23]

Terminology

The bank on whom the cheque is drawn is the paying banker and the bank who collects is the collecting banker.

Cheques and bills

Subject to a few exceptions, some of which have already been noted, the rules governing cheques are the same as those governing other bills. The principal differences are:

(1) The rules relating to acceptance do not apply to cheques.

(2) The rules relating to negotiation have little practical importance, because 97 per cent. of all cheques are not negotiated.[24]

(3) Delay in presenting a cheque for payment does not discharge the drawer, unless he suffers actual loss through the delay (s.74, *ante*, p. 285).

(4) The rules as to crossings are confined to cheques and certain other instruments and not to other bills.

(5) Payment of an order cheque bearing a forged or unauthorised indorsement discharges the paying banker, whereas in similar circumstances the acceptor of a bill would not be discharged.

(6) A number of obligations arise between banker and customer by virtue of the contractual relationship between them. This relationship must now be examined.

Banker and customer

Nature of relationship

The relationship of banker and customer is not a fiduciary one but a simple contractual relationship of debtor and creditor, with

---

[23] *Burnett* v. *Westminster Bank* [1966] 1 Q.B. 742; [1965] 3 W.L.R. 863.
[24] *Mocatta Committee on Cheque Indorsement.*

the superadded obligation of honouring the customer's cheques when there is a sufficient and available credit balance.[25]

Limitation. Formerly it was thought that the six-year limitation period ran against the customer as from the date of payment in, but in 1921 the Court of Appeal held that the customer did not have a cause of action for the recovery of his money until he had made a demand, and that the limitation period did not begin to run until demand.[26] In the case of a deposit account time will run from the moment when the cause of action accrues. Most of such accounts generally require a specified period of notice or the return of the deposit book, and the limitation period will not start to run until the requisite conditions have been fulfilled.

Duties of customer

Duty of care. The very important House of Lords case of *London Joint Stock Bank* v. *Macmillan and Arthur*[27] decided that the contract between banker and customer places on the customer a duty towards his banker to take reasonable care in drawing cheques so as to guard against alterations. The facts were:

> A clerk of M prepared a bearer cheque for signature by M. The amount appeared in figures as £2 but did not appear in words at all. M signed it. The clerk altered the figure to £120, wrote in this amount in words, and obtained payment from M's banker. The House of Lords held that the loss was caused by breach of the duty of care which M owed to his banker with the result that the banker was entitled to debit M's account with the full amount of the cheque. Lord Finlay stated that "the customer is bound to take usual and reasonable precautions to prevent forgery."

---

[25] *Foley* v. *Hill* (1848) 2 H.L.C. 28. In *Lloyds Bank* v. *Bundy* [1975] Q.B. 326 the bank persuaded a customer to charge his sole asset to the bank as security for an overdraft to the customer's son. The Court of Appeal held that (a) on the particular facts a fiduciary relationship did exist; (b) the bank should have encouraged the customer to take independent legal advice; (c) since this had not been done the transaction was voidable for undue influence. See also 124 N.L.J. 1045.

[26] *Joachimson* v. *Swiss Bank Corporation* [1921] 3 K.B. 110. In practice, of course, banks do not usually plead the Limitation Act.

[27] [1918] A.C. 777. This explains why, in the example on p. 304, the word "only" followed the amount.

The question of what is usual is, of course, one of evidence. In 1932 the case of *Slingsby* v. *District Bank*[28] came before the Court of Appeal. There:

> Executors drew a cheque in favour of John Prust & Co. There was a gap between the payee's name and the printed words "or order." A fraudulent person named Cumberbirch materially altered the cheque by writing in that gap the words "*per* Cumberbirch and Potts." He then indorsed the cheque and obtained payment. The Court of Appeal held that the executors had not been negligent in leaving the gap after the name of the payee, and were therefore entitled to recover the money from the bank.

The precaution of filling the gap after the payee's name is probably much more "usual" to-day than in 1931 so that if the unfortunate facts of *Slingsby* were to recur, it by no means follows that the result would be the same.

Pass book and statements. Formerly the banks used to send a pass book to their customer for checking and return. The practice today is to send their customer periodic statements setting out all the debits and credits during the period covered by the statement. In the United States the customer owes a duty to examine the book or statement, and if his negligent failure to detect errors causes loss, the customer bears that loss. No such duty has yet been imposed on a customer in English law.[29]

Duties of banker

General duty of care. A bank owes a contractual duty to take reasonable care in its conduct of the customer's business. If, for example, the customer is a company the bank will be liable for honouring cheques drawn by the directors for unauthorised purposes if the facts should have put the banker on inquiry.[30]

---

[28] [1932] 1 K.B. 544; [1931] 1 All E.R.Rep. 147.

[29] See, *e.g. Wealden Woodlands (Kent) Ltd.* v. *National Westminster Bank Ltd.*, *The Times*, March 14, 1983. A bank may however be estopped if the customer relies on an incorrect credit balance shown by the bank statement (*Holland* v. *Manchester and Liverpool Banking Co.* (1909) 25 T.L.R. 386).

[30] *Selangor United Rubber Estates Ltd.* v. *Cradock* (*No.* 3) [1968] 1 W.L.R. 1555; [1968] 2 All E.R. 1073. The judgment of Ungoed-Thomas J., which also deals with a number of company law and equity points, occupies 106 pages in the *Law Reports.* See also *Karak Rubber Co.* v. *Burden* (*No.* 2) [1972] 1 W.L.R. 602; [1972] 1 All E.R. 1210.

Duty to honour cheques. A banker owes a duty to his customer (but not to any other party) to honour his cheques up to the amount of his credit balance or agreed overdraft (if any). If the banker wrongly refuses to honour a cheque, the customer can claim substantial damages without proof of actual loss if the customer is a trader. Other customers can only claim nominal damages unless actual loss is proved.[31] It is not yet finally settled whether the words "refer to drawer" are defamatory.[32]

Termination of duty. By section 75:

> The duty and authority of a banker to pay a cheque drawn on him by his customer are determined by—
> (1) Countermand of payment[33]:
> (2) Notice of the customer's death.

The question of countermand was considered in *Curtice* v. *London City and Midland Bank*[34]:

> The drawer of a cheque sent to his bank a telegram countermanding payment. The telegram arrived after business hours and was placed in a box for unopened mail. For some reason this box was not cleared the following morning and the cheque was paid. The drawer sued the bank for money had and received, alleging that the bank had paid a countermanded cheque. It was held that as the banker had no actual notice of the countermand the bank was not liable [the customer did not sue the bank for negligence]. The court also observed that a countermand by telegram might justify the bank in postponing the honouring of a cheque pending an inquiry as to the genuineness of the countermand.

Apart from section 75, the banker's duty to honour his customer's cheques also comes to an end:

(a) on notice of the customer's mental disorder. This is in accordance with the general agency rule that the principal's insanity revokes the agency (*ante*, p. 61);

---

[31] *Gibbons* v. *Westminster Bank Ltd.* [1939] 2 K.B. 882; [1939] 3 All E.R. 577.

[32] See *per* Scrutton L.J. in *Flach* v. *London and South Western Bank Ltd.* (1915) 31 T.L.R. 334, 336. In *Jayson* v. *Midland Bank* [1967] 2 Lloyd's Rep. 563 a jury found that the words were defamatory.

[33] A countermand notice sent to one branch of the bank is not notice to another branch (*Burnett* v. *Westminster Bank* [1966] 1 Q.B. 742; [1965] 3 W.L.R. 863).

[34] [1908] 1 K.B. 293. The customer can of course agree with his bank that cheques shall not be countermanded; this often happens in the case of cheques covered by a "cheque card."

(b) on notice of an act of bankruptcy on which a petition can be filed;

(c) on the making of a receiving order in bankruptcy[35];

(d) if the customer is a limited company, on notice of a petition for compulsory winding up or a resolution for voluntary winding up;

(e) on service of a garnishee order nisi. Garnishee proceedings may be taken by a judgment creditor of the customer, and the garnishee order operates as a charge on moneys in the account, so that the bank cannot pay cheques drawn by their customer on that account.[36] In practice the bank should open a fresh account for subsequent receipts and payments.

Duty not to pay without authority. This is the corollary of the previous duty—the bank will be liable not only for wrongly dishonouring a cheque, but also for wrongly paying a cheque. Thus the bank will be liable if, for example:

(a) They pay a countermanded cheque, or

(b) They pay a cheque which is void for material alteration, or

(c) They pay a cheque on which the drawer's signature is forged.

In all these cases, the general rule is that the bank cannot debit the customer's account. There are, however, three exceptions to this rule:

(a) Negligence. If the wrongful payment was due to the careless manner in which the customer drew a cheque, the customer bears the loss (*London Joint Stock Bank* v. *Macmillan and Arthur, ante*, p. 306).

(b) Estoppel. A customer who discovers that his signature to a cheque has been forged is under a duty to notify his bank promptly, and if the bank is prejudiced by his failure to do so, they are not bound to repay the money. In *Greenwood* v. *Martins Bank*[37]:

---

[35] Although on adjudication the bankruptcy relates back to the commission of the act of bankruptcy (Bankruptcy Act 1914, s.37) it seems that a banker paying a cheque drawn by the debtor in favour of a third party is protected, if he pays it before the receiving order and without notice of an available act of bankruptcy (s.45 as interpreted in *Re Dalton* [1963] Ch. 336; [1963] 2 All E.R. 499).

[36] R.S.C., Ord. 49, and see Administration of Justice Act 1956, which extends garnishee proceedings to a deposit account.

[37] [1933] A.C. 51.

A husband discovered that his wife had been drawing from his account by forging his signature to cheques, but, to avoid publicity, he did not tell the bank. Subsequently the wife shot herself. After the death he sued the bank for the return of the moneys paid under the forged cheques. The effect of his failure to inform the bank earlier was that the bank's right to claim reimbursement from the wife had disappeared, owing to her death. Consequently the House of Lords held that the husband was by his conduct estopped from setting up the forgery.

Now that the right to sue the forger survives the forger's death by virtue of the Law Reform (Miscellaneous Provisions) Act 1934, it is arguable that the result of this case might now be different.

It has already been seen that there is, as yet, no estoppel arising from failure to examine the pass book or bank statements.[37a]

(c) Subrogation. If the wrongful payment by the bank satisfies a debt due from the customer to one of his creditors, the effect of the general restoration rule would be that the customer would have his bank account restored to its previous amount, and in addition the debt owed by him would be extinguished. In other words, he would make a profit from the wrongful payment. To prevent this, the bank, on restoring the money, is subrogated to the creditor's rights against the customer, *i.e.* the bank is in effect an assignee of the creditor's rights.[38]

If the bank does make an unauthorised payment (*e.g.* on a forged or countermanded cheque) the bank can recover the money from the payee and the payee's bank as money paid under a mistake of fact unless the wrongful payment has caused the payee to alter his position.[39]

The above cases of payment without authority must be distinguished from a case where a bank pays a valid cheque to the wrong person. This case, which brings in the question of statutory protection, is considered on pp. 316 *et seq.*

Joint account. Where two persons open a joint account the question has arisen as to whether the duties owed by the bank are

---

[37a] See n. 29 *supra*.

[38] *Liggett (B.) (Liverpool) Ltd.* v. *Barclays Bank* [1928] 1 K.B. 48; [1927] All E.R. Rep. 451.

[39] For a recent example see *Barclays Bank* v. *W.J. Simms Son and Cooke (Southern)* [1980] Q.B. 677.

owed to the customers jointly and not individually. In *Brewer* v. *Westminster Bank*.[40]

> Two executors opened an estate account. Cheques drawn on this account required both their signatures. One of the executors withdrew more than £3,000 by forging the signature of his co-executor to cheques drawn on the account. The co-executor brought an action for a declaration that the account had been wrongly debited. McNair J. refused the declaration, on the grounds that (1) no action could be maintained by joint contractors on a contract unless both were in a position to sue; (2) in this case the fraudulent executor was clearly not in a position to sue the bank; and (3) accordingly the co-executor had no cause of action.
>
> The decision has been forcefully criticised by academic writers and three later cases have refused to follow it. It is unlikely, therefore, to be followed in any future case.[41]

Post-dated cheques. A post-dated cheque is a curious hybrid in that it is neither a time bill nor strictly, payable on demand. It is freely negotiable[42] but it seems that a banker paying before the specified date stands to lose the money if before that date the drawer countermands. A learned writer has described the subject as "distasteful"[43] and finds it difficult to discover any valid reason for the existence of such documents.[44]

Duty of secrecy. The relationship of banker and customer is clearly a confidential one and in *Tournier* v. *National Provincial and Union Bank of England*[45] the Court of Appeal emphasised that there is a contractual duty on the banker not to divulge any facts relating to his customer which the banker discovers while acting in his capacity of banker. Thus the duty applies to all facts and not merely the state of the account. Breach of the duty will give rise to an action for damages, which will be nominal unless actual loss is proved.

The Court of Appeal pointed out that the duty was subject to exceptions, and they specified four cases where disclosure is permissible. These are:

---

[40] [1952] 2 T.L.R. 568; [1952] 2 All E.R. 650.
[41] See *Welch* v. *Bank of England* [1955] Ch. 508; [1955] 1 All E.R. 811; *Jackson* v. *White and Midland Bank Ltd.* [1967] 2 Lloyd's Rep. 68 and most recently *Catlin* v. *Cyprus Finance Corpn. (London)* (1982) 126 S.J. 744.
[42] *Hitchcock* v. *Edwards* (1889) 60 L.T. 636.
[43] The editor of *Paget on Banking*, (9th ed.), p. 187.
[44] In some countries, *e.g.* France, the issue of such a document is prohibited.
[45] [1924] 1 K.B. 461.

(a) Where the banker is compelled by law to divulge.

An example arises under section 167 of the Companies Act 1948. The Department of Trade may appoint an inspector to inquire into a company's affairs and the inspector may require the books of the company to be produced by the company's agents which by section 167(5) includes the company's banker. Another example is furnished by the Bankers Book Evidence Act 18979 which, by section 7, enables the court to make an order authorising a party in litigation to inspect, and take copies of, entries in the books of the bank. The power to make such an order is exercised with great caution.[46]

(b) Where disclosure is required in the public interest, as, for example, where the account was that of someone suspected of treasonable activities in wartime.

(c) Where disclosure is required for the banker's own protection, as where he seeks to enforce an overdraft.

(d) Where the customer consents, as where he gives his banker's name as reference. The practice of some bankers in disclosing their customer's position to other bankers making inquiries on behalf of customers may well be a breach of the duty, unless an implied consent can be proved.

Advice on investments. In modern times, many bankers advertise their willingness to discuss, and advise on, the financial problems of customers and potential customers. In *Woods* v. *Martins Bank*[47] Salmon J. pointed out that the limits of a banker's business could not be laid down as a matter of law, and that if in any particular case the giving of advice did form part of the business, the banker was under a duty to take reasonable care in giving it, and would be liable in damages if he broke that duty. In practice many bankers do give advice on investments.

Custody of valuables. Many banks accept valuables belonging to their customers for safe custody, and usually do so without making

---

[46] It was exercised in *Williams* v. *Summerfield* [1972] 2 Q.B. 512; [1972] 2 All E.R. 1334, D.C. (police inquiries). See also *Royal Bank of Canada* v. *I.R.C.* [1972] Ch. 665 for an example of a provision in the Income Tax Acts requiring disclosue and Finance Act 1975, Sched. 4, para. 5 (capital transfer tax).

[47] [1959] 1 Q.B. 55; [1958] 3 All E.R. 166. Quite apart from this there can in appropriate cases be liability in tort (*Hedley Byrne & Co. Ltd.* v. *Heller and Partners Ltd.* [1964] A.C. 465; [1963] 2 All E.R. 575) and an attempt to exclude liability would be controlled by the Unfair Contract Terms Act 1977 *post*, p. 434.

a charge. The liability of the banker is that of an ordinary bailee of goods, namely a duty to take reasonable care for their safety.[48] Further, if the goods are subsequently delivered to the wrong person, the banker will be liable for conversion, even though he acted in good faith and without negligence.

Crossings

The practice of putting crossings on cheques has been in operation for a long time. The effect of a general crossing is that the paying banker must pay the cheque to another banker[49] and not across the counter. This to some extent gives added protection to the holder in the event of theft, because not all thieves have bank accounts, and because the drawer or holder has additional time to contact the bank and stop the cheque.

General crossing

By section 76(1) a general crossing consists of two parallel transverse lines across the face of the cheque with or without the words "and company" or any abbreviation thereof.

Special crossing

By section 76(2) where a cheque bears across its face the name of a banker, the cheque is crossed specially and to that banker.

Who can cross

By section 77 a cheque may be crossed generally or specially by the drawer or by the holder.[50] The holder can also convert a general crossing into a special crossing. The section further provides that a collecting banker who receives a generally crossed cheque may cross it specially to himself (s.77(6)), and that a banker to whom a cheque has been specially crossed may again cross it specially to another banker for collection (s.77(5)).

---

[48] *Giblin* v. *McMullen* (1868) L.R. 2 P.C. 317. And see section 13 of the Supply of Goods and Services Act 1982 *ante*, p. 4.

[49] In the case of a special crossing, it must be paid to the banker named in the crossing.

[50] Thus the holder can convert an "open" cheque into a crossed cheque. He cannot, of course, convert a crossed cheque into an open cheque.

Duty of banker

The banker must pay in accordance with the crossing. Section 79 provides that:

> (1) Where a cheque is crossed specially to more than one banker except when crossed to an agent for collection being a banker, the banker on whom it is drawn shall refuse payment thereof.
>
> (2) Where the banker on whom a cheque is drawn which is so crossed nevertheless pays the same, or pays a cheque crossed generally otherwise than to a banker, or if crossed specially otherwise than to the banker to whom it is crossed, or his agent for collection being a banker, he is liable to the true owner of the cheque for any loss he may sustain owing to the cheque having been so paid.
>
> Provided that where a cheque is presented for payment which does not at the time of presentment appear to be crossed, or to have had a crossing which has been obliterated, or to have been added to or altered otherwise than as authorised by this Act, the banker paying the cheque in good faith and without negligence shall not be responsible or incur any liability, nor shall the payment be questioned by reason of the cheque having been crossed, or of the crossing having been obliterated or having been added to or altered otherwise than as authorised by this Act, and payment having been made otherwise than to a banker or to the bank to whom the cheque is or was crossed, or to his agent for collection being a banker, as the case may be.

In considering the liability of a banker who disregards a crossing (other than one which is not apparent), two possible situations must be considered.

(1) Payment to the true owner, as where a cheque owned by C is in fact paid to C. Here clearly C has no claim against the banker. It has, however, been suggested that the drawer might refuse to be debited with the payment, because payment was not made in the manner directed.[51]

(2) Payment to someone other than the true owner, *e.g.* if a cheque payable to C is paid to D. If the cheque were not a crossed cheque, the banker might escape liability to C under section 59 (if D was the holder) or under section 60 (if D was in possession under a forged or unauthorised indorsement). If, however, the cheque is a crossed one and the banker has contravened the crossing, neither section will protect him, and he will be liable to the true owner C.

---

[51] *Smith* v. *Union Bank of London* (1875) 1 Q.B.D. 31, 36 *per* Lord Cairns.

Not negotiable

These words can be placed on to a crossed cheque either at the time of the crossing or subsequently (ss.76(1), (2) and 77(4)). The effect of these words is set out in section 81:

> Where a person takes a crossed cheque which bears on it the words "not negotiable," he shall not have and shall not be capable of giving a better title to the cheque than that which the person from whom he took it had.

A "not negotiable" crossing gives considerable protection in the case of a bearer cheque (and the reader should remember that when an order cheque is indorsed in blank it becomes payable to bearer). Suppose that B is the owner of a bearer cheque. A thief steals it and delivers it to H. H, if a holder in due course, gets a good title.[52] If the cheque had been a crossed one, and the words "not negotiable" had appeared on it, H could only have acquired the same title as the thief, in other words no title.

It must be emphasised that a cheque crossed "not negotiable" can still be transferred in the usual way—but not free from defects of title. It will be recalled that a bill of exchange marked "not negotiable" is not even transferable (*ante*, p. 255). The words "not negotiable" have probably no effect at all on an uncrossed cheque.

Account payee

The words "account payee" on the face of a crossed cheque are a direction to the collecting banker to credit the payee's account with the proceeds of the cheque. The words are not even mentioned in the Act, and it was held in *National Bank* v. *Silke*[53] that a cheque bearing these words remained freely negotiable.[54] A collecting banker is put on inquiry if such a cheque is presented for collection by someone other than the payee, and collection for some other account might well be negligence.[55] The point is largely academic since most bankers do not in practice collect such cheques for any account except that of the payee.

---

[52] The words "not negotiable" may also be useful on a crossed order cheque if, for example, the drawer signs and delivers a blank cheque (see *ante*, p. 269).

[53] [1891] 1 Q.B. 435.

[54] Of course, a cheque to pay "X only" with the printed words "or order" struck out would be a non-transferable instrument.

[55] A county court judge has held that the duty of care is owed to the payee but not to the drawer (*Kenton* v. *Barclays Bank* [1977] Current Law at para. 189).

Account payee only

These words appear to have the same effect as the words "account payee."[56]

Scope of crossings rules

Besides applying to cheques, the crossings rules apply to:

(a) any document issued by a customer of a banker which, though not a bill of exchange, is intended to enable a person to obtain a payment from that banker of the sum mentioned in the document;

[Examples include a document in the form "Pay X provided he signs a receipt" and a direction to "Pay cash or order."[57]

(b) any document issued by a public officer which is intended to enable a person to obtain payment from the Paymaster-General or the Queen's and Lord Treasurer's Remembrancer of the sum mentioned in the document but is not a bill of exchange; and

(c) banker's drafts[58]; and

(d) dividend warrants.[59]

Protection of banker

This section deals with some very important statutory provisions protecting bankers against liability where a valid cheque is paid to, or collected for, a person who is not the owner.[60]

The paying banker

A banker's duty is to pay his customer's cheques and to do so quickly. In doing so, he runs the risk of paying one to the wrong person. If he does this two consequences follow:

(1) He cannot debit his customer's account;

---

[56] *Universal Guarantee Pty Ltd.* v. *National Bank of Australasia Ltd.* [1965] 1 W.L.R. 691, 696; [1965] 2 All E.R. 98, 102, P.C.

[57] *Orbit Mining and Trading Co.* v. *Westminster Bank Ltd.* [1963] 1 Q.B. 794; [1962] 3 All E.R. 565.

[58] Cheques Act 1957, s.5.

[59] Act of 1882, s.95.

[60] These provisions do not apply where the bank neither pays nor collects but merely makes two contra entries in the customer's account (*Universal Guarantee Pty. Ltd.* v. *National Bank of Australasia Ltd.* [1965] 1 W.L.R. 691; [1965] 2 All E.R. 98, P.C.).

(2) He is liable in conversion to the true owner, the damages recoverable being the face value of the cheque.[61]

The paying banker has four possible defences:

(1) By section 59 payment to the holder at or after maturity in good faith and without notice that his title is defective constitutes a valid payment which discharges the bill, absolves the banker from all liability and entitles him to debit his customer's account. This section gives the banker a good defence if he pays the bearer of a bearer cheque.[62] It does not give him a defence if he pays a person holding an order bill under a forged or unauthorised indorsement, because such person is not the holder, and payment to him would not be payment in due course. To meet this situation section 60 was enacted and this section must now be considered.

(2) By section 60 where a banker pays a cheque drawn on him in good faith and in the ordinary course of business, he is not to be prejudiced by the fact that an indorsement was forged or made without authority and he is deemed to have paid the cheque in due course.

Two points should be noted. First, section 60 only applies to cheques, whereas section 59 applies to all bills. Secondly, the banker must act in good faith (*i.e.* honestly) and in the ordinary course of business (*i.e.* in accordance with normal banking practice).

> *Example.* A draws a cheque on B Bank in favour of C. It is stolen by D who forges C's indorsement and negotiates it to E who negotiates it to F who obtains payment from B Bank. If the bank pay in good faith and in the ordinary course of business they are not prejudiced by the forgery. Consequently they can debit A's account and they are not liable in conversion to the owner C. C meanwhile cannot sue A either, because payment in due course discharges the drawer both on the cheque and the consideration.[63] C can, of course, sue E for conversion or F for conversion or money had and received. If F has to account to C, F can sue E under section 55(2)(*b*) with the result (once again) that the loss is borne by the victim of the fraud E whose sole right is against D.

---

[61] *Morison* v. *London County and Westminster Bank* [1914] 3 K.B. 356.

[62] The example on p. 298 shows how s.59 can apply to a cheque if the reference to "acceptance" is deleted and if C is the paying bank.

[63] *Charles* v. *Blackwell* (1877) 2 C.P.D. 151. This principle only applies if the cheque has reached the payee. Thus if the cheque was stolen before it reached C, C would still be able to sue A on the original debt.

(3) Crossed cheques. It will be recalled that the duty of a paying banker is to pay a crossed cheque in accordance with the crossing, and that he is liable if he fails to do so. The corollary is that if he does pay in accordance with the crossing he will be protected from liability. Section 80 provides that:

> Where the banker, on whom a crossed cheque is drawn, in good faith and without negligence pays it, if crossed generally, to a banker, and if crossed specially, to the banker to whom it is crossed, or his agent for collection being a banker, the banker paying the cheque, and, if the cheque has come into the hands of the payee, the drawer, shall respectively be entitled to the same rights and be placed in the same position as if payment of the cheque had been made to the true owner thereof.
>
> *Example.* A draws a cheque on the M Bank in favour of John Smith in settlement of a debt. John Smith receives the cheque and crosses it generally. It is stolen by a thief who goes to W Bank, pretends he is John Smith, and opens an account in that name. The W Bank present the cheque to the M Bank who pay in good faith and without negligence. *Result*: Although the spurious John Smith had no title, section 80 protects the paying bank from liability to the real John Smith, who is also debarred from suing A.

(4) Section 1 of the Cheques Act 1957. This section is widely drawn, but in view of developments which have taken place since the passing of the Act the section is likely to have little importance on the question of bankers' protection.

Before the Act there was a long-established practice whereby bankers refused to pay a cheque unless it was signed at the bank by the person who presented it for payment, and there was also a widely held belief among bankers that in the event of a wrongful payment they would not enjoy statutory protection unless this signature had been obtained. There is considerable doubt as to whether this practice was either permissible or necessary, because the Bills of Exchange Act nowhere requires indorsement of a cheque which is not negotiated.[64] At all events the tiresome practice of indorsing cheques was considered by the business community to be a waste of time and money. Bankers also found the task of examining all indorsements to be tiresome and wasteful, but they were reluctant to dispense with the indorsement of non-negotiated cheques because they felt that it might deprive

---

[64] The indorsement was more in the nature of a receipt (*Keene* v. *Beard* (1860) 8 C.B.(N.S.) 382, *per* Byles J.).

them of statutory protection. To meet the demand of both bankers and traders, section 1 of the Cheques Act 1957 was enacted and it provides as follows:

> **1.**—(1) Where a banker in good faith and in the ordinary course of business pays a cheque drawn on him which is not indorsed or is irregularly indorsed, he does not, in doing so, incur any liability by reason only of the absence of, or irregularity in, indorsement, and he is deemed to have paid it in due course.
>
> (2) Where a banker in good faith and in the ordinary course of business pays any such instrument as the following, namely:
>
> (*a*) a document issued by a customer of his which, though not a bill of exchange, is intended to enable a person to obtain payment from him of the sum mentioned in the document;
>
> (*b*) a draft payable on demand drawn by him upon himself, whether payable at the head office or some other office of his bank;
>
> he does not, in doing so, incur any liability by reason only of the absence of, or irregularity in, indorsement, and the payment discharges the instrument.

Shortly after the passing of the Act, the Committee of London Clearing Bankers, who represent all major English bankers, announced that despite the wide wording of the Act, bankers would still in practice require indorsement of cheques unless they were paid into a bank account for the credit of the payee. Accordingly, the present position depends upon how the cheque is dealt with, and three possibilities must be considered.

(a) If the payee pays the cheque into his own bank account, he will not be required to indorse it. This accounts for the overwhelming majority of all cheques.

(b) If the payee (or his transferee) presents it to the drawee banker for payment over the counter (which is, of course, only possible if the cheque is uncrossed) his indorsement will be required.

(c) If (as very rarely happens) the cheque is negotiated the collecting banker will require the indorsement of all indorsers, but not the indorsement of the person who presents the cheque for collection.

Any banker who, in the face of the Committee's decision, pays a cheque in (b) above without obtaining any requisite indorsement would not be acting "in the ordinary course of business" and could not, therefore, claim the protection of section 1 or of section 60 if a wrongful payment was made.

It will be noted that section 1 confers protection also in the case of an irregular indorsement. It is believed, however, that where the indorsement is one which is required by virtue of the Committee's decision, a banker is under a duty to ensure that the indorsement is regular. If therefore an uncrossed cheque bearing an irregular indorsement was paid across the counter the paying bank would not have paid in the ordinary course of business and would lose their statutory protection in the event of wrongful payment.

Void cheques. All the above defences are only available where the cheque in question is a *valid* cheque. They are not available if, for example, the drawer's signature has been forged, nor are they available if the cheque has become void for material alteration.[65]

Collecting banker

If a banker collects payment of a valid cheque for a person who is not the owner, he exposes himself to an action for conversion at the suit of the true owner. He can only escape liability in two cases:

(1) If section 4 of the Cheques Act 1957 protects him;
(2) If he can prove that he himself has become a holder in due course,

These matters must now be considered.

(1) Section 4, Cheques Act 1957.

This section, which replaced section 82 of the 1882 Act, provides as follows:

> (1) Where a banker, in good faith and without negligence—
> (*a*) receives payment for a customer of an instrument to which this section applies; or
> (*b*) having credited a customer's account with the amount of such an instrument, receives payment thereof for himself;
> and the customer has no title, or a defective title, to the instrument, the banker does not incur any liability to the true owner of the instrument by reason only of having received payment thereof.
> (2) This section applies to the following instruments, namely—
> (*a*) cheques;
> (*b*) any document issued by a customer of a banker which, though not a bill of exchange, is intended to enable a person to obtain

---

[65] See *Slingsby* v. *District Bank* [1932] 1 K.B. 544.

payment from that banker of the sum mentioned in the document;

(c) any document issued by a public officer which is intended to enable a person to obtain payment from the Paymaster General or the Queen's and Lord Treasurer's Remembrancer of the sum mentioned in the document but is not a bill of exchange;

(d) any draft payable on demand drawn by a banker upon himself, whether payable at the head office or some other office of his bank.

(3) A banker is not to be treated for the purpose of this section as having been negligent by reason only of his failure to concern himself with absence of, or irregularity in, indorsement of an instrument.

Various points must be noted with regard to this section.

Customer. The section only confers protection where the person for whom payment is collected is a customer. This probably means that he must be a person with an account at the bank, even if the account is opened with the very cheque which is the subject-matter of the action.[66]

Cheque. The section applies to all cheques whether crossed or not. An instrument on which the drawer's signature is forged, is not, however, a cheque, and collection of such an instrument would not be protected. It also seems that a bank collecting a "cheque" which has become void for material alteration cannot claim protection, since the instrument is a complete nullity and is no longer a cheque.[67]

Analogous instruments. It will be noted that the section also protects collection of certain other instruments. These instruments are the same as those already mentioned in the section on crossings (*ante*, p. 316).

Without negligence. Protection under section 4 is only available if the collecting banker can prove[68] that he acted without

---

[66] *Commissioners of Taxation* v. *English, Scottish and Australian Bank* [1920] A.C. 683, P.C. In *Woods* v. *Martins Bank, ante*, p. 312, a case dealing with advice on investments, Salmon J. held that the plaintiff became a customer from the time the Bank accepted instructions from him to obtain some money from a building society and to make an investment. These instructions were given before the account was opened. There is no case on the question of whether s.4 can apply before an account is actually opened.

[67] See *per* Scrutton L.J. in *Slingsby* v. *District Bank* [1932] 1 K.B. 544, 559. The point was overlooked in *Lumsden* v. *Trustee Savings Bank* [1971] 1 Lloyd's Rep. 114.

[68] The onus of proof is on him (*Lloyds Bank* v. *Savory* (*E. B.*) [1933] A.C. 201, 229, *per* Lord Wright).

negligence. The standard by which the presence of negligence is to be determined is to be ascertained by reference to the practice of reasonable men carrying on the business of bankers and endeavouring to do so in a manner calculated to protect themselves and others against fraud.[69] A banker need not be abnormally suspicious[70] but he will be held to have been negligent if the circumstances of the case should have put him on inquiry.

It is impossible to examine in detail all the cases involving negligence,[71] and the following selection is not intended to be exhaustive.

References. Failure to obtain or to follow up references when opening an account may well amount to negligence and deprive the banker of the protection of section 4, at any rate if such failure was to some extent responsible for the wrongful collection.[72]

Employer of new customer. When opening an account the banker is under a duty to inquire as to the name of his new customer's employer, where the banker knows that the customer occupies a position which involves the handling, and opportunity of stealing, his employer's cheques. Further, if the customer is a married woman, the banker should inquire as to the name of the husband's employer.[73] This duty, it seems, is not a continuing one.[74]

Misappropriation. In the *Savory* case, Lord Wright stated:

> "that the most obvious circumstances which should put the banker on his guard . . . are where a cheque is presented for collection which bears on its face a warning that the customer may have misappropriated it."[75]

---

[69] *Ibid.* at p. 221, *per* Lord Warrington.

[70] *Penmounts Estates* v. *National Provincial Bank* (1945) 173 L.T. 344, 346 *per* MacKinnon L.J.

[71] For a recent survey of the principles and their application, see *Marfani & Co. Ltd.* v. *Midland Bank* [1968] 1 W.L.R. 956; [1968] 2 All E.R. 573, C.A.

[72] *Harding* v. *London Joint Stock Bank*, reported in *Legal Decisions affecting Bankers*, Vol. 3, p. 8.

[73] *Lloyds Bank* v. *Savory, supra.* Presumably a questionnaire confined to women customers would infringe the Sex Discrimination Act 1975.

[74] *Orbit Mining and Trading Co. Ltd.* v. *Westminster Bank* [1963] 1 Q.B. 794; [1962] 3 All E.R. 565.

[75] *Ibid.* at p. 229.

A banker should not, therefore, without inquiry:

(a) Collect payment for a private account of a cheque payable to a public official.[76]

(b) Collect for an employee's private account a cheque drawn by, or in favour of, his employer.[77]

(c) Collect for an agent's private account a cheque drawn in favour of the principal[78] or a cheque drawn by the agent (on behalf of the principal) in favour of the agent personally.[79]

(d) Collect for a director's private account a cheque payable to a "one-man" company.[80]

(e) Collect a cheque marked "account payee" or "account payee only" for some other account.[81]

Indorsement. Section 4(3) which provides that the banker is not to be treated as negligent by reason only of his failure to concern himself with the absence of, or irregularity in, an indorsement must one day be construed by the courts in the light of the announcement by the Committee of London Clearing Bankers (mentioned on p. 319). It is possible that section 4(3) will be restricted to the indorsement of the person who presents the cheque for collection and will not apply to other indorsements. If this is so, if follows that where the payee negotiates an order cheque to another person, the collecting banker will still be under a duty to see that the payee's indorsement is present and regular.

Until recently there was some doubt as to whether or not the plaintiff's contributory negligence could operate to reduce his damages for conversion but it is now expressly enacted that contributory negligence is irrelevant.[82]

Collecting bank as holder in due course

The protection of section 4 applies to a collecting banker acting as such, whether he credits his customer's account before or after

---

[76] *Ross* v. *London County, Westminster and Parr's Bank* [1919] 1 K.B. 678.

[77] *Lloyds Bank* v. *Savory (E. B.)*, *supra*; *Carpenters' Co.* v. *British Mutual Banking Co.* [1938] 1 K.B. 511.

[78] *Bute* v. *Barclays Bank* [1955] 1 Q.B. 202; [1954] 3 All E.R. 365.

[79] *Midland Bank Ltd.* v. *Reckitt* [1933] A.C. 1; [1932] All E.R. Rep. 90.

[80] *Underwood Ltd.* v. *Bank of Liverpool* [1924] 1 K.B. 775; [1924] All E.R. Rep. 230.

[81] *Ladbroke* v. *Todd* (1914) 19 Com.Cas. 256.

[82] Torts (Interference with Goods) Act 1977, s.11.

receiving payment. Sometimes, however, the collecting banker may also be a holder of the cheque. This may occur in three cases:

(a) If the banker buys the cheque from the holder.[83]

(b) If the customer pays in a cheque to reduce his overdraft.[84]

(c) If the customer draws against the cheque before it has been cleared and there is an express or implied contract whereby the banker permits him to do so.[85] It is unsettled whether a bank gives value if, without any prior agreement, it allows a customer to draw against the cheque.[86]

One result of this is that if the banker can claim to be a holder in due course he will obtain a good title even if his customer had a defective title or no title and even if he was negligent. He cannot, of course, be a holder if an essential indorsement is forged. As part of the general scheme of the Cheques Act 1957, section 2 enables the collecting banker to become a holder of an order cheque, even though it is not indorsed. The section provides that:

> A banker who gives value for, or has a lien on, a cheque payable to order which the holder delivers to him for collection without indorsing it has such (if any) rights as he would have had if, upon delivery, the holder had indorsed it in blank.

In other words the unindorsed cheque is treated as if it had been indorsed so that the bank can be regarded either as the "indorsee" of an order cheque or alternatively as the bearer of a cheque which has been notionally indorsed in blank and is therefore payable to bearer.[87] In either case the bank becomes the holder and enjoys the normal rights of a holder, including a right to sue the drawer if the cheque is dishonoured.[87]

---

[83] *Great Western Railway* v. *London and County Banking Co. Ltd.* [1901] A.C. 414. The bank cashed a cheque which the payee had obtained by fraud. The House of Lords held that the bank was liable to the drawer. They were not protected by s.82 (now s.4 of the Cheques Act) because the payee was not a customer, nor were they holders in due course because the cheque was crossed "not negotiable."

[84] See s.27(3) of the Act of 1882, *ante*, p. 271.

[85] *Underwood Ltd.* v. *Bank of Liverpool* [1924] 1 K.B. 775, 804, *per* Scrutton L.J.

[86] In *Westminster Bank Ltd.* v. *Zang* [1966] A.C. 182; [1965] 2 W.L.R. 824, Salmond and Danckwerts L.JJ. took the view that the bank would be holders for value. Lord Denning M.R. took a different view. In the House of Lords, the point was left open.

[87] See *Midland Bank Ltd.* v. *Harris* [1963] 1 W.L.R. 1021; [1963] 2 All E.R. 685.

Three further points should be noted with regard to section 2. In the first place it is a direct exception to section 31 of the Bills of Exchange Act, which requires an order cheque to be indorsed before it can be negotiated. Secondly, unlike sections 1 and 4, section 2 is confined to cheques and does not apply to analogous instruments. Finally, section 2 merely deals with the absence of an indorsement and does not deal with an indorsement which is irregular. It would seem, therefore, that if the cheque is handed to the bank bearing an irregular indorsement the general rule will apply, namely, that the cheque will not be complete and regular on the face of it, so that the bank cannot be a holder in due course.

The case of *Westminster Bank Ltd.* v. *Zang*[88] is instructive on a number of points. The facts were as follows:

> Z gave a cheque to T who took it to his bank and asked his bank to credit the account of T Ltd., a company controlled by T. The account of T Ltd. was overdrawn. When the cheque (which was unindorsed) was dishonoured, the bank returned the cheque to T so that he could sue Z. The action was started but later discontinued. The cheque was then returned to the bank who sued Z claiming to be holders for value. The action failed.

Although three members of the Court of Appeal agreed that the action failed, they did so for differing reasons. Lord Denning M.R. held that as the payee had asked the bank to credit the account of a third party, the bank had not received the cheque "for collection" within section 2 and accordingly as the cheque was unindorsed the bank were not "holders." Salmon L.J. held that although the cheque had been received "for collection" the bank had not given value, so that again section 2 did not apply. Danckwerts L.J. agreed with Salmon L.J. on the "collection" point but held that the bank lost the protection of section 2 when they returned the cheque to T, and thereby lost their lien. The House of Lords unanimously held that the cheque *had* been paid in for collection but that the bank had not given value. The mere fact that the account was overdrawn did not amount to value, since interest was charged on the original amount of the overdraft unreduced by the cheque. Similarly there was no evidence of an agreement to honour cheques drawn by T Ltd. before clearance,

---

[88] [1966] A.C. 182; [1966] 2 W.L.R. 110 affirming [1965] 2 W.L.R. 824; [1965] 1 All E.R. 1023.

nor was there any evidence that such cheques had in fact been honoured.

It may sometimes occur that a banker may be a holder for value of the cheque for part of its amount and an agent for his customer as to the remainder. If he seeks to enforce the cheque any sum claimed by him in his latter capacity (*i.e.* as agent for the customer) will be subject to any defences or set-off which the person sued on the cheque may have against the customer.[89]

Paid cheque as receipt

Section 3 of the Cheques Act 1957, provides that:

> An unindorsed cheque which appears to have been paid by the banker on whom it is drawn is evidence of the receipt by the payee of the sum payable by the cheque.

Before the Act an indorsed cheque had always been evidence that the payee had received its amount, and an unindorsed cheque now has the same effect. The evidence is strong but not conclusive, and, as Lord Reid pointed out in the *Zang* case, the protection of payers has been weakened by section 2, which allows an unindorsed cheque to be collected for an account other than that of the payee.

PROMISSORY NOTES

Definition

By section 83:

> (1) A promissory note is an unconditional promise in writing made by one person to another signed by the maker, engaging to pay, on demand or at a fixed or determinable future time, a sum certain in money, to, or to the order of, a specified person or to bearer.
>
> (2) An instrument in the form of a note payable to maker's order is not a note within the meaning of this section unless and until it is indorsed by the maker.

---

[89] Chalmers *op. cit.* p. 128; *Barclays Bank Ltd.* v. *Aschaffenburger* [1967] 1 Lloyd's Rep. 387.

Example

> London
> 1st October 1983
> I promise to pay John Bloggs
> the sum of £100 value received
> M. Aker

The essential difference between a bill and a note is that the former is an order to pay, whereas the latter is a promise to pay. Both are negotiable instruments and most of the rules already discussed with regard to bills also apply to notes.

IOU

An IOU in the ordinary form is not a promissory note,[90] but it may be one if there are additional words which import a promise to pay.[91]

Collateral security

A promissory note given by a borrower of money is frequently accompanied by additional security, such as the title deeds of a house. Section 83(3) provides that:

> A note is not invalid by reason only that it contains also a pledge of collateral security with authority to sell or dispose thereof.

Alternatively, a promissory note is sometimes given *as* collateral security for a mortgage, because the relatively speedy method of enforcement is attractive to the lender.

Maker

The principal debtor on the note is, naturally enough, the person who gives the promise to pay, and he is known as the maker of the note. By section 88:

> The maker of a promissory note by making it—
> (1) Engages that he will pay it according to its tenor;

---

[90] *Akbar Khan* v. *Attar Singh* (1936) 80 S.J. 718, P.C.; [1936] 2 All E.R. 545. Lord Atkin considered that great harm would ensue if the net of negotiability were spread too wide (*ibid.* at pp. 547–548).
[91] *Brooks* v. *Elkins* (1836) M. & W. 74.

(2) Is precluded from denying to a holder in due course the existence of the payee and his then capacity to indorse.

In the case of a note payable to order, the first indorser corresponds to the drawer of an accepted bill payable to the drawer's order (s.89(2)), and subsequent indorsers are in the same position, *mutatis mutandis*, as the indorsers of a bill. If the note is a bearer note a person transferring it without indorsement will incur the usual liability of a transferor by delivery under section 58 (*ante*, p. 295).

Joint makers

Section 85 provides that:

(1) A promissory note may be made by two or more makers, and they may be liable thereon jointly, or jointly and severally according to its tenor.

(2) Where a note runs "I promise to pay" and is signed by two or more persons it is deemed to be their joint and several note.

Thus if the note reads "we promise" and is signed by two or more makers their liability is joint only, which means that there is only one debt and only one cause of action. If the note reads "I promise" it will be the joint and several note of the makers, with the result that the holder can sue the makers all together, or one by one, and an unsatisfied judgment against one will not prevent an action against the others. It will be appreciated that in either case a person who signs the note as a maker will be liable to the holder for the full amount of the note, and not merely for his share.

Presentation for payment

In order to make the maker liable, a note need only be presented for payment where the note is expressly made payable at a particular place (s.87(1)). Presentment is, however, always necessary in order to make indorsers liable (s.87(2)).

The time for presentment is dealt with by section 86:

(1) Where a note payable on demand has been indorsed, it must be presented for payment within a reasonable time of the indorsement. If it be not so presented the indorser is discharged.

This corresponds to section 45(2), *ante*, p. 285.

(2) In determining what is a reasonable time, regard shall be had to the nature of the instrument, the usage of trade, and the facts of the particular case.

(3) Where a note payable on demand is negotiated, it is not deemed to be overdue, for the purpose of affecting the holder with defects of title of which he had no notice, by reason that it appears that a reasonable time for presenting it for payment has elapsed since its issue.

It will be recalled that by section 36(3) a bill payable on demand is overdue if it has been in circulation for an unreasonable length of time, with the result that subsequent transferees can only take subject to defects of title. The reason for this difference between bills and notes is that a bill payable on demand is intended to be paid immediately, whereas a note payable on demand is intended as a continuing security and is frequently negotiated as such.

Bills and notes

Apart from the differences already noted, section 89(3) provides that the following provisions relating to bills do not apply to notes:

(a) Presentment for acceptance,

(b) Acceptance,

(c) Acceptance *supra* protest,

(d) Bills in a set.

Foreign note

Section 83(4) provides that:

> A note which is, or on the face of if purports to be, both made and payable within the British Islands is an inland note. Any other note is a foreign note.

Section 89(4) goes on to provide that where a foreign note is dishonoured, it need not be protested for dishonour. If, however, the holder is contemplating proceedings against the maker or another party in a foreign court he should bear in mind that many foreign systems of law require a dishonoured note to be protested.

Chapter Six

INSURANCE OTHER THAN MARINE

Introduction

INSURANCE today is of very great importance both in the commercial and in the personal sphere. The nature of an insurance contract is well known—it is a contract whereby a person or company ("the insurer") agrees, in return for a premium, to pay a sum of money to another person or company ("the insured") on the happening of a certain event, or to indemnify against loss caused by the risk insured against.[1]

Examples

Insurance is a very wide and diverse field, and policies can be taken out against a great variety of risks, ranging from rain on a holiday to the birth of twins. Among the more important types of insurance are:

Life and endowment assurance

Frequently a lump sum or annuity is payable on attaining a specified age or on death.

Personal accident insurance

A man may insure his limbs when embarking on a skiing holiday, and a football club may similarly insure the limbs of their leading players.

Property insurance

A man may insure his house and the contents against fire, his wife may insure her jewellery against theft and their son may insure his sports-car against damage.

Liability insurance

Many million of pounds are spent each year on insuring against legal liability. Examples include professional negligence policies,

---

[1] The benefit accruing to the insured must be of a monetary nature (*Medical Defence Union* v. *Department of Trade* [1980] Ch. 82).

householders' policies covering liability to visitors and neighbours, Road Traffic Act policies and employers' liability policies, which may cover both the employer's vicarious liability to third parties and also his personal liability to his employees. The Road Traffic Act 1972 and the Employers Liability (Compulsory Insurance) Act 1969 provides for compulsory liability insurance and the rules of a number of professions (*e.g.* solicitors and barristers) also require this.

Insurance and wager

At first sight insurance resembles a wager in that both contracts contemplate the payment of a sum of money on the happening of a future uncertain event. There is, however, a fundamental difference between the two transactions, in that a wagering contract itself *creates* the risk of loss while an insurance contract is made to *guard against* the consequences of a loss. The distinguishing feature is the interest possessed by the insured which the contract is designed to protect.[2]

Insurance business

Insurance business is carried on principally by registered friendly societies, Lloyd's underwriters and insurance companies. Insurance companies are primarily controlled by the Insurance Companies Act 1982 which consolidates earlier Acts and seeks to protect the public against small companies which may be unable to meet their liabilities. The Acts deal, *inter alia*, with minimum paid-up capital and with the margin of assets over liabilities and enables the Secretary of State to petition for windingup.[3] It is an area of law where the EEC has been very active and the Act gives effect to, a number of EEC Directives. In addition, the activities of insurance brokers are controlled by the Insurance Brokers (Registration) Act 1977 and by regulations made under that Act.

Arbitration clause

The modern insurance policy frequently contains an arbitration clause and this may help to explain the paucity of modern case law on non-marine insurance. It is noteworthy, however, that mem-

---

[2] See *per* Blackburn J. in *Wilson* v. *Jones* (1867) L.R. 2 Ex. 139, 150.
[3] For further protection of policyholders see Policyholders Protection Act 1975.

bers of the British Insurance Association and Lloyd's underwriters have agreed to refrain in general from insisting on the enforcement of arbitration clauses if the insured prefers to have the question of liability, as distinct from amount, determined by a court in the United Kingdom.

FORMATION OF CONTRACT[3a]

Form

A contract of insurance can be in any form but in practice it is embodied in a written document called a policy.

Offer and acceptance

The usual procedure followed is for the person seeking insurance to complete a proposal form which is then submitted to the insurers. If they reject the proposal, there is no contract. If they accept it, a contract may come into existence but the precise moment at which it does so is essentially a question of construction of the relevant documents. Thus if the acceptance provides (as it sometimes does) that "no insurance can take place until the first premium is received" it is clear that there is no cover until the premium is paid or tendered and it has been suggested that even if the premium is tendered the insurers are at liberty to change their minds and decide not to proceed.[4]

Temporary cover[5]

Where, as frequently occurs, a person wants immediate insurance while his proposal is being considered, temporary cover can be given in one of two ways. The first is by cover note, which is a separate contract[6] quite distinct from the policy itself, although

---

[3a] In life and health insurance there is a "cancellation period." See s.76 of the 1982 Act.

[4] *Canning* v. *Farquhar* (1886) 16 Q.B.D. 727. See *per* Lord Esher M.R., *ibid.* at p. 731. Lindley and Lopes L.JJ. were more doubtful.

[5] See Ivamy, *General Principles of Insurance Law* (4th ed.), pp. 110–115.

[6] Some motor insurance companies send out a temporary cover note when inviting renewal of the policy. This cover note is merely an offer and it requires some act by the insured to turn it into a binding contract (*Taylor* v. *Allon* [1966] 1 Q.B. 304; [1965] 1 All E.R. 557).

such of the policy's terms as are appropriate to a cover note are in practice expressly incorporated into it. The note is usually expressed to provide cover until a certain date, unless in the meantime the insurers decline the proposal. If the insured subsequently decides not to proceed with the policy, this will not rob him of the protection of the cover note.[7] The second type of temporary cover is by a slip which is initialled by a Lloyd's underwriter. A slip differs from a cover note because it places the insurer under a binding obligation to issue a policy in accordance with its terms.[8]

Loss before issue of policy

It has just been seen that if the insured has a cover note or slip he will be entitled to recover in respect of a loss occurring during the period of temporary cover but before the issue of a formal policy. Apart from this, however, the general rule is that no claim lies in respect of a loss occurring before the issue of the policy. This rule can be elaborated into the following four propositions:

(1) If unknown to both parties the loss has already occurred when the policy is made, the contract will be void for common mistake. An obvious example would be a life policy on the life of a man already dead.[9]

(2) If the fact of the loss is known only to the insured, a subsequent policy would be voidable for non-disclosure.[10]

(3) If the insurers make an offer to insure, it cannot be accepted by the insured after a loss has occurred.[11]

(4) If the insurers are bound to issue a policy on receipt of a premium, it is an implied term that there is no material change in the risk until the policy is effected.[12]

The operation of the above principles can be seen from the case of *Canning* v. *Farquhar*[13]:

---

[7] *Mackie* v. *European Assurance* (1869) 21 L.T. 102.

[8] See *Jaglom* v. *Excess Insurance Co. Ltd.* [1972] 2 Q.B. 250; [1972] 1 All E.R. 267.

[9] *Pritchard* v. *Merchants' and Tradesmens' Mutual Life Insurance Society* (1858) 3 C.B. (N.S.) 622.

[10] *Looker* v. *Law Union & Rock Insurance Co.* [1928] 1 K.B. 554.

[11] *Canning* v. *Farquhar, supra.*

[12] *Harrington* v. *Pearl Life Assurance Co.* (1914) 30 T.L.R. 613.

[13] (1886) 16 Q.B.D. 727.

The company received a proposal for life insurance which they accepted. The letter of acceptance stated "No insurance can take place until the first premium is paid." Subsequently the insured fell over a cliff and was seriously injured. The premium was tendered but refused and then C died. It was held that (1) on the facts of the case there was no contract to insure; (2) even if there had been such a contract it would have been on the implied condition that the risk was the same when the policy was called for.

Renewal

Most life policies give the insured a right to renew on payment of the premium or are entire contracts subject to forfeiture on non-payment of a premium; most other policies (*e.g.* motor) make renewal conditional on the insured obtaining the insurer's consent.

Stamp

By virtue of the Stamp Act 1891, as amended by the Finance Act 1970, life policies attract *ad valorem* duty but other policies are exempt. Insurers are liable to a penalty of £20 if they fail to issue a duly stamped life policy within one month of the receipt of the premium. This does not, however, affect the validity or enforceability of the policy.

Non-Disclosure[13a]

The general rule that "silence is golden" does not apply to a contract of insurance because, in the words of a great commercial lawyer:

> "Insurance is a contract of the utmost good faith and it is of the gravest importance to commerce that that position should be observed."[14]

The duty of disclosure is based on the idea that when a person applies for insurance he is in possession of all the information, whereas the prospective insurer knows nothing at all. To redress this balance the insured is under a duty to disclose all material facts of which he knows or ought to know. In practice the doctrine can

---

[13a] See *post*, pp. 345–346.
[14] *Greenhill* v. *Federal Insurance* [1927] 1 K.B. 65 at p. 76, *per* Scrutton L.J.

work harshly against the insured, especially as there is no duty to disclose the duty of disclosure.

The principle of full disclosure was clearly stated by Lord Blackburn as follows:

> "In policies of insurance, whether marine insurance or life insurance, there is an understanding that the contract is *uberrimae fidei* that if you know any circumstances at all that may influence the underwriter's opinion as to the risk he is incurring and consequently as to whether he will take it or what premium he will charge if he does take it, you will state what you know. There is an obligation there to disclose what you know; and the concealment of a material circumstance known to you, whether you thought it material or not, avoids the policy."[15]

The last three words are slightly inaccurate in that the effect of non-disclosure by an insured is to make the policy voidable by the insurer. No damages can be claimed for breach of the duty to disclose, since it is not based on an implied contractual term.[16] Avoidance is the only remedy and it is available either before or after the occurrence of the loss, and even though the loss was in no way connected with the non-disclosure.[17]

Examples of material facts

A fact is material if it would influence a prudent insurer in deciding whether to accept the risk and, if so, on what terms.[18] The following have been held to be material:

(1) Motor policy—previous accidents; convictions for dangerous driving[19] and for shopbreaking.[20]

---

[15] *Brownlie* v. *Campbell* (1880) 5 App.Cas. 925, 954; cited with approval in *Joel* v. *Law Union and Crown Insurance Co.* [1908] 2 K.B. 431, 438.

[16] *Glasgow Assurance Corporation* v. *Symondson* (1911) 104 L.T. 254, 258, *per* Scrutton L. J. If, however, the non-disclosure falsifies what is said there may be liability for misrepresentation, as to which, see *post*, p. 338.

[17] *Roselodge* v. *Castle* [1966] 2 Lloyd's Rep. 113 (burglary policy voidable for failing to disclose that a sales manager had been convicted of smuggling diamonds many years previously). See also [1967] 2 Lloyd's Rep. 99.

[18] *Mutual Life Insurance Co. of New York* v. *Ontario Metal Products Ltd.* [1925] A.C. 344. It is irrelvant that the insured does not consider the matter to be material.

[19] *Bond* v. *Commercial Assurance Co.* (1930) 35 Com.Cas. 171.

[20] *Cleland* v. *London General Insurance Co.* (1935) 51 Ll.L.R. 156.

(2) Fire policy—previous fires on the premises or on adjoining premises.[21]

(3) Life policy—the fact that the insured is suffering from a serious illness[22] or is a member of the Royal Naval Reserve.[23]

(4) Theft policy—the fact that an employee had a conviction for smuggling[24] or that, in the clothing trade, goods are never described as "new" unless they are Government Surplus.[25]

(5) Accident policy—the fact that the insured has recently suffered a serious deterioration of his eyesight.[26]

In some cases the fact that the proposer is a foreign national is material.[27] The fact that a previous proposal has been declined should be disclosed if it related to the same type of insurance[28] and sometimes if it related to a different type. In *Locker and Woolf* v. *West Australian Insurance*:[29]

> During negotiations for a fire policy, the proposers failed to disclose that a proposal for a motor policy had previously been turned down. It had in fact been turned down because (as the proposers well knew) their answers in the proposal form had been fraudulent. After the issue of a fire policy, a fire occurred and a claim was made. The Court of Appeal held that the previous refusal should have been disclosed, and that consequently the insurers were entitled to repudiate liability.

Proposal form

Where a proposal form is completed, the insured's duty to disclose is not confined to answering the questions in the form. The wording of the form may, of course, cut down the duty of disclosure. Thus if the proposal form contains the words "give details of illnesses during the past ten years" it is thought that the

---

[21] *Marene Knitting Mills Pty* v. *Greater Pacific General Insurance* [1976] 2 Ll.L.R. 631 P.C.

[22] *Life Association of Scotland* v. *Forster* (1873) 11 M. 351. He is, of course, only bound to disclose if he knows or ought to know that he is suffering from it (*ibid*).

[23] *Ayrey* v. *British Legal and United Provident Assurance Co.* [1918] 1 K.B. 136.

[24] See note 17 *ante*.

[25] *Anglo-African Merchants Ltd.* v. *Bayley* [1969] 2 W.L.R. 686; [1969] 2 All E.R. 421 (Government-surplus leather jerkins described as "new men's clothes").

[26] See *Lee* v. *British Law Insurance Co. Ltd.* [1972] 2 Lloyd's Rep. 49, C.A.; the case was argued as one of non-disclosure although it could equally have been based on breach of warranty.

[27] *Horne* v. *Poland* [1922] 2 K.B. 364 (burglary case).

[28] *Glicksman* v. *Lancashire and General Assurance Co.* [1927] A.C. 139.

[29] [1936] 1 K.B. 408.

insured would not be bound to disclose illnesses occurring outside this period. Further, it is always arguable that matters not mentioned in the proposal form were not material, but this will be a question of fact in each case. Conversely, the absence of a proposal form does not cut down the duty of disclosure. Thus where insurers issue a block policy for a building society and their customers the customers must disclose all facts which are relevant to the proposed insurance. In one case the customer, when completing a loan application, failed to disclose previous convictions. It was held that the insurers under a fire policy were entitled to avoid liability as against the borrower.[30]

Duration of duty

The duty of disclosure does not end when the proposal form is submitted, but continues right down to the moment when a binding contract is concluded.[31]

Renewal

If the renewal of a policy requires the insurer's consent, each renewal is in effect a new contract. It follows that all new material facts must be disclosed when applying for renewal.[32]

Agents

The duty of disclosure is also owed by any agent employed by the insured to make the policy on his behalf. In addition the principal will be deemed to have knowledge of any fact which is known to his agent, but only if the agent is under a duty to his principal to communicate such information. Thus knowledge of a fact by an agent will not be imputed to the principal so as to require disclosure if the agent himself was under no duty to disclose the fact to his principal.[33]

Fraudulent claims

If the insured makes a fraudulent claim he has broken his duty of good faith and consequently the insurer can avoid all liability,

---

[30] *Woolcott* v. *Sun Alliance* [1978] 1 W.L.R. 493; [1978] All E.R. 1253.

[31] *Looker* v. *Law Union and Rock Insurance Co. Ltd.* [1928] 1 K.B. 554.

[32] See, *e.g. Lambert* v. *Co-operative Insurance Society* [1975] 2 Ll.L.R. 485 C.A. (failure to disclose conviction of dishonesty before renewal).

[33] *Blackburn, Law & Co.* v. *Vigors* (1887) 12 App.Cas. 531.

even though he was on risk when the loss occurred. An honest but exaggerated claim, on the other hand, does not have this effect.[34]

Exceptions

The following facts need not be disclosed:

(1) Facts which the insured does not know. If, however, his ignorance was due to negligence, his ignorance will not be a defence.[35]

(2) Facts which diminish the risk, as, for example, the installation of a new burglar alarm.

(3) Facts which the insurer knows or is presumed to know. An insurer is presumed to know matters of common knowledge.

(4) Facts as to which the insurer waives inquiry. An example would arise where the insurer receives an answer which is clearly incomplete and yet makes no attempt to obtain further information.

MISREPRESENTATION[36]

A contract of insurance, like any other contract, is voidable for misrepresentation of a material fact, whether fraudulent or innocent. In order to enable the insurer to avoid liability three conditions must be satisfied:

(1) The statement must be material. The meaning of this word, and examples thereof, have already been considered.

(2) The statement must have induced the insurer to enter into the contract.

(3) The statement must be false, which is a question of construction. Thus the statement "I am in good health" will usually be construed as meaning "I am in good health to the best of my knowledge, information and belief," so that the mere fact that the insured is suffering from a disease of which he did not know will not make the statement false.[37] On the other hand in *Merchants and Manufacturers Insurance* v. *Hunt and Thorne*[38]:

---

[34] See *Norton* v. *Royal Fire & Life Ass.Co.* (1885) 1 T.L.R. 460.

[35] *Cf.* Marine Insurance Act 1906, s.18(1).

[36] See *post*, pp. 345–346.

[37] *Cf. Delahaye* v. *British Empire Mutual Life Assurance Co.* (1897) 13 T.L.R. 245.

[38] [1941] 1 K.B. 295; [1941] 1 All E.R. 123.

A proposer for a motor policy was asked: "Have you or any person who to your knowledge will drive the car been convicted of driving offences?" The answer given was "No." The proposer's son, who, as the proposer knew, would drive the car, had in fact been convicted of four such offences, although the proposer did not know this. It was held that the answer "No" amounted to a representation that there had been no convictions and as this was untrue, the insurers were not liable.

In practice the rules relating to misrepresentation are not of great importance because statements made by the insured in the proposal form are incorporated as warranties into the policy. The significance of this will become apparent in the next section.

WARRANTIES AND CONDITIONS[39]

Meaning of warranty

In the chapter on sale of goods the expression "warranty" was mainly used to refer to a collateral term of the contract not going to the root of it, in contrast to a "condition" which was a vital term. In insurance law, however, the words "warranty" and "condition" are used synonymously and both refer to vital terms going to the root of the contract.[40] This use of the word warranty is confusing and regrettable but it is probably too late to change it now.

A warranty must be distinguished from a mere definition of the risk. In *Farr* v. *Motor Traders' Mutual Insurance Society*.[41]

A proposal form for the insurance of a taxi-cab contained the following statements: (1) Is the vehicle driven solely by the proposer? (2) If not state whether driven in one or more shifts per 24 hours. The answers given were (1) No, (2) Just one. On one occasion, while another cab was being repaired, the insured used the cab for a short time in two shifts. An accident occurred while it was being used for one shift, and the insurers sought to repudiate for breach of warranty. The Court of Appeal held that the words "Just one" did not amount to a warranty that the vehicle would never be

---

[39] See also *post*, pp. 345–346.

[40] *Provincial Insurance Co. Ltd.* v. *Morgan and Foxon* [1933] A.C. 240, 253–254, *per* Lord Wright; *Dawsons Ltd.* v. *Bonnin* [1922] 2 A.C. 413, 422, *per* Viscount Haldane.

[41] [1920] 3 K.B. 669. See also Ivamy, *op. cit.* pp. 324–325 for further illustrations.

used for more than one shift, but amounted to a definition of the risk [*i.e.* that the insurers would be liable if an accident occurred when the vehicle was being used for one shift, and not liable in other cases]. Consequently the accident was within the risk and the insurers were liable.

It will be apparent from what has been said that the court must decide, as a matter of construction, whether a statement is (a) a mere representation, or (b) a warranty, or (c) a definition of the risk. To amount to a warranty no special form of words is required and the word warranty need not be mentioned. Perhaps the most common example is a clause in the policy that:

> "The answers in the proposal form shall form the basis of this contract and shall be deemed to be incorporated herein."

This clause has the effect of making the answers warranties, as also has a clause in the proposal form itself stating that the answers are to form the basis of the contract. The practice of splitting the contract in this way between proposal form and policy has been criticised[42] and it does seem that it can lead to hardship especially if a loss occurs after several years when (say) the insured no longer has a copy of the proposal form.

Breach of warranty

From the insuree's point of view the great advantage of a warranty over a mere representation is that if there is a breach of warranty he can repudiate liability under the policy without having to prove that the statement is material. Even though a particular statement is not material to the risk, it is always open to the parties to agree what facts are to be deemed material and if they do this the court must give effect to their agreement.[43] In *Dawsons Ltd.* v. *Bonnin*[44]:

> A proposal form for the insurance of a motor vehicle contained the question "State address where car will usually be garaged." A wrong address was inadvertently given. The form provided that the answers were to form the basis of the contract. Subsequently the vehicle was destroyed by fire and a claim was made under the policy. By a

---

[42] Colinvaux, *The Law of Insurance*, (4th ed.), at pp. 112.

[43] *Glicksman* v. *Lancashire and General Assurance Co.* [1927] A.C. 139. The form used by the defendants was severely criticised by four members of the House of Lords.

[44] [1922] 2 A.C. 413.

majority of three to two the House of Lords held that the insurers were entitled to avoid on account of a breach of warranty.

A warranty must be exactly complied with, so that if, for example, a motorist warranted that he had had five previous accidents whereas in fact he had had six, the insurers could avoid the policy. If, however, there is exact compliance, this is enough. In an early case a condition against working "mills" at night was held not to be broken when one single steam engine was turned on at night.[45]

Warranties may be divided into (a) warranties as to the present and (b) warranties as to the future. In the first group are statements as to age and health. Breach of such a warranty enables the insurer to avoid all liability. Examples falling in the second group are "The car will be driven by X," "There are two nightwatchmen at the factory," "No inflammable goods on the premises."[46] Clearly to give business efficacy to such a stipulation, it must be construed as meaning that the state of affairs warranted will continue. For breach of a future warranty, the insurer can repudiate as from the date of breach, but rights which have already vested in the insured before the date of breach are not affected.[47]

Where a policy is renewed it does not automatically follow that the original warranties are incorporated into the new policy. It will depend on the length of time that has elapsed and the other surrounding circumstances.[48]

Conditions

A modern form of insurance policy frequently contains a number of terms called "conditions." These may cover a wide variety of matters depending on the type of insurance in question. The performance of the conditions is frequently made a condition precedent to the insurer's liability. In the case of ambiguity, however, such a clause will be construed against the insurers and

---

[45] *Whitehead* v. *Price* (1835) 2 Cr., M. & R. 447.

[46] *Hales* v. *Reliance Fire and Accident Insurance Corporation* [1960] 2 Lloyd's Rep. 391.

[47] *Union Insurance Society of Canton* v. *Wills (George)* [1916] 1 A.C. 281, 286, *per* Lord Parmoor.

[48] See *per* Winn L.J. in *Magee* v. *Pennine Insurance Co. Ltd.* [1969] 2 Q.B. 507, 517; [1969] 2 All E.R. 895, 896.

will not allow them to escape liability. In *Re Bradley and Essex and Suffolk Accident Indemnity Society*[49]:

> A small farmer effected an employer's liability policy. This contained eight "conditions" the performance of which was said to be a condition precedent to the insurer's liability. It was conceded that some of the conditions were conditions subsequent while others were not conditions at all. One "condition" started with a statement that the premium was to be fixed by reference to the wages paid; then came a sentence requiring the insured to keep a wages book and produce it on demand; and then followed a provision for payment of an increased premium in certain cases. The insured only employed one person (his son) and did not keep a wages book. The son was injured and the insured made a claim which the insurers resisted on the ground that no wages book had been kept. A majority of the Court of Appeal held that (1) the whole clause must be read as one, (2) as such it was not a condition precedent, and accordingly (3) the insurers were not entitled to repudiate liability. [The form of policy was severely criticised by Farwell L.J.]

The wage-book clause in that case was merely a collateral stipulation, breach of which might give rise to a claim for damages but not to a right to repudiate.

Exceptions

Most policies contain a long list of exceptions, *i.e.* a list of circumstances in which the insurers will not be liable. Common examples include loss or damage caused by war, riots, civil commotion or radioactivity. If the insurers seek to rely on such a clause it must be clearly worded and any ambiguity will be construed against them.[50] Similarly if a question is ambiguous the insurers cannot repudiate if the insured has given an answer on a fair and reasonable construction of the question; otherwise the ambiguity would be a trap.[51]

---

[49] [1912] 1 K.B. 415.

[50] *Houghton* v. *Trafalgar Insurance Co.*, *post*, p. 359; Ivamy, *op. cit.* pp. 386–397 and cases there cited.

[51] *Corcos* v. *De Rougemont* (1925) 23 Ll.L.R. 164. Thus in *Taylor* v. *Eagle Star Insurance Co.* (1940) 67 Ll.L.R. 136 the insured was asked whether he had been convicted of offences "in connection with the driving of a motor vehicle" to which he replied "no." It was held that the insurers could not repudiate on the grounds that the insured had been convicted of a non-driving offence (using the vehicle while uninsured).

Waiver

Where the insurer, knowing of facts which give him a right to repudiate for breach of warranty, misrepresentation or non-disclosure, accepts a premium, he will be held to have waived the breach and will be estopped by his conduct from setting up the breach as a defence to a claim. In *Ayrey* v. *British Legal and United Provident Ass.Co.*[52]:

> The insured took out a policy of life insurance but failed to disclose that he was in the Royal Naval Reserve. Subsequently his wife informed the branch manager of the non-disclosure and he told her to continue paying the premiums which she did. Subsequently the insured died. *Held*, the insurers could not repudiate liability.

Completion of proposal form

The agent of the insurer sometimes assists the proposer in completing a proposal form which the proposer then signs. If the proposal form contains untrue statements, and the agent is aware of this, the question arises as to whether the insurer is bound by the agent's knowledge, in which case the company would be, in effect, waiving the breach as soon as premiums were paid. The general rule is that the company is not bound by the agent's knowledge because it is normally no part of the agent's duty to concern himself with the contents of the proposal form; if he completes the form he does so as agent for the insured.[53] If, however, the completion of the form is part of the agent's duty, as where he is instructed to assist illiterate proposers, the insurer is bound by the agent's knowledge that an answer is incorrect.[54]

The importance of reading the form before signing it can be seen from the recent case of *O'Connor* v. *Kirby*:[55]

> A broker filled up a proposal form for the insured. In answer to a question the insured told the broker that he had no garage, but the

---

[52] [1918] 1 K.B. 136. See also *Lickiss* v. *Milestone Motor Policies* (1966) 1 W.L.R. 1334. For the effect of delay on the right to repudiate, see *Allen* v. *Robles* [1969] 1 W.L.R. 1193; [1969] 3 All E.R. 159.

[53] *Newsholme* v. *Road Transport and General Insurance Co. Ltd.* [1929] 2 K.B. 356.

[54] *Bawden* v. *London, Edinburgh and Glasgow Ass. Co.* [1892] 2 Q.B. 534. *Stone* v. *Reliance Mutual Insurance Co.* [1972] 1 Lloyd's Rep. 469, C.A.

[55] [1972] 1 Q.B. 90; [1971] 2 All E.R. 1415, C.A. See also *Osman* v. *Ralph Moss* [1970] 1 Lloyd's Rep. 313, C.A., where a broker was liable to the insured for failing to advise him that his policy had become valueless.

broker negligently stated in the form that the car would be kept in a garage. The insured signed the form and sent it off. The car was damaged and the insurance company repudiated liability because of the incorrect answer. The insured thereupon sued the broker for negligence.

It was clearly a case where both the broker and the insured had been at fault and an apportionment under the Law Reform (Contributory Negligence) Act 1945 might have been appropriate. Rather suprisingly, however, the Court of Appeal dismissed the claim altogether on the issue of causation. They held that the broker's negligence was not a cause of the loss sustained by the insured; the loss was entirely caused by the act of the insured himself in signing and sending off the incorrect proposal form. An insurance broker is under a duty to inform his client of exceptions in the policy[56] or of other information which is relevant to the client's insurance arrangements.[57]

Statements of Practice

From the above cases and from a perusal of insurance policies one is left with an uneasy feeling that there must be many cases (some involving real hardship) when persons think they are insured when in fact they are not. As long ago as 1912 Farwell L.J. emphasised that the duty of *uberrima fides* was owed by the insurers as well as by the insured and that:

> "it is their duty to make the policy accord with and not exceed the proposal and to express both in clear and unambiguous terms."[58]

In many other areas of the law the Unfair Contract Terms Act 1977 has provided substantial protection to both business and private customers[59] but by Schedule 1 of that Act contracts of insurance are not covered by it. As a condition of granting this exemption the government required the insurance industry to draw up Statements of insurance practice. Two Statements, relating respectively to non-life and to life insurance business were

---

[56] *McNealy* v. *Pennine Insurance Co.* (1978) 122 S.J. 229.

[57] *Cherry* v. *Allied Insurance Brokers* [1978] 1 Ll.L.R. 274.

[58] *Re Bradley and Essex and Suffolk Accident Indemnity Society, supra.* The Office of Fair Trading was notified of 5,700 consumer complaints about the insurance industry in the year ending July 1980.

[59] Chapter Eight, *post*, p. 434.

published on May 4, 1977, and on July 29, 1977. They have, of course, no legally binding effect but complaints of non-compliance would presumably lead the Government to reconsider its policy of exempting insurance contracts from the 1977 Act.

One important feature of the statements is that they only apply to policyholders "resident in the U.K. and insured in their private capacity only." Thus a businessman who takes out business insurance (whether fire, fidelity, employer's liability, loss of profits or any other type) will have no protection either under the 1977 Act nor under the statements of practice.

Non-life Statement

The main provisions can be summarised as follows:

(1) The declaration at the foot of the proposal form should be restricted according to the proposer's knowledge and belief.

(2) The form should clearly spell out the duty of disclosure and the consequence of non-disclosure.

(3) Questions which the insurers have generally found to be material will be the subject of the questions in the form.

(4) So far as practicable insurers will not ask questions which require the proposer to make a value judgment or which require expert knowledge beyond that which the proposer could reasonably be required to possess.

(5) A warning as to the duty of disclosure will also be given in a renewal notice.

(6) The duty to notify claims will usually be limited to a duty to report as soon as reasonably possible.

(7) Except in cases of fraud, deception or negligence the insurer will not "unreasonably" repudiate liability

    (a) on grounds of non-disclosure or misrepresentation of a material fact where knowledge of that fact would not materially have influenced the insurer's judgment in the acceptance or assessment of the insurance; or

    (b) on the grounds of breach of warranty or condition where the circumstances of the loss are unconnected with the breach.

Life Statement

This statement is drafted is somewhat more limited terms. Thus:

1. The warning as to non-disclosure will only be given "if the

proposal form calls for the disclosure of material facts" (it should perhaps be added that there is no need to deal with renewal because the renewal of a life policy amounts to a continuation of the original contract and not to a new contract for which fresh disclosure is required).

2. The non-life provisions numbered 1. and 4. above are not reproduced in life cases.

3. Matters which insurers have commonly found to be material should be the subject of clear questions in proposal forms.

4. An insurer will not "unreasonably" reject a claim on grounds of a matter that was outside the knowledge of the proposer.

5. The duty to notify claims will be limited to a duty to notify them as soon as is reasonably possible.

Complaints and Conciliation

In Chapter Nine we shall be considering the rapid growth of Codes of Practice—one of the most important recent developments in the field of consumer protection. The statements of practice referred to above are in line with many other codes. A further significant development took place in 1981 with the setting up of the Insurance Ombudsman Bureau. Many of the large insurance companies are involved in this scheme which provides a conciliation service for their United Kingdom policyholders.

INSURABLE INTEREST

General rules

It has already been stated that the essence of an insurance contract is the protection of some interest of the insured (*ante*, p. 331). In this section it is proposed to examine the rules requiring interest and also what constitutes a sufficient interest to satisfy those rules.

The nature of insurable interest can be seen from the following working definition taken from a leading work on insurance:

> "Where the assured is so situated that the happening of the event on which the insurance money is to become payable would, as a proximate cause, involve the assured in the loss or diminution of any right recognised by law, or in any legal liability, there is an insurable

interest in the happening of that event to the extent of the possible loss or liability.[60]

Two types of interest

It is very important to distinguish sharply between insurable interest required by statute and insurable interest required by the policy. So far as statute is concerned the Life Assurance Act 1774 and the Gaming Act 1845 contain provisions designed to prevent insurance being used as a means of gaming and wagering. It will be seen shortly that a failure to comply with the statutory rules will make the policy void in some cases and illegal in others.

Interest required by policy

The question of whether the policy requires interest is essentially one of construction and there is nothing unlawful in paying on a policy where no interest exists. In practice most policies do require proof of interest because of the very important principle of indemnity. This principle is simply that a contract of insurance is a contract to indemnify the insured in respect of loss suffered by him. From this it follows that the insured must have some interest at the time of the loss, and if he has no such interest there will be nothing to indemnify and the insurers can validly refuse to pay. In practice the defence of lack of interest is frowned upon and is not often used by insurance companies.

It may be said that as a general rule all contracts of insurance are construed as contracts of indemnity (thus requiring interest) except life insurance, insurance against accident or sickness of the insured himself and certain contingency policies as, for example, those against rain. Such policies are usually[61] construed as contracts to pay a lump sum when the event occurs, regardless of actual loss.

Life Assurance Act 1774

Before the passing of this Act gambling policies of non-marine insurance were valid and enforceable. By 1774 this had been found

---

[60] *McGillivray and Parkington on Insurance Law*, (7th ed.), pp. 21–22.

[61] But not invariably. Thus an accident policy to *indemnify* the insured against medical expenses or loss of earnings would be a contract of indemnity (*Theobald* v. *Railway Passengers Assurance Co.* (1854) 10 Ex.45).

to be "mischievous" (to quote the preamble to the Act) and accordingly the Act was passed to make such policies illegal.[62] Section 1 provides that:

> No insurance shall be made by any person or persons . . . on the life or lives of any person or persons or any other event or events whatsoever, wherein the person or persons for whose use, benefit or account such policy or policies shall be made, shall have no interest, or by way of gaming or wagering.

Section 2 goes on to provide that the person for whose benefit or on whose account the policy is made must be named in the policy, while section 3 provides that no greater sum shall be recovered than the amount or value of the interest of the insured.

Section 2 as originally drawn had an unforeseen and unintended side-effect. Many large businesses run group accident schemes where the employer takes out a policy of insurance for the benefit of his employees for the time being, the object being to provide benefits on accident or death. The actual contract of insurance is made between the insurance company and the employer, so that the employee has neither a legal nor an equitable interest therein.[63] Nevertheless it is clearly for the benefit of the employees and technically it was within the restrictive provisions of section 2. Fortunately this particular problem has now been solved by statute.[64]

With regard to sections 1 and 3 the all-important time for testing the existence and extent of insurable interest is the date of the contract.[65] Thus a creditor insuring the life of his debtor would only be able to recover up to the amount of indebtedness calculated at the date of the contract. If his interest increases after that time (as, for example, in the case of a further advance) he must insure afresh.

Scope of Life Assurance Act

Section 1 of the Act refers to the "life of any person . . . or other event." This shows that, despite its name, the Act is not

---

[62] s.1 actually states that a policy contravening this section "shall be null and void" but having regard to the prohibitive words "no insurance shall be made" the courts have held such a policy to be illegal (see, *e.g. Harse* v. *Pearl Life Assurance Co.* [1904] 1 K.B. 558).

[63] *Green* v. *Russell* [1959] 2 Q.B. 226, C.A.; [1959] 2 All E.R. 525.

[64] See Insurance Companies Amendment Act 1973, s.50.

[65] *Dalby* v. *India and London Life Ass.Co.* (1854) 15 C.B. 365.

confined to policies of life insurance.[66] There are, however, certain
types of insurance to which the Act does not apply. Section 4
provides that:

> . . . nothing herein contained shall extend or be construed to
> extend to insurance bona fide made by any person or persons on
> ships, goods or merchandise.

The wording of section 1 is clearly wide enough to cover the
insurance of buildings but the Act is frequently disregarded in
practice and there appears to be no reported case in which the Act
has been held to apply to this type of insurance. A learned writer
has forcefully argued that the Act does not apply to buildings at
all.[67]

Goods

The 1774 Act, therefore, does not apply to insurance on goods,
and it has been held that this includes a policy against legal
liability arising from the use of a motor-car.[68] Gambling policies
on goods were lawful down to 1845 but the Gaming Act of that
year made all contracts by way of gaming and wagering (including
purported contracts of insurance) void.[69] Three points should be
noted about this Act. In the first place it applies to all gambling
policies and therefore overlaps with the 1774 Act. The practical
importance of the later Act, however, is that it catches goods.
Secondly, the contract is not illegal but is merely void, so that
there is no rule of law to prevent recovery of premiums paid if the
insurers have never been on risk.[70] Finally it seems clear on
principle that if the insured has no interest at the time of the
contract but has a reasonable expectation of acquiring one, the
contract will not be a wager. Even if the insured has no interest at
all, the contract is not necessarily a wager—everything depends on
the intention of the parties expressed in the policy. Thus where a

---

[66] See, e.g. Re London County Commercial Reinsurance Office [1922] 2 Ch. 67
(policy against the continuation of war).

[67] Ivamy, Fire and Motor Insurance, (3rd ed.), p. 181; Colinvaux, op. cit. treat
the Act as applying to buildings, (p. 54).

[68] Williams v. Baltic Ins.Assn. of London [1924] 2 K.B. 282 and see now s.148(4)
of the Road Traffic Act 1972, post, p. 396.

[69] s.18.

[70] Policies infringing the 1774 Act are illegal and premiums are prima facie not
recoverable, see post, p. 366.

shareholder insured timber belonging to a company in which he was the beneficial owner of all the shares, the House of Lords held that this was not a wager but a contract to pay an indemnity if interest could be proved. As it could not be proved (*post*, p. 356), an action on the policy failed.[71]

Insurable interest in lives

Own life

It is well established that a person has an unlimited interest in his own life[72] and in that of his spouse.[73] This means that he can insure his life as often as he wishes, even though he intends to assign the policies to someone without interest. If, however, the policy, while purporting to be made by and for the benefit of the life assured, is in fact made for someone else, the policy is illegal.[74] It is somewhat surprising to find that although there are stringent rules as to the interest required by the original beneficiaries, there is nothing to prevent assignment of an own-life policy to someone without interest.[75]

Friendly Societies Acts

Formerly industrial assurance companies and registered friendly societies issued policies to cover funeral expenses of near relatives. The power to issue such policies disappeared with the advent of the National Insurance Acts, and instead industrial assurance companies and registered friendly societies were given power to insure the life of a person's parent or grandparent up to an amount not exceeding £30.[76] This power still exists.

Other persons

Apart from the above cases a person can only insure the life of another if some pecuniary and legally enforceable interest can be

---

[71] *Macaura* v. *Northern Assurance Co. Ltd.* [1925] A.C. 619. Had the contract been void as a wager, the arbitrator, who made an award under an arbitration clause, would not have had jurisdiction.

[72] *McFarlane* v. *Royal London Friendly Society* (1886) 2 T.L.R. 755.

[73] *Griffiths* v. *Fleming* [1909] 1 K.B. 805.

[74] *McFarlane* v. *Royal London Friendly Society (supra)*; *Evans* v. *Bignold* (1869) L.R. 4 Q.B. 622.

[75] Assignments are further considered *post*, p. 379.

[76] Industrial Assurance and Friendly Societies Act 1948 (Amendment) Act 1958.

proved to exist. Thus in *Halford* v. *Kymer*[77] it was held that a father had no insurable interest in his son's life, even though an Act of 1774 placed the son under an obligation to support the father in his old age, while in *Harse* v. *Pearl Life Assurance Co.*[78] it was held that a son had no insurable interest in his mother's life even though she performed domestic services for him. It seems from this case that *de facto* dependency and support are not enough—there must be a legally enforceable right to support or reimbursement.

Creditors

A creditor has an insurable interest in his debtor's life.[79] The precise extent of this interest has never been decided in an English court, but in America it has been held to cover (1) the debt, (2) interest due, (3) future interest, and (4) the cost of paying annual premiums for the remainder of the debtor's life.[80] It is apparently immaterial that the debt is unenforceable by action because of absence of a written memorandum.[81] On the other hand, a debtor has no insurable interest in the life of his creditor merely because the latter gives a promise, not supported by consideration, that the debt will not be called in his (the creditor's) lifetime.[82]

Sureties

Since a surety has a right in equity to compel the principal debtor to pay the whole debt, he can insure the debtor's life for the whole debt.[83] He can also insure the life of his co-surety up to the extent of any contribution which that co-surety is liable to pay.[84] It goes without saying that the creditor can insure the surety's life as well as that of the debtor.

Employer and employee

An employee has an insurable interest in the life of his employer up to the amount of his remuneration (a term which in modern

---

[77] (1830) 10 B. & C. 724.

[78] [1904] 1 K.B. 558.

[79] *Dalby* v. *India and London Life Assurance Co.* (1854) 15 C.B. 365.

[80] *Ulrich* v. *Reinoehl* (1891) 143 Pa.238.

[81] Cf. *Hebdon* v. *West* (1863) 3 B. & S. 579. The judgment in that case does not expressly mention the point.

[82] *Hebdon* v. *West, supra.*

[83] *Branford* v. *Saunders* (1877) 25 W.R. 650.

[84] *Lea* v. *Hinton* (1854) 5 De G.M. & G. 823.

times would presumably include fringe benefits). In *Hebdon* v. *West*[85]:

> A agreed to employ B for seven years at an annual salary of £600. *Held*, this gave B an insurable interest in the life of A up to the amount of the total remuneration outstanding when the policy was effected.

Likewise an employer can insure against loss caused to him by the employee's sickness or death. Policies of so-called "key-man" insurance are becoming increasingly common,[86] especially in America.

Mere expectancy

It is a well-known principle of insurance law that to amount to insurable interest there must be some legally recognised right, so that a mere expectation of benefit in the future would not confer insurable interest. Most of the cases concern marine insurance but the principle is clearly of general application. If, however, a person enters into a transaction creating legal rights, as by selling his expectancy with a promise to repay the price if the expectancy is not realised, this may possibly give insurable interest. In *Cook* v. *Field*[87] the Court of Queen's Bench considered that such an arrangement would give the purchaser of the expectancy an insurable interest in the life of the testator. This opinion has been doubted.[88]

Capital transfer tax policies

If a person is under a legal liability to pay a sum of money on another person's death, this gives him an insurable interest in the life of that person.[89] Thus if a person makes a "chargeable transfer of value" in his lifetime he is liable to pay capital transfer tax

---

[85] *Supra*. If the contract were terminable by notice the insurable interest would probably be confined to wages down to the end of the period of notice, *cf.* the Scottish case of *Simcock* v. *Scottish Imperial*, 1902 10 S.L.T. 286.

[86] For a recent example see *Marcel Beller* v. *Hayden The Times*, December 29, 1977 where the life insured drove a car while under the influence of drink. It was held that the death was caused by his "criminal act" within an exception clause in the policy. Consequently the insurers were entitled to avoid liability.

[87] (1850) 15 Q.B. 460.

[88] McGillivray and Parkington, *op. cit.* at p. 33.

[89] It is for this reason that an insurance company which insures a life has sufficient insurable interest to enable it to reinsure.

under the Finance Act 1975 (as amended). If he then dies within three years of the disposition the rate of tax is increased and it is the transferee who must account to the Revenue for the extra tax. He can, therefore insure against the transferor dying during the three-year period.

Time

In the leading case of *Dalby* v. *India and London Life Assurance Co.*[90] the court emphasised that in life insurance cases the vital and only time for ascertaining insurable interest was the date of the contract. The facts were as follows:

> A Co., an insurance company, issued four policies under which they agreed to pay £4,000 on the death of the Duke of Cambridge. They re-insured with the defendants for £1,000. Subsequently the original policies were surrendered to A Co. whose insurable interest in the Duke's life thereupon ceased. On his death they claimed under their policy with the defendants, who contested liability and pleaded want of interest. The defence was rejected.

In giving the judgment of the Court of Exchequer, Parke B. drew a sharp distinction between life policies on the one hand and fire and marine policies on the other. The latter required insurable interest at the time of loss, since they were contracts of indemnity. Life policies, however, were not contracts of indemnity and only required insurable interest *at the time of the contract* to satisfy the Life Assurance Act 1774; such interest did not have to continue down to the date of death.

Insurable interest in property

General

Just as in life insurance, the interest must be founded on some legal or equitable right so that, again, a mere expectancy is not enough.[91] The courts, however, disapprove of the defence of lack of interest. As Brett M.R. put it in one case:

> It is the duty of the court always to lean in favour of insurable interest if possible, for it seems to me that after the underwriter has

---

[90] (1854) 15 C.B. 365.

[91] If, however, the policy is on goods the 1774 Act does not apply and if the insured has a reasonable expectancy of acquiring an interest, the policy would not be void as a wager.

received the premium the objection that there was no insurable interest is often, as nearly as possible, a technical objection and one which has no real merit, certainly as between the assured and the insurer.[92]

The interest insured may be legal or equitable, present or future and vested or contingent. Although, as already stated, a mere expectancy of itself is not sufficient, the position is otherwise where the expectancy is founded upon a legal right. Thus the owner of a business can insure against loss of profits if, for example, the business premises are put out of action by fire. Such policies are very common, but it must be remembered that profits must be specifically insured as such, so that an insurance of the business premises would not of itself cover profits.[93]

Examples

The legal owner of property can clearly insure it whether he holds it beneficially or as trustee or personal representative.[94] An equitable owner can also insure in respect of his own interest.[95] Even a person who merely has possession can probably claim to have an insurable interest since possession is equivalent to title as against anyone but the true owner and can be protected by various actions in tort (*e.g.* trespass).[96] It seems, however, that a mere *de facto* possession unaccompanied by any user or responsibility (as where the owner of land allows timber belonging to a company to lie on it) is not sufficient.[97] A bailee has insurable interest by reason of his possession, his lien and his responsibility in the event of loss or damage,[98] while a tenant of land has insurable interest by reason of his possession and his contractual right of occupation.

Sale of land

Where the owner of land contracts to sell it, both vendor and purchaser have insurable interest between contract and comple-

---

[92] *Stock* v. *Inglis* (1884) 12 Q.B.D. 564 at p. 571.

[93] *Re Wright and Pole* (1834) 1 A. & E. 621.

[94] *Lucena* v. *Craufurd* (1806) 2 Bos. & P.N.R. 269, 324.

[95] *Ex p. Yallop* (1808) 15 Ves. 60, 67. A tenant for life of settled land can of course insure up to the full value since the legal estate is vested in him.

[96] *Cf. The Winkfield* [1902] P. 42.

[97] *Macaura* v. *Northern Assurance Co.* [1925] A.C. 619.

[98] See, *e.g. Waters* v. *Monarch Life and Fire Assurance Co.* (1856) 5 E. & B. 870 and *London and North Western Ry.* v. *Glyn* (1859) 1 E. & E. 652.

tion—the vendor by reason of his ownership, possession and lien over title deeds for unpaid purchase-money, and the purchaser by reason of the risk being on him.

Mortgage of land

A mortgagee clearly has an insurable interest in the mortgaged property up to the amount of the mortgage debt. If there are several mortgagees of the same property, a situation may arise whereby the insurance company (or companies) pay out more than the sum required to reinstate the premises. The reason is, of course, that each mortgagee makes a separate contract for a personal indemnity. In *Westminster Fire Office* v. *Glasgow Provident*[99]:

> The plaintiff, a mortgagee, insured against fire with the defendants while other mortgagees of the same property insured with other companies. When a fire occurred, these companies paid sums which, when added together, amounted to more than the cost of reinstatement. No reinstatement in fact took place and the plaintiff, whose security had become insufficient, sued on his policy. The House of Lords held that he was entitled to recover.

Sale of goods

The three factors which give insurable interest under a contract for the sale of goods are property, possession and risk. If goods are still at the seller's risk or if the property has not yet passed or if the seller has possession (whether as unpaid seller or otherwise) he can insure the goods without the contract being invalidated as a wager. Likewise the buyer can insure if he has acquired property, possession or risk. In *Inglis* v. *Stock*[1] the buyer was held to have an insurable interest in goods shipped under an f.o.b. contract and forming part of a larger consignment. Although there had been no appropriation and consequently no passing of property, it was the intention of the parties that the risk should pass on shipment, and this was sufficient to confer insurable interest. Even if the buyer has not acquired property, possession or risk he can insure against loss of profit on resale as soon as he has agreed to buy the goods.

---

[99] (1888) 13 App.Cas. 699.
[1] (1885) 10 App.Cas. 263.

Creditors

In the last section it was seen that a creditor could insure his debtor's life up the amount of the debt. He has no insurable interest, however, in his debtor's property[2] unless he has some rights over it such as a charge or lien.

Shareholders

A shareholder can, of course, insure his own shares against depreciation[3] but he has no interest in the company's assets. The House of Lords in *Macaura* v. *Northern Assurance Co.*[4] rigidly applied the doctrine of separate corporate personality to defeat a claim under a policy. The facts were as follows:

> M, who owned the Killeymoon Estate, felled some timber and sold it to a company in return for £42,000 in shares. There was also a cash sum of £19,000 due to M. The shares issued to M and his nominees were the only shares issued by the company, and the timber, which lay on M's land, was virtually the sole asset of the company. M insured the timber with various companies. It was destroyed by fire. M sued on the policies and the insurers pleaded want of interest. The House of Lords held that the defence was entitled to succeed.

Time

Where the Life Assurance Act 1774 applies (as in the case of land) there must be insurable interest at the time of the contract, but if that Act does not apply (as in the case of goods) it is sufficient if there exists at that time a reasonable expectation of acquiring an interest. In either case, however, the policy, being one of indemnity, will also require proof of insurable interest at the date of the loss.

Insurance on behalf of others

The previous summary has dealt with persons insuring to protect their own insurable interest. It remains to consider how far a person can insure to protect the interest of someone else.

Insurance by person with no interest

If a person with no insurable interest at all takes out a policy of insurance, he will only be able to recover under it if he intended to

---

[2] *Macaura* v. *Northern Assurance* [1925] A.C. 619.
[3] *Wilson* v. *Jones* (1867) L.R. 2 Ex. 139.
[4] [1925] A.C. 619.

cover the interests of others. Where the Life Assurance Act 1774 applies, the persons for whose benefit the policy was made must be named in the policy.[5] If the Act does not apply, the position depends on the terms of the policy and the surrounding circumstances. Thus in *Prudential Staff Union* v. *Hall*[6] it was held that a trade union could validly insure the money of its members against theft, since it was clear that the union was insuring for the benefit of its members. If, however, the insured did not intend to protect the interests of others the contract would be void as a wager.

Amount recoverable

Where a person with no insurable interest seeks to enforce a policy taken out for the benefit of others, the amount recoverable depends on whether or not the Act of 1774 applies. If it does apply, the maximum recoverable is the amount of the insurable interest of the persons named in the policy. If it does not apply (and in the *Prudential* case a policy covering money was held to be a policy on "goods" and so outside the Act) the insured can recover the full value of the property, but must hold it on trust for the persons entitled.

Insurance by bailees

A bailee, such as a warehouseman or carrier, frequently insures goods held by him against fire, theft and other risks, and his position as bailee gives him an insurable interest up to the full value of the goods. If he takes out a policy, the question of whether he can recover the full value or merely his more limited interest as a bailee depends on the construction of the policy. In *Tomlinson (Hauliers) Ltd.* v. *Hepburn*[7] the House of Lords reviewed the authorities and Lord Reid said this:

> The fact that a bailee has an insurable interest beyond his personal loss if the goods are destroyed has never been regarded as inconsistent with the overriding principle that insurance on goods is a contract of indemnity. The question is whether the bailee has insured his whole insurable interest—in effect has taken out a goods

---

[5] s.2, *ante* p. 382. The section is often disregarded in practice (*Mumford Hotels* v. *Wheler* [1964] Ch. 117; [1963] 3 All E.R. 250).

[6] [1947] K.B. 685.

[7] [1966] A.C. 451; [1966] 1 All E.R. 418.

policy—or whether he has only insured against personal loss—has taken out a personal liability policy.[8]

Two further points should be noted. First, if the bailee recovers under a goods policy, he must hold the balance over his interest on trust for the bailor. Secondly, if the insurers can prove that the bailee did not intend to cover the interest of the bailor, the policy can be attacked as a wager.

The question of how much the bailee can recover is, therefore, one of construction. Although dicta in an early case[9] suggest that an insurance on "goods" simpliciter would merely cover the bailee's personal interest, the better view seems to be that such words are neutral, and that the nature of the conditions in the policy may well be decisive.[10] It has also been held that a policy taken out by a bailee covering "goods, his own, in trust or on commission" is a goods policy.[11] If, however, the word "commission" is followed by the words "for which he is responsible" it has been held that this is a personal liability policy only, with the result that if the bailee is not liable to the bailor there will be nothing to indemnify and the insurers will not be liable under the policy.[12]

CONSTRUCTION OF POLICY

A policy of insurance is to be construed in the same way as any other written document. Thus words must be given their ordinary and popular meaning, unless the context shows that a different meaning was intended, or unless they have acquired a different meaning by the usage of a particular trade.[13] Technical legal words, however, must be given their strict legal meaning. If there is an ambiguity the words will be construed *contra proferentem—*

---

[8] [1966] A.C. at p. 468; [1966] 1 All E.R. at p. 422.

[9] See, *e.g.* Crompton and Hill JJ. in *London and North Western Ry.* v. *Glyn* (1859) 1 E. & E. 652.

[10] See *per* Lord Reid at pp. 468 and 422 resp., Lord Hodson at pp. 472 and 424 resp.

[11] *Waters* v. *Monarch Fire & Life Assurance Co.* (1856) 5 E. & B. 870; see also *John Rigby* v. *Reliance Marine Assurance Co.* [1956] 2 Q.B. 468, [1956] 3 All E.R. 1.

[12] *North British and Mercantile Insurance Co.* v. *Moffatt* (1871) L.R. 7 C.P. 25.

[13] See *Scragg* v. *U.K. Temperance & General Provident Institution* [1976] 2 Ll.L.R. 227 where an exclusion for "motor racing" did not cover a "sprint event."

against the person who inserted them. In *Houghton* v. *Trafalgar Insurance Co.*[14]:

> An insurance policy in respect of a private four-seater car contained a clause excluding the insurer's liability if it was used to carry a load in excess of that for which it was constructed. One evening two extra passengers were carried in the car and an accident occurred. The Court of Appeal held that the clause relating to "loads" was intended to cover lorries built to carry a specified load, and did not apply to the carriage of passengers in a private car. Consequently the insurers were liable.

If two constructions are possible, the court will usually prefer a construction which will make the policy effective, rather than ineffective.[15]

Notice clause

Many policies require the insured to notify the insurers of a loss or claim within a specified time. Apart from special rules for compulsory motor insurance (*post*, p. 400) such a clause is valid and effective and is frequently construed as a condition precedent to the insurer's liability. Thus in *T. H. Adamson & Sons* v. *Liverpool and London and Globe Insurance Co.*[16]:

> A policy insuring money provided that the insurers would not be liable unless they were notified of a loss within 14 days of its occurrence. Subsequently the insured discovered that one of his employees had, over the past three years, stolen sums totalling £2,366, and immediately informed the insurers. Lord Goddard C.J. upheld the findings of an arbitrator that the claim was limited to the amount stolen in the past fourteen days.

In *Lickiss* v. *Milestone Motor Policies*[17] the court adopted a more generous construction. In that case:

---

[14] [1954] 1 Q.B. 247; [1953] 2 All E.R. 1409. See also *ante*, p. 342.
[15] Thus in *Frewin* v. *Poland* [1968] 1 Lloyd's Rep. 100 an author who insured his manuscript against "loss . . . resulting in the necessity for the assured to re-write" was held entitled to recover under the policy when a loss occurred, even though he did not in fact re-write the book.
[16] [1953] 2 Lloyd's Rep. 355. An even stronger case was *Cassel* v. *Lancashire and Yorkshire Accident* (1885) 1 T.L.R. 495, where the insured had a canoeing accident and the injury did not develop for eight months. He then immediately gave notice, but the policy required noice to be given within 14 days of the accident, and the claim accordingly failed. See also *Cox* v. *Orion Insurance Co.* [1982] R.T.R. 1 C.A.
[17] [1966] 1 W.L.R. 1334; [1966] 2 All E.R. 972.

A motor policy required the insured to inform the insurers as soon as possible of any summons served on him. This was described as a "condition precedent" to the insurer's liability. The police served a summons on the insured (who failed to inform the insurers) and at the same time the police notified the insurers that the summons had been served. A majority of the Court of Appeal held that the failure by the insured to give notice was not a breach of the notice clause because the insurers had already received the information from another source.

It has recently been suggested that the insurers may lose their right to avoid liability if they are guilty of unreasonable delay in giving notice of avoidance to the insured.[18] It is doubtful whether this reasoning is correct. The above discussion must now be read in the light of the two Statements of Practice (as to which see *ante*, p. 345).

THE RISK

It is vital for the insured to know precisely the extent of the risks which are covered. Unfortunately it cannot be said that the form of the modern policy assists him in this respect.

Negligence

In the absence of contrary agreement a policy will cover a loss due to the negligence of the insured. A common example is a comprehensive motor policy which will cover damage to the insured's car, even if the insured drove the car negligently. Another example is *Harris* v. *Poland*[19]:

A lady who had insured the contents of her house against damage by fire hid some jewellery in the grate of her fireplace to protect it against theft. Later that evening she lit a fire, forgetting that the jewellery was there, and the jewellery was damaged. It was held that the damage came within the risk covered by the policy and the insurer was liable.

Limitations on cover

Lord Sumner emphasised in *British and Foreign Marine Insurance* v. *Gaunt*[20] that even if the policy was a so-called

---

[18] *Allen* v. *Robles* [1969] 1 W.L.R. 1193; [1969] 3 All E.R. 159.
[19] [1941] 1 K.B. 462; [1941] 1 All E.R. 204.
[20] [1921] 2 A.C. 41.

"all-risks" policy there were certain types of loss which would not be covered in the absence of an express provision. The object of insurance is to guard against a fortuitous act happening from without, so that the policy will not usually cover damage caused by:

(1) *The insured's wilful act*

Thus the personal representatives of a life insured will not (unless otherwise agreed) be able to recover if the insured commits suicide when sane,[21] nor will insurers under a fire policy be liable if the insured deliberately fires the property.[22]

Where two persons are insured, the wilful misconduct of one will not prevent a claim by the other unless his interest is so inseparably connected with that of the wrongdoer that his loss or gain necessarily affects them both. Thus if a policy is taken out by two joint tenants of a house, it would seem that arson by one would preclude a claim by the other. On the other hand, the House of Lords has held that where a policy covers both the mortgagor and the mortgagee, the deliberate destruction of the property by the mortgagor does not preclude the mortgagee from suing under the policy.[23]

(2) *Inherent vice*

An accident policy would not cover death from natural causes.

(3) *Wear and tear*

A policy covering damage to a car would not cover loss of value through normal depreciation, nor the cost of replacing worn-out tyres.

It goes without saying that the policy does not cover risks which it is not lawful to cover, so that a criminal could not insure against imprisonment or execution.

Loss

Where property is insured against loss, an insured will not have a claim unless he can prove, first, that there has been a loss, and,

---

[21] See *post*, p. 384.
[22] *Upjohn* v. *Hitchens* [1918] 2 K.B. 48 at p. 58, *per* Scrutton L.J.
[23] *Samuel (P.) & Co.* v. *Dumas* [1924] A.C. 43.

secondly, that the loss was caused by the risk insured against. With regard to the meaning of loss, the following statement by Bankes L.J. is instructive:

> "Mere temporary deprivation would not under ordinary circumstances constitute a loss. On the other hand, complete deprivation amounting to a certainty that the goods could never be recovered is not necessary to constitute a loss. It is between these two extremes that the difficult cases lie. . . . "[24]

In *Holmes* v. *Payne*[25]:

> a necklace disappeared and after a thorough search could not be found. The insurers who had insured it against loss thereupon agreed to replace it. Subsequently it was found. It was nevertheless held that on the facts of the case there had been a "loss" and accordingly the insurers remained bound by their agreement to replace, although they were entitled to the necklace as salvage.

Goods may be "lost" even though the owner knows of their physical whereabouts. Thus in *Webster* v. *General Accident Fire and Life Assurance Corporation*[26]:

> The plaintiff parted with possession of his car to a rogue who falsely represented that he had a buyer for it. The rogue sold it at an auction and disappeared. The buyer at the auction acquired a good title. Parker J. (as he then was) held that there had been a "loss" of the car, and the plaintiff was entitled to recover under the policy covering loss.

On the other hand in *Eisinger* v. *General Accident Fire and Life Assurance Corporation*[27]:

> The plaintiff agreed to sell his car to a rogue in return for a cheque which was dishonoured. He claimed under a policy covering "loss" of the car, but Lord Goddard C.J. held that a person who had agreed to transfer the ownership of a car could not be heard to say that he had lost it. What he had lost was the proceeds of sale.

Causation

A loss may result from a combination of different causes, but for insurance law the "proximate" or dominant cause must be selected, and the insured will only recover if this proximate cause

---

[24] *Moore* v. *Evans* [1917] 1 K.B. 458, 471.
[25] [1930] 2 K.B. 301.
[26] [1953] 1 Q.B. 520; [1953] 1 All E.R. 663.
[27] [1955] 1 W.L.R. 869; [1955] 2 All E.R. 897.

was covered by the policy. It has been said that "the choice of the real or efficient cause from out of the whole complex of the facts must be made by applying common-sense standards."[28] The following cases illustrate:

> *Winspear* v. *Accident Insurance* (1880) 6 Q.B.D. 42.
> A man fell into a stream in the course of a fit and was drowned. It was held that the accident and not the fit was the cause of death.
> *Fidelity and Casualty of New York* v. *Mitchell* [1917] A.C. 592.
> An accident brought on latent tuberculosis which in turn caused death. The House of Lords held that the accident was the proximate cause of death.
> *Symington* v. *Union Insurance of Canton* (1928) 97 L.J.K.B. 646.
> Cork was insured against fire. When a fire started some distance away, some of the cork was thrown into the sea so as to prevent the fire spreading. It was held that the fire was the cause of the loss.
> *Gray* v. *Barr* [1971] 2 Q.B. 554; [1971] 2 All E.R. 949.
> A went into B's house and went upstairs carrying a loaded shotgun to frighten B. During a scuffle the gun went off and B was killed. It was held that the cause of death was A's deliberate act of going upstairs carrying the gun. Consequently the death was not caused by "accident" within the meaning of A's insurance policy (see also *post*, pp. 384 and 386).

Burden of proof

The onus of proving that the loss comes within the risk covered is on the insured. Thus if the goods are insured against burglary or fire, it is for the insured to prove that a burglary or fire did in fact take place. On the other hand, where the insurers seek to repudiate on the grounds of arson or fraud the burden of proving this is on them,[29] and the evidence must establish a very high degree of probability.[30]

---

[28] Lord Wright in *Yorkshire Dale S.S. Co.* v. *Minister of War Transport* [1942] A.C. 691, 706; [1942] 2 All E.R. 615. It has recently been held that heavy rainfall is not a "storm" (*Anderson* v. *Norwich Union Fire Insurance Society* [1977] 1 Ll.L.R. p. 253 C.A.) and that seepage of water is not a "flood" *Young* v. *Sun Alliance and London Insurance* [1976] 3 All E.R. 561 C.A.

[29] *Slattery* v. *Mance* [1962] 1 Q.B. 676; [1962] 1 All E.R. 525.

[30] *S. & M. Carpets (London)* v. *Cornhill Insurance Co.* [1981] 1 Ll.L.R. 667, (burden not discharged); *Watkins & Davis* v. *Legal and General Assurance Co.* [1981] 1 Ll.L.R. 674, (burden discharged).

Premium

The premium is the consideration for the risk run by the insurer.

Payment

The method and the time for payment of the premium depends on the terms of the contract express or implied. Thus payment to an agent will be sufficient if he had actual or apparent authority to receive it. In theory insurers are not bound to accept payment by cheque, but in practice they almost invariably agree to do so. If payment is made by a cheque drawn by the insured, the payment is presumed to be conditional only,[31] so that if a policy provided for forfeiture if a premium was not paid by the third of February, the receipt of a cheque on that date would not prevent forfeiture if the cheque was subsequently dishonoured.

Non-payment

The insurer can sue for the premium if there is a binding contract to issue the policy in respect of which the premium is payable.[32] In practice many policies provide that the insurers are not to be on risk until the premium is paid.

Renewal

If renewal of a policy requires the insurer's consent, as it does in virtually all types of insurance except life insurance, the insurers are not bound to accept a renewal premium. In the case of life policies, however, the insured is usually given an absolute right to renew and his renewal premium must be accepted, providing that it is tendered in accordance with the conditions of the policy. Alternatively a life policy may take the form of a continuing insurance, subject to forfeiture on non-payment of a premium.

Days of grace

Many policies, to avoid practical difficulties and hardship, provide for a number of extra days (or days of grace), within which a renewal premium may be paid. A question sometimes arises where during the days of grace but before the premium has been

---

[31] *Cf.* the position where a seller of goods is paid by cheque, *ante*, p. 170.
[32] *General Accident Insurance Corporation* v. *Cronk* (1901) 17 T.L.R. 233.

paid, a loss occurs. The insurers' liability will depend on the type of policy and on the wording of the policy. In the case of policies other than life the cover will usually come to an end at the expiration of the original term of insurance, and if loss occurs subsequently the insurers will not be on risk. The sending of a premium during the days of grace is simply an offer to renew, and if it is accepted by the insurers in ignorance of a loss having occurred the new policy will be either voidable for non-disclosure (if the loss was known to the insured) or void for common mistake. In the case of life policies giving a right to renew on payment of a premium within the days of grace, the position where death occurs before renewal but within the days of grace is uncertain,[33] but in practice the policy expressly provides that the insurers will remain liable during the days of grace. Finally it was held in *Stuart* v. *Freeman*[34] that where a life policy took the form of a continuing contract, subject to forfeiture on non-payment of a premium, no forfeiture was possible during the days of grace and consequently the insurers remained on risk during that time.

Recovery of premiums

Subject to special rules as to fraud and illegality, the principle is that in the absence of contrary agreement the premium is recoverable if the risk has never attached, the reason being that there has been a total failure of consideration. The rule is an old one and in the eighteenth century Lord Mansfield regarded it as well established.[35] Most of the case law has been evolved in marine cases where the matter is now governed by statute,[36] and with the paucity of case law in non-marine cases the precise extent of the principle set out above cannot be regarded as finally settled. It seems clear, however, that in the absence of contrary agreement the premium is recoverable in the following cases:

(1) Where the contract is void for common mistake. This is merely an illustration of the general rule that money paid under a mistake of fact is recoverable.[37]

---

[33] See dicta of Willes J. in *Pritchard* v. *The Merchants and Tradesmen's Mutual Life Insurance Society* (1858) 3 C.B. (N.S.) 622 at p. 643, and contrast dicta of Matthew L.J. in *Stuart* v. *Freeman* [1903] 1 K.B. 47, 55.

[34] [1903] 1 K.B. 47.

[35] *Stevenson* v. *Snow* (1761) 3 Burr. 1237, 1246.

[36] Marine Insurance Act 1906, s.84.

[37] *Kelly* v. *Solari* (1841) 9 M. & W. 54.

(2) Where the contract is avoided for innocent misrepresentation or non-disclosure not amounting to fraud.[38]

(3) Where the policy is avoided by the insurers for breach of a present warranty (such as an untrue statement by the insured that he is of temperate habits).[39] If, however, the warranty relates to the future (as in the case of a warranty not to engage in motor racing) the insurers will be on risk until the breach occurs,[40] so that a premium paid in respect of such period will not be recoverable. On the other hand a premium paid in respect of a period occurring after the breach is recoverable[41] unless the contract otherwise provides, as it frequently does.

Fraud

If the policy was obtained by the fraud of the insured, he clearly cannot sue to recover his premium, since he cannot be allowed to take advantage of his own wrong. If, however, the insurers take the initiative and seek the equitable remedy of rescission for misrepresentation or non-disclosure, the court may, in its discretion, put them on terms as to return of premium, the principle being that "he who seeks equity must do equity."[42]

Gaming Act 1845

There appears to be no direct authority as to whether premiums can be recovered where the contract is void as a gaming contract under the Gaming Act 1845. On principle it should be recoverable since the insurers have not been on risk, and the contract is not illegal. In marine insurance, however, section 84(3)(c) of the Marine Insurance Act 1906 prohibits the recovery of premiums in the case of a gaming or wagering contract.

Illegal policies

Policies which are illegal, *e.g.* for want of insurable interest, are governed by the general rule of contract—*in pari delicto potior est*

---

[38] See, *e.g. Biggar* v. *Rock Life Assurance Co.* [1902] 1 K.B. 516 at p. 526, *per* Wright J.

[39] *Thomson* v. *Weems* (1884) 9 App.Cas. 671. Presumably, if there is fraud, the rules governing fraud will apply.

[40] *Ante*, p. 341.

[41] *Sparenborg* v. *Edinburgh Life Assurance Co.* [1912] 1 K.B. 195, 204, *per* Bray J.

[42] *London Assurance* v. *Mansel* (1879) 11 Ch.D. 363, 372. *Cf. Lodge* v. *National Union Investment Co.* [1907] 1 Ch. 301 (moneylending case).

conditio defendentis. Thus premiums paid under an illegal contract cannot be recovered.[43] To this rule there are three exceptions:

(1) Where the insured was induced to effect the policy by a fraudulent mispresentation by the insurer's agent that the policy was lawful, premiums are recoverable because the parties were not *in pari delicto.*[44]

(2) Premiums are recoverable if the insured was unaware of the facts making the contract illegal, as where, in an early case, the insured believed that he was the owner of the property insured, whereas in fact he was not.[45]

(3) Premiums are recoverable if the insured abandons the contract before the risk has started to run. This is an illustration of the general contract rule which encourages repentance by allowing a *locus poenitentiae.*

Apportionment

Premiums are generally indivisible, and the Apportionment Act 1870 does not apply.[46] Thus the insured cannot claim a return of part of a premium on the grounds that for part of the period of insurance the risk did not attach. If the property is over-insured the insured can recover a proportion of the premium in the case of marine insurance (Marine Insurance Act 1906, s.84(3)(*e*)),and a learned writer has suggested that a similar rule applies to non-marine insurance, provided that the insured acted honestly.[47]

Quite apart from this, the policy sometimes gives the insurers an option to cancel the policy and provides that if such option is exercised a rateable proportion of the premium must be returned.

---

[43] *Harse* v. *Pearl Life Assurance Co.* [1904] 1 K.B. 558, C.A.

[44] *Hughes* v. *Liverpool Victoria Friendly Society* [1916] 2 K.B. 482. If the misrepresentation is innocent, however, the general rule applies (*Harse* v. *Pearl Life Assurance Co., supra*). It is thought that the agent could be liable in negligence since his expertise was being relied upon (*cf. Hedley Byrne* v. *Heller & Partners* [1964] A.C. 465; [1963] 2 All E.R. 575).

[45] *Routh* v. *Thompson* (1809) 11 East 428.

[46] s.6.

[47] Ivamy, *General Principles of Insurance Law*, (2nd ed.), p. 163.

INDEMNITY

The indemnity principle

It will be recalled that most contracts of insurance are construed as contracts of indemnity, the major exceptions being life insurance and insurance against accident or sickness of the insured himself.[48] Under an indemnity contract there is one fundamental rule, namely that the insured cannot recover or retain for his own benefit more than his actual loss.[49] In *Darrell* v. *Tibbitts*[50]:

> A landlord of property received £750 under a fire insurance policy when the property was damaged by fire. Subsequently the tenant, who had covenanted to repair, did so. *Held*, since the contract of insurance was one of personal indemnity of the landlord the insurance moneys were repayable to the insurers since the landlord had suffered no loss.

The only exception to the basic rule arises in the case of a so-called valued policy. In order to fix with certainty the sum payable in the event of a loss, the parties sometimes agree at the time of the contract on the value of the subject-matter of the insurance. The main feature about such an agreement (which corresponds roughly with a contractual provision as to liquidated damages) is that where a total loss occurs a sum representing the agreed value is recoverable by the insured, even though it exceeds his actual loss. In such a case the valuation is conclusive as between the parties, so that the insurers cannot claim that the insured value was not the true value[51] unless the overvaluation was so excessive as to amount to a wager[52] or, of course, unless there was something in the nature of misrepresentation or non-disclosure. The most common type of valued policy to be found in non-marine insurance is a policy insuring against loss of profits. Valued policies are very rare in fire insurance. It has been suggested that where the Life Assurance Act 1774 applies, a claim

---

[48] *Ante*, p. 347.

[49] See *Castellain* v. *Preston* (1883) 11 Q.B.D. 380 at p. 386 *et seq.*, *per* Brett L.J. For a full discussion of the indemnity principle see (1949) 49 *Columbia Law Review* 818 *et seq*.

[50] (1880) 5 Q.B.D. 560. The tenant could presumably have taken advantage of s.83 of the Fires Prevention (Metropolis) Act 1774 as to which see *post*, pp. 373–374.

[51] *Bruce* v. *Jones* (1863) 1 H. & C. 769.

[52] *Lewis* v. *Rucker* (1761) 2 Burr. 1167.

based on an overvaluation could be challenged under section 3 of that Act, which limits the amount recoverable to the interest of the insured at the time of the contract.[53] While this may be correct from the literal reading of the section, a bona fide valued policy is certainly outside the mischief of the Act and the court is free to take the opposite view by holding that the "interest" of the insured is determined by the agreed valuation. The objection based on section 3 is not in practice relied upon.[54]

The amount recoverable

It has just been seen that under a valued policy the property is insured at an agreed valuation. In other cases the parties agree on a maximum figure up to which the insurance is to operate. The premium payable is assessed by reference to this maximum figure. This maximum figure is somewhat misleadingly spoken of as the sum insured, and the cardinal point is that the insurer's liability can never exceed this figure. It may, however, be less than that figure since the contract is to pay the sum insured or the loss suffered by the insured, whichever is less.

Three basic rules

Applying the above rules to particular situations three basic rules can be formulated. The first basic rule is that in the event of a total loss, the insurers under an unvalued policy are liable to pay the market value of the property at the time and place of the loss or the sum insured, whichever is less.[55] Thus if a car is insured for £800 and the market value at the time of loss is only £600, the insurers are only liable to pay £600 although they have been receiving premiums based on a figure of £800. This is a common source of misunderstanding among motorists who fail to reduce the sum insured as the car advances in age. Conversely, if a car insured for £800 increases in value to £1,000, the insurer's liability is limited to £800, the sum insured. It should also be noted that if the insured has only a limited interest in the property the insurer's liability to indemnify him will not exceed the value of that interest.

---

[53] *Ante*, p. 348, Colinvaux, *op. cit.* p. 9.
[54] Thus in *Elcock* v. *Thomson, infra,* the section was not pleaded.

The case of *Re Wilson and Scottish Insurance Co.*[55] turned on special facts:

> W owned a Studebaker car and insured it for *inter alia* damage or loss "up to full value." In his proposal form he stated the present value as £250 and the premium was based on this figure. The premium was paid at the original rate on each renewal. Some months after a renewal the car was destroyed and the arbitrator found its then value to be £400. On the question of how much was recoverable by the insured, Astbury J. held that (1) the insured must be taken to have repeated his statement as to value on each renewal; (2) accordingly if the increase from £250 to £400 occurred since the last renewal, W was entitled to £400, whereas if it had occurred before the renewal he was only entitled to £250. The matter was referred to the arbitrator for his finding on this point.

Two observations can be made. The first is that, unlike most policies, there was no "sum insured" operating as a ceiling on the insurer's liability. The second point is that if the increase had occurred before the renewal, the insurers could presumably have escaped liability by pleading misrepresentation or non-disclosure. They did not plead this, no doubt feeling that having received a premium based on £250 they should honour their obligations up to that amount.

Normally, therefore, the indemnity is based on the market value of the property and not the cost of its purchase or production[56] or reinstatement.[57] If, however, the property has no market value—as in the case of a valuable but unsaleable machine—the second basic rule is that the insurers are liable to pay the cost of reinstatement or the sum insured, whichever is less.[58] The third basic rule is that in the case of a partial loss—as where a car is merely damaged—the insurer's liability is essentially based on the

---

[55] [1920] 2 Ch. 28. If the insurers contest liability and are found liable, the court may exercise its power of awarding interest under the Law Reform (Miscellaneous Provisions) Act 1934 (*Burts & Harvey Ltd. and Alchemy* v. *Vulcan Boiler and General Insurance Company Ltd.* [1966] 1 Lloyd's Rep. 354.

[56] *Aubrey (Richard) Film Productions* v. *Graham* [1960] 2 Lloyd's Rep. 101. In view of ever-increasing costs it is clearly advisable to base house and contents insurance on the cost of reinstatement and replacement and to keep it under annual review, a number of policies contain automatic index linking provisions.

[57] *Leppard* v. *Excess Insurance Co.* [1979] 1 W.L.R. 512 C.A.

[58] See *per* Lord Selborne in *Westminster Fire Office* v. *Glasgow Provident Investment Society* (1888) 13 App.Cas. 699, 713.

cost of repairs or the sum insured, whichever is the less.[59] An alternative formula, sometimes used in fire insurance, is that the insurers are liable for the difference between the value before the fire and the value after the fire.[60]

Mere sentimental value is not to be taken into account[61] and it has already been pointed out that the insurance of property against "loss" will not cover loss of profits or use. In other words, profits must be insured as such.[62]

Valued policy

Where a partial loss occurs in the case of a valued policy, it seems that the insurers are liable for a proportion of the agreed valuation corresponding to the diminution of the actual value. In *Elcock* v. *Thomson*[63]:

> A mansion house was insured against loss or damage by fire. It was a valued policy and the value was agreed at £106,850. The house was damaged by fire. In an action on the policy the actual value before the fire was found to be £18,000 and the value after the fire £12,600. It was not reinstated. Morris J. held that the insured was entitled to recover a proportion of the agreed value corresponding to the diminution of the actual value. Since this diminution was 30 per cent. the correct award was 30 per cent. of £106,850, *i.e.* £32,055.

His Lordship left open the question of whether the sum required for reinstatement could have been claimed if reinstatement had taken place. On principle there seems no reason why such sum should not be recovered up to the sum insured.

Excess clause

Many policies require the insured to bear a proportion of each claim (*e.g.* "excess of £100 for each and every claim"). If, for example, a builder agrees to repair defects over a five year period he cannot avoid the full effects of an "excess" clause under a

---

[59] See *Scottish Amicable Heritable Securities Association* v. *Northern Assurance* (1883) 11 R.(Ct.of Sess.) 287, 295, *per* Lord Craighill.

[60] *Westminster Fire* v. *Glasgow Provident, supra.* McGillivray and Parkington, *op. cit.* p. 643 *et seq.*

[61] *Re Egmont's Trust* [1908] 1 Ch. 821, 826, *per* Warrington J.

[62] *Maurice* v. *Goldsborough Mort & Co.* [1939] A.C. 452; [1939] 3 All E.R. 637, P.C.

[63] [1949] 2 K.B. 755; [1949] 2 All E.R. 381.

liability policy by combining various repairs into a single claim against the insurers.[64]

Average clause

If the insured insures for less than the full value of the property, the insurers are nevertheless liable to indemnify the insured right up to the sum insured. In the case of a total loss, there is no difficulty—the insured will receive the sum insured and bears the remaining loss himself. If, however, there is a mere partial loss, the insurers are prima facie liable to indemnify the insured right up to the sum insured, even though they have only received a small premium and even though they must have calculated that a partial loss would not exhaust the full insurance moneys. To guard against under-insurance, it is very common, especially in the case of fire policies, where the risk of partial loss is high, to find an "average clause." The words "subject to average" in a Lloyd's policy incorporate the following standard clause:

> "Wherever a sum insured is declared to be subject to average, if the property shall at the breaking out of any fire be collectively of greater value than such sum insured, then the insured shall be considered as being his own insurer for the difference and shall bear a rateable share of the loss accordingly."

In *Acme Wood Flooring Co.* v. *Marten*[65]:

> Timber worth £36,000 was insured for £12,000 under a policy containing an average clause. Damage was caused totalling £12,000. It was held that the insurers were only liable to pay—

$$\frac{£12,000}{£36,000} \times £12,000 = i.e. \ £4,000$$

[Had there been no average clause, the full £12,000 would have been payable.]

Reinstatement

Option clause

It will be apparent from what has been said that the primary obligation of the insurers is to provide a cash indemnity. In

---

[64] *Trollope & Colls* v. *Haydon* [1977] 1 W.L.R. 244 C.A.
[65] (1904) 90 L.T. 313.

practice, however, many policies give the insurers an option to replace or to reinstate the property as an alternative to paying its value. This power to reinstate may substantially reduce the insurer's liability. In *Westminster Fire* v. *Glasgow Provident*, the facts of which were set out on p. 335, the various insurance companies had to pay out an aggregate sum in excess of the cost of reinstatement. Had the companies jointly exercised their contractual option to reinstate, the cost of so doing would have exhausted their liability.

Once the insurers have elected to exercise their option to reinstate a building, they are bound to put it into substantially the same condition as it was before the fire, and this obligation is not limited to the sum insured.[66] It follows that if, during the reinstatement, building costs rise so that the insurers are compelled to spend more than the sum insured they are not excused from liability. If, however, the task of reinstatement becomes commercially impossible owing to some unforeseen circumstance occurring without the fault of either party, the doctrine of frustration would apply to prevent the insurers being liable for damages for failure to build.[67] In such a case the insured would have to be content with an indemnity in cash. An example of this situation would be where the proposed reinstatement was contrary to the local by-laws and hence not possible. Insurers who reinstate will also be liable if the work is done badly or if there is unreasonable delay.[68]

Fires Prevention (Metropolis) Act 1774

Section 83 of this Act opens with the following preamble:

> And in order to deter and hinder ill-minded persons from wilfully setting their house or houses or other buildings on fire with a view of gaining to themselves the insurance money, whereby the lives and fortunes of many families may be lost or endangered.

To prevent such macabre schemes, the section provides that where an insurance office has insured a house or other building against loss or damage by fire the company is bound, at the request

---

[66] *Times Fire Assurance Co.* v. *Hawke* (1858) 1 F. & F. 406.

[67] Cases like *Brown* v. *Royal Insurance Co.* (1859) 1 E. & E. 853 must now be read in the light of the doctrine of frustration. Colinvaux, *op. cit.* p. 177.

[68] McGillivray and Parkington, *op. cit.* p. 696.

of any person interested, to lay out the insurance money as far as it will go in reinstatement. Likewise, the insurance office is bound to apply the money in reinstatement where it suspects fraud or arson on the part of the owner-occupier, or other person insuring the property.[69] The duty to reinstate does not, however, arise if within sixty days of the claim the party claiming the insurance money gives a sufficient security to the directors of the office that the money will be used for reinstatement, or if within that time the money is settled and disposed of among the contending parties to the satisfaction of the directors.

Several points in this section require attention. The first is that, after earlier doubts, it was held in *Re Quicke's Trusts*[70] that the section was of general application and not confined to London. Secondly, it was suggested in *Portavon Cinema* v. *Price and Century Assurance Co.*[71] that the section only applied to insurance companies and not to Lloyd's underwriters—if this is so it is difficult to see why it should be. Thirdly, the power to compel reinstatement is vested in "any person interested," so that it includes persons who are strangers to the contract of insurance, provided only that they have an interest in the subject-matter.[72]

The provisions of the Act differ in many ways from the power of reinstatement contained in the option clause. The main difference is that in the former case the right to insist on reinstatement is given to persons interested, whereas in the latter case it is the insurers who can enforce this right. Then, again, the Act is confined to insurance of buildings against loss or damage by fire. Finally the statutory obligation of the insurance company is limited to the insurance money, so that if the cost of reinstatement exceeds the sum insured, the insurance company is not liable in any way in respect of such excess.

Enforcement

It is clear that a person interested can obtain an injunction against the insurance company restraining them from paying over

---

[69] If the insurers can *prove* fraud or arson they will repudiate liability altogether.
[70] [1908] 1 Ch. 887 following *Ex p. Gorley* (1864) 11 L.T. 319.
[71] [1939] 4 All E.R. 601.
[72] *Sinnott* v. *Bowden* [1912] 2 Ch. 414 (mortgagee); *Wimbledon Park Golf Club Ltd.* v. *Imperial Insurance Co.* (1902) 18 T.L.R. 815 (lessee).

the insurance money without obtaining from the insured a sufficient security to reinstate.[73] Whether he can go further and obtain a mandatory injunction requiring the money to be laid out in reinstatement is a point which has produced a conflict of judicial opinion,[74] but on principle there seems no reason why such remedy should not be available.

Position of mortgagee

Although a mortgagee's insurable interest is limited to the sum secured by the mortgage, he is entitled to have his security kept undiminished. If a mortgage was made securing a loan of £2,000 on a house worth £5,000, an insurance for £2,000 might prove inadequate, since other persons interested could apply under the 1774 Act to have the money used in reinstatement and the partially rebuilt house might then be an insufficient security. To obtain full protection, therefore, a mortgagee can (and should) insure up to the full amount of the property. If he were to make a claim, however, it is thought that it would be limited to the amount of his interest.

Subrogation

The cardinal rule of indemnity insurance is that the insured cannot recover more than an indemnity. In the words of Lord Blackburn:

> "When there is a contract of indemnity . . . and a loss happens, anything which reduces or diminishes that loss reduces the amount which the indemnifier has to pay, and if the indemnifier has already paid it, then if anything which diminishes the loss comes into the hands of the person to whom he has paid it, it becomes an equity that the person who has already paid the full indemnity is entitled to be recouped by having that amount back."[75]

---

[73] *Wimbledon Park Golf Club Ltd.* v. *Imperial Insurance Co., supra.*

[74] See Page Wood V.-C. in *Simpson* v. *Scottish Union Insurance Co.* (1863) 1 H. & M. 615 (remedy available); Wright J. in *Wimbledon Park Golf Club Ltd.* v. *Imperial Insurance Co.* (1902) 18 T.L.R. 815 (remedy not available); doubted in *Sun Insurance Office* v. *Galinsky* [1914] 2 K.B. 545.

[75] *Burnand* v. *Rodocanachi* (1882) 7 App.Cas. 333 at p. 339. Note that an insurer who pays an agreed value is deemed to have paid a full indemnity and can recover from the insured any damages which the insured recovers up to that amount, even though the agreed value is less than the true value (*Thames & Mersey Marine Insurance* v. *British & Chilian S.S. Co.* [1916] 1 K.B. 30).

This quotation summarises perfectly the doctrine of subrogation. An insurer who has paid an indemnity is subrogated to the rights of the insured against any third party who is liable to the insured in respect of that loss or damage. Thus if a house insured against fire is damaged by a fire caused by the negligence of X, the insurers having paid on the policy can sue X to recoup themselves. The action is in fact brought in the name of the insured, who can be compelled to lend his name to the proceedings, on tender of a suitable indemnity as to costs.[76] Once the insurers have themselves been indemnified in respect of the sum paid by them and costs, any additional damages belong to the insured.

If the insured person succeeds in proceedings against a third party he may be awarded interest on the judgment under the Supreme Court Act 1981 as compensation for having been kept out of his money. In reality, however, it is the insurers who have been kept out of their money; accordingly he must account to his insurers for any interest accruing due since they indemnified him.[77]

The right of subrogation goes beyond the mere enforcement of rights of action. In *Castellain* v. *Preston*[78]:

> The owner of a house which was insured against fire contracted to sell it. After contracts had been exchanged but before completion a fire occurred and the insurance company paid the vendor. Subsequently the purchase was completed. It was held that since the vendor had received the full purchase price, he could not be said to have suffered any loss as a result of the fire and was bound to repay the insurance moneys to the company.

If the insured receives a sum from a third party in respect of the loss or damage covered by the policy, the principle of subrogation requires him to hold this sum on trust for the insurers, to the extent of any sum paid by them. This principle can apply even to a purely voluntary payment, but it does not apply where a payment expressly relates to any loss not covered by the policy.[79]

If the insured compromises his rights against a third party (as, for example, by giving a tenant a release under seal from his

---

[76] *Edwards* v. *Motor Union* [1922] 2 K.B. 249, 254, *per* McCardie J.

[77] *H. Cousins & Co. Ltd.* v. *D. & S. Carriers* [1971] 2 Q.B. 230; [1971] 1 All E.R. 55.

[78] (1883) 11 Q.B.D. 380. The position today might be different if the purchaser could claim an interest in the moneys. See s.47 of the Law of Property Act 1925 *post*, p. 381.

[79] *Burnand* v. *Rodocanachi, supra.*

covenant to repair) he in effect destroys or modifies his insurers' right of subrogation and he is liable to them for any loss which he causes them.[80] If a contract is made in respect of goods consigned to a carrier, any agreement between the insured and the carrier which reduces the carrier's legal liability is a material fact requiring disclosure, since it affects the insurer's rights of subrogation.[81]

Three final points should be noted. First, the insurers will not be subrogated to any right unless it is incidental to the loss which they have indemnified. Thus if a motor-cyclist has insured his vehicle against damage and it is damaged in an accident caused by the negligence of M, the insurers who have paid will be entitled to damages recovered in respect of the vehicle but not damages recovered for personal injuries. Secondly, the equitable doctrine of subrogation can only be invoked if the insurers have indemnified the insured.[82] In practice, however, many liability policies give express rights of subrogation to the insurers and these can be enforced even before payment. An example of this can be seen in the case of *Lister* v. *Romford Ice and Cold Storage Co. Ltd.*, where the policy gave the employers' insurers a right to claim indemnity from a negligent employee.[83] Finally, subrogation only applies to contracts of indemnity and not to life policies.

Contribution

A person can generally insure as often as he pleases, but if the contract is one of indemnity he cannot recover in the aggregate more than his actual loss. If there has been a double insurance of the same interest against the same risk, an insurer who has paid more than his share can bring an action to recover rateable contribution from the others. In order to give rise to a claim for contribution, the contract must be one of indemnity, and in addition the following conditions must be satisfied:

---

[80] *Phoenix Assurance Co.* v. *Spooner* (1906) 22 T.L.R. 695, C.A.

[81] *Tate* v. *Hyslop* (1885) 15 Q.B.D. 368, 377.

[82] Thus if the insured, having left his car with a garage for repair, is dissatisfied with the work done and takes the car away, the insurers cannot be said to have "indemnified" their insured if they pay the garage without his consent (*Scottish Union and National Insurance Co.* v. *Davis* [1970] 1 Lloyd's Rep. 1, C.A.).

[83] [1957] A.C. 555; [1957] 1 All E.R. 125 in practice such subrogation is not enforced without the employer's agreement. For judicial disapproval of subrogation in the employment context see *Morris* v. *Ford Motor Co. Ltd.* [1973] Q.B. 792; [1973] 2 All E.R. 1084.

(1) The risk which has occurred must be common to both policies.[84]

(2) Insurances must have a common subject-matter.[84] Thus where A drives B's car with B's consent while A's car is being repaired, A's legal liability to third parties may be covered under his own policy covering him while driving other cars, and also under B's policy covering persons driving with B's consent, and a case for contribution might arise.

(3) The policies must cover the same interest. In *North British and Mercantile Insurance Co.* v. *London, Liverpool and Globe Insurance Co.*[85]:

> A bailee of grain insured his interest, and the owner insured his interest with a different company. A fire took place, in circumstances where the bailee was liable to the owner. The owner's insurance company paid. It was held that (1) since different interests were covered, there was no question of contribution; (2) since the bailee was liable to the bailor (*i.e.* the owner) the bailor's insurance company were entitled, on payment of the claim, to be subrogated to the bailor's rights against the bailee; and (3) accordingly the entire loss was borne by the bailee's insurers.

(4) Each policy must be enforceable at the date of loss.

Rateable proportion clause

Contribution proceeds on the principle that an insurer is liable to pay, and does pay, more than his share of the loss. In practice, however, the policy almost invariably contains a rateable proportion clause, which, in effect, restricts the insured's claim under the policy to a rateable proportion of the damage.

> Example. Goods are issued with A. company for £10,000 and with B. company for £100,000. Each policy contains a rateable proportion clause. Damage is caused amounting to £5,000 and a claim is made against A. company.

In the previous edition of this work it was stated that A. company would have to pay an amount which was rateable to the total sum at stake, *i.e.* $\dfrac{£10,000}{£110,000} \times £5,000$.

---

[84] *American Surety Co. of New York* v. *Wrightson* (1910) 27 T.L.R. 91.
[85] (1877) 5 Ch.D. 569.

In a recent case, however, the Court of Appeal has rejected this approach and has held that the two insurers must bear the loss equally.[86]

Some policies go even further and exclude all liability if another policy is in force against the same risk. If a risk is covered by two policies, both of which contain this clause, the two exemption clauses cancel each other out and both policies are effective.[87]

Salvage

If there is a total loss and the insurers pay or reinstate, they are entitled to the damaged goods as salvage, or the value of the goods if sold. Thus the mangled remains of a car which has been smashed beyond repair must, if the insurers pay a total loss or elect to replace, be handed to the insurers. The salvage principle is yet another illustration of the indemnity rule, because it prevents the insured from retaining more than his actual loss. As an example of salvage see *Holmes* v. *Payne, ante*, p. 362.

ASSIGNMENT AND TRANSFER

The word assignment in insurance is used in two different senses. It is sometimes used to mean assignment of the policy moneys, and sometimes to mean assignment of the policy itself. In this Chapter the word "assignment" will be confined to the former situation, while the word "transfer" will be used to refer to the latter.

Life policies

A life policy is not merely a contract. It is a chose in action,[88] and as such it is capable of being assigned. In practice a life policy is frequently assigned either to secure a bank overdraft or as collateral security on a mortgage. A legal assignment which enables the assignee to sue in his own name is possible under the Policies of Assurance Act 1867 and also under section 136 of the Law of Property Act 1925. Under the 1867 Act, which only applies

---

[86] *Commercial Union Assurance* v. *Hayden* [1977] 2 W.L.R. 272; [1977] 1 All E.R. 441.

[87] *Weddell* v. *Road Transport and General Insurance Co. Ltd.* [1932] 2 K.B. 563 see also *National Employers Mutual* v. *Hayden* [1980] 2 Lloyd's Rep. 149.

[88] *Re Moore* (1878) 8 Ch.D. 519, 520, *per* Jessel M.R.

to life policies, assignment is possible by means of indorsement on the policy or by a separate instrument.[89] In either case it must be duly stamped and must be in the form scheduled to the Act, which is as follows:

> I [AB] of   in consideration of   do hereby assign unto
> [CD] of   , his executors, administrators and assigns the policy
> of assurance   . In witness, *etc.*

The assignee must give written notice to the company at its head office and if there are competing assignments, priority is governed by the date on which such notice is received.[90] It follows that an intending assignee should inquire at the head office whether previous notices have been received, and should also give immediate notice when the assignment has been completed.

The Act of 1925 also provides for a legal assignment, which will enable the assignee to sue in his own name, provided that the assignment is absolute and not by way of charge and provided also that the assignment is in writing under the hand of the assignor. This Act is of general application and is not confined to life policies. Again, to perfect the assignee's title, written notice must be given to the insurers, although in this case a notice to a branch office, or to an agent authorised to receive it, is sufficient. Finally, if for some reason the assignment is ineffective at law it may still take effect in equity. An equitable assignment can be completely informal, as, for example, by a mere deposit of the policy.[91] Notice is not strictly essential,[92] but again is highly desirable, to preserve priority and to prevent the insurer from paying the assignor. Under an equitable assignment the assignee cannot sue without joining the assignor—as plaintiff if he consents and as defendant if he does not. The assignee of a life policy need have no insurable interest. A person may thus validly effect a policy on his own life and then assign it to a person without interest. Such a policy is perfectly valid, even if it was effected for the express purpose of such assignment.[93] If, however, the insured merely lends his name to another person under a previous arrangement, and that person

---

[89] s.5.
[90] s.3.
[91] *Shaw* v. *Foster* (1872) L.R. 5 H.L. 321.
[92] See, *e.g. Holt* v. *Heatherfield Trust* [1942] 2 K.B. 1; [1942] 1 All E.R. 404.
[93] *McFarlane* v. *Royal London Friendly Society* (1886) 2 T.L.R. 755.

pays all premiums and enjoys the sole benefit of the policy, this will amount to fraudulent evasion of the Life Assurance Act 1774 and the policy will be illegal.[94]

It goes without saying that a life policy cannot be transferred.

Indemnity policies

Assignment

An indemnity policy may be validly assigned either equitably or under section 136 of the Law of Property Act 1925. Thus a mortgagor who has insured his house can assign to his mortgagee the right to recover under the policy if he (the mortgagor) suffers loss. As the basis of the assignment is the continuing insurable interest of the assignor, it follows that if he parts with the property the assignment will become valueless.[95]

Transfer

An insurance policy being a personal contract, can only be transferred with the insurer's consent—a clearly reasonable rule, because otherwise they might find themselves covering a man of straw with a bad record instead of a man of substance with a spotless reputation.[96] If they do consent to hold the transferee insured, a new contract comes into existence, and the transferee is now the insured.

Sale of land

The question of transfer assumes practical importance where contracts are exchanged on the sale of land. The purchaser can, and very often does, effect his own insurance. Alternatively he can take a transfer of the vendor's policy and give immediate notice to the vendor's insurers, who are not, of course, bound to consent to the transfer. In addition he may be able to take advantage of section 47 of the Law of Property Act 1925 which provides that

---

[94] *Shilling* v. *Accidental Death Insurance Co.* (1857) 27 L.J.Ex. 16.

[95] *Ecclesiastical Commissioners* v. *Royal Exchange Assurance Commission* (1895) 11 T.L.R. 476.

[96] *Peters* v. *General Accident Fire & Life Assurance Corporation Ltd.* [1938] 2 All E.R. 267, C.A. (motor policy not transferable to buyer of car without insurer's consent). *Bromley L.B.C.* v. *Ellis* (1970) 114 S.J. 906, C.A. (brokers liable in negligence for wrongfully telling the buyer of a car that he was covered.

where insurance money becomes payable to a vendor after the date of the contract for sale or exchange of any property under a policy maintained by him against damage to or destruction of that property, the money shall on completion of the contract be held or receivable by the vendor on behalf of the purchaser and shall be paid by the vendor to the purchaser. The section, however, only takes effect subject to:

(1) any stipulation to the contrary contained in the agreement,

(2) any necessary consent of the insurers, and

(3) the payment by the purchaser of the proportionate part of the premium from the date of the contract.

Thus this right, like that of transfer, is dependent on the consent of the insurers, and is not often relied on in practice.[97]

SPECIAL TYPES OF INSURANCE

Life insurance

Life insurance may be defined as any insurance in which the insurer's liability is dependent upon human life. A policy against death by accident is for many purposes[98] regarded as a life policy, and an endowment policy will be regarded as a life policy if the insurer's liability is altered by death.[99]

Section 11 policies

General. A married person sometimes takes out a policy on his or her own life and expressed to be for the benefit of his or her spouse and/or children. By section 11 of the Married Women's Property Act 1882 such a policy creates a trust for the specified beneficiaries, and the policy moneys do not, while any object of the trust remains unperformed, form part of the insured's estate, nor are they subject to the insured's debts. If the beneficiaries are named in the policy, as in a policy "for my wife Mary and my

---

[97] Presumably the purchaser would be a "person interested" for the purpose of the Fires Prevention (Metropolis) Act 1744, *ante*, p. 373, but there is no direct authority on the point.

[98] *e.g.* assignment under the Policies of Assurance Act 1867 (*ibid.* s.7) but not for purposes of Stamp Duty (Stamp Act 1891, s.98(1)).

[99] *Joseph* v. *Law Integrity Insurance Co.* [1912] 2 Ch. 581; *Gould* v. *Curtis* [1913] 3 K.B. 84, C.A.

daughter Jane" they acquire an immediate vested interest which will pass to their personal representatives if they die before the policy moneys become payable.[1] If, however, they are not named, as in a policy "for my husband and children" the trust is presumed to be in favour of those members of the class who are alive when the policy moneys become payable and they will take in equal shares.[2]

Effect of divorce. A vested interest in favour of a named spouse is not divested *ipso facto* on divorce, although the divorce court has power to vary the trusts, since the policy is a "settlement" within section 24 of the Matrimonial Causes Act 1973.[3] If, however, the spouse is unnamed, a divorce will destroy the contingent interest of the spouse, because the spouse will no longer be the spouse of the insured when the policy moneys become payable. In default of other beneficiaries, the policy moneys will revert to the insured or his estate.

Advantages. The practical advantages of a section 11 policy include the following:

(1) There is a saving of income tax on premiums paid.[4]

(2) Capital transfer tax will not be payable on the premiums if they are paid out of income as part of the normal expenditure of the insured.[5]

(3) As the moneys do not form part of the insured's estate, they can be paid immediately without waiting for a grant of probate or letters of administration to his estate.

(4) The policy moneys are not available for the creditors of the insured, although if the creditors can prove that the insured effected the policy and paid the premiums with intent to defraud them, they are entitled to recover the amount of the premiums out of the policy moneys (proviso to section 11).

Scope. The section covers not only normal life policies, but policies against death by accident[6] and endowment policies, if the

---

[1] *Cousins* v. *Sun Life Assurance Society* [1933] 1 Ch. 126.
[2] *Re Browne's Policy* [1903] 1 Ch. 188; but see *Re Griffith's Policy* [1903] 1 Ch. 739.
[3] *Gunner* v. *Gunner* [1949] P. 77; [1948] 2 All E.R. 771.
[4] Income and Corporation Taxes Act 1970, s.19 (as amended).
[5] Finance Act 1975, Sched. 6, para. 4.
[6] *Re Gladitz* [1937] Ch. 588.

policy money is payable on the death of the insured. It does not matter that the interest of the spouse is conditional on her surviving the insured.[7]

Murder and manslaughter

It will be recalled that a policy of insurance is designed to guard against the consequences of fortuitous events, so that it will not cover a loss caused by the wilful act of the insured.[8] This is a rule of construction and it exists side by side with another rule, based on public policy, that the person entitled to the policy cannot recover for loss due to his intentional criminal act. These two principles can be seen in action in two cases. The first is *Amicable Society* v. *Bolland*,[9] where the life insured committed forgery and was executed. It was held that his personal representatives could not recover under the policy. The second is *Cleaver* v. *Mutual Reserve Fund Life Association*,[10] where a man took out a section 11 policy for the benefit of his wife who poisoned him. It was held that where the beneficiary murdered the insured the policy moneys were payable but neither the murderer nor his estate could benefit. The last rule can apply equally where the person entitled to the policy moneys kills the insured by manslaughter, the principle being that "a man shall not slay his benefactor and thereby take his bounty."[11] In the most recent case, however, it was pointed out that "manslaughter is a crime which varies infinitely in its seriousness"; accordingly the extent to which public policy would bar a claim must depend on the particular facts of the case.[12]

The above rules of public policy also govern the question of whether the killer can recover an indemnity under his own legal liability policy (*post*, p. 386).

Suicide

Until 1961 suicide while sane was a felony, and the above principle of public policy prevented the personal representatives of the deceased from claiming the policy moneys, even if the policy

---

[7] *Re Fleetwood's Policy* [1926] Ch. 48.
[8] *Ante*, p. 361.
[9] (1830) 4 Bligh (N.S.) 194.
[10] [1892] 1 Q.B. 147.
[11] *Re Hall* [1914] P. 1.
[12] See *Gray* v. *Barr*, *ante*, p. 363, and *post*, p. 386. See also 89 L.Q.R. 235.

contained an express clause for payment in this event.[13] Since the Suicide Act 1961, however, suicide is no longer a crime, and therefore the question of public policy no longer arises. There is, however, the other rule, which is common to all policies (see *ante*, p. 361, that the risk does not cover loss due to the wilful act of the insured, unless it expressly so provides. This point of construction may still enable the insurers to reject a claim, unless the policy expressly provides for recovery, in which case they are presumably liable. If, however, the insured commits suicide when insane, his act will not be treated as wilful and the policy moneys will be payable, unless the policy otherwise provides.[14]

Sane suicide could cause hardship to innocent third parties, such as an assignee for value of the policy, and it is quite usual to find a clause providing that on a sane suicide the policy shall become void unless the policy is at that time in the hands of an assignee for value. Such a clause is valid quite apart from the Act of 1961.[15]

Fire insurance

The main principles of fire insurance including the amount recoverable, the importance of the average clause and the principles of reinstatement have already been considered. It remains to add that the word "fire" must be construed in its popular sense, so that damage caused by an explosion will not be covered by a policy against damage by "fire" unless the explosion itself was caused by fire in the popular sense.[16] It goes without saying that if an explosion causes or intensifies a fire, the insurers will be liable for damage due to that fire, unless the policy expressly excludes damage from explosion.[17]

There must be actual ignition, so that damage due to heat would not be covered,[18] nor in the absence of ignition would damage caused by lightning or electricity.

---

[13] The leading case was *Beresford* v. *Royal Insurance Co. Ltd.* [1938] A.C. 586; [1938] 2 All E.R. 602.

[14] *Horn* v. *Anglo-Australian Life Assurance Co.* (1861) 30 L.J.Ch. 511.

[15] See *per* Lord Atkin in *Beresford's* case, *supra*.

[16] *Everett* v. *London Assurance* (1865) 19 C.B. (N.S.) 126.

[17] *Stanley* v. *Western Ins.Co.* (1868) L.R. 3 Ex. 71.

[18] *Austin* v. *Drewe* (1816) 6 Taunt. 436 considered in *Harrris* v. *Poland* [1941] 1 K.B. 462; [1941] 1 All E.R. 204.

Many policies contain express conditions requiring any alteration in the fire risk to be notified to the insurers and prohibiting the storing of articles which are likely to increase the fire risk.

Liability insurance[19]

General

The practice of insuring against legal liability has become of great importance in recent times, and in the case of motor insurance and employers' liability insurance it has been made compulsory. There is no doubt whatever that a policy against liability for negligence is perfectly valid and enforceable. On the other hand, as already stated, an insured cannot, on the grounds of public policy, recover for the consequences of an intentional criminal act, even though he was unaware that the act was in fact a crime.[20] Thus in *Gray* v. *Barr*, the facts of which appear on page 363, the Court of Appeal held that, even if there had been an "accident," a claim by A under a policy covering his liability for accidents would have failed on grounds of public policy. In the words of the trial judge:

> "The logical test, in my judgment, is whether the person seeking the indemnity was guilty of deliberate, intentional and unlawful violence, or threats of violence. If he was, and death resulted therefrom, then, however unintended the final death of the victim may have been, the court should not entertain the claim for indemnity."

It is submitted that this principle also applies where the insured intentionally commits a tort, such as defamation.[21] If the insured commits an act of criminal negligence (such as reckless driving) or

---

[19] For a recent case on a solicitor's negligence policy, see *Forney* v. *Dominion Insurance Co. Ltd.* [1969] 1 W.L.R. 928; 3 All E.R. 831.

[20] *Haseldine* v. *Hosken* [1933] 1 K.B. 822, where a solicitor had entered into a champertous agreement. *Hardy* v. *Motor Insurers' Bureau* [1964] 2 Q.B. 745; [1964] 2 All E.R. 742, C.A.

[21] See McGillivray and Parkington *op. cit.* at p. 825. S.11 of the Defamation Act 1952 provides that an agreement to indemnify a person against civil liability for libel is not to be unlawful unless at the time of publication that person knows that the matter is defamatory and does not reasonably believe there is a good defence to an action brought upon it.

a statutory offence (such as speeding) this will not prevent him from recovering under an indemnity policy.[22]

The contract is one of indemnity, and the insured can enforce it as soon as he has furnished satisfactory proof of his liability.

Legal liability

It must be appreciated that the insurer's liability to pay is based on the insured being legally liable in respect of the damage. An important statute in this connection is the Law Reform (Husband and Wife) Act 1962 which enables a husband and wife to sue each other in tort. Thus if a husband negligently injures his wife there will be a legal liability, in respect of which the husband can claim indemnity under his legal liability policy.

Many policies expressly reserve to the insurers the right to conduct litigation on behalf of (and in the name of) the insured, both to dispute liability, and to enforce subrogation rights (see, for example, *Lister* v. *Romford Ice and Cold Storage Co. Ltd.*, *ante*, p. 377). Another very common clause provides that the insured shall pass on all claims to his insurers and shall not make any admission of liability. An admission in breach of this term might enable the insurers to repudiate all liability.[23]

In the case of professional men, a claim in the courts for negligence is likely to be very damaging, whether successful or not. Hence it is common to find a "Queen's Counsel clause" whereby the insurers agree to pay any third party claim without disputing liability, unless leading counsel advises that it can be successfully contested.

Knock-for-knock agreement

Where an accident takes place between two persons, both of whom are insured with different companies, the insurance companies sometimes try to enforce a "knock-for-knock" agreement, made between themselves. This agreement provides that each company will pay the damage of their insured and will not

---

[22] *Tinline* v. *White Cross Insurance Co.* [1921] 3 K.B. 327; *James* v. *British General Insurance Co.* [1927] 2 K.B. 311; both cases were doubted by the Court of Appeal in *Haseldine* v. *Hosken*, *supra*, but they have not been overruled, and they were treated as good law in *Gray* v. *Barr (supra)*. If they are wrong, many thousands of claims have been wrongly paid.

[23] This is restricted in compulsory motor insurance cases, *post*, pp. 399–400.

take legal proceedings against the other party involved. It is of the greatest importance to appreciate that such an agreement is in no way binding on the insured who was not a party to it. Thus an insured who wishes to preserve his no-claim bonus can simply sue the other motorist in the courts. Again, he may recover only a limited sum from his insurers[24] and can then proceed against the other party, even if the insurers request him not to do so. He will, of course, hold the damages in trust for the insurers to the extent of the sum which they have paid.[25]

If the insured makes a claim under the policy and then brings an action for damages against the person responsible for the damage, the amount of the lost no-claims bonus can be recovered as part of the damages.[26]

Injured party

If the person causing the damage is insured, the injured party usually conducts negotiations with the insurance company. Where these negotiations are protracted, as where the extent of the injury is uncertain, the advisers of the injured party must not allow the claim to become statute-barred.

Statutory subrogation

The injured part, being a stranger to the contract of insurance, has no rights under it. This formerly caused hardship where the insured, having incurred a liability covered by the policy, became bankrupt, or (being a company) went into liquidation. In such a case the policy moneys merely formed part of the estate for all the creditors. To remedy this, the Third Party (Rights against Insurers) Act 1930 was passed. The Act applies in any of the following events:

(1) If the insured becomes bankrupt.

---

[24] Some policies contain an "excess clause" whereby the insured bears the first part of any damage (*e.g.* the first £20) and the insurers are only liable for the excess.

[25] *Morley* v. *Moore* [1936] 2 K.B. 359; [1936] 2 All E.R. 79. Thus an action may not be worth while if damages are likely to be reduced under the Law Reform (Contributory Negligence) Act 1945.

[26] *Ironfield* v. *Eastern Gas Board* [1964] 1 W.L.R. 1125; [1964] 1 All E.R. 445. The loss of the benefit of any unexpired premium can also be recovered. See *Patel* v. *L.T.E.* [1981] R.T.R. 29.

(2) If the insured makes a composition or arrangement with creditors.

(3) If the insured is a company and
    (a) A winding-up order is made, or
    (b) A resolution is passed to wind up voluntarily (otherwise than merely for reconstruction or amalgamation with another company), or
    (c) A receiver or manager of the company's business or undertaking is duly appointed or possession is taken, by or on behalf of debenture holders secured by floating charge, of any property comprised in or subject to the charge.

In any of the above events the Act provides that if the insured, being insured against liability to third parties, incurs such liability, either before or after the happening of the event, his rights against the insurer are transferred to the third party (section 1(1)). Further, where the insured becomes bankrupt, or a winding-up order is made or resolution passed, no agreement between the insurer and the insured made after the commencement of the bankruptcy or winding up and after liability has been incurred to a third party can affect the third party's rights under the Act, nor can these rights be affected by any waiver, disposition or assignment made by the insured, nor by any payment made by the insurers to the insured, after such commencement (s. 2).

Since the insured has no right to be indemnified until he has provided proof of his liability, it has recently been held that the third party must establish that liability (whether by agreement[27] or litigation or arbitration) before he can take advantage of his rights under the Act.[28] Once the liability of the insured has been established, the third party can sue the insurers direct and they are under the same liability as they would have been to the insured. Thus if they were in a position as against their insured to repudiate for non-disclosure or breach of warranty, they can lawfully repudiate as against the third party.[29] They can also rely on any

---

[27] In practice an admission of liability may well be a breach of the terms of the policy.

[28] *Post Office* v. *Norwich Union Fire Insurance Society, Ltd.* [1967] 2 Q.B. 363; [1967] 1 All E.R. 577.

[29] See *Farrell* v. *Federated Employers Insurance Co.* [1970] 1 W.L.R. 1400; [1970] 3 All E.R. 632, C.A.

arbitration clause contained in the policy.[30] If the amount of the claim is less than the sum insured, the Act does not affect any rights of the insured as to moneys over and above the amount of the claim (section 1(4)). In the converse case, where, for example, a man insured up to £10,000 incurs liability of £12,000 the insurers cannot, of course, be compelled to pay more than the sum insured (*i.e.* £10,000) and section 1(4) provides that:

> "nothing in this Act shall affect the rights of the third party against the insured in respect of the balance."

In considering these "rights" it will be recalled that unliquidated damages in tort are not provable in bankruptcy,[31] and it may well be that a similar rule applies in the liquidation of an insolvent company.[31a] The injured party must therefore sue the debtor[32] and obtain judgment for a liquidated amount, which will then be provable in the bankruptcy or liquidation.

It remains to add that this Act applies to all forms of liability insurance, including compulsory motor insurance, and cannot be excluded by agreement (s. 1(3)).

Motor insurance

General

The modern form of motor-vehicle insurance policy is an elaborate document with a large number of restrictions and limitations.

What risks are covered. There are, of course, a great many different kinds of motor-vehicle policies. Some cover only the risks which have to be covered by virtue of the Road Traffic Act 1972, *viz.* legal liability for causing death or bodily injury to a third party, but many others go much further than this and cover

    (1) damage to a third party's property,

---

[30] *McCormick* v. *National Motor and Accident Insurance Union* (1934) 40 Com.Cas. 76.

[31] Bankruptcy Act 1914, s.30(1).

[31a] In *Re Berkeley Securities Ltd.* [1980] 1 W.L.R. 1589, Vinelott J. held that unliquidated damages *were* provable but in *Re Islington Metal and Plating Works Ltd., The Times,* March 26, 1983, Harmon J. refused to follow this decision. See also *The Times,* June 9, 1983 for further discussion of the point.

[32] In the case of a company which is being compulsorily wound up leave of the court is necessary (Companies Act 1948, s.231).

(2) damage to the vehicle itself[33] and its contents, and

(3) injury to the insured himself and passengers.

Other drivers and other cars. The main cover operates when the insured himself is driving a specified car, but many policies extend their cover to:

(1) persons driving the insured's vehicle with his consent, and/or

(2) the insured himself while driving some other vehicle not owned by him or held by him under a hire-purchase agreement.

The policy, however, only remains effective while the insured has an interest in the specified vehicle. In *Tattersall* v. *Drysdale*[34]:

> A policy with reference to a specified car, contained an extension covering the insured while driving other cars. The insured sold the specified car and drove another one. It was held that as soon as he sold the specified car, the policy ceased to be effective.

This case and the earlier case of *Rogerson* v. *Scottish Automobile and General Insurance Co.* were both concerned with a comprehensive policy covering damage to the vehicle itself as well as the owner's legal liability. More recently a Divisional Court had to consider the position where the policy merely covered legal liability. In *Boss* v. *Kingston*[35]:

> The owner of a Triumph motor-cycle had a policy covering his legal liability to third parties. The policy also purported to cover him when driving another motor-cycle not owned or hired by him. The policy required him to maintain the Triumph in an efficient condition and to give the insurers access to it. The insured sold the Triumph. While driving a motor-cycle belonging to a friend he was prosecuted for using an uninsured vehicle in contravention of the Road Traffic

---

[33] If the insurers instruct a garage to do repairs, the insured may be able to sue the garage if they have been guilty of unreasonable delay (*Charnock* v. *Liverpool Corporation*) [1968] 1 W.L.R. 1498; [1968] 2 All E.R. 473). If the insurers fail to pay (*e.g.* because of insolvency) the question of whether the garage can recover their charges from the insured is a question of construction of the particular arrangement. For a case where the garage's claim failed see *Brown & Davis* v. *Galbraith* [1972] 1 W.L.R. 997.

[34] [1935] 2 K.B. 174, following *Rogerson* v. *Scottish Automobile and General Insurance Co.* (1931) 146 L.T. 26, H.L. Conversely, the seller of the car cannot, without the insurer's consent, transfer the policy to the buyer (*Peters* v. *General Accident* [1938] 2 All E.R. 267, *ante*, p. 381).

[35] [1963] 1 W.L.R. 99; [1963] 1 All E.R. 177.

Act 1960. He pleaded that the policy was still effective. The plea failed and he was found guilty.

In arriving at their decision the Divisional Court purported to distinguish the *Rogerson* and *Tattersall* cases by pointing out that in those cases the vehicle itself was covered so that when the insured sold the vehicle he ceased to have any insurable interest in it, and they considered that the policy lapsed on that ground. In the present case the policy did not require the insured to have an insurable interest in the vehicle. Nevertheless, as a matter of construction, the policy was only intended to be effective while the owner retained the Triumph, especially as the conditions as to maintenance and access could not be carried out once the cycle was sold. It is thought that the insurable interest point is irrelevant to the issue of lapse which is in every case one of construction of the terms of the policy.

The policy cannot be renewed if the sale of the specified car has brought it to an end.[36]

Death. If a policy covers the insured and persons driving with his permission, the House of Lords has held, by a bare majority, that a permission given by the insured before his death can continue after his death, so that the policy continues to be effective after the death of the insured.[37] The decision is a startling one, especially as every one of the judgments was concerned solely with the word "permission" and not with the basic principle that a contract of insurance is of a personal nature. The facts of the case were, however, rather special. The insured could not drive and the policy was not operative if he did drive. On these facts, therefore, the personal element was not very strong. If, however, the decision is of general application, it leads to the anomalous position that a policy in this form lapses on a disposal of the car[38] but does not lapse on death.

User clause. The policy invariably specifies the user in respect of which the insurers will be on risk. In *Wood* v. *General Accident, Fire and Life Assurance Corporation*[39]:

---

[36] *Wilkinson* v. *General Accident, Fire & Life Insurance Co.* [1967] 2 Lloyd's Rep. 182.

[37] *Kelly* v. *Cornhill Insurance Co.* [1964] 1 W.L.R. 158 [1964] 1 All E.R. 321.

[38] *Smith* v. *Ralph* [1963] 2 Lloyd's Rep. 439; *Peters* v. *General Accident, supra.*

[39] (1948) 65 T.L.R. 53. It seems that a claim will fail even if only one of the purposes was a business purpose (see *Seddon* v. *Binions, Zurich Insurance Co. (Third Party)* (1977) 122 S.J. 34.

A policy on a Daimler car only covered its use for "social domestic and pleasure purposes." The insured made a journey with the object of making a business contract at the end of it. An accident occurred. It was held that the accident was not covered because the journey (although no doubt pleasurable) was not within the user clause.

Hire or reward. A policy frequently excludes liability if the vehicle is being used "for hiring" or "for hire or reward." In *Wyatt* v. *Guildhall Insurance Co. Ltd.*[40] Branson J. held that such a policy did not cover an accident which occurred where the insured carried a passenger for a lump-sum payment, while in *Bonham* v. *Zurich General Accident and Liability Insurance Co.*[41] a majority of the Court of Appeal held that an insured who warranted that he would not carry persons for hire or reward had broken the warranty by regularly giving lifts to persons who paid him the equivalent of the train fare, even though he never asked for payment and even though there was no contractual obligation to pay. On the other hand, a mere sharing of out-of-pocket expenses will not take the car outside the policy.[42]

Unroadworthy condition. Another very common clause is one excluding liability if the vehicle is used in an unroadworthy condition. In *Clarke* v. *National Insurance and Guarantee Corpn. Ltd.*[43]:

A motor policy excluded liability while the car (a four-seater Anglia) was being driven in an unsafe or unroadworthy condition. During a journey in which there were eight passengers an accident occurred and the car was destroyed. The insurers repudiated liability. The Court of Appeal, reversing the decision of Davies L.J., held that (1) as the overloading seriously affected the steering, braking and control of the car it was unroadworthy; (2) the car was in an unroadworthy condition at the time of the accident even though it could have been safely driven at a low speed; (3) accordingly the insurers were entitled to repudiate liability (but see *post*, p. 399).

---

[40] [1937] 1 K.B. 653; [1937] 1 All E.R. 792.

[41] [1945] K.B. 292; [1945] 1 All E.R. 427.

[42] *McCarthy* v. *British Oak Insurance Co.* (1938) 159 L.T. 215; [1938] 3 All E.R. 1.

[43] [1964] 1 Q.B. 199; [1963] 3 All E.R. 375. A breach of duty to keep a vehicle in a roadworthy condition (or "efficient condition" which means the same thing) enables the insurers to avoid liability even though the accident was not caused by the breach (*Conn* v. *Westminster Motor Insurance Association Ltd.* [1966] 1 Lloyd's Rep. 407).

Road Traffic Act 1972

History. The arrival of the motor-car inevitably brought a very sharp increase in the number of road accidents, and a great many of these were caused by the negligence of persons who were unable to pay compensation. In order to remedy this and to give an effective remedy to injured persons, the Road Traffic Act 1930 made it compulsory for the users of motor-vehicles to insure against certain risks. This Act and later ones were consolidated by the Road Traffic Act 1960. Another Act was passed in 1971 to make passenger insurance compulsory and the Acts of 1960 and 1971 were then consolidated by the Road Traffic Act 1972. In the remainder of this chapter a reference to a section is to that section in the 1972 Act.

What insurance is compulsory. By section 143 it is unlawful for any person to use[44] or cause or permit any other person to use a motor-vehicle on a road[45] unless there is in force a policy, issued by an authorised insurer, covering legal liability for death or bodily injury to a third party.[46] This must be read subject to section 145 which provides that the policy need not cover:

(1) Liability to a person employed by the insured, in respect of death or injury arising out of and in the course of his employment.

(2) Any contractual liability.

The words "arising out of and in the course of his employment" are the same as those used in the old Workmen's Compensation Act and in the present Social Security Act 1975. Presumably such injuries were excluded from compulsory cover because it was thought unreasonable to saddle employers, who were already paying workmen's compensation, with the additional burden of insurance premiums. It will be appreciated that this exclusion will only be of practical importance to the injured employee if the employer is personally unable to pay his claim and if he has failed to insure under the Employers' Liability (Compulsory Insurance) Act 1969.

---

[44] The word "use" is wider than "drive" so that a criminal offence can be committed if, *e.g.* a person assists in "push-starting" an uninsured car (*Leathley* v. *Tatton* [1980] R.T.R. 21) or if it is parked in a street while the engine is being repaired.

[45] "Road" means a thoroughfare to which the public have access *Cox* v. *White* [1976] R.T.R. 248 D.C.; *Deacon* v. *A.T. (a minor)* [1976] R.T.R. 244.

[46] Certain vehicles are exempt, *e.g.* invalid chairs.

An injury caused by an intentional criminal act comes within the scope of compulsory insurance, even though the criminal himself cannot recover an indemnity under the policy.[47]

Passengers. It has already been seen that injury to passengers has now been brought within the area of compulsory insurance. The rights of the injured passenger against the insurance company will only arise if he can establish legal liability on the part of the person using the vehicle. Before December 1, 1972 (when passenger insurance became compulsory), it was open to the parties to make an agreement excluding liability to the passenger.[48] Now, however, section 148(3) makes such an agreement void.[49]

Emergency treatment. Section 155 contains provisions enabling a qualified medical practitioner to obtain payment of a specified amount from the user of the vehicle in respect of emergency treatment given at the time of the accident and section 145(3)(b) requires the policy to cover such liability. In addition, if the insurers make a payment in respect of a person who to their knowledge has received hospital treatment, the insurers are liable (subject to a statutory maximum) to pay the charges of the hospital for giving such treatment.[50]

Certificate of insurance. A policy is of no effect for the purpose of the above provisions of the Act until a certificate of insurance is delivered to the insured (section 147). Alternatively, the owner may deposit £15,000 with the Accountant General of the Supreme

---

[47] *Hardy* v. *Motor Insurers' Bureau* [1964] 2 Q.B. 745; [1964] 2 All E.R. 742.

[48] See *Bennett* v. *Tugwell* [1971] 2 Q.B. 267; [1971] 2 All E.R. 248 (windscreen notice that passengers travelled at their own risk) and *Birch* v. *Thomas* [1972] 1 W.L.R. 294; [1972] 1 All E.R. 905.

[49] The wording of the section is wide: "the fact that a person so carried has willingly accepted as his the risk of negligence on the part of the user shall not be treated as negativing any such liability of the user." This could effect cases like *Dann* v. *Hamilton* [1939] 1 K.B. 509; [1939] 1 All E.R. 59 (accepting lift from drunken driver) and *Nettleship* v. *Weston* [1971] 2 Q.B. 691; [1971] 3 All E.R. 581 (duty owed by learner driver to instructor). Presumably the provisions of the Law Reform (Contributory Negligence) Act 1945 would be unaffected.

[50] s.154. The limits are £200 for an in-patient and £20 for an out-patient. See also *Barnet Group Hospital Management Committee* v. *Eagle Star Insurance Co.* [1960] 1 Q.B. 107; [1959] 3 All E.R. 210.

Court in which case the Act will not apply when the vehicle is driven under his control.[51]

What must be covered. The Act requires that the policy must cover the liability of the user of the vehicle, but not necessarily the liability of the driver. If the owner of a car drives it himself, he is the user and his liability must be covered. On the other hand if a vehicle is driven by an employee in the course of his employment, the policy need only cover the vicarious liability of the employer and not the personal liability of the employee.[52]

It has already been seen that the compulsory insurance provisions are only operative if the vehicle is being used on a "road." (*ante*, p. 394). It has recently been held that a vehicle can be on a road even though the rear wheels are still on private land.[53]

Who can enforce the policy. Section 148(4) provides that:

> Notwithstanding anything in any enactment[54] a person issuing a policy under section 145 of this Act shall be liable to indemnify the persons or classes of persons specified in the policy in respect of any liability which the policy purports to cover in the case of such person or persons.

It has already been seen that the cover given by a motor policy is frequently extended to cover not only the insured but another person driving with his consent. Apart from section 148(4), such other person could not sue the insurers on the policy, because he was not a party to the contract, nor had he given consideration, nor was his name mentioned in the policy as required by section 2 of the Life Assurance Act 1774 (*ante*, p. 348). Section 148(4), however, enables such persons to sue the insurers. The subsection is not confined to those risks which must be covered under the Act but applies to all risks which are in fact covered. Thus in *Digby* v. *General Accident Fire and Life Assurance Corporation*[55]:

---

[51] s.144.

[52] *Ellis* v. *Hinds* [1947] K.B. 475.

[53] *Randall* v. *Motor Insurers' Bureau* [1968] 1 W.L.R. 1900; [1969] 1 All E.R. 21.

[54] *i.e.* the Life Assurance Act 1774, *ante*, p. 348.

[55] [1943] A.C. 121. The case was decided at a time when passenger insurance was not compulsory. Note that s.148(4) does not give rights to the injured third party; it merely gives rights to the persons who are covered by the policy. The right of the injured third party to sue the insurers in compulsory insurance cases is dealt with in s.149, *post*, p. 398.

The actress Merle Oberon took out a motor policy whereby the insurers agreed to indemnify her against "claims by any person." The policy similarly covered any person driving with her consent. One day, while she was a passenger in her chauffeur-driven car, she was injured owing to the chauffeur's negligence. She recovered damages from him. The House of Lords held (1) the words "claims by any person" in relation to the chauffeur included a claim by the policy holder herself, and (2) accordingly, as he was covered against the risk which had taken place, he could claim an indemnity from the insurers under what is now section 148(4).

Special rules as to compulsory insurance

The matters about to be discussed only apply to compulsory insurance, and it must be appreciated that in the case of a mixed claim, as where the insured kills a third party and also destroys the third party's car, the insurance policy may be effective for the personal injury part of the claim but not for the damage to the car. The object of the rules about to be discussed is to make sure that the injured third party will be duly compensated. The general position is that an injured third party is now certain to receive his money provided that:

   (i) insurance is compulsory, and

   (ii) he has complied with the rules as to notice, and

   (iii) legal liability on the part of the user can be established.

If the policy is valid and effectual, the injured party can sue the insurers on a judgment obtained against the insured (section 149, *infra.*). If there is no policy, or the risk for some reason is not covered, the Motor Insurer's Bureau have agreed to pay if the driver fails to do so or if he cannot be traced (see below).

Failure to insure. A criminal offence is committed by anyone who uses a motor-vehicle on a road without compulsory insurance, or by anyone having the care, management or control of the vehicle[56] who causes or permits it to be so used.[57] In the latter

---

[56] *Lloyd* v. *Singleton* [1953] 1 Q.B. [1953] 1 Q.B. 357; [1953] 1 All E.R. 291. In *Macleod* v. *Buchanan* (1940) 84 S.J. 452, H.L.; [1940] 2 All E.R. 179 the owner of a car insured for business purposes only, gave another person a general permission to use it. He was held guilty of an offence when the vehicle was used for private purposes.

[57] A seller of a car who allows a buyer to take it away uninsured is not such a person (*Peters* v. *General Accident Fire and Life Assurance Corporation* (1938) 158 L.T. 476; [1938] 2 All E.R. 267, on the other hand a bona fide belief that the driver has a valid licence is no defence (*Baugh* v. *Crago* [1975] R.T.R. 453.

case, the person who "causes or permits" will also be liable in tort
for breach of statutory duty if:
  (i) the driver tortiously injures a third party,
  (ii) the injury is one against which it is compulsory to insure,
       and
  (iii) the third party can prove that the driver cannot pay.[58]

Direct enforcement. Section 149 provides that where a third
party has obtained judgment against the insured, the insurers are
liable to pay the amount of the judgment and costs provided that:
  (a) the judgment is in respect of a compulsory risk, and
  (b) the liability is covered by the policy,[59] and
  (c) a certificate of insurance has been delivered to the insured,
      and
  (d) notice of the action in which the judgment was obtained
      was given to the insurers before or within seven days after
      its commencement.
The section goes on to provide that the insurers are liable to the
third party even though as between themselves and the insured
they were entitled to cancel or avoid the policy, *e.g.* for breach of
warranty, although in such a case they can claim an indemnity
from their insured. There are, however, three cases where the
insurers are not liable to satisfy the judgment and these are:
  (1) If execution is stayed pending an appeal;
  (2) If the policy was cancelled *before the accident* and the
certificate was surrendered, or the holder made a statutory
declaration that it was lost or destroyed, or the insurers com-
menced proceedings in respect of failure to surrender it not later
than 14 days after its cancellation; or
  (3) If in an action started not later than three months from the
commencement of the proceedings in which the judgment was
obtained, the insurers obtain a declaration that, apart from any
provisions contained in the policy, they are entitled to avoid the
policy for non-disclosure or misrepresentation.[60] Notice of the

---

[58] *Monk* v. *Warbey* [1935] 1 K.B. 75. But if the third party has allowed a claim
against a driver who was able to pay to become statute-barred, no damage flows
from the breach of duty and no action is maintainable (*Daniels* v. *Vaux* [1938] 2
K.B. 203; [1938] 2 All E.R. 271).
[59] Thus the section would not apply if an accident occurred while a car, insured
for private purposes, was used for business purposes.
[60] As to whether the policy is voidable see *ante*, pp. 335 and 338.

declaration proceedings must be given to the third party within seven days of the commencement of these proceedings. It will be appreciated that section 149 will not assist the third party where the injury or damage is non-compulsory. In such a case he will have no rights against the insurers, unless the Third Party (Rights against Insurers) Act 1930 (*ante*, p. 388) can be invoked.

Void conditions. By section 148(1) a third party can recover from the insurers in respect of a compulsory risk notwithstanding any clause in the policy limiting the insurers' liability by reason of certain specified matters. The insurers then have a statutory right to recover from the insured any sum which they have had to pay by virtue only of this subsection. The subsection includes a clause relating to:

(a) the age or physical or mental condition of persons driving the vehicle,
(b) the condition of the vehicle,
(c) the number of persons that the vehicle carries,
(d) the weight or physical characteristics of the goods that the vehicle carries,
(e) the horse power or cylinder capacity or value of the vehicle,
(f) the times at which or the areas within which the vehicle is used.

> The operation of this subsection can be seen by a further examination of *Clarke* v. *National Insurance and Guarantee Corpn. Ltd.* (*ante*, p. 393). Besides the destruction of the car, a passenger was injured and another motorist was killed. With regard to the car and the passenger, the exemption clause was effective because, at that time, neither risk was compulsory; but with regard to the death of the other motorist (a compulsory risk) the clause was void under section 148(1). Consequently the insurers were bound to meet the claim by the deceased motorist's personal representatives; having done so, they were entitled to an indemnity from their insured. If the facts had occurred after December 1, 1972, the injury to the passenger would also have been covered by section 148(1).

Any limitation not covered by section 148(1) (*e.g.* a clause restricting use for social domestic and pleasure purposes only) remains valid and effective.[61]

Section 148(2) also makes void as regards compulsory risks a clause in the policy relieving the insurer from liability in respect of

---

[61] See, *e.g. Wood* v. *General Accident Insurance Co.*, *ante*, p. 392.

some act or omission occurring after the accident. Common examples would be clauses excluding liability if the insured failed to notify a claim, or admitted liability,[61a] or if criminal proceedings were brought against the insured. The subsection does not give the insurers a statutory right to recover from the insured any sum which they are compelled to pay to a third party, but the policy may give them such a right.

Motor Insurer's Bureau agreements

Compulsory motor insurance was first introduced in 1930 with the object of giving an effective remedy to persons injured by negligent driving. By 1945 there was considerable public concern that in a large number of cases drivers were still uninsured, so that injured parties often obtained worthless judgments. Accordingly discussions took place between the Government and motor insurers and this led to the setting up of the Motor Insurers' Bureau. In 1946 the Bureau entered into an agreement with the Minister of Transport which was designed to plug the gap which had emerged. The agreement was varied from time to time and at present there are two agreements in force. Both were made on November 22, 1972; one relates to uninsured drivers while the other relates to untraced drivers.

(1) Uninsured drivers. The Bureau has agreed with the Secretary of State for the Environment that it will satisfy any judgment (including interest and costs) which is not satisfied in full within seven days for any reason, provided that:

(a) the judgment was obtained in respect of a compulsory risk, and

(b) notice of the action is given before or within seven days of its commencement, and

(c) if so required by the M.I.B., and subject to full indemnity by the M.I.B. as to costs, the person bringing the proceedings has taken all reasonable steps to obtain

---

[61a] In non-compulsory cases an admission may prevent the insured recovering under his policy (see *Terry* v. *Trafalgar Ins. Co.* [1970] 1 Lloyd's Rep. 524) and *ante*, p. 387.

judgment against all the tortfeasors[62] responsible for the injury or death of the third party, and

(d) the judgment or judgments (including any obtained under (c) above) are assigned to the M.I.B.

This agreement, which is of great practical importance, could be invoked if, for example,

(a) there is no policy, or
(b) the policy has been validly avoided under section 149, or
(c) the accident is caused by a thief driving a stolen car, or
(d) the accident is caused while the vehicle is used for an unauthorised purpose, or
(e) the policy is an owner-driver-only policy and the vehicle is driven by someone else, or
(f) the insurance company goes into liquidation.

Notice. If there is a policy in existence, even though the insurer may be in a position to repudiate, the third party can give the usual notice under section 149 (*ante*, p. 398) and the insurer will then handle the claim, either on his own behalf if the policy is effective, or on behalf of the Bureau if it is not. If, on the other hand, there is no policy at all, or if the insurer cannot be traced or has gone into liquidation, notice of the proceedings must be given to the Bureau.

Enforcement. The theoretical difficulty of allowing a person to sue on the Motor Insurers' Bureau Agreement, although he is a stranger to that agreement, has no practical importance because the Bureau, whether in litigation or in arbitration, does not take the point.[63]

(2) Untraced drivers. The foregoing provisions as to compulsory insurance have no value unless there is someone who can be sued. Consequently they do not assist the victim in "hit-and-run cases" because he will not be able to trace the driver. The second M.I.B.

---

[62] Thus where the owner permits the vehicle to be used when uninsured, the M.I.B. can compel the third party to bring a "*Monk* v. *Warbey*" claim against the owner. It follows from this that the M.I.B. agreement in no way affects the *Monk* v. *Warbey* principle (*ante*, p. 398).

[63] In *Hardy* v. *M.I.B.* Lord Denning M.R. commented "No point is taken by the Motor Insurers' Bureau that [the agreement] is not enforceable by the third person. I trust no such point will ever be taken." [1964] 2 Q.B. 745, 757; [1964] 2 All E.R. 742, 744.

agreement is designed to deal with such cases[64] and clearly it is of great practical importance. It applies if:

(1) the accident occurred on or after December 1, 1972[65];
(2) the person responsible for the death or injury cannot be traced;
(3) on a balance of probabilities the untraced person would be liable to pay damages to the injured person;
(4) the liability comes within the compulsory insurance provisions of the Road Traffic Act 1972;
(5) the death or injury was not caused by the use of the vehicle as a weapon[66] and
(6) the application for payment is made to the Bureau within three years of the accident.

If these conditions are satisfied the Bureau will pay to the applicant an amount equal to the damages which would have been awarded by the court. If the Bureau receive an application for payment they will investigate the matter and they will notify the applicant of their decision and the amount of the award (if any). If the application is rejected, or if the applicant is dissatisfied with the amount of the award, he can appeal to an arbitrator to be selected from a panel of Queen's Counsel appointed by the Lord Chancellor. The applicant cannot sidestep this appeal procedure by bringing an action in the courts.[67]

---

[64] It has been estimated that there are at least 3,000 of such cases in each year. The scheme also applies if the driver cannot be fraud because, *e.g.* he gives a false name and address (*Clarke* v. *Vedel* [1979] R.T.R. 26 C.A.).

[65] Accidents occurring between May 1, 1969, and December 1, 1972, are governed by an earlier agreement.

[66] If, of course, the driver can be traced, the injured third party would have rights under s.149 (*ante*, p. 398) or under the Uninsured Drivers Agreement (*ante*, p. 400).

[67] *Persson* v. *London Country Buses* [1974] 1 W.L.R. 569; [1974] 1 All E.R. 1251, C.A.

CHAPTER SEVEN

BAILMENTS AND CARRIAGE OF GOODS

INTRODUCTION

BAILMENTS[1] have been touched upon in some of the earlier chapters of this book and it is now necessary to examine them somewhat more closely. In the fragmentary development of the common law, the concept of bailment was developed much earlier than that of contract, and there is considerable early case law, much of which is very confused. With the growth of the law of contract there was much less litigation relating to bailments as such and there is a dearth of modern case law on the subject. The reason for this is that most modern bailments form part of a contract and the courts have been more concerned with the rights and duties of the parties under the particular contract than with their position under the general law of bailment.

It will be apparent from the above that bailment is essentially a common law subject although statutes have been passed from time to time dealing with particular aspects.[2]

Definition

The following definition, taken from a leading work,[3] brings out all the essential features of a bailment.

> "Any person is to be considered as a bailee who otherwise than as a servant either receives possession of a thing from another or consents to receive or hold possession for another upon an undertaking with the other person either to keep and return or deliver to him the specific thing or to convey and apply the specific thing according to the directions antecedent or future of the other person."[4]

---

[1] For a comprehensive survey of this subject, see Paton, *Bailment in the Common Law* (1952).
[2] Examples include the Hire-Purchase Act 1965, the Torts (Interference with Goods) Act 1977 and the whole mass of statute law relating to carriage of goods.
[3] Pollock and Wright, *Possession*, at p. 160.
[4] The "other person" is called the bailor.

403

It will be seen from this definition that there are two essential features of every bailment, namely:

(1) A transfer of possession to the bailee, and

(2) An obligation on the part of the bailee to deal with the very thing bailed in accordance with the direction of the bailor.

The following are among the more important types of bailment.

(1) Hire.[5]

(2) Custody.

(3) Carriage.

(4) Pledge.

(5) Loan of chattel for use.

(6) Delivery of chattel for treatment, as where a car or suit is delivered for repair.

Bailment and contract

Before examining the two essential features of a bailment, it is worth emphasising that bailment exists independently of contract,[6] although frequently there is a contract governing the rights and duties of the parties. The most obvious illustration of this is the gratuitous bailment—a bailor may lend a chattel for use without reward, and conversely a bailee may receive goods for storage without reward. In either case there is no legally binding contract because of the absence of consideration, but nevertheless a bailment comes into existence. Again, a minor may be a bailee of goods even if the "contract" under which he obtained them is void.[7]

Pure personalty

The concept of bailment is only concerned with pure personalty and not with land.

---

[5] If an option to purchase is also given to the bailee it is, of course, a hire-purchase agreement (*Helby* v. *Matthews*) [1895] A.C. 471).

[6] For a recent example of bailment without contract, see the interesting case of *Morris* v. *C. W. Martin & Son, Ltd.* [1966] 1 Q.B. 716; [1965] 2 All E.R. 725, C.A. A bailment is possible even though the bailee does not know the identity of the bailor (*ibid.*).

[7] *Ballett* v. *Mingay* [1943] K.B. 281; [1943] 1 All E.R. 143.

TRANSFER OF POSSESSION

General

The courts have refrained from a precise definition of possession,[8] and the term is used somewhat differently in various branches of the law. The essential features are control and an intention to exclude others. A person can sometimes have possession of a chattel even if he is unaware of its existence. Thus the occupier of land possesses chattels which are embedded in or under that land.[9] If, therefore, a dispute arises as between the occupier and a finder, the occupier will have a superior right to the chattel and can claim it from the finder.[10]

Licence

A number of modern cases have been concerned with the distinction between a bailment and a licence. They have mainly been concerned with vehicles being left on land either gratuitously or on payment of a small charge. It seems clear from these cases that where a vehicle is parked on land without transferring the key, it will usually amount to a mere licence to leave the vehicle on that land, and not to a bailment imposing a duty of care. In *Ashby* v. *Tolhurst*[11]:

> The plaintiff left his car in the defendant's car park on payment of 1s., in return for which a "Car Park Ticket" was handed to him. This ticket purported to absolve the defendant from any liability for loss of or damage to cars. Owing to the admitted negligence of the defendant's servant a stranger was permitted to take the car away. It was never recovered. An action by the plaintiff against the defendant failed. The Court of Appeal held that: (1) Having regard to the terms of the ticket and to the fact that possession did not pass to the defendant, there was no bailment but merely a licence imposing no

---

[8] See *per* Lord Jowitt in *U.S.A. and Republic of France* v. *Dollfus Mieg et Cie, S.A., and Bank of England* [1952] A.C. 582, 605; [1952] 1 All E.R. 572, 581.

[9] *South Staffordshire Waterworks Co.* v. *Sharman* [1896] 2 Q.B. 44 at p. 47, *per* Lord Russell C.J.

[10] *London (City of) Corporation* v. *Appleyard* [1963] 1 W.L.R. 982; [1963] 2 All E.R. 834.

[11] [1937] 2 K.B. 242; [1937] 2 All E.R. 837; followed in *Tinsley* v. *Dudley* [1951] 2 K.B. 18; [1951] 1 All E.R. 252 and *Halbauer* v. *Brighton Corporation* [1954] 1 W.L.R. 1161; [1954] 2 All E.R. 707. It is thought that the Occupiers' Liability Act 1957 has not altered the position, since that Act does not apply to risks such as theft. See also *post*, p. 435.

duty of care. (2) Even if there were a bailment the defendant would be absolved from liability by the wording of the clause.

If the plaintiff does hand over the key, it is much more likely that the court will find that there has been a transfer of possession and a bailment.[12]

The problem of distinguishing between bailment and licence is not confined to vehicles. In *Ultzen* v. *Nicols*,[13] where a waiter took a customer's coat and placed it on a peg, it was held that the restaurant had become bailees. On the other hand in *Deyong* v. *Shenburn*[14] it was held that an actor who left his clothes in his dressing room did not constitute the theatre owners bailees of the clothes.

No delivery

A bailment can arise without actual delivery, as where the seller of goods agrees to store them for the buyer under a separate contract of storage. A mere agreement to postpone delivery will not, however, make the seller a bailee.[15]

Double possession

A bailment may be for a fixed term or at will, *i.e.* terminable at the will of the bailor. In the former case the bailee alone has possession, with the result that he alone can sue a third party for trespass or conversion if the third party in some way interferes with possession. In the latter case, however, it appears from the cases that the bailor retains possession[16] or an immediate right to

---

[12] See, *e.g. Adams (Durham)* v. *Trust Houses Ltd.* [1960] 1 Lloyd's Rep. 380. The delivery of the key is not, however, conclusive. See *B.G. Transport Services* v. *Marston Motor Co.* [1970] 1 Lloyd's Rep. 371.

[13] [1894] 1 Q.B. 92; and see *Samuel* v. *Westminster Wine Co. Ltd.* [1959] C.L.Y. 173.

[14] [1946] 1 K.B. 227; [1946] 1 All E.R. 226.

[15] This distinction was thought to be important under s.8 of the Factors Act 1889 and section 24 of the Sale of Goods Act 1979, but in the light of the case of *Worcester Works Finance Co. Ltd.* v. *Cooden Engineering Co. Ltd.* this may no longer be so. See *ante*, p. 154.

[16] *Lotan* v. *Cross* (1810) 2 Camp. 464 (gratuitous bailment), *Wilson* v. *Lombank Ltd.* [1963] 1 W.L.R. 1294; [1963] 1 W.L.R. 1294; [1963] 1 All E.R. 740 (bailment for reward), Lord Porter in *United States of American and Republic of France* v. *Dollfus Mieg et Cie, S.A., and Bank of England* [1952] A.C. 582, 666; [1952] 1 All E.R. 572, 585.

possess equivalent to possession,[17] with the result that the possessory remedies of trespass and conversion are available to him as well as to the bailee. The concept of double possession has been criticised.[18]

Before leaving this question of rights against third parties, it is worth mentioning that a bailee can sue a third party in tort, even though, as between himself and the bailor, the bailee is not liable. The leading case is *The Winkfield*[19]:

> A ship called the *Mexican* was negligently struck and sunk by another ship called the *Winkfield*. The *Mexican* was carrying mails from South Africa to England at the time of the Boer War. The Postmaster-General, as bailee of these mails, claimed £5,000 damages from the owners of the *Winkfield*. It was held that even though he was not legally liable for the loss to the owners of the mails, he was entitled to recover.

SPECIFIC MANDATE

A transaction only amounts to bailment if the person receiving possession is under an obligation to deal with the subject-matter in a particular way, either by returning it (as in the case of hire or loan) or in some other way (as in the case of carriage). Thus an ordinary loan of money will not amount to a bailment because the borrower is merely bound to return an equivalent amount and not the identical coins.[20] For the same reason a delivery of goods for consumption will not amount to bailment.[21] On the other hand, the delivery of money with a specific direction to pay those particular coins into, say, a bank account, would no doubt be a bailment,[22] and likewise a person who receives goods to sell on behalf of another is, it seems, a bailee of the proceeds of the sale.[23] This sort of problem has become less important since the passing

---

[17] Lord Jowitt in the *Dollfus Mieg* case, note 8, *supra*.

[18] Paton, *op. cit.* Preface and p. 6 *et seq.*

[19] [1902] P. 42. He must, of course, account to the bailor for any sum above his own interest.

[20] *R. v. Hassall* (1816) Le. & Ca. 56 at p. 63.

[21] *South Australian Insurance Co. v. Randell* (1869) L.R. 3 P.C. 101, where a farmer delivered wheat to a mill-owner on the terms that he could claim, at his option, either an equivalent amount of the same quality, or a cash sum.

[22] The example is taken from Paton, *op. cit.* at p. 28.

[23] *R. v. De Banks* (1884) 13 Q.B.D. 29; Stephen J. dissented.

of the Theft Act 1968 which has, *inter alia*, abolished the crime of larceny by a bailee.

Finders

It is somewhat unreal to describe the finder of a chattel as being in any sense a bailee, since there is clearly no specific mandate. Nevertheless such a person is sometimes treated as a bailee if he takes the chattel in order to save it for the true owner, on the somewhat dubious ground that he has the owner's implied consent. The cases show that initially a finder owes no duty of care with regard to a chattel found by him, but that if he actually takes the chattel into his custody he will be liable if it is lost or damaged as a result of his negligence.[24]

Involuntary bailees

This expression is used to refer to a person who receives possession of goods against his will, as where a person has goods sent to him by mistake or by a tradesman anxious to boost sales. What (if any) are the legal obligations of such a person? In the early case of *Howard* v. *Harris*,[25] when an author sent his manuscript to a theatrical producer who had not asked for it, it was held that the producer was under no duty of any kind with regard to its safe custody. If this case is correct, an involuntary bailee can never be liable for mere negligence. With regard to liability for conversion, this tort is normally one of strict liability,[26] but where the defendant is an involuntary bailee he will only be liable if he acted intentionally or negligently. In *Elvin and Powell* v. *Plummer Roddis*[27]:

> X fraudulently ordered coats worth £350 from plaintiffs to be sent to defendants. He then telegraphed to defendants: "goods sent in error, sending van to collect." The defendants acted on this telegram and sent the coats to X. On a finding by the jury that the defendants acted without negligence, the plaintiffs' action against them was dismissed.

---

[24] *Newman* v. *Bourne and Hollingsworth* (1915) 31 T.L.R. 209.

[25] (1884) C. & E. 253. For a criticism, see *Beven on Negligence*, at pp. 928–929 where it is suggested that the case may have been misreported.

[26] *Hollins* v. *Fowler* (1875) L.R. 7 H.L. 757.

[27] (1933) 50 T.L.R. 158; contrast *Hiort* v. *Bott* (1874) L.R. 9 Ex. 86, but see (1960) 76 L.Q.R. 386.

The position with regard to unordered goods was radically altered by the Unsolicited Goods and Services Act 1971. This provides in effect, that where a person receives unsolicited goods in the circumstances specified in the Act, the transferee can treat the goods as a gift to him if (1) the transferor does not take or demand possession within six months of the transferee receiving the goods or (2) not less than 30 days before the end of that six-month period the transferee gives a notice in writing to the transferor, and the transferor fails to collect or demand the goods within 30 days of the giving of such notice.[28]

The above statutory provisions only apply if the goods were sent to the recipient (a) with a view to his acquiring them without his having agreed either to acquire or return them and (b) without his having any reasonable cause to believe that they were sent with a view to being acquired for the purpose of a business.[29]

DUTIES OF THE BAILOR

Title

Under a contract of hire the hirer can sue the bailor if his possession is disturbed on the ground *inter alia* that the bailor has no right to transfer it (Supply of Goods and Services Act 1982, s.7 *ante*, p. 126). The measure of damages would be governed by the normal contractual rules of *Hadley* v. *Baxendale*.[30] In hire-purchase all sums paid are recoverable, because the essence of the agreement is the option to purchase, so that there is a total failure of consideration if the person letting out the goods is unable to confer this option.[31] In simple hire, on the other hand, a hirer who has had some use cannot allege total failure of consideration, but can recover for his actual loss.

Quality and fitness

In the case of non-contractual bailment (such as a gratuitous loan) it seems from an early case that the only duty on the part of

---

[28] s.1.
[29] *Ibid.*
[30] (1854) 9 Ex. 341.
[31] *Warman* v. *Southern Counties Car Finance Corporation* [1949] 2 K.B. 576; [1949] 1 All E.R. 711.

the bailor is to disclose defects of which he actually knows.[32] It may well be, however, that the widening concept of negligence as formulated in *Donoghue* v. *Stevenson*[33] might now impose liability where the defect was one of which the bailor ought to have known. Such a duty may also arise in relation to other bailments (as where goods are delivered for storage or repair).

In the case of hire of goods on or after January 4, 1983 the matter is now governed by section 9 of the Supply of Goods and Services Act 1982 (*ante*, p. 126) under which the bailor will incur the same strict liability as a seller or transferor of goods (*ante*, pp. 114 and 126).

DUTIES OF THE BAILEE

Duty of care

A bailee is under a duty to take reasonable care[34] of the chattel bailed to him. Many of the earlier cases, notably the leading case of *Coggs* v. *Bernard*[35] in which Lord Holt classified bailments according to the terminology of the Roman law, draw a sharp distinction between (1) bailments of the bailor's benefit only, such as deposit, (2) bailments for the benefit of both parties, such as hire, and (3) bailments benefiting the bailee only, such as gratuitous loan. According to these earlier cases, the bailee in the first case was only liable for gross negligence, whereas in the second case it was his duty to take reasonable care, and in the third case, to quote Lord Holt:

> "the [bailee] is bound to the strictest care and diligence . . . so as if the bailee be guilty of the least neglect he will be answerable."[36]

In more recent times, however, both the use of the term "gross negligence" and the clear-cut division of bailments into three categories have received judicial disapproval. It has repeatedly

---

[32] *Coughlin* v. *Gillison* [1899] 1 Q.B. 145.
[33] (1932) A.C. 562.
[34] There is a substantial overlap between this duty and the duty to exercise reasonable care and skill under a contract for the performance of a service (see Supply of Goods and Services Act 1892, s.13 *ante*, p. 4.
[35] *Coggs* v. *Bernard* (1703) 2 Ld.Raym. 909 at p. 915.
[36] *Ibid.*

been affirmed that gross negligence is ordinary negligence with a vituperative epithet,[37] and, more recently, in a case not dealing with bailments, Lord Goddard had this to say:

> "the use of the term gross negligence is always misleading . . . the words should never be used in any matter to which the common law relates."[38]

The nature of the bailee's duties was examined and discussed in *Houghland* v. *R. Low (Luxury Coaches) Ltd.*[39] where the facts were as follows:

> The defendants provided a coach for an old peoples' outing. On the return journey the passengers loaded their suitcases into the boot of the coach at Southampton and then got into the coach which moved off. During a break for tea the coach broke down and a new one was sent for. When it arrived, the luggage was transferred from the first coach to the relief coach. The removal from the first coach was unsupervised while the restacking into the new coach was supervised by an employee of the defendants. On arrival a suitcase belonging to the plaintiff was missing. In an action against the defendants for its loss, the Court of Appeal held that (1) as bailees the defendants were liable unless they could show that they had not been negligent; (2) on the facts they had failed to prove this and were therefore liable.

Few would quarrel with this unexceptional decision, particularly as there was no supervision when the luggage was taken from the first coach. More important than the decision, however, are the observations of Ormerod L.J. on bailments in general. The county court judge had found that the bailment was a gratuitous one and that the defendants were accordingly only liable for gross negligence. Dealing with these findings Ormerod L.J. expressed himself as follows:

> "For my part I have always found some difficulty in understanding just what was gross negligence, because it appears to me that the standard of care required in a case of bailment or any other type of case is the standard demanded by the circumstances of the particular

---

[37] See, *e.g.* Willes J. in *Grill* v. *General Iron Screw Collier Co.* (1866) L.R. 1 C.P. 600 at p. 612.

[38] *Pentecost* v. *London District Auditor* [1951] 2 K.B. 759, 766; [1951] 2 All E.R. 330, 333.

[39] [1962] 1 Q.B. 694; [1962] 2 All E.R. 159. If the contract was made on or after July 4, 1983 Section 13 of the 1982 Act (*ante*, p. 4) would apply.

case. It seems to me that to try and put a bailment for instance into a water-tight compartment, such as gratuitous bailment on the one hand and bailment for reward on the other, is to overlook the fact that there might well be an infinite variety of cases which might come into one or the other category."

This is a considerable simplification of the law as compared with the elaborate classification of Lord Holt, and as such it is to be welcomed.[40] It equates the duty of every bailee with the duty owed by any person in the law of negligence, namely, a duty to take reasonable care in the circumstances of the case. There is, however, one major difference. In general a plaintiff suing for the tort of negligence must prove that the defendant has broken the duty of care owed to the plaintiff. In bailment, however, the position is reversed and it is for the bailee to disprove negligence.[41]

Relevant circumstances

What then are the relevant circumstances which are taken into account in deciding whether the bailee has been negligent? The court is likely to have regard, *inter alia*, to the following matters:

(1) The nature of the bailment. Although a clear-cut distinction between gratuitous bailments and bailments for reward is now out of favour, the fact that the bailee is being paid for his services, or is receiving a benefit in some other way, is clearly highly relevant. It must also be borne in mind that section 13 of the 1982 Act (*ante*, p. 4) only applies to a *contract* for the provision of a service. Consequently if the transaction is entirely gratuitous the common law rules set out above will continue to apply.

It should be noted in this connection that an apparently gratuitous bailment has often been treated as a bailment for reward, on the grounds that it formed part of a larger business transaction. In *Andrews* v. *Home Flats Ltd.*[42]:

---

[40] It is therefore regrettable that in *Morris* v. *C. W. Martin & Sons Ltd.* [1966] 1 Q.B. 716; [1965] 2 All E.R. 725 Lord Denning M.R. and to a lesser extent Diplock L.J. appeared to reaffirm the *Coggs* v. *Bernard* classification.

[41] *Joseph Travers Ltd.* v. *Cooper* [1915] 1 K.B. 73.

[42] 173 L.T. 408; [1945] 2 All E.R. 698. This is another case where, on similar facts, the 1982 Act would not apply—there appears to have been no *contract* between the landlord and the tenant's wife.

A landlord of a block of flats provided a box-room in which trunks could be stored without charge by tenants and members of their families. There was no system requiring production of a ticket when the trunks were collected. A trunk belonging to the plaintiff, who was the wife of a tenant, was stored there and lost. In an action against the landlord the Court of Appeal held that (a) since the provision was part of the service provided by the landlord and assisted him in finding tenants, he must be treated as a bailee for reward, and was accordingly required to show the standard of care required of such a person, and (b) on the facts he was guilty of negligence and therefore liable.

Other decisions are to the same effect.[43]

(2) Skill of bailee. It is a well-established principle of the law of negligence that if a person holds himself out as possessing a particular skill he will be liable to a plaintiff who suffers injury or damage by his failure to show it.[44] The Supply of Goods and Services Act 1982 (*ante*, p. 4) is declaratory of the common law in this respect.

(3) Subject-matter of the bailment. It is clear on principle that the subject-matter of the bailment is a relevant factor in considering the duty owed by a bailee. Thus if the goods bailed were, to his knowledge, of great value or fragile, a high degree of care would be required.[45]

Conversion

A bailee must not convert the goods of the bailor to his own use. If he does so convert them, he is liable. What is the position, however if the goods are stolen by the bailees' employee? Prima facie the bailee is not liable since the thief was not acting in the course of his employment. Nevertheless, if the goods are stolen by the very employee who was entrusted with their safe custody, the bailee will be liable, on the ground that an employer is liable

---

[43] See, *e.g. Martin* v. *L.C.C.* [1947]. 1 K.B. 628; [1947] 1 All E.R. 783; *Samuel* v. *Westminster Wine Co.* [1959] C.L.Y. 179.

[44] See *Salmond and Heuston on Torts* (18th ed.), pp. 207–208. In *Argyll* v. *Beuselinck* [1972] 2 W.L.R. the interesting suggestion was made that a person employing a solicitor of high standing and great experience is entitled to expect more than ordinary competence.

[45] See, *e.g. British Road Services* v. *Arthur V. Crutchley & Co.* [1968] 1 All E.R. 811 (theft of whisky from warehouse).

where his employee does dishonestly an act which he was employed to do honestly.[46]

Notice of loss

The bailee must also take reasonable steps to try to recover goods which have been lost, and if he fails to take such steps he will be liable unless he can prove that such steps would not have led to the recovery of the goods. Thus in *Coldman* v. *Hill*.[47]:

> The defendant was a bailee of cattle belonging to the plaintiff. Two of these cattle were stolen *without any fault on the defendant's part*. The defendant failed to notify the plaintiff or the police. On discovering the facts the plaintiff sued him for negligence. The Court of Appeal, reversing the decision of a Divisional Court, held that the onus was on the defendant to prove that even if notice had been given the cows would not have been recovered, and on the facts of this case this onus had not been discharged. Accordingly the defendant was liable.

Exemption Clauses

The subject of exemption clauses and the effect of the Unfair Contract Terms Act 1977 will be considered in the next chapter. Here it is sufficient to point out that the party relying on the clause can only do so if he can show that the loss or damage was covered by the precise wording of the clause. If therefore a carpet is accepted for cleaning at "owner's risk" these words will be wide enough to protect the cleaning company from liability for negligence; if however the carpet is lost in unexplained circumstances the company may well be liable quite apart from the 1977 Act.[48]

Personal performance

Where the bailee undertakes to do work or perform a service such as storage, carriage or repair, the question as to whether he can delegate performance to another will depend on the terms of

---

[46] *Morris* v. *C. W. Martin & Sons Ltd.* [1966] 1 Q.B. 716; [1965] 2 All E.R. 725, applying *Lloyd* v. *Grace, Smith & Co.* [1912] A.C. 716 and overruling *Cheshire* v. *Bailey* [1905] 1 K.B. 237. Presumably the 1982 Act would also impose liability if the employer was negligent.

[47] [1919] 1 K.B. 443.

[48] See the pre-Act case of *Levison* v. *Patent Steam Carpet Cleaning Co.* [1978] Q.B. 69.

the contract and on the type of bailment. In *Davies* v. *Collins*[49] a dyer and cleaner contracted to clean a uniform and to exercise every care in doing so. It was held that the language of this contract gave the cleaner no right to have the work done by a sub-contractor. The storage of furniture is also a contract where the personal skill of the bailee is of the essence, so that delegation would amount to a breach of contract unless expressly authorised.[50]

Performance within a reasonable time

This has already been considered (*ante*, p. 4).

Duty to return

It is the duty of a bailee other than a carrier to return the goods to the bailor at the end of the agreed period. If he fails to do this, he will be liable to the bailor unless he can prove:

(a) That he has lost the goods without negligence on his part, or

(b) That the contract validly exempts him from liability, or

(c) That the refusal was legally justified, as where he lawfully exercises a lien or a right of sale.

Estoppel of bailee

If the bailor claims the return of the goods, it will generally be no defence for the bailee to plead that the bailor is not the owner because at common law a bailee is estopped from denying his bailor's title.[51] This estoppel rule does not, however, apply where the bailee defends the action with the authority of the true owner.[52] It follows that a bailee faced with competing claims brought by the bailor and a third party is clearly in a dilemma. If he denies the third party's claim he will be liable to the third party in conversion, if the latter can establish an immediate right to

---

[49] (1945) 114 L.J.K.B. 199; [1945] 1 All E.R. 247. A similar result was reached in *Garnham, Harris & Elton Ltd.* v. *Alfred W. Ellis (Transport) Ltd.* [1967] 1 W.L.R. 940; [1967] 2 All E.R. 940 (wrongful delegation by carrier).

[50] *Edwards* v. *Newland (E. Burchell Ltd., Third Parties)* [1950] 2 K.B. 534; [1950] 1 All E.R. 1072.

[51] See, *e.g. Rogers Ltd.* v. *Lambert* [1891] 1 Q.B. 318.

[52] *Biddle* v. *Bond* (1865) 6 B. & S. 225, and see *ante*, p. 21.

possess,[53] while if he tries to deny his bailor's title he will generally be unable to do so. His best course is to take interpleader proceedings under Order 17 of the Rules of the Supreme Court.

Breach of duties[54]

If a bailee wrongfully departs from the terms of the bailment by doing an act inconsistent with those terms, he takes upon himself the risk of so doing, except where the risk is inherent in the property itself. In *Lilley* v. *Doubleday*[55]:

> A bailee who agreed to store goods in a particular building stored them in a different one. The goods were destroyed in an accidental fire. It was held that as the bailee had departed from the terms of the bailment he was strictly liable for the loss.

Another case which brings out the difference between the bailee's position during the bailment and after its termination is *Edwards* v. *Newland* (*E. Burchell Ltd., Third Parties*).[56] There:

> The defendant agreed to store furniture for the plaintiff for reward. Subsequently, without the plaintiff's knowledge, he agreed with the third party for storage by them. The third party's premises were damaged by a bomb and they asked that the furniture should be removed. There was a dispute about unpaid charges and when eventually the plaintiff removed the furniture some items were found to be missing. The Court of Appeal held that (1) the plaintiff was entitled to recover from the defendant because by sub-contracting he had departed from the terms of the bailment; (2) the defendant was not entitled to recover against the third party because the latter (being a bailee) had not, on the facts, been negligent.

LIEN AND POWER OF SALE

Lien

It is a very old principle of the common law that a bailee has a lien if he has spent skill and labour on the improvement of the

---

[53] But a qualified refusal pending inquiries is not actionable in tort (*Clayton* v. *Le Roy* [1911] 2 K.B. 1031).

[54] Where there is no contract between the parties the claim against the bailee is one of tort, so that, *inter alia,* the tort limitation periods apply (*Chesworth* v. *Farrar and Another* [1967] 1 Q.B. 407; [1966] 2 All E.R. 107).

[55] (1881) 7 Q.B.D. 510. Presumably the position would have been different if the original building was destroyed so that it became essential to store the goods elsewhere.

[56] [1950] 2 K.B. 1 All E.R. 1072. See also *Mitchell* v. *Ealing L.B.C.* [1979] Q.B. 1.

chattel bailed.[57] Thus a repairer has a lien, but not someone who merely stores the goods or maintains them in their existing condition.[58] The general rule can be (and frequently is) varied by contract, and a lien can also be acquired by trade usage. Such usages have been established in the case of solicitors, bankers, factors and wharfingers. It should be mentioned in passing that the bankers' lien does not extend to valuables deposited for safe custody,[59] nor to the contents of a locked box left with the banker.[60]

Particular and general

Liens may be either particular, *i.e.* in respect of a debt arising from the particular transaction, or general, *i.e.* in respect of a general balance of account. The law does not favour general liens, since they tend to give the creditor an unfair advantage over other creditors. Thus a bailee's lien is a particular lien only unless it is enlarged by contract or by usage. An example of a contractual general lien is to be found in the Railway Board's Conditions of Carriage. Usages establishing a general lien have been recognised in the case of solicitors, factors and bankers[61] and in some, but not all, cases involving warehousemen.

Part performance

Although in general a lien only arises on completion of the work, an early case shows that where a bailee is ordered to do work for a lump sum and subsequently the bailor countermands the order, the bailee has a lien for the work actually done.[62]

Who is bound

The general rule is that a lien binds only the person who created it or anyone who authorised him to do so. Thus if an agent without actual or apparent authority delivers goods for repair his principal

---

[57] *Scarfe* v. *Morgan* (1838) 4 M. & W. 270.

[58] *Hatton* v. *Car Maintenance Co. Ltd.* [1915] 1 Ch. 621 at p. 624; *Re Southern Livestock Producers Ltd.* [1964] 1 W.L.R. 24; [1963] 3 All E.R. 801 (maintenance and servicing of pigs).

[59] *Brandao* v. *Barnett* (1846) 12 Cl. & F. 787.

[60] *Leese* v. *Martin* (1873) L.R. 17 Eq. 224.

[61] For cases see *ante*, pp. 32–34.

[62] *Lilley* v. *Barnsley* (1844) 1 Car. & Kir. 344.

is not bound by any lien which may be claimed by the repairer.[63] A bailee who is entitled to use the chattel has implied authority to do acts incidental to such user, and this will frequently include authority to have it repaired, with the result that the repairer's lien will be binding on the bailor.[64] The question then arises as to the effect of a clause prohibiting the bailee from creating liens. The point arose in *Albemarle Supply Co.* v. *Hind & Co.*[65] where the garage knew that the car was on hire-purchase but did not know of the restriction. The Court of Appeal held that the owner had conferred ostensible authority on the hirer to have it repaired and, despite the clause, the garage's lien was binding on the owner. If, however, the bailment is brought to an end before the goods are transferred to the repairer the bailee's possession becomes unlawful and he cannot transfer lawful possession on which a lien can be based.[66]

Termination of lien

A lien is based on possession, and surrender of possession by the bailee will terminate his lien, unless the goods are transferred to the bailor for a temporary purpose only and on the understanding that the lien is to continue.[67]

Apart from this a lien is also lost:

(1) If the debt is paid.

(2) If the bailee refuses a tender of the sum due. The bailor must tender the sum in respect of which the lien is exercisable and if this is refused the bailee's lien is at an end. If the bailee has a larger claim than that covered by his lien (as where a garage has a repairer's lien but has also spent money on maintenance and storage) and the bailee informs the bailor that he will not return the chattel until the larger sum is satisfied, the bailor is in the same

---

[63] For a recent case where an owner was not bound by a warehouseman's lien see *Chellaram & Sons (London)* v. *Butlers Warehousing & Distribution Ltd.* [1978] 2 W.L.R. 412 C.A.

[64] *Tappenden* v. *Artus* [1964] 2 Q.B. 185; [1963] 3 All E.R. 213, C.A., where the earlier cases are reviewed.

[65] [1928] 1 K.B. 307.

[66] *Bowmaker Ltd.* v. *Wycombe Motors Ltd.* [1946] K.B. 505; [1946] 2 All E.R. 113.

[67] As in *Albemarle Supply Co.* v. *Hind, supra*, where the owner of cabs which were garaged with a bailee who had a lien for repairs was allowed to take them away during the daytime.

position as if he had made a lawful tender—in other words, the lien is at an end.[68]

(3) If the bailee takes a security inconsistent with the lien. The matter is one of construction of the arrangement.[69]

(4) If the bailee misuses the goods, as by selling them to a third party. In this case, of course, the bailee will be liable in conversion unless he had some legal justification for the sale.[70]

(5) By agreement.

Right of sale

A lien is basically possessory only and confers no right of sale. If legal proceedings are taken, however, the High Court has a discretion to order the sale of goods if it considers it just.[71] Such a power might well, for example, prove useful in a dispute concerning perishable goods.

A right of sale can, of course, be conferred by the terms of the contract or by statute, and perhaps the most important recent statute on this topic is the Torts (Interference with Goods) Act 1977 which replaces the Disposal of Uncollected Goods Act 1952 and which must now be briefly considered.

Scope

Section 12 (which applies equally to private and to commercial bailments) confers a power of sale where goods are in the possession or under the control of a bailee and:

(1) the bailor is in breach of an obligation to take delivery of the goods or, if the terms of the bailment so provide, to give directions for their delivery; or

(2) the bailee could impose such an obligation by giving notice to the bailor but is unable to trace or to communicate with the bailor; or

(3) the bailee can reasonably expect to be relieved of any duty to safeguard the goods on giving notice to the bailor but is unable to trace or communicate with the bailor.

---

[68] *Per* Scrutton L.J. in the *Albemarle* case, *op. cit.* at p. 318.
[69] *Cf.* the similar rules governing an agent's lien (*ante*, p. 33) and an unpaid seller's lien (*ante*, p. 173).
[70] See, *e.g. Mulliner* v. *Florence* (1878) 3 Q.B.D. 484.
[71] R.S.C., Ord. 29, r.4.

Obligation to take delivery

Part I of Schedule 1 enables the bailee to serve a written notice on the bailor to compel him to take delivery. The notice can be served on the bailor (1) personally, or (2) by leaving it at his "proper address" or (3) by post (in which case it can be combined with a "sale" notice under Part II of Schedule 1 as to which see below). It can be given when the bailee has carried out his task of repair or treatment or valuation or when his duty as a custodian is at an end.

The notice must give the name and address of the bailee, the whereabouts of the goods, the fact that they are ready for collection and the amount of any sums which became due from the bailor to the bailee before the giving of the notice.

Sale notice and sale

The power of sale conferred by Section 12(3) is available if:

(a) the bailee has given notice of intention to sell in accordance with Part II of Schedule 1; or

(b) the bailee has failed to trace or communicate with the bailor in order to give him such a notice after having taken reasonable steps for that purpose; and

(c) in either case the bailee is reasonably satisfied that the bailor owns the goods. The notice, which must be served by registered post or by recorded delivery, must indicate (1) the name and address of the bailee, (2) the whereabouts of the goods, (3) the date on which the bailee intends to sell the goods and (4) the amount of any sums which became due from the bailor to the bailee before the giving of the notice.

The object of these provisions is to give the bailor a reasonable opportunity to collect the goods so as to prevent a sale and the interval between the giving of the notice and the proposed sale date must be long enough for this purpose. Further, if sums are due under (4) above, the period must be not less than three months.

The Act does not specify the manner of sale (*e.g.* auction) but the bailee will be well advised to obtain the best possible price because he must account to the bailor for the proceeds of sale (less any expenses of the sale and less any sums due under (4) above) and by section 12(5)(*a*):

the account shall be taken on the footing that the bailee should have adopted the best method of sale reasonably available in the circumstances.

A sale will give the purchaser a good title as against the bailor but not against the true owner, if this is someone other than the bailor (s.12(4)).

CARRIAGE OF GOODS BY LAND AND AIR

This vast subject cannot be adequately covered in a book of this size but in any work on commercial law some reference to it is essential because it is so often linked to contracts for sale of goods. It is proposed therefore to deal with the subject in broad outline and to refer the reader for more detailed treatment elsewhere.[72]

Carriage generally

The carriage of goods by land and air is governed partly by the common law and partly by statutory provisions (some of which incorporate international conventions into English law). The common law rules, which were developed at a time when the main form of transport was the horse, have little significance in these days of standardised contracts, nationalisation and, international conventions. There has also been a considerable amount of transport legislation.

Carriage by road—domestic

Structure of industry. The road transport industry is divided between private and public enterprise. The carriage of goods by road is carried on partly by private firms and partly by an organisation known as the National Freight Company Limited which has taken over the business of the former National Freight Corporation (See Transport Act 1980, s.45–51 and regulations made thereunder). There is also an elaborate licensing system for goods vehicles, which applies equally in the public and private sectors of the industry.

---

[72] See in particular Professor Kahn-Freund's excellent book entitled *The Law of Carriage by Inland Transport* (4th ed.) and *Chitty on Contracts* (25th ed.), Vol. 2. pp. 333–464.

Common carriers. The common law draws a sharp distinction between common carriers and private carriers. A common carrier is one who professes willingness to carry for reward the goods of all persons that desire to employ him.[73] His profession or willingness may be confined to certain places or to certain types of goods, but subject to that he must be willing to carry for everyone. If, therefore, he reserves the right to reject any particular consignment on the ground that the customer's offer is not sufficiently attractive, he will be a private carrier and not a common carrier.[74] In early times when "carriage" meant the mail coach and the stage coach, common carriers were important, and when the railways arrived they were also given the status of common carriers. Since then, however, everything has changed. The mail coach has disappeared, the furniture remover and long-distance road-haulier is hardly ever a common carrier because he nearly always reserves the right to reject offers, and the railways are no longer common carriers because section 43 of the Transport Act 1962 expressly so provides. The subject of common carriers therefore is virtually bereft of all practical importance.[75]

Duties of common carrier. A common carrier is under two special common law duties, both of which spring from what the late Professor Kahn-Freund has called "the leitmotiv of the history of transport law," namely, "the assumption, tacit or explicit, that the carrier is a potential or actual monopolist."[75] The first of these special duties is a duty to accept all goods for carriage at a reasonable charge. Refusal to accept goods renders the carrier liable to an action for damages, unless he can prove that the refusal was justified for some reason, *e.g.* that the vehicle was full[76] or that the goods were badly packed or otherwise not fit to be carried.

---

[73] *Belfast Rope Work Co.* v. *Bushell* [1918] 1 K.B. 210.

[74] A few common carriers remain. Thus in *Hunt and Winterbotham* v. *B.R.S.* (*Parcels*) *Ltd.* [1962] 1 Q.B. 617 the defendants did not deny they were common carriers. See also *Eastman Chemical International A.V.* v. *N.M.T. Trading and Another* [1972] 2 Lloyd's Rep. 25 and *A. Siohn & Co.* v. *R. H. Hagland and Son Transport* [1976] 2 Ll.L.R. 428 where the defendants were found to be common carriers.

[75] See (1963) 26 M.L.R. 174 for a survey of the law culminating in the Transport Act 1962.

[76] *Spillers and Bakers Ltd.* v. *G.W.R.* [1911] 1 K.B. 386 and cases there cited.

The second main duty concerns the safety of the goods. In the absence of contrary agreement and subject to the protection conferred by the Carriers Act 1830 a common carrier is strictly liable[77] for loss of or damage to goods in transit unless he can prove that the loss was caused by one of the four excepted perils and that he took all reasonable care. The perils are act of God, act of the Queen's enemies, inherent vice and the consignor's own fault. Whether the Law Reform (Contributory Negligence) Act 1945 applies to the last named of these has not yet been decided.

The duty can be excluded by agreement, but clear wording is required to exclude liability for negligence as well as the strict liability.[78] Further, the Carriers Act 1830 provides that where a package containing certain specified types of valuable or breakable goods is handed to a common carrier on land and the total value of these goods exceeds £10 the carrier is generally not liable at all for loss of or injury to the valuable or breakable goods unless the consignor at the time of consignment makes a special declaration of value and pays or agrees to pay an increased charge. Finally, an exemption clause may cease to be operative if the entire subject-matter of the contract is destroyed.[79]

Lien. A common carrier has a particular and possessory lien over the goods in respect of unpaid freight. This lien takes priority over the unpaid seller's right of stoppage in transit,[80] but in the absence of contrary agreement the unpaid seller's right takes priority over any additional general lien which the contract purports to give the carrier as against the buyer.[81]

Private carrier. Most carriers by road are private carriers and their rights and duties are governed by the general principles of bailment outlined earlier and by the terms of any contract between the carrier and his customer. Thus there is no common law obligation to accept all goods for carriage, nor does liability extend

---

[77] *i.e.* his liability goes beyond the duty of reasonable care and skill (as to which see *ante*, p. 4).

[78] *Rutter* v. *Palmer* [1922] 2 K.B. 87, 90, *per* Bankes L.J.

[79] Consider *Eastman Chemical International A.G.* v. *N.M.T. Trading and Another* [1972] 2 Lloyd's Rep. 25. Presumably there must be some fault on the part of the defendant.

[80] *Booth S.S. Ltd.* v. *Cargo Fleet Iron Ltd.* [1916] 2 K.B. 570.

[81] *U.S. Steel Products Co.* v. *G.W.R.* [1916] 1 A.C. 189, *ante*, p. 176.

beyond the normal liability of a bailee (as to which see, *ante*, p. 410), nor does the Carriers Act 1830 apply in the case of valuables and breakables. A private carrier has no lien over the goods unless his contract gives him one.

Exemption clauses. A private carrier can, and frequently does, limit or exclude his liability by contract,and the standard conditions of the Road Haulage Association contain a clause providing that in the event of loss or damage the carrier's liability should be limited to a fixed sum. A majority of the Court of Appeal has recently held that this clause can apply even where the goods are stolen by a person for whose acts the carrier is responsible, and even where the carrier was negligent in employing that person without proper references.[82] If, however, the carrier deviates from the contract in some essential respect (*e.g.* by a wrongful delegation to a sub-contractor) he becomes strictly liable for loss or damage and it has been held that the exemption clause does not apply to that situation.[83]

Who can sue the carrier. The general rule is that the contract of carriage is made between the carrier on the one hand and the owner of the goods on the other, so that it is the owner who can sue for loss, damage or delay,[84] and conversely it is the owner who will be primarily liable for freight. In the great majority of cases the carriage takes place in pursuance of a contract of sale and if the consignee is the owner of the goods[85] the consignor will be regarded as making the contract as agent for the consignee. If, however, the consignor contracts on his own behalf he can sue the carrier on the contract and in addition the owner may have an action in tort.[86]

---

[82] *John Carter (Fine Worsteds) Ltd.* v. *H. Hanson Haulage (Leeds) Ltd.* [1965] 2 Q.B. 495; [1965] 1 All E.R. 113 but see now Unfair Contract Terms Act 1977, ss. 2 and 3 *post*, pp. 437 *et seq.*

[83] *Garnham, Harris & Elton Ltd.* v. *Alfred W. Ellis (Transport) Ltd.* [1967] 1 W.L.R. 940; [1967] 2 All E.R. 940.

[84] In the absence of contrary agreement the carrier is bound to deliver within a reasonable time. See, *e.g. Briddon* v. *Great Northern Ry.* (1858) 28 L.J.Ex. 51. and now Supply of Goods and Services Act 1982, s.14 *ante*, p. 4.

[85] The very act of delivery to the carrier may transfer the property (Sale of Goods Act 1979, s.18, rule 5(2), *ante*, p. 134).

[86] *Lee Cooper* v. *Jeakins (C.H.) and Sons* [1967] 2 Q.B. 1; [1965] 1 All E.R. 280.

Carriage by road—international

This topic is governed by an International Convention (the CMR convention) which was made part of English law by the Carriage of Goods by Road Act 1965 and which is set out in the Schedule to that Act. One important feature is that the normal six year limitation period under the Limitation Act 1980 is replaced by a one year limitation period under Article 32 of the Convention. The Court of Appeal has stated that traditional English rules as to the construction of statutes are not necessarily relevant when construing the terms of an international convention.[87]

Carriage by rail

Structure of industry. When the railways were nationalised by the Transport Act 1947, they were vested in the British Transport Commission. This Commission has now ceased to exist and its railway services were transferred to two Boards—the Railways Board and the London Board. The former provision requiring an integrated service (*i.e.* as between road and rail) for the carriage of goods has been repealed.[88]

Carriage by Railways Board. The Board are not under any common law[89] or statutory duty to accept goods for carriage and the terms on which they accept them are entirely a matter of contract. In practice, however, they will usually be carried under the General Conditions of Carriage. Apart from special conditions for the carriage of animals and fuel, the General Conditions are divided into two main sections—carriage at Board's risk and carriage at owner's risk, a higher rate being charged for the former. If goods are carried at Board's risk the Board's liability for loss or damage approximates to some extent with that of a common carrier, except that the list of excepted perils is considerably wider. In the case of delay the Board will be liable unless they can disprove negligence. There are also provisions limiting the Board's liability to £2,000 per tonne of gross weight of

---

[87] *James Buchanan & Co.* v. *Babco Forwarding and Shipping Co.* [1977] 3 W.L.R. 907 H.L.
[88] Transport Act 1980, Schedule 9.
[89] The Act of 1962 provides that they are not common carriers (s.43(6)).

the consignment in the event of a total loss or a proportionate sum in the event of a partial loss.

Where goods are carried at owner's risk[90] the position depends on the nature of the loss. In the case of non-delivery of an entire consignment or of one separate package forming part thereof, the position is the same as in carriage at Board's risk. In any other case, however, the Board are only liable upon proof of wilful misconduct[91] by themselves or their servants.

In practice the Railways Board makes Board's risk charges compulsory for most freight and parcel traffic and the scope of owner's risk terms is accordingly very limited.

Other conditions. The General Conditions, at both owner's risk and Board's risk, give the Board a general lien coupled with a right of sale. There are also detailed provisions governing the time for notifying a loss, and the time for making a claim.

Carriage by air

Internal organisation. The carriage of goods by air in Great Britain is carried out partly by British Airways, a public corporation, and partly by private operators licensed by the Air Transport Licensing Board, which was set up under the Civil Aviation (Licensing) Act 1960. The Corporation is liable for loss or damage as an ordinary bailee and the Crown Proceedings Act 1947 does not apply to a claim brought against it.[92]

Inernational organisation. The International Civil Aviation Organisation was set up in 1947 to look after international civil aviation affairs and its members include all the major aviation countries. There are also a number of private international bodies, and the most important of these at the present time is the International Air Transport Association, to which the corporation belongs.

---

[90] This may sometimes be a breach of a seller's duty to make a reasonable contract of carriage (see *ante*, p. 167).

[91] For the meaning of this, see *Horabin* v. *B.O.A.C.* [1952] 2 All E.R. 1016, 1019, *per* Barry J.

[92] *Moukataff* v. *B.O.A.C.* [1967] 1 Lloyd's Rep. 396. See also the Civil Aviation Act 1971 which makes a number of structural and organisational changes.

Warsaw Convention.[93] In view of the intrinsically international character of aviation, it is clear that innumerable problems and disputes would arise between the countries if each one had its own different aviation rules. Accordingly in 1929 the Warsaw Convention was drawn up and it has been ratified by a great number of countries, including the United Kingdom. The Convention, which lays down uniform rules for the international carriage of passengers, luggage and goods, was incorporated into English law by the Carriage by Air Act 1932 and was set out in the Schedule to the Act. In 1955 a protocol was drawn up amending the Warsaw Convention in certain respects and the text of the Convention in its amended form appears in the Schedule to the Carriage by Air Act 1961 which came into force on June 1, 1967. This original Schedule has recently been replaced by a new one which gives effect to two further protocols (see the Carriage by Air and Road Act 1979). Where the contract of carriage is made with one airline but the goods are carried by another airline, the Convention regulates the rights and liabilities of both the contractual carrier and the actual carrier.[94]

What carriage is international. The Convention only applies to international carriage which is defined as "any carriage in which according to the agreement between the parties the place of departure and the place of destination, whether or not there be a break in the carriage or a transhipment are situated either within the territories of two High Contracting Parties[95]; or within the territory of a single High Contracting Party, if there is an agreed stopping place within the territory of another State even if that State is not a High Contracting Party.[96]

A journey from country A (a party to the Convention) to country B (not a party to the Convention) would not be international carriage for the purpose of the Convention.

Loss, damage or delay. If the journey is international the Convention (as amended) sets out a number of mandatory provisions which cannot be excluded or varied in any way,

---

[93] See [1966] J.B.L. 335.
[94] Carriage by Air (Supplementary Provisions) Act 1962.
[95] *i.e.* parties to the Convention. See the Carriage by Air (Parties to Convention) Order. 1975 (No. 430).
[96] Art.1(2).

although they can be supplemented by other terms not inconsistent with them. The Convention provides that the carrier will be liable for loss, damage or delay during the carriage by air[97] but that he can escape liability by providing that he and his agents took all possible measures to avoid the damage or that it was impossible for him or them to take such measures. Even if there is liability, it is limited by reference to "special drawing rights" per kilogram unless the consignor makes a special declaration and pays a supplement if required.[98] The carrier cannot, however, take advantage of this limit if he is guilty of wilful misconduct[99] or if he fails to issue a proper consignment note[1] for the goods as required by the Convention. There are very strict time limits; thus, for example, a complaint alleging loss of baggage (including now partial loss of baggage) must be notified within seven days. The servants or agents of the carrier can also claim the benefit of this financial limit if they were acting within the scope of their employment.[2]

Non-international carriage. An Order in Council made in 1952 provides that, subject to a few modifications, the Warsaw Convention is to apply to non-international carriage.[3]

---

[97] Arts. 18 and 19.

[98] Art. 22A *Cf.* For special drawing rights and their sterling value see s.6 of the 1979 Act and Article 22A(3).

[99] For a recent example see *Rustenburg Platinum Mines and Others* v. *South African Airways and Pan American Airways* [1979] 1 Ll.L.R. 19 C.A.—goods stolen by loaders—carriers fully liable.

[1] See *Corocraft* v. *Pan-American Airways Inc.* [1969] 1 Q.B. 616, where the Court of Appeal compared the English and the French text of the Convention.

[2] See the Act of 1962. s.4; In the words of Professor Kahn-Freund, "The legislative technique used in order to achieve this result is not distinguished by its simplicity" (Kahn-Freud, *op.cit.* at p. 707).

[3] The Carriage by Air (Non-International Carriage) (U.K.) Order, 1952.

CHAPTER EIGHT

EXEMPTION CLAUSES

INTRODUCTION

IN the previous seven chapters we have examined the obligations of suppliers of goods and services. In this chapter it is proposed to consider the extent to which these obligations can be modified or excluded by agreement between the parties. This has been a very live topic in the past century—especially with the explosion of mass-marketing and standard form contracts. It is essentially an aspect of consumer protection which is dealt with more fully in the next chapter, but it will be seen that the rules protect business customers (whether sole traders or partners or companies) as well as private customers—although the extent of control is more limited in certain cases.

THE ROLE OF THE COURTS

Before considering the various statutory controls the courts must deal with two preliminary matters, namely

(1) Was the clause incorporated into the contract?

(2) Does the clause, on its true construction, cover the event which has occurred?

As a practical matter these questions are unlikely to be of importance if the clause is wholly void. There are however many cases where the clause will be valid if it is "reasonable" and there are also cases where the clause is not subject to any statutory controls at all (as in the case of insurance contracts, *ante*, p. 344). In these cases the two preliminary questions referred to above are vitally important and they must now be briefly examined.

Incorporation

The general principles governing this matter have been well-established for some time. The cases show that:

(1) If the contractual document is signed this operates as an incorporation of all the terms which appear on that document or which are referred to in it.[1]

(2) If a contractual document is not signed the clause will only be effective if reasonable steps have been taken to bring it to his notice *before* the contract was made.[2] In deciding this question the courts will pay particular regard to three questions namely:

    (a) the nature of the document (if any) containing the clause

    (b) the nature of the liability which it is sought to exclude and

    (c) the previous course of dealing between the parties.

Dealing first with the nature of the document the courts will enquire whether it is of a kind on which the customer can reasonably expect to find conditions. A railway ticket has been held to be such a document[3] but not a deck-chair receipt.[4]

Turning now to the nature of the liability, the point was vividly illustrated by *Thornton* v. *Shoe Lane Parking Co. Ltd.*[5]

> Mr. Thornton, who was described by the Master of the Rolls as a trumpeter of the highest quality, went to park his car at a multi-storey car park. On arriving opposite a ticket machine a ticket popped out, the light turned from red to green and Mr. Thornton went through and parked his car. The ticket referred to conditions displayed on the premises. These conditions excluded *inter alia*, liability for personal injury caused by negligence. There was an accident caused partly by the defendants' negligence and Mr. Thornton was injured.

The Court of Appeal had no difficulty in holding that the defendants were liable on the basis that they had not taken reasonable steps to bring the exemption clause to Mr. Thornton's notice. In the words of Lord Denning, M.R.

> "It is so wide and destructive of rights that the court should not hold any man bound by it unless it is drawn to his attention in the most explicit way. . . . In order to give sufficient notice, it would need to be printed in red ink with a red hand pointing to it—or something equally startling."

---

[1] The leading case is *L'Estrange* v. *Graucob* [1934] 2 K.B. 394.

[2] See *Olley* v. *Marlborough Court Hotel* [1949] 1 K.B. 532 (notice in hotel bedroom; contract made at reception desk; notice not incorporated).

[3] *Thompson* v. *L.M.S.* [1930] 1 K.B. 41.

[4] *Chapelton* v. *Barry U.D.C.* [1940] 1 W.L.R. 532.

[5] [1971] 2 Q.B. 163. The exemption clause in this case would now be void under section 2(1) of the Unfair Contract Terms Act 1977 *post,* p. 437.

Megaw L.J. added that:

> "It does not take much imagination to picture the indignation of the defendants if their potential customers . . . were one after the other to get out of their cars leaving the cars blocking the entrance to the garages in order to search for, find and peruse the notices!"

In contracts between businessmen the question of incorporation merges with a closely related problem—the so-called battle of the forms. An example will illustrate the point.

> 1. In answer to an enquiry from B, S sends to B a quotation for the supply of machine-tools. The quotation states that "the seller's conditions of business shall govern the contract and any attempt by the buyer to introduce different terms shall be null and void." The conditions include an exemption clause.
>
> 2. B places an order which states that "the buyer's conditions of business shall govern the contract and any attempt by the seller to introduce different terms shall be null and void." The conditions do not include an exemption clause.
>
> 3. S sends to B a confirmation of the order which again includes the condition in 1 above.
>
> 4. The market for the goods collapses and B cancels his order.

On general contractual principles it would seem that the cancellation is valid because S's counter-offer has never been accepted. If no cancellation had taken place and if *e.g.* B complained that the goods delivered to him were faulty the courts would probably hold that S's conditions (including the exemption clause) prevailed.[6]

Does the clause cover the event which has occurred?

Even if the clause has been duly incorporated into the contract it is not automatically effective. The courts have developed a number of techniques to counter their effect.

(1) *Privity*

After earlier doubts the House of Lords have held that an exemption clause in a contract between A and B could not protect C—even if C was an employee or contractor employed by B to

---

[6] *B.R.S. Ltd.* v. *Crutchley Ltd.* [1968] 1 All E.R. 811. *Contra* if S signs a tear-off slip on the order form agreeing to be bound by B's terms (*Butler Machine Tool Co. Ltd.* v. *Ex-Cell-O Ltd.* [1979] 1 W.L.R. 401 C.A.).

perform the contract.[7] It seems however that this ruling can be outflanked by having a clause whereby a party contracts, as agent for his employees, etc., that they shall have the benefit of the clause. As a matter of strict legal analysis this can create a new contract between the employees and the other party and the performance of the main contract will provide the consideration for it.[8]

(2) *Strict construction and the "contra proferentem" rule*

A party seeking the protection of an exemption clause must prove that the wording is clear enough to cover the alleged breach; any ambiguity is construed against him. In *Wallis Son and Wells* v. *Pratt and Haynes*[9]

> A commercial contract for the sale of seed excluded "all warranties." The seller supplied seed of a different description; the buyer claimed damages and the seller argued that he was protected by the clause. The House of Lords held that (a) the seller had broken a *condition* of the contract; (b) this breach was not covered by a clause which only referred to *warranties*; (c) the mere fact that the buyer was compelled under the Sale of Goods Act to treat the breach as a breach of warranty (*ante*, p. 100) was irrelevant; (d) accordingly the sellers were not protected by the clause and were liable.

In *White* v. *John Warwick & Co. Ltd.*[10]

> A hired out a tradesman's tricycle to B at "owner's risk." The saddle tipped forward throwing B to the ground. B claimed damages and succeeded. It was held that the exemption clause only covered A's strict liability in contract (as to which see *ante*, p. 126) and not his concurrent liability for negligence.

A final illustration is provided by the case of *Houghton* v. *Trafalgar Insurance Co. Ltd.* the facts of which have already been given.[11]

(3) *Misrepresentation*

The courts will not allow a party to rely on an exemption clause if he has misrepresented its effect.[12]

---

[7] *Scruttons* v. *Midland Silicones Ltd.* [1962] A.C. 446.
[8] *New Zealand Shipping Co. Ltd.* .v *Satterthwaite* [1975] A.C. 154.
[9] [1911] A.C. 394.
[10] [1953] 1 W.L.R. 1285; [1953] 2 All E.R. 1021.
[11] [1954] 1 Q.B. 247; [1953] 2 All E.R. 1409, *ante*, p. 359.
[12] *Curtis* v. *Chemical Cleaning and Dyeing Co.* [1951] 1 K.B. 805 [1951] 1 All E.R. 631.

(4) *Later oral promise*

An exemption clause will be ineffective if it is displaced by a later oral promise. In *Couchman v. Hill*[13]

> An auctioneer at a cattle auction said to a prospective but hesitant buyer of a heifer "I warrant she is unserved." This induced the buyer to buy but the statement was incorrect. It was held that the auctioneer was liable to the buyer and that he could not shelter behind a small-print exemption clause.

To prevent this type of over-enthusiastic statements by sales staff some sellers expressly provide that "no employee has any authority to vary these conditions" or "no employee has any authority to make representations." In *Overbrooke Estates Ltd. v. Glencombe Properties Ltd.*[14] the Court of Appeal upheld the effectiveness of such a provision on the grounds that the agent had neither actual nor apparent authority to make representations in such a case. The practical implications could be horrendous.

> Suppose that S's agent A negotiates a sale to B who informs A that he is only interested in buying the goods if A will vary the payment terms so as to give B more time to pay. A does so. The conditions of trading expressly deny A authority to alter the terms in any way. Several weeks later, having spent £10,000 on the transaction S discovers what A has done and sues immediately for the full price.

On one construction there may be no contract at all because S and B never agreed on the terms. No doubt the court would strain to avoid such a result—perhaps on the basis that S did not do enough to bring the restriction on A's authority to the notice of B.

(5) *Fundamental breach and breach of a fundamental term*

The twin doctrines of "fundamental breach" and "breach of a fundamental term" were widely used by the courts in recent years as a weapon to protect the consumer against unreasonable exemption clauses. The two terms are often used interchangeably but there is a difference between them. A fundamental term has been described by Lord Devlin as "something narrower than a condition—something which underlies the whole contract so that if it is not complied with the performance becomes totally different

---

[13] [1947] K.B. 554; [1947] 1 All E.R. 103.
[14] [1974] 3 All E.R. 811.

from that which the contract contemplates."[15] A fundamental breach on the other hand is a serious breach of contract with disastrous consequences for the innocent party. An obvious example would be the theft by a bailee of goods entrusted to him for carriage, storage, cleaning or repair.

In a number of cases (all decided at a time when the Unfair Contract Terms Act 1977 had not been passed) the Court of Appeal laid down the highly questionable rule that an exemption clause could never cover a fundamental breach.[16] This rule was exploded by the House of Lords on two occasions[17] and with the arrival of the 1977 Act it can be confidently predicted that the doctrine of fundamental breach has had its day. In a very recent case the House of Lords has warned that the courts should not re-introduce the doctrine when construing an exemption clause.[17a]

UNFAIR CONTRACT TERMS ACT 1977

Although there are many statutes which strike down exemption clauses there is no doubt that the Unfair Contract Terms Act 1977 is by far the most important.

The Act came into force on February 1, 1978 and case law is beginning to trickle through. The Act operates in five overlapping areas, namely:

 (a) negligence;
 (b) contractual obligations;
 (c) terms implied in contracts for sale of goods, hire-purchase, hire and quasi-sales (*ante*, pp. 103–126);
 (d) guarantees and indemnities;
 (e) misrepresentation.

Before considering these areas it is necessary to mention some preliminary points.

---

[15] *Smeaton Hanscomb & Co. Ltd.* v. *Setty (Sassoon) Son & Co. (No.* 13) [1953] 1 W.L.R. 1468.

[16] See, *e.g. Karsales (Harrow) Ltd.* v. *Wallis* [1956] 1 W.L.R. 936.

[17] *Suisse Atlantique* v. *N.V. Rotherdamsche Kolen Centrale* [1967] 1 A.C. 361; *Photo Production* v. *Securicor Transport* [1980] A.C. 107 [1980] 1 All E.R. 556.

[17a] *George Mitchell (Netherhall) Ltd.* v. *Finney Lock Seeds Ltd., The Times,* July 1, 1983. H.L.

Preliminary matters

(1) The Act does not create new duties—it merely controls clauses which cut down a duty which would otherwise exist or which exclude or modify the remedies available on breach of this duty.

> Let us suppose that Richard parks his car in a car park and keeps the key. There is a large notice at the entrance—"The company is not liable for any loss or damage to the vehicle or to its contents whether or not due to the negligence of the company or of its servants or agents." When Richard comes back to collect his car it cannot be found.

It will be recalled that this transaction amounts to a licence and not to a bailment (*ante*, p. 405). Under the general law there is no duty on the licensor to guard against theft and the Unfair Contract Terms Act does not create one.

(2) The name of the Act is misleading—it is both too narrow and too wide. It is too narrow because it only refers to "contract"; the Act also applies to negligence both at common law and under the Occupiers' Liability Act 1957. On the other hand it is too wide because it does not control all "unfair terms"; it merely controls certain exemption clauses and notices.

(3) With very minor exceptions the key provisions of the Act (ss.2–7) only apply to "business liability." By section 1(3) this means: liability for breach of obligations or duties arising—

(a) from things done or to be done by a person in the course of a business (whether his own business or anothers); or

(b) from the occupation of premises used for business purposes of the occupier.

By section 14 the term "business' is widely defined so as to include a profession and the activities of any government department or local or public authority. There are, of course, bound to be borderline cases as to whether or not a particular activity constitutes a "business."[18] What about a landlord who lets a block of flats? What about a bazaar run by a charity? The tax cases show that the key factors include the frequency of the transaction, the manner of operation and the profit motive. It is felt that, on these criteria, a charity bazaar would not be a business

---

[18] The term is also relevant in relation to supply of services (*ante*, p. 4), sale of goods (*ante*, p. 114) and unsolicited goods and services (*ante*, p. 409).

whereas a landlord might well be carrying on a business—especially if he provided services for the tenants.

(4) Sections 2–4 do not apply to certain contracts listed in Schedule 1. They include (a) contracts of insurance (b) any contract so far as it relates to (i) the creation, transfer or termination of an interest in land or in intellectual property, (ii) the formation or dissolution of a company or partnership and (iii) the creation or transfer of any securities or any interest therein.

(5) The Act repeatedly refers to a clause which "excludes or restricts" liability. This clearly covers a clause providing that:

> no liability is accepted for any loss or damage howsoever caused

or

> liability shall be limited to the cost of replacing the appliance and all liability for consequential loss is excluded.

Then when we turn to section 13(1) we find that:

> To the extent that this Part of this Act prevents the exclusion or restriction of any liability it also prevents
> (a) making the liability or its enforcement subject to restrictive or onerous conditions;
> (b) excluding or restricting any right or remedy in respect of the liability, or subjecting a person to any prejudice in consequence of his pursuing any such right or remedy;
> (c) excluding or restricting rules of evidence or procedure.

Thus the following would be caught:
(a) "all claims within seven days";
(b) "before starting proceedings the customer must pay £1,000 into a joint bank account;
(c) "no rejection";
(d) "the report by our engineer shall be conclusive."

Section 13(1) then concludes with these words:

> and (to that extent) sections 2 and 5 to 7 also prevent excluding or restricting liability by reference to terms and notices which exclude or restrict the relevant obligations or duty.

What does this mean? How can the Act control a clause which prevents a duty from arising? The probable answer is to adopt the approach of Lord Denning M.R. in *Karsales (Harrow) Ltd.* v. *Wallis*[19] by looking at the contract or activity apart from the

---

[19] [1956] 1 W.L.R. 936.

clause. If for example it is a contract giving rise to a condition of reasonable fitness or a duty of reasonable care the Act would control a clause or notice providing that "no condition of fitness is implied herein" or "the occupier shall be under no duty of care."[20]

Two final points can be made on this topic. First, an agreement in writing to submit present or future disputes to arbitration is not a clause excluding or restricting liability (see s.13(2)). Secondly, it is thought that the Act would not apply to a genuine "liquidated damages" clause nor to a genuine settlement out of court ("I accept £100 (or a credit note) in full and final settlement of all claims").

The five areas affected by the Act

(a) *Negligence*
    Section 1(1) defines negligence as the breach:

    (a) of any obligation, arising from the express or implied terms of a contract to take reasonable care or to exercise reasonable skill[21];
    (b) of any common law duty[22] to take reasonable care or to exercise reasonable skill (but not any stricter duty)[23];
    (c) of the common duty of care imposed by the Occupiers Liability Act 1957.

We can now consider section 2—one of the most important sections of the Act. It reads as follows:

    (1) A person cannot, by reference to any contract term, or to a notice given to persons generally or to particular persons exclude or restrict his liability for death or personal injury resulting from negligence.

---

[20] In *Hedley Byrne & Co. Ltd.* v. *Heller & Partners Ltd.* [1964] A.C. 465; [1963] 2 All E.R. 575 the House of Lords held that the bank owed no duty of care in the giving of a reference because it had expressly disclaimed responsibility. It is felt that this position has now changed, the disclaimer will be a section 13 exemption clause and the reference will be controlled in section 2 (*post*, p. 438).

[21] *e.g.* under a contract for the provision of a service (Supply of Goods and Services Act 1982, s.13, *ante*, p. 4).

[22] *e.g.* the duty of a bailee (*ante*, p. 410).

[23] *e.g.* common carriers, *ante*, p. 423.

(2) In the case of other loss or damage, a person cannot so exclude or restrict his liability except in so far as the term or notice satisfies the requirement of reasonableness.

(3) Where a contract term or notice purports to exclude or restrict liability for negligence a person's agreement to or awareness of it is not of itself to be taken as voluntary acceptance of any risk.

The scope of section 2 is wide. Examples include architects, builders, cinemas, cleaners, decorators, garages, promoters of sporting events, restaurants and holiday tour operators. In all these cases—and there are many more—an exemption clause or notice will be totally void if the negligence results in death or personal injury. If the negligence results in damage to property or economic loss the clause or notice will only be effective if it satisfies the reasonableness test (as to which see s.11, *post*, p. 443). In view of the astronomic nature of potential claims it is vital for the person providing the service to have adequate insurance arrangements.

(b) *Contractual obligations*

The other really far-reaching provision in the Act—and one bristling with problems—is section 3. It reads as follows:

(1) This section applies as between contracting parties where one of them deals as consumer or on the other's written standard terms of business.

(2) As against that party, the other cannot by reference to any contract term—
  (a) when himself in breach of contract, exclude or restrict any liability of his in respect of the breach; or
  (b) claim to be entitled.
      (i) to render a contractual performance substantially diffe-rent from that reasonable expected of him or
      (ii) in respect of the whole or part of his contractual obligations, to render no performance at all.

except in so far as (in any of the cases mentioned above in this subsection) the contract term satisfies the requirement of reasonable-ness.

This section is based on the recommendation of the Law Commission in their Second Report on Exemption Clauses (Law Com. No. 69) and it is discussed on pages 52–62 of that Report. It applies to a contract between a businessman and a person dealing as consumer; it also applies to a contract between two businessmen where it is made on the standard written terms of one of them—and presumably this would include the standard terms of a trade association to which the party relying on the clause belonged.

When does a person "deal as consumer?" Section 12 provides the answer.

> (1) a party to a contract "deals as consumer" in relation to another party if—
> (a) he neither makes the contract in the course of a business nor holds himself out as doing so; and
> (b) the other party does make the contract in the course of a business; and
> (c) in the case of a contract governed by the law of sale of goods or hire-purchase or [any other contract under which ownership or possession of goods pass] the goods passing under or in pursuance of the contract are of a type ordinarily supplied for private use or consumption.

If a solicitor ordered a carpet or car for his private use, and if the order was given on business notepaper, the solicitor would "hold himself out" as buying in the course of a business and he would *not* be dealing as consumer. Conversely it seems that a holding company which has no business can "deal as consumer" for the purposes of the Act.[24]

Section 12(1)(c) could cause problems in the case of "do-it-yourself" materials such as wiring, cement and builders' tools. If these items are not normally supplied for private use or consumption the do-it-yourself enthusiast would not "deal as consumer" in relation to these items.

If section 3 does apply it will subject three types of clause to the scrutiny of the reasonableness test. The first is a clause excluding or restricting liability for breach (for example "damages limited to £1,000"). The second type of controlled clause is where the trader claims a right to render a contractual performance substantially different from that which was reasonably expected of him. The Law Commission in their report cited the case of *Anglo-Continental Holidays Ltd.* v. *Typaldos Lines (London) Ltd.*[25]

---

[24] *Rasbora Ltd.* v. *J.C.C. Marine Ltd.* [1977] 1 Ll.L.R. 645—a case on a similar provision in the Supply of Goods (Implied Terms) Act 1973.

[25] [1967] 2 Ll.L.R. 61 C.A.

where a holiday brochure contained the words "Steamers, Sailing Dates, Rates and Itineraries are subject to change without notice." The third type of controlled clause (and potentially the widest of them all) is a clause which authorises a party to offer no performance at all. Thus a clause giving a right of cancellation could be caught and so also could a *force majeure* clause ("the seller shall not be liable for non-delivery if delay is caused by strikes, lockouts or other acts beyond the seller's control.")

(c) *Implied terms*

In Chapter Three we examined the various terms as to title, description, quality, fitness and sample which were implied into contracts of sale, "quasi-sale," hire-purchase and hire (*ante*, p. 103). It is now necessary to consider the extent to which such terms can be excluded. Since the rules governing these various contracts are now virtually identical they can conveniently be considered together.

(1) Title. The rules governing this topic can be summarised as follows:

    (a) In the case of sale and hire-purchase the statutory terms as to title etc. cannot be excluded.[26]

    (b) A similar rule applies in the case of a "quasi-sale" in the course of a business.[27]

    (c) Where goods are hired out by the owner in the course of a business a clause excluding his "title" obligations is controlled by the reasonableness test.[28]

    (d) the controls in (b) and (c) above do not apply to non-business transactions but the practical impact of this is likely to be small.

Turning now to description, quality, fitness and sample, the rules are virtually[29] identical for all four types of contract—sale, hire-purchase, quasi-sale, hire. Thus:

---

[26] See Act of 1977, s.6(1). There is no distinction here between business and non-business transactions (s.6(4)).

[27] *Ibid.* s.7(3A) added by section 17 of the Supply of Goods and Services Act 1982.

[28] *Ibid.* s.7(4).

[29] The only minor difference is that in sale of goods and hire-purchase the controls apply equally to business and non-business transactions (Act of 1977, s.6(4)). It must of course be borne in mind that in the case of quality and fitness the obligation only arises where the seller is acting in the course of a business.

1. If the buyer, etc., deals as consumer (*ante*, p. 439) the exemption clause is void,[30] and
2. If the buyer, etc., does not deal as consumer the exemption clause is valid in so far as it satisfies the test of reasonableness.[31]

One further point can usefully be mentioned here. If a buyer under a "work and materials" contract has a complaint it may be important to know whether it relates to the materials or to the work. In the former case there may well be strict liability (*ante*, p. 122) and an exemption clause will be wholly void if the buyer deals as consumer. If, however, the complaint relates to the work the claim must be based on failure to exercise reasonable care and skill (*ante*, p. 4) and an exemption clause will be controlled by the reasonableness test under section 2 of the 1977 Act (unless personal injury has been caused).

(d) *Guarantees and indemnities*

(i) Perhaps one of the most unreasonable clauses imaginable was formerly used by a ferry company. It said in effect "if we (the company) incur liability to a third party in carrying your car you (the consumer) must indemnify us—even if the liability was entirely due to our negligence." Not surprisingly such clauses are now controlled—perhaps the only surprising thing is that they are not subject to an outright ban. Section 4(1) provides that:

> A person dealing as consumer cannot by reference to any contract term be made to indemnify another person (whether a party to the contract or not) in respect of liability that may be incurred by the other for negligence or breach of contract, except in so far as the contract term satisfies the test of reasonableness.

It will be observed that the section only applies where an indemnity is sought from a person dealing as consumer. It may well be, therefore, that a business-to-business indemnity is fully valid and enforceable and is not controlled by the Act.

(ii) Guarantees. Most purchasers of cars and other expensive consumer goods have come to expect manufacturers' guarantees as part of the transaction. Until fairly recently many guarantees actually took away from the customer more than they gave to him.

---

[30] Act of 1977, s.6(2), 7(2).
[31] *Ibid*. s.6(3), 7(3).

In return for an agreement to replace defective parts the guarantee excluded the customer's right to claim damages in tort if a defect in the product resulted in injury or damage. Lord Denning M.R. severely criticised such clauses in *Adams* v. *Richardson*.[32] In ringing tones he declared:

> Instead of heading it boldly GUARANTEE he should head it NON-GUARANTEE for that is what it is.

Fortunately this type of problem should now be a thing of the past because section 5 of the 1977 Act nullifies a large number of such clauses. By section 5(1):

> In the case of goods of a type ordinarily supplied for private use or consumption, where loss or damage—
> (a) arises from the goods proving defective while in consumer use: and
> (b) results from the negligence of a person concerned in the manufacture or distribution of the goods:
> liability for the loss or damage cannot be excluded or restricted by reference to any contract term or notice contained in or operating by reference to a guarantee of the goods.

(e) *Misrepresentation*

Exemption clauses relating to misrepresentation have been subject to statutory control for more than 15 years. The relevant law is still to be found in section 3 of the Misrepresentation Act 1967 although the section has been redrafted by section 8 of the 1977 Act so that it now reads as follows:

> If a contract contains a term which would exclude or restrict
> (a) any liability to which a party to a contract may be subject by reason of any misrepresentation made by him before the contract was made; or
> (b) any remedy available to another party to the contract by reason of such a misrepresentation
> the term shall be of no effect except in so far as it satisfies the requirement of reasonableness as stated in section 11(1) of the Unfair Contract Terms Act 1977; and it is for those claiming that the term satisfies that requirement to show that it does.

The first point to notice here is that section 3 of the 1967 Act applies to *all* contracts (both business and non-business), including

---

[32] [1969] 1 W.L.R. 1647.

those contracts which are outside the main provisions of the 1977 Act. Most of the decided cases on section 3 have been concerned with sale of land. Secondly, the section will only apply if there is both a misrepresentation and a contractual attempt to exclude liability for it. Consider the following facts.[33]

> A advertises land for sale with "15000 square feet of lettable office space." At the foot of the particulars there is a clause which states "the accuracy of these particulars cannot be guaranteed and a prospective purchaser should make his own enquiries."

The sellers might try to argue that the concluding words meant that there was no misrepresentation at all. In a recent case however, the Court of Appeal have rejected this appoach. The court will of course consider all the evidence and if they are satisfied that the buyer *was* induced by the letting figure to enter into the contract they will decide that there was an actionable misrepresentation and that the words of disclaimer (if they are contractual at all) are controlled by section 3.[33]

The reasonableness test

Sections 2, 3, 4, 6, 7 and 8 all refer to the reasonableness test. The concept is not a new one; it has applied to misrepresentation since 1967 and it has applied to the implied terms in sale of goods and hire purchase since 1973. Section 11 draws a distinction between contractual clauses and non-contractual notices. In the case of contract the person claiming that the term is reasonable must prove that:

> the term shall have been a fair and reasonable one to be included having referred to the circumstances which were, or which ought reasonably to have been, known to or in the contemplation of the parties when the contract was made.

Thus the critical date is the date of the contract. For example, a limitation of damages clause which was reasonable at the date of the contract will be upheld even though by the time of the hearing it has become hopelessly inadequate by reason of inflation or by reason of the plaintiff's losses being far greater than expected.

If we turn now to non-contractual notices we find that the party relying on the notice must prove that:

---

[33] *Cremdean Properties Ltd.* v. *Nash* [1977] 244 E.G. 547.

it should be fair and reasonable to allow reliance on it having regard to the circumstances obtaining when the liability arose or (but for the notice) would have arisen.

Statutory guidelines

There is no doubt that the court has a wide discretion and presumably the party relying on the clause or notice must plead the facts upon which he relies to support his claim of reasonableness. Schedule 2 contains a non-exhaustive list of guidelines which are expressed to apply only to cases within sections 6 and 7 but which will no doubt be considered by the court in other cases as well. The court must consider:

(a) The bargaining strength of the parties (including the alternatives (if any) available to the customer);

(b) Any inducement given to the customer and whether he had an opportunity of entering into a similar contract with other persons without the disputed clause;

(c) Whether the customer knew or ought to have known of the existence of the term;

(d) Where the term excludes or restricts liability if some condition is not complied with, whether it was reasonable at the time of the contract to expect that compliance would be practicable; and

(e) Whether the goods are manufactured, processed or adapted to the special order of the customer.

Limitation of damages clauses

A further guideline is provided by section 11(4) which was introduced to deal with the fears of small traders (including travel agents) who had visions of being driven out of business by enormous claims. It reads as follows:

> Where by reference to a contract term or notice a person seeks to restrict liability to a specified sum of money, and the question arises (under this or any other Act) whether the term or notice satisfies the requirement of reasonableness, regard shall be had in particular to
> (a) the resources which he could expect to be available to him for the purpose of meeting the liability should it arise and
> (b) how far it was open to him to cover himself by insurance.

Some points from decided cases

The first few cases confirm that the critical factors will be bargaining power, knowledge and choice—plus, in appropriate cases, the seriousness of the breach. On the question of bargaining power it will be interesting to see whether the courts will follow the advice given by Lord Wilberforce in the pre-Act case of *Photo Productions Ltd.* v. *Securicor Transport Ltd.*[34] cases where an employee of the defendants intentionally started a small fire on the plaintiff's premises. The fire got out of control and enormous damage was caused. After holding that the defendants were protected by an exemption clause, Lord Wilberforce said this:

> After [The Unfair Contract Terms Act] in commercial matters generally, when the parties are not of unequal bargaining power, and when risks are normally borne by insurance, not only is the case for judicial intervention undemonstrated but there is everything to be said, and this seems to have been Parliament's intention, for leaving the parties free to apportion the risks as they think fit and for respecting their decisions.

These words refer to cases where the parties *knowingly* decide on who bears the risks.[35] In the vast majority of cases, however, the exemption clause is not negotiated at all and no steps are taken to bring it to the notice of the other party. In such cases the clause may well be struck down. This can be illustrated by the two following cases:

(1) *Walker* v. *Boyle* [1982] 1 W.L.R. 495. During negotiation for the sale of V's house V told P that there was no boundary dispute. This was an innocent misrepresentation which induced P to buy. On discovering the facts P refused to proceed whereupon V claimed specific performance and relied on Condition 17 of the National Conditions of Sale which provided that "no misdescription shall annul the sale." It was held that (1) the clause was unreasonable and accordingly (2) P could reject the claim for specific performance and could also claim the interest foregone on his deposit.

(2) *George Mitchell* v. *Finney Lock Seeds, The Times*, July 1, 1983[35] farmers ordered 30lbs of cabbage seed at a price of £192 but the sellers supplied a totally useless product which was not cabbage seed in any commercial sense. The sellers sought to rely on a non-negotiated limitation of damages clause limiting their liability to £192. The House of Lords held that the clause was unreasonable and

---

[34] [1980] 2 W.L.R. 283; [1980] 1 All E.R. 556 H.L. The facts took place before February 1, 1978 when the 1977 Act came into force.

[35] See also *R. W. Green Ltd.* v. *Cade Bros. Farm* [1978] 2 LL.L.R. 602 where potato seed was infected by a hidden virus; there was no negligence on the seller's part; the clause had been negotiated by trade associations of seller and buyer; the clause was upheld.

that the buyers should be entitled to recover their actual loss *i.e.* £61,513.

On the question of choice the county court case of *Woodman* v. *Photo Trade Processing Ltd.*[36] is highly significant as a pointer for the future.

> Mr. Woodman took photographs at a friend's wedding. The shop to which he brought the film for development displayed a notice limiting their liability to the cost of the film. The film came back ruined and Mr. Woodman claimed damages. The action was successful and damages of £75 for disappointment were awarded.

The significant feature of the case (a test case with support from the Consumer's Association) is the reason why the limitation clause was struck down as being unreasonable. The learned judge considered that it should have been possible to offer the public a choice—development under the present arrangements at a very low price or a more specialised service at a higher price. This clearly points the way to double-priced quotations—£X with the exemption clause or £Y without it.

OTHER LEGISLATION

It remains to add that the Unfair Contract Terms Act 1977 is not the only Act which controls exemption clauses. Apart from the Misrepresentation Act 1967 which has already been considered the list of Acts includes the following.

Defective Premises Act 1972
Occupier's Liability Act 1957
Hire-Purchase Act 1965
Consumer Credit Act 1974
Solicitors Act 1974
Companies Act 1948
Carriage of Goods by Road Act 1965
Road Traffic Act 1972
Transport Act 1962

---

[36] *Times Business News* June 20, 1981.

CHAPTER NINE

FAIR TRADING AND CONSUMER PROTECTION

THE term "consumer protection" can be used to describe rules of law which recognise the bargaining weakness of the individual consumer and which ensure that that weakness is not unfairly exploited. In recent years the growth of vast national and international companies and the standardisation of their methods of production and distribution has led to an increased demand for consumer protection and there has been quite a lot of activity both in Parliament and elsewhere. In this chapter it is proposed to examine briefly the main types of consumer protection in force at the present time.

In the eighteenth and nineteenth centuries the common law of contract was built on the two pillars of "freedom of contract" and "sanctity of contract." This was obviously right in the case of genuine bargains between equals. With the development of standard form "take-it-or-leave-it" contracts for the purchase of a mass-produced article there was clearly a strong case for modifying the "freedom of contract" principle to fit the economic facts. Unfortunately the common law courts felt themselves unable to shake off the "freedom of contract" principle and in view of this their contribution towards consumer protection has been disappointing. The courts have endeavoured to limit the scope of exemption clauses but their approach has been based on a construction of words rather than on policy; consequently their decisions could generally be outflanked by a skilful draftsman. There have been times when the common law was more robust. Thus, in the turbulent days of the early Middle Ages, when liability without proof of fault was almost unheard of, the courts held that an innkeeper was liable without proof of fault for loss of his customers' belongings—a clear rule to discourage conspiracies between innkeepers and thieves.

In modern times, the task of protecting the consumer has been largely left to Parliament, which has performed this function in various ways.

1. Direct regulation of contracts and enforcement of small claims

Examples include the Bills of Sale Acts, the Unfair Contract Terms Act 1977 (*ante*, pp. 434–446) and the Consumer Credit Act 1974, *ante*, Chapter Four.

A statute conferring rights is of no value unless adequate machinery exists for its enforcement. Many customers have been deterred in the past from enforcing their rights where the amount involved has been relatively small. One reason has been that the cost of doing so might be greater than the amount of compensation recoverable in proceedings. Even if legal aid was available there was always the danger that the Law Society's charge (see now Legal Aid Act 1974, s.9(6)) would eat up any moneys recovered. There was the further point that the technical rules of procedure and evidence could act as a strong deterrent to a dissatisfied consumer bringing proceedings without the aid of a solicitor. Finally, there was the risk of having to pay the costs of the other side if the claim was unsuccessful. Two procedural changes are designed to make it easier for small claims to be enforced in the county court. The first change relates to costs; where the amount claimed does not exceed £500 no costs will normally be awarded. Thus the plaintiff will not normally run the risk of having to pay the defendants' costs if he loses the case (although conversely he will not get an order for payment of his own costs and this will make the litigation uneconomic for him unless he is prepared to conduct his own case without the help of a solicitor). The second change extends the power of the county court to order arbitration. A claim for £500 or less will nearly always be referred to arbitration (C.C.R. 1981, Ord. 19, r. 2(3)). In many cases the registrar himself will act as the arbitrator; the hearing will be informal and the rules of evidence will be relaxed.

2. The criminal law

A statute conferring civil rights can be useful to the consumer but in many cases the customer may be unable or unwilling to enforce these rights for reasons such as fear, lethargy, ignorance or expense. Accordingly a number of statutes have been passed creating criminal offences in consumer transactions and vesting enforcement powers in public authorities. Examples include the Food and Drugs Act 1955, the Trade Descriptions Act 1968–1972 and the Consumer Credit Act 1974.

The further question then arises as to whether a breach of the statute gives rise to an action for damages. Apart from a few statutes which expressly deal with the matter[1] the courts must decide, as a matter of construction, whether an action lies. On the whole their attitude has been disappointingly negative, but the Criminal Justice Act 1972 introduced an entirely new principle which is now to be found in section 35 of the Powers of Criminal Courts Act 1973. It provides in effect that on any criminal conviction the court can award compensation to a victim. This discretion (which extends far beyond consumer protection) is immensely wide; the only practical difficulty is that no machinery appears to exist whereby the victim is given a right to notice of the proceedings and a right to be heard; the onus therefore lies on the person claiming compensation to inform the prosecutor and the clerk of the court. It has recently been held that if there are several victims of the crime the court can choose which of them are to receive compensation.[2]

The cases show that the power to award compensation is designed for simple and straightforward cases and the criminal court must not allow itself to get bogged down with difficult problems of causation and remoteness of damage.[3] The means of the convicted person must be taken into account and an order will not be made if it would cast an excessive burden upon him or if it would be counter-productive.[4] The award can be payable by instalments.

The provisions of section 35 are supplemented and modified by the following provisions of the Act:

> (1) No such order can be made in respect of injury or death arising from the presence of a motor vehicle on a road (s.35(3)).
> (2) In the magistrates' court there is a ceiling of £1,000 for each conviction (s.35(5) as amended by section 40 of the Magistrates' Courts Act 1980).
> (3) Application can be made, at any time before payment, to have the award varied on the ground that (a) a civil court has assessed the

---

[1] See, e.g. Consumer Safety Act 1978, s.6(1).

[2] R. v. Arrey, The Times January 6, 1983.

[3] e.g. R. v. Thomson Holidays [1974] Q.B. 592. (Offence under Trade Descriptions Act 1968—company ordered to pay a fine and compensation to a holiday-maker.)

[4] R. v. Daly [1974] 1 W.L.R. 133; [1974] 1 All E.R. 290; R. v. McIntosh [1973] Crim.L.R. 387, C.A.; R. v.Oddy [1974] 1 W.L.R. 1212; [1974] 2 All E.R. 666.

loss at a smaller amount or (b) property in respect of which the award has been recovered (s.37).

(4) In subsequent civil proceedings the compensation order must be disregarded in assessing the loss but the civil court cannot award any sum which has already been paid under the order and it is not enforceable as regards any sum which is payable under the order (s.35).

Competition law

There is a school of thought which believes that the best way to protect the consumer is by encouraging and maintaining free and undistorted competition. Here again the contribution made by the common law has been minimal and the relevant law is almost entirely statutory. The principal statutes are the Restrictive Trade Practices Acts 1956–68, the Resale Prices Act 1964, the Fair Trading Act 1973 and the Competition Act 1980.[5] In addition, the philosophy of free competition is central to the Treaty of Rome and the competition rules based on Article 85 are much stricter than the present English domestic law (*post*, p. 552).

4. Supervision by administrative agency

The Fair Trading Act[6] broke new ground by appointing a Director-General of Fair Trading (hereafter referred to as "the Director") and charging him with, *inter alia*, keeping under review consumer trade practices and investigating practices which may adversely affect the economic interests of consumers. The Director is assisted by a Consumer Protection Advisory Committee consisting of persons appointed by the Secretary of State and having specialist knowledge of consumer matters. The Act is a long one and many of its provisions relate to restrictive practices, monopolies and mergers. In the remainder of this chapter it is proposed to summarise the main provisions relating to consumer practices.

Functions of the Director-General

The functions of the Director-General under the Fair Trading Act can be summarised as follows:

---

[5] For a recent account of his activities see his 1981 Annual Report at pp. 26–47.

[6] For a fuller account of the 1973 Act, see Lowe and Woodroffe *Consumer Law and Practice* Chapter 14.

(1) He must, so far as appears to him to be practicable, keep under review the carrying on of commercial activities in the United Kingdom relating to the supply of goods or services to consumers, and collect information with respect to such activities in order to discover practices which may adversely affect the economic interests of consumers in the United Kingdom (s.2(1)(*a*)). In other words he must take the initiative to find out about these harmful practices.

(2) He must, so far as appears to him to be practicable, receive and collate evidence relating to the matters specified in (1) above and which appears to him to be evidence of practices adversely affecting the interests of consumers in the United Kingdom (whether they are economic interests or relate to health, safety or other matters) (s.2(1)(*b*)). Thus on matters of health and safety (such as inflammable nightwear or defective harnessing for children's seats in cars) the Director's duty is a passive one—to receive and collate.

(3) At the request of the Secretary of State, or on his own initiative, he must supply information to the Secretary of State together with a recommendation for action in appropriate cases (s.2(3)).[7]

(4) He can refer certain harmful consumer trade practices to the Committee (Part II, *infra*).

(5) He can on his own initiative take proceedings against persons who are trading unfairly (Part III), *infra*).

(6) He can arrange for information and advice to be published for the benefit of consumers (s.124(1)).

(7) He must encourage trade associations to prepare and circulate codes of practice for guidance in safeguarding and promoting the interests of consumers in the United Kingdom (s.124(3)). The development of these codes (which are considered *post*, p. 458) are among the most important developments in the past few years.

Prohibition of Harmful Consumer Trade Practices (Part II, ss.13–33)

In the past the only way of abolishing an undesirable trade practice was to pass an Act of Parliament to ban it. This is a slow,

---

[7] The Price Marking (Bargain Offers) Order 1979 (S.I. 1979 No. 364) made under the Prices Act 1974, resulted from a section 2(3) recommendation.

hazardous and cumbersome procedure and there is always the risk that pressure of parliamentary time will lead to serious delays or the loss of the Bill altogether. In many cases prompt action is highly desirable and Part II of the Act provides machinery whereby a harmful consumer practice can be banned by order without the need for an Act of Parliament. Before explaining how the new machinery works some key definitions must be briefly examined.

(a) "Consumer" is defined in section 137 as a person (i) to whom goods or services are supplied, or are sought to be supplied, in the course of a business carried on by the supplier and (ii) who does not receive or seek to receive them in the course of a business carried on by him.

(b) "Goods" includes buildings; thus unfair practices by estate agents and builders can fall within Part II.

(c) "Consumer trade practice" is exhaustively defined in section 13 as a practice carried on in connection with the supply of goods or services to consumers relating:

(1) to the terms or conditions (whether as to price or otherwise) on or subject to which goods or services are or are sought to be supplied, or

(2) to the manner in which those terms or conditions are communicated to the persons to whom the goods or services are, or are sought to be, supplied, or

(3) to promotion (by advertising, labelling or marking of goods, canvassing or otherwise) of the supply of goods or services, or

(4) to methods of salesmanship employed in dealing with consumers, or

(5) to the way in which goods are packed or otherwise got up for the purpose of being supplied, or

(6) to methods of demanding or securing payment for goods or services supplied.

Examples would include exemption clauses, the size of print, doorstep selling, double pricing and misleading packaging, *e.g.* false bottoms on bottles giving a false impression of size.

The Part II Procedure

The Director or the Secretary of State or any Minister can refer a consumer trade practice to the Committee under section 14; the Committee must then decide whether it is harmful to the economic interests of consumers and must report to the Director.

The important provision in Part II is section 17 under which a reference to the Committee by the Director can be accompanied by proposals for action. This is only possible if the Director considers that the practice has the effect, or is likely to have the effect:

(a) of misleading consumers as to, or withholding from them adequate information as to, or an adequate record of their rights and obligations under relevant consumer transactions, or

(b) of otherwise misleading or confusing consumers with respect to any matter in connection with relevant consumer transactions, or

(c) of subjecting consumers to undue pressure to enter into relevant consumer transactions, or

(d) of causing the terms or conditions on or subject to which consumers enter into relevant consumer transactions to be so adverse to them as to be inequitable.

As already stated, the reference can be accompanied by proposals for action. Schedule 6 contains a non-exhaustive list of such proposals, including (a) the prohibition of particular terms; (b) the giving of information to consumers; (c) implication of certain terms into contracts; and (d) the size of print. These provisions are similar to those adopted in the hire-purchase legislation and now in the Consumer Credit Act 1974 (*see* Chapter Four).

If a section 17 reference is made the procedure is as follows:

(1) It must be published in the London, Edinburgh and Belfast *Gazettes* (s.17(4)).

(2) The Committee must consider representations by interested persons or bodies; subject to this the Committee can regulate its own procedure (s.81).

(3) The Committee must report to the Director within three months or such longer period as the Secretary of State may allow (s.10). In their Report the Committee must indicate whether the practice does adversely affect the economic interests of consumers and, if so, whether (a) they agree with the Director's proposals or (b) they would do so if they were modified in a certain way or (c) they do not agree with the proposals (s.21).

(4) In cases (a) and (b) above the Secretary of State can make an order giving effect to the original or modified proposals; such an order then requires an affirmative resolution of each House of Parliament (s.22).

Thus the practice will only be regulated under Part II if this course is approved by the Director, the Committee, the Secretary of State, the House of Commons and the House of Lords. It has been estimated that the whole process could take six months—a long time but not as long as an Act of Parliament normally takes.

Once an order has been made non-compliance is an offence punishable (a) on summary conviction by a fine of up to £1,000 and (b) on indictment by a fine or imprisonment up to two years or both (s.23 as amended by the Criminal Law Act 1977). No direct civil consequences flow from such an offence (s.26) but presumably the Powers of Criminal Courts Act 1973, s.35 will allow the criminal court to make an award of compensation in appropriate cases. The task of enforcement is given (as under the Trade Descriptions Acts and Consumer Credit Act) to local Weights and Measures authorities.

Part II in operation

So far the use made of Part II has been surprisingly and disappointingly small—only four references have been made in more than nine years and only two of these have resulted in meaningful Orders. These two Orders will now be briefly examined.

(a) **Continued use of certain void exemption clauses.** We have seen that a seller cannot exclude the duties which he owes to a consumer under sections 12–15 of the Sale of Goods Act 1979 (section 6 of the Unfair Contract Terms Act 1977 *ante*, p. 440). Despite all the media publicity on consumer affairs and despite the many excellent publications issued by the Office of Fair Trading many consumers remain woefully ignorant of their legal rights. In particular many of them are unaware of their right to reject faulty goods and to get their money back from the retailer. Retailers may be tempted to preserve this ignorance by putting up notices stating that "no goods can be returned" or "no cash can be refunded under any circumstances." Such matters are now governed by the Consumer Transactions (Restrictions on Statements) Order 1976 No. 1813 as amended by S.I. 1978 No. 127[8] and the main provisions of this important Order can be summarised as follows:

---

[8] In 1981 local authorities brought 26 successful prosecutions under the Order.

1. A criminal offence is committed where a notice containing a "section 6" void exemption clause is displayed at any place where consumer transactions are effected (Art. 3).

2. An offence is also committed where such a clause is included in an advertisement, catalogue, circular or document, or on any goods or their containers, relating to a consumer transaction (*ibid.*).

3. Where goods or their container or a document are supplied with a statement as to the consumer's rights against the supplier in relation to defects, fitness for purpose or correspondence with description, an offence is committed unless there is, in close proximity, a clear and conspicuous statement to the effect that the statutory rights of the consumer are not affected (*ibid.* Art. 4).

4. A similar obligation is imposed on a third party (*e.g.* manufacturer) in a case where the goods or their packaging or a document contain a statement setting out the obligations accepted by him. Thus a manufacturer who agrees in his guarantee to replace defective parts within 12 months commits a criminal offence unless the guarantee also states clearly and conspicuously that these rights do not affect in any way the statutory rights of the consumer against the supplier.

It should be noted that the Order only refers to one particular type of void exemption clause—namely a clause which is void under section 6 of the 1977 Act. The Director-General of Fair Trading has asked for reports as to the continued use of other void clauses or notices so that he can consider whether further Part II references are required.[9]

(b) Disclosure of business status. A consumer seeing a "small ad" in a newspaper or magazine may have no idea that the person offering to supply the goods is a trader. If the goods are faulty he may find himself in serious difficulties (quite apart from problems of tracking down the supplier) because any claim under section 14 of the Sale of Goods Act will fail unless he can prove that the goods were supplied in the course of a business (*ante*, p. 114). To deal with this type of problem the Business Advertisements

---

[9] 1981 Annual Report of Director-General at p. 24. The Director-General already exercises control over such clauses and notices in exercising his wide discretionary licensing powers under the Conumer Credit Act (*ibid.* and *ante*, p. 212).

(Disclosure) Order 1978 requires business sellers of goods to make it clear in advertisements directed at consumers that they are traders.[10]

The Director has said that he prefers to act by persuasion rather than compulsion. It may be therefore, that the real value of the Part II machinery is the fact that it is there, in reserve, to be used if necessary.

Part III—Action against Individual Traders

Part II is concerned with the banning of general practices which will presumably be notified to the Director by bodies who meet them in practice (Consumer Groups, Citizens Advice Bureaux and others). Part III on the other hand gives the Director power to take proceedings against individual traders or companies who are trading unfairly. An unscrupulous trader may be tempted to supply goods which infringe the Trade Descriptions Act, or the statutory rules as to merchantable quality, or the common law rules as to negligence, in the hope that consumers will be prevented by ignorance, apathy, poverty and fear from doing anything about it. The trader might also calculate that his profit will greatly exceed any fines and/or compensation and/or damages that he may have to pay. It is this type of case which falls within Part III (ss.34–43) of the Act.

The Director can invoke his powers under Part III if it appears to him that a person carrying on a business has persisted in a course of conduct which is detrimental to the interests of consumers in the United Kingdom and is "unfair" *i.e.* in breach of civil or criminal obligations (s.34). The Director must then use his best endeavours to obtain a satisfactory written undertaking by the trader to refrain from such conduct in future. If he fails to obtain such an undertaking, or if the undertaking is given and broken, the Director can take proceedings against the trader in the Restrictive Practices Court or, in certain cases, the county court (ss.35 and 41). If the court is satisfied that (a) the trader has been trading unfairly and (b) such conduct is likely to continue, the court can make an order restraining him from doing so (s.37). Alternatively the court may accept an undertaking from the trader to refrain from such conduct. In either case non-compliance will constitute

---

[10] In 1981 local authorities brought 158 successful prosecutions under the Order.

contempt of court. Legal aid is available for the proceedings (s.43) and appeal lies to the Court of Appeal (s.42).

If the defaulting trader is a company the provisions of Part III set out above also apply to an officer or controlling shareholder who consented to or connived at the unfair trading (s.38). Finally, if the company is a member of a group of interconnected bodies section 40 closes an obvious loophole by enabling the court to extend its order so as to bind other companies in the group.

Part III in action

In the period 1973–81 a total of 291 Part III assurances, undertakings or orders have been obtained and the breakdown as between trades is as follows:

Cars and motoring	65
Home improvements	53
Mail order	45
Electrical	40
Carpets and furniture	15
Food and catering	15
One-day and doorstep sales	12
Other	46

One of the deterrent features of the Part III procedure is the publicity given to the proceedings—the traders are all named in the Director-General's Annual Reports and in press releases. The following random illustrations are taken from the 1981 Annual Report.

(1) Peter David John Hammett of The Bungalow, Burnett's Lane, West End, Southampton, trading as Hammett Motors of the same address gave an assurance that he would refrain from:

(a) Committing offences under section 1 of the Trade Descriptions Act 1968 by applying a false trade description to motor cars or by supplying or offering to supply motor cars to which a false trade description is applied; and

(b) committing breaches of contract with consumers by supplying motor cars which do not correspond with the description by which they are sold as required by subsection 1 of the amended section 13 of the Sale of Goods Act 1979.

(2) R & G Associates (London) Ltd., a body corporate, trading as Bodycare (registered office 31, High Street, Rayleigh, Essex, by its director Stanley Dennis Rogers and by its secretary Pearl Leslie Rogers gave an assurance that it would refrain from:

(a) committing breaches of contract with consumers by failing to deliver goods ordered within the time agreed and/or within any reasonable time and/or at all; and

(b) in breach of a duty other than a contractual duty, failing to return to consumers money to which they are legally entitled, being money which has been paid in respect of goods which have never been delivered.

Stanley Dennis Rogers and Laxmi Nath Gupta (a former director) each gave assurances under section 38 with regard to this course of conduct.

(3) Dan Colin Cooper gave the following undertaking to the West London County Court:

(a) That he would exercise all due diligence not to commit breaches of contract with consumers by failing to provide holiday accommodation in accordance with the terms of a contract therefor; and

(b) that he would not commit breaches of contract by failing to return within a reasonable time money paid by way of a returnable deposit.

Information and Advice

The Office of Fair Trading has been extremely active in publishing numerous booklets and leaflets which seek to make consumers and traders aware of their legal rights and duties.

Codes of Practice[11]

The task of encouraging trade associations to issue Codes of Practice for their members has been energetically pursued and no less than 20 voluntary codes have been adopted. They cover a very large sector of consumer services including cars, electrical goods, laundries, shoe repairs, furniture, photographic equipment, postal services, funeral services, holidays and double glazing. The codes lay down recommended standards of service—including, in a number of cases the retention of an adequate supply of spare parts. In addition (and this is of considerable importance for consumers) they contain provisions for the settlement of disputes by conciliation or, if this fails, by a fairly inexpensive arbitration conducted by a member of the Chartered Institute of Arbitrators.

---

[11] For fuller treatment see Lowe and Woodroffe *op. cit.* at pp. 121–144 and appendices. For the "code" relating to Insurance see *ante*, p. 345.

This can, in appropriate cases, provide a convenient alternative to the hazards of litigation.

The Codes of Practice are not legally enforceable but they can have an indirect legal effect by indicating what is "reasonable"; thus for example the Association of British Launderers and Cleaners recommend that their members should not exclude liability for negligence. A launderer who did exclude his negligence liability might well find that the clause would fail to pass the test of reasonableness (see *ante*, p. 443).

Apart from encouraging the introduction of Codes the Office of Fair Trading is also active in monitoring them and in pressing for improvements to be made. There is no doubt that Codes represent a major growth area and many more of them are likely to be introduced in the next few years.

CHAPTER TEN

EXPORT SALES[1]

THIS subject, the importance of which needs no emphasis, can be conveniently divided into three sections—the contract of sale, payment, and carriage of goods by sea. It is proposed to consider these topics in that order.

THE CONTRACT OF SALE

How are orders obtained?[2]

The English exporter can obtain export contracts in a number of ways. First, he can, if his business is large enough, set up a branch or a subsidiary company in the foreign country. Secondly, he can appoint agents to obtain orders. Thirdly, he can enter into what is called an "exclusive sales" agreement with a foreign importer whereby the importer agrees to buy exclusively from the exporter and to use his best endeavours to create a market for the exporter's goods, and in return he is given exclusive selling rights within a particular territory. The following points should be noted with regard to exclusive sales agreements:

(1) The exporter should ensure that the agreement does not contravene the law relating to restraint of trade and restrictive practices. In particular, an exclusive sales agreement may sometimes infringe Article 85 of the Treaty of Rome which is much stricter than English domestic law.[3]

(2) The agreement should make it clear that orders are placed by the foreign buyer as principal and not as agent. The advantage of the agreement from the seller's point of view is that he can deal

---

[1] For a fuller treatment, see C. M. Schmitthoff, *The Export Trade*, (7th ed.).
[2] For a recent discussion of the topic see (1983) 133 N.L.J. 663.
[3] The Restrictive Trade Practices Act 1956 exempts exclusive sale agreements from its operation, provided that a trade association is not involved. See also *post*, p. 553.

with one firm which is well known to him, rather than with a large number of unknown firms whose solvency may be doubtful.

(3) The agreement should specify precisely the goods covered, the territory covered, the obligations of the parties and the duration of the arrangement. A seller might, to make the arrangement worth while, require the buyer to place orders up to a specified amount within a certain period. A clause requiring the buyer to do this should state that this obligation is not dependent on the buyer himself having obtained orders for the goods.[4]

Having dealt with the methods by which orders are obtained, it is now possible to consider the actual contracts of sale between the English seller and the foreign buyer, and the obligations to which they give rise.

Which law applies?

Since an export sale involves a foreign element, it will not necessarily be governed by English law. The matter is more fully dealt with in the next chapter and it need only be stated here that an English exporter who wishes, as he usually does, to have the contract governed by English law should insert a stipulation to that effect. He should also stipulate where any litigation or arbitration is to take place.[5]

It should also be mentioned that English domestic law is sometimes expressly modified in relation to export sales. Thus for example the protection provisions of the Unfair Contract Terms Act 1977 (*ante*, p. 434) will not apply if the contract is an "International Supply Contract" as defined by Section 26 of that Act. The remainder of this chapter states the position on the assumption that English law applies.

Types of contract

A number of different types of contract can be concluded, and the question of which is best will usually depend on the type and size of business which the exporter carries on.[6] The terms of many

---

[4] *Cf. James Shaffer Ltd.* v. *Findley, Durham & Brodie* [1953] 1 W. L. R. 106.
[5] A clause referring disputes to arbitration in England is strong evidence of an implied choice of English law but it is not conclusive (see *post*, p. 507).
[6] It should be added that some of the contracts can also be used in non-export sales.

of the contracts about to be discussed have become standardised, but the interpretation of these terms is not uniform throughout the world.

Ex works

An ex works contract approximates most closely to a domestic sale. The seller is bound to make available goods of the contract description at the agreed time and place, and the buyer's duty is to collect them.[7] In the absence of contrary agreement the price is payable on delivery[8] and the property and risk will usually pass to the buyer when the goods are unconditionally appropriated to the contract.[9] Where the buyer requires documents, such as an export licence, which are obtainable in the seller's country, it is the duty of the seller to assist the buyer to obtain them.

F.O.R. (free on rail)

Here the seller's obligations are slightly more extensive. He must see that the goods are loaded onto the railway authority's collecting vehicle and, at his own expense, he must give immediate notice to the buyer that this has been done. The presentation of an invoice or advice note is sufficient for this purpose. Once the goods have been delivered to the railway authority the risk passes to the buyer[10] and the price becomes payable. The duty to assist the buyer with regard to the obtaining of documents is the same as on an ex works contract. The buyer must, of course make his own arrangements for carriage and must pay the freight. He must also inform the seller of the destination of the goods.

F.O.T. (free on truck)

This contract is the same as the previous one, except that the seller is bound, at his own expense, to load the goods onto the railway truck and not merely onto the railway collecting vehicle.

---

[7] See *International Chamber of Commerce Trade Terms* (Incoterms) (1953), as revised in 1980.

[8] Sale of Goods Act 1979, s.28 (*ante*, p. 161). The price will naturally be lower than under a c.i.f. or f.o.b. contract, because the seller's duties are less extensive.

[9] *Ibid.* ss.18(5) and 20.

[10] See Incoterms *op. cit.* The seller bears the risk of damage while the goods are being loaded onto the collecting vehicle (*Underwood* v. *Burgh Castle Brick & Cement Syndicate* [1922] 1 K. B. 343, *ante*, p. 131).

F.A.S. (free alongside)

Under this contract it is the duty of the seller to place the goods, at his own expense,[11] alongside a ship named by the buyer. The buyer, for his part, must nominate a ship and give adequate notice to the seller, and the loading of the goods onto the ship is also the buyer's responsibility.[12] Property and risk pass when the goods have been placed alongside.

Export licence. "It may well seem strange," said Viscount Simonds in the leading case, "that in a world in which restrictions on export are a commonplace, the elementary precaution is not taken of providing that any necessary licence should be got by one or the other of the parties."[13] These words emphasise the importance to the exporter of inserting a clause in the contract dealing with the duty to obtain any export licence, and also regulating the position if the licence cannot be obtained. If the contract is silent on the point, the position will turn on the facts of the particular case. In the words of Lord Somervell of Harrow,[14] "This is an area in which it is impossible to lay down general rules." In one case where both parties carried on business in England and after the making of the contract an Act was passed requiring an export licence, the Court of Appeal held that, on the facts, it was the buyer's duty to obtain the licence since he alone was in possession of the necessary information.[15] In another case[16] oil was sold by an English company to an American company f.a.s. Lisbon. An export licence was required and this could only be applied for by the seller's Portuguese suppliers. These suppliers applied for a licence but it was refused. The House of Lords held that, on the facts, it was the duty of the seller to do their best to

---

[11] Thus dock dues and porterage are generally payable by the seller.

[12] The responsibility for loading is the main difference between this contract and the f.o.b. contract (*infra*).

[13] *Pound (A. V.) & Co.* v. *Hardy (M.) & Co. Inc.* [1956] A. C. 588, 608; [1956] 1 All E. R. 639, 648.

[14] *Ibid.* at pp. 611 and 650, respectively.

[15] *Brandt (H. O.) & Co.* v. *Morris & Co.* [1917] 2 K. B. 784. Under an f.o.b. contract the act of exporting is the buyer's responsibility and it has therefore been suggested that it will be the buyer's duty to obtain any necessary export licence in the absence of a term of the contract express or implied (Schmitthoff *op. cit.* at p. 24).

[16] *Pound (A. V.) & Co.* v. *Hardy (M.) & Co. Inc., supra.*

obtain the licence, and that on failure to obtain it the buyers were excused further performance.[17]

F.O.B. (free on board)

Under this contract, which is of great commercial importance, still further obligations are undertaken by the seller. These obligations are not always uniform.

Strict f.o.b. The strict form of f.o.b. contract requires the seller, at his own expense, to place the goods on board a ship nominated by the buyer. The buyer, for his part, must nominate a ship and inform the seller in good time.[18] The price quoted by the seller does not take into account freight and insurance, because these are a matter for the buyer. In connection with insurance, however, the provisions of section 32(3) of the Sale of Goods Act 1979 should be borne in mind. It provides that:

> Unless otherwise agreed, where goods are sent by the seller to the buyer by a route involving sea transit, under circumstances in which it is usual to insure, the seller must give such notice to the buyer as may enable him to insure them during the sea transit, and, if the seller fails to do so, the goods shall be deemed to be at his risk during such sea transit.

In *Wimble* v. *Rosenberg*[19] a majority of the Court of Appeal (Hamilton L.J. dissenting) held that this subsection applied to an f.o.b. contract. It also appears from this case that the seller's liability will depend on whether his failure to supply information prevented the buyer from insuring the very goods in question. Thus if the buyer already has sufficient information to enable him to effect such a policy, the seller will not be liable. On the other hand, both Buckley and Vaughan Williams L.JJ. pointed out that the buyer will not be prevented from relying on section 32(3) merely because he could have effected a general cover policy.

Additional duties. The strict division of duties is sometimes commercially impracticable. In these cases it is common to find

---

[17] The House did not have to decide whether the contract was frustrated or whether the sellers were liable in damages.

[18] The time for nominating an effective ship is normally of the essence of the contract (*Olearia Tirrena S. P. A.* v. *N. V. Algemeene Oliehandel* [1972] 2 Lloyd's Rep. 341).

[19] [1913] 3 K. B. 743.

contracts for sale f.o.b. which impose additional duties on the seller, such as the duty to obtain shipping space, make the contract of carriage and to insure.[20] In this type of contract, which is fairly close to a c.i.f. contract, it may be important to decide whether the seller undertakes these additional obligations as principal or as agent for the buyer.[21] The seller is entitled to charge the buyer for these additional services.

Export licence. The position is the same as on an f.a.s. contract, and express provision should always be made.

Failure to nominate. The contract should also contain a clause that on failure to nominate a ship the buyer shall become liable for the price. In default of such clause, it seems that the seller's only remedy is to sue for damages.[22]

Passing of risk. The risk passes to the buyer when the goods have been lifted over the ship's rail. The goods are then both commercially and legally "on board,"[23] and if they are subsequently damaged while the loading is being completed the buyer bears the loss.

Passing of property. It is generally accepted[24] that property passes to the buyer when the goods have been handed over the ship's rail; in other words, at the same time as the risk. If, of course, the contract goods form part of a larger consignment so that at the moment of shipment they are still unascertained, no property passes until they are ascertained.[25] It should be noted that the risk in such a case may pass before the property, so that if the entire consignment were accidentally damaged after being lifted over the ship's rail, the loss would fall on the buyer, if this was the intention of the parties.[26] Since the essence of the contract

---

[20] "The f.o.b. contract has become a flexible instrument," *per* Devlin J. (as he then was) in *Pyrene Co., Ltd.* v. *Scindia Navigation Co.* [1954] 2 Q. B. 402, 424; [1954] 2 All E. R. 158, 167.

[21] See Sassoon, *British Shipping Laws*, Vol. 5, (2nd. ed.), pp. 362, 380.

[22] *Colley* v. *Overseas Exporters* [1921] 3 K. B. 302. For the measure of damages see s.50 of the Sale of Goods Act 1979 (*ante*, p. 181) and *Harlow & Jones* v. *Panex International*) [1967] 2 Lloyd's Rep. 509.

[23] See *per* Devlin J. in the *Pyrene* case, *supra*, at pp. 414 and 161 respectively.

[24] See, *e.g.* Schmitthoff, *op. cit.* at p. 21 Sassoon, *op. cit.* at pp. 363–364.

[25] s.16 of the Sale of Goods Act 1979; *Re Wait* [1927] Ch. 606, *ante*, p. 189.

[26] *Inglis* v. *Stock* (1885) 10 App. Cas. 263.

is the delivery of goods rather than documents, it would seem on principle that the passing of the property is not delayed by the fact that the seller retains the bill of lading, or has the bill made out to his own order. The point, however, is not free from doubt,[27] and it may be that where the contract makes the seller responsible for arranging the shipment, property will not pass until the bill of lading is transferred to the buyer.[28]

C.I.F. (cost, insurance, freight)

The nature of this contract, which like the previous one is of great importance in international trade, was described by Lord Porter as follows[29]:

> "The obligations imposed upon a seller under a c.i.f. contract are well known, and in the ordinary case include the tender of a bill of lading covering the goods contracted to be sold and no others, coupled with an insurance policy in the normal form and accompanied by an invoice which shows the price and, as in this case, usually contains a deduction of the freight which the buyer pays before delivery at the port of discharge. Against tender of these documents the buyer must pay the price."

The essential feature of the c.i.f. contract is that it is "a contract for the sale of goods to be performed by the delivery of documents."[30] This emphasis on the shipping documents— insurance policy, bill of lading and invoice—can be seen from the case of *C. Groom Ltd.* v. *Barber*[31] where it was held that on tender of the documents the buyer is bound (unless otherwise agreed) to pay for the goods, even if they have already been lost. He will normally[32] have a claim in respect of the loss under the contract of carriage or the contract of insurance.

---

[27] See the full discussion of the point by Sassoon, *op. cit.* at pp. 363–371.

[28] See *The President of India* v. *Metcalfe Shipping Co. Ltd.* [1969] 2 Q. B. 123; [1969] 1 All E. R. 861 where, on the particular facts, it was held that property did not pass until the bill of lading was handed over. See also s.19(2) of the Act of 1979, *ante*, p. 136 and Schmitthoff *op. cit.* at pp. 78–79.

[29] *Comptoir d'Achat et de Vente du Boerenbond Belge S. A.* v. *Luis de Ridder Limitada* (*The Julia*) [1949] A. C. 293, 309; [1949] 1 All E. R. 269, 274.

[30] *Arnhold Karberg & Co.* v. *Blythe* [1916] 1 K. B. 495 at pp. 510, 514, *per* Bankes and Warrington L. JJ.

[31] [1915] 1 K. B. 316.

[32] But not necessarily; the loss may be caused by a risk expressly excluded by the bill of lading and the policy. Here the buyer (unless he has himself insured) is without a remedy.

Before considering the duties of the parties, it must be emphasised that if a contract does not possess this "sale of documents" character, it will not be a c.i.f. contract, even though the parties give it that name. In the leading case of *Comptoir d' Achat* v. *Luis de Ridder* ("The Julia")[33]:

> Argentinian sellers sold rye to Belgian buyers c.i.f. Antwerp, payment in exchange for documents. A delivery order (which the sellers were entitled to deliver in lieu of a bill of lading) was sent to the buyers, but this order did not entitle them to obtain possession of the rye (which was on a ship chartered by the seller) until a number of conditions were satisfied. There was also an insurance policy covering a bulk consignment of rye on this ship and the delivery order stated that the buyers had a share in this policy. When the delivery order was sent to the buyers they paid the price. While the ship was on its way to Antwerp, that town was occupied by the Germans, whereupon the rye was taken to Lisbon and sold. The buyers claimed the return of the price as money paid for a consideration which failed.

Had this been a true c.i.f. contract the action would have failed. The House of Lords held, however, that this was not a true c.i.f. contract at all but a contract to deliver at Antwerp—in other words it approximated to an ex ship contract. The buyer had paid the price for the goods and not for the documents, and were, accordingly, entitled to recover the price when the goods did not arrive.

Duties of seller. The main duties of the seller under a genuine c.i.f. contract can be summarised[34] as follows:

(1) He must ship goods of the contract description within the agreed time, or if no time is agreed, within a reasonable time. Time for delivery is usually of the essence in commercial contracts.[35]

(2) He must make a contract for the carriage of goods by sea which is consistent with his contractual obligations and which is reasonable and usual in the particular trade.

---

[33] [1949] A. C. 293; [1949] 1 All E. R. 269.
[34] See Incoterms *op. cit.*
[35] *Reuter* v. *Sala* (1879) 4 C. P. D. 239. It should be noted that "shipment" under an English contract generally means "placing on a ship" (*Mowbray Robinson & Co.* v. *Rosser* (1922) 91 L. J. K. B. 524).

(3) He must insure the goods with reputable insurers under a policy of marine insurance which is to be available for the buyer and covers the transit contemplated by the contract.[36] The terms of the policy must be no less favourable than those current in the trade and the goods must be covered up to an amount representing their reasonable value.[37]

(4) Finally he must tender the shipping documents to the buyer.

Shipping documents. The original practice was to tender the invoice, bill of lading and insurance policy, and in the absence of contrary agreement there is no need for a buyer to accept an insurance broker's cover note[38] or an insurance certificate. In modern commercial practice, however, it is common to find a clause giving the seller the right to tender delivery orders and insurance certificates. The reason for this is that the bill of lading issued by the carrier to the seller frequently covers a large number of consignments which are being sent to different buyers, while the seller's insurance policy is often a so-called "floating policy" covering all goods sent out by the seller up to a specified amount.

It should perhaps be added that where a bill of lading is tendered to the buyer, it must relate only to the goods which the buyer has agreed to buy; if it covers other goods as well, the buyer may refuse the tender.[39]

The bill of lading may take the form of an acknowledgement that the goods have been shipped, or merely that they have been received by the carrier for shipment. How far a bill in the latter form is good tender is doubtful.[40]

Duty of buyer. On tender of the correct shipping documents the buyer must pay the price.[41] It will be seen shortly that he does not thereby lose the right to reject the goods and to recover the price

---

[36] See *Promus S. A.* v. *European Grain and Shipping* [1979] 1 Ll.L.R. 375 for a recent case where the policy did not conform with the contract with the result that the buyer was entitled to reject it.

[37] *Biddell Bros.* v. *E. Clemens Horst Co.* [1911] 1 K. B. 214, 220.

[38] *Wilson Holgate & Co.* v. *Belgian Grain Produce Co.* [1920] 2 K. B. 1.

[39] *Re Keighly Maxted & Co. and Bryan, Durant & Co.* (1894) 70 L.T. 155.

[40] See *Weis* v. *Produce Brokers Co.* (1921) 7 Ll. L. R. 211, *United Baltic Corpn.* v. *Burgett and Newsam* (1921) 8 Ll. L. R. 190 and contrast *Diamond Alkali Export Corpn.* v. *Fl. Bourgeois* [1921] 3 K. B. 443.

[41] This is an illustration of s.28 of the Sale of Goods Act 1979 if "delivery" is understood as meaning "delivery of documents."

if, on arrival, it is discovered that the seller has broken a condition of the contract.

Risk. The risk under a c.i.f. contract passes to the buyer when the goods have been lifted over the ship's rail, even though the property may not have passed.[42] This is an example of a case where the risk passes before the property, contrary to the general rule contained in section 20 of the Sale of Goods Act (*ante*, p. 137). If the goods deteriorate, the buyer must bear this loss unless the parties otherwise agree or unless the seller is in breach of section 14(2) of the Sale of Goods Act 1979. Under a normal c.i.f. contract the seller's obligation as to quality is determined at the place of shipment,[43] but it may well be that the goods will be classified as unmerchantable if they are unable to withstand a normal journey.[44] The precise position with regard to c.i.f. contracts is not, however, finally settled and it has been suggested that there may be a distinction between a sale of perishable goods (such as potatoes) and other goods (such as skins).[45]

Property. The question of when property passes is as always a question of intention, and to avoid doubts, the exporter should expressly stipulate that no property is to pass until payment of the price. Even if there is no such clause, a seller who retains control over the bill of lading will usually retain the property in the goods.[46] Thus, it will be recalled that where the bill is made out to the order of the seller or his agent, the seller is prima facie deemed to have reserved the right of disposal (Sale of Goods Act 1979, s.19(2), *ante*, p. 136). If the bill is made out to the order of the buyer, but is retained by the seller as security for the price no property passes to the buyer until payment or tender of the price.[47] Finally, it has been suggested that even if the bill is delivered to the

---

[42] *Biddell Bros.* v. *E. Clemens Horst Co.* [1911] 1 K. B. 214, affd. [1912] A. C. 18.

[43] See *Oleificio Zucchi S. P. A.* v. *Northern Sales Ltd.* [1965] 2 Lloyd's Rep. 496, 518, *per* McNair J.

[44] Consider *Mash & Murrell* v. *Emanuel Ltd.* [1961] 1 W. L. R. 862; [1961] All E. R. 485; reversed on the facts [1962] 1 W. L. R. 16; [1962] 1 All E. R. 77.

[45] *Cordova Land Co.* v. *Victor Bros. Inc.* [1966] 1 W. L. R. 793, *per* Winn J.

[46] See *Cheetham & Co. Ltd.* v. *Thornham Spinning Co. Ltd.* [1964] 2 Lloyd's Rep. 17. It is submitted that the references to "specific goods" were incorrect.

[47] *Arnhold Karberg & Co.* v. *Blythe, Green, Jourdain & Co.* [1915] 2 K. B. 379, 387, *per* Scrutton J.

buyer, no property passes if the buyer fails to pay or tender the price.[48]

Inspection. It will be recalled that, by section 34 of the Sale of Goods Act 1979, a seller tendering delivery must generally give the buyer a reasonable opportunity of examination. This rule, however, gives way to a contrary agreement, and a c.i.f. contract is an example of such contrary agreement, so that a buyer cannot refuse to pay on tender of documents merely because he has had no chance to inspect the goods.[49]

Rejection. The buyer's right to reject was considered in the case of *Kwei Tek Chao* v. *British Traders and Shippers*[50] and from the illuminating judgment of Devlin J. three points emerge:

(1) The property which passes on delivery of the bill of lading is a conditional property only, and the buyer has a right to reject if the goods do not conform with the contract.

(2) There are two quite distinct rights to reject—a right to reject the documents and a right to reject the goods.

(3) A dealing with the "conditional property" such as the pledging of the bill of lading does not amount to an acceptance of the goods within section 35 and does not, therefore, destroy the right to reject them.

If, however, the buyer takes up and pays for the shipping document he may thereby be estopped from later rejecting the goods on the ground of a defect (*e.g.* late shipment) which was apparent from the documents.[51]

C. and F. (cost and freight)

This as the name implies is similar to a c.i.f. contract except that the seller does not undertake responsibility for insurance. Since insurance is the buyer's responsibility the provisions of section 32(3) of the Sale of Goods Act 1979[52] are relevant.

---

[48] See *Ginzberg* v. *Barrow Haematite Steel Co. Ltd.* [1966] 1Lloyd's Rep. 343.
[49] *Biddell Bros.* v. *E. Clemens Horst* [1912] A. C. 18.
[50] [1954] 2 Q. B. 459; [1954] 1 All E. R. 779.
[51] *Panchaud Frères S. A.* v. *Etablissements General Grain Co.* [1970] 1 Lloyd's Rep. 53, C. A.
[52] *Ante*, p. 464.

Ex ship contract

This is the most onerous contract from the seller's point of view, because it is his duty to ship the goods to the buyer at his (the seller's) own risk and to make delivery at a named port. The property and risk do not pass, nor is the price payable, until delivery is actually made. It follows that a price paid in advance is recoverable if the goods do not arrive.[53]

As the goods are at the seller's risk during transit he is under no duty to insure. If he does insure it will be for his own benefit only, so that the buyer will have no right of action against the insurer if a loss occurs.[54]

PAYMENT

Cash

The seller may, of course, require payment in cash and contracts providing for "cash against documents" are commonly found. Often, however, the buyer is anxious to obtain the goods on credit, so that he can pay for them out of the proceeds of a resale. It has already been seen in Chapter Five how the bill of exchange admirably filled the gap between sale and resale because it gave the buyer time to pay and at the same time it enabled the seller to obtain immediate funds by discounting the bill.

Credit

Although the system of sending bills of lading to buyers together with bills of exchange is still quite widely used, it has one defect from the seller's point of view, namely the practical difficulties that might arise if the buyer failed to honour the bill of exchange. These difficulties might well be considerable if the goods had already been shipped and the market was falling. To eliminate this risk the practice of payment by banker's commercial credit was evolved. This practice has great advantage from the exporter's point of view and at the present time a very large proportion of the export trade is financed in this way. The banking practice relating

---

[53] Cf. *The Julia, ante*, p. 467.
[54] *Yangtse Insurance Assn.* v. *Lukmanjee* [1918] A. C. 585.

to documentary credits is standardised by the Uniform Customs and Practice for Documentary Credits 1974.

Nature of credit

Looked at from the exporter's viewpoint the essential feature of the transaction is that he can look to a bank[55] for payment of the price, thereby eliminating virtually all risk of not receiving payment. Credits take a variety of forms, but in all of them the seller delivers the shipping documents to the bank and the bank thereupon pays, accepts or negotiates bills of exchange drawn by the seller on the buyer or on the bank. The bank will then look to the buyer for reimbursement.

Procedure

There are three (and sometimes four) stages in the opening of a credit.

Buyer and seller

The first stage, of course, is the contract of sale itself. This may, and frequently does, provide for payment by banker's commercial credit, and may require the buyer to open a credit within a certain time. In many cases the type of credit is also specified. Thus the seller may, and should, require payment by confirmed irrevocable credit, an expression which will become clear when the different types of credit have been examined.

The exact obligations of the buyer depend on the wording of the contract. In the absence of express stipulation as to time the buyer must open the credit within a reasonable time having regard to the date fixed for shipment.[56] Where the seller is given a choice to ship during a certain period, *e.g.* January or February, the credit must be available throughout the whole of that period.[57]

---

[55] The opening of a credit is a conditional payment only (compare payment by negotiable instrument, *ante*, p. 170) so that the seller can still sue the buyer if, for some reason, the bank fails to pay (*W. J. Alan & Co. Ltd.* v. *El Nasr Export and Import Co. Ltd.* [1972] 2 Q. B. 189; [1972] 2 All E. R. 127, *per* Lord Denning M.R.).

[56] *Sinason-Teicher Inter-American Grain Corporation* v. *Oilcakes and Oilseeds Trading Co.* [1954] 1 W. L. R. 935; [1954] 2 All E. R. 492.

[57] *Pavia and Co., S. A.* v. *Thurmann-Nielsen* [1952] 2 Q. B. 84; [1952] 2 Q. B. 84; [1952] 1 All E. R. 492, 494. Schmitthoff, *op. cit.* at p. 254, suggests that the seller must be put into a position of knowing that the credit has been opened before he sends the goods to the docks.

If the buyer is unable to open a credit, the position depends on the wording of the contract. If the contract is expressed to be "subject to the opening of a credit," then there is no contract if the credit is not obtained.[58] In practice, however, the contract does not take this form and the buyer will be liable in damages for breach of his contractual obligation to open the credit. Such damages may be higher than damages for non-acceptance of goods because they are not governed by section 50(3) of the Sale of Goods Act 1979 and they may include the seller's loss of profit on the transaction.[59]

Buyer and issuing bank

The second stage is a communication by the buyer to his bank requesting the bank to open a credit in favour of the seller. The buyer signs a form of application addressed to the banker specifying the type of credit, the amount and full details of the documents to be handed over by the seller. The form also contains:

(a) An undertaking by the buyer to reimburse the bank;
(b) A statement that the bank is entitled to hold the documents as security for repayment of the principal sum, interest, commission and charges;
(c) A clause conferring on the bank a power of sale in order to realise the security.

Issuing bank and correspondent bank

Sometimes the bank instructed by the buyer, which would normally be a bank in the buyer's country, notifies the seller that the credit has been opened. In many cases, however, this arrangement is not convenient to the seller who would naturally prefer to deal with a bank in his own country. To meet this situation the buyer (or issuing bank) appoints as its agent a bank in the seller's country, and it is this bank, known as the intermediary or correspondent bank, which deals with the seller. The relationship between the issuing and the correspondent bank is that of principal and agent so that if the correspondent bank has paid in

---

[58] *Trans Trust S. P. R. L.* v. *Danubian Trading Co.* [1952] 2 Q. B. 297, 304; [1952] 1 All E. R. 970, 976, *per* Denning L. J.
[59] *Trans Trust* case, *supra*.

accordance with instructions it is entitled to be indemnified by the issuing bank.[60]

Bank and seller

The final stage is a communication by the issuing or correspondent bank to the seller that a credit has been opened in his favour and setting out the conditions for its operation.

Nature of contract. The nature of the first three of the above transactions gives rise to no difficulty but there has been some speculation among academic writers as to the nature of the relationship between the banker and the seller. In business circles the essence of the transaction is the letter of credit sent by the bank to the seller, and it is taken for granted that the bank is bound as soon as the letter of credit is sent. In law, however, two questions have to be asked: how does the sending of the letter amount to a binding contract and what is the consideration for the letter? No definite answer has yet been given but it has been persuasively argued that the buyer who negotiates the credit is, for some purposes, the seller's agent, and that he makes on the seller's behalf an offer to hand over the shipping documents, and that the contract is concluded as soon as the bank communicates the acceptance of this offer to the seller by sending him the letter of credit.[61]

Types of credit

Credits can be classified in various ways according to the obligations undertaken by the bank. It is only necessary here to examine two of these classifications.

Revocable and irrevocable

The distinction between revocable and irrevocable credits is fundamental from the seller's point of view. If the credit is a revocable one the bank merely informs the seller that they have authority to pay or accept bills of exchange in return for the

---

[60] For the right of reimbursement where the payment is unauthorised, see *Bank Melli Iran* v. *Barclays Bank* (*Dominion, Colonial and Overseas*) [1951] 2 T. L. R. 1057 1063, *per* McNair J.

[61] Gutteridge and Megrah, *Law of Bankers Commercial Credit*, at pp. 22 *et seq.* where the various theories are fully reviewed.

documents, but the bank does not undertake that they will in fact do so. Further the bank is entitled, as against the seller,[62] to cancel the credit at any time, and although it is their usual practice to give the seller notice of cancellation it has been held that they are under no legal obligation to do so.[63] It is not surprising therefore that revocable credits are seldom used.

In the case of an irrevocable credit, on the other hand, the bank binds itself to honour the seller's draft if the seller complies with his obligations with regard to the shipping documents. The buyer cannot, in such a case, cancel his original instructions. In *Hamzeh Malas & Sons* v. *British Imex Industries Ltd.*[64]

> Buyers bought goods to be delivered by instalments, payment to be by irrevocable credit. The credit was duly opened and the first instalment was shipped. Buyers complained that the goods were of inferior quality and applied for an injunction restraining the sellers from drawing further on the credit. The Court of Appeal refused to grant the injunction.

Confirmed and unconfirmed

An irrevocable credit may be confirmed or unconfirmed, and this distinction also is of great importance to the seller. Under a confirmed credit the correspondent bank undertakes personal liability to the seller, whereas under an unconfirmed credit it merely acts as agent but without incurring personal liability for the price. The disadvantage of the latter is that if for some reason the bank defaults, the seller may have to start litigation in the buyer's country to enforce his rights against the issuing bank. Hence it is usual for the contract to stipulate for payment by confirmed credit.

---

[62] And against a third party to whom the seller has negotiated the bill. Such third party is deemed to have notice of the terms of the credit (*Chartered Bank of India, Australia and China* v. *Macfadyan* (*P.*) & *Co.* (1895) 1 Com. Cas. 1).

[63] *The Cape Asbestos Co.* v. *Lloyds Bank* [1921] W. N. 274. The seller had shipped goods in reliance on the credit which, unknown to him had been cancelled. It was held that he had no claim against the bank when payment was refused.

[64] [1958] 2 Q. B. 127. Sellers L. J., however, suggested that the court might interfere at the instance of the buyer if there was fraud. The basic rule was confirmed by the House of Lords in *United City Merchants* (*Investments*) v. *Royal Bank of Canada, The Times*, May 21, 1982.

If the contract does provide for this, the seller need not deliver the goods if the buyer opens a credit which is unconfirmed.[65]

Duties of seller

A seller wishing to avail himself of a credit must tender to the bank documents corresponding exactly with those specified in the letter of credit. A correspondent bank which has accepted documents differing from those agreed upon cannot claim reimbursement from the issuing bank, and likewise an issuing bank accepting such documents cannot claim reimbursement from the buyer, unless in either case the person from whom reimbursement is claimed has ratified the breach of duty.[66]

The duty to tender correct documents is strict. "There is no room," said Lord Sumner in one case, "for documents which are almost the same, or which will do just as well."[67] In *Rayner* v. *Hambros Bank*[68]:

> A credit in favour of the plaintiffs called for documents covering a shipment of Coromandel groundnuts. Sellers tendered a bill of lading showing that machine-shelled groundnut kernels had been shipped. The bank refused the tender and the Court of Appeal held that they were justified in doing so.

How far it is necessary for the description in the bill of lading to correspond word for word with that in the credit has not been finally decided. Gutteridge and Megrah[69] take the view that a bill of lading is good tender for this purpose if the description does not conflict with that in the credit and carries such shipping marks as enable the goods to be identified with those specified in the credit. Some of the forms of application for credits to be opened contain the following clause:

> "It is agreed that the bills of lading themselves need only contain a general description of the relative goods and it will be sufficient if

---

[65] *Panoutsos* v. *Raymond Hadley Corpn. of New York* [1917] 2 K. B. 473. Confusion is caused by the fact that "irrevocable" and "confirmed" are used interchangeably in some of the cases. Although in the vast majority of cases a credit which is irrevocable is also confirmed, this is not strictly necessary.

[66] For an example of such ratification see *Bank Melli Iran* v. *Barclays Bank* (*Dominion, Colonial and Overseas*) [1951] 2 T. L. R. 1057.

[67] *Equitable Trust Co. of New York* v. *Dawson & Partners* [1927] 27 Ll. L. R. 49 at p. 52.

[68] [1943] 1 K. B. 37.

[69] *Op. cit.* at pp. 86–87.

documents tendered under the credit taken as a whole contain the description required by the credit."

It seems that such a clause merely confirms the general position.[70]

The question of what documents constitute good tender under a credit overlaps to a large extent with the question of what documents have to be delivered to a buyer under a c.i.f. contract. It seems that, as a general rule, banks are entitled to insist on a "clean" bill of lading, that is to say a bill acknowledging without qualification that the goods have been received in apparent good order and condition.[71]

It should finally be added that a bank sometimes accepts defective documents accompanied by an indemnity from the seller. Whether such an indemnity enures for the benefit of the buyer has not been settled.[72] What is clear is that where documents, appearing on the face of them to be in strict conformity with the credit, turn out to be forgeries the issuing bank which has paid out on these documents can recover the money from the buyer.[73] It is also clear that the bank can refuse to pay if it knows that the bills are fraudulent (*United City Merchants (Investments)* v. *Royal Bank of Canada* [1981] Com.L.R. 98).

Duty of banker

A bank which has issued an irrevocable credit is bound to honour it, and it has already been seen that the buyer cannot instruct the bank not to pay. If the bank wrongfully refused to perform its duties under the credit, the seller can claim damages. The assessment of damages will be governed by the usual *Hadley* v. *Baxendale* rules[74] and the seller's claim is not necessarily confined to the amount of the debt and interest. The seller will be able to recover his loss of profit on the transaction if the bank ought to have foreseen that this would be the result of its breach of

---

[70] *Midland Bank* v. *Seymour* [1955] 2 Lloyd's Rep. 147, 152.
[71] *British Imex Industries Ltd.* v. *Midland Bank Ltd.* [1958] 1 Q. B. 542; [1958] 1 All E. R. 264.
[72] See the question discussed in Gutteridge and Megrah, *op. cit.* at pp. 115–125.
[73] *Gian Singh Ltd.* v. *Banque de L'Indochine* [1974] 1 W. L. R. 1234, P. C.
[74] (1854) 9 Ex. 34.

duty.[75] It is vitally important to appreciate that the credit creates a contract between the seller and the issuing and/or confirming bank which is entirely distinct from the underlying contract of the sale. The underlying principle is similar to that relating to negotiable instruments—namely that the business community should be entitled, so far as possible, to regard them as the equivalent of cash. Thus the supply of defective goods under the contract of sale does not entitle the buyer to instruct the bank not to honour the credit.[76]

Bank as pledgee

The buyer must reimburse the bank in accordance with the terms of the contract between them. The bank, meanwhile, will retain the documents of title as security and can, as pledgees, sell them if the buyer defaults. Sometimes, however, an arrangement is made whereby the bank releases the document to the buyer in return for a letter of trust executed by the buyer, whereby the buyer acknowledges that he holds the bills of lading, the property represented thereby, and the proceeds of sale on trust for the bank. Such an arrangement, which is sometimes used to enable the buyer to sell the goods or to deliver them to a purchaser, is perfectly valid, so that where the buyer sells the goods and then becomes bankrupt the proceeds of sale belong to the bank and not to the buyer's creditors.[77] The disadvantage of the arrangement is that the bank may lose its security if the buyer is dishonest.[78]

Factoring

Before leaving the subject of finance, a word should be said about a new system known as factoring which is becoming increasingly important. Where a seller sells goods, he assigns to the factor (who may be a finance house, a merchant bank or a confirming house) the price payable by the buyer, and notifies the buyer that the price should be paid to the factor. The factor, who charges a commission to the seller, pays the price in return for the

---

[75] Cf. *Trans Trust S. P. R. L* v. *Danubian Trading Co.*, [1952] 2 Q. B. 297, 306; [1952] 1 All E. R. 970, 977, *per* Denning L. J. *Ian Stach Ltd.* v. *Baker Bosley Ltd.* [1958] 2 Q. B. 130, 145; [1958] 1 All E. R. 542, 549, *per* Diplock J.

[76] See *Discount Records Ltd.* v. *Barclays Bank* [1975] 1 W. L. R. 315.

[77] *North Western Bank* v. *Poynter, Son and Macdonalds* [1895] A. C. 56, H. L.

[78] *Lloyds Bank* v. *Bank of America* [1938] 2 K. B. 147, *ante*, p. 149.

assignment and then proceeds to recover it from the buyer. The advantages from the seller's point of view are as follows:

(1) He is spared the trouble of maintaining a detailed sales ledger, since he invoices all goods to the factor.

(2) He has one debtor whose credit is unassailable, rather than a great many whose credit is dubious and from whom recovery may prove difficult.

(3) He is not affected by the buyer's insolvency, whereas under the system of bankers' commercial credits the bank usually has a right of recourse against the seller, as drawer of a bill of exchange, in the event of default by the buyer.

The factoring system can also be used in inland sales where it is particularly useful for a merchant setting up business in England for the first time and trading with many unknown firms. In the export trade the factor is frequently someone in the buyer's country.

CARRIAGE OF GOODS BY SEA

The subject of carriage was touched upon when considering the obligations of seller and buyer under the various contracts. It is a vast subject which cannot be adequately summarised here,[79] but it may be useful to examine more fully the nature and effect of a bill of lading in view of its great importance in connection with the international sale of goods.

Bill of lading

Nature of bill of lading

The bill of lading is a receipt for the goods signed by or on behalf of the shipowner and is also evidence of the contract of carriage. It must, however, be emphasised that the contract itself is made before the bill is issued and although the bill is excellent evidence of the terms of the contract[80] it is not conclusive. In *The Ardennes*[81]:

---

[79] Readers are referred to *Scrutton on Charterparties* and to *Carver on Carriage of Goods by Sea*, which must, however, be read in the light of the Carriage of Goods by Sea Act 1971
[80] *Per* Devlin J. in *Heskell* v. *Continental Express* [1950] 1 All E. R. 1033, 1037.
[81] [1951] 1 K. B. 155; [1950] 2 All E. R. 517.

Sellers exporting mandarins from Spain to England informed the carriers that the goods had to be delivered before December 1 (the date on which an import duty was being imposed). The carriers undertook to do this. Bills of lading were issued containing no reference to this undertaking. The ship arrived after December 1. Lord Goddard C.J. held that the bill of lading did not contain the whole contract and awarded the sellers damages.

Apart from this, there is a third function of a bill of lading, and perhaps it is the most important one of all. The bill of lading is a document of title which represents the goods. As Bowen L.J. put it:

"It is the key which in the hands of a rightful owner is intended to unlock the door of the warehouse, floating or fixed, in which the goods may chance to be."[82]

Again in the words of Lord Wright:

"By mercantile law the bills of lading are the symbols of the goods."[83]

It is usual to prepare bills of lading in two or more parts and to send them to the consignee by separate mails. The object of this practice is to guard against loss in transit.

Accuracy

Since a bill of lading is likely to be acted upon by buyers and by banks under commercial credits, it is of the greatest importance that the terms should be accurate, and from the statute law and case law five principles emerge. In the first place a person who negligently issues a bill of lading in respect of goods which have not been shipped may be liable in tort for negligence. Formerly it was thought that in the absence of a contractual or special relationship there was no liability for careless statements causing financial loss, and in accordance with this principle Devlin J. held in *Heskell* v. *Continental Express*[84] that a firm of ship brokers issuing a bill were not liable to a seller who was not in contractual relationship with them but who had acted upon the bill and had suffered damage. Now, however, the House of Lords has

---

[82] *Sanders* v. *Maclean* (1883) 11 Q. B. D. 327, 341.
[83] *Ross T. Smyth Ltd.* v. *T. D. Bailey, Son & Co.* [1940] 45 Com. Cas. 292; [1940] 3 All E. R. 60, 67.
[84] [1950] 1 All E. R. 1033, 1037.

emphatically stated that there can be tortious liability for careless statements[85] and Lord Devlin himself considered that his own decision in *Heskell* v. *Continental Express* could no longer be regarded as authoritative.[86]

Secondly, where a ship's agent signs a bill of lading which incorrectly states the quantity of goods shipped, the agent impliedly warrants his authority to make that representation and is liable to the holder of the bill for any breach of this warranty. This liability can arise even if the agent acted without negligence and the damages can include the value of the unshipped goods.[87]

Thirdly, the Carriage of Goods by Sea Act 1971 which applies to nearly all[88] outward shipments from Great Britain and Northern Ireland provides as follows:

> Art. III. 3. After receiving the goods into his charge, the carrier, or the master or agent of the carrier, shall, on demand of the shipper, issue to the shipper a bill of lading showing among other things—
>
> (a) The leading marks necessary for the identification of the goods as the same are furnished in writing by the shipper before the loading of the goods starts, provided such marks are stamped or otherwise shown clearly upon the goods if uncovered or on the cases or coverings in which such goods are contained, in such a manner as should ordinarily remain legible until the end of the voyage;
>
> (b) Either the number of packages or pieces, the quantity, or weight as the case may be, as furnished in writing by the shipper;
>
> (c) The apparent order and condition of the goods:
>
> Provided that no carrier, master or agent of the carrier, shall be bound to state or show in the bill of lading any marks, number, quantity, or weight which he has reasonable ground for suspecting not accurately to represent the goods actually received or which he has had no reasonable means of checking.
>
> 4. Such a bill of lading shall be prima facie evidence of the receipt by the carrier of the goods therein described in accordance with paragraphs 3(a)(b) and (c).

---

[85] *Hedley Byrne & Co. Ltd.* v. *Heller & Partners* [1964] A.C. 465; [1963] 2 All E. R. 575.

[86] *Ibid.* at pp. 532 and 612 respectively.

[87] *V/O Rasnoimport* v. *Guthrie & Co. Ltd.* [1966] 1 Lloyd's Rep. 1.

[88] Except shipments of (a) live animals, and (b) cargo, which by the contract of carriage is stated as being carried on deck and is so carried (Schedule, Art. 1 (c)).

Fourthly, section 3 of the Bills of Lading Act 1855 provides that in certain circumstances statements in a bill of lading are to be *conclusive* evidence of their accuracy. The section reads as follows:

> Every bill of lading in the hands of a consignee or indorsee for valuable consideration, representing goods to have been shipped on board a vessel,[89] shall be conclusive evidence of such shipment *as against the master or other person signing the same*,[90] notwithstanding that such goods or some part thereof may not have been so shipped, unless such holder of the bill of lading shall have had actual notice at the time of receiving the same that the goods had not in fact been laden on board. Provided that the master or other person so signing may exonerate himself in respect of such misrepresentation by showing that it was caused without any default on his part and wholly by the fraud of the shipper, or of the holder, or some person under whom the holder claims.

Finally a person who has made an incorrect statement in a bill of lading may be estopped at common law from denying its accuracy to someone who has acted on it to his detriment.[91]

Clean and claused bills

The carrier will issue a clean bill of lading if the goods are shipped in apparent good order and condition. In the words of one learned judge this phrase means that:

> "apparently, and so far as met the eye, and externally they [the goods] were placed in good order on board this ship."[92]

If the goods were not so shipped, the shipowner may issue a "claused" bill setting out the defects, such as, for example, "cans leaking". A claused bill clearly may be an embarrassment to the shipper, who may be unable to transfer it or to use it for the purposes of a banker's commercial credit. To avoid this result, the shipowner sometimes agrees to issue a clean bill in return for an indemnity against any liability which might result. This practice is

---

[89] The section does not apply to bills which merely state that goods have been received for shipment (*Diamond Alkali Export Corpn.* v. *Fl. Bourgeois* [1921] 3 K. B. 443, 450).

[90] It seems that signature by the master of the ship does not prevent the shipowner from pleading non-shipment (*Scrutton on Charterparties*, (18th ed.), at p. 108; *Thorman* v. *Burt* (1886) 54 L. T. 349).

[91] *The Skarp* [1935] P. 134. *Cf. Cremer* v. *General Carriers* [1974] 1 W. L. R. 341.

[92] Sir R. Philimore P. in *The Peter der Grosse* (1875) 1 P. D. 414, 420.

highly dangerous and if the effect of the arrangement is to defraud the consignee the indemnity cannot be enforced. In *Brown Jenkinson & Co. Ltd.* v. *Percy Dalton (London) Ltd.*[93]:

> Exporters loaded on board a ship 100 barrels of orange juice which were described by the tally clerks as old and frail, with some barrels leaking. Exporters then persuaded loading brokers acting for the shipowners to issue clean bills of lading in return for an indemnity. The Court of Appeal (Lord Evershed M. R. dissenting) held that the indemnity could not be enforced.

Referring to indemnities, Pearce L. J. said (at p. 659):

> "In trivial matters and in cases of bona fide disputes where the difficulty of ascertaining the correct state of affairs is out of proportion to its importance, no doubt the practice is useful. But here the plaintiffs went outside those reasonable limits."

Through bills

It frequently occurs that the ship on to which the goods are loaded only performs part of the journey, and that the goods have at some point to be transferred to another carrier for the journey to be completed. In such cases the original carrier often issues "through" bills of lading, which may take one of two forms. The carrier may either sign on behalf of himself and as agent for the other carriers (named or unnamed) or he may simply agree to carry the goods to a particular point and then to make arrangements for their transhipment. If the former form is adopted, it would seem that when the goods are transhipped a contract comes into existence between the shipper and the new carrier. In the latter case, there would appear to be no contractual relationship between them, and the liability of the new carrier for loss or damage would turn on the normal rules of negligence.

Transfer of bill

It will be recalled from Chapter Five that a negotiable instrument has two main features:

(a) It can be transferred by delivery or by indorsement completed by delivery, and

(b) The transferee, if a holder in due course, may obtain a better title than his transferor.

---

[93] [1957] 2 Q. B. 621; [1957] 2 All E. R. 844.

The first, but not the second of these applies to bills of lading which can therefore be described as quasi-negotiable. The following rules govern the form of transfer:

(1) A bill of lading directing delivery of the goods "unto bearer" is transferable by delivery.

(2) A bill directing delivery "unto X or order" or "unto X or assigns" is transferable by indorsement completed by delivery.

(3) If the space before "unto order" or "unto assigns" is left blank, the shipper can transfer the bill by completing the blank with the name of the transferee and then delivering it to him. Alternatively he can transfer the bill without completing the blank.

(4) If the bill directs delivery to a named person and the printed words "or order" or "or assigns" are deleted, the bill cannot be transferred by that person.

It has already been seen that transfer of the bill operates to transfer the property in the goods if this is the intention of the parties. If such property does pass, section 1 of the Bills of Lading Act 1855 also vests in the consignee or indorsee the rights and liabilities arising under the contract of carriage.[93a] Thus the holder of the bill can sue the shipowner for short delivery and conversely the shipowner can sue the holder for freight. This rule does not affect any rights of stoppage in transit or right of action against other parties.[94] Thus if the transferor of the bill is liable for freight he continues to be liable even though under section 1 the transferee is now also liable.

It should perhaps be added that the passing of property depends not only on the intention of the parties but also on whether the transferor is able to pass it. The basic rule of *nemo dat quod non habet* applies, subject to statutory exceptions under sections 2, 8 and 9 of the Factors Act 1889 and sections 25 and 47 of the Sale of Goods Act 1979. These have already been considered.[95]

[93a] Even if the buyer is not the owner he may still have a claim in tort (*Schiff und Kohlen GmbH* v. *Chelsea Maritime Ltd.* [1982] 1 All E.R. 48 and see Todd [1983] J.B.L. 42).

[94] *Ibid.* s.2.

[95] See *ante*, pp. 147–157 and 177.

Delivery of goods

It is the duty of the carrier to deliver the goods to the person presenting the bill of lading and to no one else and if he fails to perform his duty an exemption clause is unlikely to protect him. In *Sze Hai Tong Bank* v. *Rambler Cycle Co.*[96]:

> English exporters of bicycle parts gave the bill of lading to a bank and told them to release the bill to the buyers in return for the price. The buyers, who did not have the bill of lading, persuaded the carriers to deliver the goods to them in return for an indemnity from themselves and the S Bank. When the exporter sued the carriers, the latter claimed that they were protected by a clause in the bill that their responsibility should cease absolutely after the goods were discharged from the ship. They also brought in the S Bank as third parties and claimed indemnity. The Judicial Committee of the Privy Council held that (1) the clause was not intended to cover, and did not cover, a carrier who deliberately disregarded his obligations; and (2) the bank was liable on the indemnity.

Where a bill is issued in a set (*i.e.* in several parts) the carrier may safely deliver to the first person presenting the bill unless he had notice of other claims to the goods or knowledge of any other circumstances raising a reasonable suspicion that the claimant is not entitled to the goods.[97]

UNIFORM LAWS ON INTERNATIONAL SALES

In an attempt to unify the laws of different countries relating to International Sales, two Conventions were signed at The Hague in 1964 and they have been ratified by a number of countries including the United Kingdom. The texts of these Conventions appear in the First and Second Schedules to the Uniform Laws on International Sales Act 1967. The principal Convention relates to the rights of buyer and seller under an international sale of goods. There is also an ancillary Convention known as the Uniform Law on the Formation of Contracts for the International Sale of Goods. Despite its name it deals solely with the question of offer and acceptance. It differs at some points from English law but it is not

---

[96] [1959] A. C. 576; [1959] 3 All E. R. 182. As explained in the *Suisse Atlantique* case (*ante*, p. 434).

[97] *Scrutton on Charterparties, op. cit.* at p. 293.

possible to examine it in detail here.[98] In the remainder of this chapter it is proposed to examine briefly the main provisions of the sales convention.

Scope

At present the scope of the Uniform Law is narrow. Article 1 provides that it can apply where the parties have their places of business or habitual residences in different Contracting States,[99] while Article 4 enables the Uniform Law to be expressly chosen in any other case. The United Kingdom has, however, exercised its right to declare that the Uniform Law shall *only* apply if expressly chosen by the parties. No other Contracting State has so far exercised this right and there is no doubt that difficult problems could arise.

> A in England sells goods to B in Italy. No mention is made of the Uniform Law. The English seller can argue that by English law the Law does not apply because the parties have not chosen it. The Italian buyer could reply that by Italian law the Law does apply because the parties have not excluded it.

Presumably an English court would resolve the difficulty by referring the matter to the proper law of the contract (see *post*, p. 504).

Even if the Uniform Law does apply, its scope is more limited than the Sale of Goods Act. In particular, it does not deal at all with questions of transfer of property and transfer of title. Similarly it does not deal with questions of capacity, formation, illegality and discharge. Thus, despite the provisions of Article 2 that "rules of private international law shall be excluded for the purposes of the application of the present Law . . . " there are still many areas where these rules must be applied. The rules of private international law are considered in the next chapter.

Arrangement

The Law is divided into the following six Chapters:
  1. Sphere of Application

---

[98] See Graveson, Cohn and Graveson, *Uniform Laws on International Sales* for a very helpful commentary on the two conventions.

[99] This comprises (at present) West Germany, Italy, Israel, the Netherlands, Belgium, San Marino and the United Kingdom (see S. I. 1972 No. 973).

2. General Provisions
3. Duties of Seller
4. Duties of Buyer
5. Matters Common to Buyer and Seller
6. Passing of Risk.

This is certainly a logical arrangement, especially as the Articles imposing duties are closely followed by Articles setting out the remedies available for breach of the duties. The remedies of damages and rejection have been discussed in Chapter Three but it should be mentioned that in many continental countries the remedy of specific performance is available much more readily than in this country. The Uniform Law deals with this point by enabling a court to refuse specific performance if it would have done so in a similar case not governed by the Law (Art. 16).

Fundamental breach

The concept of fundamental breach is central to the Law; it is as the name implies a breach of a serious character and it enables the innocent party to "declare the contract avoided," *i.e.* treat it as repudiated. Article 10 reads:

> For the purposes of the present Law a breach of contract shall be regarded as fundamental whenever the party in breach knew, or ought to have known, at the time of the conclusion of the contract, that a reasonable person in the same situation as the other party would not have entered into the contract if he had foreseen the breach and its effects.

In a forceful criticism of this provision[1] Graveson, Cohn and Graveson make the point that a trivial breach may be fundamental in a buyer's market but non-fundamental in a seller's market. The definition is certainly a highly artificial one and it could well cause as much difficulty and trouble to legal advisers as the English doctrine of fundamental breach has done over the years.[2] In one respect, however, the concept of "fundamental breach" is superior to that of "breach of condition". It will be recalled that under English law a buyer can reject for breach of condition even though he has suffered no loss at all (*Arcos* v. *Ronaasen*, *ante*, p. 111). The Uniform Law rejects this rigid approach and substitutes the

---

[1] At pp. 55–57.
[2] The doctrine has been dealt with *ante*, pp. 433–434.

more flexible test of the "intermediate stipulation" (*ante*, p. 99); thus the court must consider the effect of the breach in deciding whether the other party can "avoid" the contract.

Delivery

Articles 19 to 49 deal in considerable detail with the seller's duty of delivery and with the various remedies available to the buyer if the duty is not performed. The key definition appears in Article 19(1):

> delivery consists in the handing over of goods which conform with the contract.

If this Article is read together with Article 33 it becomes clear that the various duties under English law (to supply goods of the right description, of merchantable quality, corresponding to sample, fit for the buyer's purpose, etc.) are all treated under the Law as part of the basic duty of delivering goods conforming with the contract.

If the seller's failure to delivery on time amounts to a fundamental breach, Article 26 places the buyer under a positive duty to inform the seller within reasonable time whether he is insisting on performance or avoiding the contract; if the buyer fails to do this the contract is automatically avoided (although damages can still be claimed).

Lack of conformity

It will be recalled that under English law a buyer loses the right to reject goods for breach of condition if, *inter alia*, he retains the goods beyond a reasonable time without intimating rejection.[3] Articles 38 and 39, read with Article 11, go much further; a buyer loses *all* rights to complain of lack of conformity (*i.e.* even a right to damages) unless he examines the goods and informs the seller of the defect within as short a period as possible, in the circumstances, from the moment when the act could reasonably be done. Quite apart from this, Article 49 imposes a one-year limitation period in lack of conformity cases.

---

[3] *Ante*, p. 100.

Payment

Articles 57–64 deal with the buyer's duty to pay the price and the seller's remedies on non-payment. Perhaps the most interesting point here relates to resale. Under English law a seller can sue the buyer for the price and he is not bound to resell the goods. Under Article 61, however, a seller who can reasonably resell is, in effect, bound to do so and cannot sue for the price: " . . . the contract shall be *ipso facto* avoided as from the time when such resale should be effected."

Two-way lien

Under English law an unpaid seller can refuse to deliver if *inter alia* the buyer is insolvent.[4] Article 73(1) is much wider. It reads:

> Each party may suspend the performance of his obligations whenever, after the conclusion of the contract, the economic situation of the other party appears to have become so difficult that there is good reason to fear that he will not perform a material part of his obligations.

Damages

The rules as to damages in Articles 82–88 are fairly similar to those under English law except that Article 83 gives an automatic right to interest in some cases.

Risk

Unlike English law the risk will prima facie pass with delivery.[5]

Exclusion

Article 3 provides that the parties can expressly or by implication exclude the whole or any part of the Law.

The future

The Uniform Law rules (including those in the Formation of Contract Convention) will in due course be replaced by new rules contained in the United Nations Convention on Contracts for the International Sale of Goods. This was concluded in Vienna in 1980 but it has not yet been incorporated into English law.

---

[4] *Ante*, p. 171.
[5] Art. 97.

Chapter Eleven

CONTRACTS WITH A FOREIGN ELEMENT

Introduction

THE first nine chapters have dealt with rules of English law relating to a number of commercial contracts. These rules will be applied by English courts where no foreign element is involved. If, however, a case does contain a foreign element, as where A in England agrees to send goods on a Dutch ship to B in South Africa, the court will not necessarily apply the same law as it would do if there was no foreign element. The branch of English law which deals with cases containing a foreign element is called the Conflict of Laws, and it deals with three questions:

(1) Has the English court jurisdiction to hear the case at all?

(2) If it has jurisdiction, what country's system of law is to be applied to it?

(3) To what extent will the English courts recognise and enforce a judgment obtained abroad?

As a result an English judge may very well find himself directed by the English conflict rules to the application of a foreign system of law. It must be appreciated that every system of law prevailing outside England and Wales is a foreign law—Scots law is just as foreign as Hungarian law. If a provision of foreign law is in issue, it must generally be proved as a fact by an expert, and if no evidence is forthcoming the foreign law is presumed to be the same as English law.[1]

The rules set out in this chapter will soon have to be read subject to a Convention made between the original six Member states of the EEC. The Convention is set out in Schedules 1–3 to the Civil Jurisdiction and Judgments Act 1982. When it is brought into force it will make radical changes to English law in EEC cases but it will not affect other cases. The Convention is examined on p. 555.

---

[1] *De Reneville* v. *De Reneville* [1948] P. 100; [1948] 1 All E.R. 56. For the method of proof see Civil Evidence Act 1972, s.4.

DEFINITION OF TERMS

Domicile[2]

Although a precise definition is impossible[3] a person is regarded as domiciled in a territory if he lives in it and intends to do so permanently.[4] On birth each child acquires a domicile of origin, namely the domicile of the father if the child is legitimate and that of the mother if the child is illegitimate. The domicile of origin is tenacious—it may in due course[5] be replaced by the acquisition of a new domicile of choice, but as soon as that domicile is abandoned the domicile of origin revives until another domicile is acquired.[6] Domicile is chiefly of importance in matters of personal status such as marriage, legitimacy and succession, and apart from Convention matters (as to which see *post*, p. 557), it has very limited importance in the field of commercial contracts.

Lex fori

This means the law of the court in which the case is tried. Thus the *lex fori* of any case tried in the English courts is English law.

Lex loci solutionis

This means the law of the place of performance of the contract.

Lex situs

This means the law of the place where the property lies.

Lex loci contractus

This means the law of the place where the contract is made.

SOURCES OF LAW

In an area of law where many points are unresolved the courts frequently refer to the leading textbooks and in particular to Dicey

---

[2] This Section deals with domicile as part of the general law. For the special meaning of domicile in "Convention" cases, see *post*, p. 556.

[3] *Doucet* v. *Geogeghan* (1878) L.R. 9 Ch.D. 441, 456, *per* Sir George Jessel M.R.

[4] *Ramsay* v. *Liverpool Royal Infirmary* [1930] A.C. 588.

[5] *Udny* v. *Udny* (1869) L.R. 1 Sc. & Div. 441, H.L.; *Re Flynn* [1968] 1 W.L.R. 103.

[6] *Princess Thurn and Taxis* v. *Moffitt* [1915] 1 Ch. 58.

and Morris and to Cheshire. They will be referred to in appropriate places in this chapter.

JURISDICTION

Preliminary

The general rule is that any person can sue and can be sued in the English courts, but there are two main exceptions. The first is that an alien enemy cannot sue. It is important to appreciate that the test of enemy alien status is not nationality but whether the alien resides or carries on business in the enemy country. Thus a foreigner who is permitted to reside in England despite a state of war between his country and England can sue in the English courts,[6] and so also can a national of the enemy country who resides in a neutral country not in enemy occupation.[7] Conversely the Court of Appeal has held that:

> "for the purpose of determining civil rights a British subject or the subject of a neutral state who is voluntarily resident or who is carrying on business in hostile territory is to be regarded and treated as an alien enemy."[8]

In the case of a company registered in England the courts are prepared to lift the veil of incorporation and if they find that the controllers of the company are enemy aliens the company will be accorded enemy status and will not be able to sue.[9]

The second exception, based on general principles of public international law, relates to foreign Governments and Heads of State. This matter is governed by the State Immunity Act 1978 and the immunities conferred by that Act are considerably narrower than the common law immunities which were replaced by the Act. In particular:

> 1. Immunity can be waived by agreement or by the State[10] taking a step in the proceedings (other than claiming immunity.)[11]

---

[7] *Re Duchess of Sutherland* (1915) 31 T.L.R. 394.

[8] *Porter* v. *Freudenberg* [1915] 1 K.B. 857, 869.

[9] *Daimler Co.* v. *Continental Tyre and Rubber (Great Britain) Co.* [1916] 2 A.C. 307, H.L.

[10] This term includes the Head of State, the Government and any Government Department.

[11] s.2.

2. Commercial transactions only enjoy immunity if the parties to the dispute (*a*) are States or (*b*) have agreed in writing that immunity shall apply.[12]

3. Immunity does not apply to a contract of employment between the State and an individual where the contract was made in the United Kingdom or where the work was to be wholly or partly performed there.[13]

4. There is no immunity in respect of (a) acts or omissions causing death, injury or damage in the United Kingdom,[14] (b) any interest or obligation of the State relating to land in the United Kingdom[15] or (c) any alleged infringement of a patent or trade mark by the State in the United Kingdom.[16]

Apart from the 1978 Act there are a number of other important statutory provisions. One is the Diplomatic Privileges Act 1964 which confers varying degrees of immunity on:

(a) a diplomatic agent and members of his family forming part of his household,

(b) members of the administrative and technical staff of the mission,

(c) members of the service staff of the mission.

The immunity conferred under this Act can be waived by the sending state.[16] The waiver must be express, but where an action is started by a member of the protected class, this precludes him from pleading immunity in respect of any counterclaim directly connected with the principal claim.[17] It is important to appreciate that if such a person waives his immunity as regards proceedings, he does not thereby waive his immunity as regards execution of the judgment. Such execution can only be levied if a separate waiver is forthcoming.[18]

Apart from the above, the International Organisations (Immunities and Privileges) Act 1950,[19] confers various privileges and immunities on international organisations and on officials of, or

---

[12] s.3.
[13] s.4.
[14] s.5.
[15] s.6.
[16] See Sched. 1, Art. 32, para. 1.
[17] *Ibid.* para. 3.
[18] *Ibid.* para. 4.
[19] The Act has been slightly amended by the Act of 1964.

delegates to, such organisations. The precise scope of the immunity, and the organisations and persons to which the immunity applies, are specified by Orders in Council. Finally the Diplomatic Immunities (Conferences with Commonwealth Countries and the Republic of Ireland) Act 1961 confers immunity on representatives of certain Commonwealth countries and of the Republic of Ireland who attend conferences in the United Kingdom.

The basic rule[20]

"The foundation of jurisdiction," said Holmes J., "is physical power."[21] This principle is reflected in the English rules governing jurisdiction in matters of contract. The basic rule can be stated very simply: the English court has jurisdiction if the defendant (or in certain circumstances his agent) can be served with the writ. For valid service to be effected the defendant must usually be present in England or Wales at the time of service. If he is not present the court can only hear the case if

(a) he submits to the jurisdiction of the court, or

(b) the case falls within Order 11 of the Rules of the Supreme Court and the court in its discretion grants leave for the writ (or notice of the writ if service is to take place outside Scotland, Northern Ireland, the Channel Islands or the Isle of Man) to be served abroad.

The questions of presence, submission and Order 11 will now be separately examined.

Presence

If the defendant is present in England or Wales at the time of the service of the writ, the court has jurisdiction to hear any action against him in respect of a contract. This is so even if the contract has no connection whatever with England.

> Suppose that X and Y, both of whom are domiciled and resident in Spain, agree for the sale of sherry from X to Y at a price of 10,000

---

[20] *McDonald* v. *Mabee* (1917) 37 Sup.Ct. 343.

[21] Apart from the 1968 Convention there are also special jurisdiction rules as between the courts of England, Scotland and Northern Ireland (see Civil Jurisdiction and Judgments Act 1982, ss.16 and 17 read with Schedules 4 and 5). Thus for example a party domiciled in England can be sued in Scotland on a contract which is to be performed there.

pesetas, delivery to take place in Madrid. The contract is in the Spanish language and form and provides that all disputes are to be governed by Spanish law. X comes to England for a week on business and while he is here Y comes here for a few hours. X can serve Y with a writ claiming damages for breach of contract and the court will have jurisdiction.

It appears, therefore, that the defendant can be served if he is here, however short his stay.[22] If, however, he was tricked into coming here, service may be set aside.[23] So far as corporations are concerned, a company or other body incorporated in England is deemed to be present in England, even though all its business is done abroad.[24] A company incorporated abroad is present in England if it carries on business in England. Where the business of an individual is carried on by an agent, a distinction must be drawn between an agent who accepts orders in England and thereby binds his foreign principal, and an agent who merely transmits orders for acceptance by the foreign principal. In the former case the principal carries on business *in* England and is present, while in the latter case he merely carries on business *with* England and is not present. In *Dunlop Pneumatic Tyre Co.* v. *Aktien Gesellschaft für Motor.*[25]

> A German company had a stand for the sale of their cycles at an exhibition at the Crystal Palace, lasting nine days. Their agent at the stand demonstrated the models, encouraged the public to buy them, and accepted orders. He had power to bind the company by accepting the orders. *Held*, the company was present here during the exhibition so that a writ served on the agent during that time gave the English court jurisdiction to hear an action by a buyer for delivery of the goods.

It should also be noted that where a company incorporated outside England sets up a place of business here, it must file with the Registrar of Companies the name of a person authorised to accept service on its behalf.[26]

---

[22] *Maharanee of Baroda* v. *Wildenstein* [1972] 2 Q.B. 283; [1972] 2 All E.R. 689 (service at race meeting at Ascot). The rule is criticised in Cheshire and North (10th ed.), p. 80.

[23] *Watkins* v. *North American Lands, etc., Co.* (1904) 20 T.L.R. 534.

[24] See Companies Act 1948, s.437.

[25] [1902] 1 K.B. 342.

[26] Companies Act 1948, s.407. See also R.S.C., Ord. 65, r. 3, for the practice governing service on a corporation.

Presence of agent

To obviate possible procedural difficulties which might arise when attempting to serve the foreign principal of an agent who carries on business here, Order 10, rule 2(1), gives the court a discretion to authorise service of the writ on the agent instead of the principal. It reads as follows:

> Service of writ on agent of oversea principal:
> 2.—(1) Where the court is satisfied on an *ex parte* application that—
> (*a*) a contract has been entered into within the jurisdiction with or through an agent who is either an individual residing or carrying on business within the jurisdiction or a body corporate having a registered office or a place of business within the jurisdiction, and
> (*b*) the principal for whom the agent was acting was at the time the contract was entered into and is at the time of the application neither such an individual nor such a body corporate, and
> (*c*) at the time of the application either the agent's authority has not been determined or he is still in business relations with his principal
> the Court may authorise service of a writ beginning an action relating to the contract to be effected on the agent instead of the principal.

Submission

A person outside the jurisdiction of the court may submit to the jurisdiction, and if he does this the court can hear a case brought against him. Submission will occur where a defendant who has been improperly served enters an acknowledgment of service[27] and does not use the machinery which is available to have the service of the writ set aside.[28] Where a party appears before the court as plaintiff, this normally amounts to a submission[29] giving the court jurisdiction to hear a counter-claim but not an entirely separate action.[30] If the parties agree that the court is to have jurisdiction and if they also specify the method of service that

---

[27] As to which see Ord. 12, r. 1.
[28] See Ord. 12, r. 8.
[29] *Yorkshire Tannery* v. *Eglinton* (1884) 54 L.J. Ch. 81.
[30] *Factories Insurance Co.* v. *Anglo-Scottish General Commercial Insurance Co. Ltd.* (1913) 29 T.L.R. 312.

method may be followed, but leave of the court to serve the writ out of the jurisdiction is still required.[31]

Order 11

The basic rule, therefore, is that, apart from submission, no action can be heard here unless the defendant is in England or Wales at the time of service. This could lead to hardship where a person who had incurred an obligation in this country left the jurisdiction, so that it could not be enforced against him. This, perhaps, was the motive force behind Order 11, rule 1, of the Rules of the Supreme Court. This order[32] creates many exceptions to the general rule, by allowing the court to grant leave for service abroad. It must be appreciated, however, that the jurisdiction is a discretionary one. A plaintiff seeking leave must first bring his case within one of the paragraphs of the rule. If he does this the court may, in its discretion, allow him to serve the writ (or notice of the writ) abroad.

Although the object of the rule was to avoid hardship for the plaintiff, the courts have emphasised that the rule can equally cause hardship to the defendant by putting him to the trouble and expense of defending an action in England. This has led the courts[33] to lay down the following four principles for the guidance of judges considering their discretionary powers:

(1) The court should be extremely careful before it allows a writ to be served on a foreigner out of England.[34]

(2) Any doubt should be resolved in favour of the foreigner.

(3) Since the application for leave is made *ex parte*, a full disclosure must be made.

(4) The courts should refuse leave unless the case comes within the spirit as well as the letter of the appropriate rule.

Contract cases within Order 11, rule 1

Rule 1 is subdivided into 12 paragraphs bearing letters (*a*) to (*l*). Six of these paragraphs, (*b*) (*c*) (*f*) (*g*) (*i*) and (*j*), are relevant to actions brought in respect of a contract.

---

[31] R.S.C., Ord. 10, r. 3.

[32] The corresponding County Court Order is Ord. 8, r. 2.

[33] See *The Hagen* [1908] P. 189, 201 (Farwell L.J.); *Aaronson Bros. Ltd.* v. *Maderera Del Tropico S.A.* [1967] 2 Lloyd's Rep. 159.

[34] See observations of Winn J. in *Cordova Land Co.* v. *Victor Bros. Inc.* [1966] 1 W.L.R. 793.

(1) *Order* 11, *rule* 1 (*b*)

This rule enables leave to be obtained if

> a contract . . . affecting land situated within the jurisdiction is sought to be construed, rectified, set aside or enforced.

The precise scope of this rule is not entirely clear. It has been held to cover an action against the assignee of a tenant for breach of a repairing covenant[35] but not an action brought by a landlord against the tenant's assignee for rent due under the lease,[36] presumably because the claim was in effect one for the recovery of a debt rather than for enforcement of a contract.[37]

(2) *Order* 11, rule 1(*c*)

This paragraph applies:

> if in the action begun by the writ leave is sought against a person domiciled or ordinarily resident within the jurisdiction.

It will be recalled that domicile involves residence coupled with the intention to remain permanently. It is this intention which distinguishes domicile from residence. The expression "ordinarily resident" connotes residence with some degree of permanence[38] and must be distinguished from mere temporary presence.

The scope of paragraph (*c*) is wide.

> Suppose that A, domiciled in England, is sent by his firm to Germany for a year. While there he contracts to buy an expensive Mercedes car but fails to pay. Since A retains his English domicile the court can grant leave for notice of the writ to be served on him abroad.

(3) *Order* 11, *rule* 1(*f*)

This paragraph and the following one are important as they deal specifically with contract, It applies:

> if the action . . . is brought against a defendant not domiciled or ordinarily resident in Scotland to enforce, rescind, dissolve, annul or otherwise affect a contract or to recover damages or obtain other

---

[35] *Tassell* v. *Hallen* [1892] 1 Q.B. 321.

[36] *Agnew* v. *Usher* (1884) 14 Q.B.D. 78.

[37] See *Kaye* v. *Sutherland* (1887) 20 Q.B.D. 147, 151.

[38] *Peel* v. *C.I.R.* (1928) 13 Tax Cas. 443; *Stransky* v. *Stransky* [1954] P. 428; [1954] 2 All E.R. 536.

relief in respect of the breach of a contract being (in either case) a contract which

    (i) was made within the jurisdiction, or

   (ii) was made by or through an agent trading or residing within the jurisdiction on behalf of a principal trading or residing out of the jurisdiction, or

  (iii) is by its terms, or by implication, governed by English law.

In deciding where a contract is made for the purpose of (i) the normal English rules are applied. A contract concluded by correspondence is "made" where the acceptance is posted,[39] while a contract by Telex is "made" in the country where the acceptance is received.[40]

Case (ii) covers a case where the agent merely transmits an order to his principal as well as the case where he makes a contract himself.[41]

Case (iii) applies where English law is the proper law of the contract.[42] This is considered below (see *post*, p. 504 *et seq.*).

(4) *Order* 11, *rule* 1 (*g*)

This paragraph applies:

> If the action . . . is brought against a defendant not domiciled or ordinarily resident in Scotland or Northern Ireland in respect of a breach committed within the jurisdiction of a contract made within or out of the jurisdiction and irrespective of the fact, if such be the case, that the breach was preceded or accompanied by a breach committed out of the jurisdiction that rendered impossible the performance of so much of the contract as ought to have been performed within the jurisdiction.

In *International Corporation Ltd.* v. *Besser Manufacturing Co. Ltd.*[43]:

> By a contract made in the United States the defendants (an American company) appointed the plaintiff (an English company) as their sole agents for the sale of their products in England and Europe

---

[39] *Benaim* v. *Debono* [1924] A.C. 514. The same applies to telegrams (*Cowan* v. *O'Connor* (1888) 20 Q.B.D. 640).

[40] *Entores Ltd.* v. *Miles Far East Corporation* [1955] 2 Q.B. 327; [1955] 2 All E.R. 493 affirmed by the House of Lords in *Brinkibon Ltd.* v. *Stahag Stahl und Stahlwarenhandel-gesellschaft* [1982] 2 W.L.R. 264; [1982] 1 All E.R. 293.

[41] *National Mortgage and Agency Co. of New Zealand* v. *Gosselin* (1922) 38 T.L.R. 832.

[42] For a recent case on the proper law and on the discretion of the court, see *Mauroux* v. *Soc. Com. Abel Pereira* [1972] 1 W.L.R. 962.

[43] [1950] 1 K.B. 488; [1950] 1 All E.R. 355.

and agreed to pay commission of 15 per cent. on all sales. The plaintiff applied for leave to serve abroad a writ claiming an account and commission due. *Held*, leave should be granted. The place of payment was England and the breach, *i.e.* non-payment, occurred in England.

The closing words of paragraph (*g*) were inserted to deal with cases like *Johnson* v. *Taylor Bros.*[44] In that case a seller under a c.i.f. contract had failed to deliver the shipping documents in England, but leave was refused because the really substantial breach, namely, failure to ship the goods at all, had occurred abroad. Leave in such a case could now be granted. Likewise if A, a French company, employing a man in England, wrote a letter from Paris wrongfully dismissing him no breach would have occurred in England,[45] but a subsequent non-payment of salary in England would amount to such a breach.[46] On the other hand if goods are shipped from New York c.i.f. Hull, and the buyer alleges that they are unmerchantable, the breach (if any) has not taken place in England so that leave under paragraph (*g*) cannot be granted.[47]

(5) *Order* 11, *rule* 1 (*i*)

This paragraph applies where an injunction is sought ordering the defendant to do or refrain from doing anything within the jurisdiction. It could be used, if, for example, an employee absconded to Scotland with lists of the employer's English customers and the employer sought an injunction to restrain the employee from using the lists.

(6) *Order* 11, *rule* 1 (*j*)

This paragraph applies:

> if the action . . . being properly brought against a person duly served within the jurisdiction, a person out of the jurisdiction is a necessary or proper party thereto.

An example is furnished by the case of *Massey* v. *Heynes*[48] where an English agent made a contract on behalf of a foreign

---

[44] [1920] A.C. 144.
[45] *Holland* v. *Bennett* [1902] 1 K.B. 867.
[46] Dicey and Morris, (10th ed.), p. 211, illustration (1).
[47] *Cordova Land Co.* v. *Victor Bros. Inc.* [1966] 1 W.L.R. 793.
[48] (1888) 21 Q.B.D. 330.

principal, which contract the principal afterwards repudiated. The other contracting party sued the agent and was allowed to join the foreign principal because he claimed in the alternative (a) against the principal if the agent had authority, and (b) against the agent for breach of warranty of authority if he had no authority.

Order 11, rule 2

This rule enables the court to grant leave to serve a writ abroad if the action is brought in respect of a contract containing a term that the court shall have jurisdiction. This rule overlaps with Order 11, rules 1(f) and (g) (ante, pp. 498–499) but at the same time is potentially wider than either of these rules because it can be used even though the defendant is domiciled or ordinarily resident in Scotland or Northern Ireland.

Interim relief

Important powers as to the granting of interim relief (e.g. an injunction to restrain a defendant removing his assets out of the jurisdiction) are conferred by sections 24 and 25 of the 1982 Act.[48a] Thus relief can be granted if the only issue is one of jurisdiction or if proceedings are taking place in another part of the United Kingdom.

Foreign jurisdiction clause

A clause referring all disputes to a foreign tribunal does not automatically oust the jurisdiction of the English court.[49] Nevertheless, although the English courts have a discretion in the matter, they will usually exercise it by granting a stay of the English proceedings unless a strong case can be made out by the party opposing the stay.[50]

CHOICE OF LAW

If the English court has jurisdiction to hear the case the next problem is to decide which law is to be applied to it. This process is

---

[48a] In the remainder of this chapter, unless otherwise stated, "the 1982 Act" means the Civil Jurisdiction and Judgments Act 1982.

[49] *The Fehmarn* [1958] 1 W.L.E. 159; [1958] 1 All E.R. 333.

[50] *The Eleftheria* [1970] P. 94; [1969] 2 All E.R. 641 and cases there cited. For a recent case where a stay was refused see *The El Amria* [1981] 2 LL. L.R. 339.

called choice of law, and the choice depends on how the problem before the court is classified. It is necessary, therefore, to say something about the process of classification before the various choice of law rules can be examined.

Classification

When a problem arises in practice, the lawyer who is asked to advise "classifies" the problem, *i.e.* he places it, in popular language, in its correct legal pigeon hole. When his client has told him the facts he will know whether the matter is one of contract law, tort, landlord and tenant, matrimonial law and so on. He will also have made a more detailed classification. If the problem is one of contract, the particular point may, for example, be one of mistake, or consideration, or illegality. In the conflict of laws this problem of classification is of great importance, because until the problem has been classified it is not possible to select the correct system of law to be applied to it. To take a very simple example from another field, suppose a man has died intestate domiciled in Italy leaving movable and immovable property in England, and the court is asked to decide which law governs the succession to his property. The problem is "classified" into (1) succession to immovable property and (2) succession to movable property. Having done this, the law then applies the conflict rules applicable to these situations, *viz.* (1) intestate succession to immovables is governed by the *lex situs* of those immovables, which in this case is English law, and (2) intestate succession to movables is governed by the law of the last domicile of the deceased, which in this case is Italian law.

Where a dispute concerning a commercial contract comes before the court it will be classified according to the following categories:

> 1. Capacity. This covers such matters as the power of minors and mentally disordered persons to bind themselves by contract.
> 2. Formation. This covers offer and acceptance, consideration, intention to create legal relations and factors operating to negative consent, such as mistake, misrepresentation and duress.
> 3. Formal validity. This covers such matters as the need for a seal, or a written memorandum. In this case, however, a further classification has to be made—namely a classification of the rule imposing the formality. If non-compliance makes the contract void,

the rule is said to be one of substance,[51] whereas if non-compliance merely makes the contract unenforceable by action, the rule is said to be one of evidence or procedure.

4. Essential validity. This covers a contract which may be void under a positive rule of law, such as the Gaming Act 1845.

5. Illegality. This would include such matters as a contract to defraud the Revenue by dressing up salary as "expenses", life insurance without insurable interest (*ante*, p. 348) and transfer of money in contravention of Exchange Control regulations.

6. Interpretation and legal effect. This covers the meaning of the words used by the parties and the express or implied obligations to which their contract gives rise.

7. Manner of performance. This covers matters such as the currency in which the debt has to be paid (see *post*, p. 526) and the meaning of "normal business hours" at the place fixed for performance.

8. Discharge. This covers such matters as accord and satisfaction, frustration and the effect of moratorium legislation.

9. Procedure and Evidence. A matter will be classified as procedural if it relates solely to the remedy and not to the substance of the obligation. Examples include a rule of law which makes a contract unenforceable by action, the method by which proceedings must be brought, and a rule of limitation which bars the remedy only but not the right.

It will be appreciated that a dispute between two persons may well give rise to more than one of the above problems. A defendant sued for breach of contract may set up a defence that the contract was not in writing as required by the *lex loci contractus* and also that it was illegal by the *lex loci solutionis*.

The process of classification and the selection of the appropriate rule of choice of law may very well differ from country to country, so that a rule classified by country A as one of substance may be classified by country B as one of procedure. In any case coming before the English courts, English law, which in this case means the English conflict of laws rules, is applied to classify the problem.[52] It should be noted, however, that these rules are not necessarily the same as those which are applied where no foreign element is involved. For instance, the time-honoured distinction between realty and personalty is discarded in favour of the

---

[51] *Bristow* v. *Sequeville* (1850) 5 Exch. 275.

[52] For classification problems in other fields, see *Re Martin* [1900] P. 211; *Re Wilks* [1935] Ch. 645.

internationally valid distinction between immovables and movables. Leasehold land and land held under an immediate binding trust for sale is regarded by English internal law as personalty, but is classified by English conflict of laws rules as immovable.

The proper law

Having classified the problem, the final function of the conflict of laws rules is to allocate the problem to a particular system of law. The conflict of laws has now been resolved, and it only remains for the judge to apply the system of law which has been selected.

In the case of a commercial contract the system of law which governs most, but not all, of the above problems is called the proper law of the contract and it may be convenient at this stage to indicate how the proper law is ascertained.

It is commonly said that there are two views on the ascertainment of the proper law—the "subjective" view originally supported by Dicey and the "objective" view supported (among others) by Westlake and by Cheshire. According to the subjective view:

> "the term 'proper law of contract' means the law or laws by which the parties intended, or may fairly be presumed to have intended, the contract to be governed."[53]

The keystone here is intention. The objective view can be seen from the judgment of Denning L.J. (as he then was) in *Boissevain* v. *Weil*.[54]

> "the proper law of the contract depends not so much on the place where it is made, nor even on the intention of the parties or on the place where it is to be performed, but on the place with which it has the most substantial connection."

It is submitted that this difference of approach is largely a verbal one, with little practical importance. In the great majority of cases the parties do not expressly choose what law is to govern their contract, and the court must then decide on the proper law. If the

---

[53] Dicey (5th ed.), p. 628. The current edition does not adopt this view in its entirety (*post*, p. 505).

[54] [1949] 1 K.B. 482, 490; [1949] 1 All E.R. 146; see also *Bonython* v. *Commonwealth of Australia* [1951] A.C. 201, and especially *Re United Railways of Havana* [1961] A.C. 1007; [1960] 2 All E.R. 332.

parties do expressly select the proper law, they will usually select a system with which the contract is substantially connected, and in this situation the chosen law will, on any view, be accepted as the proper law. Thus the only situation where the two views diverge is one which is unlikely to arise often in practice—namely, the express selection by the parties of a system of law with which the contract is not substantially connected. Dicey and Morris in its most recent edition, adopts an intermediate position which, it is thought, accurately represents the present law:

> The proper law of a contract means the system of law by which the parties intended the contract to be governed, or, where their intention is neither expressed nor to be inferred from the circumstances, the system of law with which the transaction has its closest and most real connection.[55]

Express choice

Where the parties have expressly chosen the law which is to govern their contract the court will usually give effect to their intention. In the words of Lord Atkin.[56]:

> "The legal principles which are to guide an English court on the question of the proper law of a contract are now well settled. It is the law which the parties intended to apply. Their intention will be ascertained by the intention expressed in the contract, if any, which will be conclusive."

The next question is how far it is necessary for the chosen law to have some connection with the contract. In *Vita Food Products Incorporated* v. *Unus Shipping Co.*[57]:

> A company incorporated in New York agreed with a company incorporated in Nova Scotia that the latter company, who owned a motor-vessel, would carry a consignment of herrings from Newfoundland to New York. The bills of lading stated that "this contract shall be governed by English law."

The Judicial Committee of the Privy Council,[58] on appeal from Nova Scotia, decided that English law was the proper law of the

---

[55] Dicey and Morris (10th ed.), p. 747; see *Whitworth Street Estates Ltd.* v. *Miller and Partners* [1970] A.C. 583; [1970] 1 All E.R. 796, H.L., for a discussion of the principles involved.

[56] *R.* v. *International Trustee* [1937] A.C. 500, 529; [1937] 2 All E.R. 164.

[57] [1939] A.C. 277; [1939] 1 All E.R. 513.

[58] Lords Atkin, Porter, Russell of Killowen, Macmillan and Wright.

contract. Lord Wright, who delivered the judgment of the Board, had this to say:

> "It might be said that the transaction . . . contains nothing to connect it in any way with English law and therefore the choice could not be seriously taken. Their Lordships reject this argument both on grounds of principle and on the facts. *Connection with English law is not as a matter of principle essential.*"[59] (Italics supplied.)

The freedom to choose any law is not, however, entirely unqualified. In the passage immediately preceding the one just quoted Lord Wright said:

> "But where the English rule that intention is the test applies, and where there is an express statement by the parties of their intention to select the law of the contract, it is difficult to see what qualifications are possible, *provided the intention expressed is bona fide and legal and provided there is no reason for avoiding the choice on the ground of public policy.*" (Italics supplied.)

What his Lordship had in mind was an attempt to evade a provision of the law with which the contract was closely connected by selecting a system of law with which it was not connected.[60]

> Suppose that A and B make an essentially English contract of sale excluding the seller's obligations as to fitness and merchantable quality. The contract (which has no connection with France) contains a clause that French law is to be the proper law.

It would be open to the courts to find that the choice of French law was not bona fide as it was an attempt to exclude the non-excludable implied terms. In fact, the Unfair Contract Terms Act 1977 covers this very point; it provides that the statutory controls are to apply in such a case if the court is satisfied that the main object of the clause was to evade the provisions of the Act.[61]

Those who favour the "most real connection theory" argue that

---

[59] *Ibid.* at pp. 290 and 521 respectively. His Lordship also observed that the contract did have a connection with England because the ship was registered under the Merchant Shipping Act and because the underwriters were likely to be English. In practice many standard form contracts used in international trade refer disputes to English law or English arbitration.

[60] A dictum of Upjohn J. that "this court will not necessarily regard [the parties' choice of law] as being the governing consideration where a system of law is chosen which has no substantial connection with the contract looked on as a whole" (*Re Helbert Wagg* [1956] Ch. 323, 34; [1956] 1 All E.R. 129, 136) was presumably directed at this question of evasion.

[61] s.27(2).

while the parties have full freedom to select the law which governs such matters as performance, interpretation and discharge, the preliminary question of whether a valid and binding contract has come into existence must be determined quite independently of the parties' intentions, by referring to the system of law with which the putative contract is most closely connected.[62]

No express choice

Where, as is more usual, the parties have not made an express choice, the court must examine the surrounding circumstances to see whether they indicate an implied choice of law.[63] Some earlier cases seek to discover the proper law by reference to "the presumed intention of the parties." This, however, is somewhat artificial and unreal, because the truth of the matter is that the parties did not consider the matter at all, and had they done so they would probably have been unable to agree.[64] In *The Assunzione*,[65] Birkett L.J., after stating that he had been confronted with a sense of unreality, described the duty of the court as follows:

> "This court has therefore to examine the facts of the case and to consider what inference or presumption arises from these facts, and then, regarding the parties as just and reasonable people, to say after that full consideration what is the reasonable inference to be drawn and what was the probable intention of the parties."

In deciding on the proper law all circumstances connected with the contract must be taken into account. In the following passage Lord Atkin sets out the relevant principles clearly and accurately:

> "In coming to its conclusion the court will be guided by rules which indicate that particular facts or conditions leads to a prima facie inference, in some cases an almost conclusive[66] inference as to the

---

[62] Cheshire and North *op. cit.* pp. 212–213.

[63] *Re United Railways of Havana and Regla Warehouses Ltd.* [1961] A.C. 1007 [1960] 2 All E.R. 332.

[64] Compare the so-called "implied term" theory of the doctrine of frustration.

[65] [1954] P. 150; [1954] 1 All E.R. 278.

[66] It was formerly thought that a clause referring disputes to the courts or arbitration of a particular country raised an "irresistible inference" of a choice of that country's law (*Tzortzis* v. *Monark Line A/B* [1968] 1 W.L.R. 406; [1968] 1 All E.R. 949, C.A.), but this must now be modified in the light of observations made by the House of Lords in *Compagnie D'Armement Maritime* v. *Compagnie Tunisienne* [1971] A.C. 572; [1970] 3 All E.R. 71.

intention of the parties to apply a particular law, *e.g.* the country where the contract is made; the country where the contract is to be performed; if the contract relates to immovables the country where they are situate; the country under whose flag the ship in which goods are contracted to be carried, sails.[67] But all these rules but serve to give prima facie indications of intention, however difficult it may be in some cases to find such. The principle of law so stated applies equally to contracts to which a sovereign state is a party as to other contracts."[68]

Thus no one factor is conclusive and the court must consider not only the matters set out above but also any other relevant matters such as the residence and domicile of the parties, and the form of the contract. Thus if a contract contains legal clauses which are well known in country A but are meaningless in country B this is some evidence that the law of country A governs,[69] but the mere fact that, as is very often the case, a bill of lading is drawn up in the English language will not be strong evidence that English law is to apply, especially if the contract is otherwise not connected with England.;[70]

As an illustration of how a modern court tackles the choice of law problem where no express choice is made the case of *The Assunzione* is instructive:

> Under an exchange agreement between the Italian and French Governments, French brokers acting on behalf of shippers agreed with brokers for Italian shipowners that the Italian ship *Assunzione* should carry wheat from Dunkirk to Venice. The court had to decide whether French or Italian law was the proper law. Counsel for the shippers argued that French law should apply because (1) the charterparty was headed "Paris" (although in fact this was purely fortuitous since negotiations had been carried out by correspondence), (2) the charterparty which was in English had a supplement in French, (3) the bill of lading was in the French language, and (4) the brokers were acting on behalf of the French Government. Counsel for the shipowners argued that the contract should be governed by

---

[67] In modern times, particularly with the arrival of flags of convenience, the flag is of far less importance. (See *The Assunzione* [1954] P. 150; [1954] 1 All E.R. 278) but it can still be used as a last resort (*Coast Lines Ltd.* v. *Hudig and Vider Chartering N.V.* [1972] 2 Q.B. 34; [1972] 1 All E.R. 451, C.A.).

[68] *R.* v. *International Trustee* [1937] A.C. 500, 529; [1937] 2 All E.R. 164, 166.

[69] *James Miller and Partners* v. *Whitworth Street Estates Ltd.* [1970] A.C. 583; [1970] 1 All E.R. 796, H.L.

[70] *The Metamorphosis* [1953] 1 W.L.R. 543, 549; [1953] 1 All E.R. 723, 727.

Italian law because (1) the ship was an Italian ship, (2) Italy was the place of delivery, (3) payment of freight and demurrage was to be made in Italy in Italian lire. The Court of Appeal, upholding Willmer J., held that although the facts were very evenly balanced, the provision for payment tipped the scales in favour of Italian law.

If the intention of the parties cannot be gleaned from the circumstances the court must find the legal system with which the contract has its closest and most real connection. Thus, in the leading case of *Re United Railways of Havana and Regla Warehouses, Ltd.*[71]

> To finance the purchase of railway rolling stock for use in Cuba, an English company borrowed 6,000,000 dollars from a Pennsylvania Corporation. The machinery of the transaction was complicated. The first stage was, as Lord Denning put it, comparable to a modern hire-purchase agreement financed through a finance company in that the rolling stock was vested in the Pennsylvania Corporation who leased it to the company. At the same time 6,000 trust certificates were issued and it was agreed that the rentals under the lease should be paid to the Corporation in Pennsylvania, and would be received by the Corporation as trustees for the holders of the trust certificates. The House of Lords held that the lease was governed by Pennsylvanian law because, there being no express choice of law, Pennsylvanian law was the law with which the contract had its closest and most real connection.

Presumptions

During the last century certain presumptions as to the proper law were developed by the courts. Having regard to the language used in the more modern cases, however, it is probably true to say that the presumptions are very weak and should only be used as a last resort, when other attempts to discover the proper law have failed. The presumptions can be summarised as follows:

(1) Where an ordinary contract is made which does not contain a foreign element, the parties clearly intend their rights to be governed by the law of the country in which it is made—the *lex loci contractus*. This presumed intention also applies, although less strongly, where a foreign element is involved. Thus there is an initial presumption in favour of the *lex loci contractus*.[72] This

---

[71] [1961] A.C. 1007; [1960] 2 All E.R. 332.
[72] *P. & O. Steam Navigation Co.* v. *Shand* (1865) 3 Moo.P.C.(N.S.) 272. P.C.

presumption is particularly strong if the contract is to be substantially performed in the country in which it is made. In some cases, however, the place of contracting is purely fortuitous. If there has been lengthy correspondence between A in London and B in Belgium with offers, counter-offers and more counter-offers, it may be quite fortuitous whether the final letter of acceptance is posted in London or in Belgium. In such a case, or in a case where a contract is concluded between two businessmen in a train, ship or plane, the presumption in favour of the *lex loci contractus* is not strong.[73]

It will be apparent from what has just been said that English law applies its own domestic rules in identifying the place of contracting. Thus a contract concluded by correspondence will be "made" in the country where the acceptance is posted (unless a contrary intention appears), while a contract made by instantaneous communication such as telephone or Telex is made in the country where the acceptance is received.[74]

(2) Where a contract is made in one country and is wholly or substantially to be performed in another country, there is a presumption that the law of the place of performance is the proper law. In *Benaim* v. *Debono*,[75] the court was of the opinion that the contract had its closest connection with Gibraltar, being the *lex loci solutionis*, and therefore the law of Gibraltar was held to be the proper law to the exclusion of Maltese law, the *lex loci contractus*.

Sometimes the *lex loci solutionis*, while not being the proper law, nevertheless governs the rules as to the mode and manner of performance, such as the method by which money has to be paid or by which notice has to be given. In such a case, however, the substance of the obligation as, for example, whether "pounds" means English or Australian pounds[76] and whether performance is excused by frustration[77] will be governed by the proper law.

---

[73] See *Benaim* v. *Debono, post*, p. 519.
[74] *Entores Ltd.* v. *Miles Far Eastern Corporation* [1955] 2 Q.B. 327; [1955] 2 All E.R. 493.
[75] [1924] A.C. 514, *post*, p. 519.
[76] *Bonython* v. *Commonwealth of Australia* [1951] A.C. 201, *post*, p. 522.
[77] *Jacobs* v. *Credit Lyonnais* (1884) 12 Q.B.D. 589, *post*, p. 520.

Another illustration of the limits of the role of the proper law is provided by the recent case of *James Miller and Partners Ltd.* v. *Whitworth Street Estates (Manchester).*[78] In that case:

> A appointed B to carry out some work on a factory in Scotland. The contract, which was in the English RIBA form, contained an arbitration clause and in due course a Scottish arbitrator was appointed to conduct an arbitration in Scotland. By Scots law he could not be required to state a case for the opinion of the court. The House of Lords held (a), by a majority of 3–2, that English law was the proper law of the contract; (b), unanimously, that nevertheless the law of the place where the arbitration took place (*i.e.* Scots law) governed the conduct and procedure of the arbitration; (c), that the right to ask for a case stated was a procedural matter arising out of the arbitration and was governed by Scots law.

(3) There is a presumption that a contract relating to immovable property is governed by the law of the country in which the immovables are situate (the *lex situs*).

(4) Contracts for the carriage of goods by sea are presumed to be governed by the law of the ship's flag. This presumption is perhaps the least strong and is very easily displaced.[79]

Incorporation of foreign law

Having ascertained the meaning of the proper law it is now proposed to deal with the individual aspects of a contract and to examine which law applies. Before doing so, however, it might be useful to point out that the parties sometimes incorporate into their contract a specified system of law. Thus on a contract for the sale of goods, the contract might contain the following clause:

> "The rights and duties of the parties hereto with regard to delivery, acceptance and payment shall be those contained in the Sale of Goods Act 1979."

In this case the position is the same as if the parties had expressly written into their contract the relevant sections of the Sale of Goods Act. The importance of the distinction between incorporation and the selection of the proper law is that in the former case the parties incorporate the law *as it stands at the time of the contract*, while if a proper law is chosen, the parties agree to be

---

[78] [1970] A.C. 583; [1970] 1 All E.R. 796.
[79] See *ante*, p. 508, n. 67.

bound by that law as it exists from time to time, so that a change in the law, which may operate to alter, avoid or discharge the contract, will be binding on the parties.[80] If any question arises as to whether the incorporation is valid or invalid, this will be a matter for the proper law.

Choice of law rules

Capacity

In view of the great number of young people who visit this country from overseas, it is surprising that the question of capacity to make a commercial contract is completely without any modern authority. In the early case of *Male* v. *Roberts*,[81] where a minor bought goods in Scotland, Lord Eldon stated that Scots law governed capacity as being "the law of the country where the contract arose." This decision, given at a time when the Conflict of Laws was for obvious reasons still in its infancy, would not seem to be conclusive of how a case would be decided in the latter part of the twentieth century. There are also wide dicta in some cases that capacity to contract is governed by the law of the person's domicile,[82] but all these cases concern either marriage or marriage settlements and are therefore of no more than persuasive authority on the question of commercial contracts. Further, the selection of the domiciliary law could cause hardship and inconvenience to any trader dealing with visitors from overseas. Probably the most satisfactory rule would be to uphold a contract made by a person if he had capacity *either* by the law of his domicile and residence *or* by the law of the place with which the contract is most closely connected. This view is put forward by Dicey and Morris.[83]

Immovables. Where there is a contract for the sale or mortgage of immovable property, it was held in *Bank of Africa* v. *Cohen*[84] that capacity was governed by the *lex situs*. The decision has been criticised.[85]

---

[80] *Re Helbert Wagg Ltd.* [1956] Ch. 323; [1956] 1 All E.R. 129.
[81] (1800) 3 Esp. 163. It is noteworthy that Scots law was almost certainly the proper law as well.
[82] See, *e.g. Sottomayer* v. *De Barros* (*No. 1*) (1877) 3 P.D. 1, *per* Cotton L.J.
[83] *Op. cit.*, at p. 778.
[84] [1909] 2 Ch. 129.
[85] Morris, *The Conflict of Laws*, 2nd ed., p. 293.

Formation

The question of what law determines the formation of the agreement is uncertain. Dicey and Morris state that it is the law which would be the proper law if the contract were a valid one, while Cheshire and North prefer the law of the country with which the "contract" is most closely connected. In many cases these two views will lead to the same result.[86]

In English internal law a contract comes into existence if there is an offer and acceptance, an intention to create legal relations and (unless the contract is under seal) valuable consideration. In the conflict of laws, however, the word "contract" may have a wider meaning. In *Re Bonacina*[87];

> X, who carried on business in England, owed money to Y. Subsequently he became bankrupt and obtained his discharge in bankruptcy. After obtaining his discharge he executed a document in Italy, by which he agreed to pay the debt. Both X and Y were Italians. It was held that, despite the absence of consideration, there was a valid contract by Italian law, which was the proper law of the agreement. Accordingly on the death of X, Y was entitled to prove for the debt against X's estate.

This decision in favour of the proper law may well be applied to other aspects of the contract, such as offer and acceptance. As a matter of principle, however, there is much force in the view that *for this purpose* the proper law should be ascertained objectively. In the words of a famous American judge;[88]

> "Some law must impose the obligation and the parties have nothing whatsoever to do with that, no more than with whether their acts are torts or crimes."

Further, Dicey and Morris[89] admit that some matters (such as the question of whether silence amounts to acceptance) must depend on the law of the residence or place of business of the party concerned.

---

[86] See *Albeko Schuhmaschinen AG.* v. *Kamborian Shoe Machine Co. Ltd.* (1961) 111 L.J. 519.

[87] [1912] 2 Ch. 394.

[88] Learned Hand J. in *E. Gerli & Co.* v. *Cunard S.S. Co.* 48 F. (2d) 115 (1931), Cheshire and North, *op. cit.*, supports this view.

[89] *Op. cit.*, at p. 776.

Formal validity

If the parties have made a genuine agreement, the next problem is whether the agreement is formally valid. Most modern systems of law do not impose many formalities for commercial contracts, and this may help to explain the almost total absence of authority. It is clearly established that compliance with the forms required by the *lex loci contractus* is sufficient[90] and most writers seem to be agreed that compliance with the formalities required by the proper law should be equally effective.[91]

It is important, however, to distinguish between matters of form and matters of evidence and procedure, because all procedural matters are governed by English law as the *lex fori*. To take an example:

> A orally agrees in Ruritania to sell a piece of land in Tomtopia to B. By both Ruritanian and Tomtopian law no formalities are required. A repudiates the contract and B wishes to claim damages in the English courts.

It seems that B cannot sue A unless there is a written note or memorandum as required by section 40 of the Law of Property Act 1925 because, this section says "no action shall be brought" and is therefore an imperative rule of procedure applicable in the English courts.[92]

Whether a rule of law is classified as formal or procedural depends on the effect of non-compliance. If non-compliance makes the contract void, the rule will be classified as one of substance, and if the contract fails to satisfy either the *lex loci contractus* or the proper law, the contract will not be enforced.[93] If, on the other hand, the rule merely makes a contract unenforceable by action, the rule will be ignored as procedural unless it is an English rule.[94]

---

[90] *Guépratte* v. *Young* (1851) 4 De G. & Sm. 217.

[91] *Cf. Van Grutten* v. *Digby* (1862) 31 Beav. 561, a case relating to a marriage settlement.

[92] *Cf. Leroux* v. *Brown* (1852) 12 C.B. 801, a case on the Statute of Frauds 1677. The application of this Act to a foreign contract is criticised in Cheshire and North, *op. cit.* at pp. 692–693.

[93] *Alves* v. *Hodgson* (1797) 7 T.R. 241 (unstamped document void by *lex loci* and not enforced in England).

[94] *Bristow* v. *Sequeville* (1850) 5 Ex. 275.

Essential validity

A contract which has the outward appearance of having been validly concluded with due formalities and with full and free consent, may nevertheless be wholly or partly void by reason of some substantive rule of law. Thus, to take two examples discussed earlier in this book, section 18 of the Gaming Act 1845 declares all contracts of gaming and wagering to be absolutely void, and section 6 of the Unfair Contract Terms Act 1977 makes void a clause excluding terms implied by sections 12–15 of the Sale of Goods Act 1979 in consumer sales (*ante*, p. 441). Where such a provision is in issue the problem is said to be one of essential validity and, subject to the rules as to illegality discussed below, it is governed by the proper law of the contract. Thus in *Saxby* v. *Fulton*[95]:

> A lent money to B for gambling at Monte Carlo. By the law of Monte Carlo (the proper law) gambling is valid. The loan was therefore held to be recoverable in England.

Again in *Hamlyn* v. *Talisker Distillery*:[96]

> A contract which was to be mainly performed in Scotland contained a clause referring disputes to an English arbitrator. By Scots law the arbitration clause was void. The House of Lords, sitting as a Scottish court of appeal, held that English law was the proper law and accordingly the arbitration clause was valid.

Illegality

Since the courts will not enforce a contract which is void by its proper law, *a fortiori* they will not enforce one which is illegal by its proper law. Thus in *Kahler* v. *Midland Bank*:[97]

> Shares belonging to the plaintiff were deposited by a Czech bank with an English bank. When the plaintiff claimed them, the English bank pleaded that it could not release them without infringing Czech exchange control legislation. The House of Lords, holding that Czech law was the proper law of the contract of deposit, dismissed the plaintiff's claim, because, in the words of Viscount Simonds, "the

---

[95] [1909] 2 K.B. 208.
[96] [1894] A.C. 202; see also *Re Missouri Steamship Co.* (1889) 42 Ch.D. 321, 330, where an exemption clause in a charterparty was upheld because it was valid by the proper law although void by the *lex loci contractus*.
[97] [1950] A.C. 24; [1949] 2 All E.R. 621. For criticism see F.A. Mann, 11 M.L.R. 479 and 13 M.L.R. 206–212.

courts of this country will not compel the performance of a contract if by its proper law performance is illegal."

The question of illegality is not, however, left exclusively to the proper law and a number of other systems of law have to be considered. In the first place, quite apart from any question of proper law, the English courts will not enforce a contract which contravenes an English statute, if on its true construction the statute applies to the contract. In *Boissevain* v. *Weil*:[98]

> In 1944 the respondent, who was a British subject involuntarily resident in Monaco during the war, borrowed 960,000 French francs from the appellant, a Dutch subject, and agreed to repay the loan as soon as possible after the war. At the time of the loan a Defence Regulation made under the Emergency Powers (Defence) Act 1939 was in force in England, and it provided that no person other than an authorised dealer should buy or borrow foreign currency. The Act provided that regulations made under it should, with certain exceptions, apply to all British subjects. An action in England to recover the loan failed, because the contract was illegal. Lord Radcliffe (with whom the other members of the House of Lords concurred) emphasised that the transaction clearly fell within the express prohibition of the regulation.

In such a case it will always be necessary to examine the statute to discover whether it has extra-territorial operation and whether it applies even though the contract is governed by a foreign system of law.

Secondly, and this is a similar point to the previous one, the English courts will not enforce a contract which is valid by its proper law, if it violates a distinctive rule of English public policy. Here again it will be necessary to examine the relevant rule and to decide whether the contract comes within the mischief at which the rule is aimed. Thus a contract to pay a sum of money to a lady in consideration of future immoral cohabitation would clearly not be enforced in England, even though the contract is governed by a foreign law. Again in *Dynamit Aktiengesellschaft* v. *Rio Tinto Co., Ltd.*:[99]

> By a contract governed by German law and made in 1910 an English company agreed to deliver minerals to a German company. The contract provided for suspension in the event of war. In 1916

---

[98] [1950] A.C. 327; [1950] 1 All E.R. 728.
[99] [1918] A.C. 292.

(*i.e.* during the First World War) the English company brought proceedings for a declaration that the contract was not merely suspended, but was discharged, on the ground that by English law it was illegal for an English firm to be in contractual relationship with the enemy in time of war. The declaration was made.

Just as the courts will not enforce in times of war a contract which involves trading with the enemy, so they will not enforce in times of peace a contract tending to prejudice this country's relations with a friendly foreign state. If an English contract is made with the object of violating the laws of such a state it will not be enforced. Thus in *Regazzoni* v. *K.C. Sethia* (1944), *Ltd.*:[1]

> Under a contract governed by English law, A agreed to sell jute bags to B c.i.f. Genoa. Both parties knew that (1) the bags would be obtained from India, (2) the ultimate destination of the bags was South Africa, (3) it was illegal by Indian law to export goods from India directly or indirectly to South Africa. A failed to deliver and B sued him. It was held that the contract was illegal and could not be enforced.

Thirdly, a contract of which English law is the proper law will not be enforced if it is illegal by the *lex loci solutionis*. In *Ralli Bros.* v. *Compania Naviera Sota y Aznar*:[2]

> X chartered a Spanish ship to carry jute from Calcutta to Barcelona. Under the contract, which was governed by English law, X agreed to pay part of the freight in Barcelona. Before the jute arrived, a Spanish law was passed making it unlawful to pay more than 875 pesetas per ton for jute delivered in Spain. This maximum was less than the agreed freight. X offered to pay 875 pesetas per ton but he refused to pay more, on the grounds that to do so would violate Spanish law. The shipowner sued X in England for the excess. It was held that X was not liable.

It is uncertain whether this is merely a rule of English domestic law (*i.e.* an example of frustration[3]) or whether there is a more general rule that even if a contract is valid by its proper law, the English courts will not enforce it if performance is illegal by the *lex loci solutionis*. On principle, it would seem that the question of

---

[1] [1958] A.C. 301; [1957] 3 All E.R. 286. There appears to be no authority indicating whether this principle also applies to a contract not governed by English law.

[2] [1920] 1 K.B. 287.

[3] The frustration cases are dealt with in the judgment of Scrutton L.J.

how illegality at the place of performance affects the contract should be left for the proper law to decide.[4]

Lex loci contractus. Fourthly, it now appears to be generally accepted that illegality by the *lex loci contractus* will not prevent the enforcement of a contract which is valid by its proper law. It is true that in *Re Missouri Steamship Co.*[5] Lord Halsbury stated *obiter* that the English courts would not enforce a contract which infringed a mandatory rule of the *lex loci contractus*, and a decision of the Court of Appeal supports this view.[6] This decision, however, was disapproved of by Lord Wright in delivering the judgment of the Judicial Committee of the Privy Council in the *Vita Food* case (*ante*, p. 505), and there appears to be no other case where a contract valid by its proper law has not been enforced merely because it infringed the *lex loci contractus*. Looked at in general terms, there appear to be two relevant principles:

(a) If the parties make a genuine choice of the proper law, this law and not the *lex loci contractus* should govern legality.

(b) If the parties make a contract which is illegal at the place of contracting and they then attempt to evade the illegality by selecting a favourable proper law, it is submitted that the selection would not be bona fide and that the contract would not be enforced.

Finally a contract which is not illegal by virtue of any of the rules discussed above is enforceable in England, even if it is illegal by the law of the country where a party resides or carries on business. In *Kleinwort Sons v. Ungarische Baumwolle Aktiengesellschaft.*[7]

> An English bank opened a credit in favour of a Hungarian firm X & Co. When the credit expired X & Co. refused to pay in London because by Hungarian law it was illegal for them to do so. It was held that since the promise to pay was not governed by Hungarian law, nor was it to be performed in Hungary, the illegality was no defence and accordingly X & Co. were liable.

---

[4] Dicey and Morris, *op. cit.*, at p. 795; Morris, *op. cit.* p. 234. *Contra*, Graveson, *The Conflict of Laws*, (7th ed.), pp. 436–437.

[5] (1889) 42 Ch. D. 321 at p. 336.

[6] *The Torni* [1932] P. 78.

[7] [1939] 2 K.B. 678; [1939] 3 All E.R. 38. See also *Power Curber International* v. *National Bank of Kuwait SAK* [1981] 1 W.L.R. 1233 C.A.

Interpretation and effect

If a contract valid in all respects has come into existence the interpretation of the terms used by the parties and the legal effect of the contract are both governed by the proper law.

Interpretation. A technical term may have a different meaning in different countries, and it is for the proper law to apply its own rules of construction to decide which meaning should be given to it. Thus if under a contract of carriage from country A to country B a carrier stipulates that he is to be under "no liability" it will be for the proper law to decide whether these words are wide enough to exclude liability for negligence.

Effect. The proper law deals with the legal effect of the contract and the rights and liabilities of the parties to it. Thus in *Benaim* v. *Debono*:[8]

> Maltese buyers bought anchovies from sellers in Gibraltar f.o.b. Gibraltar. On arrival in Malta the buyers complained of the quality of the anchovies, but nevertheless tendered them to sub-purchasers who refused to accept them. Buyers then sought to repudiate the contract made with the sellers. By Maltese law they could do this but by Gibraltar law, they could not. It was held that the law of Gibraltar was the proper law and as this law governed the rights of the parties the buyers were not entitled to reject.

The proper law will also decide such matters as the following:
(1) What conditions are implied in the contract?
(2) Has the risk passed?
(3) Whose duty is it to obtain the export licence?
(4) Where is the place of delivery?
(5) What are the unpaid seller's rights?
(6) Can a hirer put an end to the hiring?
(7) Is an employer bound to provide work?
(8) Does an insurance policy expressed to be for the benefit of a named person confer on that person a legally enforceable right?
(9) Has an agent earned his commission?
(10) Is time of the essence?

Manner of performance. While matters of substance are governed by the proper law, matters of detail are sometimes

---

[8] [1924] A.C. 514.

governed by the law of the place of performance.[9] Thus the proper
law would decide whether the seller was under any duty to send
the goods to the buyer, but if the contract provided that the buyer
was to collect the goods "during usual business hours," the
meaning of these words would be determined by the *lex loci
solutionis*.[10]

Discharge

The previous section showed that performance was governed by
the proper law. The question of discharge is also governed by the
proper law, as it logically should be since the overwhelming
majority of contracts are discharged by performance. The proper
law, however, applies to all forms of discharge, whether it be
performance, accord and satisfaction, frustration or breach. In
Jacobs v. *Credit Lyonnais*:[11]

> A company trading in England agreed to sell to an English firm
> 20,000 tons of Algerian esparto grass to be shipped from Algeria and
> paid for in London. After some deliveries the sellers failed to
> complete delivery and when sued by the buyers pleaded that there
> had been an insurrection in Algeria and that under a clause of the
> French Civil Code which applied in Algeria they were excused
> performance. The Court of Appeal held that since the contract was
> governed by English law the sellers were liable and the French law
> was irrelevant.

Countries who are faced with economic difficulties sometimes
attempt to preserve the value of their currency by passing a
so-called *moratorium* on debts payable in foreign currency abroad.
In *Re a claim by Helbert Wagg*:[12]

> A German company owed a debt to an English company under a
> contract governed by German law. The debt and interest were to be
> payable in sterling in London. The German Government made a law
> ordering the payments to be made in marks to an office of the
> German Government, and when the payments had been made the

---

[9] See Lord Wright in *Mount Albert P.C.* v. *Australasian, etc., Life Insurance
Society, Ltd.* [1938] A.C. 224, 240; [1937] 4 All E.R. 206, 215; Morris, *op. cit.* at
pp. 236–238.

[10] This example is given in Dicey and Morris, *op. cit.* at p. 813.

[11] (1884) 12 Q.B.D. 589. At the time of the decision the doctrine of frustration
had not been fully developed. If the facts occurred today it is conceivable that
under English law the contract would be held to have been frustrated.

[12] [1956] Ch. 323; [1956] 1 All E.R. 129.

debt was by German law extinguished. Upjohn J. held that the debt was discharged "The power of legislation to affect a contract by modifying or annulling some terms thereof is a question of discharge of the contract, which in general is governed by the proper law."

On the other hand in *National Bank of Greece and Athens* v. *Metliss*:[13]

> The NM Bank borrowed money and issued bonds guaranteed by the N Bank. Both the banks were Greek, but the contract of loan and the bonds were governed by English law. In 1941 the Greek Government imposed a *moratorium* suspending payments under the bonds. In 1953 the Greek Government made a decree which (1) dissolved the N Bank; (2) amalgamated it with another bank to form the National Bank of Greece and Athens; and (3) provided that this bank should be the universal successor to the rights and liabilities of the dissolved N Bank. An action was brought against the new bank on the bonds. The House of Lords held (1) the new bank had succeeded to the obligations of the old one (this being a matter of status and therefore governed by the law of domicile, *i.e.* the law of the country of incorporation); (2) the *moratrium* was ineffective because Greek law was not the proper law of the bonds; and (3) accordingly the bank was liable.

After the decision in this case, the Greek Government passed a further decree retrospectively relieving the new bank of its obligations under the guarantee. In *Adams* v. *National Bank of Greece S.A.*[14] the House of Lords held that this decree, too, was inoperative for the same reason—the problem was one of discharge, and was governed by English law (the proper law) and not the law of Greece.

Limitation. When a defendant pleads that his obligation has been discharged by virtue of a statute of limitations, it is necessary to make a distinction already referred to on p. 514 between substance and procedure, and to decide whether the statute extinguishes the right altogether or (as is more usual) merely takes away the remedy. Three points should be borne in mind:

(1) If, on its true construction, the foreign rule bars the right altogether, it will operate as a valid discharge of the debt. This is only so, of course, if the rule is that of the proper law.

---

[13] [1958] A.C. 509; [1957] 3 All E.R. 608.
[14] [1961] A.C. 255; [1960] 2 All E.R. 421.

(2) If, however, the foreign rule merely takes away the remedy, it will be classified as procedural and ignored in an action brought in the English courts.[15]

(3) In any action in England the provisions of the Limitation Act 1980, will apply, because the provisions of that Act relating to contracts are procedural.

Procedure and evidence

It has already been seen that in any action brought in England all questions of procedure and evidence are governed by English law as the *lex forti*.

Monetary obligations

With the dramatic fluctuations in the value of currencies, particularly during the present century, the rules governing monetary obligations in international contracts are of the greatest importance. There are four basic problems:

(1) What currency has the debtor agreed to pay?

(2) What constitutes legal tender of that currency?

(3) How much money (measured in units of that currency) does that debtor have to pay? This is called the money of account.

(4) In what currency does the debtor have to pay the agreed amount? This is called the money of payment.

Which currency? Where the parties use ambiguous words like "pounds" and "francs" which are capable of referring to different currencies, the contractual currency will be determined by the proper law of the contract. In *Bonython* v. *Commonwealth of Australia*:[16]

> The Government of Queensland borrowed £2,000,000 and issued debentures in "pounds sterling" repayable at the holder's option in Australia or England. Over half the loan was obtained in England. After the Australian pound had been devalued, a number of debenture holders claimed that they were entitled to be paid in London the nominal amount of the debentures in English pounds, or, if payment was made in Australia, a sum in Australian pounds

---

[15] *Huber* v. *Steiner* (1835) 2 Bing. N.C. 202.

[16] [1951] A.C. 201. Lord Simonds pointed out that where one of the contracting parties is the government of a state, there is a strong presumption that it was contracting with reference to its own currency.

equal in value to the nominal value in English pounds. The Commonwealth of Australia, who had taken over the debt, opposed this view and contended that "pounds" in the debentures meant Australian pounds. The Judicial Committee of the Privy Council dismissed the claim of the debenture holders and held that the meaning of the word "pound" must he determined by Queensland law as being the proper law of the contract.

Legal tender. Having ascertained the contractual currency, the question of what coins, notes or chattels constitute legal tender in that currency is governed by the law of the country whose currency it is (*lex pecuniae*) even if the law of that country is not the proper law.[17] Thus if a contract for the export of goods from England to Switzerland provides for payment in French francs, and the French Government replaces its existing franc with a new currency, it is for French law to say what constitutes "francs."

Money of account. The question of how much the debtor has to pay is governed by the proper law of the contract. It is important to appreciate that virtually every system of law applies the principle of nominalism, that is to say it fixes the debtor's liability by reference to the nominal amount of the currency which he has agreed to pay. This may create great hardship to the creditor where the chosen currency depreciates or is devalued. Thus in *Re Chesterman's Trusts*:[18]

> A German national mortgaged his interest under an English trust to a Dutch bank as security for a loan of 31,000 marks (£1,500). The deed creating the mortgage was expressly made subject to English law. At the time of the loan the lender was entitled to be repaid in gold marks, but in the economic depression following the First World War the German Government decreed that any obligation to pay a sum in marks should be satisfied by the delivery of paper marks. These paper marks were virtually valueless. The lender brought an action in the English courts.
>
> The court had to decide the case in accordance with the principles already stated. English law, as the proper law, applied the principle of nominalism, while German law, as the *lex pecuniae*, stated that "marks" meant "paper marks." Accordingly the lender was only entitled to be repaid the sterling equivalent of 31,000 paper marks (worth approximately 5p).[19]

---

[17] *Pyrmont Ltd.* v. *Schott* [1939] A.C. 145; [1938] 4 All E.R. 713.

[18] [1923] 2 Ch. 466.

[19] See *post*, p. 524 for the abolition of the former rule that judgment has to be given in sterling.

Two schemes have been devised to guard against such risks. The first is called revalorisation. This is a provision in the law of certain countries (not including England) whereby the court is permitted to depart from the principle of nominalism and to award the creditor a larger sum representing a sum of the depreciated currency equal in value to the nominal amount of the original currency.

Revalorisation is a process whereby the debt itself, and not the currency, is revalued[20] and therefore is only possible if the law which provides for revalorisation is the proper law of the contract.[21] Thus in the case of *Re Chesterman's Trusts* a revalorisation provision in the German Civil Code would not have availed the lender, because German law was not the proper law of the contract.

The second method of guarding against fluctuation is one which is frequently adopted by the parties to an international contract, namely a gold clause. There are two main types of such clauses:

(a) A gold coin clause, which requires the debtor to make payment in gold.

(b) A gold value clause whereby the debtor agrees to pay at the due date an amount of the contractual money which is equal to a specified quantity of gold.

The distinction between the two is of particular importance, because in times of economic trouble the government of a state is far more likely to prohibit payment in gold than payment in the national currency ascertained in relation to the value of gold. Thus the two main questions for the court are:

(1) Is the clause a gold-coin clause or a gold-value clause?

(2) Is the clause valid?

The first of these is a matter of construction and is governed by the proper law of the contract. In the leading case of *Feist* v. *Société Intercommunale Belge d'Electricité*[22]:

> Loan Bonds issued by a Belgian company provided for repayment of capital and for payment of interest in sterling gold coin of the

---

[20] Although most of the cases are concerned with currencies which are devalued, the principles apply equally where a currency is revalued, *i.e.* where its value is increased.

[21] *Anderson* v. *Equitable Assurance Society of the United States* (1926) 134 L.T. 557.

[22] [1934] A.C. 161.

United Kingdom of or equal to the standard of weight and fineness existing on the first day of September 1928.The contract was made subject to English law. The House of Lords (reversing the decision of the Court of Appeal) held that the contract did not require delivery of gold coins and that the clause was a gold-value clause.

Once the meaning of the clause has been ascertained the proper law decides whether effect can be given to it. In *R.* v. *International Trustee*:[23]

> The British Government issued in America certain gold notes which were convertible into gold bonds. The holders could elect whether to be repaid in London or in New York, and in the latter case the sum payable was to be ascertained in accordance with a gold-value clause. Subsequently a Joint Resolution of Congress provided that all gold-value provisions were contrary to public policy and that every obligation containing such provision should be discharged upon payment, dollar for dollar, in any coin or currency which at the time of payment was legal tender. The House of Lords held that the contract was governed by New York law and accordingly the gold-value clause was rendered ineffective by the resolution.

It is noteworthy that the House was prepared to hold New York law to be the proper law, even though one of the contracting parties was the British Government. If the proper law had been English law, the result of the case would presumably have been the same, having regard to the rule that where English law is the proper law, the courts will not compel performance if performance is illegal by the *lex loci solutionis*.[24] A point which has not been settled is the position where the gold clause is invalidated by the *lex loci solutionis*, where the proper law of the contract is that of some other country and is not English law. Dicta in one case suggest that the provisions of the *lex loci solutionis* would govern,[25] but this has been criticised[26] and appears to be contrary to principle.

Quite apart from the above, the contract may simply provide for adjustment of the price in the event of devaluation or revaluation. Where a party claims that, as a result of a breach of contract, he

---

[23] [1937] A.C. 500; [1937] 2 All E.R. 164.

[24] See the *Ralli Brothers* case, *ante*, p. 517.

[25] Lord Romer in *New Brunswick Ry.* v. *British and French Trust Corporation* [1939] A.C. 1 at pp. 43–44; [1938] 4 All E.R. 747, 770.

[26] Cheshire and North, *op. cit.* at p. 247.

has suffered damage by reason of devaluation this is a problem of remoteness of damage and is governed by the proper law.[27]

Money of payment. When the value of the debt has been ascertained the final problem is to discover in what currency this sum is to be paid, and this matter is governed by the law of the place of payment. It is important to distinguish clearly between money of account and money of payment. In the *Bonython* case (*ante*, p. 522) the law of Queensland fixed the money of account, *viz.* the nominal value of the debentures, in Australian pounds. If, say, debentures for £1,000 were repayable in England, English law would decide whether the debtor could lawfully tender one thousand Australian pounds, or whether he would have to pay the sterling equivalent of one thousand Australian pounds.

Where the place of performance is England payment can be made either in he contractual currency or in its sterling equivalent according to the rate at which the currency can be bought in London in a recognised and accessible market, and irrespective of any official rate of exchange.[28] For many years it was generally accepted that an English court could only give judgment in sterling and that the date for conversion into sterling was the date on which the debt became due.[29] The House of Lords has recently held, however, that this is no longer so.[30] They also held that a judgment for a foreign currency debt is convertible into sterling at the date when the court authorises enforcement.[30] Such an order can be made not only where the proper law is the law of the foreign currency but also where English law is the proper law.[31]

Negotiable instruments

As the currency of foreign trade, the subject of negotiable instruments bristles with Conflict of Laws problems. It is, of course, highly desirable to unify the conflict rules of the countries engaged in international trade, and there have been a number of

---

[27] *Aruna Mills Ltd.* v. *Dhanrajmal Gobindram* [1968] 1 Q.B. 655; [1968] 1 All E.R. 113, and see *ante*, p. 187.

[28] *Marrache* v. *Ashton* [1943] A.C. 311; [1943] 1 All E.R. 276.

[29] *The Teh Hu* [1970] P. 106; [1969] 3 All E.R. 1200.

[30] *Miliangos* v. *George Frank* (*Textiles*) *Ltd.* [1975] 3 W.L.R. 758; [1975] 3 All E.R. 801, affirming [1975] 2 W.L.R. 555; [1975] 1 All E.R. 1076.

[31] *Barclays Bank International* v. *Levin Bros.* (*Bradford*) *Ltd.* [1977] Q.B. 270.

conventions which have attempted to do this. Most of these, however, have not been adopted by the United Kingdom.

The English conflict rules relating to negotiable instruments are largely, but not exclusively, contained in a statutory provision, section 72 of the Bills of Exchange Act 1882 (hereinafter referred to as section 72).[32] It will be seen that these rules differ materially from those governing other contracts, the chief difference being that the Act in many cases refers the problem to the *lex loci contractus*, and does not enable the parties to select their own system of law. In other words, the doctrine of the proper law has little or no place in the field of negotiable instruments.

Readers of Chapter Five will have appreciated that negotiable instruments involve not one but several distinct contracts. There is the original contract when the bill is issued by the drawer to the payee, another contract when the bill is accepted, another contract when the bill is indorsed, another when it is accepted for honour *supra* protest, and so on. It is important to keep this in mind when reading the following pages.

Negotiability

It will be recalled that by English law a negotiable instrument has two special features:

(a) It can be transferred by delivery or by indorsement completed by delivery, and

(b) The transferee (if a holder in due course) can obtain a good title free from earlier defects.

Both these special features concern the transfer or "negotiation" of the document and if the court, in a Conflict of Laws case, is asked to decide whether a document is negotiable, it refers the matter to the law of the country where the alleged "negotiation" took place. If the alleged negotiation took place in England, the document will only be recognised as negotiable if it is treated as such by the mercantile community in England, or if an Act of Parliament makes it negotiable. In *Picker* v. *London County Banking Co.*[33]:

---

[32] Section 72(4), which related to bills expressed in a foreign currency, was repealed by Section 4 of the Administration of Justice Act 1977.
[33] (1887) 18 Q.B.D. 515.

A owned certain Prussian bonds. They were stolen from A in England and pledged with an English bank. The bank claimed to be entitled to retain the bonds as holders of a negotiable instrument. By Prussian law the bonds were negotiable but the English mercantile community did not regard them as such. The Court of Appeal held that since the transaction had taken place in England, English law applied, and accordingly the bonds were not negotiable and the bank was not entitled to retain them as against A.

Capacity

Section 72 is silent on the question of capacity to become a party to a negotiable instrument, and the point does not appear to be covered by authority. Dicey and Morris[34] suggest that to avoid doubts and to enable negotiable instruments to be freely negotiated, all matters of form, formation and capacity should be governed by the same system of law, and that since form is expressly referred to the *lex loci contractus* (see below), capacity should also be governed by that law. There is much force in that argument which is supported by a Canadian decision.[35]

Formalities

In the case of bills of exchange and promissory notes,[36] the question of formalities is dealt with by section 72, which provides as follows:

"Where a bill drawn in one country is negotiated, accepted, or payable in another, the rights, duties, and liabilities of the parties thereto are determined as follows:—

(1) The validity of a bill as regards requisites in form is determined by the law of the place of issue, and the validity as regards requisites in form for the supervening contracts, such as acceptance, or indorsement, or acceptance *supra* protest, is determined by the law of the place where such contract was made.

Provided that—

(a) Where a bill is issued out of the United Kingdom it is not invalid by reason only that it is not stamped in accordance with the law of the place of issue.

---

[34] *Op. cit.* at p. 884.

[35] *Bondholders Securities Corporation* v. *Manville* [1933] 3 W.W.R. 1, where a married woman domiciled in Saskatchewan signed a promissory note in Florida. By Florida law a married woman had no capacity to do this. It was held that the question was governed by the law of Florida as the *lex loci contractus* and the note was therefore void.

[36] s.89 states that, subject to exceptions, the rules as to bills apply to notes.

(b) Where a bill, issued out of the United Kingdom, conforms, as regards requisites in form, to the law of the United Kingdom, it may, for the purpose of enforcing payment thereof, be treated as valid as between all persons who negotiate, hold, or become parties to it in the United Kingdom."

Thus the maxim *locus regit actum*—the place governs the transaction—is the general rule. It must, however, be appreciated that the country in which a bill or note is signed is not necessarily the *locus contractus*, because a bill is not issued until it is delivered, complete in form, to a person who takes it as a holder,[37] and because every contract on a bill is normally incomplete until delivery.[38] If A in London draws a bill on B in France and sends it to C, the payee, in Belgium, Belgian law governs the form of the original contract. When C presents the bill to B, who accepts it and returns it to C, Belgian law again governs the form of the acceptance.

Provisos. The first of the two provisos, relating to stamping, is based on a rule of the English conflict of laws that the courts of this country will not enforce the Revenue laws of another. The wide language of the subsection suggests that the failure to stamp will be ignored even if the *lex loci contractus* makes the unstamped bill completely void.[39]

The second proviso is clearly based on commercial convenience. If A in France draws a bill on B in England and B accepts, whereupon A indorses the bill to an English bank, the English bank can sue B on his acceptance if the bill is formally valid by English law, and can safely disregard any formal invalidity by French law.

Interpretation

Section 72(2) provides that:

Subject to the provisions of this Act, the interpretation of the drawing, indorsement, acceptance, or acceptance *supra* protest of a bill, is determined by the law of the place where such contract is made.

---

[37] Act of 1882, s.2.
[38] *Ibid.* s.21.
[39] If, of course, the failure to stamp merely makes the contract unenforceable, the foreign rule to this effect would in any event be classified as procedural and ignored.

> Provided that where an inland bill[40] is indorsed in a foreign country the indorsement shall *as regards the payer* be interpreted according to the law of the United Kingdom.

The *lex loci contractus* therefore governs interpretation. In *Haarbleicher and Schumann* v. *Baerselman*:[41]

> A foreign bill which was payable in England was indorsed in Germany. The indorser added the words "für mich" [for me]. By English law this was a restrictive indorsement, by German law not. It was held that German law, as the law of the country where the indorsement took place, governed the matter.

If the bill in this example had been an inland bill and an indorsee had sought to enforce payment against the acceptor, the proviso would have applied and English law would have governed.

Scope of section 72(2). The point which has aroused great controversy among writers is the meaning of the word "interpretation." Does it cover not only the meaning of the words but also their legal effect?[42] A case which lends some authority to the view that it does is *Koechlin* v. *Kestenbaum*[43]:

> A bill drawn in France in favour of M was indorsed in France by E, who was M's authorised agent. The indorsement by E did not show this, and the English acceptors refused to pay, on the ground that the indorsement by E did not comply with section 32(1) of the 1882 Act. The Court of Appeal held that: (1) the problem was either one of form and governed by section 72(1) or of interpretation and so governed by section 72(2). (2) In either case French law, as the *lex loci*, governed the matter, and since by French law the indorsement was valid, the acceptors were liable.

Legality

The Act of 1882 does not deal expressly with the question of the legality of a bill or note, and the matter is therefore governed by the general common law rules discussed earlier (see *ante*, p. 515) which are preserved by section 97 of the Act. A cheque cannot,

---

[40] For definition, see *ante*, p. 291.
[41] (1914) 137 L.T.J. 564.
[42] See Dicey and Morris, *op. cit.* pp. 895–896: Cheshire, *op. cit.* pp. 551–554; Morris, *op. cit.* p. 316. The question posed in the text is answered in the affirmative by the draftsman of the Act—see Chalmers, *Bills of Exchange*, (13th ed.), at p. 241.
[43] [1927] 1 K.B. 616, 889.

therefore, be enforced in England if it is illegal by its proper law. In *Moulis* v. *Owen*:[44]

> A borrowed money for gaming in Algiers and gave the lender a cheque drawn on an English bank. The Gaming Acts 1710–1835, provide that a cheque given as security for money lent for gaming is deemed to have been given for an illegal consideration. It was held that as the cheque was governed by English law, it could not be enforced. It is noteworthy that by Algerian law both the loan and the cheque were valid. If the lender had sued on the loan and not on the cheque, he would have succeeded because Algerian law was the proper law of the loan.[45]

Transfer

The law which governs the proprietary, as opposed to the purely contractual, aspects of a negotiable instrument is not finally settled. The following problem illustrates:

> A cheque drawn in Roumania and owned by A in Roumania is stolen by B, who forges A's indorsement and transfers the bill to C in Vienna. C in turn transfers it to D in London. A sues D for conversion.

The question is: did C get a good title through the forged indorsement? In a case on these facts[46] the Court of Appeal held that the matter should be governed by Austrian law as the law of the country where the transfer took place, and by that law he did get a good title. It is not clear, however, whether the decision was arrived at on the general principle that the transfer of a tangible movable is governed by the *lex loci actus* (*i.e.* the law of the country where the transfer takes place) or whether the court gave a very wide and artificial meaning to the word "interpretation" in section 72(2) and held that Austrian law applied by virtue of this subsection. The distinction is not purely academic.

> Suppose that in the *Embiricos* case the bill had been drawn in England on an English drawee. Suppose further that D sued the English acceptor:
> If the matter is governed by the general law, D would succeed since the *lex loci actus* gave C a good title. If, however, the matter is

---

[44] [1907] 1 K.B. 746.
[45] *Société Anonyme des Grand Etablissements du Touquet Paris-Plage* v. *Baumgart* (1927) 96 L.J.K.B. 789.
[46] *Embiricos* v. *Anglo-Austrian Bank* [1905] 1 K.B. 677.

governed by section 72(2), the bill is an inland bill and accordingly the proviso to that subsection will require D's rights to be ascertained by English law. Since section 24 prevents any title from being acquired under a forged indorsement, D would have no title and his action would fail.

Duties of holder

Section 72(3) provides that:

> The duty of the holder with respect to presentment for acceptance or payment and the necessity for or sufficiency of a protest or notice of dishonour, or otherwise, are determined by the law of the place where the act is done or the bill is dishonoured.

According to Cheshire "this obscure section verges perilously on the unintelligible."[47] It would seem that the rules regulating the manner of, and time for, presentment for acceptance and payment are governed by the law of the country in which presentation is made,[48] and that the steps (if any) to be taken on dishonour are governed by the law of the country where dishonour takes place.[49] There is some authority for the view that the question of whether presentment is necessary at all is not governed by this subsection.[50] If this is correct the question will be decided by the law governing the contract in question. Thus if an action were brought against a drawer the question of whether the drawer is liable even though no presentment for payment had been made would depend on the law governing the contract made by the drawer, *i.e.* the law of the place of issue.

Maturity

By section 72(5):

> Where a bill is drawn in one country and is payable in another, the due date thereof is determined according to the law of the place where it is payable.

ENFORCEMENT OF FOREIGN JUDGMENTS

Having considered the question of jurisdiction and choice of law, it remains to consider the third branch of the conflict of laws, *i.e.* the

---

[47] Cheshire and North *op. cit.* at p. 256.
[48] See Dicey and Morris, *op. cit.* at pp. 898–899.
[49] *Horne* v. *Rouquette* (1878) 3 Q.B.D. 514.
[50] *Cornelius* v. *Banque Franco-Serbe* [1942] 1 K.B. 29; [1941] 2 All E.R. 728.

rules relating to the enforcement in England of a judgment obtained abroad. For obvious reasons of territorial sovereignty a judgment obtained in, say, Norway cannot automatically be enforced in England. Nevertheless the judgment creditor is not without a remedy. He has two possible remedies:

(1) If certain conditions are satisfied he can sue on the foreign judgment treating the sum awarded as a simple contract debt due from the judgment debtor.

(2) Under certain statutory provisions he may be able to register the judgment in an English court and then enforce it as if made by that court.

Formerly a third alternative was available—the judgment creditor could ignore the judgment altogether and sue on the original causes of action. This anomalous rule has been largely abolished by section 34 of the 1982 Act although it still applies if for some reason the judgment is not enforceable or entitled to recognition in the United Kingdom.

These remedies will now be separately considered.

Action on judgment

An action can[51] be brought in England[52] on a judgment obtained abroad if three conditions are satisfied:

(1) The foreign court was competent;

(2) The judgment is final; and

(3) In the case of an action *in personam* (including an action brought in respect of a contract) the judgment is for a liquidated sum of money.

It is proposed to examine these conditions and then to consider what possible defences are open to the defendant.

Competent court

A judgment obtained abroad will not be actionable in England unless the English court, applying its own rules of private international law, decides that the foreign court had jurisdiction to

---

[51] Within six years of the judgment (*Re Erroll Flynn, decd. (No. 2)* (1968) 112 S.J. 804).

[52] If the judgment is registrable under the 1933 Act no action is allowed (*post*, p. 554).

hear the case.[53] The rules governing this question ("competence") are basically those already discussed in connection with the jurisdiction of the English court. It will be recalled that in an action *in personam*, such as an action arising out of a contract or tort, the whole matter revolves around the ability to serve the writ on the defendant, which normally requires presence or submission.

If, therefore, the defendant was present in the foreign country so that he could be served, the English courts will regard the foreign court as competent even though the defendant was only in the country for a short time.[54]

For this purpose a corporation will be regarded as present in the country if it has a more or less permanent place of business within the jurisdiction. In *Littauer Glove Corpn.* v. *F.W. Millington,* (1920) *Ltd.*[55]:

> A director of an English company went on business to New York. The company had no place of business in America but the director sometimes used that of one of the company's biggest American customers. A summons was served on him there as director of the defendant company. He ignored it and judgment was signed against the company. An action on the judgment was then brought in England. *Held,* (1) The company was not present in America, (2) consequently the New York court was not competent, and (3) consequently the action must fail.

Submission

Similarly, a defendant who submits to the jurisdiction of the foreign court renders that court competent. Submission may take place where the person against whom the judgment is given (a) appears before the court as plaintiff, or (b) files an acknowledgment of service without protest or (c) makes a contract containing an agreement to submit.[56] What is to be said, however, of the

---

[53] Note however that a judgment obtained in another part of the United Kingdom is enforceable in England even though the court did not have jurisdiction according to the English rules of private international law discussed below (Act of 1982, s.19).

[54] *Carrick* v. *Hancock* (1895) 12 T.L.R. 59.

[55] (1928) 44 T.L.R. 746; *cf. ante*, pp. 494–497.

[56] In matters of contract, a submission to the jurisdiction must be express: *Vogel* v. *Kohnstamm Ltd.* [1973] Q.B. 133; [1971] 2 All E.R. 1428 not following *Blohn* v. *Desser* [1962] 2 Q.B. 116; [1961] 3 All E.R. 1, which indicated that the act of trading in a foreign country was an implied submission to the jurisdiction of the courts of that country.

person who, when sued, merely appears in order to contest the jurisdiction of the court? Until recently there was some authority for the remarkable proposition that such action did amount to submission[57] but fortunately this strange rule has been swept away by section 33 of the 1982 Act which makes it quite clear that there is no submission in these circumstances.

Two questions on the competency of the foreign court remain unsettled. The first is whether the court is competent merely because the defendant is a national of the country concerned. Dicta in *Emanual* v. *Symon*[58] and other cases[59] suggest that this is sufficient, but there seems to be no reason on principle why this should be so, and the suggestion has been criticised.[60] The second unsettled point is how far the English courts will enforce a judgment where jurisdiction was based neither on presence, nor on submission but on rules of the foreign court similar to those under Order 11. Denning L.J. has stated *obiter* that such a judgment should be recognised,[61] and on principle there is much to be said for the view, expressed in a matrimonial case, that

> "our courts . . . should recognise a jurisdiction which they themselves claim."[62]

Breach of jurisdiction agreement

A further exception to the basic rule as to jurisdiction is to be found in section 32 of the 1982 Act, the broad effect of which is that a foreign judgment will not be recognised or enforced in the United Kingdom if:

---

[57] *Harris* v. *Taylor* [1915] 2 K.B. 580.

[58] [1908] 1 K.B. 302, 309.

[59] *e.g. Harris* v. *Taylor, op. cit.* p. 591.

[60] Cheshire and North *op. cit.* at p. 641.

[61] In *Re Dulles' Settlement* [1951] Ch. 842, 851; [1951] 2 All E.R. 69. But see *Schibsby* v. *Westenholz* (1870) L.R. 6 Q.B. 155 where the foreign rules for service were very different.

[62] *Travers* v. *Holley* [1953] P. 246, 251; [1953] 2 All E.R. 794, 797, *per* Somervell L.J., but see *per* Hodson L.J. in *Re Trepca Mines* [1960] 1 W.L.E. 1273, 1281; and more recently the judgment of Widgery J. in *Société Co-operative Sidmetal* v. *Titan International* [1966] 1 Q.B. 828; [1965] 3 All E.R. 494, where the view was expressed (*obiter*) that the principle of *Travers* v. *Holley* did not apply. In the matrimonial field the question of recognition is now largely governed by the Recognition of Divorces and Legal Separations Act 1971 (as amended).

(a) the proceedings were contrary to an agreement that the dispute was to be settled otherwise than by proceedings in the courts of that country; and

(b) they were not brought with the consent of the judgment debtor; and

(c) the judgment debtor did not counterclaim or otherwise submit to the jurisdiction of the court.

Internal competence

The foreign court must have been competent in its own country as well as internationally, so that if, for example, a decree of nullity is granted by a court having no power to grant such decree, it will not be recognised in England.[63] In the commercial field this would prevent enforcement of a judgment pronounced by a civil court if the subject-matter could only be dealt with by a commercial court. On the other hand, a mere error by the foreign court with regard to its own rules of procedure will not prevent enforcement.[64]

Judgment final

No action lies in England on a foreign judgment unless it is final, in the sense of being unalterable by the court pronouncing it. Thus no action lies on an interlocutory judgment,[65] nor on an order for maintenance if the court has power to vary the amount of past and future instalments,[66] nor on a judgment which is not a final adjudication of the matter in dispute. In *Nouvion* v. *Freeman*[67]:

> A sold land to B in Spain and brought an "executive action" for the price in the Spanish courts. An executive action was a proceeding

---

[63] *Papadopoulos* v. *Papadopoulos* [1930] P. 55. If, however, the proper court pronounced the decree, the court will not admit evidence to the effect that the decree is wrong in law and is void by the local law, *Merker* v. *Merker* [1963] P. 283; [1962] 3 All E.R. 928. Cf. *Adams* v. *Adams* [1971] P. 188.

[64] *Pemberton* v. *Hughes* [1899] 1 Ch. 781.

[65] *Patrick* v. *Shedden* (1853) 2 E. & B. 14.

[66] *Harrop* v. *Harrop* [1920] 3 K.B. 386. If the power to vary relates only to future instalments, sums already due can be recovered by action in England (*Beatty* v. *Beatty* [1924] 1 K.B. 807).

[67] (1889) 15 App. Cas. 1. Similarly in *Blohn* v. *Desser* (*ante*, p. 534) a foreign judgment against a partnership could not be enforced against an individual partner without a separate action in which the partner could raise personal defences. It was held that the original judgment was not "final."

of a summary nature, with only a limited number of available defences and if successful it resulted in a "remate" judgment. This was final as between the parties but it did not preclude "plenary" proceedings being taken in the same court and in respect of the same subject-matter. In these proceedings all possible defences could be raised and the remate judgment could not be used to support a plea of *res judicata*. A remate judgment was obtained, and A sought to enforce it in England. The House of Lords held that he could not do so because it was not a final judgment.

The mere fact that an appeal can be brought against the judgment[68] or that an appeal is actually pending,[69] does not prevent the judgment from being final.

Similarly a judgment obtained in an American state will be regarded as final and conclusive, even though it is unenforceable in sister states until all possibilities of appeal have been exhausted.[70]

Fixed sum

To be enforceable in England a judgment in an action *in personam* (such as contract or tort) must be for a fixed sum of money. If therefore a plaintiff recovers judgment for £X less the defendant's taxed costs, no cause of action arises until the costs have been taxed because until then there is no fixed sum.[71] A sum which can be ascertained by a simple calculation is a fixed sum for this purpose.[72]

Defences

If a competent court has given a final judgment for a fixed sum of money, the judgment is conclusive in England, which means that (subject to one exception) the defendant cannot reopen the merits of the case. Thus he cannot plead that the foreign court took a wrong view of the facts or law or that he has evidence which might have led to a different result. The English court will not sit as a court of appeal from the foreign court, and this is so even

---

[68] *Beatty* v. *Beatty, supra.*
[69] *Scott* v. *Pilkington* (1862) 2 B. & S. 11. The court will usually exercise its discretionary power to order a stay of execution.
[70] *Colt Industries Ltd.* v. *Sarlie* (*No.* 2) [1966] 1 W.L.R. 1287, C.A.
[71] *Sadler* v. *Robins* (1808) 1 Camp. 253.
[72] *Beatty* v. *Beatty, supra.*

though the judgment sued upon was based on a mistaken view of English law. In *Godard* v. *Gray*[73]:

> The plaintiffs, a French firm, chartered a ship from the defendants, an English firm, under a charterparty containing the following clause:
> "Penalty for non-performance of this agreement estimated amount of freight." The defendants having broken the agreement, the plaintiffs brought proceedings in the French courts. No one informed the court that the clause was by English law a penalty and that the plaintiffs were only entitled to recover their actual loss. The judge therefore awarded them the full freight. When sued in England on the judgment, the defendants sought to attack it by setting up the mistake made by the court. *Held*, they could not do so.

Although a defendant cannot (usually) attack the merits of the judgment sued upon, he has three possible defences to the action. The first is fraud.

> "Although it is not permitted to show that the court was mistaken, it may be shown that they were misled."[74]

This is a well-known general rule of English domestic law and applies where, for example, documents put in evidence are afterwards shown to have been forgeries.[75] In this type of case the evidence of fraud must not have reached the plaintiff until after the hearing. In the case of actions to enforce a foreign judgment, however, the Court of Appeal has on two occasions reached the startling conclusion that a defendant can set up the defence of fraud in respect of a matter which was not only known to him at the time of the hearing but was actually investigated by the foreign court. In *Vadala* v. *Lawes*[76]:

> An Italian firm sued the defendant in Italy on certain bills of exchange which appeared to have been accepted on the defendant's behalf by his agent acting under a power of attorney. The defendant alleged that these bills were fraudulent and were simply given by the agent in connection with certain gambling transactions between the plaintiffs and the agent. The defence failed. When sued in England

---

[73] (1870) L.R. 6 Q.B. 139. A misapplication of the local law is equally irrelevant: *Merker* v. *Merker*, *supra*.

[74] *The Duchess of Kingston's Case* (1776) 2 Sm. L.C. 644, *per* Grey C.J.

[75] *Cole* v. *Langford* [1898] 2 Q.B. 36.

[76] (1890) 25 Q.B.D. 310. And see *Abouloff* v. *Oppenheimer* (1882) 10 Q.B.D. 295.

on the judgment the defendant again raised the fraud. *Held*, he was entitled to do so.

This is the one case where the court will reopen the merits. In the words of Lindley L.J.[77]:

> "if the fraud upon the court consisted in the fact that the plaintiff has induced that court by fraud to come to a wrong conclusion, you can reopen the whole case, even though you will have in this court to go into the very facts which were investigated and which were in issue in the foreign court."

In the most recent case on the point[78] the Court of Appeal went so far as to allow a defendant to plead a fraud of which he was fully aware at the time of the original proceedings but which he had not brought to the notice of the court. The decision has been severely criticised.[79]

The second defence is that the judgment infringes English ideas of public policy. In this way a judgment ordering a putative father to maintain his illegitimate child indefinitely is not enforceable.[80] Nor can an action be brought on a penal judgment[81] or one in respect of a foreign revenue demand.

The final defence is that the judgment was obtained in a manner contrary to natural justice. This means, in effect, that the party now sued on the judgment was denied an opportunity to present his case, or was denied a fair hearing. The problem is likely to arise where a defendant for some reason does not receive notice of the proceedings. The modern case law—all of it on the recognition of foreign divorce decrees—shows that if the rules of the foreign court as to service are properly observed the mere fact that for some reason the defendant does not receive notice does not of itself make the proceedings contrary to natural justice.[82]

---

[77] (1890) 25 Q.B.D. 310, 316–317.

[78] *Syal* v. *Heyward* [1948] 2 K.B. 443; [1948] 2 All E.R. 576; criticised in 65 L.Q.R. 84; 12 M.L.R. 106.

[79] Professor Graveson in 12 M.L.R. 106.

[80] *Re Macartney* [1921] 1 Ch. 552.

[81] See *Schemmer and Others* v. *Property Resources Ltd. and Others* [1975] Ch. 273. See also *Raulin* v. *Fischer* [1911] 2 K.B. 93 as to enforceability of the non-penal part of a partly penal judgment.

[82] *Igra* v. *Igra* [1951] P. 404; contrast *MacAlpine* v. *MacAlpine* [1958] P. 35; [1957] 3 All E.R. 134 (fraud on the court preventing service; decree not recognised).

The plea that the trial was unfair is clearly not an easy one to establish and it cannot be put forward if the alleged unfairness was unsuccessfully challenged by the defendant in the foreign proceedings themselves.[83]

Direct enforcement

Various statutes allow a foreign judgment to be registered in England and then enforced as if made by the English court.

United Kingdom judgments

Section 18 of the 1982 Act (read with Schedules 6 and 7) enables a judgment obtained or entered in one part of the United Kingdom to be enforced in other parts. The basic procedure is that the party seeking to enforce the judgment can apply for a certificate (in the case of a money judgment) or for a certified copy of the judgment (in the case of a non-money judgment). The certificate or copy can then be registered in another part of the United Kingdom. When this has been done the judgment can be enforced as if it were a judgment obtained in the court of registration.

These provisions (which replace earlier legislation) do not apply to bankruptcy or winding-up proceedings but the Bankruptcy Act 1914 and the Companies Act 1948 contain appropriate provisions for recognition.[84]

Administration of Justice Act 1920

This Act enables a judgment obtained in the courts of certain Commonwealth countries to be registered in the High Court in England or Ireland or the Court of Session in Scotland. Application for registration must be made within 12 months, whereupon the court hearing the application may order registration:

> "if in all the circumstances of the case they think it just and equitable that the judgment should be enforced in the United Kingdom."[85]

Unlike the provisions which have just been considered registration is not available as of right, but is a matter for the discretion of

---

[83] *Jacobson* v. *Frachon* (1928) 138 L.T. 386.
[84] See Bankruptcy Act 1914, s.121; Companies Act 1948, s.276.
[85] s.9

the court. The judgment must be given by the courts of a country to which the provisions of the Act have been applied by Order in Council, the principle being that the Act will only be applied to those countries which are prepared to afford similar treatment to judgments obtained in the United Kingdom. Many Orders in Council have already been made, including Orders in respect of Jamaica, Kenya, New Zealand and most of the Australian States.

The Act (as amended by Section 35(2) of the 1982 Act) also enables the judgment creditor to obtain a certified copy of a judgment obtained in the High Court and he can then register this in one of the relevant Commonwealth courts.

Restrictions. No registration is possible if:

(a) The judgment does not provide for payment of a sum of money; or

(b) The original court acted without jurisdiction; or

(c) The judgment debtor did not voluntarily submit to the jurisdiction of the adjudicating court, unless he was carrying on business or was ordinarily resident within that jurisdiction; or

(d) The judgment debtor was not served and did not appear in the proceedings; or

(e) The judgment was obtained by fraud; or

(f) An appeal is pending; or

(g) The cause of action was one which for reasons of public policy, or for some other similar reason, could not have been entertained in England.

Effect of registration. Once the judgment is registered it is enforceable as if made by the registering court.

Foreign Judgments (Reciprocal Enforcement) Act 1933[86]

This Act, as its name implies, is designed to facilitate the reciprocal enforcement of English and foreign judgments. It provides that the judgments of a country to which the Act has been extended by Order in Council may be registered as of right in the High Court. The Orders in Council are made in the case of countries which are prepared to provide similar facilities for the registration of an English judgment. This Act applies to both Commonwealth and non-Commonwealth countries and, in order

---

[86] As amended by Schedule 10 of the 1982 Act.

to standardise registration procedure, section 7 provides that, as soon as an Order in Council is extended to a Commonwealth country or territory the provisions of the Administration of Justice Act 1920 shall cease to have any effect with regard to that country. The Act has been extended to France, Belgium, India, Pakistan, the Australian Capital Territory, Norway, Austria, Western Germany, Israel, The Netherlands, Guernsey, Jersey, the Isle of Man and West Berlin.[87] The Conventions made between the United Kingdom and these countries contain a number of detailed provisions relating to mutual recognition and enforcement.

An application for registration can be made to the High Court within six years and if the conditions laid down in the Act are satisfied the court must order registration.[88] The conditions are that the judgment must have been granted by a "recognised"[89] court, and must require payment of a sum of money to the applicant (other than a sum in respect of taxes or in respect of a fine or other penalty) and (*a*) it must be final and conclusive as between judgment creditor and judgment debtor *or* (*b*) it must require the latter to make an interim payment to the former. The fact that an appeal is possible or pending does not prevent the judgment from being final.[90] Thus the conditions are very similar to those required at common law for an action on the judgment (see *ante*, p. 533). There are, however, a number of cases where registration must be set aside, and one case where it may be set aside. Registration must be set aside in any one of the following six cases:

(1) If the judgment is not one to which the Act applies.

(2) If the foreign court acted without jurisdiction.

(3) If the judgment debtor, being the defendant in the original proceedings, did not (despite service of process in accordance with the foreign law) receive notice in sufficient time to enable him to defend and did not appear.

(4) If the judgment was obtained by fraud.[91]

---

[87] The Orders relating to EEC countries will be superseded by the EEC Convention (*post*, p. 555).

[88] s.2.

[89] The former requirement that the judgment had to be that of a superior court no longer applies (Act of 1982, Schedule 10, para. 1(2)).

[90] s.1(3).

[91] The rules are the same as at common law. *Syal* v. *Heyward, ante*, p. 539, was a case under the Act.

(5) If enforcement of the judgment would be contrary to public policy.

(6) If the rights under the judgment are not vested in the applicant.[92]

The one case where registration may be set aside is where the court is satisfied that the subject-matter of the judgment has already been the subject of a final and conclusive judgment by a court having jurisdiction in the matter.[93]

The Act contains elaborate rules to decide whether the foreign court had jurisdiction. They are similar to those discussed earlier in relation to enforcement by action (*ante*, p. 533). The court is deemed to have had jurisdiction in an action *in personam* in the following cases:

> (i) If the judgment debtor, being defendant in the original court, submitted to the jurisdiction by voluntarily appearing in the proceedings otherwise than for the purpose of contesting the jurisdiction or of protecting, or obtaining the release of, property seized or threatened with seizure, in the proceedings.
>
> (ii) If the judgment debtor was plaintiff in the original case.
>
> (iii) If the judgment debtor, being defendant, had previously agreed to submit to the jurisdiction.
>
> (iv) If the judgment debtor, being defendant, was, at the time of the institution of the proceedings, resident in the foreign country, or, being a corporation, had its principal place of business in that country.
>
> (v) If the judgment debtor, being defendant, had an office or place of business in the foreign country and the original action was brought in respect of a transaction effected through or at that office or place.

It has recently been held that this list is exhaustive and that there is no room for any principle that the foreign court must be deemed to have had jurisdiction if it acted under powers corresponding to Order 11 of the Rules of the Supreme Court.[94]

---

[92] s.4(1)(*a*).

[93] s.4(1)(*b*).

[94] *Société Co-operative Sidmetal* v. *Titan International* [1966] 1 Q.B. 828; [1965] 3 All E.R. 494.

Effect of registration. Once a judgment is registered it operates as if it had been granted by the High Court.

Effect of statutory provisions on other remedies

The question finally to be considered is how far the statutes just mentioned affect the creditor's rights to sue on the judgment. As a result of the changes made by the 1982 Act the position can be summarised as follows:

(1) Where a judgment obtained in another part of the United Kingdom is enforceable in England by registration (*ante*, p. 540) it cannot be enforced in England in any other way—see Section 18(8) of the 1982 Act.

(2) If the Administration of Justice Act 1920 applies, the creditor can still sue on the judgment but section 9(5) provides that he is not to recover any costs of such action unless registration is refused or unless the court otherwise orders.

(3) If the Foreign Judgments (Reciprocal Enforcement) Act 1933 applies, no action lies on any judgment which is registrable under the Act.[95]

Under section 8 of the 1933 Act a judgment to which the Act applies, or would apply if a sum of money were payable under it, is conclusive between all parties thereto in English proceedings and can be set up by way of defence and counterclaim. Thus if a court in (say) Germany decided that a contract was valid and awarded a sum of money by way of damages the debtor could not argue in England that the contract was not valid. If, however, the foreign judgment merely decides that the foreign limitation rules bar the remedy in the foreign court it has recently been held by the House of Lords that this judgment is not a bar to an action on the merits in England.[96]

---

[95] s.6.

[96] *Black-Clawson International Ltd.* v. *Papierwerke Waldtrof-Aschaffenburg A.G.* [1975] 2 W.L.R. 513; [1975] 1 Al E.R. 810. Varying interpretations of the precise effects of section 8 were expressed in this case.

CHAPTER TWELVE

THE IMPACT OF THE EEC

On January 1 1973, the United Kingdom became a member of three communities—the European Coal and Steel Community, Euratom and (most important), the European Economic Community. The changes to English law resulting from accession to the Treaties of Paris and Rome are fundamental and far-reaching but it will take time before the full impact of membership is felt. Since the European Economic Community (EEC) is primarily concerned with economic and commercial matters it must clearly be dealt with in a book on commercial law. It is proposed to consider first the objects of the EEC, then to examine briefly the institutions and the sources of law, and finally to examine two of the areas where major developments have taken place—the law governing competition and the Convention on Jurisdiction and the Enforcement of Judgments. It is not proposed to consider problems arising from Euratom and the European Coal and Steel Community.

HOW IT ALL BEGAN

Although the Treaties are economic their roots are political. France and Germany have fought each other three times between 1870 and 1945. Consequently when Europe began to recover from the devastation of the Second World War the politicians looked for ways of ensuring that it would never happen again. It was felt that one way of achieving this result was by merging the coal and steel industries of France and Germany and in 1950 the Treaty of Paris setting up the European Coal and Steel Community was signed by six countries. The Community prospered and in 1957 the far more ambitious Treaty of Rome setting up the European Economic Community was signed by the same six Signatories. It provided for the elimination of customs barriers, the free movement of capital, labour, goods and services, measures to prevent the distortion of competition, and the harmonisation of laws regulating commercial activity. In this way a true "common market" could be set up. Here again political thinking played a prominent part; as the countries of the EEC became more and more integrated they could rival the super-powers of the U.S.A. and the U.S.S.R. and in this way the countries of Western Europe could enjoy again (albeit collectively) the power which they enjoyed before the outbreak of the Second World War. Movement towards political integration has been slow but progress in other directions has been more rapid.

1. Objects and Activities of the EEC

Article 3 reads:

> For the purposes set out in article 2, the activities of the Community shall include, as provided in this Treaty and in accordance with the timetable set out therein:
>
> (a) The elimination, as between Member States, of customs duties and of quantitative restrictions on the import and export of goods, and of all other measures having equivalent effect;
>
> (b) the establishment of a common customs tariff and of a common commercial policy towards third countries;
>
> (c) the abolition, as between Member States, of obstacles to freedom of movement for persons, services and capital;
>
> (d) the adoption of a common policy in the sphere of agriculture;
>
> (e) The adoption of a common policy in the sphere of transport;
>
> (f) The institution of a system ensuring that competition in the common market is not distorted;
>
> (g) the application of procedures by which the economic policies of Member States can be co-ordinated and disequilibria in their balances of payments remedied;
>
> (h) the approximation of the laws of Member States to the extent required for the proper functioning of the Common Market;
>
> (i) the creation of a European Social Fund in order to improve employment opportunities for workers and to contribute to the raising of their standard of living;
>
> (j) the establishment of a European Investment Bank to facilitate the economic expansion of the Community by opening up fresh resources;
>
> (k) the association of the overseas countries and territories in order to increase trade and to promote jointly economic and social development.

It is an ambitious programme and a great deal is being done. The areas in which the impact of the EEC has been felt most strongly are agriculture, competition law, company law, employment law (including related questions of social security law) transport law and the rights of individuals, firms and companies to establish themselves in other Member States. In addition, major changes have been made to the rules governing the jurisdiction of the English Courts in civil and commercial matters and in the enforcement of foreign judgments. A consumer protection programme has been drawn up and the EEC Commission have added their voice to those advocating strict liability on the manufacturer of products. Recent legislation which is based wholly or partly on EEC directives have included the Companies Acts 1980–81, the Insurance Companies Act 1981 and the Transfer of Undertakings (Protection of Employment) Regulations 1981.

Apart from these basic questions of substantive law the English lawyer must adapt his thinking in various fundamental respects. In particular he must realise that:—

(a) EEC and EEC-inspired legislation must be construed consistently throughout the EEC.

(b) Judges in other EEC states (and Judges of the European court) adopt a much broader purpose-based approach to the interpretations of statutes than the traditional English approach.

(c) A client may have rights under EEC law which are co-extensive with, or wider than, his rights under an English statute.[1] Thus it has been held that the "equal pay" rights conferred by Article 119 of the Treaty of Rome are wider than those conferred by the Equal Pay Act 1970 and indeed that the Equal Pay Act had failed to implement EEC law correctly.

(d) By section 3 of the European Communities Act 1972 an English Court must take judicial notice of the Treaties, the Communities' Official Journal and the judgments of the European Court.

2. INSTITUTIONS AND SOURCES OF LAW

The Community is administered by four main bodies—the Assembly, the Council of Ministers, the Commission and the Court of Justice (see Art. 4).

---

[1] See the equal pay case of *Snoxall* v. *Vauxhall Motors* [1978] Q.B. 11 and the Sex Discrimination case of *Garland* v. *British Rail* [1982] 2 W.L.R. 918.

Assembly (European Parliament)

As is generally known, the Parliament has no legislative powers and the Ministers who make up the Council of Ministers are not members of, nor responsible to, the Assembly. In extreme cases the Assembly can dismiss the Commission (Art. 144) and it has recently been given powers in connection with the approval of the Community Budget. Its opinions (*e.g.* on the statute for the proposed European company) now tend to carry more weight than in the past.

Council and Commission

The power structure of the Community is based on a dialogue between the Commission in Brussels and the Council of Ministers. The Commission has 13 Commissioners and a staff of well over 6,000. In the words of two learned writers:

> "It is possible to categorise the functions and powers of the Commission into three broad groups; it is an initiator and co-ordinator of Community policy; it is the executive agency of the Communities; it is the guardian of the Community Treaties."[2]

Thus although many decisions have to be taken by the Council the forward planning and the preliminary spadework is done by the Commission. It also has very extensive executive power; an important example of this can be seen in the development and enforcement of the rules relating to competition (see *post*, p. 551).

The Council consists of one Minister from each Member State. Although it has power to take decisions (Art. 145) it can normally do so only on a proposal from the Commission. Apart from competition law and certain other areas it is with the Council that the real power lies.

The Court

The Court of Justice in Luxembourg, consisting of one judge for each Member State, is charged with the task of ensuring that "in the interpretation and application of this Treaty the law is observed" (Art. 164). The procedure of the Court differs in many ways from the procedure in England and four examples of this can be given. First, the Court relies far more on written documents

---

[2] Lasok and Bridge, *An introduction to the Law and Institutions of the European Communities* 2nd ed. at p. 112.

and far less on oral argument. Secondly, the Court is assisted by an Advocate-General, who presents legal argument at the conclusion of the evidence. Thirdly, the court interprets the Treaty by reference to its broad economic objectives and not merely literally. Fourthly, the Court is not bound by its own decisions.

There are various Articles which deal with the jurisdiction of the Court.[3] In particular:

1. A court or tribunal in any Member State can ask the Court for a "preliminary ruling" on a question concerning the interpretation of the Treaty or the validity of acts done by institutions of the Community (Art. 177). Further, if the court or tribunal considers that a ruling on this matter is necessary for its own decision, and if there is no appeal from that court or tribunal it *must* refer the matter to Luxembourg (*ibid.*). It will be appreciated that Article 177 can affect not only the House of Lords and the Supreme Court but also lower courts and tribunals (*e.g.* a social security tribunal where a question arises concerning the rights of a foreign worker).[4]

2. The Commission can bring a Member State before the Court for breach of its duties under the Treaty (Art. 169).

3. Similarly, a Member State, after reporting the matter to the Commission, can take proceedings against another Member State for breach of Treaty obligations (Art 170). No case has been heard under this Article and, in view of the political damage which such litigation would cause, this is hardly surprising.

4. A Member State, the Council, the Commission and sometimes a natural or legal person can bring proceedings before the Court challenging the acts of Communities institutions on the grounds of, *inter alia* infringement of the Treaty, lack of competence or abuse of powers (Art. 173).

5. If a dispute arises as to the interpretation of the Treaty the Court has exclusive jurisdiction (Art. 219).

---

[3] See Chapter 2 of an excellent book, *Judicial Remedies in the European Communities* by Brinkhorst and Schermers.

[4] For the principles to be applied by an English judge in deciding whether to refer a case to Luxembourg see the judgment of Lord Denning M.R. in *H.P. Bulmer Ltd.* v. *J. Bollinger S.A.* [1974] 3 W.L.R. 202 which is analysed and discussed by Mr. Richard Plender in *A Practical Introduction to European Community Law* (1980) at pp. 17–22.

Other bodies

A number of other bodies assist in the running of the Community. They include the Economic and Social Committee, a Monetary Committee and the European Investment Bank.

Sources of law

Section 2(1) of the European Communities Act 1972 provides that:

> All such rights, powers, liabilities, obligations and restrictions from time to time created or arising by or under the Treaties, and all such remedies and procedures from time to time provided for by or under the Treaties, as in accordance with the Treaties are without further enactment to be given legal effect or used in the United Kingdom shall be recognised and available in law and be enforced, allowed and followed accordingly.

In *H.P. Bulmer Ltd.* v. *Bollinger S.A.*[5] Lord Denning M.R. explained the position in his characteristically colourful way when he said:

> "The Treaty is like an incoming tide. It flows into the estuaries and up the rivers. It cannot be held back . . . it is equal in force to any statute."

One of the central questions is the extent to which the Treaty itself, and laws made under it, create rights and duties enforceable in the English courts. The position can be summarised as follows:

1. Some provisions of the Treaty itself confer rights and duties enforceable in the English courts. Thus if A sues B in the High Court claiming damages for breach of contract, B could file a defence that the contract is void under Article 85 of the Treaty because it distorted competition in the Common Market.

2. Any regulation made by the Council or by the Commission is "binding in its entirety and directly applicable in all Member States" (Art. 189). In other words a regulation made in Brussels will automatically form part of English law and create rights and duties which will be enforceable in the English courts.[6] At the present time the overwhelming majority of regulations relate to agriculture.

---

[5] [1974] 3 W.L.R. 202.
[6] See Wyatt and Dashwood *The Substantive Law of the EEC* (1980), pp. 33–36 for further discussions.

3. Any directive made by the Council or by the Commission will bind this country to give effect, in its own way, to the result to be achieved (Art. 189). If therefore, the Council issue a directive requiring an amendment to English company law or employment law it will be left to the Government to decide whether to achieve this result by Act of Parliament or by statutory instrument in accordance with section 2(2) of the 1972 Act. Directives are widely used in connection with the harmonisation of national laws and they sometimes confer rights which an individual can enforce directly in his national courts.[7]

4. A decision issued by the Commission or the Council binds the persons to whom it is addressed (Art. 189).

5. A judgment of the Court of Justice interpreting the provisions of the Treaty will bind all English courts.

6. The objects of the Community would clearly be thwarted if Member States had the power to legislate in a manner contrary to the rules of the Treaty or to rules made under powers conferred by the Treaty and it is generally accepted that each Member State must refrain from passing such legislation.

3. COMPETITION

It has already been seen that free competition on a community-wide basis is central to the philosophy of the Community and the Commission has been very energetic in developing and enforcing a body of rules in this field.

The general position

There are four basic rules:

1. Agreements falling within Article 85(1) are prohibited and void[8] and heavy fines can be imposed by the Commission.

2. The Commission (and *only* the Commission) can grant an exemption if certain conditions are satisfied (Art. 85(3)).

---

[7] *Van Duyn* v. *Home Office* [1975] 2 W.L.R. 760, European Court. The case was concerned with a directive restricting the powers of national Governments to interfere with the free movement of workers.

[8] See (1983) L.S. Gaz. 272 for a valuable discussion as to the enforcement of EEC competition law in the English courts.

3. In order to obtain the exemption, *notice* of the agreement must be given to the Commission (Regulation 17 of 1962).
4. Article 86 prohibits an abuse by one or more undertakings of a dominant position within the Common Market so far as it may affect trade between Member States.

What agreements are caught by Article 85?

Article 85(1) reads as follows:

> The following shall be prohibited as incompatible with the Common Market, all agreements between undertakings, decisions by associations of undertakings and concerted practices which may affect trade between Member States and which have as their object or effect the prevention, restriction or distortion of competition within the Common Market, and in particular those which:
> (a) directly or indirectly fix purchase or selling prices or any other trading conditions;
> (b) limit or control production, markets, technical development, or investment;
> (c) share markets or sources of supply;
> (d) apply dissimilar conditions to equivalent transactions with other trading parties, thereby placing them at a competitive disadvantage;
> (e) make the conclusion of contracts subject to acceptance by the other parties of supplementary obligations which, by their nature or according to commercial usage, have no connection with the subject of such contracts.

The Article only applies to arrangements which "may affect trade between Member States." Thus an exclusive sales agreement between two English firms relating solely to trade in England would not be caught.[9] The word "effect" has been construed by the Commission as applying only to arrangements which are likely to affect trade to an appreciable extent. In 1970 the Commission stated that an agreement would not be caught by Article 85(1) if:

(a) the aggregate annual turnover of the firms taking part in the agreement does not exceed 15 million dollars in the case of manufacturing firms and 20 million dollars in the case of commercial firms *and*

(b) the products covered by the agreement represent not more than five per cent. of the total value of business in identical

---

[9] Exclusive sale agreements are also outside the Restrictive Trade Practices Act 1956.

products in that part of the Community where the agreement is intended to be effective.[10]

Examples of agreements caught by Article 85(1):

(1) A manufactures electrical goods. He appoints a sole distributor in each EEC country and each distributor agrees not to export outside his own territory. This, in effect, carves up the "common" market into 10 separate markets and thereby distorts competition.[11]

(2) A owns a trade mark for shaving cream. He gives B the right to use it in Italy and C in Germany. C then indirectly exports the cream into Italy and undercuts B. The trade mark is being used by A as a method of carving up the common market; the arrangement is therefore invalid.[12]

Conditions for exemption

The first condition for exemption is that the agreement must be notified to the Commission. If this has been done Article 85(3) enables the Commission to grant exemption if the agreement fulfils *four* conditions—two positive and two negative. The conditions are that:

(1) the agreement, etc., contributes to improving the production or distribution of goods or to promoting technical or economic progress;

(2) it allows consumers a fair share of the resulting benefit;

(3) it does not impose on the undertaking any restrictions which are not indispensable to the attainment of these objectives;

(4) it does not afford to such undertakings the possibility of eliminating competition in respect of a substantial part of the products in question.

Exemption can be granted in respect of *inter alia* any "agreement or category of agreements" and in 1967 the Commission made a very important regulation (No. 67/67) under which exclusive distributorship agreements were exempted without formalities (*i.e.* without the need to notify) provided that certain conditions were satisfied. This regulation has recently been replaced by two

---

[10] See [1972] J.B.L. 280.
[11] Consider the *Consten and Grundig* case [1966] C.M.L.R. 418.
[12] *Sirena* case [1971] C.M.L.R. 1260. See also *Deutsche Grammophon* v. *Metro* [1971] C.M.L.R. 631.

new ones relating to exclusive distribution agreements[12a] and exclusive purchasing agreements.[12b]

The question of whether an agreement or arrangement infringes Article 85 can be decided not only by the Commission and European Court but also by domestic courts, but only the Commission can grant exemption under Article 85(3). A notification to the Commission does not normally make the agreement provisionally valid.[13]

Co-operation

In 1968 the Commission issued a Communication indicating that certain practices involving co-operation between undertakings did not infringe Article 85(1).[14]

Abuse of dominant position

The other main plank of the competition policy of the EEC is Article 86 which declares that the abuse of a claimant's position in the common market (or in a substantial part of it) is incompatible with the Common Market. The Article then goes on to set out four examples of such abuse. They are:

> (1) The direct or indirect imposition of any purchase or selling price or of any other trading conditions which are inequitable.
> (2) The limitation of production, markets or technological development to the prejudice of consumers.
> (3) The application of unequal conditions to parties undertaking equivalent engagements in commercial transactions, thereby placing them at a competitive disadvantage.
> (4) Making the conclusion of a contract subject to the acceptance by the other party to the contract of additional obligations which by their nature or according to commercial usage, have no connection with the subject of such contract.

In deciding whether these has been an infringement of Article 86 it is first necessary to identify the "market" in respect of which the dominant position is alleged to exist. Thus if X Ltd. is the sole

---

[12a] See Commission Regulation (EEC) No. 1983/83.
[12b] See Commission Regulation (EEC) No. 1984/83.
[13] *Brasserie de Haecht* v. *Wilkin* (No. 2) [1973] C.M.L.R. 287.
[14] For the text of this see Cawthra, *Restrictive Agreements in the EEC* at p. 127.

supplier of bananas in a particular area the question arises as to whether bananas constitute a separate "market" as distinct from the general market for fresh fruit. In the leading case of *United Brands Co.* v. *The Commission* the European Court said this:

> "For the bananas to be regarded as forming a market which is sufficiently differentiated from other fruit markets it must be possible for it to be singled out by such special features distinguishing it from other fruits that it is only to a limited extent interchangeable with them and it is only exposed to their competition in a manner that is hardly perceptible.[15]

The Commission surprised many people when they decided in the *Continental Can* case that an abuse had occurred when an American company, which enjoyed a dominant position, bought up its one remaining major EEC competitor and thereby changed the structure of competition in the market irreversibly. The company appealed to the European court who allowed the appeal ([1973] C.M.L.R. 199) on the ground that the evidence of the Commission fell short of the "dominant position" required by Article 86. The Court did not, however, dissent from the view that buying up a competitor could amount to "abuse." Other examples of abuse can include unfair pricing policies, onerous trading terms, loyalty rebates and refusal to deal with another undertaking.[16]

4. Convention on Jurisdiction and Enforcement of Judgments[17]

Article 220 of the Treaty provides that:

> Member States shall, so far as is necessary, enter into negotiations with each other with a view to securing for the benefit of their nationals . . . the simplification of formalities governing the reciprocal recognition and enforcement of judgments of courts or tribunals and of arbitration awards.

The original six members of the EEC negotiated with each other and the result was a Convention extending far beyond the limited

---

[15] [1978] E.C.R. 207, 277. See also *Hoffman-La-Roche* [1976] 2 C.M.L.R. 25 and *General Motors Continental* [1976] C.M.L.R. 95. In all three cases the above test resulted in a finding that there *was* a separate market for the goods or services in question.

[16] See Wyatt and Dashwood *op cit.* at pp. 307–319 for further examples.

[17] See (1983) L.S. Gaz. 547.

object laid down in Article 220. This Convention was supplemented by his Protocols and some amendments were made by a further Convention dated October 9, 1978 which provided for the accession to the Convention of the United Kingdom, Denmark and Ireland.

The Conventions and Protocols, which are printed in Schedules 1, 2 and 3 to the Civil Jurisdiction and Judgments Act 1982 and they are given the force of law by section 2 of that Act. Judicial notice must be taken of any judgment of the European Court as to the meaning and effect of the Conventions (Section 3(1)). Further, section 3(3) breaks entirely new ground in the English law relating to interpretation of statutes it reads:

> Without prejudice to the generality of subsection (1) the following reports (which are reproduced in the Official Journal of the Communities) namely—
> (a) the reports by Mr. P. Jerard on the 1968 Convention and the 1971 Protocol; and
> (b) the report by Professor Dr. Peter Schlosser on the Access Convention.
> may be considered in ascertaining the meaning or effect of any provision of the conventions and shall be given such weight as is appropriate in the circumstances.

Terminology

A difficulty appears right at the beginning of the Convention. Article 2, which appears under the heading "General Provisions," states that:

> Subject to the provisions of this Convention, persons domiciled in a Contracting State shall be answerable to the courts of that State whatever their nationality.

The difficulty, of course, is to decide what is meant by "domicile." In the case of a company, it means the place where the company has its registered office (Art. 53). In the case of an individual, the term is given a meaning which is much wider than its usual meaning for other purposes of English Law.[18]

Basic principles of jurisdiction

When the Convention was drawn up in 1968, each of the Six had its own rules as to jurisdiction. These individual rules will continue

---

[18] Act of 1982 section 41.

to exist side by side with the Convention rules, but only as regards persons who are not covered by the Convention. Thus, the present basis of jurisdiction (presence of the defendant)[19] would no longer be sufficient in Convention cases but it would remain valid for other cases.

As regards the Contracting States the basic rule is that each one assumes jurisdiction over any defendant who is domiciled in that State and declines jurisdiction over any defendant who is domiciled in another Contracting State (see Arts. 3 and 19). Thus a person domiciled in France cannot normally be sued in Belgium. This basic rule, which differs radically from the present English law, is only modified in a few cases. In particular:

(1) A party to a contract can be sued in the Contracting State where the contract was to be or has been performed.

(2) Where a dispute relates to a firm's branch or agency, the case can be heard by the Contracting State where the branch or agency is situated.

(3) An insured person has a number of options open to him in proceedings arising out of an insurance policy. If for example the insurer is domiciled in a Contracting State the insured person can sue him in the Contracting State where the insurer[20] or the insured is domiciled (a prospect which is hardly likely to prove popular with British insurance companies).

(4) Similarly the buyer under a hire-purchase or credit-sale agreement has a number of options open to him.

(5) The parties may agree that disputes arising out of a particular legal relationship are to be heard by the courts of a particular Contracting State. Such agreements must be in writing or confirmed in writing.

In cases arising under (3) or (4) above the contractual power to vary the Convention rules is considerably restricted.

(6) A defendant who enters a voluntary appearance in the courts of a Contracting State thereby makes that State competent. This is similar to the present rules of English law (*ante*, p. 496).

---

[19] See *ante*, p. 494.
[20] An insurer who has a branch or agency or other establishment in a contracting state is treated for these purposes as being domiciled in that state (Art. 8).

It will be appreciated that these rules are much narrower than the present rules of English jurisdiction. Many cases falling within R.S.C., Ord. 11 would not fall within the Convention.

Enforcement

The provisions for the recognition and enforcement of judgments are based on the concept of the EEC as a single country. A judgment obtained in one Contracting State is to be enforced in any of the others, subject only to a very few qualifications and conditions. It should be noted that the rules as to enforcement apply to any judgment obtained in a Contracting State even if the defendant was not domiciled in that State or in any other Contracting State. Thus if a Hungarian is sued in France (under internal French rules relating to jurisdiction) a judgment obtained against him in France can be enforced in England.

Under the Foreign Judgments (Reciprocal Enforcement) Act 1933, there are detailed rules for ensuring that the court giving the judgment was a competent court (*ante*, p. 543). Under the Convention this is only so in a limited class of case (*e.g.* insurance, hire-purchase and credit-sale). In all other cases the enforcing court will assume that the adjudicating court was competent.

If the judgment is duly registered in the High Court it can be enforced as if made by that court. There is a right of appeal against the grant or refusal of registration (see Arts. 36–41 and section 6 of the 1982 Act).

INDEX